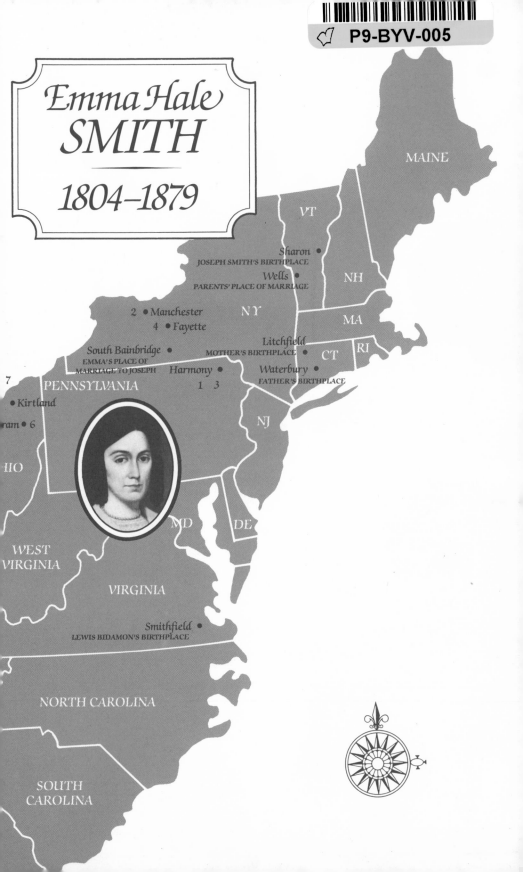

Emma Hale SMITH

1804–1879

MAINE

VT

NH

Sharon •
JOSEPH SMITH'S BIRTHPLACE

Wells •
PARENTS' PLACE OF MARRIAGE

2 • Manchester   N Y
4 • Fayette

MA

South Bainbridge •
EMMA'S PLACE OF
MARRIAGE TO JOSEPH

Litchfield
MOTHER'S BIRTHPLACE

RI

Harmony •   CT

7   PENNSYLVANIA   1 3

Waterbury •
FATHER'S BIRTHPLACE

• Kirtland

ram • 6

NJ

HIO

MD   DE

WEST
VIRGINIA

VIRGINIA

Smithfield •
LEWIS BIDAMON'S BIRTHPLACE

NORTH CAROLINA

SOUTH
CAROLINA

Mormon Enigma:
Emma Hale Smith

Mormon Enigma: Emma Hale Smith

Prophet's Wife, "Elect Lady,"
Polygamy's Foe, 1804–1879

Linda King Newell
and
Valeen Tippetts Avery

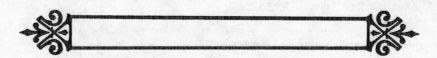

Doubleday & Company, Inc., Garden City, New York

To our children,
Christine, Jennifer, Eric, and Heather Newell, and
Christopher, Maureen, Nathan, and Thad Avery

Designed by Virginia M. Soulé

Library of Congress Cataloging in Publication Data

Newell, Linda King.
  Mormon enigma.

  Bibliography: p. 369
  Includes index.
  1. Smith, Emma Hale. 2. Mormons—United States—
Biography. I. Avery, Valeen Tippetts. II. Title.
BX8695.S515N48 1984   289.3′092′4 [B]
ISBN: 0-385-17166-8

Library of Congress Catalog Card Number 80–2400

Oh, what a commingling of thought filled my mind for the moment, again she is here, even in the seventh trouble—undaunted, firm, and unwavering—unchangeable, affectionate Emma!

Joseph Smith, Jr., about his wife,
August 16, 1842

I never saw a day in the world that I would not almost worship that woman, Emma Smith, if she would be a saint instead of being a devil.

Brigham Young about Emma,
October 1, 1866

My mother was one of the best poised women I ever met. Of the purest and noblest intentions herself, she never submitted to be made a party to anything low, wrong, or evil, was absolutely fearless where the right was concerned; and was a just and generous mother. Her heart never changed toward her children, and her fidelity to them never wavered. It's needless to say that we *loved her*.

Joseph Smith III about his mother,
January 17, 1893

Contents

List of
Illustrations

Genealogical Charts

following page 9

Introduction

Many women who have become influential in religious and women's history have been known initially because of their association with prominent men. Emma Hale Smith Bidamon (1804–1879) is a case in point. Although she was not the leader of a religious movement herself, she was closely associated with three controversial men who were. She was the wife of Joseph Smith, who is claimed as founder by both the Church of Jesus Christ of Latter-day Saints (LDS or Mormon), headquartered in Salt Lake City, Utah, and by the Reorganized Church of Jesus Christ of Latter Day Saints (RLDS), headquartered in Independence, Missouri. She was a onetime friend and longtime antagonist of Brigham Young, who led the Mormons on their trek west from Illinois in 1846 and guided their colonization of the Great Basin. And she was the mother of Joseph Smith III, leader of the Reorganization that brought together church members scattered in the Midwest. Emma's descendants have led that church from 1860 to the present.

Yet Emma Smith was far more than an appendage and helpmeet to prominent men. She was also a capable, articulate, and influential individual in her own right who profoundly affected the development of the religious movements with which she was associated. From her initial elopement with the young would-be prophet Joseph Smith in 1827, through seventeen years of marriage and repeated moves through five states, she became a force to be reckoned with, especially in financial and other practical matters affecting the Mormon church. Deeply in love with her husband, she quietly but vigorously opposed the polygamous beliefs and practices which he sought to introduce into Mormon practice in Illinois in the early 1840s. Following her husband's assassination in 1844 and the migration westward of the main body of Mormons under Brigham Young in 1846, Emma remained behind in the nearly deserted town of Nauvoo, Illinois. There she continued to live thirty-two more years as the wife of Lewis C. Bidamon, who never embraced Mormon doctrines. When a group of individuals dissatisfied with Brigham Young and polygamy founded a church which Emma's son Joseph Smith III would lead after 1860, she gained a new status.

Because of the complexity of Emma's role in the Mormon movement, few dispassionate accounts of her life have appeared. On the one hand, members of the Reorganized Church have chiseled a careful image of her: perpetually patient, always valiant, silently stoic, the mother of the Reorganization. On the other hand, Utah Mormons, while celebrating her role as Joseph Smith's wife and the first president of the Relief Society, have generally been highly critical. Early leaders in Utah castigated Emma from their pulpits for opposing Brigham Young and the practice of polygamy, and for lending support to the Reorganization. As these attitudes filtered down through the years, Emma was virtually written out of official Utah Mormon histories. In this biography, we have attempted to reconstruct the full story of this remarkable and much misunderstood woman's experiences.

Emma left no diary or journal. Some family papers mention her only briefly. Joseph Smith's diary refers to Emma and their children, and twenty-two letters written between them are extant. A few letters written after 1844 and one page of "blessings" she desired to be hers represent her only personal statements. Thus we reconstructed Emma's story from other original documents and other evidence collected over eight years.

We found documentation illustrating her life to be extensive but widely scattered. These sources are listed in the Notes and Bibliography. We added minimal punctuation but retained the original spelling. Dialogue in the narrative is taken from accounts reporting it.

Although we each have roots that penetrate deep into Mormon history and culture, we have written neither to support nor to dispute doctrine and have used accounts both favorable to and critical of the new religion that Joseph Smith established. We also recognize the difficulty of maintaining balance in describing historical events that many people hold sacred. The solution Brigham H. Roberts expressed in the Preface to the *Comprehensive History of the Church* became ours: "to frankly state events as they occurred, in full consideration of all related circumstances, allowing the line of condemnation or justification to fall where it may; being confident that in the sum of things justice will follow truth."

In a collaboration that has spanned nearly nine years and encompassed research in archives from coast to coast as well as visits to the location of each of Emma's homes and other historical sites in Pennsylvania, Ohio, Missouri, Illinois, and Iowa, it becomes difficult to assign credit in the various elements of the project to one author or the other. Suffice it to say, neither of us could have done it alone; it has been an all-absorbing labor for both of us. In the end a flip of a coin determined the order in which the authors' names appear.

We owe a debt of gratitude to the librarians and staff of the Beinecke Rare Books and Manuscripts Library at Yale University, New Haven, Connecticut; the Henry E. Huntington Library and Art Gallery, San Marino, California; the Stanford University Libraries, Palo Alto, California; and the Bancroft Library at the University of California at Berkeley. We owe much to Dennis Rowley, Hyrum L. Andrus, and LeGrand Baker for their help at the Harold B. Lee Library at Brigham Young University, Provo, Utah; and also to Melvin T.

Smith at the Utah State Historical Society, and Everett L. Cooley and Della
Dye at the University of Utah's Marriott Library, both located in Salt Lake
City, Utah. Madelon Brunson and Patricia B. Struble of the RLDS Library-
Archives, Independence, Missouri, gave us assistance and friendship. At the
Historical Department of the Church of Jesus Christ of Latter-day Saints in
Salt Lake City, Utah, James L. Kimball, Jeffery O. Johnson, Donald T.
Schmidt, William W. Slaughter, and Ronald G. Watt gave us direction and
help with manuscript materials and photographs. We are indebted to the
members of the Joseph Fielding Smith Institute for Church History at Brig-
ham Young University: Leonard J. Arrington, Maureen Ursenbach Beecher,
Jill Mulvay Derr, Ronald K. Esplin, Dean C. Jessee, and Carol Cornwall Madsen.

Many other scholars and collectors also shared their own research with us
or have guided us to other documents: James B. Allen, Danel W. Bachman,
Irene M. Bates, Lyndon W. Cook, Dorothy Danhaus, Gracia Denning, An-
drew F. Ehat, Robert B. Flanders, Donna Hill, Edythe H. Hindley, Robert D.
Hutchins, Scott G. Kenney, Edward Luce, D. Michael Quinn, Gene Sessions,
Jan Shipps, E. Gary Smith, Kenneth Stobaugh, Richard S. Van Wagoner,
Marcia Vogel, and Buddy Youngreen.

We are indebted to Alma Blair, Richard L. Bushman, Peter L. Crawley,
Paul M. Edwards, Ronald K. Esplin, Max H. Parkin, Larry C. Porter, and
William D. Russell, who read parts of the work. Patricia Aikens edited the
early stages of the book. James L. Clayton, Lawrence Foster, Marvin S. Hill,
L. Jackson Newell, and W. L. Rusho read the entire manuscript and offered
insights and suggestions. We especially appreciate the editing skills of Lavina
Fielding Anderson and the indexing skills of Gary Gillum. We also thank Jean
Anne Vincent, Senior Editor, and her assistants, Doreen DeFlorio and Susan
Cass at Doubleday & Company, Inc., for their patience and assistance, and
Robert Breinholt and Del Jenks for their enthusiastic encouragement.

To Maxine Wood Campbell and Marilyn Damron White we owe a debt
of gratitude that only writers with fine, competent typists can appreciate.
Their husbands, Ralph E. Campbell and Leland R. White, proofread the
manuscript. Jean Robbins, William H. Kehr, Karen Post, Patricia Shimmins,
and John and Rose Harmon have each been of great help.

And, finally, our greatest appreciation goes to our husbands, L. Jackson
Newell and Charles C. Avery, and our children. For both the Averys and the
Newells, this has been a family effort. We are grateful to each one of them.

Although all these people have made our task easier, we accept responsibility for statements and conclusions expressed herein.

1

Emma and Joseph

1825–1827

When Emma Hale awoke on a Thursday morning, January 18, 1827, she did not plan to be married by evening. The day before she had left her home in Harmony, Pennsylvania, to be a guest of the Josiah Stowell family across the state line in southern New York; the handsome Joseph Smith was there also. Emma stood tall, about five feet, nine inches. Men had decorously described her as "well turned, of excellent form . . . with splendid physical development."[1] Large brown eyes complemented her olive complexion. She usually brushed her long dark hair to a shine, then parted it in the middle and fastened it snugly against the nape of her neck. Her speech was lively, spirited, and witty. Joseph, who had just turned twenty-one, had asked for Emma's hand twice and had been rebuffed—not by Emma, but by her father, who Emma said was "bitterly opposed to him."[2] Isaac Hale could see no good in a man who dug for buried treasure or had "visions." Six months past her twenty-second birthday, Emma was old enough to know her own mind and was determined to see Joseph even without her father's knowledge.

An acquaintance of Emma's family, W. L. Hines, remembered seeing the couple after they left Hales'. "Jo stole his wife . . . while [Isaac] Hale was at Church. My wife and I saw him on an old horse with Emma on behind as they passed our house on their way to [be] . . . married."[3] "I had no intention of marrying when I left home," Emma recalled, but the next day, at the Stowells', Joseph's arguments, accompanied by Mr. Stowell's support, were persuasive. Emma weighed the situation and made her decision. "Preferring to marry him to any other man I knew," she said, "I consented."[4] One of her mother's friends, who described Emma as "intelligent," said that her marriage to Joseph Smith "can only be accounted for by supposing 'he had bewitched her.' "5

Before nightfall Emma and Joseph stood nervously in Esquire Zachariah Tarbell's parlor in South Bainbridge, New York and repeated their marriage vows. Not willing to face her father long enough to return home for her personal possessions, Emma escaped Isaac Hale's indignation by fleeing with Joseph seventy-five miles north to the groom's home at Manchester, New York. The decision to elope would not have been easy. She had grown up in the stable and well-ordered home that Isaac and Elizabeth Hale provided for their nine children, but her marriage to Joseph Smith, the man who would become the prophet of the Mormon church, would lead her halfway across the United States and embroil her in controversy over the Mormon practice of plural marriage that would endure for more than a century after her death. Emma followed the man she loved, leaving the Hales, and Harmony, and the Susquehanna River behind her.

The Susquehanna River dominates the physical landscape of Harmony (now Oakland), Pennsylvania. Emma had grown up along its banks in comfort and security. In the late eighteenth century the river's long valley in southern New York and northern Pennsylvania was heavily forested. Oquago Mountain sloped south and east to the river, but the famed Ichabod Swamp, near the Pennsylvania-New York border, held all the mystery. An early settler described it as "a dreadful swamp, thick with hemlock and laurel, and full of paths of wild animals—bears, wolves and panthers."6 Captain Ichabod Buck once became lost in the thicket and fought his way through its tangles to the river with a jackknife as his single weapon. The swamp had claimed only his name. The land was fertile, though heavy stands of oak, pine, beech, hemlock, maple, and hickory stood as silent obstacles to the farmers' attempts to sow wheat and corn.

Two men had arrived on the banks of the Susquehanna with their young wives in 1791: Emma's parents, Isaac and Elizabeth Lewis Hale, together with Elizabeth's brother Nathaniel and his bride Sarah Cole. In Vermont they had piled their belongings onto a cart hitched to a yoke of oxen and headed for the Susquehanna Valley. On their arrival, Isaac and Elizabeth Hale bought land and an "improvement"—perhaps a log cabin. Nathaniel and Sarah Lewis settled the adjacent property. The two couples became the first permanent settlers in the area.

Isaac killed deer and elk in the higher elevations and rubbed the carcasses down with salt. He piled the meat into wooden troughs which he skidded over the snow like a sled. He traded his kill for help on his farm, but as often as not the meat appeared unannounced on the doorsteps of his needy neighbors.

Isaac and Elizabeth were members of the first informal Methodist Episcopal "class" in Harmony, meeting in private homes until a church could be built. Elizabeth's brother, Nathaniel Lewis, became a well-known lay preacher. Uncle Nathaniel's popular style marked him as the family's resident religious authority. Elizabeth remained a faithful member of the Methodist Episcopal Church for fifty years but Isaac could see that dependence upon God alone did not fill the haymow or fell the trees or move the logs. Isaac became deistic in his religious philosophy, trusting his own judgment. His decisions resulted in a solid reputation among his neighbors, a full pantry, a sturdy barn, a good house, and food on the table for his five sons and four daughters.

Emma, the third girl and seventh child in this family, was born July 10, 1804. According to a family spokesman, Isaac owed his return to traditional religious fealty to this daughter. He was in his early fifties when he stopped at the edge of a small clearing in the woods where he saw Emma, seven or eight years old, praying that her father might return to the orthodox Christianity she understood. Moved by the simple faith and love of this child, Isaac soon found his way back to the fold and brought Emma's seventeen-year-old brother David with him.[7] She attended church with her parents and sang the hymns in her lyric soprano voice.

Emma had more interests than religion. Tall and gangly, with dark hair and strong arms, she mastered her canoe well enough to make the Susquehanna her personal thoroughfare. Her older brother David was a pilot on the river and undoubtedly an indulgent observer as she maneuvered the canoe on the water. Her brothers taught Emma to handle horses and she rode with self-confidence and skill. Jesse, David, Alva, and Isaac, and two sisters, Phoebe and Elizabeth, were older than Emma. A sister named Tryal was two years younger, and Reuben trailed by four more years. The four elder brothers gave Emma an opportunity to deal with young men, for in her eyes they must have always seemed grown. Her quick wit, remarked upon by friends when she became an adult, was shaped by her family in these early years.

Both Jesse and David were tax collectors. Still, Isaac complained of his own taxes and forwarded a document to the authorities protesting, "Year after year thousands of dollars are wrung from the pockets of our citizens in the shape of taxes."[8]

Though Isaac worked hard and steadily, Elizabeth also contributed to the family income. She opened her home to boarders, operating an inn or tavern, to provide the family with extra cash to augment produce from the garden, farm crops, and meat from the wilds. She taught her daughters to make candles from tallow, cure sausages for the winter, and dry fruit from the orchards. They learned to knit and sew, to patch and mend. Quite likely the results of their homemaking skills appeared as entries in the annual agricultural fair.

Elizabeth Lewis Hale saw that her children could read and write, probably teaching them herself through the long winter months. When Emma was nine the townspeople built a log schoolhouse and furnished it with rough log benches. But they hired the best schoolmaster available. Caleb Barnes, educated in Boston, taught his first year in Harmony when Emma was twelve. Perhaps it was with him that Emma developed a fluency in the written language that was evident throughout her life. All of the Hale children were considered bright, but Emma was exceptional. Undoubtedly with great pride her father was able to send her away to a girls' school for an additional year of study, a marked contrast to the experience of her mother, who had struggled for an education amidst the poverty of her growing-up years.

Elizabeth Lewis had married Isaac Hale when she was twenty-three and he was twenty-seven. Both the Hales and the Lewises were old New England families.[9] John Heald, the first ancestor to come to the New World, arrived as an indentured worker from England in 1635. Six years later he became a freeman in Concord, Massachusetts, and twenty years after his arrival he realized the immigrant's dream of holding land of his own, a mark of respectability to the Hales. John's son Gershom moved to Springfield, Massachusetts, in 1700 and persuaded the town fathers to grant him twenty acres in an area known as the "feeding hill" or common.

Gershom Hale's grandson, Reuben Hale, settled first in New Hartford, Connecticut. With Diantha Ward he "entered into ye marriage covenant" on August 29, 1759, in Oxford, Massachusetts. He was recommended and admitted to the church at Hartland Township in 1772. A few years later Reuben Hale enlisted in the Revolutionary Army, serving six years. He bought and sold land over the years and apparently had some mechanical ability which augmented his farming.

Reuben's and Diantha's second son, Isaac, was Emma's father. He was born in 1763 at Waterbury, Connecticut, but his grandfather, Arah Ward, took him to Wells, Vermont, while he was still a child, presumably at the death of his mother. When Isaac was seventeen he also joined the Revolutionary Army and marched under Colonel Ebenezer Allen. At that same age he inherited his Grandfather Ward's land in Wells, Vermont, with the provision that he take "into his care his Grandmother Phoebe Ward in her old age, to keep and provide for during her life." She probably lived four more years, for in 1784 Isaac deeded some of her land to his brother.

For Isaac the frontier pulled stronger than the inherited acres in Vermont. After a summer in Connecticut he traveled to southern New York, where he hunted wild game to fulfill a boarding agreement: Isaac furnished the meat and Ichabod Buck provided the breadstuff. He returned briefly to New England for the one vital commodity he was not able to hew out of the raw country—a wife.

Isaac Hale met Elizabeth Lewis in his hometown of Wells, Vermont. One of her ancestors, John Howland, left England on the *Mayflower* at age twenty-eight. Twelve years later, in 1632, George and Sarah Lewis and their family arrived in Plymouth Colony with a group of Pilgrims led by a Rev. Mr. Lathrop. After two years in Plymouth, George was among a number who were dismissed from the church and who moved to Scituate, a few miles north. The records do not indicate a reason for the dismissal, but clearly George Lewis did not lack character, being "an honest good man, [who] got his living by his labor; a sincere Christian, living in peace, and avoiding suits at law. He did not hold that the chief end of man was to gather riches, but, rather, to do good, and to train his children in righteous ways to grow to be honest, industrious men and useful and respected citizens." George completed his economic servitude and became a freeman in January 1636.

After three years the Lewises located across the bay in Barnstable on Cape Cod, again with the Rev. Mr. Lathrop, following a custom of the times of attaching themselves to a religious leader. George was then a planter but he also surveyed highways, became a juryman and then a constable. In the New World his children also obtained an education.

The Lewis family remained in the Barnstable area for almost a hundred years. George Lewis's great-grandson Gershom was born there in 1704. At eighteen he faced a delicate problem in courting fourteen-year-old Sarah Steele. When her father made out his will he bequeathed several pieces of property to his two daughters with this provision: "In case . . . my said daughter Sarah shall at any time, match and marry with Gershom Lewis now living in Farmington, which she knows is a thing very cross and contrary to my mind . . . the bequest and legacy I have here given her shall be utterly null and void. . . . My will further in that case is that . . . I . . . bequeath to my said daughter Sarah, the sum of 5 pounds, personal estate and no more."[10] In less than a month he was dead. Whether the romance shriveled naturally or whether Sarah simply chose to keep her legacy is a matter of speculation, but no wedding took place.

At thirty-one Gershom Lewis married Mary Maltby in Guilford, Connecticut. Emma's grandfather, Nathaniel Lewis, was their third child, born in 1740. He married Esther Tuttle in 1767, then moved to Wells, Vermont. By the time he served in the Revolutionary War, he and Esther had six children, the eldest being Elizabeth, Emma's mother. Soon after Nathaniel moved his family to Vermont the first Methodist preacher visited Wells and asked someone to direct him to the poorest family in town. The Lewises fitted that description. The preacher organized a small class that met in the Lewis home with the father as leader. Elizabeth Lewis was then thirteen. Her brother, Nathaniel, Jr., a year and a half younger, began his lifelong interest in preaching.

As a young woman Elizabeth was a prize for any man, particularly one like Isaac Hale, who needed a wife to take to the wilderness. She was tall and well built and a frontiersman could see that her sons would probably inherit strong bodies fit for felling trees and plowing land. Her education gave her an intangible asset: no child born to Elizabeth Lewis Hale would be raised an illiterate. With particular pride Elizabeth later watched her daughter Emma

return from girls' school to teach in Harmony, probably in the same log structure where she sat as a wiggly child.

As a young woman, Emma was physically and emotionally strong, with a
streak of independence. Her demeanor for the most part was quiet but sociable. She had a delightful sense of humor. Evidence suggests that she judged
people's characters quite accurately and acted upon her own instincts regardless of other opinions. She moved with slow precision but was capable of doing
"an amazing amount of work" in little time.[11]

Emma was nearly twenty in the spring of 1824. One evening in May a
neighbor named Jason Treadwell came to the Hales' house.[12] Treadwell, who
lived with his wife and child in part of his father's house, was a local ne'er-do-
well with an appetite for liquor. According to the county history, his father
worked his seventy-five acres with little help from the son, thereby supporting
both families. Jason was a strong, powerfully built man, about thirty. Heavy
eyebrows that met over his nose gave him a savage appearance. His practical
jokes bordered on the sinister.

On this night Isaac noticed that Jason seemed agitated. Either through
concern or curiosity, Mr. Hale asked, "Jason, what has been the matter with
you today?"

"Nothing that I know of," Treadwell replied, then parried the rest of the
conversation and gave Isaac no information.

The following day horrifying news spread through town. Someone had
found Oliver Harper—shot dead—up on a hill by the roadside. A man of
about fifty, Harper owned and worked a large farm just north of Harmony. He
also operated an extensive lumbering business and, the previous day, had been
down the Susquehanna on a raft with a load of lumber. He had set out to walk
back home with eight hundred dollars in his pocket. When Isaac Hale reported the conversation with Treadwell, Jason became a likely suspect. But the
authorities found no weapon or money and, therefore, no motive. Then a Mr.
Welton came forward with a strange story that further implicated Treadwell.
Welton had passed over the same road, near the place the body was found,
only an hour or so before Harper's death. He spotted someone lying by a log
and partially hidden by underbrush. The person looked up and frightened
Welton. The stranger had blackened his face with coal dust and Welton feared
for his life when he saw the obvious disguise. He quickly thought of a way to
insure his safety.

"Here, come with me," he invited. "I have got something with me that
will help you." The whiskey he produced tempted the man, who followed him,
swigging from the bottle as he walked. At the edge of the woods Welton
continued on his way, much relieved that the man with the blackened face had
turned back. But Mr. Welton remembered a scar under the chin of his new
acquaintance. Confident of his memory, he later promised to pick the man out
of any crowd. Already under arrest by virtue of Isaac Hale's testimony, Jason

Treadwell was placed in the midst of the men at Munson's tavern in Hickory Grove. A carefully guarded Treadwell stood at the bar drinking whiskey when Welton singled him out, exclaiming, "This is the man! By that scar I know he is the man!"

A motive then became apparent. Another neighbor, John Comfort, had earlier called Treadwell down for drinking, laziness, and general dissolution. Treadwell, angered and insulted at Comfort's interference, repeatedly threatened him. Comfort had also made a trip down the river and planned to return home the same day as Oliver Harper. The two men resembled each other in size and appearance and were dressed much alike. A man with killing on his mind and alcohol in his blood, hiding nervously in the bushes, could easily mistake one for the other.

If the suspicions of the townspeople were correct, Jason Treadwell killed the wrong man. He had lain in ambush to take revenge on John Comfort and murdered Oliver Harper instead. After his gun was found hidden in a log and a partial confession was taken, Treadwell was tried, convicted, and hanged. The constable in charge later submitted a bill for twelve and one half cents to the County Board of Supervisors to cover the price of whiskey and "a small file . . . for taking Irons off of Treadwell."[13]

Isaac Hale thus found himself testifying against his neighbor's son, who was near the age of his own boys, Jesse and David. Bizarre as the Treadwell case was, both the murderer and his victim would figure in the future lives of the Hale family. Years later Emma's older brother, Alva, would see one of his daughters married to Jason Treadwell's son; but it was an easy-money scheme of Oliver Harper's that profoundly changed Emma's life.

Not long before Harper's death a distant relative of Emma's, William Hale, had approached Isaac with a peculiar story. A woman claiming to have powers that enabled her to see underground had told William Hale that great treasures were concealed in a hill just northeast of Isaac's house.[14] Persons with such powers were commonly called "peepers" and many people took them seriously. William Hale began digging in the specified area. The work was slow and difficult for a man who had an aversion to hard physical labor. Not wealthy enough himself to hire help, yet sure there would be riches to share with a partner, he talked Oliver Harper into financing the dig. Harper's untimely death suspended the operation for a time, but exciting rumors about buried treasure still swept through Harmony.

Josiah Stowell lived across the river in South Bainbridge, New York. He was one of the many men of good reputation and adequate means who convinced himself that treasure did, indeed, lie hidden beneath the soil. Stowell became William Hale's new partner. Certain that the early Spanish explorers had discovered a silver mine and covered it with earth to hide it, Josiah worked on the site with William Hale but realized that progress would be faster if they hired men to help. For some time Stowell had known a farmer by the name of

Smith who lived farther north in New York and he believed that one of Smith's sons had extraordinary powers. The men in that family were at least six feet tall, strong, and with reputations as hard workers. The combination seemed ideal to William Hale and Josiah Stowell.[15]

Because Elizabeth Hale's tavern was close to the work site, Josiah Stowell made arrangements with her to board some men and left for northern New York to hire them. Each previous fall he had traveled to the Smith home to buy their wheat. This year a letter preceded his visit outlining the digging operation and offering employment to the Smith men.[16] When Stowell returned to Harmony after his buying trip to upstate New York a new group of boarders came with him and entered the Hale house in November 1825. One tall, fair, blue-eyed man named Joseph Smith stood among them. These were the money diggers.

Boarders at the Hale house meant income above the wages of Emma's brothers and revenue received from farm produce and wild game. By November heavy outdoor work was almost completed for the year, and the warm kitchen became the social and economic center of the farmstead. Men with hearty appetites filled the room with banter and conversation. Elizabeth Hale, aided by her daughters, efficiently presided over the kitchen. While Emma moved from hearth to table, helping her mother serve the men, she no doubt noticed the remarkable resemblance between the Smith father and son. The senior Smith stood two inches above his six-foot-tall son and they both had similar coloring and strong, well-proportioned bodies.

The younger Joseph's hair was changing from the sandy color of his youth to light brown. Emma quite likely thought he was nice-looking, perhaps even handsome if one observed him straight on. From the side the slope of his forehead gave his nose the appearance of being too large. He limped slightly as he walked. Later, when they were better acquainted, Joseph probably told her how he acquired the limp and related accounts of his childhood, his family, and his work. He also must have described to her an unusual experience of having a vision several years earlier in a grove of trees near his father's farm.

Joseph's background of English ancestry was similar to Emma's and, by coincidence, his parents, too, had married in Vermont. Lucy Mack brought a dowry of a thousand dollars cash to her marriage to Joseph Smith, Sr., in contrast to Elizabeth Lewis's poverty. The Smiths farmed the rocky soil of Vermont with high optimism until the drought and hard frosts forced them to sell the farm near Randolph and relocate on the rented acreage of Lucy's parents near Sharon, Vermont. They paid their debts with Lucy's money and began again but without capital. On December 23, 1805, Lucy gave birth to their fifth child, a son whom they named Joseph after his father. Their first child died at birth, but Alvin, Hyrum, and Sophronia were older than Joseph. Samuel Harrison, another son Ephraim who lived only eleven days, and William were all born to the Smiths before the family moved to Lebanon, New Hampshire, in 1811.

This move seemed propitious until a typhoid epidemic swept the region in 1812. Seven-year-old Joseph was ill with the fever and developed complications that left him nearly crippled and caused the limp apparent to Emma years later. The bone had become infected until the only alternative seemed to be amputation, but Lucy would not hear of such a drastic measure and the child bravely suffered without anesthetic through an operation that enabled him to keep his leg.[17]

Lucy had given birth to two more children, Katherine and Don Carlos, by 1816 when the "year without a summer" forced a mass migration of ruined farmers who left Vermont in such numbers that the dearth was felt for decades. Joseph, Sr., went to western New York and settled in Palmyra. Lucy sold what belongings she could and followed with the children. Caleb Howard, the man her husband had hired to drive his family to Palmyra, New York, turned out to be irresponsible and was short-tempered with the children. When they reached Utica, New York, Howard had used up most of the money. Seeing no more profit in the venture, he began throwing Lucy's belongings out of the wagon. Joseph watched as his mother confronted Howard in front of a crowd. She forbade him to touch her team, dismissed the man, and took charge herself, financing the remainder of their journey by selling their household goods along the way. Lucy finally reached her husband with few belongings and two cents in cash.

The senior Joseph had found a place to house his family temporarily near the center of Palmyra. Lucy painted designs on oilcloth and baked cakes, gingerbread, and other pastries to sell with beer and boiled eggs. The sign by the door, CAKE AND BEER SHOP, advertised the little business. Young Joseph and the smaller children sold the cakes from a small cart in the streets of Palmyra. Family members hired out for various kinds of farm work. Within a year they had made almost all the down payment on a hundred acres of land about two miles south of Palmyra. The Smiths agreed to pay one hundred dollars a year to a New York City land speculator. The last payment was due by the end of 1825, setting the total cost for the farm at around nine hundred dollars. The Smith family moved into a small log cabin on their own land.

It took most settlers a year to clear the first ten acres of land and have it ready for crops. Lucy remembered that her husband, aided by the three older boys, Alvin, Hyrum, and Joseph, cleared "something like thirty acres of land . . . that first year." Over the next few years those acres increased to sixty. The farm had an abundance of sugar maple trees. Their yearly production of sugar was about a thousand pounds. Joseph, Sr., saw a market for sap buckets and barrels and put his skill as a cooper to work in the winter when the farm work was not so demanding. On this farm Lucy gave birth to their ninth and last child, named Lucy, in 1821.

John Heald, d.1662

Dorothy Andrews

John Vinton, 1620-1664

Ann, d.1664

John Hodge, 1643-1692/4

Henry Denslow, d.1676

William Bunnell
Ann Wilmot, d.1654
Peter Mallory, d.1697/1701
Mary Preston, 1629-1690
Andrew Ward, 1597-1659
Hester Sherman, 1606-1665
John Meigs, 1612-1672
Thomasine Fry
Thomas Beach, d.1662
Sarah Platt, b.1670
Jonathan Royce, d.1690
Mary Spinning, d.1658

Richard Towner, d.1727

Mary

Thomas Barnes, 1623-1693
Mary
John Frost, 1642-1707
Mercy Paine
George Lewis
Sarah Jenkins
Henry Cobb, 1596-1679
Patience Hurst, d.1648
Thomas Huckins, d.1679
Rose Hullier, 1616-1687
John Chipman, 1614/21-1708
Hope Howland, 1629-1683
John Maltby
Mary Williamson

Thomas Lord, 1585-1667
Dorothy Bird, 1589-1676
Wm. Buckland, d.1683
Mary Bosworth, 1611-1687
William Tuttle, d.1673
Elizabeth, 1612-1684
Thomas Powell, d.1681
Priscilla
Samuel Hotchkiss, d.1663
Elizabeth Clevery, d.1681
Robert Talmage, d.1662
Sarah Nash, b.1648
William Bradley, d.1690
Alice Prichard, d.1692

John Chedsey, 1611-1688
Elizabeth, d.1688
John Thompson, 1645-1692/3
Priscilla Powell, d.1726

├ Gershom Heald, 1647-1717

├ Ann Vinton, 1656-1698

├ Thomas Hodge, 1669-1712

├ Susanna Denslow, b.1646

├ Benjamin Bunnell, 1642-1696

├ Rebecca Mallory, 1649-1691

├ Andrew Ward, 1645-1690

├ Tryal Meigs, 1646-1690

├ John Beach, 1655-1709

├ Mary Royce, b.1658

├ Judith Bunnell, b.1672

├ William Ward, 1678-1769

├ Lettice Beach, b.1679

├ Samuel Towner, 1691-1784/5

├ Thomas Barnes, 1653-1712

├ Abigail Frost, 1670-1746

├ Edward Lewis, d.1703

├ Hannah Cobb, 1639-1736

├ John Huckins, 1649-1678

├ Hope Chipman, 1652-1728

├ William Maltby

├ Mary

├ Rebecca Barnes, 1691/2-1728

├ John Lewis, 1666-1738/9

├ Elizabeth Huckins, 1671-1741

├ John Maltby, 1670-1727

├ William Lord, 1623-1678

├ Lydia Brown

├ Thomas Tuttle, 1635-1710

├ Hannah Powell, 1641-1710

├ Samuel Hotchkiss, 1645-1705

├ Sarah Talmage, b.1652

├ Isaac Bradley, 1651-1712/3

│ Elizabeth, 1656-1712/3

├ Ebenezer Chedsey, 1665/6-1726

├ Priscilla Thompson, 1671-1728

├ Hannah Lord, b.1670/78

├ Caleb Tuttle, 1674-1751

├ Mary Hotchkiss, 1679/80-1723

├ William Bradley, 1682-1727

├ Elizabeth Chedsey, b.1693

ANCESTRY OF EMMA HALE SMITH (1804-1879)

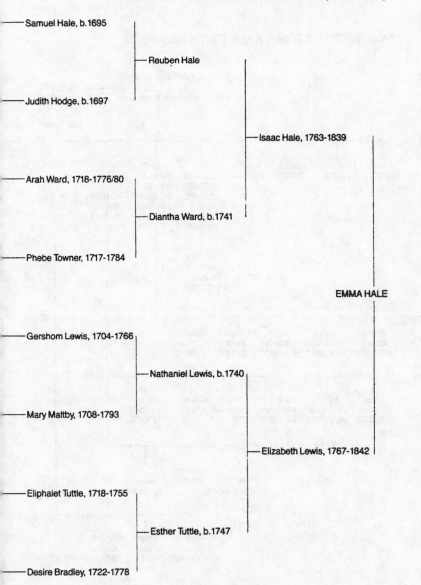

Samuel Hale, b.1695

Reuben Hale

Judith Hodge, b.1697

Isaac Hale, 1763-1839

Arah Ward, 1718-1776/80

Diantha Ward, b.1741

Phebe Towner, 1717-1784

EMMA HALE

Gershom Lewis, 1704-1766

Nathaniel Lewis, b.1740

Mary Maltby, 1708-1793

Elizabeth Lewis, 1767-1842

Eliphalet Tuttle, 1718-1755

Esther Tuttle, b.1747

Desire Bradley, 1722-1778

POSTERITY OF EMMA HALE SMITH (1804-1879)

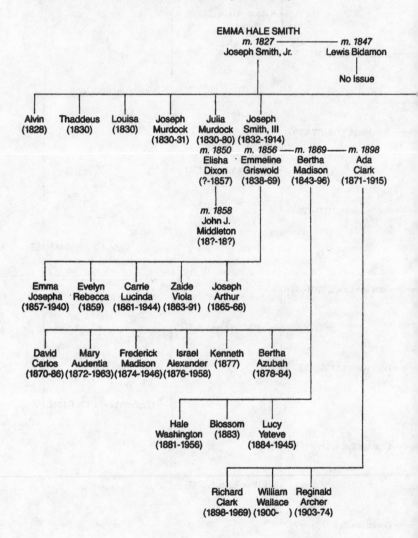

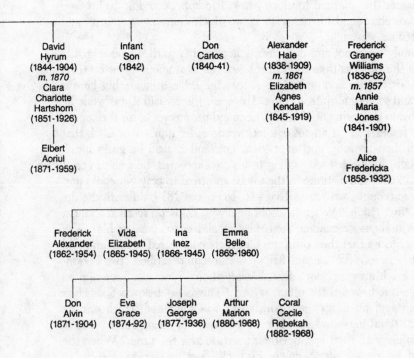

David
Hyrum
(1844-1904)
m. 1870
Clara
Charlotte
Hartshorn
(1851-1926)

Infant
Son
(1842)

Don
Carlos
(1840-41)

Alexander
Hale
(1838-1909)
m. 1861
Elizabeth
Agnes
Kendall
(1845-1919)

Frederick
Granger
Williams
(1836-62)
m. 1857
Annie
Maria
Jones
(1841-1901)

Elbert
Aoriul
(1871-1959)

Alice
Fredericka
(1858-1932)

Frederick
Alexander
(1862-1954)

Vida
Elizabeth
(1865-1945)

Ina
Inez
(1866-1945)

Emma
Belle
(1869-1960)

Don
Alvin
(1871-1904)

Eva
Grace
(1874-92)

Joseph
George
(1877-1936)

Arthur
Marion
(1880-1968)

Coral
Cecile
Rebekah
(1882-1968)

When the Smiths arrived in Palmyra, the entire family was influenced by the religious excitement there. The whole area of western New York gained a reputation for periodic revivals throughout the first half of the nineteenth century, and historians labeled the area west of the Catskill and Adirondack mountains the "Burned-over District." Longing to "feel and shout like the rest," Joseph later remembered wanting to belong but even at his young age could not overcome his reservations. He watched as various ministers vied for different family members and said he could not understand how so many people professing the same God could create such division within the community. Two issues that plagued fourteen-year-old Joseph, according to his own writings, revolved around his desire to know which church was "right" and how one became "saved."

The family could not afford to pay a schoolteacher so they held school at home, using the Bible as their text. Joseph was not as studious as his brothers and sisters. His mother said he had never read the Bible through, but he was thoughtful and sometimes introspective. However, Joseph said it was while he read the Bible in the spring of 1820 that he found the answer to his theological dilemma in James 1:5. "If any of you lack wisdom, let him ask of God, that giveth to all men liberally, and upbraideth not; and it shall be given him." Simple enough, Joseph felt. According to his own accounts, he walked across the road and knelt near a stump in the woods and tried to pray but could not.

Joseph's accounts, written in 1831–32, 1834, and 1839, differ in the details of this "first vision." When he could finally pray, Joseph recalled seeing a pillar of fire or light descending from heaven and encompassing him. The earliest account says that the Lord Jesus Christ then appeared to him and told him his sins were forgiven. In the 1838 version Joseph described "two Personages, whose brightness and glory defy all description." One addressed him by name and gestured toward the other, saying, "This is my beloved Son. Hear him!" Joseph said he asked them which sect was right and which one he should join. "I was answered that I must join none of them, for . . . they draw near to me with their lips, but their hearts are far from me." When the vision ended, he found himself lying on his back, "looking up into Heaven."[18]

Joseph did not tell his family immediately, but he did tell a Methodist preacher he had met at earlier revival meetings. To Joseph's astonishment, the minister reacted with shock and contempt. William Smith indicated that they had not been aware of animosity from the townspeople until after Joseph let it be known that he had seen a vision. Whether that incident was actually the catalyst or whether Lucy had unknowingly caused the bitter feelings herself is open to speculation. A sociable person, raised in a family with comfortable means, Lucy did without finery in her marriage, although she seldom complained. When the ladies in the community invited her to their tea circles, she was obviously pleased. But when some of the merchants' wives expressed their sympathy because she lived in a small log cabin instead of the finer house "she deserved," Lucy reacted strongly. "I am the wealthiest woman that sits at this table," she said. "I have never prayed for riches of the world, as perhaps you have, but I have always desired that God would enable me to use enough wisdom and forbearance in my family to set good precepts & examples before my children." She went on: "We owe no man; we never distressed any man which circumstance almost invariably attends the Mercantile life so I have no reason to envy those who are engaged. Beside there is none present who have this kind of wealth that have not lately met with a loss of children or othe[r] friends." But unfortunately she spoke personally. "Now as for Mrs. the Minister's lady, I ask you how many nights of the week you are kept awake with anxiety about your sons who are in habitual attendance at the Grog Shop & gambling house."[19] Lucy's report of the incident indicates that she did not intend her remarks to be unkind—only pointed—but they undoubtedly ruffled the feathers of the minister's wife.

Whatever the initial cause, controversy developed around the Smith family. When the minister circulated the vision story, Joseph seemed unprepared for the furor that developed. "Though I was hated and persecuted for saying that I had seen a vision, yet it was true. . . . I was led to say in my heart, why persecute me for telling the truth?" Joseph remained adamant. "I had seen a vision, I knew it, and I knew that God knew it, and I could not deny it, neither dare I do it."[20] Surprisingly, being rebuffed and ridiculed did not make Joseph withdrawn or aloof. Acquaintances described him as a good-natured lad with a "jovial" easy way who seemed to enjoy a host of friends.[21]

More than three years elapsed before he experienced another spiritual manifestation. Then one night he lay awake.[22] He remembered the room suddenly getting lighter and lighter until he could see "a personage" standing in the air near his bed. Dressed in a "loose robe of most exquisite whiteness," the personage said he was a messenger from God. He told Joseph there was a "book deposited, written upon gold plates, giving an account of the former inhabitants of this continent, and the sources from whence they sprang . . . the fullness of the everlasting Gospel was contained in it."[23]

Joseph said he saw the hiding place of the plates as though in a vision, while the messenger named Moroni gave him instructions. The visitor returned twice more that night and appeared in the fields the next day. He told the boy to tell no one but his family of his experience.

According to Joseph's account, he went immediately to the place Moroni had shown him, a hilltop about two miles south of his home. He reported that he then pried up a large rounded stone to find a box underneath made of stone slabs cemented together. Inside he recognized the gold record and "interpreters" called the Urim and Thummim. Joseph said he impulsively assessed the gold and realized financial security lay within his reach, but when he attempted to take the gold plates the messenger appeared and chastised him for wanting "to obtain riches." He told Joseph to return annually for instructions, which Joseph said he did.

Joseph and his older brothers hired out for wages. The extra income from these sons financed the construction of a larger family home which Alvin supervised, but before the house was finished he became ill. A physician medicated him with an overdose of calomel, which lodged in his upper bowel and caused gangrene. He died after a poignant farewell to his family.[24] Joseph would remember this brother in fond and reverent terms, perhaps because Alvin had shown a keen interest in Joseph's visions.

Joseph and Alvin had also worked together. While they were digging a well for a neighbor, Willard Chase, Joseph had found a smooth smoky-colored stone the size of an egg, though not that shape, with light stripes running through it. Chase said *he* had found the stone, not Joseph, and when he believed Joseph could see things in it he wanted it back. Dispute over the stone rankled Chase and he later reentered Joseph's life to exact vengeance.

Money digging, or treasure hunting, was widespread among the rural areas of New York and New England as well as the area of Pennsylvania near the Hales'. The phenomena influenced Joseph, too. Those around him who believed in glass-looking and divining treasures were religious people who easily mixed folk magic and treasure seeking with Christianity. For example, Willard Chase was a devout Methodist—his obituary said he was a minister; Josiah Stowell was a respected member of the Presbyterian Church and a reputable man in his community; the Smiths also were buffeted by the prevailing folklore. The discovery of the seer stone and the reported visit of Moroni came in fairly close succession, perhaps making it difficult for them to sort out the differences between the spiritual and the superstitious. Most of those who would accuse Joseph of money digging were participators themselves but claimed the Smiths were an indolent family and what little income they had came from hiring out as money diggers.

Although the family worked in a variety of ways for economic support, their wheat crop provided their basic income. They contracted yearly with buyers like Josiah Stowell for its sale. He knew that Joseph also had a peep stone and wanted the young man to work for him because "he possessed certain keys, by which he could discern things invisible to the natural eye."[25] William Hale wrote to the Smiths about digging for him, then Stowell, followed the letter with a visit. Lucy remembered young Joseph trying to talk Stowell out of the enterprise, but the man insisted. Joseph, Sr., seemed more enthusiastic about the prospects of digging than his son. Another payment on the farm was due and Stowell offered high wages. So father and son, along with several others, accompanied Josiah Stowell to the Hale farm in Pennsylvania. And although Joseph would never locate a buried treasure in Harmony, Pennsylvania, he did find Emma Hale.

Isaac Hale viewed the money-digging activities with conflicting emotions. On the one hand, his farming experience taught him that the earth rarely harbored great riches. But when his neighbor, Josiah Stowell, believed peep stones could reveal hidden treasures and invested money in the enterprise, Isaac suspected Josiah knew something he did not. Both men were comfortably well off, but neither was wealthy. If Josiah Stowell found a fortune under Isaac's nose, the subtle social structure existing among the local farmers would be altered in Stowell's favor. It would humiliate Isaac if his lazy relative, William Hale, found a treasure. Isaac Hale guarded both his options. He allowed the money digging to take place under his watchful eye but kept himself a respectable distance from the operation.

On November 1, 1825, Isaac witnessed an agreement between the workers and Josiah Stowell which formed a digging company. The Smiths' share amounted to two elevenths of the findings, whether it be in ore or "coined money and bars or ingots of Gold or Silver."[26]

As the money digging progressed with no sign of treasure, Isaac seemed to place the responsibility for the whole operation on Joseph. Isaac said, "Young Smith gave the moneydiggers great encouragement, at first, but when they had arrived in digging too near the place where he had stated an immense treasure would be found—he said the enchantment was so powerful that he could not see it." Several years later Isaac referred to his son-in-law as a "careless young man—not very well educated, and very saucy and insolent to his father."[27] There is no account of Joseph's father ever registering that complaint against his son. What Isaac interpreted as insolence may have been a disagreement over whether or not to continue with the digging operation. According to his mother's account, Joseph had not wanted to participate in the first place. Soon he succeeded in getting Stowell to end the project.

Emma did not see Joseph from the same perspective as her father. She found him pleasant, thoughtful, and open, without being rowdy. Josiah Stowell believed "he was a fine likely young man & at that time did not Profess religion he was not a Profain man although I did once in a while hear him Swair he never gambled to my knowledge. . . . I well know he was no Horse Jocky for he was no Judge of Horses I sold him one that is old. . . . I never new him to git drunk I believe he would now and then take a sip. . . . I state this for fact that any thing from what I have said about Joseph Smith that is wors than I say is fals & untru."[28]

When Josiah Stowell abandoned the digging enterprise, Emma did not have to say good-bye to Joseph, for Stowell hired him as a farmhand and to cut timber.[29] He crossed the Susquehanna River to visit her. Probably acutely conscious of the difference between his education and Emma's, Joseph found time to go to school while he lived at the Stowells'. When Josiah did not have work for him he traveled three miles along the river to Colesville to work for Joseph Knight, who thought Joseph was "the best hand he ever hired."

Emma had attracted Joseph's interest from their first meeting. "Fine looking, smart, [and] a good singer," is how a visitor at the Hales described her, "and she often got the power."[30] What the "power" was the visitor did not elaborate upon, but Emma did have deep faith and knew the Bible well. When Joseph told her of his vision in the woods she believed him.

Once Emma and Joseph agreed to marry, they sought Isaac's approval. Apparently anticipating the young man's approach, Isaac gave a thundering refusal. His reason was that Joseph was a stranger.[31] It may be that Emma's father had his eye on a neighbor's son for his daughter and that he disapproved of Joseph's money digging. Isaac Hale's "no" was absolute.

If Emma was pleading her case with her father, Joseph's arrest and subsequent trial at Bainbridge, New York, in March 1826 did not help. Mrs. Stowell's nephew had formally charged Joseph with being a disorderly person and an impostor. While the disorderly complaint was not addressed at the trial, Joseph's professed ability to peer through his stone and divine the location of buried treasure was. Joseph testified "that he had a certain stone, which he occasionally used to locate hidden treasures in the bowels of the earth," and lost property, but that he had given up the activity because it made his eyes sore. He said he did not solicit that business and would prefer to have nothing to do with it.

When Josiah Stowell took the stand he enthusiastically endorsed Joseph's ability to use the stone, stating he "positively knew that the prisoner could tell, and professed the art of seeing those valuable treasures through the medium of [the] stone."[32] Other witnesses testified that Joseph's actions were designed to deceive. One source said the Court found the defendant guilty, another indicated he was acquitted. Still another stated, ". . . because he was a minor . . . they hoped he might reform [and] he was allowed to escape."[33] Joseph's involvement in money digging continued to plague his reputation. Of this period in his life he wrote, "During this time, as is common to most, or all youths, I fell into many vices and follies; . . . I have not . . . been guilty of wronging or injuring any man or society of men; and those imperfections to which I alude, and for which I often had occasion to lament, were a light, and too often, vain mind, exhibiting a foolish and trifling conversation."[34] After the trial ended Joseph turned his mind to Emma. If she hoped Joseph's employment with Josiah Stowell would change his standing in Isaac's eyes, it was in vain. Joseph was less welcome in the Hale home than he had ever been. Emma's brothers joined forces with her father and teased Joseph so incessantly while on a fishing trip that he threw off his coat and offered to fight them.[35]

The couple had their allies, however. One wintry day Emma saw a high-stepping horse pull a cutter to a stop in front of her house. The tall, well-dressed driver was Joseph. Joseph Knight had outfitted him with a new suit of clothes and loaned him the horse and sleigh, enabling him to visit Emma in more style than was his previous custom. Joseph asked again for Emma's hand in marriage and Isaac again refused. When Josiah Stowell and Joseph Knight went north to Palmyra for wheat in the fall, Joseph, still stinging from the rebuff, went home with them.

He arrived in time to see his brother Hyrum marry Jerusha Barden—who was the same age as Emma—on November 2, 1826. The wedding undoubtedly stirred Joseph's emotions. He missed Emma and was determined to have her. Lucy recalled: "He had felt so lonely ever since Alvins death that he had come to the conclusion of getting married if we had no objections and he thought that no young woman that he ever was acquainted with was better calculated to render the man of her choice happy than Miss Emma Hale . . . whom he had been extremely fond of since his first introduction to her."[36] Joseph's father remembered Emma from his own brief stay at her house and was pleased with his son's choice. He not only gave his blessing but invited Joseph to bring her home to live with them.

When Joseph went that fall to the hill named Cumorah, the "personage" told him he could have the record the following September "if he brot with him the right person" and indicated that Joseph would know who that was. Joseph Knight, in whom Joseph later confided the story, said the young man "looked into his glass and found it was Emma Hale Daughter of old Mr. Hale of Pensulvany."[37]

The last payment on the farm was soon due. Stowell and Knight had agreed to advance the Smiths the price of next year's wheat, but Joseph, Sr., had to go to Pennsylvania for the money. Lucy said about her husband and son, "They then concluded to set off together—one for money, the other for a wife." Part way to Pennsylvania a letter containing disturbing news interrupted their travel. Calvin Stoddard, the carpenter the Smiths had hired to finish the house, had convinced the land agent that the two Josephs had run away to escape the debt. Stoddard had thereupon offered to pay the full price for the land in exchange for the deed and the agent accepted. Joseph and his father turned back to Palmyra immediately. Eventually the senior Smith persuaded the agent to sell the farm to a third-party buyer who would allow them to live there as tenants. In an unusual twist the carpenter, Calvin Stoddard, soon fell in love with Sophronia Smith and married her on December 30, 1827.

As soon as the situation settled at home, Joseph returned to Pennsylvania for some unfinished business of his own. Emma accepted his proposal at Stowell's on January 18, 1827. After their hasty marriage the couple traveled north to Palmyra and moved in with the Smith family. Hyrum's wife, married almost three months, had smoothed the way for Emma's entry into the family. Lucy said Jerusha was "one of the most excellent of women, with whom I had seen much enjoyment." When Emma arrived, Lucy remembered, "I hoped for as much happiness with my second daughter-in-law, as I had received from the society of the first, and there was no reason why I should expect anything to the contrary."[38]

Emma gave her father time to calm his anger before she wrote from New York and asked for her clothes, furniture, and cows. Isaac replied that they were safely cared for and at her disposal. In August she and Joseph hired Peter Ingersoll to drive them to Harmony to get her belongings. The reunion was not pleasant. Isaac's eyes brimmed with tears as he leveled his gaze at his new son-in-law: "You have stolen my daughter and married her. I had much rather have followed her to her grave."[39]

Isaac never forgave Joseph for the affront to his family name, although he managed to reconcile himself somewhat when he secured a promise from Joseph that the money digging was over. Emma and Joseph left Harmony with her property and an invitation from Isaac to return to the Hale farm. The offer, though appreciated, was not nearly so attractive then as it would be in December when they would need a refuge.

While he and Emma rode in Peter Ingersoll's wagon as it bumped along the rutted roads toward Manchester, Joseph told Ingersoll that he intended to keep his promise to Isaac Hale. "It will be hard for me," he said, "for they will all oppose, as they want me to look in the stone for them to dig money."[40]

Not long after their return from Harmony, Joseph went to Manchester village on business for his father but did not return at the appointed time. Lucy explained to Emma that several years earlier someone had shot at Joseph in front of the house, but the bullet missed its intended target. Who fired the shot or why was unknown, but the family was uneasy whenever Joseph was late. Now Emma and the others waited with apprehension. When Joseph finally arrived and sank into a chair exhausted, his father asked where he had been. Joseph answered soberly, "I have taken the severest chastisement that I have ever had in my life. As I passed by the hill of Cumorah, where the plates are, the angel met me, and said that I had not been engaged enough in the work of the Lord; that the time had come for the Record to be brought forth."[41] Nobody doubted his word.

On September 20, 1827, Josiah Stowell and Joseph Knight arrived at the Smiths' home to buy their usual load of wheat. Emma, eager for news from home, inquired about her family and friends. When the guests retired that night, Emma and Joseph quietly retreated to their own room to prepare to go out. Joseph slipped downstairs to find his mother working in the kitchen. He asked her for a chest with a lock and key and Lucy was concerned when she did not have one.

"Never mind," he assured her, "I can do very well for the present without it—be calm—all is right." A few minutes later Emma came out in her bonnet and riding dress. She joined Joseph outside and Mr. Knight's horse and wagon lurched forward down the road toward the hill Cumorah. There Emma waited with the wagon while he climbed up the hill and disappeared in the darkness. Before long Joseph reappeared carrying a bundle wrapped in his coat, and Emma saw the outline of what he told her was a book of thin gold sheets inscribed with ancient characters. He climbed into the wagon beside her and turned the horse toward home, stopping halfway there. Emma watched again as he disappeared into the blackness of the forest with the bundle in his arms. He hid the treasure in a hollowed-out log, then covered the hole with pieces of bark.

The venture took several hours and by the time Emma and Joseph rode into the yard Lucy had tried to placate everyone. Joseph Knight was certain some thief had stolen his horse and wagon and Joseph, Sr., kept asking where Joseph was and why he did not join them for breakfast. The clatter of horse and wagon outside the kitchen door relieved everyone.

Emma and Joseph said nothing about where they had been. Lucy worried that her son had broken some commandment and had been denied the plates. Her anxiety mounted until she left the room to avoid blurting out her questions. Joseph followed his mother to reassure her and show her what she described as the "interpreter." It consisted of "two smooth three cornered diamonds set in glass, and the glasses were set in silver bows, which were connected with each other in much the same way as old-fashioned spectacles." The breastplate which held the interpreter was concave in shape, with two metal straps fastening it to the hips and shoulders. It appeared to have been made to fit a very large man.

Joseph said the messenger, Moroni, had charged him with the safety of the plates when he retrieved them from Cumorah. When his father asked to see them, Joseph explained that Moroni forbade showing them until he translated the characters, but later Emma and the family would handle the plates through the wrappings and riffle the thin metallic pages. William Smith said they were heavier than wood or stone, estimating their weight at around sixty pounds.

Soon the neighborhood heard that Joseph now had the gold plates. Some people would eventually sign affidavits that the plates were a hoax; others believed Joseph. A neighbor stated, "Yes; I rather think he did [have them]. Why not he find something as well as anybody else. . . . In Illinois and Ohio, in mounds there, they have discovered copper plates since. . . . Now, I never saw the Book of Mormon—don't know anything about it, nor care; and don't know as it was ever translated from the plates . . . but all this don't prove that Smith never got any plates."[42] Willard Chase, who had argued earlier about the peep stone, heard about them and organized his friends to take them by force. Joseph, Sr., inadvertently overheard the plans. Joseph was digging a well for a widow in the nearby town of Macedon. In his absence Joseph, Sr., anxiously asked Emma if his son had moved the plates or if she knew their whereabouts and told her about Chase's plotting. Emma suggested that if the

Lord meant Joseph to have the plates the manipulations of men would be unsuccessful, but she volunteered to warn Joseph. William Smith caught the only horse available—a stray, marked as the law required with a hickory branch bent around its neck. Emma, newly pregnant, mounted and rode to the work site. When Emma told Joseph about Willard Chase's plans, he borrowed a horse and rode back with her to retrieve the plates from their hiding place in the woods. He returned to the house battered, exhausted, and with a dislocated thumb, explaining that he had been attacked three different times on his way back. Joseph hurriedly secured the plates in a chest his brother Hyrum supplied and hid them under the hearthstone. The immediate crisis passed after Chase and his looters searched the house in vain.

During October and November bands of curious, skeptical people disrupted the Smith household with threats, rumors, and evening raids. Former partners of Joseph claimed a share in the mysterious bounty. Willard Chase's sister peered into her peep stone to locate the plates. Joseph moved them to a pile of flax in the loft of his father's cooper shop, then put the empty chest under the floorboards. Directed by the peep stone, Willard Chase's group ransacked the shop and smashed the chest without finding the plates.[43]

Martin Harris, a well-to-do farmer who lived on the other side of Palmyra, had been a close and trusted friend of the family. He had shown a particular interest in the story of the plates, and when he heard that Joseph had them he enthusiastically climbed Cumorah's slopes and dug holes, looking for more treasure. Joseph's mother said Mrs. Harris was peculiar, hard of hearing, and somewhat suspicious. Dolly Harris made a nuisance of herself in the Smith house by badgering Joseph about the plates and burdening the family with her strange dreams. She gave twenty-eight dollars to Joseph, who accepted the money but made sure he signed a note for the amount.

Clearly, Joseph could never translate under such chaotic conditions. Isaac Hale's offer to live at Harmony now seemed attractive. In December Emma's brother Alva came to help them move. When Alva accompanied Joseph to Palmyra on business, Martin Harris approached Joseph with a small bag of silver. "Here, Mr. Smith, is fifty dollars. I give this to you to do the Lord's work with." He paused. "No, I give it to the Lord for his own work." Joseph insisted on giving Harris a promissory note and asked Alva to sign with him. But Harris would not accept a note and called on bystanders to witness that he gave the money freely. When word spread that Joseph was leaving, Willard Chase and others united in a final effort to get the "gold Bible" before it was out of their reach. Their scheme broke down when the men squabbled over who should take charge.[44]

At Harris's suggestion, Emma and Joseph left two days earlier than planned. For extra security, Alva Hale helped Joseph cut large clubs for each of them. With loaded wagon, Alva as their driver, and the plates hidden in a barrel of beans, Emma and Joseph began the trek to Harmony and Emma's girlhood home.

2

The "Elect Lady"

1827–1830

Returning to the tranquil scene of her childhood, Emma anticipated peace in the Hale home, which had not been searched by marauders or been invaded by the curious, as had the Smith home. Undoubtedly she saw Alva's help with the move down from New York as an indication that her father had forgiven her, but her illusion of peace soon shattered. Alva told his father Joseph had found gold plates and brought them with him to translate. A skeptical Isaac asked to see them. "I was shown a box in which it is said they were contained, which had to all appearances, been used as a glass box of the common window glass," he said. "I was allowed to feel the weight of the box . . . [but] I was not allowed to look. . . . After this, I became dissatisfied, and informed him that if there was any thing in my house of that description, which I could not be allowed to see, he must take it away; if he did not, I was determined to see it."[1]

Emma could see that living in her parents' home would be difficult. She and Joseph moved nearby into the house her brother Jesse left when he moved to Illinois. The sturdy frame structure built by Isaac and his sons had ample room for two people awaiting the birth of a first child. Emma had modest comfort and a degree of privacy, two things she would often live without. She and Joseph negotiated to buy the house and thirteen acres of land from Isaac Hale for two hundred dollars. Isaac did not expect immediate payment but the two men agreed to the terms. The confrontation with Isaac over the gold plates destroyed Joseph's hope of acceptance by Emma's family. In good faith, he had assured Isaac the summer before that he had given up money digging. But no matter how Emma and Joseph explained the plates, to Isaac the whole thing smacked of treasure hunting. No doubt hoping to convince Isaac of his acceptability, Joseph then made a move that further embarrassed himself and the Hales.

Emma's uncle, Nathaniel Lewis, preached as a lay minister of the local Methodist Episcopal church. His congregation met in the homes of the members for Sunday services. On Wednesdays a regular circuit preacher visited Harmony. In the spring or summer of 1828 Joseph asked the circuit rider if his name could be included on the class roll of the church. Joseph "presented himself in a very serious and humble manner," and the minister obliged him.

When Emma's cousin, Joseph Lewis, discovered Joseph's name on the roll, he "thought it was a disgrace to the church to have a practicing necromancer" as a member. He took the matter up with a friend, and the following Sunday, when Joseph and Emma arrived for church, the two men steered Joseph aside and into the family shop. "They told him plainly that such character as he . . . could not be a member of the church unless he broke off his sins by repentance, made public confession, renounced his fraudulent and hypocritical practices, and gave some evidence that he intended to reform and conduct himself somewhat nearer like a christian than he had done. They gave him his choice to go before the class, and publicly ask to have his name stricken from the class book, or stand a disciplinary investigation." Joseph refused to comply with the humiliating demands and withdrew from the class. His name, however, stayed on the roll for about six more months, either from oversight or because Emma's brother-in-law, Michael Morse, who taught the class, did not know of the confrontation. When Joseph did not seek full membership, Morse finally dropped his name.[2]

As winter settled in, Joseph turned his attention to translating the plates. Although Emma never saw the plates, she believed he had them. "They lay in a box under our bed for months but I never felt at liberty to look at them," she reported in later years.[3] She said they were sometimes on a table in her living room, "wrapped in a small linen table cloth, which I had given him to fold them in. I once felt of the plates, as they thus lay on the table, tracing their outline and shape. They seemed to be pliable like thick paper, and would rustle with a metallic sound when the edges were moved by the thumb, as one does sometimes thumb the edges of a book." Emma lifted and moved the plates as she dusted around them.[4]

If Emma's faith in Joseph was remarkable, so was Joseph's faith in Emma. He told her that no one would be allowed to see the plates until they were translated, yet he did not hide them from her. If the plates were a hoax, she could have easily exposed Joseph as an impostor. "I believe he was everything he professed to be," she would say at the age of seventy-four.

When Joseph began the translation he needed someone to write for him as he dictated. Emma began her role as scribe. The schoolteacher in Emma recognized Joseph's struggle with written English. "He could not pronounce the word Sariah," she said. Although Joseph's own reading of the scriptures had been sporadic at best, Emma knew the Bible well and read it often. Once, as he translated, the narrative mentioned the walls of Jerusalem. Joseph stopped. "Emma," he asked, "did Jerusalem have walls surrounding it?" Emma told him it did. "O, I thought I was deceived,"[5] was his reply.

Emma recalled that at first Joseph used the interpreters, called the Urim and Thummim, but later he placed a smooth dark stone in his hat, then put his face in the hat to block the light. When asked if Joseph could have written the story privately, then dictated it, pretending he was translating from the plates, Emma retorted, "Joseph Smith could neither write nor dictate a coherent and well-worded letter; let alone dictating a book like the Book of Mormon . . . it is marvelous to me . . . as much as to any one. . . . I am satisfied that no man could have dictated the writing of the manuscripts unless he was inspired; for, when [I was] acting as his scribe, [he] would dictate to me for hour after hour; and when returning after meals, or after interruptions, he would at once begin where he had left off, without either seeing the manuscript or having any portion of it read to him." Emma continued, "It would have been improbable that a learned man could do this; and, for one so ignorant and unlearned as he was, it was simply impossible."[6]

When Emma's household duties required her attention, her brother Reuben occasionally acted as scribe. The rest of the Hale family apparently remained skeptical, if not outright hostile, and Reuben's involvement was brief. The whole affair was more than Isaac could abide. "The manner in which he pretended to read and interpret," Isaac stated, "was the same as when he looked for the money-diggers."[7]

By midwinter Emma's and Joseph's stores had dwindled. To ask Emma's family for assistance was out of the question, so they made the twenty-eight-mile trip up the Susquehanna to Colesville to see their friend Joseph Knight, Sr., who wrote, "He Could not translate But little Being poor and nobody to write for him But his wife and she Could not do much and take Care of her house. . . . His wifes father and familey ware all against him and would not help him." Ignoring resistance to Joseph from his own family, Knight gave them "some little provisions and some few things out of the Store apair of shoes and three Dollars in money to help him a little."[8]

Martin Harris visited Emma and Joseph in the winter. Willing to help financially, Harris "looked to make money from the venture, but also said he expected it to resolve many controversial points of doctrine."[9] He suggested that Joseph let him take a sample of his work to scholars who could verify it. Joseph agreed. On an eight-by-eleven-inch piece of unlined paper he copied vertical lines of characters in brown ink and signed his name.[10] Harris said he then traveled to New York City and showed the copy to two men, a Dr. Mitchill, probably Samual Latham Mitchill, who was both a classical scholar and a scientist, and Charles Anthon of Columbia College, a professor of ancient languages. According to Harris, Anthon pronounced the characters authentic and correctly translated and gave Harris a certificate. When Harris told him divine intervention was involved, he took the statement back and tore it up. Anthon said he remembered the visit from Harris, but he had not verified the translation. Nonetheless, Martin Harris reported his findings to Joseph and returned home to put his affairs in order so he could go to Harmony and assist in the translation.

Harris's homecoming was less than joyous. His wife, Dolly, suspected that Martin would throw his money away in helping Joseph and insisted on going to Harmony too. They arrived at Emma's and Joseph's home in April. Dolly immediately "commenced ransacking every nook and corner of the house— chests, trunks, cupboards" in search of the plates until Joseph hid them outside. She concluded that Joseph had buried them so she searched outdoors. When she came back to Emma's kitchen empty-handed she had an excuse. "Are there any snakes around here in the winter?" she asked.

"No," was Emma's reply.

"I have been walking around in the woods," Dolly reported, "and a tremendous black snake stuck up his head before me, and commenced hissing at me."[11]

Emma may have warned Dolly that she was intruding where she had no right, for Mrs. Harris took lodging with a neighbor for a while before returning home. But she told the neighbor Joseph was an impostor with designs upon her husband's property. Undoubtedly the word reached the Hales, who were not accustomed to having their family objects of gossip and ridicule.

By June, Joseph and Martin Harris brought the number of translated pages to one hundred sixteen. Perhaps, Harris reasoned, if his wife could see what they had accomplished she would believe the work was worthwhile. He begged Joseph to let him take the manuscript back to Palmyra with him. Finally Joseph said he had asked the Lord three times and Harris could take the translated pages if he promised to show them to no one but his family. Harris agreed.

On June 15, 1828, the day after Harris left, Emma went into labor that was long and extremely difficult. Her first child, a son, lived only three hours. The saddened parents named him Alvin, after Joseph's deceased brother,[12] and buried him east of the house. The midwife who attended Emma, her sister-in-law Rhoda Skinner, indicated that this first child had birth defects. Sophia Lewis, probably a cousin of Emma's, also said that she "was present at the birth of this child, and that it was still-born and very much deformed."[13] For over two weeks Emma hovered near death while Joseph kept vigil at her bedside.

As Emma gained strength Joseph became anxious about the manuscript. He did not mention his concern to Emma "for fear of agitating her mind too much for the health of her body," but his despondency worried her. "I shall not be at ease until I know something about what Mr. Harris is doing,"[14] she said, and urged him to go to Palmyra. At first he protested but Emma insisted and Joseph, "seeing her so cheerful and so willing to have him leave," finally decided to go.

Joseph found Harris in distress; he had lost the manuscript. Lucy reported Joseph's reaction as he clenched his hands together. "My God!" he cried. "All is lost, all is lost. . . . Must I . . . return to my wife with such a tale as this? I dare not do it lest I should kill her."[15] Despite his promise to Joseph, Martin Harris had shown the prized manuscript to everyone who came by until he opened the drawer one day and found it gone. The prime suspect was his vindictive wife. Joseph returned to Emma empty-handed and told her that he had been severely chastised by the messenger, Moroni, who explained that he was not to retranslate the same material but use a second account to avoid being trapped by inconsistencies.

As autumn's red and gold faded from the hills around Harmony, Joseph's parents arrived, anxious over Emma's health and without news for more than two months. It was Lucy's first trip to Harmony. "Emma writes for me," Joseph told his mother, "but the angel said that the Lord would send me a scribe." Lucy satisfied herself that all was well with her son and his wife, then found Emma's family "pleasantly situated and living in good style," and deemed them "intelligent and highly respectable." After three months the senior Smiths returned to Palmyra confident that their son had married well.[16]

In the spring Joseph's younger brother, Samuel, came to help with the tilling and planting and brought with him a young schoolteacher named Oliver Cowdery who had boarded with the Smith family. Cowdery was twenty-two. About five feet, five inches tall, he carried his slight frame with a loose, easy walk. His Roman nose gave balance to his clean-shaven face with its prominent lower jaw. He had dark brown eyes, a high forehead, and a quick smile. Two days after his arrival Oliver Cowdery was at work with quill in hand. At last Joseph had a full-time scribe.

Early spring is a lean season for those who work the land, but Joseph was especially pressed in 1829. Supplies were now scarce and he had yet to harvest a crop. Joseph and Oliver walked again to Colesville, New York, to see Joseph Knight, Sr., only to find him gone. After several discouraging days inquiring for work, they returned home to find the generous Mr. Knight ahead of them, unloading supplies. The tired men hefted the food into the large basement room and stacked it along the stone wall. Emma gratefully surveyed ten bushels of grain, six bushels of potatoes, a barrel of mackerel, and a pound of tea. Knight had even remembered lined paper. Isaac Hale's face may have been grim if he watched free provisions arrive at the door of a son-in-law who, he felt, neglected his farm.

With adequate supplies stored away and Samuel working the farm, Joseph and Oliver resumed work on the plates. They could do only a few pages each day, according to Emma, but as the story unfolded on the heavy foolscap paper she was intrigued with it. It was an account of an ancient people who migrated to America from Jerusalem about 600 B.C., drifting with the prevailing ocean and wind currents. They divided into two major factions called the Lamanites and the Nephites. Wars and contentions persisted throughout their history. They kept meticulous records of their conflicts, social structure, economic life, religious beliefs, and faith. At one time Jesus Christ visited and taught the Nephites, and for two hundred years thereafter peace prevailed. Later devastating wars almost annihilated the Nephites, but one man remained to write the final words of this ancient record. This was Moroni, last keeper of the record and son of Mormon, after whom the book would be named. Joseph explained that the Lamanites were ancestors of the American Indians and the book's purpose was to be a witness for Christ.

Gossip spread about Joseph's translating; neighbors in Harmony began subtle harassment prompted by rumors Dolly Harris had spread earlier. Emma's uncle, Nathaniel Lewis, listened intently to the young man's claims, then baited him. "Joseph," he said, "can anybody else translate strange languages by the help of them spectacles?"

"Oh, yes," was the answer.

"Well, now," said Mr. Lewis, "I've got Clarke's Commentary and it contains a great many strange languages; now if you will let me try the spectacles, and if, by looking through them, I can translate these strange languages into English, then I'll be one of your disciples."[17] Not willing to antagonize Emma's family any further, Joseph let the conversation drop.

Work under these circumstances was difficult. Sometime in the latter part of May 1829, Oliver wrote to a friend named David Whitmer in Fayette, New York, and asked if they could go there to finish the translation. To Emma's and Joseph's surprise, David Whitmer pulled up to their house in his wagon early in June to offer them a place to live and help with the translation. He indicated that his friends were eager to meet Joseph and hear of his work first hand. The men drove one hundred thirty-five miles to Fayette, leaving Emma to care for affairs at home. The situation may well have fueled Isaac's wrath. Now he could claim that Joseph neglected the farm, and Emma as well. In Fayette, Oliver Cowdery, David Whitmer, and Martin Harris asked Joseph to inquire of the Lord if they could see the plates. When the answer was affirmative, Joseph showed the three men the gold plates, commenting, "I feel as if I was relieved of a burden which was almost too heavy for me to bear, and it rejoices my soul, that I am not any longer to be entirely alone in the world."[18] Mrs. Whitmer also claimed she saw the plates in a vision, a privilege afforded her for her hard work on behalf of the men. Ironically, Emma's untiring efforts to support Joseph did not receive the same reward. She soon came to Fayette and she and Joseph occupied the room to the right of the head of the stairs in the crowded Whitmer house.

Emma and Oliver were scribes but the translating did not always go smoothly. One morning Emma did something that angered Joseph. When he went upstairs to work "he could not translate a single syllable" so long as he was irritated with his wife. He finally walked outside and into the orchard where he "made supplication to the Lord." When he came back about an hour later he asked Emma to forgive him. The translation then proceeded, but Joseph had learned that the Lord watched out for Emma's interests too.[19]

On June 11, 1829, Joseph obtained a copyright for the Book of Mormon. Oliver had copied the manuscript by August and, with Emma and Joseph, took the transcript to E. B. Grandin, the publisher in Palmyra. Funding publication of the book became the next hurdle. Martin Harris applied for a thirteen-hundred-dollar loan but was refused when the banker learned its purpose. Hyrum Smith urged Joseph to sell the copyright for his book to raise the needed cash. According to David Whitmer, Joseph used the seer stone to learn that Hyrum Page, the Whitmer's brother-in-law, and Oliver Cowdery were to travel to Toronto, where someone would meet them ready to buy the copyright. The two men made the trip but returned empty-handed and disillusioned. When they confronted Joseph, he replied, "Some revelations are of God, some are of man, and some are of the devil."[20] Emma would one day conclude the same thing about a particular revelation concerning a new order of marriage.

Finally Martin Harris mortgaged his farm for three thousand dollars to guarantee five thousand copies of the book and had to sell part of it to meet the bill. His wife left him, complaining, "Martin Harris was once industrious, attentive to his domestic concerns, and thought to be worth about ten thousand dollars. . . . Whether the Mormon religion be true or false, I leave the world to judge, for its effects upon Martin Harris have been to make him more cross, turbulent and abusive to me."[21]

Oliver Cowdery supervised the printing process, organizing and punctuating the text as the printer set the type. Sometimes he spotted errors as the pages rolled from the press and stopped to make corrections. This resulted in differences among the copies of the first edition. In his Preface Joseph allowed for inconsistencies: "And now, if there are faults they are the mistakes of men; wherefore, condemn not the things of God." Emma and Joseph returned to Harmony, where Emma could now tell her family the book actually would be published.

Through the winter Joseph left Emma twice while he went to Palmyra to deal with problems related to the book. When the last Book of Mormon came off the press in March 1830, Emma and Joseph were elated. Joseph contemplated the next step—the establishment of a church organization that would enable him to teach the new gospel formally. His interest in organizing a church kept him away from her and the farm with increasing frequency and for longer periods of time.

Joseph met with friends and neighbors in the home of David Whitmer's father, Peter, on Thursday, April 6, 1830. The service consisted of prayers, blessings of some already baptized, and the Lord's Supper, which they termed the Sacrament. During the business part of the meeting, Joseph organized the Church of Jesus Christ with six members as required by New York law. Apparently Emma had remained in Harmony on the farm, for accounts that name the other women present make no mention of her. A number of people were baptized into the church that same day, including members of Joseph's family, but Emma's baptism took place two months later.

Believing the church to be a restoration of all blessings, powers, and ecclesiastical authority given by Jesus Christ, they named themselves "latter-day" saints as opposed to the "former-day" saints of biblical times, often referring to themselves simply as "Saints." Outsiders, in derision, called the members Mormons or Mormonites, but acceptance of the nickname by church members soon took the sting out of the epithet.

When the people questioned who would be their leader, some insisted Joseph ask the Lord. When the meeting ended, Joseph announced that the Lord had revealed that he himself should be called "a seer, a translator, a prophet, an apostle of Jesus Christ."[22] From this time Joseph was called "the prophet," even by those outside the church, with varying degrees of respect. But to his followers he became the leader of Christ's church and the mouthpiece of God. These people believed they were establishing much more than a church: they were building the kingdom of God on earth.

The procedures of the fledgling church originated with Joseph's statements, which he continued to attribute to the inspiration of God. He referred to their arrival as "having a revelation." These instructions usually came in answer to specific problems or questions. They covered varied aspects of life, often called the recipient by name, exhorted him to do good, and gave explicit instructions. When talking of these revelations, Joseph used the word "received," implying that they did not originate in his own mind but that God prompted him to speak or think a certain way about a subject at hand. When instructions changed as new commandments came or when policies were reversed, his followers believed the Lord gave these additional words through Joseph. They acted upon them and sometimes judged others' acts by the terms of the revelation.

For those who witnessed Joseph's receiving of a revelation, the experience left a lasting impression. One witness wrote, "At once his countenance changed [and] he stood mute . . . there was a search light within him, over every part of his body. I never saw anything like it on earth. . . . He got so white that anyone who saw him would have thought he was transparent."[23]

Joseph viewed these revelations as "light bursting upon the world." His position would become more powerful, extending into the temporal realm as well as the spiritual. David Whitmer wrote in subsequent years that he was uneasy about so much power being placed in one man, though he participated in the spiritual feast "with great joy." In years to come, those followers who saw Joseph as a *man* with a prophetic calling generally remained faithful, while those who saw him *only* as a prophet and deified him almost invariably found themselves disillusioned.

After the organization of the church, Joseph returned to Harmony. Emma drove back to Colesville with him where a number of those who had been at the organizational meeting of the church were anticipating baptism. Emma, too, wanted to be baptized. On Saturday, June 26, the group piled rocks and logs across a nearby stream to dam water for a small pond to be used for baptisms the following morning. This ordinance represented the cleansing of sins, and assured the recipients that sins that burned their conscience (with the exception of shedding innocent blood) would be forgiven by a merciful God. The next step was for the elders of the church to lay hands on the head of every man and woman for confirmation as members of the church.

Sometime Saturday night a group of townspeople crossed a field under cover of darkness and destroyed the dam. The next morning several of them slipped into the meeting. Afterward they cornered those heading toward the creek for baptism to talk them out of such nonsense.

In this atmosphere of contention Emma and Joseph rose early on Monday morning, June 28, 1830. Before their enemies knew of it, Joseph and his friends had repaired the dam. While enough water backed up behind the rough structure to start baptizing the thirteen converts who had planned to have the ordinance the day before, a mob gradually assembled. Oliver Cowdery and Emma stood waist deep in the pond. Raising his right hand until his arm formed a square, he said, "Emma Hale Smith, having been commissioned of Jesus Christ, I baptize you in the name of the Father, and of the Son, and of the Holy Ghost. Amen." The cool water rushed around Emma's head as Oliver submerged her, then lifted her out again. She had taken the official step that made her a part of her husband's work. The mob jeered, "Have you been washing sheep?" when the rest were baptized. Emma and the others walked back to the Knights' home with the crowd of nearly fifty milling around and harassing them.

That evening, as friends began to gather for the confirmation ordinance, Emma was astounded to see a constable on the doorstep with a warrant for Joseph's arrest. He charged Joseph with "being a disorderly person and setting the country in an uproar by preaching the Book of Mormon." She watched anxiously as the officer led her husband away. Emma made arrangements to stay with her sister Elizabeth, who had married Benjamin Wasson and was living between Colesville and Harmony. During the two days she waited in

Elizabeth's home, the women in the area occasionally met at a church member's home to pray for Joseph's freedom. When Emma finally saw her husband again, he had eaten only crusts of bread and had been through two bizarre, impromptu trials at South Bainbridge and Colesville. Between Joseph's trials, his lawyer, John S. Reid, rode up to see Emma. He said Emma's face was "wet with tears . . . [and] her very heartstrings [were] broken with grief."[24] The local judicial systems were unable to convict him, but nevertheless Joseph had received rough and contemptuous treatment and been persecuted for what he believed and taught. Dismayed and shaken by the ordeal, Emma and Joseph went quietly back to Harmony.

Emma, through Joseph, became the recipient of a revelation directed exclusively to her after their return from the Colesville arrest. Although Joseph occasionally mentioned women in his revelations, this one, which would be called the "Elect Lady revelation," is the only one addressed solely to a woman. Whether she heard it first as Joseph spoke the words, or whether he dictated the verses for Oliver Cowdery to write, Emma believed it to be a communication from God to her.

The revelation addressed Emma warmly. "Hearken unto the voice of the Lord your God while I speak unto you, Emma Smith, my daughter," it began, then in recognition of her acceptance of the gospel it further explained, "all who receive my gospel are sons and daughters in my kingdom."

"Thy sins are forgiven thee," the Lord assured her, "thou art an elect lady, whom I have called." She would learn God's will for her life and, "if thou art faithful and walk in the paths of virtue before me, I will preserve thy life, and thou shalt receive an inheritance in Zion."

Probably in reference to others' viewing of the plates while Emma was not allowed to see them, the instructions continued, "Murmur not because of the things which thou hast not seen, for they are withheld from thee and from the world."[25] That single line urging Emma to "murmur not" would later give rise to speculation that Emma had complained of not seeing the record. Future writers would use that phrase to condemn Emma, but nothing in the Elect Lady revelation approaches the chastisements Joseph occasionally received.[26]

The revelation outlined Emma's responsibilities toward Joseph. "Let thy soul delight in thy husband and the glory which shall come upon him . . . go with him at the time of his going . . . be for a comfort in . . . his afflictions, [and offer] consoling words in the spirit of meekness. . . . Thou shalt be ordained under [Joseph's] hand to expound scriptures and to exhort the church," the words continued. "Thy time shall be given to writing and to learning much.

"Lay aside the things of this world, and seek for the things of a better," the revelation said, then it gave Emma two specific assignments. The first was to act as scribe for her husband. The second gave Emma responsibility "to make a selection of sacred hymns . . . which is pleasing unto me, to be had in my church. My soul delighteth in the song of the heart; yea, the song of righteousness is a prayer unto me."

The revelation ended with a phrase of hope: "Lift up thy head and rejoice, and cleave unto the covenants which thou hast made." It urged Emma to beware of pride and to keep the commandments continually. "A crown of righteousness thou shalt receive. And except thou do this, where I am you cannot come."

The Elect Lady revelation singled Emma out and marked her as worthy of particular approbation from the Lord. It fitted her natural talents and abilities. Her intellect, combined with her education, qualified her to act as Joseph's scribe—now most likely penning letters, revelations, and blessings. Her compassionate nature would express itself in her care for Joseph and others. The instructions to "expound the scriptures" and to "exhort the church" hinted of her future development as a leader. Emma sang as she worked and sang when she worshiped; compiling a hymnal would be a pleasure.

Meanwhile, Isaac Hale had grown increasingly impatient with Joseph. He obviously knew that much of Emma's and Joseph's sustenance came from the kindness of friends. To see his daughter living off charity would not have set well with the old hunter, particularly when her husband was "chasing angels and gold books." Furthermore, two years earlier Joseph had contracted with Isaac to buy the thirteen-acre farm where they were living. He still had not paid the two hundred dollars. Isaac may have finally asked if or when he intended to make good on the mortgage, and in August Joseph paid in full.[27] Where he got the money is unclear. Perhaps income from the Book of Mormon sales materialized, or friends intervened, but Isaac no doubt suspected it was not from Joseph's labors in the fields.

Isaac Hale's disapproval did not interfere with Emma's and Joseph's practice of their faith. When Joseph Knight's son Newel and his wife Sally visited in Harmony, the two couples held a small religious service at home. The unruly crowd in Colesville had interrupted the service after Emma's baptism and she had not been confirmed. After sharing sacramental wine and bread, the men laid their hands on Emma's and Sally's heads and confirmed them members of the church. Afterward Joseph said, "The Spirit of the Lord was poured out upon us, we praised the Lord God, and rejoiced exceedingly."[28]

About this same time a disgruntled Methodist preacher agitated against Joseph and his church. Some explanation for his opposition may be seen in interviews given by two of the Smiths' neighbors. Ezra Pierce said, "I pulled sticks with Joe for a gallon of brandy once at a log rolling; he was about my age." In answer to the query, "Did young Joe drink?" Pierce answered, "Everybody drank them times. . . . They would have it at huskings, and in the harvest field, and places of gathering; the Smiths did not drink more than others."[29] While this neighbor looked upon the use of alcohol with some tolerance, the Hales were probably inclined to follow the Methodist Church's position, which supported abstinence from alcoholic drinks as opposed to the temperance advocated by many societies of the decades between 1820 and 1850. In 1816 the Methodist General Conference had moved that "no station or local preacher shall [use] spirituous or malt Liquor without forfeiting his ministerial character among us."[30]

Another neighbor commented that it was "common then for everybody to drink, and to have a drink in the field; one time Joe, while working for some one after he was married, drank too much boiled cider. He came in with his shirt torn; his wife felt bad about it, and when they went home, she put her shawl on him."[31]

Joseph claimed that the Methodist minister paid Isaac a visit after hearing that Emma's father had promised to protect her and Joseph from violence or slander. He repeated falsehoods "of the most shameful nature, which turned the old gentleman and his family so much against us, that they would no longer promise us protection nor believe our doctrines."[32] With this final erosion of family support the minister had found fertile ground for his rumors and innuendos. Life for Emma and Joseph became increasingly difficult in Harmony.

Late in August 1830 Newel Knight's wagon rumbled into the yard again. He had come to help move Emma and Joseph to the Whitmer farm in Fayette, New York. They loaded a few belongings in the wagon, locked the door behind them, and left the rest of their furniture inside.

Emma bade farewell to her parents. It was a difficult parting for her. She loved the peaceful Susquehanna, the lore of Ichabod Swamp, and the hardwood forests. She had come back nearly two years earlier anticipating much. The baby who had stirred inside her then lay buried near the house. Hope for a reconciliation between her father and her husband had evaporated. Emma would never see Harmony, her mother, or her father again.

General excitement and a warm welcome greeted Emma and Joseph in Fayette where Lucy and Joseph, Sr., soon joined them. Strife in Manchester had caused them to leave.[33]

Emma was pregnant again, and ill. Her mother-in-law kept watch over her and noted that "Emma's health at this time was quite delicate, yet she did not favor herself on this account, but whatever her hands found to do, she did with her might, until she went so far beyond her strength that she brought upon herself a heavy fit of sickness, which lasted for weeks. And, although her strength was exhausted, still her spirits were the same, which, in fact, was always the case with her, even under the most trying circumstances."[34] When the older Smiths arrived, Emma and Joseph needed the furniture left behind in Harmony and sent a friend to get it.

That fall Emma sewed clothing for four missionaries who were to preach

through Ohio and Missouri. The success of that journey would draw Emma to
Ohio.The first hint of the move came a few months later at a meeting in the
elder Smiths' home. Two strangers entered the room and found seats. When
Joseph finished his sermon one of them stood up. He was Edward Partridge, a
hatter from Kirtland, Ohio. His companion was Sidney Rigdon, formerly Partridge's Campbellite minister, now a new convert to the Mormon church.

Partridge said he and Rigdon had been to Manchester and Palmyra looking for Joseph and had inquired into the character of the man. The Smiths'
neighbors told him that the family had a good reputation in the community
until their son deceived them about his discovery of the Book of Mormon
plates. Partridge had walked around the farm in Manchester and noticed the
obvious signs of thrift and industry. The only objections he found among the
neighbors were related to the family's religious beliefs, which he was now ready
to embrace, "if," he said, "Joseph will baptize me." Joseph soon obliged.

The two men explained that Parley P. Pratt, one of the missionaries
Emma had sewn for, had visited his friends Sidney and Phoebe Rigdon in
Kirtland. Rigdon was thirty-seven and a handsome man, above average in
height and a little portly. A compelling speaker and trained minister of the
Disciples of Christ, he was a follower of Alexander Campbell, who attempted
to reform Baptist theology and return to the "ancient order of things." When
Parley Pratt announced that the Book of Mormon opened the door to divine
authority, Sidney Rigdon allowed some Mormon missionaries to address his
congregation. Within two weeks Pratt had baptized Rigdon, and in a month a
nucleus of one hundred thirty church members lived in the county, many of
whom came from Rigdon's former congregation.

Sidney Rigdon approached Edward Partridge about his new faith. He and
his wife Lydia were respected members of the community with relatively large
property holdings. The couple had joined the Campbellite church through the
influence of Rigdon; now he introduced them to the new restored church.[35]
Lydia was baptized, but Edward wanted to know more about Joseph Smith
before he made his commitment. Determined to see the leader of this new
religion for themselves, Sidney Rigdon and Edward Partridge traveled through
unusually cold weather to Fayette,[36] where they stayed through December and
into January listening to Joseph's teachings. Their enthusiastic report about
the new converts in Ohio beckoned Emma and Joseph westward.

3

Gathering in Ohio

1830–1834

The winter of 1830–1831 was one of the most severe recorded in the eastern United States. The December snows were soft and deep; what little melting occurred was soon covered over by storms that maintained a four-foot level through February. Freezing rains in January enabled the wolves to run on the crust while heavier game sank through helplessly. Deer and elk could not find browse of twigs and shrubs. That winter the elk disappeared from the plains of Illinois and Missouri—never to return. A storm covered the breadth of the United States, blizzards whirled snow until familiar landmarks disappeared, and streams could be recognized only by breaks in the forests. Newspapers suspended publication when the mails could not go out. Human life maintained a precarious balance.

On January 2 of that winter, Joseph announced at a church conference that he had received new revelations commanding the entire group to sell or rent their farms and move three hundred miles to Kirtland, Ohio. The revelations promised them "power from on high . . . great riches, a land of milk and honey, and an inheritance for them and their children forever."[1] The village of Kirtland, which lay northeast of Cleveland, boasted a gristmill, a sawmill, a hotel, and the Gilbert and Whitney Mercantile store. Most of the thousand or so settlers were of New England stock.

Before long Emma sat with Joseph, Sidney Rigdon, and Edward Partridge in a crowded sleigh, gliding over the frozen roads toward Kirtland. She was now twenty-six years old, uncomfortable from her pregnancy, and still weak from an extended illness in December. They rested briefly at the home of her sister-in-law, Sophronia Smith Stoddard, but for the remainder of the month-long journey the travelers sought public houses or relied on the hospitality of farmers.

On February 1, 1831, the sleigh came to a stop in front of the Gilbert and Whitney store in Kirtland. Joseph jumped out, strode into the store, and thrust his hand out to the proprietor. "Newel K. Whitney, thou art the man!" he boomed.

The astonished Whitney parried for time. "You have the advantage of me," he replied. "I could not call you by name as you have me."

"I am Joseph, the prophet," came the response. "You have prayed me here, now what do you want of me?"

A few evenings earlier Newel and Elizabeth Whitney had prayed fervently for religious instructions. Elizabeth said a voice told them to "prepare to receive the word of the Lord, for it is coming."[2] They accepted Joseph as the embodiment of the Lord's instruction.

Whitney's partner, Algernon Sidney Gilbert, invited the Smiths to stay with his family and, while new friends helped transfer the travelers' belongings to a wagon, Joseph went ahead with him. Emma's driver started the horses down the hill toward the Gilberts' house. Suddenly the wagon slid sideways, lurched, and overturned, throwing Emma in the snow. Her scream brought Joseph bolting from Gilbert's home to help. She was not hurt and when the wagon was righted she and Joseph went to the house to choose a room. Emma could see that the family was already crowded. Henry Rollins, his mother, and his sister Mary Elizabeth also lived there. Emma declined the Gilbert's offer, and Elizabeth Whitney took the Smiths into her own home for several weeks. Disappointed that Emma and Joseph found other lodging, Henry Rollins reported that none of "our rooms suited her."[3]

A generous warmhearted woman, Elizabeth Ann Whitney became Emma's first friend in Kirtland. Six-year-old Sarah Ann Whitney and young Mary Elizabeth Rollins came to regard their "Prophet Joseph" with awe and wonderment. Emma, not suspecting the role the two young girls would eventually play in her life, watched as Joseph gave eleven-year-old Mary Elizabeth Rollins his appreciative attention when he discovered she had eagerly read a Book of Mormon and had begun to memorize part of it.[4]

Newel and Elizabeth Whitney felt pleased and honored to have Emma and Joseph in their home, but Elizabeth's elderly Aunt Sarah pursed her lips at the thought of a self-appointed preacher under her roof. After a month Joseph became increasingly conscious of Emma's impending confinement and he announced a revelation. It stated, "It is meet that my servant Joseph Smith, Jun. should have a house built, in which to live and translate."[5] In obedience to the commandment, Isaac Morley began building a cabin on his land several miles north of Kirtland. Emma and Joseph moved into it in early spring. Though small, the single room was private, and it was Emma's. She began housekeeping with few provisions and little furniture, for they had abandoned almost everything in New York.

On April 30, 1831, Emma gave birth to twins in the cabin. The "gentle Morley girls" assisted with the delivery and helped with the housework. The infants, a boy and a girl, were probably premature and lived only three hours. Emma and Joseph named the twins Thaddeus and Louisa, then buried them. In a six-month period Emma had made the difficult break with her parents, endured a strenuous trip, adjusted to a new town, and established her own home. After only four years of marriage, all three of her children lay in graves.

The day after Emma's twins died, Julia Clapp Murdock died in childbirth, leaving her newborn twins and three other young children motherless. John Murdock considered the grim difficulties of caring for his five small children alone and concluded that he must divide his family among his friends.[6] The survival of his newborn twins, named Joseph and Julia, depended on a woman who could nurse them. When they were nine days old Emma took them as her own. This adoption did not separate the natural father from his children, as John Murdock boarded at Emma's home periodically over the years. Nevertheless, Emma and Joseph did not tell the children they were adopted and the community recognized and accepted the children as Smiths.

The same evening that Emma received her new twins, she greeted her mother-in-law with surprise and relief, for she had thought that Lucy was dead. Local newspapers had reported a boat loaded with immigrating members of the church from Colesville, New York, had sunk in Lake Erie with all drowned.[7] Lucy led this group in much the same way as she had led her family to New York when Joseph was still a child. He had often seen his mother in this role, and Emma would learn that he expected her to exercise similar responsibility—much to the chagrin of some of his associates, who would bristle to see Emma make decisions on her own.

Lucy's Colesville immigrants arrived in Kirtland almost penniless. The influx of destitute Saints taxed the resources of those with property. Economically, no room existed for a large group of displaced people. Pressure to find another place to settle mounted against the Mormons in Kirtland until Joseph finally found a solution: Zion.

Emma had frequently heard Joseph discuss an unknown gathering place he called "Zion." Parley P. Pratt and Oliver Cowdery described Missouri in glowing terms. Joseph mulled over the reports, decided to investigate the area himself, and told the Colesville Saints to leave immediately for the eight-hundred-mile trek to Missouri. They prepared to move again on faith and little else. Joseph, Sidney Rigdon, Martin Harris, Edward Partridge, and Sidney Gilbert and family also left. Gilbert expected to establish a new store for dry goods and groceries in Missouri, while his partner Newel Whitney continued with the store in Kirtland. William W. Phelps, who would become Emma's associate in a publishing venture, also joined the group.

In Missouri Joseph saw space for a Mormon community in the midst of the rough frontier settlements. By revelation he announced that this area was Zion and that the Mormons who came there should purchase property, build homes, and prepare to stay. He dedicated a site for a temple near the small town of Independence and laid the cornerstone for the future building. The designation of the area as Zion and the temple site induced Mormons to immigrate to Missouri. The Colesville Saints arrived in July, and for the next eight years the Mormon settlements and interests would be separated by the eight hundred miles between Ohio and Missouri.

Emma remained in the cabin at the Morley settlement throughout the summer. Certainly the twins demanded care, but this may have been her first opportunity to work on the hymnbook mentioned as her responsibility in the Elect Lady revelation. When her husband returned from Missouri in September 1831, much of the social life in Kirtland again revolved around Emma and Joseph. A stream of visitors—the skeptics, the curious, the seekers, and the believers—came to see Joseph. He gradually developed a strong style of oratory that could hold audiences captive for hours. They sometimes laughed, sometimes cried, and often accepted his message.

Word spread that spiritual phenomena, including miraculous healings, were part of this new religion. Curiosity about this brought John and Elsa Johnson to Emma and Joseph. At a meeting someone drew attention to Elsa's withered arm, long rendered useless by rheumatism. "Here is Mrs. Johnson with a lame arm; has God given any power to man now on the earth to cure her?"

Joseph rose and walked to her. Taking her arm gently in his hands, he said, "Woman, in the name of the Lord Jesus Christ I command thee to be whole." Elsa raised her arm above her head and moved it around with no pain. The next day she washed clothes with full use of the arm. As a result, the Johnson family, as well as a Methodist minister, Ezra Booth, joined the church.[8]

By the time Emma and Joseph met the Johnsons, Joseph had begun compiling his revelations. He believed that some sections of the Bible had either been lost or misinterpreted over the centuries of translations. He labored over revisions in the biblical text while Sidney Rigdon wrote the corrections in the margins and between the lines. But people frequently interrupted Joseph's work in the crowded cabin at the Morley settlement. Dissatisfied with living the revealed Law of Consecration, a communal system designed to care for the destitute who straggled into Kirtland with no means of support, church members came to Joseph to complain. Members of the church signed over their assets to a group represented by a lay bishop. Each had promised to labor faithfully and was promised in return the receipt of supplies according to need. With increasing frequency, Joseph was called on to arbitrate disputes. When

John and Elsa Johnson offered Emma and Joseph quarters in their large farm-house thirty-six miles south of Kirtland near a settlement called Hiram, the Smiths accepted.

John Johnson had built the large New England colonial-style house five years earlier, but instead of chimneys at either end he had built a central complex of fireplaces. Johnson's acreage and buildings showed evidence of hard work and good care from his four grown sons, John, Jr., Luke, Olmstead, and Lyman, and one daughter, Nancy Marinda, age sixteen. Only Olmstead had refused to join the church.

Emma, Joseph, and the twins moved in with the Johnson family on September 2, 1831. They lived in two rooms, one on either side of the giant kitchen on the main floor. Emma and Joseph slept in the south room, and the twins occupied the room to the north. Emma soon cleaned, cooked, and mended alongside Elsa and Nancy Marinda.

Emma baked in the brick bustle oven built in the fireplace wall. She shoveled hot coals into the oven, then stoked them to a flame. Once the fire was roaring, she shoved the door forward against the lintel, forcing the smoke and fumes up the flue. To test the temperature she held her hand in the oven and counted slowly. If her hand felt uncomfortably hot in twelve seconds, the oven was "hot," it was "quick" in eighteen seconds, "moderate" at twenty-four seconds, and "warm" at thirty seconds.[9] When the oven was hot Emma removed the coals and placed her bread dough on the bricks inside. Then she pushed the door in as far as possible, closing the oven and shutting off the flue. Although cooking required effort, one ate well at the Johnsons'.

But the quiet peace of the Johnson farm was an illusion. In November Ezra Booth charged Joseph with "a want of sobriety, prudence, and stability . . . a spirit of lightness and levity, and temper of mind easily irritated, and an habitual proneness to jesting and joking."[10] To Booth, these actions were unbecoming in a prophet. He accused Joseph of having revelations too conveniently for them to originate from God. Booth's friend Simonds Ryder, misunderstanding the Law of Consecration, claimed to have found papers outlining a plot to take people's property from them and place it under Joseph's control. When the Johnson boys saw farmers sell their holdings and consecrate their profits to the church, they feared that their expected inheritance would go the same way. John Johnson was respected in the community, but the neighbors grew bold and devised a way to circumvent Johnson and reach Joseph Smith in Johnson's own house. A barrel of whiskey fortified their courage one night as winter's hold began to break.

In the big white farmhouse Emma and Joseph tended the eleven-month-old twins, who had been feverish for days with a hard case of measles. Neither parent had slept much and on the night of March 24, 1832, Emma insisted that Joseph take their son to the children's room and rest with him on the trundle bed. Emma stayed in her own bed with Julia beside her. Exhausted, she fell into a heavy sleep, undisturbed by a light tapping at the window. She did not hear the front door open nor did she hear the Johnson boys creep upstairs to bar the entrance to their father's room so he could not get out.[11]

Suddenly the door burst open. Emma woke with a start, then screamed when she saw a mob of men with blackened faces attempting to carry her husband out of the house. The group, led by Ezra Booth and Simonds Ryder, numbered about fifty or sixty. They overpowered the struggling, kicking Joseph and staggered into the yard with him. An undocumented account says the terrified Emma grabbed both babies and ran to the barn to hide, perhaps fearing rape by the violent, drunken men. Whether she remained in the house or hid in the barn, Emma could hear oaths and heavy grunts as Joseph fought to free himself in the yard. One man held a flickering lantern fashioned from a gallon can. The light bobbed and swung as it lit up portions of the men's faces. The delicate diamond-, heart-, and crescent-shaped perforations in the tin glowed softly in contrast to the ugly brutality silhouetted by the lantern.[12]

Joseph managed to get one leg free and kicked so hard he sent a strong man sprawling. The man picked himself up and shook a bloody fist in Joseph's face. "God damn ye, I'll fix ye!" He grabbed Joseph by the throat and choked him into unconsciousness. The mob moved out of the yard until the light flickered in a field and the curses were muffled by the distance.

Joseph regained consciousness to see Sidney Rigdon on the ground where the men had dragged him by his heels over the frozen earth. Joseph assumed he was dead. Fearing the same fate, he pleaded for his own life.

"God damn ye, call on yer God for help, we'll show ye no mercy!" was the reply.

The violent men carried him farther into the field, never letting his feet touch the ground for fear he would have leverage to free himself. They tore his clothes from his body, leaving only his collar, then laid him out on the frozen ground and called for a Dr. Dennison. Dennison, a respected physician, had been induced to come along for the purpose of castrating Joseph, but when he saw the helpless man stretched out before him he refused to perform the mutilation.

Joseph overheard snatches of the conversation and concluded they were deciding whether or not to kill him. One man dug at Joseph's flesh with his fingernails, muttering, "God damn ye, that's the way the Holy Ghost falls on folks."

Another cried, "Simonds, Simonds, where's the tar bucket?"

"I don't know where 'tis, Eli's left it," came the answer.

They sent someone to fetch the crude bucket made from a hollowed-out log with a rope handle.

"Let's tar up his mouth."

Joseph wrenched his head away when they attempted to jam the tar paddle into his mouth. Someone tried to force a vial between his lips, but it shattered, breaking one of Joseph's teeth. They poured tar over his head, smeared it down his body, rolled him in an open feather tick, and then left him lying on the frozen ground. Joseph later said that "his spirit seemed to leave his body, and during the period of insensibility he consciously stood over his own body, feeling no pain, but seeing and hearing all that transpired."[13] Joseph clawed the tar from his nose and mouth until he could breathe better, then lay motionless until the vertigo diminished. In the distance he discerned two lights and stumbled toward them.

In the house Elsa and John Johnson freed themselves from the bedroom. John was too late to help Joseph; Elsa calmed Emma and helped with the feverish babies. When Joseph appeared at the dimly lit doorway the tar looked like blood to Emma. Thinking he had been "torn to pieces," she fainted. Joseph called for a blanket, wrapped it around himself, and went inside. Throughout the night friends softened the tar with lard and scraped it from Joseph's battered body. The next morning Emma watched as he calmly delivered his usual Sunday sermon from the front steps of the Johnson home, the broken tooth adding a sibilant lisp to his words. Among the crowd gathered in the yard were several men who had raided the house the night before, including one who had supplied the mob with a barrel of whiskey to "raise their spirits." That afternoon Joseph baptized three people. Several of the mob would eventually be baptized.

When Joseph visited Sidney Rigdon the next day he found him delirious and calling for his razor, threatening to kill his wife and Joseph. Rigdon did not regain his strength for some time, and there were those who believed that the blows he received on his head affected him for the rest of his life.

The victim who suffered most, however, was not Joseph with his bruises and scratches, or the delirious Sidney Rigdon. It was the adopted baby, Joseph. Already weakened by a difficult case of measles and the accompanying high fever, the cold night air aggravated the child's condition. Through the next six days and nights Emma hovered over her baby with growing apprehension. On Friday, March 29, 1832, Emma realized her worst fears as she watched life ebb from his tiny body. She and Joseph buried the fourth of their first five children.

Emma grieved alone for the dead child. Joseph had delayed his departure for church conference in Missouri and now, three days after the baby's death, he left with Newel K. Whitney and Sidney Rigdon. The Johnson home was still in turmoil over the violence of March 24; Joseph and Newel assured Emma that she should stay at the Whitney home while they were gone. Unfortunately, Newel neglected to tell his wife.

When Emma arrived, Elizabeth Ann Whitney was ill in a bed at the back of the house. Her elderly Aunt Sarah answered the door and turned Emma away. Elizabeth's aunt had always lived with them, and she assumed by right of years that she had a say in the family affairs. While the Whitneys regarded Emma's and Joseph's presence in their home as the fulfillment of a vision,

Aunt Sarah looked with skepticism at all preachers and did not want Joseph to make her family the dupes of "priestcraft." When Elizabeth Ann learned what her aunt had done she was chagrined. "I would have shared the last morsel with either of them," she said.[14] Humiliated, Emma found another place to stay and said nothing for fear it would "injure feelings." She told Lucy thirteen years later, and even then she was not able to conceal her mortification.[15]

Emma spent the summer of 1832 shuttling between the homes of Frederick G. Williams, Reynolds Cahoon, and the senior Smiths. Oblivious to Emma's circumstances, Joseph chided her in a letter: "Sister Whitney wrote a letter to her husband which was very Chearing and being unwell [myself] at that time and filled with much anxiety it would have been very Consoling to me to have received a few lines from you but as you did not take the trouble, I will try to be contented with my lot knowing that God is my friend in him I shall find Comfort."[16] But Lucy commented, "During Joseph's absence [Emma] was not idle for she labored faithfully for the interest of those with whom she staid cheering them by her lively and spirited conversation . . . her whole heart was in the work of the Lord and she felt no interest except for the church and the cause of truth. Whatever Her hands found to do she did with her might and did not aske the selfish question shall I be benefited any more than anyone else? . . . Her countenance always wore a happy expression of zeal and let her own privations be what they might."[17] What Emma may not have revealed until it became obvious was that she was pregnant again.

When Martin Harris carried word to Missouri that the families in Kirtland were well, Joseph wrote to Emma that the news "greatly Cheared our hearts and revived our Spirits we thank our heavenly Father for his Goodness unto all of you."[18] Hyrum's family was not so fortunate. Jerusha had followed Hyrum to Kirtland with the Colesville Saints. Late in May her daughter Mary, not yet three, became ill and her health steadily failed. She died in Hyrum's arms on May 29, 1832. Joseph wrote to Emma, "I was grieved to hear that Hiram had lost his little Child. I think we can in Some degree Simpathise with him but we all must be reconsiled to our lots and Say the will of the Son be done." Four years later, in January 1836, he would receive a comforting revelation for parents who lost children in death: "And I also beheld that all children who die before they arrive at the years of accountability, are saved in the celestial kingdom of heaven."[19]

While in Missouri, Joseph called a meeting to discuss publishing efforts of the church. His revelations would appear in a Book of Commandments, supplementary scripture to the Book of Mormon and the Bible. He assigned W. W. Phelps to correct and print hymns that Emma had selected.

After the meeting Joseph started home to Kirtland with Newel Whitney and Sidney Rigdon. Partway through Ohio the stagecoach horses bolted and Whitney leaped from the door. His leg caught in the wheel spokes and broke in several places. Rigdon went on ahead while Joseph remained with Newel in an inn and cared for him until the leg mended. At some time during their four-week stay Joseph became very sick and vomited so hard he dislocated his jaw. He believed he had been poisoned and that Newel healed him by laying hands on his head in the name of the Lord. Joseph would suspect poisoning again in his life, but this may have been food poisoning or the beginning of a chronic illness.

On his return Joseph and Emma again lived briefly at the Johnson farm, but they needed a place of their own. Newel Whitney offered them three storage rooms above his store. This arrangement left Emma space enough to take in boarders and, except for infrequent intervals, she would earn money in this way for the remaining forty-seven years of her life. Emma also began a lifelong practice of taking in domestic helpers, usually young women who needed a place to live. They washed clothes and did household chores in return for board and room. Emma's friendship with these women usually became landmarks in their lives.

In the early fall Joseph and Newel went to New York City. Concerned over Emma as she entered the last few weeks of her pregnancy, Joseph asked Hyrum to watch over her until he returned. In October Emma received a letter from the Pearl Street Boarding House in New York City. "This day I have been walking through the most Splended part of the City of New Y[ork]," Joseph began, but he said he did not waste time contemplating the sights. The thought of two hundred thousand unconverted souls walking around in close proximity filled him with determination to preach. Joseph also found himself excited by the tall buildings and strange inventions and concluded that God was not displeased with luxury but rather that the Lord would rejoice in works calculated to make men comfortable and wise and happy. Joseph reasoned that the only iniquity involved in enjoying luxury would be to deny God the glory. This attitude would remain with him from that time: earth and its legitimate pleasures were to be enjoyed.

Joseph also wrote of his homesickness. "After beholding all that I had any desire to behold I returned to my room to meditate and calm my mind and behold, the thoughts of home, of Emma and Julia, rushes upon my mind like a flood and I would wish for moment to be with them. My breast is filled with all the feelings and tenderness of a parent and a Husband." Sensing Emma's apprehension at the impending birth of their child, Joseph expressed his concern. "I feel as if I wanted to say something to you to comfort you in your peculiar triel and presant affliction. I hope God will give you strength that you may not faint. I pray God to soften the hearts of those around you to be Kind to you and take the burdon of your shoulders as much as posable and not afflict you. I feel for you for I Know your State and that other do not, but you must cumfort yourself Knowing that God is your friend in heaven and that you have one true and living friend on Earth your Husband."[20] Joseph and Newel

Whitney traveled to Kirtland on the first of November, having had no recent news of home.

On November 6, 1832, Emma lay exhausted in an upstairs room over the Gilbert and Whitney store. She had ended a painful labor and delivery at two o'clock that morning. The women who came in and out freshened the room and cared for the new baby. If Emma heard the baby cry and fret, the sound of life would be reassuring. A disturbance on the street and staircase signaled Newel's and Joseph's arrival from New York. "You have a son," someone said to Joseph. And this one would live. Emma and Joseph named their baby Joseph. Then the community began sorting out the names. Joseph, Sr., became Father Smith; Joseph, Jr., was already "Brother Joseph"; this baby would become "young Joseph," and later Joseph III. From the first this child resembled his mother with his brown eyes, dark hair, and olive skin.

Two days after young Joseph's birth three men arrived in Kirtland and inquired after Joseph at the Whitney store. They were directed through the neighborhood until the sound of chopping led them to Joseph, who was cutting trees. Two brothers, Brigham and Joseph Young, and their friend Heber C. Kimball had come in search of a prophet; that they found one cutting wood may have surprised them. Emma was resting with the two-day-old baby at her side when Joseph took Brigham and the others to meet her. Brigham Young was thirty-one when he arrived in Kirtland. Born in Whitingham, Vermont, in 1801, he was the ninth child of a stern moralistic father who fought the rocky soil of Vermont with no more success than the Smiths had, but he refused to leave. Because the family lived close to poverty, young Brigham mastered many trades in order to earn a penny. His skilled hands built furniture, repaired clocks, and made windows. He was a compact, powerfully built man with gray eyes, deep-set under a wide forehead. His hair was sandy brown and his face clean-shaven. His wife had died earlier that year, leaving him two daughters.

When preaching in the area Samuel Smith had left a Book of Mormon with another of Brigham's brothers; Brigham borrowed it and read it, then converted his brother. Brigham and Joseph struck up an immediate friendship. The evening the three men arrived a group came to Joseph's house and conversed freely on topics dealing with the doctrines of the kingdom. When Joseph asked Brigham Young to pray, Brigham spoke in tongues, using strange sounds and unfamiliar words. The others looked at Joseph in some perplexity, for this type of spiritual phenomenon was not common to them. It was Joseph's first experience with the puzzling speech and he called it "pure Adamic" and stated that it was "of God."[21] Speaking in tongues spread through the Pennsylvania branches of the church first, then occurred in Mendon, New York. Brigham Young brought it to Kirtland. The practice became a part of the Saints' worship—particularly among women—until well into the next century. After meeting Joseph, Brigham arranged his affairs and moved his two daughters to Kirtland along with Vilate and Heber C. Kimball.

As the church expanded the missionary efforts increased. Joseph established a school to train men in the new doctrines as well as English, Latin, and geography. This "School of the Elders" met, according to Brigham Young, "in a small room situated over [Emma's] kitchen." While the men's desire for more education could not be faulted, the more mundane aspects of human affairs invariably appeared. Young said that "When they assembled together in this room after breakfast, the first thing they did was to light their pipes, and while smoking, talk about the great things of the kingdom, and spit all over the room, and as soon as the pipe was out of their mouths a large chew of tobacco would then be taken. Often when the Prophet entered the room to give the school instructions he would find himself in a cloud of tobacco smoke."[22]

The situation in the room was probably an example of the conditions that the Kirtland Temperance Society opposed. Founded in 1830, it was not predominantly Mormon, but some were among its members. Temperance societies worked to abolish "ardent spirits" and also condemned the use of alcohol, tobacco, and the eating of too much meat. Without question this larger social movement affected the Mormons.

Thus Emma, faced almost daily with "having to clean so filthy a floor" as was left by the men chewing tobacco, spoke to Joseph about the matter. David Whitmer's account supports Brigham Young's description. "Some of the men were excessive chewers of the filthy weed, and their disgusting slobbering and spitting caused Mrs. Smith . . . to make the ironical remark that 'It would be a good thing if a revelation could be had declaring the use of tobacco a sin, and commanding its suppression.' " Emma had support among the women. Whitmer further reports, "The matter was taken up and joked about, one of the brethren suggested that the revelation should also provide for a total abstinence from tea and coffee drinking, intending this as a counter dig at the sisters." Joseph made the issue the subject of prayer, and the "Word of Wisdom" was the result.[23] Joseph's revelation came, "showing forth the order and will of God in the temporal salvation of all saints in the last days." It advised against the use of strong drinks or tobacco and would someday mark the Mormons quite distinctively in their religious habits.[24]

The Word of Wisdom sometimes made Emma's role as the prophet's wife take an interesting turn, for new members expected her standards to meet their own expectations. On one occasion an old lady drove up to the prophet's house, wanting to look at "God's mouthpiece" before she had even washed the dust from her eyes. Emma offered her a cup of strong tea to revive her, for she had traveled far over rutty roads. "And to be sure she did smack her lips over the cup, but when she went about town she whispered that Emma did not keep the Word of Wisdom, and if Joseph couldn't control his own household . . . She left the Church and left it in company."[25]

Other defections had more serious consequences for Emma. Doctor Philastus Hurlbut established himself as a physician, but his name, "Doctor," came from his parents in the superstitious belief that as the seventh son he possessed supernatural powers. Hurlbut went on a mission but the church disfellowshipped him for using obscenity to a young girl. When Joseph allowed him a hearing, he confessed, was reestablished, then boasted that he had outsmarted Joseph Smith's God. The Council cut him off from the church.

Hurlbut declared himself an enemy of the Mormons and went back to the Palmyra and Harmony areas, where he located about a hundred residents willing to sign statements against the Smiths.[26] Joseph read the publicized statements and denounced them as the efforts of Satan. In return, Hurlbut publicly threatened Joseph's life. Hurlbut sold his affidavits to Eber D. Howe, editor of the Painesville, Ohio, *Telegraph*, for five hundred dollars. Howe then corresponded with Emma's father, Isaac Hale. In an apparent attempt to rid his family of the stigma of Joseph's reputation, Isaac had already published his own denunciation in a local newspaper, the *Susquehanna Register*, on May 1, 1834. He gave Howe permission to use it. Hale reiterated his view that Joseph did not keep his promise to avoid peep stones and work on his farm. "I conscientiously believe that the whole 'Book of Mormon' (so called) is a silly fabrication of falsehood and wickedness, got up for speculation, and with design to dupe the credulous and unwary—and in order that its fabricators may live upon the spoils of those who swallow deception,"[27] he stated. When Howe published his collection as *Mormonism Unvailed* (sic), he included Isaac's judgment. The book opened old wounds for Emma. Circulation of the denunciation from Joseph's father-in-law had great impact on those unfamiliar with the previous struggle between the two men. No doubt existed in Emma's mind that her father considered her duped.

While Hurlbut stirred up animosities in Kirtland, life became increasingly difficult for the Saints in Missouri. Tensions had been building there for some time that would affect Emma and the church. As President Andrew Jackson's policies expelled Indians from their ancestral lands along the Ohio River, they moved through Missouri to the high arid plains beyond the Mississippi. To the original settlers, these Indians were savages crossing their land. The Mormons, on the other hand, saw part of the literal gathering of Israel in the western migration of the Indians and felt free to befriend them. W. W. Phelps's enthusiastic editorials in the Mormon newspaper, the *Evening and Morning Star*, concerning the religious implications of the gathering Indians only fueled the settlers' growing anger.

Some Missouri citizens had come from the South and brought slaves with them. They passed laws designed to keep free blacks out of the state. When free black members of the church tried to gather in "Zion" with the other Saints, white authorities refused them entry across the border unless they could prove citizenship in another state. William W. Phelps attempted to explain the law in an editorial in his paper in July 1833. He printed an extract from the state law and exhorted, "Great care should be taken [to obey the law]. The Saints must shun every appearance of evil." But his next sentence infuriated the local populace. "As to slaves, we have nothing to say; in connection with the wonderful events of this age much is doing towards abolishing slavery, and colonizing the blacks in Africa."[28]

Anti-Mormon sentiment exploded. Before the month was over a manifesto circulated through the countryside. Signers of the document agreed to rid themselves of the Mormons "peacably if we can, by force if we must," and declared the formation of a military unit. They labeled the Mormons fanatics, "tampering with our slaves and endeavoring to sow dissensions and raise seditions among them. . . . We agree to use such means as may be sufficient to remove them, and to that end we each pledge each other our bodily powers, our lives, fortunes and sacred honors." Over a hundred people signed the document, including many public officials.[29] The group met on Saturday, July 20, 1833, at the Independence courthouse. Men then swarmed up the street to the press office of the *Evening and Morning Star*. A mob shoved William Phelps and his family into the street and threw their household belongings after them. Phelps watched several men hoist his press through a second-story window and toss trays of type after it. They ransacked his office and destroyed his papers, including the pages for the Book of Commandments.

The crowd moved on and pillaged the store. Men grabbed bolts of colorful cloth and flipped them into streamers through the town square. Nine-year-old Emily Partridge and her sister Eliza, thirteen, were at a spring drawing water when the mob arrived at their house. From a short distance the girls watched angry men surround their father and envelop him in their midst, then move back toward town. Emily watched from the window. Finally she saw two men walk down the road. One carried a hat, coat, and vest. The other was a grotesque figure and Emily ran upstairs to hide. The second man was her father, covered with tar mixed with acid and rolled in feathers. A few days later the family watched their large haystack burn as roaming bands struck fear through the Mormon settlements.[30]

In November violence broke out again; the mob wrestled down and beat several Mormon men while women and children cowered in adjacent thickets. They tied some men to trees and whipped them until blood ran down their bodies. Thirty or forty night riders came late in the evening of November 1 to David Bennett's home. He and his wife were both critically ill. They dragged Bennett from his bed and beat him to death with his own gun while his wife and children fled. Another night men with painted faces surrounded the house of Nancy and Edward Larkey, fired guns at random, and told them to leave or be killed. Their young daughter buried her face in her mother's skirts and cried, "Oh, Ma; what shall we do; what shall we do!"

Nancy Larkey held her close and calmly told her, "Do not fear, if they kill us we will go to God, where they cannot come."[31]

By November the Mormons took up arms. A force led by David Whitmer left two men dead in a cornfield. When Lieutenant Governor Lilburn Boggs requested that both sides give up their arms, the Mormons complied, but the Missouri settlers did not. Through November Mormon refugees gathered along the banks of the Missouri. The ferries could not keep up with the influx of homeless people, who made shelters of poles and blankets. In desperation the church members appealed to the Kirtland settlement for help. Joseph Smith announced a revelation that the members in Kirtland should help redeem Mormon losses in Missouri, prompting the organization of a strange military campaign: Zion's Camp.

On February 24, 1834, the newly organized High Council—a governing body within the church—met at Emma's and Joseph's home and selected Joseph as commander-in-chief of the "Armies of Israel." The purpose of the army was the "redemption of Zion": they were going to Missouri to redeem Mormon lands, spiritual life, loyalty, political power, and church organization. Emma cared for her boarders and prepared supplies for the campaign while Joseph left for a trip to New York to recruit for Zion's Camp until March. She and the other women outfitted the army with food and clothing and gathered provisions for the homeless Missouri Mormons.

Joseph's cousin, George A. Smith, joined the group. At seventeen, George A.'s clothes for the journey were "a pair of pantaloons made of striped bed ticking, two cotton shirts, a straw hat, a cloth coat and vest, a blanket and a pair of new boots, and . . . a knapsack . . . made of apron check." His father proudly gave him a Queen's Arm musket to complete the outfit.[32]

The advance camp left Kirtland May 1, 1834. Two hundred and four men, eleven women, and seven children in some twenty-four wagons eventually joined the trek. Emma and probably every other woman, child, and old man saw them off. The first file marched out carrying a white bandanna inscribed "Peace." Then came armed men bearing every sort of weapon; most of the guns and swords were inherited from their Revolutionary War grandfathers. Those without muskets brandished huge butcher knives. Their plan, however, was to travel as farmers so that the Missourians would not learn of their march. Along with their weapons, they carrried rakes, pitchforks, axes, and other farm implements. Brigham Young captained one company of twelve armed with a gun, a bayonet, a dirk, an ax, and some farm tools. Joseph, accompanied by a big bulldog, was the best equipped. He carried a pair of brass-barreled horse pistols with silver mountings, a fine sword, and a rifle, and traveled under the alias of "Squire Cook."

After the first day's march George A.'s striped pantaloons hung in tatters and he had sat on his straw hat. A chronic eye infection made him squint and tilt his head back to see. He did not look like a soldier, and possibly for that reason Joseph appointed him to speak to outsiders. In spite of the image he portrayed, George possessed "a very tenacious and powerfully retentive memory—any person, or thing, he ever saw, or heard, once committed to memory . . . he seemed never to forget."[33]

News of the company in the form of a thousand rumors raced ahead of them. The *Missouri Intelligencer and Boon's Lick Advertizer* reported that six hundred Mormons armed with "every kind of instrument of destruction from scalping knives to double-barreled rifles" marched toward Missouri. Citizens across western Missouri began arming themselves.

Emma waited in Kirtland for news of the camp's progress and sent letters to Joseph with friends traveling to Missouri. She received a letter from Joseph in May. "I sit down in my tent to write a few lines to you to let you know that you are on my mind and that I am sensible of the dutes of a Husband and Father and that I am well and I pray God to let his blesings rest upon you and the Children and all that are a round you until I return to your society," he told her. "The few times you wrote and sent by the hand of Brother Lyman gave me satisfaction and comfort and I hope you will continue to communicate to me by your own hand for this is a consolation to me to convirse with you in this way in my lonely moments which is not easily discribed. . . . I must close for I cannot write on my knees sitting on the ground. . . . O may the blessings of God rest upon you is the prayer of your Husband until death."[34]

The next time Emma heard from Joseph he sent her money and advised her: "I want you to make use of the money I send you in wisdom, for such things as you need, and make yourselves as comfortable and contented as you can and continue to pray to the Lord to hasten the day when we shall be permitted to behold each other's face again and enjoy the blessing of the family Circle in peace and in righteousness." Joseph dictated much of his letter and his style became more flowery and less personal: ". . . our thoughts linger with inexpressible anxiety for the wives and our children our kindred according to the flesh who are entwined around our hearts; and also our brethren and friends; our whole journey would be as a dream, and this would be the happiest period of all our lives. We learn [on] this journey how to travel, and we look with pleasing anticipation for the time to come, when we shall retrace our steps, and take this journey again in the enjoyment and embrace of that society we so much love."[35]

Inside the camp, all did not always go as smoothly as Joseph described to Emma. Forty days of muddy roads, poor food, sporadic military discipline, fatigue, and petty bickering eroded their morale and shortened tempers. A sham battle near Decatur, Illinois, perked up almost everybody's spirits but Heber C. Kimball's. He had grabbed somebody's unsheathed sword and cut his hand.

As Zion's Camp entered Missouri a series of anticlimaxes prevented an actual battle with the Missourians, who outnumbered the forces from Kirtland. Rain soaked ammunition and a storm of huge hailstones discouraged the men. The Missourians dispersed and the men of Zion's Camp prepared to stay temporarily at Rush Creek, five miles from Liberty. But there, on June 20, cholera stalked the camp, choosing its victims with capricious and terrifying abandon.

Cholera scourged the world from 1832 to 1834. No one understood how the bacteria spread and travelers unwittingly carried it with them. Zion's Camp passed through infested communities where death carts were common sights, and bought food, accepted provisions, and drank from the polluted streams. Sometimes the terrific toxins in cholera brought agonizing suffering crowded into the few hours between the crisis of the disease and death. Other times, victims seldom lost consciousness until the merciful end came. Joseph, like many others, regarded disease and deformity as punishments meted out by an angry God. He called the camp together and told them that, in consequence of disobedience, God had decreed that sickness should come upon the camp, and that if they did not humble themselves they should die like sheep with the rot. Death by cholera was an unbelievably severe sentence for minor pseudomilitary infractions. The sufferers' cries and moans filled the whole camp. Men on guard fell with their guns in their hands. Joseph said he tried to heal the victims by the laying on of hands, but the disease seized him "like the talons of a hawk." Fourteen members of the camp fell victim to the plague.

Joseph disbanded the camp. Each man received $1.14 and was to make his own way home to Kirtland. As the men sought help, people closed doors in their faces in fear of the disease. In despair they buried their friends on the bank of a small creek—unknowingly polluting the stream.

What little news reached Emma in Kirtland was erroneous and slow arriving. On July 12 the Chardon *Spectator* announced that "a body of well-armed Mormons, lead on by their great prophet, Joe Smith, lately attempted to cross the river into Jackson county . . . a battle ensued, in which, Joe Smith was wounded in the leg, and the Mormons obliged to retreat; . . . Joe Smith's limb was amputated, but he died three days after the operation."[36] Until word filtered back, or until Joseph arrived in Kirtland two weeks later, Emma may have believed him dead.

4

"Seas of Tribulation"

1834–1838

Emma greeted Joseph with relief when he returned in good health on August 1, 1834. Zion's Camp had not redeemed lands in Missouri for the Mormons, although it assured the members there that the Kirtland Saints cared for their welfare. Some church members viewed the expedition as Joseph's personal quest for empire. These men nursed their grievances and waited. For others, the experience created firm and lasting bonds. From among his most faithful supporters in Zion's Camp Joseph organized a quorum of twelve apostles, often referred to simply as "the Twelve," who were to take the gospel to "all nations, kindreds, tongues and people." Among the first members of that quorum were Brigham Young, Heber C. Kimball, Orson Hyde, William E. McLellin, Parley P. Pratt, and William Smith; each would have an effect on decisions Emma would make later.

Emma and the Saints anticipated the construction of an unusual building that would provide a physical sanctuary for their spiritual needs. On June 1, 1833, Joseph had revealed the dimensions of the Kirtland temple. Many saw in it expressions of the beauty lacking in most of their own homes. When Joseph pointed out the site, Hyrum Smith enthusiastically grabbed a scythe and cut the wheat growing on it. He and Reynolds Cahoon dug the foundation trench, and George A. Smith hauled the first load of stone from nearby quarries. One woman "drove two yoak of cattle and haled rock,"[1] while others helped in more traditional ways. Some made and mended clothing for the men laboring on the temple, some sewed curtains and wove carpets. "Well, sisters," observed Joseph, "you are always on hand. Mary was the first at the resurrection; and the sisters now are the first to work on the inside of the temple."[2]

Emma supported the temple construction at some personal sacrifice by taking in the workers as boarders. Lucy described the crowded scene in her daughter-in-law's home: "How often have I, with my daughters and daughter-in-law, parted every bed in the house for the accomodation of the brethren. And then Joseph would take his cloak and lay down on the hard floor with no other bed or bedding, and Emma place herself by his side and share his comfort while My husband and myself l[o]dged in the same room with a single blanket for bed & bedding." She continued, "This was our rest for 2 weeks together and we labored hard every day but those who were accomodated by our privations did not know how we fared for Emma nor I never either of [us] suffered them to know that we took such [unwearied] pains for them."[3]

To add to the confusion, a certain Michael Chandler arrived in July with a traveling exhibit of four Egyptian mummies together with some rolls of papyrus covered with hieroglyphic figures. He had heard that Joseph Smith could translate unknown languages. Church members at Kirtland purchased them, but the mummies ended up on display in Emma's home, drawing a steady stream of visitors. Emma conducted tours, explaining the characters on them, as she had heard Joseph do.[4]

An unexpected minor disruption around Emma's premises was the love-sick Oliver Cowdery. Oliver's wife, David Whitmer's sister Elizabeth, had left for a visit to her parents in Missouri and the separation began to grind on him. "I live at bro. Joseph's and am treated with brotherly kindness," he wrote his wife, "but that is not like living with a family of one's own, when the Lord has given him one."[5]

Oliver Cowdery passed some of his lonely hours in the evening gatherings where Joseph Smith, Sr., pronounced promises and blessings upon the heads of the faithful. As patriarch, his duties required him to communicate to the Saints the individual blessings to which they were each entitled as the children of God. When he blessed Emma, Oliver Cowdery was present and acted as scribe. This blessing offered her both approval and comfort. "For thy faithfulness and truth, thou shalt be blessed with thy husband and rejoice in the glory which shall come upon him . . . thy whole soul has been drawn out in prayer for his deliverance; rejoice, for the Lord has heard thy supplication." In reference to the Hale family, she was told, "Thou hast grieved for the hardness of the hearts of thy father's house, and thou hast longed for their salvation. The Lord will have respect to thy cries, and by his judgments he will cause some of them to see their folly and repent of their sins; but it will be by affliction that they will be saved." One promise Emma would remember at the end of her life was, "Thou shalt see many days; yea, the Lord will spare thee till thou art satisfied, for thou shalt see thy redeemer. Thy heart shall rejoice in the great work of the Lord, and no one shall take thy rejoicing from thee." The blessing also recognized her grief at the deaths of her children.

Thou hast seen much sorrow because the Lord has taken from thee three of thy children: in this thou art not to be blamed, for he knows thy pure desires to raise up a family, that the name of my Son might be blessed. And now, behold, I say unto thee, that thus says the Lord, if thou will believe, thou shalt yet be blessed in this thing and thou shalt bring forth other children, to the joy and satisfaction of thy soul, and to the rejoicing of thy friends. Thou shalt be blessed with understanding, and have power to instruct thy sex, teach thy family righteousness, and thy little ones the way of life, and the holy angels shall watch over thee: and thou shalt be saved in the kingdom of God, even so, Amen.[6]

Social gatherings like those surrounding the giving of patriarchal blessings granted Emma an occasional reprieve from work, but some quiet evenings at home had their lighter moments. Shortly after a school opened for the men, Joseph spent all day in class. He came home one evening, decided to teach his family grammar, gathered them all around the fire, and proceeded to do so. Emma, the schoolteacher, must have smiled. Another family occasion began joyfully and ended on a somber note. A December sleigh ride with Emma, Julia, and young Joseph soured when a passerby bawled out to Joseph, "Do you get any revelations lately?"

On Thursday night, October 29, 1835, Emma prepared dinner for the Whitneys, Partridges, and several others. The conversation turned to hopes for the future. Newel Whitney looked at his friends and said, "I expect that in one year all the party present will be seated around a table in the land of Zion."

Emma responded, "I hope that will be the case, and that not only you but the rest of the company present might be seated around my table in that land of promise!"[7]

After dinner Emma went to a High Council meeting with Joseph. The matter of business was the trial of a couple charged with whipping their daughter unreasonably. Lucy Mack Smith began to testify about matters that Joseph believed had long since been settled by the church, and he objected to his mother's comments. William Smith rose and charged Joseph with invalidating her testimony. Joseph told William he was out of order and asked him to sit down. Enraged, William said he would not sit down until Joseph knocked him down. Joseph threatened to walk out of the meeting, but Father Smith intervened and they returned to the issue at hand. The erring parents were finally reprimanded for raising a daughter who required the whip at fifteen years.

The Smith family fight did not diminish with the end of the meeting. Two days later Joseph, William, and Hyrum met at Emma's house to settle their differences. William said Joseph always tried to carry out his own plans whether they were right or wrong—a charge Joseph regarded as an insult. When Hyrum attempted to make peace William rushed outdoors, bent upon vengeance. The argument upset Emma and the other Smiths two full months. Though the disagreement had begun over a relatively minor matter, the fury that sustained it came from a deeper source and would continue to disrupt the two brothers' relationship.[8]

A week after the argument with William, Joseph came home from Sunday services and scolded Emma for leaving the meeting before the Sacrament was passed. His words brought Emma to tears. "She made no reply," his history stated, "but manifested contrition by weeping." But he apparently attempted to ease some strain for Emma. On October 17, 1835, he called his family together, "arranged domestic concerns," and dismissed his boarders.[9]

While the crowded conditions in Emma's home were difficult, housing space and food available to the immigrants who steadily arrived in Kirtland were far worse. Elizabeth Ann Whitney and Emma solicited help from others in the community and held a feast for the newcomers. Special invitations went to the poor, the lame, the halt, the deaf, the blind, the aged, and the infirm. The "feast" was simple food since there was no other kind in Kirtland, but the spirit of sharing compensated for the lack of abundance.

Evidence suggests that Emma and Elizabeth Whitney shared not only a close friendship but also a common bond of compassion for those who suffered. Emma's keen sense of others' needs endeared her to church members. One example was the Crosby family. Caroline Barnes Crosby arrived in Kirtland with her husband Jonathan in January 1836. They moved about, living with other families, until they finally found a place of their own. Jonathan called it "a cold place to live in winter, a loos floor, & none over head." There Caroline gave birth to a son. "Being in a cold house my wife took cold & was sick with a sore brest nearly all winter. She could not nurse the boy, & we had to beg milk from the nabors."[10] Jonathan took a job working "on br Joseph's house as he was building tolerably large," and worked on for several days alone when Joseph ran out of money and could not pay the workmen. After Jonathan and Caroline went to bed hungry one night, they decided to ask "Sister Emma" for help. He worked several hours the following day, unable to bring himself to ask for charity even though money was due him for labor. Emma saw him and asked if he had enough provisions. He told her he was without and had no money; Emma gave him a twenty-pound ham and a sack of white flour from her own stores. Caroline wrote, "He came home rejoicing, considering it a perfect God send . . . nothing ever tasted half as good."[11]

Not all of the new converts who filtered into Kirtland came in family units as did the Crosbys. Loyalty to conviction was often pitted against loyalty to family. Emma understood that challenge, as she had faced it herself when she said farewell to a saddened mother and embittered father several years earlier. However, Emma corresponded with her parents while she lived in Kirtland. A former neighbor who ran the stone quarry recalled, "When I first saw Emma on the streets in Kirtland, she threw her arms around me and I think kissed me, and inquired all about her father's family. I brought her letters and took some later to Mr. Hale from her."[12]

Meanwhile, Samuel Smith had visited Boston on a missionary journey and befriended two young girls, Mary Bailey and Agnes Coolbrith, who would both become Emma's sisters-in-law. Samuel baptized Mary before leaving Boston. When opposition to the Mormons grew, Mary and Agnes left their families and traveled a thousand miles alone, arriving in Kirtland in 1833. They boarded with Joseph and Lucy Smith on a farm outside of town and worked on clothing for the laborers on the temple. Mary undoubtedly kept her eye on the handsome Samuel, and he looked no farther for a wife than in his mother's kitchen. Samuel married Mary Bailey in August 1834. Don Carlos, nineteen years old and a young giant at six feet, four inches, married Agnes Coolbrith in July 1835. She was twenty-four.

Converts continued to stream into Kirtland wanting to see Joseph. They came with an idea of how he should look and act, and invariably Joseph surprised them. "I thought he was a quear man for a Prophet, at first," said Jonathan Crosby, "he didn't appear ecactly as I exspeced to see a Prophet of God, however I was not stumbled at all. I found him to be a friendly cheerful pleasant agreable man. I could not help liking him."[13]

In 1835, with a press now operating in Kirtland, Joseph published the Book of Commandments under a new name, the Doctrine and Covenants, and the faithful accepted it as scripture. The High Council met on September 14 and decreed again that Emma Smith be appointed to make a selection of sacred hymns as she had been commanded in the Elect Lady revelation. Her first collection had most likely been destroyed with Phelps's printing press in Missouri three years earlier. Phelps was assigned to edit and arrange the songs for printing.

Phelps was forty-three in 1835 when he boarded at Emma's house. "He was quite a singular man, spare of flesh, already sufficiently aged to wear spectacles, was methodical and studious in his habits, and not very prepossessing in appearance though of good brain and judgment."[14] A poet in his own right, he contributed twenty-six hymns to Emma's collection. She also included a number of hymns written by others such as Eliza R. Snow, Parley P. Pratt, and Edward E. Partridge. Emma may have been a contributor herself, for several hymns are of unknown authorship. She chose forty-two songs from other denominations.

Emma's hymnal came off the press early in 1836 although it bears an 1835 date.[15] A small, pocket-size book—about three by four inches—bound in leather, the front and back covers were unadorned, but gold lettering on the spine read simply, "Hymns." The title page noted, "A collection of SACRED HYMNS, for the Church of the Latter Day Saints. Selected by Emma Smith, Kirtland, Ohio: Printed by F. G. Williams & Co. 1835." This volume contained ninety hymns. The first was "Know Then That Ev'ry Soul Is Free," and the last one became the stirring anthem of Mormonism, "The Spirit of God Like a Fire Is Burning," written by W. W. Phelps. The words were printed in stanzas without music. The chorister announced the name of the tune to which the hymn would be sung and the congregation was expected to know it. Some hymns fitted several tunes.

As the temple neared completion Phelps and Williams worked diligently to have the hymnal completed in time for the dedication. The temple was a monument to the faith of both the men and the women, and they saw symbols of their own personal growth in its quality and perfection. Standing on the hill in defiance of rumor, division, prejudice, and disruption, it became a triumphant statement that they could accomplish something of beauty. The church councils planned the dedication carefully to express their reverence and to be as impressive as the building itself.

By 7 A.M. on March 27, 1836, several hundred people waited at the doors. In groups, in pairs, and one by one, they climbed the wide front stairs and quietly filed through the two towering front doors. Men and women separated upon entering. Emma and the other women lifted the hems of their skirts to climb the staircases and take their places in the balcony. The men walked straight ahead and into the pews on the main floor, pulling closed the small gate on the aisle as each bench filled.

Sunlight filtered through the wavy glass and illuminated the people's faces. Their eyes traced the lines of the graceful Ionic columns and the intricately carved woodwork of the stately pulpits. Men who had brought stone from the quarries sensed the strength built into the foundation. With pride they viewed the results of their pounding, carving, plastering, and painting. Women who had sewn draperies and carpets saw that the interior was warm and inviting, while the outside walls glistened with bits and pieces of their china ground fine and mixed with the plaster. For these Saints it was a glorious day and their hearts echoed the silent prayer, "Lord, accept our offering."

At nine o'clock the service began with psalm reading and a hymn. Emma's soprano voice joined with the others; all six hymns sung at the ceremonies were from her hymnal—either the book itself had come off the press early enough to be used that day or they used type sets from the *Messenger and Advocate.* When Joseph gave the dedicatory prayer, he asked God to accept the building as fulfillment of the commandment to construct it. He prayed that the Lord would confound and bring shame and confusion upon those who had spread lying reports abroad, "against Thy servant, or servants," and asked the Lord's assistance in building up the church. When the prayer ended the assembled saints broke into joyous song:

> "The Spirit of God like a fire is burning;
> The latter day glory begins to come forth;

The visions and blessings of old are returning; .
The angels are coming to visit the earth.

"We'll sing and we'll shout with the armies of heaven;
Hosanna, Hosanna to God and the Lamb!
Let glory to them in the highest be given,
Henceforth and forever: amen and amen!"

Don Carlos Smith blessed the bread and wine for the Lord's Supper. Frederick G. Williams rose and stated that an angel entered through the window and took a place between himself and Father Smith and remained there during the meeting. The congregation shouted, "Hosanna, Hosanna, Hosanna to God and the Lamb," three times, sealing it each time with "Amen! Amen! Amen!" Brigham Young spoke in tongues; David W. Patten interpreted, and at four o'clock in the afternoon the dedication was over.

The women found the services inspiring. Nancy Naomi Alexander Tracy sat through the seven-hour dedication holding her six-month-old son, Lachoneus Moroni. "They were two of the happiest days of my life," she said. "It was verily true that the Heavenly Influence rested down upon that house. . . . Heavenly beings appeared to many. . . . Solemn assemblies were called. Endowments were given. The Elders went from house to house, blessing the Saints and administering the sacrament. Feasts were given. Three families joined together and held one at our house. We baked a lot of bread and had the best of wine."[16]

The evening of the dedication four hundred and sixteen male members of the church met in the temple and Joseph instructed them about the ordinance of washing of feet. As the meeting progressed, George A. Smith rose and began to prophesy, and Joseph reported hearing a noise "like the sound of a rushing mighty wind, which filled the Temple."[17] George A. later described the men's meeting and an unexpected result of it. "The Lord poured out his spirit upon us and gave us some little idea of the law of anointing, and conferred upon us some blessings. . . . He told us to wash ourselves, and *that* almost made the women mad, and they said, as they were not admitted into the temple while this washing was being performed that some mischief was going on. And some of them were right huffy about it."[18] According to another report, the sisters who had worked to weave the veils were not invited "to share in all the joyful manifestations, and they were not pleased. Emma, although she may have felt slighted, tried to explain that there were many privileges not accorded women and they must not complain."[19] But Prescindia Huntington described a meeting when the entire congregation knelt and prayed softly and both she and her sister Zina heard "a choir of angels singing most beautifully" overhead and toward one corner of the room. Neither of them saw the angels, but "myriads of angelic voices seemed to be united in

singing some song of Zion." On another day she was at home when a child
came to the door and told her there was a meeting on top of the temple.
Prescindia wrote, "I went to the door, and there I saw on the temple angels
clothed in white covering the roof from end to end. They seemed to be
walking to and fro; they appeared and disappeared. The third time they appeared and disappeared before I realized that they were not mortal men. Each
time in a moment they vanished, and their reappearance was the same. This
was in broad daylight, in the afternoon. A number of children in Kirtland saw
the same."[20]

Each church member responded differently to the spiritual gifts and extraordinary religious manifestations. Emma apparently did not speak in
tongues or experience mystical phenomena, yet she did not seem to doubt
those who did. Her letters to Joseph and later to her children clearly show that
she relied on both faith and prayer. She was a practical woman and her religious commitment served her, as she in turn served others, in that light.

Emma was pregnant through the winter and spring of 1835–1836 and on
July 20, 1836, gave birth to another son whom they named Frederick Granger
Williams Smith after the publisher of Emma's hymnal. Joseph soon left for
the East.

Accounts of the purpose of the trip conflict. Joseph's letters mention his
renting a home in Salem, Massachusetts, teaching, preaching, and visiting.
Ebenezer Robinson, who boarded at Emma's, said that Joseph had read in the
Painesville (Ohio) Telegraph that a treasure lay buried beneath a house in
Salem and a man had offered to guide him to it. Pressed by debts and needing
capital to build Kirtland, on the one hand, and, on the other, pained by the
earlier problems about money digging and peep stoning, Joseph kept his intentions from all but a few. In a note to Emma, Joseph made a veiled reference to
the secret project: "With regard to the great object of our mission, you will be
anxious to know. We have found the house . . . very luckily and providen-
tially. . . . [It] is occupied, and it will require much care and patience to rent
or buy it. We think we shall be able to effect it."[21]

The search for the treasure was unsuccessful. Perhaps the revelation he
dictated at the close of the expedition quieted some criticism. "I, the Lord
your God, am not displeased with your coming on this journey, notwithstanding your follies. I have much treasure in this city [Salem] for you, for the
benefit of Zion. . . . I will order all things for your good, as fast as ye are able
to receive them." Joseph returned to Kirtland empty-handed. Ebenezer Robinson noted sadly, "We speak these things with regret."[22] But the episode
brought to a close the money-digging chapter of Joseph's life.

Meanwhile Emma, now thirty-two, had a new friend enter her life. Eliza
R. Snow was the same age but had never married. She lived in Mantua, Ohio,
about thirty miles from Kirtland. Slightly above medium height, Eliza was
slender with auburn hair. She was "graceful and dignified," with a "noble

countenance, the forehead being unusually high and expansive, and the features of a slightly Hebrew cast," setting off her striking brown eyes. Eliza had published poetry and verse from the time she was twenty-two. A member of the Campbellite church, she had failed to receive a desired reassurance that this religion was correct. Sometime around 1831 Joseph Smith had visited her home. Eliza had scrutinized Joseph's face and decided it was "honest," but almost five years passed before she joined the church on April 5, 1835. She came to Kirtland for the temple dedication. Shortly afterward, at Emma's and Joseph's invitation, Eliza boarded with them and began to teach a "select school" for young ladies. Emma now had a friend who was an intellectual equal.

Eliza was not fond of teaching school, but living in Emma's home offered a compensation: Eliza watched Joseph. "[I] had ample opportunity to mark his 'daily walk and conversation,' as a prophet of God; and the more I became acquainted with him the more I appreciated him as such," she wrote. "His lips ever flowed with instruction and kindness; and although very forgiving, indulgent, and affectionate in his temperament, when his God-like intuition suggested that the welfare of his brethren, or the interests of the kingdom of God demanded it, no fear of censure—no love of approbation could prevent his severe rebuke."

Significantly, Eliza's life sketch made few references to Emma, except as "the family of the Prophet." Nor did she comment on Emma's advanced pregnancy, nor on the birth of Frederick, events that would be of natural interest to most women. Eliza joined Emma's and Joseph's thrice-daily devotions, "these precious seasons of sacred household service truly seemed a fortaste of celestial happiness."[23] To have a husband like Joseph Smith must have seemed heaven to the unmarried Eliza.

Emma nursed Joseph through a serious illness during the summer of 1837. Mary Fielding, a convert who had arrived from Canada in 1834, wrote that "our beloved Brother Joseph Smith appeared to be so far gone that [we doubted he would] live till next morn." Joseph's illness was serious enough to scare even him. As he lay helpless he asked Emma to pray for him. Afterward Mary said Joseph "was blessed at time[s] with such glorious visions as made him quite forget that his body was afflicted."[24]

Thirty-six-year-old Mary would soon be associated with the family in a new role. Hyrum Smith went to Missouri that fall of 1837. His wife Jerusha was expecting their fifth child in October. When the baby Sarah was born, Jerusha's health failed, even under Lucy's and Emma's care. For eleven anxious days the family watched and worried. On October 13, 1837, Jerusha Barden Smith called her older four children to her side, kissed them good-bye, and said, "Tell your father when he comes that the Lord has taken your mother home and left you for him to take care of."[25] With Jerusha's death, Emma lost a sister-in-law and a friend. They had been new brides together and had shared much since 1827. At Joseph's insistence, Hyrum Smith married Mary Fielding on December 24, 1837, two and a half months after Jerusha's death. His immediate remarriage probably prompted critics who believed that he had not allowed the proper lapse of time since his wife's death. He explained, "It was not because I had less love or regard for Jerusha, that I married so soon, but it was for the sake of my children."[26]

Mary's marriage to Hyrum came at the most chaotic of times. Construction of the temple had temporarily boosted the economy of Kirtland, but after the dedication the economy declined as poor converts arrived in ever increasing numbers. The old settlers attempted to keep them out of Kirtland by economic pressures, but the Mormon population increased twentyfold while the landholdings only quadrupled. In November 1836 Joseph and other church leaders drew up articles for a bank to provide capital for investments. It was a desperate gamble. Oliver Cowdery went to Philadelphia for plates to print bank notes, and Orson Hyde went to the legislature in Columbus with a petition for a bank license. It was refused. Oliver returned with plates for the Kirtland Safety Society Bank, but Orson Hyde came back without a charter. The plates were so expensive that they printed some specie anyway, writing in "Anti" before the word "Bank" and "ing" after it. The notes read, "Kirtland Safety Society Anti-Banking Company," and the paper passed as legal tender from a joint-stock company. At first the money circulated wildly. When merchants and businessmen who were more sophisticated than the Mormons began to redeem their notes, Joseph could see that a run would ruin the bank. After one month he and Sidney Rigdon resigned as officers but the bank failed. This affected Joseph's status.

People who were convinced that Joseph had intended a swindle at the outset attacked him verbally and threatened him physically. This disruption forced Joseph to leave the city frequently. As a consequence, Emma again took in boarders. Whether they paid in cash or kind, the results benefited the family. In Joseph's absence Emma earned their income and decided how to spend it. She bought, sold, bartered, and traded. Her letters to Joseph reveal that she wrote as a business partner, clearly expecting that he would consider what she had to say. She negotiated with men in solving her financial difficulties, and though she did not always succeed, she became a person to be dealt with, not ignored.

In April 1837 Joseph went into hiding without seeing Emma before he left. When she wrote on April 25 her sense of humor had not failed. "Your letter was welcomed both by friends and foes," she told him. "We are glad enough to hear that you was well, and our enemies think they have almost found you, by seeing, where the letters were mailed." On a more serious note she wrote, "I cannot tell you my feelings when I found I could not see you before you left, yet I expect you can realize them, the children feel very anxious about you because they don't know where you have gone." She continued, "I have got all the money that I have had any chance to, and as many goods as I could. . . . I verily feel that if I had no more confidence in God than some I could name, I should be in a sad case indeed but I still believe that if we humble ourselves, and are as faithful as we can be we shall be delivered from every snare that may be laid for our feet, and our lives and property will be saved and we redeemed from all unrenderable encumbrances."[27]

Eight days later Emma wrote again. While she believed that "unrenderable encumbrances" would soon cease, she still struggled with financial problems. "I do not know what to tell you," she began in frustration, "not having but a few minutes to write, the situation of your business is such as is very difficult for me to do anything of any consequence, partnership matters give everybody such an unaccountable right to every particle of property or money that they can lay their hands on, that there is no prospect of my getting one dollar of current money or even get the grain you left for our bread, as I sent to the French place for that wheat and brother Strong says that he shall let us only have ten bushel, he has sold the hay and keeps the money." She continued, "Dr. Cowdery tells me he can't get money to pay the postage of the office. . . . Brother Parish has been very anxious for some time past to get the little mare, and I do not know but it would be your will to have him have her, but I have been so treated that I have come to the determination not to let any man or woman have anything whatever without being well assured, that it goes to your own advantage." Emma probably would have bested Josiah Stowell, who gloated at having sold Joseph an old horse in Harmony.

"It is impossible for me to do anything," she wrote, "as long as every body has so much better right to all that is called yours than I have. . . . If you should write after you get this, I want you to let me know as much as possible about the situation of your business, that if possible I can benefit by the information." Business and church affairs demanded resolution. She advised him with cool aplomb, "If you should give anyone a power of attorney, you had better give it to brother Knight, as he is the only man that has not manifested a spirit of indifference to your temporal interest. I mean the only one I have had occasion to say much to about business. You may be astonished because I have not accepted some but when I see you I will tell you the reason, be assured I shall do the best I can in all things, and I hope that we shall be so humble and pure before God that he will set us at liberty to be our own masters in a few things at least, Yours for ever."

Emma also cared for an unnamed boarder. Remembering that measles had already taken one of her children, she confided to Joseph, "[The] young man . . . is here yet and is very sick with the measles which makes much confusion and trouble for me, and is also a subject of much fear and anxiety unto me, as you know that neither of your little boys have ever had them, I wish it could be possible for you to be at home when they are sick, you must remember them for they all remember you, and I could hardly pacify Julia and Joseph when they found out you was not coming home soon."[28]

In the same letter Emma mentioned Oliver Cowdery's nephew. In November 1836 Warren Cowdery had indentured his son Hervey to Emma and Joseph for five years. According to the terms of the contract, the boy would work for his board, room, and education. Emma spoke of the boy with warmth and asked Joseph to write "some words of encouragement to Hervey, for he is very faithful not only in business, but in taking up his cross in the family."[29]

Emma and Joseph had moved into their new home on the west side of the street that ran from the temple down to the Chagrin River. While watching the big boys catch a few small fish, five-year-old Joseph asked to try his luck. Emma outfitted a little pole with a piece of thread and a bent pin. The boy tossed it in without bait and, by some miracle that follows children, hooked a six-inch horned chub. He dropped the pole, gathered up the fish, and ran to the house to show Emma. "I've got one! I've got one!" he shouted.[30]

The pleasant aspects of Emma's life, however, were being overshadowed by rumors that Joseph had an unconventional view of marriage. His and Emma's abrupt departure from Harmony in 1830 may have been because her cousin, Hiel Lewis, accused Joseph of improper conduct with women. Fifty years later he repeated thirdhand stories that Joseph attempted "to seduce E.W. (Eliza Winters)," and that Joseph and Martin Harris had said "adultery was no crime."[31] However, Josiah Stowell's daughters insisted, in the 1830 Bainbridge court trial, that Joseph had always behaved properly toward them.

Joseph's ideas about changes in marital practices came during a season of unprecedented religious activity. By the time he left the Johnson home in 1832 he had received more than half of the revelations that would eventually appear in print. The Book of Mormon provided only vague references to the Lord's acceptance of plural wives but hinted of acceptance by stating, "For if I will, saith the Lord of Hosts, raise up seed unto me, I will command my people; otherwise they shall hearken unto these things."[32]

The Bible contained more explicit examples, and Joseph had revised it extensively, completing Genesis, Chapters 7 to 19, in February or early March of 1831.[33] Mormons believe that Joseph asked the Lord why plural wives were acceptable in the day of Abraham, Isaac, and Jacob but not in his day. Thirty to fifty years later several of Joseph's contemporaries would state that he had received a revelation approving plural marriage in 1831. In 1869 Orson Pratt said, "[Joseph] had inquired of the Lord [if] the principle of taking more wives than one is a true principle, but the time had not yet come for it to be practiced."[34] In 1882 Hyrum Smith's son, Joseph F. Smith, dated a revelation approving plural marriage in 1831 and added, "The Lord showed him [Joseph] those women . . . and at that time some of these women were named and given to him, to become his wives when the time should come that this principle would be established."[35]

Apparently Joseph introduced the subject through a revelation received near Jackson County, Missouri, on July 17, 1831, stating, "For it is my will, that in time, ye should take unto you wives of the Lamanites and Nephites [Indians] that their posterity may become white, delightsome and just, for even now their females are more virtuous than the gentiles." The copy of the revelation is in the handwriting of William W. Phelps, who adds, "I asked brother Joseph, privately, how 'we,' that were mentioned in the revelation could take wives of the 'natives' as we were all married men? He replied instantly, 'In the same manner that Abraham took Hagar and Keturah; that Jacob took Rachel, Bilhah and Zilpah; by revelation—the saints of the Lord are always directed by revelation.' "[36]

Evidence suggests that although Joseph believed he was commanded by God through revelation to establish plural marriage as part of the "restoration of all things," questions undoubtedly arose. For example, who would perform the marriages? Could Joseph officiate in his own behalf? Who should be told of the doctrine? How would Emma and others react to such an unorthodox practice? There is no record that Joseph received immediate instructions in these matters, making his early attempts to instigate plural marriage most difficult for Emma when she encountered them.

Mary Elizabeth Rollins claimed that Joseph had a private conversation with her in 1831; she was then twelve years old. She said Joseph "told me about his great vision concerning me. He said I was the first woman God commanded him to take as a plural wife."[37] Although she did not become a plural wife of Joseph's until a number of years later, that early conversation planted a seed that Mary Elizabeth long remembered.

Within six months of Joseph's conversation with Mary Elizabeth Rollins, he and Emma had moved into the John Johnson home. Orson Pratt later quoted Lyman Johnson as saying that "Joseph had made known to him as early as 1831 that plural marriage was a correct principle," but remarked also that "the time had not yet come to teach and practice it."[38] Perhaps Joseph was not discreet in his discussions about plural marriage, because rumor and insinuation fed the fury of the mob that tarred and feathered him. When the Johnson boys joined the mob that entered their own home, they clearly suspected an improper association between Joseph and their sixteen-year-old sister, Nancy Marinda.[39]

Undoubtedly members of the Johnson family retold the tar-and-feathering story with all its ramifications. William E. McLellin, a member of the Twelve wrote in an 1872 letter about an incident related to him by Frederick G. Williams in 1838. McLellin wrote that Joseph "committed an act with a Miss Hill—a hired girl": near the time of Joseph III's birth. "Emma saw him and spoke to him . . . he desisted, but Mrs. Smith refused to be satisfied. [Joseph] called in Dr. Williams, O. Cowdery, and S. Rigdon to reconcile Emma. But she told them just as the circumstances took place. He found he was caught. He confessed humbly, and begged forgiveness. Emma and all forgave him. She told me this story was true."[40] McLellin's secondhand account, written forty years after it allegedly happened and twenty-five years after he discussed it with Emma, has similarities to another incident that occurred around the time of the birth of Emma's second son, Frederick.

Emma took nineteen-year-old Fanny Alger into her home early in 1835. Fanny's parents and brother were members of the church. Benjamin F. Johnson said she was "A varry nice & Comly young woman about my own age. towards whoom not only mySelf but every one Seemed *partial* for the ameability of her character and it was whispered eaven then that Joseph *Loved her.*" But Joseph loved her indiscreetly, for Warren Parrish told Benjamin Johnson "That He himself & Oliver Cowdery did know that Joseph had Fanny Alger as a wife for They were *spied upon* & found together."[41]

William McLellin told his account of Joseph and Fanny Alger to a newspaper reporter in 1875. "[McLellin] . . . informed me of the spot where the first well authenticated case of polygamy took place, in which Joseph Smith was 'sealed' to the hired girl. The 'sealing' took place in a barn on the hay mow, and was witnessed by Mrs. Smith through a crack in the door! . . . Long afterwards when he visited Mrs. Emma Smith . . . she then and there declared on her honor that it was a fact—'saw it with her own eyes.'" In an 1872 letter McLellin gave other details of the story. He said that Emma missed both Fanny and Joseph one night, and went to look for them. She "saw him and Fanny in the barn together alone. She looked through the crack and saw the transaction!!! She told me this story too was verily true."[42] Joseph's theology may have allowed him to marry Fanny, but Emma was not ready to share her marriage with another woman. When Fanny's pregnancy became obvious, Emma forced her to leave.[43] Perhaps, in his old age, William McLellin confused the hired girl, Fanny Alger, with the Fanny Hill of John Cleland's 1749 novel and came up with the hired girl, Miss Hill.[44]

The incident drove a serious wedge between Oliver Cowdery and Joseph. Oliver wrote to his brother Warren from Missouri on January 21, 1838, "When [Joseph] was here we had some conversation in which in every instance I did not fail to affirm that what I had said was strictly true. A dirty, nasty, filthy affair of his and Fanny Alger's was talked over in which I strictly declared that I had never deviated from the truth in the matter . . . just before leaving, he wanted to drop every past thing, in which had been a difficulty or difference—he called witnesses to the fact, gave me his hand in their presence."[45]

But handshakes and gentlemen's agreements are pitiful dams in the face of flooding gossip. In an 1886 statement a Mrs. Alexander repeated rumors she had heard in Kirtland. While there is little corroborating evidence for much of what she said, one of her more colorful stories illustrates the type of rumor with which Emma contended. She said Emma hired a jovial, talkative, two-hundred-pound lady to work for her. Everyone liked Polly Beswick because she was "very agreeable in conversation," a colorful gossip. Polly told her friends that "Jo Smith said he had a revelation to lie with Vienna Jacques, who lived in his family," and that Emma told her "Joseph would get up in the night and go to Vienna's bed." According to Polly, "Emma would get out of humor, fret and scold and flounce in the harness," then Joseph would "shut himself up in a room and pray for a revalation . . . state it to her, and bring her around all right." Polly said Emma was a "very fine woman."[46]

Emma's front against her talebearing neighbors was a quiet reserve, but her anxiety showed through. She wrote to Joseph and closed her letter with a quiet plea. "I pray that God will keep you in *purity* and safety till we all meet again." And in another letter, "I hope that we shall be so humble and *pure* before God that he will set us at liberty to be our own masters."[47]

Emma was not the only one upset by the prevailing rumors. Attempting to make the Mormons' position on marriage very clear, W. W. Phelps had introduced an "Article on Marriage" at a general assembly of the church on August 17, 1835, while Joseph was in Michigan. In his absence the assembly voted unanimously to print it in the Doctrine and Covenants, where it remained in all editions until 1876, when LDS Church officials removed it. The statement read in part, "Inasmuch as this church of Christ has been reproached with the crime of fornication, and polygamy; we declare that we believe, that one man should have one wife; and one woman but one husband, except in case of death, when either is at liberty to marry again."[48] The statement did little to stem rumor and gossip, but it reassured church members.

All the discordant elements of the Kirtland era fomented to a head in the fall and winter of 1837. William E. McLellin believed "the Presidency to a great extent [were] absolved in temporal things." Although his observations may have been colored by bitterness, he wrote in 1872 that the "presidency and leading men," about fifteen couples, hired expensive carriages and drove to Cleveland "to show Big." McLellin said some became intoxicated and "smashed things up generally" before coming home the next day still under the influence. "But no confessions were ever required or made."[49] If McLellin's picture was accurate, this event further eroded Joseph's standing among the people.

Joseph had spent much of the year absent from Kirtland, finding with each return that the situation was worse. Inflated real estate prices, failure of the bank, and disillusionment with Joseph's leadership brought on a crisis. David Whitmer, Oliver Cowdery, Martin Harris, and W. W. Phelps spoke against Joseph. They organized a rival church with David Whitmer as president and intended to use the temple. "They Say they will have it if it is by the shedding of blood," wrote Hepsibah Richards.[50] Six of the Twelve Apostles rebelled. In a meeting in the temple in December 1837, Joseph and Sidney

Rigdon led one faction of the church and Oliver Cowdery and the Whitmers led another. Brigham Young declared Joseph was still a prophet and in favor with God. On the morning of December 22 a mob of dissenters hounded Brigham Young out of Kirtland in return for his support of Joseph. The halcyon days that Mary Fielding described as "a quiet, comfortable waiting upon God in his House" were over. As the storm gathered, Eliza R. Snow reflected:

> For see, ah, see! in yonder eastern land—
> In Kirtland City, a promiscuous band,
> Where wheat and tares to such a height had grown
> That Saints could scarce from hypocrites be known![51]

Caroline Crosby heard that her neighbors were leaving the church: "We had taken sweet counsel together, and walked to the house of God as friends. [But] they came out baddly against the prophet." Hepsibah Richards's letters illuminated those volatile months. "I care not how soon I am away from this place," she wrote. "I have been wading in a sea of tribulation ever since I came here. . . . [The] people have been tempest tost; and at times the waves have well nigh overwhelmed us."[52]

A leader in the anti-Mormon faction, Grandison Newell, formally charged Joseph with fraud. At ten o'clock in the evening on January 12, 1838, Joseph and Sidney Rigdon left Kirtland on the fastest horses they could find. Emma, now thirty-three, packed her wagon, knowing whatever she left behind would become common plunder. She made a place for Julia, six, and Joseph, five, and eighteen-month-old Frederick among the scanty provisions. Emma left Kirtland in much the same way as she had arrived: pregnant, and in the dead of winter. Zion in Missouri lay eight hundred miles away.

Behind her in Kirtland, Hepsibah Richards woke at one o'clock in the morning to see the eerie light of burning buildings flickering on the walls. The printing office went up in flames; the temple stood badly scorched. "I am not pained at the thought of leaving K[irtland]," mused Hepsibah, "for I have never felt at home here. . . . I believe there are *good* people in K[irtland] but [it] is not a good place to make Mormons."[53]

5

Strife
in Missouri

1838–1839

Joseph's departure from Kirtland signaled an end to the Mormon efforts to build up a settlement in Ohio, and most of the members prepared to follow him to Missouri, hoping in vain to receive fair prices for their property. Apparently Emma and Joseph received nothing for their home. Emma traveled with the Rigdon family sixty miles south to Norton, Ohio, arriving only thirty-six hours after Joseph and Sidney, a remarkable achievement considering that the men rode without baggage.

Brigham Young and his family also waited there with Joseph. Four days after Joseph had fled Kirtland, they left on the second leg of their journey to Far West, Missouri. Armed mobs followed them for two hundred miles. Often Joseph and Brigham lay in the back of the wagon, hidden by hanging blankets. Twice their pursuers ate in the same roadhouse unaware of their quarry. One night as Emma settled her family for the evening in a hostelry she heard men's voices through the thin walls. Their pursuers were staying the night in the same house, bragging about their plans to catch Joseph and Brigham. Late that evening several men barged into the room but failed to recognize the Smith and Young families.

Joseph tried unsuccessfully to find work cutting cordwood and sawing logs in Dublin, Indiana. Finally he turned to Brigham for help. Brigham contacted a local church member who had been trying to sell his "tavern-stand." This man soon received a generous offer that Brigham said "was the hand of the Lord to deliver President Joseph Smith from his present necessity." The man gave the prophet three hundred dollars, enough money to continue on for more than two months.[1] At five years of age, young Joseph remembered the trek as half lark and half terror. When the trail changed from dirt to rough log corduroy, riding in the pitching wagon tired the passengers more than walking. Young Joseph recalled stepping over the rigid poles, holding tightly to his mother's hand, the dog, Major, bounding beside them.

By February they had reached Quincy, Illinois, on the banks of the Mississippi, and were dismayed to find the ice dangerous to cross because it had broken up, then frozen over. Brigham Young remembered pulling the teams through an abandoned flatboat onto the ice, stringing out both wagons and teams to distribute the weight. Joseph's horse, Charlie, broke through "at every step for several rods."

A few days into Missouri the wagons came to the banks of the Salt River. The old ice had "sunk" and a foot of new ice had frozen over the top. Brigham said, "By plunging our wagons 2½ or 3 feet into the water [at the edge], we could gain the solid ice." The men balanced a canoe over open water from shore to ice. Emma, six months pregnant, walked gingerly through the unsteady canoe, crossed the ice, and repeated the process on the far bank.[2] One hundred twenty miles east of Far West a group of exuberant Saints met the travelers with fresh teams, a carriage, and money. Eight miles from town, a brass band met them with an enthusiastic salute. Emma must have smiled. It was exactly the kind of gesture Joseph loved.

In Far West, Missouri, Lucinda Morgan Harris and her husband George welcomed Emma and Joseph into their home. Lucinda Harris was three years older than Emma, a pretty woman with fair hair and blue eyes. She had once been married to a prominent Mason named William Morgan whose disappearance in western New York was highly publicized at the time Emma and Joseph lived there. By the time Joseph brought Emma to Far West he had become close friends with Lucinda and her second husband and had often stayed in their home while in Missouri. Two months later Joseph and Emma moved into their own house on the town square in Far West. She set up a leach in her yard by piling ashes from the hearth into a perforated hollow log and pouring water over them. The resulting pungent liquid contained lye, which Emma mixed with waste fat to make soap.

While they planted their garden, Joseph stood in the hand-turned furrows and reflected on the luxury of town life in Ohio: "All we had to do back in Kirtland was put out the fire and call the dog, but settling is a different thing."

Thinking the surrounding woods harbored peace, Emma answered, "I prefer settling."[3] On June 2, 1838, Emma gave birth to another son. This one would have his father's blue eyes and light hair. According to tradition, Emma teased that he was born in a "Hale" storm and named the child Alexander Hale Smith. Lucinda Morgan Harris probably cared for Emma, as Joseph left two days after the birth for a small Mormon settlement twenty-five miles from Far West named Adam-ondi-ahman.

Joseph designated Adam-ondi-ahman in Daviess County as the settling place for the Kirtland Saints, and they soon streamed into the area. Far West, in Caldwell County, had fifteen hundred people, and the Mormons spilled over into Daviess, Ray, and Carroll counties. When they purchased land contiguous to one another, this settlement pattern afforded a natural power bloc. Joseph planned a great city and taught that the Mormons would have a temple and become a mighty people. The ragged Saints quickly grasped the concept of future glory and announced to their neighbors with enthusiasm that this was the land of their inheritance and would be theirs forever. The Missourians were angered to see the land taken up. Some began to say that the country was not big enough to hold them both; the Mormons would have to go. Both Mormons and Missourians made rash charges, riders harassed Mormon outposts, and the Saints turned inward in mutual defense.

While the tensions fomented between the two groups, serious conflict appeared between Joseph and some of the other church leaders. Before Joseph's arrival, two of the Whitmer brothers, David and John, and William W. Phelps had sold their property in Jackson County contrary to Joseph's orders. On March 10 a church court in Missouri excommunicated them. Complaints against Oliver Cowdery for "vexatious law suits . . . falsely insinuating that [Joseph Smith] was guilty of adultery . . . selling his lands in Jackson County . . . leaving his calling . . . for the sake of filthy lucre, and turning to the practice of law" led to his excommunication on April 12, 1838.[4] Lyman Johnson soon followed. When Sidney Rigdon rode into Far West and learned that these former church leaders still lived among the Saints, he exploded with anger.

Two weeks after Emma gave birth to Alexander, Sidney Rigdon harangued the church members over their laxity in allowing excommunicated leaders to remain in the area. Eventually eighty-three Mormons signed an ultimatum giving the dissenters three days to get out of Far West. While Oliver Cowdery, the Whitmers, and Lyman Johnson rode to Liberty for legal aid, their families were thrown into the street and their belongings strewn about by the Mormons. Oliver was stunned and blamed Rigdon for influencing Joseph to become an enemy. Oliver had lived in Emma's home and she, in turn, had received warm hospitality from the Whitmer and Johnson families. She could only have been saddened by this brutal treatment.

Emboldened by Joseph's tolerance of such actions, Sampson Avard and Jared Carter soon organized a secret society of male members. Called the "Sons of Dan," they quickly shortened the name to "Danites." They were bound together by oaths and secret signs and signals, and sworn to uphold the church and each other to the point of death. These men encouraged each other to a harsh militarism that would haunt the church for another forty years.[5]

On the Fourth of July the Mormons celebrated with a public show of military strength and invited their neighbors to watch. A brass band marched to the central square in Far West. Behind the band came the "infantry," then the church leaders, followed by women and children, Emma most likely among them. A cavalry brought up the rear. Mormon determination showed in every step. The Missourians watched in a confusion of anger, puzzlement, and mockery.

Sidney Rigdon gave the oration, beginning with the text, "Better, far better, to sleep with the dead than be oppressed with the living." He built his patriotic ideas carefully at first, then frenzy overcame him. "We are wearied of being smitten," he cried to the impoverished Mormons, "and tired of being trampled upon. . . . But from this day and hour, we will suffer it no more. . . . And that mob that comes on us to disturb us, it shall be between us and them a war of extermination." The Mormons stood rapt. Gone was the reference to the other cheek. "We will follow them till the last drop of their blood is spilled or else they will have to exterminate us; for we will carry the seat of war to their own houses and their own families. . . . We this day then proclaim ourselves free, with a purpose and a determination that never can be broken—No never! no never!! NO NEVER!!!"[6] Sidney's rhetoric brought an "Amen!" that reverberated like thunder. Joseph himself shouted "Hosannah!" and the crowd broke out in wild cheering. Publication of the speech enraged the Missouri press, which then heaped abuse on the Mormons.

William P. Peniston, colonel of the Daviess County militia and candidate for the state legislature, picked up the gauntlet and initiated a free-for-all at the Gallatin polling place on election day. The fight lasted only a few minutes. The Mormons voted and left, but exaggerated rumors of the altercation flew to both Joseph and the Missouri authorities. Roving mobs soon hit isolated Mormon settlements. Hyrum Smith reported that they frequently took "men, women, and children prisoners, whipping them and lacerating their bodies with hickory scythes and tying them to trees, and depriving them of food until they were compelled to gnaw the bark from the trees."[7]

The Missourians perfected a technique for pulling down houses. One or two lariats snaked out in the night and looped around a cabin ridgepole. Horses leaned into the ropes and, with a sharp crack, the roof swung free, leaving an open shell. If the mob worked quietly enough, the cracking roof was the first sign of attack to a sleeping family. Few Mormons dared to rebuild but gathered what they could carry and left. Armed men approaching an isolated cabin were a fearful sight, but when they came in shapeless blanket coats with their faces blackened with charcoal, they could rape women and kill children and not be identified in court.

After the Missourians laid siege to it, the Mormons abandoned DeWitt and traveled to Far West without provisions. The crowded town offered "no habitations or houses to shelter them, and [they] were huddled together, some in tents and others under blankets" with almost no supplies. Lyman Wight, a bold and loyal supporter of the church, wolfed down a piece of Emma's bread.

"Why, Sister Emma," he said, "with a chunk of corn bread like this in my hand, I could go out of doors and stand at the corner of the house in the northwest wind and eat myself into a sweat."[8]

The experiences of Emma's two sisters-in-law brought the seriousness of the situation home to her and the Smith family. Mary Bailey, Samuel's wife, was forced to leave her home with a four-day-old baby and her small children beside her in an open lumber wagon. An eleven-year-old boy drove them the thirty miles to Far West. Lucy said when Mary arrived "She was entirely speechless and stiff with the cold. . . . I continued to employ every means that lay in my power for her recovery, and in this I was much assisted by Emma." The family soon learned that Don Carlos's wife, Agnes Coolbrith, had fared no better. While her husband was on a mission in Virginia a mob turned her out of her house on October 17. She waded the waist-deep Grand River with a babe in arms and a two-and-a-half-year-old child, then walked through three inches of snow to find Lyman Wight's house at eleven o'clock at night.[9]

Wight, furious that a mob would treat a woman so, stormed into the headquarters of the Mormon-controlled militia and demanded, "How long must we suffer this violence?" He was told to arm the Mormons and disperse the mobs around Adam-ondi-ahman. On October 18 Lyman Wight and David Patten marched at the head of forty men to retaliate by raiding farms, burning houses, and carrying off food. Emma's and Joseph's home in Far West became the clearinghouse for defense against the mobs. To Emma's door came rumors and accounts of burnings, plunderings, killings, and brutality. A young drummer boy, Arthur Millikin, had been shot in both legs and was carried to Emma to nurse back to health. Arthur would later marry Joseph's youngest sister, Lucy.[10] Word spread throughout Missouri that the Mormons were armed and would fight back. A Captain Bogard led a militia group that engaged seventy Mormon men led by David Patten. The battle left Patten mortally wounded, two other Mormons dead, and one Missourian killed. Patten's wife rushed to see him before he died.[11] A few days later Vilate Kimball and her daughter Helen visited Patten's widow, Phebe Ann. Helen recalled that a bowie knife hung from her belt and a cauldron of water boiled on the stove. Mrs. Patten carried a dipper, "intending, she said, to fight if any of the demons came there."[12] On October 27, 1838, two days after the battle at Crooked River, Governor Lilburn W. Boggs issued an order to Major General John B. Clark that repeated Sidney Rigdon's rhetoric of less than four months earlier. It read in part: "Your orders are, therefore, to hasten your operations. . . . The Mormons must be treated as enemies and *must be exterminated* or driven from the state."[13] Armed with an open license to hunt, the mobs roamed through the Mormon counties.

Three days after the extermination order, the mob ravaged a little settlement called Haun's Mill, where fifteen or twenty families had settled along

Shoal Creek. Several companies of Missouri militia converged upon the mill on October 30, 1838, at four o'clock in the afternoon. Some people ran to the woods, others fled to the blacksmith shop. The militia shot through the cracks in the logs and picked off the crouching Mormons, including young boys, at will.[14]

William Huntington stumbled onto the tragedy. When he asked for directions to Haun's Mill he was told that it was "three miles Beyond Hell, and if I would go on I should get in to Hell before night." When some men threatened to tie him to a tree to "chaw bark," Huntington took the advice whispered by a woman and left quickly, "as she new thare intentions was to kill all Mormons who were Not out of the county that day."[15]

Emma heard of outrages at Haun's Mill as the survivors straggled into Far West numb with shock and fear. The same day that the Haun's Mill massacre erupted, scouts reported that an army was marching toward Far West. Two thousand armed men milled in the flat, bent on killing the Mormons, who spent a sleepless night. The Mormons barricaded the town with logs and hefted wagons and carts on top. Men tested guns and ammunition while the women packed, ready to leave if a flight was allowed. Joseph estimated they were outnumbered five to one. Rather than take up arms, some Mormon men quietly disappeared. They were regarded as cowards, but they believed they had preached moderation and could not make themselves heard.

The next day fifteen hundred reinforcements arrived for the Missouri troops. Besieged and outnumbered, Joseph decided to surrender. Toward evening, October 31, Emma kissed him good-bye, then he, Sidney Rigdon, and Parley P. Pratt walked out with a flag of truce. They were immediately surrounded and taken prisoner; the mob now had its pawns. A court-martial deliberated through the evening. Its decision, handed to Brigadier General Alexander W. Doniphan, read:

> Sir: You will take Joseph Smith and the other prisoners into the public square of Far West and shoot them at 9 o'clock tomorrow morning.
>
> Samuel D. Lucas
> Major-General Commanding

Doniphan told Joseph of the order, and rumor flashed it to Emma, who had only to look out her window to see the place Lucas designated. In an act of insubordination for which he was never called to task, Doniphan refused to execute the command. In a terse note to his superior officer he stated: "It is cold-blooded murder. I will not obey your order. My brigade shall march for Liberty tomorrow at 8 o'clock and if you execute these men, I will hold you responsible before an earthly tribunal, so help me God."[16]

The men of Far West gave up their arms as part of the negotiations, then troops from the Missourians' camp ran wild in the town. They drove Emma and the children into the street and pillaged the house. Had they known who the victims were, they might well have raped Emma as a means of insulting Joseph. Several cases of "ravishment at Far West" were reported.[17]

On Friday, November 2, a cold rain poured down as the militia marched Joseph and the other prisoners to the town square in Far West to prepare to take them to jail in Independence. The officers allowed Joseph to enter his house with a guard. Julia, Joseph, and Frederick grasped his legs and held to his clothing, afraid to let him out of their sight. Joyful to see him alive, desperately afraid to see him leave, Emma lost her composure and sobbed along with the children. The guard allowed no moment for private parting and forced Joseph into the street.

Young Joseph still clung to his father's leg. "Father," he cried, "is the mob going to kill you?"

Emma watched a guard slam the child away with the side of his sword. "You little brat, go back. You will see your father no more."[18]

Parley P. Pratt and Hyrum Smith bade their wives farewell under the same conditions. Mary Fielding Smith would soon give birth to her first child. A guard told her she need never think that she would see Hyrum alive again. Joseph and the other prisoners soon sat in the wagon surrounded by guards. Joseph, Sr., and Lucy embraced each of the prisoners in silence, hands clutched through the wagon cover. Joseph's anguished "God bless you, Mother," came muffled through the canvas, then the wagon rumbled off.

Joseph was in General Moses Wilson's care during the march toward Independence. He protected Joseph from lynching but soon learned he had an unusual man in his charge. "I carried him in to my house a prisoner in chains, and in less than two hours my wife loved him better than she did me," Wilson reported. Joseph later asked him to return the horse and saddle that Bogard had confiscated and that Wilson now owned. Wilson retaliated against his remarkable prisoner by keeping the horse.[19]

The prisoners arrived at Independence, Missouri, on Sunday, November 4. Joseph wrote to Emma that same day. "My dear and beloved companion, of my bosam, in tribulation, and affliction," she read. "I would inform you that I am well, and that we are all of us in good Spirits as regards our own fate." In a lighthearted attempt to ease Emma's fears he related their entry into the town with a touch of humor. "We have been protected by the Jackson County boys, in the most genteel manner, and arrived here in the midst of a Splended perade."

Emma learned something of the conditions under which Joseph wrote, even though his account had to be restrained. "[I] can only pray for deliverance . . . and take everything as it comes with patience and fortitude." The letter also informed her that the men were lodged in a house instead of a jail. "If we are permited to Stay any time here, we have obtained a promise that we may have our families brought to us . . . I want you to stay where you are until you here from me again, I may Send for you to bring you to me."

His attempts to present a cheerful picture soon gave way to anxiety for Emma and the children: "Conduct all matters as your circumstances and necessities require, may God give you wisdom and prudance and Sobriety which I have every reason to believe you will, those little children are Subjects of my meditation continually, tell them that Father is yet alive, God grant that he may see them again." Joseph expressed his hope that Emma would not have to leave the area and be farther away. "Oh Emma for God sake do not forsake me nor the truth but remember me," he entreated. "If I do not meet you again in this life may God grant that we may meet in heaven, I cannot express my feelings, my heart is full, Farewell Oh my kind and affectionate Emma. I am yours forever."[20] The comfort of the house in Independence was short-lived. The prisoners were soon taken to the jail in Richmond where Emma's answer to Joseph's letter reached him. Her reassuring letter is no longer extant but it brought a rush of emotion from Joseph: "I received your letter which I read over and over again, it was a Sweet morsal to me. Oh God grant that I may have the privalidge of Seeing once more my lovely Family, in the enjoyment, of the Sweets of liberty . . . to press them to my bosam and kiss their lovely cheeks would fill my heart with unspeakable grattitude." Joseph described the conditions under which they were being held: "We are prisoners in chains, and under Strong guards for Christ Sake and for no other causes. . . . Brother Robison is chained next to me, he has a true heart and a firm mind, Brother Whight is next, Bro. Rigdon, next, Hyram Next; Parley next; Amasa, next; and thus we are bound together in chains, as well as the cords of everlasting love."

Mindful of the situation in which the children had last seen him, Joseph wrote:

Tell the children that I am alive and trust I shall come and see them before long. Comfort their hearts all you can, and try to be comforted yourself. . . . Tell little Joseph he must be a good boy; Father loves him with a perfect love; he is the Eldest [and] must not hurt those that are Smaller than him but comfort them. Tell little Frederick, Father loves him with all his heart; he is a lovely boy. Julia is a lovely little girl; I love her also, She is a promising child; tell her, Father wants her to remember him and be a good girl . . . Little Alexander is on my mind continualy. Oh my affectionate Emma, I want you to remember that I am a true and faithful friend to you; and the children, forever. My heart is entwined around yours forever and ever; Oh, may God bless you all.[21]

Joseph asked her to visit him and bring the children if she could. In Far West, Emma gathered what supplies were available for the coming winter and prepared to leave on a moment's notice, should the opportunity arise to see Joseph. Jeremiah Willey had stopped by Emma's house "To see and comfort [Joseph's] wife in distress." She promptly enlisted his services to carry messages to Joseph.

On November 30 Joseph and five of his fellow prisoners entered the Liberty jail, twenty-five miles to the west of Richmond in Clay County. Five other men arrested at the same time as Joseph remained in the Richmond jail. Emma heard of the move from Joseph: "My Dear companion, I take this opportunity to inform you that we arrived in Liberty and committed to jail this Evening but we are all in good Spirits. Captain Bogard will hand you this line. My respects to all. remain where you are at present."[22]

Immediately after receiving this letter Emma took young Joseph and Sidney Rigdon's wife Phoebe to the prison to see Joseph. They found the men locked in a dungeon with dirt floors. A low ceiling rested on thick stone walls. The temperature inside was cold as the outside. When the prisoners built a fire the smoke choked them, for there was no chimney. Rough guards allowed the three visitors inside and the hinges creaked when the heavy door swung shut behind them. Emma, young Joseph, and Phoebe spent the night in the damp, half-lit cellar with Joseph and his companions but had to leave the following day. Emma returned soon. On December 20 she entered the cell again. This time she spent two days confined with Joseph along with the wives of Caleb Baldwin and Reynolds Cahoon. As the year ended, she returned to Far West.[23]

Emma had probably left her children home with friends during this last visit, but she entered her house to find that it had been sacked. A trunk stood open with its contents strewn about, a gold ring gone, and a sealed letter opened. A roll of linen cloth, some valuable buttons, a piece of cashmere, and a number of prized books were missing. Hyrum reported that Emma had been robbed of all she had. John Lowe Butler's journal records that William McLellin and another man "went into brother Joseph's house and commenced searching over his things and Sister Emma asked him why he done so." McLellin's answer was, "Because I can." Butler stated, "He took all his julery out of Joseph's box and took a lot of his cloths and in fact, plundered the house and took the things off." Emma received word from Joseph that they suffered from the cold and he asked for quilts and bedding. John Butler recorded, "My wife was up there when the word came and she said that Sister Emma cried and said that they had taken all of her bed cloths except one quilt and blanket and what could she do? So my wife with some other sisters said, 'Send him them and we will see that you shall have something to cover you and your children.' My wife then went home and got some bed cloths and took them over to her."[24] Emma pressed charges with the help of James Mulholland, Joseph's clerk, but apparently nothing was returned.

The following month Emma went again to Liberty jail, taking Mary Fielding to see Hyrum. Mary had been bedridden since the premature birth of her son on November 13. Her sister Mercy, who cared for her, nursed the new baby, and watched over Hyrum's five children by Jerusha Barden, also had her own eight-month-old baby. Emma saw that Mary, still weak and ill, was loaded into a wagon bed with the two small babies tucked in beside her. Young Joseph found a warm place among the blankets. Mercy accompanied Emma to help care for Mary, and the women set out on the forty-mile trip. The bitter cold weather made them "suffer much"; they arrived at Liberty jail January 21, 1839.

The bleakness of the prison faded away for Joseph, who had his son and wife again, and for Hyrum, who could see Mary's firstborn son. Caleb Baldwin, Alexander MacRae, Sidney Rigdon, and Lyman Wight shared the cramped quarters with Joseph and Hyrum, but no one slept that night. Instead they had a spiritual feast that six-year-old Joseph would remember always. The six-foot, six-inch Alexander MacRae, who could not stand upright in the low-ceilinged room, forgot the stiffness in his shoulders when the familiar words of "The Massacre at River Raisin" rang out. Probably hoping the guards eavesdropped, the visiting Erastus Snow launched a mischievous parody to the tune of "Hunters of Kentucky" and called it "Mobbers of Missouri." Before the night was over Joseph had decided to give his son a blessing, perhaps because Hyrum blessed his new son. Joseph laid his hands on young Joseph's head and pronounced on the boy all the blessings to which he himself was heir through his progenitors. In later years young Joseph would not remember the content of the blessing, only that it had occurred. No one in the jail cell with Joseph ever recorded having witnessed the event. Neither Joseph nor Hyrum mentioned it in his journal, but apparently it was a tender father's blessing, loving and personal.[25] Joseph would bless this son again in ways that had more public implications.

The harsh grating sound of the door closing between Emma and Joseph probably remained in her thoughts long after her departure. But Emma left with hope this time. Sheriff Samuel Hadley, who was in charge of the jail, told her, "All the authorities are waiting for is for you to get out of the state . . . [and] the prisoners will be let out. . . . There is no reason for detaining them other than the unreasonable orders given." The Sheriff knew that Joseph would go to Emma as soon as he was released and would risk harm or rearrest. If Emma were in another state, Missouri law could not touch him.[26] She returned to Far West to prepare to leave it again.

Pressure from the mobs steadily increased. "If you will forsake your Mormon prophet . . . we will become your brothers, and will fight for you and we will protect you . . . but if you will not, why we will fall upon you."[27] It was that simple in the eyes of many Missourians, but most Mormons stuck to their faith. As Nathan Knight trudged out of Far West he tallied the worth of his losses: "1 cow shot, 40 dollars; 1 horse taken and spoiled, 80; wearing apparel, 46; bedding 60; one ox, 7; one gun, 10; umbrella, razor, bake oven, 7.77; for being shot through lungs and finger, 5,000; for being compelled to leave Mo., 1,000."[28]

In conference with Joseph and the others, Brigham Young made the decision to move the Mormons east, back through Missouri and across the Mississippi River to Illinois. Emma was in Far West for only about ten days after she left Liberty jail. The elder Smiths packed a wagon, then unpacked again, "because Emma wanted the wagon," Lucy said. Emma filled the wagon with supplies and her four children, but one item remained. While Joseph was imprisoned, his scribe, James Mulholland, had stayed in Emma's home and kept Joseph's papers. When the local men became unruly, Mulholland gave the papers to his sister-in-law, thinking a woman might escape search. "Immediately on taking possession of the papers," Ann Scott related, "I made two cotton bags of sufficient size to contain them, sewing a band around the top ends of sufficient length to button around my waist; and I carried those papers on my person in the day-time, when the mob was round, and slept with them under my pillow at night. . . . I gave them to sister Emma Smith. . . . on the evening of her departure for Commerce."[29]

The following morning, February 7, 1839, Emma and her children left Far West with a group headed by Stephen Markham. A friend drove her team and cared for her horses. One afternoon Emma stopped at a log farmhouse. Young Joseph recalled that a yelping pack of dogs met them at the gate, but the farmer and his wife made Emma and the children comfortable. A great fire warmed one end of the double-log home and the family slept safely on the floor.

The Mississippi had frozen over before Emma arrived. Fearful of the thin ice, she separated the two horses, put Charlie on her wagon and trailed Jim behind, then walked apart with two-and-a-half-year-old Frederick, and eight-month-old Alexander in her arms. She had Julia hold tightly to her skirt on one side, positioned young Joseph on the other, and, with the heavy bags of Joseph's papers fastened securely to her waist, Emma walked across the frozen river to safety. Of this trek she later wrote: "No one but God, knows the reflections of my mind and the feelings of my heart when I left our house and home, and almost all of everything that we possessed excepting our little children, and took my journey out of the State of Missouri, leaving [Joseph] shut up in that lonesome prison. But the reflection is more than human nature ought to bear, and if God does not record our sufferings and avenge our wrongs on them that are guilty, I shall be sadly mistaken."[30]

6

Sanctuary
in a Swamp

1839–1841

Emma walked up the east bank of the Mississippi and into the outskirts of a small town named Quincy on February 15, 1839. She was now thirty-four. One year earlier she had crossed the ice in the opposite direction with Joseph and Brigham Young on their way to Missouri. But Zion now lay in shambles. A week after Emma left Far West the elder Smiths joined Brigham Young's company and soon arrived in Quincy. They were joined by other Saints throughout the winter.

The citizens of Quincy responded to the Mormons' needs with extraordinary compassion. Sarah Kinsley Cleveland and her husband John took Emma and her children into their home three miles from town. Every other shelter available filled with refugees.

On March 9, 1839, Emma wrote to Joseph, "I shall not attempt to write my feelings altogether, for the situation in which you are, the walls, bars, and bolts, rolling rivers, running streams, rising hills, sinking vallies and spreading prairies that separate us, and the cruel injustice that first cast you into prison and still holds you there, with many other considerations, places my feelings far beyond description." She credited "the direct interposition of divine mercy" in helping her "endure the scenes of suffering that I have passed through but I still live and am yet willing to suffer more if it is the will of kind Heaven, that I should for your sake." Emma told Joseph with maternal pride that little Alexander was "one of the finest little fellows, you ever saw in your life" and was learning to walk by pushing a chair around the Cleveland house. She expressed appreciation for the help that the Quincy people offered. Then, embarrassed at her handwriting, she explained that hard work stiffened her hands, and her "heart convulsed with intense anxiety" over his welfare. She closed her letter with "I am ever yours affectionately."[1]

Joseph and his companions in jail acknowledged, "We received some letters last evening—one from Emma, one from Don C. Smith, and one from Bishop Partridge—all breathing a kind and consoling spirit . . . they were to our souls as the gentle air is refreshing."[2] Emma's and Joseph's correspondence reveals that her love, affection, and loyalty helped sustain him through those winter months, yet he worried. "Do you think that my being cast into prison renders me less worthy of your friendship?" he asked, then answered himself, "No, I do not think so."[3]

In the meantime, the guards heaped verbal abuse and foul language on the men confined in the cell until Joseph finally stood one night and "in the name of God" rebuked them to silence. He prayed in despair and the response was, "My son, peace be unto thy soul; thine adversity and thine afflictions shall be but a small moment."[4]

With spring came new hope, and Joseph directed Emma to speak to the church in his behalf on March 21. "I have sent an Epistle to the church directed to you because I wanted you to have the first reading of it. . . . I want all the church to make out a bill of damages and apply to the United States Court as soon as possible however they will find out what can be done themselves you expressed my feelings concerning the order and I believe that there is a way to git redress for such things." He also expressed concern for Emma. "I very well know your toils and simpathise with you," he told her. "If God will spare my life once more to have the privelege of takeing care of you I will ease your care and indeavour to cumfort your heart. Tell me all you can and even if old Major [the dog] is alive yet and what those little prattlers say that cling around you[r] neck," he requested. "Do you tell them that I am in prison that their lives might be saved?"[5]

Emma heard rumors that Joseph might be set free.[6] Whenever she could persuade someone to go to the wharf and make inquiry, she did. One day in April, Dimick Huntington rode three miles into town at Emma's request. He lounged around the boat landing while the Quincy ferry docked about eight o'clock in the morning. A disheveled traveler leaned against the side rail with his head turned away. Ragged pants were tucked inside old boots full of holes. He wore a blue cloak with the collar turned up to hide his face, and a wide-brimmed black hat drooped down over his unkempt beard. His skin was pale and his body wasted. Dimick approached the ferry as the man guardedly raised his head. "My God!" Huntington exclaimed. "Brother Joseph, is that you?"

Alarmed, Joseph hushed Dimick and immediately asked about Emma and the children. Huntington explained that they were several miles away and asked if he did not want to find his parents first. Impatient at any delay, Joseph insisted, "Take me to my family as quick as you can." Dimick located a second horse and Joseph slouched in the saddle to avoid detection as they negotiated the back streets of town. Joseph did not realize that Mormons could hold their heads up in Quincy.

As they approached the Cleveland house Dimick hung back, suspecting that a reunion worth observing might be at hand. Emma glanced through the door at the stranger stopping at the yard and recognized him before he had time to dismount. She ran through the door and was in Joseph's arms before he was halfway to the front gate.[7]

Joseph explained that the Missourians had decided to set some of the men free and found a most unusual way to do it. During a move to another prison, the sheriff told the astonished prisoners, "I'll take a good drink of grog and go to bed, and you may do as you have a mind to." Three guards slaked their thirst with whiskey and honey while a fourth saddled the horses for the Mormons. Joseph and Hyrum and the others rode off before the guards could change their minds.[8] After five months they were finally free.

Soon after Joseph's arrival Wandle Mace of Quincy heard him speak for the first time. Mace watched him carefully and observed that even after six months in prison "he was a fine looking man, tall and well proportioned, strong and active, light complexion, blue eyes, and light hair, and very little beard. He had a free and easy manner, not the least affectation, yet bold and independent, and very interesting and eloquent in speech."[9] Before long Mace and his family requested baptism into the church.

During the next month Joseph turned his attention to finding a permanent settlement for his people. While most of the Mormons from Missouri had gone to the ferry crossing at Quincy, a small group traveled farther north where they discovered some old military barracks at Montrose, Iowa, on the west side of the river. They found Isaac Galland, the owner, across the river at a settlement called Commerce. Galland offered to sell the Mormons his interests on both sides, but his deeds of conveyance were shaky at best.[10] The church authorities believed they had purchased the lands outright, when in fact no clear titles existed to any land parcels in that area. Galland watched the eager Mormons begin again that spring of 1839 and made his own prophecy of doom: the Saints would continue to buy out the settlers and build up their area "until they again acquire a sufficient quantity of 'Honey-comb' to induce the surrounding [people] to rob them again; at which time they will no doubt have to renounce their religion; or submit to a repetition of similar acts of violince, and outrage as have already been."[11]

Oblivious to Galland's forecast, Emma and Joseph moved from Quincy to Commerce, fifty miles north on the east bank of the Mississippi. Joseph soon changed the name to Nauvoo, a name that he said meant "the city beautiful." The town site lay on the peninsula of a horseshoe bend in the river. High bluffs ran along the east side of the area, while the peninsula itself was low and flat. The soil was so wet from springs that a man could hardly walk on it and teams found it impossible. But despite these drawbacks the location offered exclusive access to the river. Nauvoo could become an important terminus for river traffic. Though it was a swamp, it was a spectacular site for the building of a city.

On May 9, 1839, Emma moved her family into a small two-story log house which they called the Homestead. It overlooked the Mississippi to the south. The single lower room had a fireplace in the west end; a staircase led to a second room above. Drinking water came from a well in the yard. Joseph, Sr., and Lucy Smith moved into a summer kitchen connected to the main building by a shed roof, while several small outbuildings scattered near the house provided shelter for other families. In a letter, Emma and Joseph told Sarah and John Cleveland that they had chosen a lot for them across the street from their own. Joseph also set aside the lot next to Cleveland's for Lucinda and George Harris.[12]

Soon after Emma moved she purchased a cow from a nearby farmer. Mr. Hibbard taught young Joseph a principle of human nature he would remember all his life. Emma assigned her son to milk the cow, but halfway through, the cow would bolt for the Hibbard place, leaving the boy fuming. The wily old cow had learned she could outmaneuver a boy with a bucket between his legs. Young Joseph frequently appeared at the Hibbard farm to get his cow and the old man and the boy became acquainted. The farmer, who appeared to be hard of hearing, was called "Deaf" Hibbard. Joseph's troubles with his cow probably made him laugh. One day Hibbard called Joseph to him and asked in a low voice, "Is there anyone near?"

"No, Mr. Hibbard," Joseph shouted loudly back.

"I can hear you very well, Joseph," Hibbard said. "When there is no one near you needn't speak so loud to me. When somebody is about, then speak loud." The man then explained that his wife was a perpetual scold but that he turned a deaf ear to her storming. Joseph realized that Hibbard had been shamming for many years, but he never forgot to yell when others were present or to speak quietly when they were alone. It was an enlightening experience about hearing only what one wanted to hear.[13]

In the midst of the house building, plowing, and planting, many fell ill with the "meanest of all diseases." The Mormons called it the ague, but it was malaria. The swamps harbored the anopheles mosquito. The unsuspecting Mormons walked into the situation with their resistance already weakened by their miseries of the past winter. Oliver Huntington's mother became the third fatality in Nauvoo. The rest of the family were too sick to work. "We were a pitiful set and none to pitty us but God and his prophet; Brother Joseph seeing that we still grew worse, told William that we would all die if we stayed there, and that he must take the team and bring us down to his own house. So he took us all into his own family."[14] Joseph also found a child named Jane and brought her home "as his wife Emma was a good nurse."

Elizabeth Ann Whitney described her family as "all sick with ague, chills and fever, and [we] were only just barely able to crawl around and wait upon each other. Under these trying circumstances my ninth child was born. Joseph, upon visiting us and seeing our change of circumstances, urged us at once to come and share his accommodations. [We] went to live in the Prophet Joseph's yard in a small cottage."[15]

The sick filled every bed in Emma's house and spilled over onto makeshift bedrolls outside. She and Joseph moved into a tent in the yard. When they could free themselves from nursing duties in their own home, they "would ride on horseback, from place to place visiting the sick, anointing with oil, and lay hands on them, and heal them and relieve their wants."[16] Young Joseph carried water to the sick until he caught the disease himself. When he became impatient waiting for his mother to come to his bed, he crawled out of it and immediately fainted. Emma replaced her child in bed and explained that he was not the only one sick, that she would come to him when she could.

The unseen plague seemed to have no identifiable cause. People blamed the night air, vapors from putrid vegetable and animal matter, grief, fear, unripe fruit, and "intense thought." No amount of human compassion seemed to stay the disease. Some believed the powers of Satan were at work to destroy the people. By July 22 Joseph himself was down with malaria. Emma included him in her daily rounds and gave direction to others who were well enough to help her. Young Benjamin F. Johnson assisted with Joseph's care and served Emma's thin gruel of meal and water to the sick. Wandle Mace converted a coffee grinder into a portable mill that worked so well a ten-year-old boy could grind a bushel of wheat in an hour for Emma.

While malaria was no laughing matter, a grim sense of humor enabled many Mormons to bear it with some grace. One sufferer, Charles Lowell Walker, wrote an "Ode to the Ague" that makes up in color for what it lacks in medical terms.

> Dear sufferer, it is for your sake
> I give the description of a shake;
> You first feel cold and very queer,
> And then you shake, oh dear, oh dear;
> Next, fever burns with glowing heat
> And you are parched from head to feet.
> All those that shake say this is true,
> And so does C.L.W.[17]

In September some members of the Quorum of the Twelve left for missions to England. John Taylor and Wilford Woodruff answered Joseph's missionary call first, followed by Brigham Young and Heber C. Kimball. The latter were so sick that others had to boost them into the wagon. As it pulled away Heber commented to Brigham, "This is pretty tough but let us rise and give them a cheer." They swayed to their feet, waved their hats, and yelled, "Hurrah, hurrah, hurrah for Israel!" Their two sick wives leaned against the door and watched as long as they were able.

In spite of the sickness Joseph sent a group of men back to Far West for the Mormon printing press. The press and all the type had been buried for safekeeping and was now brought to Nauvoo, where the only place for it was an underground room with a stream of water flowing through it. Joseph assigned his brother Don Carlos and Mercy Fielding's husband, Robert B. Thompson, to help Ebenezer Robinson publish a newspaper, the *Times and Seasons,* and print missionary pamphlets.

When the cool fall air killed the mosquitoes, the malaria gradually decreased and Emma turned her attention to bringing some order to her house. She took in two young girls, Julia and Savilla Durfee, to work for her, Julia as seamstress and teacher, Savilla as maid. Emma's kitchen duties were probably similar to the other women's. They dried fruits and vegetables and cured meat. They wrapped rock-hard maple sugar loaves and hung them from rafters in the smokehouses, then hammered off small pieces as needed. Most of the milk was made into cheese which drained from cloth bags or perforated buckets hung from tree limbs or rafters. Kitchen utensils were simple homemade wooden cutting boards, rolling pins, spoons, and doughboxes. Emma might have beaten eggs with a whisk made of birch twigs tied together. A wringer and a washboard always stood nearby. For clothing to be very clean, the white things were boiled with homemade soap, making washday a daylong affair.[18]

Cookstoves were available, but few Mormons could afford the price. Instead, Emma made "ash cakes" in her fireplace by adding salt to sifted cornmeal mixed with boiling water. The ubiquitous cornmeal appeared in hasty pudding, corn dodgers, and corn bread. Sweetened with maple sugar or honey, it also made the dessert. While Emma became adept at making variations on the basic menu derived from cornmeal, her family still found the daily fare monotonous. On one occasion Hyrum's son John came with young Joseph to dinner. With a boy on each side, Joseph examined the food laid out on the table, then prayed, "Lord we thank thee for this jonnycake, and ask thee to send us something better, Amen."

The corn bread was cut and served, but before they could finish it a man at the door asked for Joseph. "I have brought you some flour and a ham," he said.

Joseph took the proffered gifts, blessed the man for bringing them, then turned to Emma with a sly and mischievous grin. "I knew the Lord would answer my prayer."[19]

While Emma became absorbed in her domestic responsibilities Joseph's desire to make somebody pay for the outrages in Missouri prompted him to go to Washington to seek compensation. Sidney Rigdon and two other men went with him. Just outside of Springfield, Illinois, Joseph's party met a company of seven wagons traveling from Canada to Nauvoo led by William Law, a new convert to the church. Fate would twist the lives of Law, Emma, and Joseph together before their association ended.

Emma first met William Law in Nauvoo when he handed her a letter from Joseph. He was a tall, well-built man with a pleasant manner. He found Emma's household full of sickness in spite of the High Council's resolution on October 20 that was also published in the *Times and Seasons*, that "Joseph Smith, Jun.; and his family be exempt from receiving in future such crowds of visitors as have formerly thronged his house."[20] Emma described her situation in a letter to Joseph. Someone had brought Orson Hyde and his wife, Nancy Marinda Johnson, to Emma the day Joseph left. She said they both had a "ravaging disease." The next day James Mulholland's wife brought her sick husband to Emma, hoping her expert nursing would save his life. Emma nursed him for five weeks, then wrote to Joseph, "His spirit left its suffering tenement for a better mansion than he had here."[21] Emma's own children were also sick; Frederick's fever broke shortly after his father left, then young Joseph started with what Emma termed the "chill fever." He suffered through two bouts of it, then lost a great deal of blood from a nosebleed. His slow recovery kept Emma worried.

Joseph wrote, "I shall be filled with constant anxiety about you and the children until I hear from you and in a perticular maner little Fredrick it was so painful to leave him sick." Unable to restrain himself from offering instruction, Joseph went on, "I hope you will wach over those tender offspring in a manner that is becoming a mother and a saint and try to cultiveate their minds and learn them to read and be sober do not let them be exposed to the wether to take cold and try to get all the rest you can it will be a long and lonesome time during my absense from you and nothing but a sense of humanity could have urged me on to so great a Sacrafice."[22] A small prick of conscience may have reminded Joseph that this was not a good time to leave Emma alone. She was pregnant again. When Emma wrote to Joseph in December she told him, "Business does not go on quite as well since you left as when you were here . . . much business remains unattend[ed] to, in consequence of it; though Hyrum has put Robert B. Thompson, in his office; yet he has done nothing towards adjusting the business as yet, nor do I think he will. Carlos requests me to have you inform us, what became of the letter, which Mr. John T. Green, sent Ebenezer Robinson containing the names of a number of subscribers."

Emma did not neglect to relay the concerns of Joseph's friends to him: "There is manifested, far great anxiety for you in this place; that you may be prospered in the mission whereunto you are sent." Needing to be frugal with her candles and lamp oil, she closed with reluctance, "As the night is fast approaching, I must reserve my better feeling untill I have a better opportunity to express them, Yours affectionately, Emma Smith."[23]

When Joseph reached Washington he presented his case in person to

Martin Van Buren. The President read the letter Joseph gave him, looked up, and remarked, "What can I do? . . . If I do anything I shall come in contact with the whole state of Missouri."[24] The President insisted, "Your cause is just, but I can do nothing for you."[25] Van Buren's dismissal of the Mormon claims angered Joseph, whose outspoken accusations against the state of Missouri activated the fury of its governor, Lilburn Boggs. Not content to have the Mormons out of Missouri, Boggs began an active campaign to have Joseph arrested and brought back for trial.

Joseph and Sidney Rigdon brought new clothes from the East for their families. Joseph had three new suits, Sidney had four, and each one had clothing for their wives and children. Almon Babbitt, a lawyer who would eventually alienate both Joseph and Emma as well as Brigham Young, accused Joseph of extravagance. He probably expected Joseph and Emma to set an example of the gracious poverty worthy of poorly paid clerics. In reality, Emma had faced her losses with remarkable grace, and Joseph's gifts to his family were undoubtedly in recognition of their personal sacrifices. Still, some Mormons looked on their own poverty with remarkable humor and cheerfulness. The unmarried Abigail Pitkin wrote to a sister in Ohio:

> With chairs we're blessed with only Two
>   Missouri claims the remaining few;
>
> For old Missouri's wicked clan
>   Our cupboard kept, and warming pan,
> We have a heifer very small
>   At present gives no milk at all;
> And fowls which throng our door
>   But lack of corn will keep them poor,
> Poor things, they'll have to make up meat
>   When we have nothing else to eat.
>
> In dress and manners we appear
>   Much as we did when you were here.
> Our names we keep but rather would
>   Exchange for better if we could
>
> We've many friends and many foes,
> Many wants and many woes,
> But still I am content to be
>   A Mormon!—not a Pharisee.[26]

While the citizens of Nauvoo built up the city, Brigham Young, in England, incurred Joseph's displeasure. The incident involved Emma's responsibility to collect hymns, a prerogative of hers that Joseph guarded closely. Rather than ship books to England, Brigham and the other missionaries planned to publish the Book of Mormon and a hymnal that probably included Emma's selections as well as songs Joseph and the Twelve had chosen. On October 27, 1839, five weeks after Brigham and others left for England, the High Council met and *"Voted,* that Sister Emma Smith select and publish a Hymn-Book for the use of the Church, and that Brigham Young be informed of this action and he not publish the Hymns taken by him from Commerce."[27] Unfortunately, the instructions never reached Brigham and he wrote to his wife Mary Ann in June 1840, "We are printing 3,000 copes of a hym book 5,000 copes of the Book of Mormon. . . . I have now got through with the hym book. I have had perty much the whole of it to doe mey self . . . so it has made my labor so hard that it seems as though it would be imposable for me ever to regane my helth." Brigham then instructed Mary Ann to "Tell *Br* Joseph Smith that I send as much love to him and Emma and famely . . . as I can get carid a cross the water."[28]

When Brigham wrote to his wife again in November he had received a letter from Joseph. The tone distressed him: "In Brother Joseph letter he sent to the twelve he said he had somethings aganst them, according to what I could lern from the letter it was because we did not wright to him upon the subject of printing the hymbook . . . all I have to say about the matter as to my self is I have don all that I could to due good and promote the cause that we are in."[29] Brigham was not aware that other church members had printed hymnals. David White Rogers, chairmaker of some means, published a hymnal in New York in 1838 and plagiarized the preface from Emma's 1835 collection. Forty-nine of eighty-nine songs came from her hymnal. The same conference authorizing Emma to make a new selection of hymns also resolved that "D. W. Rogers's [hymnbook] be utterly discarded by the Church."[30] In the spring of 1840 one Thomas Grover accused Rogers of several areas of misconduct, among them, "compiling a hymn-book, and selling it as the one compiled by Sister Emma Smith. . . . After many observations and explanations, it was . . . resolved, that D. W. Rogers be forgiven and the hand of fellowship be continued towards him."[31] Another man, Benjamin C. Elsworth, published a hymnal a year after Rogers. He lifted Emma's preface and used sixty-six hymns from her collection plus all but one of the remaining forty from the Rogers book, adding only seven to make one hundred twelve in all. He apparently escaped condemnation.[32] Brigham and the Twelve survived the controversy generated over their hymnal relatively unscathed. Still thoughtful of Emma, he sent a copy of the hymnbook published in England to her and checked on its safe arrival through another letter to Mary Ann the following January.[33]

Emma's expanded collection would come off the press in 1841, printed by Ebenezer Robinson. Emma often sang as she worked, and surely some of the songs her family heard were in her collection. A young man named William Holmes Walker heard her sing the first time he visited the Smith home in Nauvoo. "I arrived at his [Joseph's] house about nine o'clock, just as his family was singing, before the accustomed evening prayer. His wife Emma, leading in the singing. I thought I had never heard such sweet, heavenly music before."[34] When William's mother died the following year he, his younger brother Lorin, and his sisters, Lucy and Catherine, would find a home with Emma and Joseph.

Lucy Walker was then fifteen and a half. Later in her autobiographical sketch she recalled Emma's and Joseph's kindness. "The Prophet and his wife introduced us as their sons and daughters. Every privilege was acorded us in the home. Every pleasure within reach was ours." When Lucy's eight-year-old sister Lydia became "stricken with brain-fever, [Joseph] told the boys to drive down to the Mississippi river, then took her in his arms and baptised her. When [Lydia was] brought in, Sister Emma, noble woman that she was, helped change her clothing. And all that loveing hearts and willing hands could do, was done." In spite of the best efforts of both Emma and Joseph, the girl died a few days after. "Here let me say," Lucy wrote, "that our own father and mother could scarsely have manifested greater solicitude for her recovery than did the Prophet and his wife—Emma. They accompanied us to her last resting place beside her Mother." The rest of the Walker children, with the exception of the baby, came to Emma's crowded home where she mothered them all for nearly two more years. William Walker married in November 1843 and brought his bride to live at Emma's for six months until he took the five youngest of the Walker children to live with him and his new wife.[35]

Taking in children in times of need was already an established pattern for Emma. In the spring of 1840 she gave a home to two of Edward and Lydia Partridge's daughters. Bishop Edward Partridge died on May 27, 1840. Lydia kept the small children with her, but Emma opened the first permanent door to Emily, sixteen, and Eliza, twenty, when she invited them to live with her. "We did not work for wages but were provided with the necessities of life," Emily remembered. "Joseph and Emma were very kind to us; they were almost like a father and mother, and I loved Emma and the children."[36] These sisters would remain in the Smith household for the next three years until circumstances unexpected by them all forced a separation.

During the spring Joseph constructed a large room on the back of the Homestead. A great fireplace in the north end allowed the extension to be used as a kitchen and the two original rooms became sleeping quarters. A special retreat lay hidden under the house. Part way down the steps leading to the cellar, Joseph cut the timbers bearing the steps, then hinged the stairs so a couple of them could be lifted forward. This gave entry to a small vaulted room with a dry brick floor and bricked walls large enough for two people to occupy either sitting or lying down. Ventilation came from spaces around the stairs.[37]

On June 14, 1840, another son was born to Emma and Joseph. They named him Don Carlos after his strapping uncle. Probably one of several midwives who practiced in Nauvoo attended Emma in this birth. These women carried their medical instruments in small black "baby satchels." They used "scalpels, needles, scissors, tweezers, saw blades, a small hammer, a spool of heavy thread, a few obstetrical instruments, plus a package of scorched cloths which had been oven-sterilized." Tradition states that Joseph blessed these women and set them apart as midwives.[38] Evidence suggests that Emma occasionally helped at births.

During these months Emma faced the challenges of domestic life. Her growing children sometimes displayed a streak of independence, a rightful inheritance in that family. Once Julia watched one of Sidney Rigdon's small daughters get what she wanted by banging her head on the floor and kicking the furniture. Julia decided to try the same approach. "Don't you go Lacy Rigdon on me," Emma scolded, and picked her child up from the floor.[39]

Another case involved Alexander and his older brother, Joseph. In the middle of a quarrel between the two the younger child bit the older. When Emma learned of the incident she calmly examined the teeth marks on Joseph's arm, rolled up Alexander's sleeve, and bit him in the same place. Emma taught Julia to sew and cook, and to read, for there were no schools in Nauvoo for the first year or so. Emma later gave Julia the responsibility for teaching the boys their letters.[40] From both their parents, the children learned generosity.

One morning as Emma prepared breakfast the family heard a hesitant knock. Young Joseph answered the door. A black man named Jack stood waiting to see the Mormon leader. When invited in, he said he preferred to wait until the meal was over. Jack had lost one arm just below the elbow when a cannon discharged prematurely during a Fourth of July celebration. The illness and fever that followed kept the man from working, and he had used up all his savings. Now he stood before the Smiths' door and explained that he could not get work because he looked so shabby. Joseph brought out a handsome buckskin suit that was his pride and gave it to the black man, who soon found a position on a steamer. Long before the suit wore out, he pressed payment for it on Joseph, who refused to accept it. The suit had been a gift.[41]

Emma's household remained lively with a constant flow of visitors while Nauvoo swelled with a steady number of converts filtering into the area. By far the largest group were immigrants from England who began to arrive in the city as converts of the Twelve. The first organized company sailed from Liverpool on June 6, 1840. Their experiences would be repeated in various forms until forty-seven hundred of them eventually represented a third of the population of Nauvoo.

Two of these converts, Jane and John Mellen, could not afford to come together. Jane remained in England while John sailed to the United States, found work, and saved enough to bring his family over. Four months after he left, Jane gave birth to her third baby, who died at ten months of age. Eventually she docked in New Orleans with her two surviving children and four dollars in her purse. She worked for a riverboat captain to secure passage up the Mississippi River to Nauvoo where she was told her husband was dead. Emma took in Jane and her family for two weeks. Early one morning as Jane walked down the street to do a day's washing she met her husband face to face. The story of his death had been a rumor. The couple rented a house and began a new life.[42]

At this time Emma's concern for her husband's safety had resurfaced. Governor Lilburn Boggs of Missouri had sent a message to the governor of Illinois, Thomas Carlin, requesting the return of Joseph, Sidney Rigdon, Parley P. Pratt, and others as fugitives from justice. When Carlin did not comply, Boggs sent his own men to Illinois to arrest Joseph. Joseph had been in and out of hiding several days. His father's health worsened throughout the summer of 1840. When the old patriarch began to vomit blood, Lucy sent for her children. After blessing each one, Joseph Smith, Sr., died on September 14, 1840.[43] For Emma the loss was great, as he had been a father to her in the years since her estrangement from Isaac Hale. The family buried their father on September 15. Joseph made himself inconspicuous at the funeral, for he had had word that the Missourians were looking for him. He went into hiding later that same day and managed to keep clear of the Missouri officials long enough to discourage them.

Not long after his father's death Joseph reorganized the presidency of the church, realigning the priesthood powers. Hyrum Smith became patriarch in place of his father; William Law took Hyrum's place in the first presidency, along with Joseph and Sidney Rigdon. At the same time Joseph became sole trustee-in-trust for the church, a decision that affected Emma. Joseph and other church leaders had bought several large tracts of land, and while it was clear that these men were purchasing land on which members of the church could dwell, they pledged their personal credit to do so. Soon Joseph, with the encouragement and consent of others in the church hierarchy, would transfer smaller pieces of land to Emma and the children. Joseph's private business and the affairs of the church were becoming intertwined, and Emma often assisted him in buying and selling land.[44] Eventually the intermingling of church and private land would provide controversy strong enough to alienate Emma from some of her longtime friends.

The year of Joseph, Sr.'s death, John Cook Bennett arrived in Nauvoo, joined the church, and found a temporary place to live in Emma's home. About five feet, nine inches tall, a handsome man with graying dark hair and black eyes, he was broad-shouldered, with a trim waist and hips. His face was rather thin, his mouth tight-lipped, and his manner ingratiating and smoothly polite. He had an air about him that annoyed Emma, and young Joseph recalled that she disliked him from the very first. Although Bennett made much of his abilities as a physician when he came to Nauvoo, Emma distrusted him enough to refuse to take his prescribed medicine during an illness. He lost further influence with her when he pulled young Joseph's tooth with a "turn key" and the boy bled severely before a solution made of saltpeter on leather shavings finally checked the bleeding. Bennett had better luck with the community as a whole when he offered the suffering Mormons quinine for their malaria.

After he had found another place to live, he still took many of his meals at Emma's house. Young Joseph recalled that his mother would set a loaf of her bread in front of the fire until the end was toasted brown, then cut off a thin slice and replace the loaf. Thus she prepared Bennett's supper of toasted bread and milk, "just as he liked it." He expounded on a new food just coming into vogue, claiming that the "love apple" or tomato, had beneficial medicinal qualities.[45]

Bennett seemed to know something about almost everything. This impressed Joseph, who needed an urbane representative for the church. He hoped to have Nauvoo chartered under the state of Illinois. Bennett offered to guide the proposed documents through the legislature and did his job well by developing sympathy for the Mormons through graphic descriptions of the Missouri persecutions. The charters passed without so much as a complete reading, giving the elected officers of the city broad powers.[46] The city council could pass any ordinance not conflicting with the federal or state constitutions. The council could also act as the municipal court and could organize a militia that answered exclusively to the mayor. The mayor held a position of supreme power, for he formulated laws as a member of the city council, interpreted laws as a member of the court, and enforced them through the militia, known as the Nauvoo Legion.

Triumphant from his session with the Illinois legislature, which passed the charters on December 16, 1840, John C. Bennett returned to Nauvoo in time to be elected the city's first mayor on February 1 of the new year. Few Saints knew Bennett. That he secured such a high office so rapidly suggests that Joseph trusted him implicitly and had spoken on his behalf.

Bennett wasted no time setting up an efficient military organization, complete with officers, ranks, and military drills, which attracted almost every able-bodied man in Nauvoo. Governor Thomas Carlin commissioned Joseph lieutenant general of the Legion, and Joseph immediately made John C. Bennett second in command with the rank of major general. Joseph wore a blue coat, gold-colored epaulets, high black boots, and a sweeping hat topped with ostrich feathers. He carried an impressive sword. Only John C. Bennett outshone him, resplendent in gold braid, buttons, and tassels. Emma and the wives of "other distinguished officers [often] accompanied their companions on parade." One woman later wrote of Emma's fondness for horses and said she "could manage them well in riding or driving. Many can recall seeing her mounted on horseback beside her husband in military parade and a grander couple could nowhere be found. She always dressed becomingly, and a riding costume showed off her shapely figure to the best advantage."[47]

The Mormons saw in the Legion strength and power that had been denied them earlier when they faced roving mobs. The Legion drilled regularly. Even the children, young Joseph included, marched behind the men. The boys brandished wooden swords and carried an impressive banner that announced, "Our fathers we respect; our mothers we'll protect."[48] They regarded the hated Missourians with much bravado from the safe side of the river. The Legion inspired boys' games in the meadow near the river. They had mock guns, wooden bowie knives, and wild imaginations. Sometimes they were horse thieves, at other times explorers, pioneers, river pirates, or hunters. When young Joseph joined the group the game became "Mormons and Missourians" and the play was sometimes rough. He described the games to his mother with much enthusiasm. Emma listened with concern because ideas of revenge and violence were becoming real to her boys. She reasoned with her son, forbade that particular game, and repeatedly watched reason fail. Finally, willow in hand, Emma marched young Joseph to a secluded spot and applied firmer reason in a lower place. She had to take him to the same place two more nights, then he played with Frederick and remained in her sight.[49]

Joseph planned two large buildings for Nauvoo—a temple and a hotel. He wanted the Nauvoo temple to be the most splendid building on the Mississippi. On a hill overlooking the city, workers dug the foundation and on April 6, the eleventh anniversary of the founding of the church, they laid the cornerstone with appropriate ceremony. This provided the Nauvoo Legion with its first opportunity for an impressive review. At seven-thirty in the morning artillery fire announced the arrival of Brigadier Generals William Law and Don Carlos Smith in front of their cohorts. As a grown woman, Samuel Smith's daughter Mary wrote, "I have heard Aunt Emma say that [Don Carlos] was the handsomest man she ever saw—That when in uniform and on horse back that he was magnificent—And Aunt Emma was not given to undue laudations."[50] Half an hour after Don Carlos's entry, Major General John C. Bennett was conducted to his post while the cannon fired. At nine-thirty Lieutenant General Joseph Smith appeared on the grounds with his guard, staff, and field officers. Emma rode sidesaddle on her horse Charlie and, with a group of women, presented a silk American flag to Joseph. The cannon fired again. At noon the procession squared up on the temple site for Sidney Rigdon's oration. It reminded every man and woman present of the trials and hardships encountered on the long road from the organization of the church at the Whitmer farm to the present ceremonies. The military band marched on the field, then combined with a choir, and music rang through the half-completed streets of the Mormon city. The day ended with Emma and the women serving a turkey dinner to the honored guests and officers.

One guest watched the proceedings with increasing apprehension and anger. Whatever he saw or interpreted that day, Thomas C. Sharp, editor of the Warsaw *Signal*, went away a determined enemy of Joseph and the Mormons. Within three years Sharp would launch a concerted attack against the Mormons, using polygamy as his focal point. Unknown to Sharp at this time, Joseph Smith had already begun the practice of plural marriage in Nauvoo. Just the evening before he had secretly married Louisa Beaman.

7

A New Order
of Marriage

1841–1842

On the evening of April 5, 1841, Joseph Bates Noble crossed the river from Montrose, Iowa, and met Joseph Smith under an elm tree. Twenty-six-year-old Louisa Beaman, dressed in a man's hat and coat, stood at Joseph's side. With Joseph telling him the words of the ceremony, Noble married his wife's sister to the Mormon prophet.

The previous fall Joseph had approached Noble, a close friend, confiding in him the "principle of celestial marriage." He said that God had revealed the doctrine to him in Kirtland but that an angel of the Lord had now appeared to him, commanding that he introduce this "new order of marriage." That Joseph began teaching plural marriage in Nauvoo to Noble, who was not a member of the ranking councils of the church, is not surprising, since Hyrum Smith and Sidney Rigdon had expressed their distaste for Joseph's involvements in Kirtland, and the Twelve were still in England on their missions. Joseph swore Noble to secrecy, saying, "I have placed my life in your hands, therefore do not in an evil hour betray me to my enemies."[1] Similar statements would accompany Joseph's instructions to others, indicating that he recognized plural marriage would bring upheaval to his people and perhaps result in his own death.

Joseph kept his relationship with Louisa Beaman secret from all but a select few. He also kept it secret from Emma. His earlier attempts to begin the practice in Kirtland had presented severe trauma for Emma, and Joseph knew that she would not willingly share him with another woman. Early in that summer of 1841, however, Joseph publicly tested the water for this new order of marriage. Emma sat in a Sunday morning service in the grove of trees used as a meeting place and listened to Joseph preach the "restoration of all things" as they were in the times of Abraham, Isaac, and Jacob. "Suppose we send one of our Elders to Turkey or India . . . where they practiced polygamy and he would say to them, 'Your laws are not good, you should put away your plural wives; what would they do to him?' They would [ask] . . . 'Elder, is there not a land of Zion, a place where the saints should gather to?' The Elder should not lie to him. He shall say, 'Yes, Brother, there is a land of Zion where saints of God are required to gather to . . . the laws in Zion are such that you can bring your wives and enjoy them here as well as there,' the Elder shall say to that Brother."[2]

One church member, Joseph Lee Robinson, heard the speech and later recorded it in his journal, adding, "This was to me the first intimation that I ever received that polygamy would ever be practiced or lawful with this people." His brother Ebenezer later wrote of Don Carlos Smith's reaction, "Any man who will teach and practice the doctrine of spiritual wifery will go to hell, I don't care if it is my brother Joseph." Joseph Robinson said the prophet went home to dinner but "several of the first women of the church collected at the Prophet's house with his wife," saying, "Oh Mister Smith, you have done it now. It will never do, why it is all but blasphemy. You must take back what you have said today. It is outrageous. It would ruin us as a people." Helen Mar Kimball, Vilate's and Heber's daughter, later identified several of the women, including her mother and Emma, who were so persuasive.

"I will have to take that saying back and leave it as though there had been nothing said," Joseph acquiesced, interrupted his dinner, and returned to the grove to address the congregation again in the afternoon. Minimizing his morning message, he told them the time for plural wives was in the future and admonished his listeners not to be concerned. He promised them that the Lord would help them to understand the purpose and do His will if they were faithful.[3] But the "future" would be for the general membership. Not only had Joseph already taken plural wives, but over the next few months he would initiate the practice among a handful of his most trusted followers.

The confrontation with Joseph over his sermon in the grove opened old issues for Emma. They certainly must have had conversations about plural marriage in Kirtland, but there is no record of how he might have alleviated Emma's fears that the problem would resurface, or if he explained to her a theological structure that would allow men more than one wife. Whatever he said to her, Emma's love for Joseph, together with her own pious upbringing, left no room for such a doctrine.

Throughout her childhood Emma heard the conservative Methodist theology as it was preached by her Uncle Nathaniel, but she accepted Joseph as her prophet as well as her husband and embraced an unorthodox religious belief as she did so. After the difficulties in Kirtland, she had faith that God had led Joseph in the paths that took them to Missouri and finally to Illinois.

Emma had apparently believed that the issue of other wives was closed and hoped that it lay forever at rest. With quiet confidence, she had proceeded to remake her life in Nauvoo.

Observers and writers have speculated about Joseph's motivation for initiating a practice that violated local laws and went against the prevailing Christian teachings of his time, postulating that he was either a brilliant impostor or that he suffered from some mental disorder.[4] Many concluded that the practice of polygamy stemmed from his own insatiable sexual drive, fueled by a quest for power. In an effort to defuse that charge somewhat, others have intimated that Emma was frigid and unresponsive, implying that if Joseph had a problem it must have been Emma's fault. Intimate details of their married life will remain unknown, for Emma and Joseph were no more likely to reveal their personal intimacies than anyone else, but some aspects of their marital relationship may be worth considering. In 1841 she and Joseph had been married fourteen years and she had given birth to seven children and would bear two more in the next three years. From many sources, one can conclude that Emma experienced considerable discomfort, which ranged from fainting spells to severe nausea during her pregnancies. These symptoms sometimes lasted throughout her pregnancies, rather than diminishing, as other women's often do. But, as her mother-in-law indicated, Emma was not one to pamper herself or complain and at times pushed herself to exhaustion. If Joseph found her unattractive or less desirable in the advanced stages of pregnancy, his own writings give no hint of it. He frequently referred to her as "my affectionate Emma," an endearment that he used almost exclusively with her, even though he often stated his love for many of his friends and supporters.

The majority of faithful Mormons would give little consideration to Joseph's own physical drives or to other charges. With "an almost compulsive emphasis on unquestioning loyalty to the Priesthood authority as the cardinal virtue," they would maintain simply that God commanded plural marriage through the prophet Joseph Smith.[5]

If Joseph knew prior to 1840 that the "restoration of all things," particularly plurality of wives, included marriage that would continue past death, there is no record that he included the concept in his conversations. He signed his early personal letters to Emma, "Your affectionate Husband until Death," "O may the blessings of God rest upon you is the prayer of your Husband until death," or "Your Husband until death." Not until 1842 would his letters hint of marriage for eternity, saying, "Yours in haste, your affectionate husband until death, through all eternity, and for evermore."[6]

While Joseph was in Philadelphia early in 1840, Parley P. Pratt recalled one of the earliest known accounts of Joseph's teaching eternal marriage. He said Joseph talked about the "idea of eternal family organization, and the eternal union of the sexes." Until this time Pratt had believed close affections to be "something from which the heart must be entirely weaned" before one was prepared for heaven. "It was from [Joseph] that I learned that the wife of my bosom might be secured to me for time and all eternity; . . . while the result of our endless union would be an offspring as numerous as the stars of heaven, or the sands of the sea shore." Pratt added one last significant remark: "Joseph Smith had barely touched a single key; had merely lifted a corner of the veil and given me a single glance into eternity."[7]

When Brigham and others of the Twelve returned to Nauvoo from England in July 1841, Joseph began immediately to teach them the new doctrine of marriage. Only this time he brought the concept of plural marriage together with eternal marriage into what would become known as "celestial" or "patriarchal" marriage. The combination did not bring forth the same euphoria that Pratt had experienced a year and a half earlier. In looking back on the occasion, Brigham Young said, "It was the first time in my life that I had desired the grave, and I could hardly get over it for a long time." Heber C. Kimball begged Joseph "to remove the requirement" or he would leave the church. And John Taylor indicated that the Twelve "seemed to put off as far as we could, what might be termed the evil day" when they would take plural wives. Despite the reaction, Joseph was so relieved not to carry the burden alone that he reportedly clapped his hands and danced like a child.[8]

Joseph explained the doctrine to some of the Twelve together, presumably the three above mentioned, and Willard Richards, George A. Smith, and Orson Pratt. He encouraged them not to delay in putting their new knowledge into practice. From July 1841 to April 1842 Joseph and the Twelve began educating themselves and various women to the acceptance of the plural wife doctrine. Joseph Lee Robinson commented, "It could not be expected that they could enter into this new order of things without difficulty and some severe trials for it is calculated in its nature to severely try the women, to nearly tear their heart strings out of them, and also it must severely try the men as well."[9]

From 1841 until his death Joseph would continue to take more plural wives. Twentieth-century historians disagree on the number. Andrew Jensen documented twenty-seven, from statements and affidavits of the women themselves or from witnesses to the marriages. Fawn Brodie later added other sources to total forty-eight. Stanley S. Ivins claimed eighty-four. None of these writers attempted to assess whether these were connubial wives, sealed to Joseph only for eternity, or linked merely by name.[10] Emma would eventually know about some of Joseph's plural wives; her knowledge of seven can be documented conclusively,[11] and some evidence hints that she may have known of others.[12] Persistent oral and family traditions insist that Joseph fathered children by at least four of his plural wives. Mary Elizabeth Rollins Lightner's comments illustrate the secrecy surrounding the birth of these children. As late as 1905 she commented, "I knew he had three children. They told me. I think two of them are living today but they are not known as his children as they go by other names." Demographic studies of Nauvoo suggest that babies appeared as members of the household who were not born to the family, perhaps indicating that children born in plurality were absorbed into trusted families. Josephine R. Fisher signed an affidavit in 1915 stating that, on her deathbed, her mother told her she was Joseph's child but admonished her to keep it secret.[13] Most of the women who later stated that they were wives of Joseph steadfastly refused either to confirm or deny whether they had given birth to his children.

How did Joseph determine who his plural wives would be? How did he and other men approach the women? What was the women's reaction to these unusual proposals? How did Emma finally come to her knowledge that Joseph both taught and practiced a new order of marriage, and what was her reaction both to the principle and to the women she encountered as his wives? The answers to these questions unfold over the next three years.

It was one thing for Joseph to announce to the men that they were now to marry additional women, but it was another for those men to tell their wives. He told some of these men to keep plural marriages a secret from their first wives. For example, Mary Ann Young had retired to bed when men's voices outside the house awakened her. Joseph was explaining plural marriage to Brigham, who objected, but Joseph argued that it was a test of faith, and the more wives Brigham took, the greater would be his glory in heaven. Overhearing this and knowing Brigham had never faltered in his loyalty to his prophet, Mary Ann lay back on the bed, sick at heart.[14] She eventually accepted plural marriage, but how she came to her decision is unknown.

Emma's friend Vilate Kimball came about her knowledge of plural marriage in a different manner. Heber Kimball had honored Joseph's charge to keep the doctrine from his wife but appeared troubled. Helen said her mother began praying to know what was causing so much anxiety in Heber. The plan of celestial marriage was made known to her "in a vision"; she told him she knew about his dilemma and that he should obey. Kimball took Sarah Peake Noon, an Englishwoman with two children, as his first plural wife.[15]

Initial reaction of those who left accounts almost universally described "shock, horror, disbelief, or general emotional confusion," followed by a "period of inner turmoil lasting from several days to several months." People prayed and fasted, hoping for enlightenment, and often reported "a compelling personal experience" that brought them to accept plural marriage as a true principle.[16] Vilate Kimball described Parley Pratt's conversion in an 1843 letter to Heber. "J . . . . h has taught him some principles and told him his privilege, and even appointed one for him, I dare not tell you who it is, you would be astonished and I guess some tried. . . . Sister Pratt has ben rageing against these things, she told me her self that the devel had been in her until within a few days past, she said the Lord had shown her it was all right . . . they are so ingagued I fear they will run to fast." In closing Vilate told her husband to burn the letter,[17] suggesting one reason so few contemporary documents concerning plural marriage are extant.

No record exists of Joseph teaching the full theological backdrop for plural marriage before coming to Nauvoo, and two years would pass before he attempted to explain it to Emma. He would do it then only after she had confirmed her suspicions about him and had confronted him. Emma's friends learned from their husbands that Joseph had received a revelation outlining a new order of marriage, but Emma came to it piecemeal over a number of years through circumstances that hurt and shocked her.

Emma knew Joseph as no other mortal did, seeing him as both prophet and husband. In February 1843 Joseph told a visitor "a prophet was a prophet only when he was acting as such." That same day he recorded in his journal, "I went out with my little Frederick, to exercise myself by sliding on the ice."[18] George Q. Cannon, a contemporary of Emma and Joseph, wrote: "Prophets must, like other men, eat drink and wear apparel. They have the physical necessities and the affections and enjoyments which are common to other men. And it is this petty human fact . . . which leaves him 'without honor in his own country.' "[19]

Joseph Lee Robinson quoted Joseph as saying "that God had revealed unto him that any MAN that EVER COMMITTED ADULTERY . . . could never be raised to the highest EXALTATION in the CELESTIAL GLORY and that he felt anxious with regard to himself." Robinson went on to say that Joseph "inquired of the Lord, that the Lord told him that he Joseph had never committed ADULTERY."[20] Why should Emma not question some of Joseph's actions when he questioned them himself? If Robinson's statement is true, it may indicate, as one writer suggests, Joseph's reluctance to leave behind the old monogamous system of marriage, or it may mean that he had some difficulty with the new standard he was teaching.

After Joseph converted the Twelve to plural marriage, another problem arose. It still remained for married men to ask women to marry them. Would a prospective wife accept the teachings with understanding? Would she reject them out of hand and make public accusations? Or would she quietly decline but remain silent out of loyalty? When Joseph approached Hiram Kimball's wife, Sarah Melissa Granger, early in 1842, Sarah said, "I asked him to teach it to someone else. He looked at me reprovingly . . . [saying] 'I will not cease to pray for you.' "[21] Sarah learned that Joseph also wanted Rachel Ivins for a wife and forewarned her friend, who refused to meet with him. Both women remained in the church and kept their own counsel. In the few cases that did become public knowledge, the women's reputations were defamed by church leaders and family members alike.[22]

Mary Elizabeth Rollins Lightner indicated that Joseph had first commented in 1831 that she would one day become his wife. Joseph approached her again in 1834 but, afraid of the unusual arrangement, she married Adam

Lightner on August 11, 1835. Early in 1842 Joseph again reminded her that he had been commanded to take her as a wife. By this time, Mary Elizabeth said, she had been dreaming for a number of years that she was his wife. She commented to Joseph, however, "Well, don't you think it was an angel of the Devil that told you these things?"

"No, it was an angel of God," Joseph reassured her. "The angel came to me three times between the year 1834 and 1842 and said I was to obey that principle or he would slay me." Mary Elizabeth said Joseph told her that the last time the angel had come with a drawn sword and threatened his life. "Joseph said I was his before I came here and all the Devils in Hell should never get me from him." This extraordinarily powerful psychological and theological argument placed her in a contest between good and evil. Joseph held out one final argument that carried much weight in the eyes of those people who intended to live their lives by the word of God in order to inherit His kingdom. He offered salvation to Mary Elizabeth if she would accept his proposal. "All that [God] gives me I shall take with me for I have that authority and that power conferred upon me."

Mary Elizabeth said she would not be married to him until she too had a witness. "If God told you that why does he not tell me?"

"You shall have a witness," Joseph promised. Then he asked Mary Elizabeth if she was going to be a "traitor."

"I . . . shall never tell a mortal I had such a talk from a married man," she replied. Mary Elizabeth, who had been in Emma's home often and had taught painting to Julia, was mindful of another complication. She asked if Emma knew about her. Joseph neatly sidestepped the issue with an incomplete answer: "Emma thinks the world of you."

After making Joseph's proposal the subject of prayer, Mary Elizabeth said "an angel" passed silently through her room and out the window one night. After telling Joseph of the experience, she asked him why, if it was "an angel of light," it did not speak to her.

"You covered your face," he told her, "and for this reason the angel was insulted."

"Will it ever come again?"

Joseph thought for a moment, then said, "No. Not the same one, but if you are faithful you shall see greater things than that." He then predicted three signs that would take place in her family. "Every word came true," she wrote. Brigham Young officiated at her marriage to Joseph.[23]

The next three years would prove to be a most difficult time, not only for Emma, but also for the small group to whom Joseph taught the new order. Most converts came into the church with a strong religious background and regarded immorality with abhorrence. Joseph's teachings for the exaltation of his people required a change in their cultural behavior as well as a religious conversion. New revelation was now the basis for their religion, and Joseph insisted that the revelations that he received from God were absolute and he expected them to be obeyed.

Unaware that Joseph was teaching the Twelve and others the principles of plural marriage, Emma dealt with other problems: death stalked the Smith family. The summer heat brought mosquitoes and with them the fever and chills of malaria. Don Carlos Smith caught the disease and died on August 7, 1841. His partner, Robert Thompson, Mercy Fielding's husband, followed him in death a fortnight later. In September Emma's fourteen-month-old baby, Don Carlos, suffered also from malaria and died on the fifteenth. This was Emma's fourth child to die and was perhaps the most difficult death, for her own health was "delicate"; she expected another baby in the winter. Hyrum Smith's second son, who had lost his own mother in Kirtland, died of malaria or typhoid thirteen days after his little cousin Don Carlos. Emma's sister-in-law, Mary Bailey Smith, and her infant daughter died on January 25, 1842.[24] By April Samuel remarried and Levira Clark became stepmother to his four children. Lucy Mack Smith, crippled with arthritis, had become extremely ill. Most of that winter her daughters Sophronia and Lucy helped Emma care for her.

The Hale family also lost members during this period. Emma's father had died January 11, 1839. His tombstone bore the inscription, "The body of Isaac Hale, the hunter, like the cover of an old book, its contents torn out and stripped of their lettering and gilding, lies here, food for worms, yet the work itself shall not be lost, and it will appear once more in a new and beautiful edition, corrected and amended."[25] Isaac's will left the farm to his son Alva with the stipulation that he maintain his mother "in a kind comfortable & proper manner during her life." Elizabeth Hale died three years later, on February 16, 1842. Isaac Hale's will stipulated that, after paying each brother twenty dollars, Alva was also to "pay his sisters such sums as would be right & proper." Emma seems to be included without discrimination on Isaac's part.

Throughout these months of sorrow Emma also took on additional responsibilities. She and Joseph had particular interest in three of the building projects in Nauvoo. The temple was planned for the spiritual rejuvenation of the Saints; the anticipated Nauvoo House hotel, across the street to the east from the old Homestead, would help provide income and accommodations for visitors; and Joseph's red brick store, which would be the setting for many events in Emma's life, neared completion at the end of 1841. The upstairs rooms would soon become a central meeting place, the nerve center of Nauvoo. The two-story building was "somewhat spacious for a country store," Joseph commented, with the main room ten feet high. An English artisan painted the counters to look like marble and grained the pillars with a feather to resemble fine mahogany and maple. A door from this room opened to a small hall with steps to the upper floor, a cellar on the left, and a private room on the right. The stairs led to a large open room and Joseph's private office. A south window overlooked the river, offering a retreat from the bustle of the street in front. The store stood on the corner of Granger and Water streets, through the lot to the west from the Homestead house where Emma and Joseph lived.

In the middle of December Emma and Joseph unpacked thirteen wagonloads of goods. The shelves bulged with a wide variety of items that tempted the frugal citizens.[26] Most of the supplies had been ordered by Joseph's representatives on the East Coast and sent to the shipping head at St. Louis. Emma had power of attorney. Joseph wrote Edward Hunter in Pennsylvania: "Your message is delivered to Mrs. Smith, and she will be glad to have returns on her letter of attorney, as speedily as circumstances will permit, according to the understanding thereof. . . . P.S. You will endeavor to have the money on your letter of attorney from Mrs. Smith, ready to furnish a supply of goods early in the spring."[27]

On January 5, 1842, Joseph opened the red brick store. He stood behind the counter selling goods, dispensing supplies, bantering with his friends, and enjoying his position at the head of his mercantile establishment, but he took in very little cash. His easygoing manner with his followers made it difficult to demand payment when the Saints were destitute. The store's daybook began to fill with IOUs.

Joseph sat in council with either the city government or the church officials almost every evening in rooms above the store. His history for Saturday, January 22, indicated that he spent the day "very busy in appraising tithing property."[28] The following Saturday he again spent the day "much engaged with the tithings." By Monday, January 31, he called Emma to assist with the tithing appraisals. Much of this tithing was not in cash but in kind. Emma learned to evaluate acreage, city lots, and goods of various kinds in order to give the donor proper credit.

Perhaps Emma overworked herself, for on February 6, 1842, she gave birth to a son who did not survive. Only five months had passed between the death of her baby, Don Carlos, and this child. Emma buried her infant in the middle of winter, undoubtedly with her reserves drained.[29]

As Joseph watched Emma grieve, he no doubt recalled that the Murdock twins had eased her sorrow eleven years earlier. He talked with Anna and William McIntire about their three-month-old twin girls; he wanted to borrow a baby. The McIntires agreed to let Joseph take one of the twins during the day for Emma to nurse if he would bring her home in the evening. This Joseph did punctually every day. His attachment to the child became as strong as Emma's. Few people could tell the twins apart, but Joseph always recognized the one named Mary. One time Anna McIntire found Joseph trotting the baby on his knee because he did not want to return a fussy baby to its mother. When Emma regained her health she no longer kept the baby regularly but continued to drop in to see her. When the child died at age two, both Emma and Joseph grieved with her parents.[30]

The Nauvoo years became a time for implementing doctrine. Sometimes Emma worked with Joseph in the office while he "translated, revised, and read letters in the evening."[31] Although many revelations seemed to come forth spontaneously, others seem to have come piecemeal, building "line upon line, precept upon precept." Many revelations of the latter kind culminated in the Mormon temple ordinances, including baptism for the dead,[32] an extension of the concept that baptism is necessary and, therefore, should be available by proxy to the dead. Sometime in 1841 Emma was baptized in the Mississippi River in behalf of her father, and a year later for her mother, her sister Phoebe, her Uncle Reuben Hale, her Aunt Esther Hale, and her Great-Aunt Eunice Cady.[33]

Other temple ordinances were washings and anointings, celestial marriage (or sealing for eternity), the endowment, and a higher ordinance sometimes referred to as the "second anointing." Emma would eventually participate in all of these ordinances. It becomes important, then, to know something of these practices that Joseph gradually introduced.

On March 15, 1842, Joseph began an association with Masonry. The Illinois Grand Master Mason presided over the installation of a Masonic Lodge in Nauvoo and inducted Joseph "on Sight." The following day, Joseph's history says, "I was with the Masonic Lodge and rose to the sublime degree." Just over six weeks later, on May 4, he began the endowment ceremony,[34] an ordinance of religious instruction committing the recipient to God and the church. Washings and anointings and a partial endowment took place in the Kirtland temple, but at that time they were exclusively for men. Joseph would introduce the full endowment ceremony first to nine men in May 1842 and then, a year later, to Emma and a few other women, mostly first wives of the male group. By June 1844 Joseph would admit over sixty-five men and women into the "Endowment Council" or "Anointed Quorum."[35]

Some scholars have suggested that Joseph drew heavily from Freemasonry for the endowment, while others argue that he recognized ancient temple rites in the Masonic order and restored them to a more perfect form. Both views may have validity. Evidence of temple rites throughout Jewish, Christian, and Moslem cultures may point to a common origin. Some American Indian religious ceremonies possess remarkable similarities to Mormon temple rites.[36] Whether they came from a common source or developed independently will continue to be a point of debate.

Many who received their endowments were aware of the close parallels to Masonry, and their writings reflect Joseph's attitude. Heber C. Kimball wrote Parley P. Pratt, "Thare was near two hundred been made Masons [here]. . . . All of the Twelve apostles have become members Except Orson Pratt . . . there is a similarity of preas[t]Hood in Masonry. Bro. Joseph Ses Masonry was taken from preasthood, but has become degenerated. But menny things are perfect."[37] Joseph Fielding, Mary's brother, wrote in his journal, "Many have joined the Masonic Institution. This seems to have been a stepping stone for preparation for something else, the true origin of Masonry."[38]

Joseph recognized that women did not participate in traditional American Masonry. An unorthodox French Masonry included orders for women and filtered into America. In one type, the leading woman was referred to as the "Elect Lady," a title by which Emma had been known since 1830 and by which she would become increasingly identified. This is also a biblical term.[39]

Over the next few months Joseph organized the women into a select society as the first step toward introducing them to higher ordinances. His communications to the women would contain references to Masonry. He would speak of being good Masons, ancient orders, keys, tokens, examination, order of the priesthood, degrees, secrets, candidates, lodges, signs, and rules, in preparation for an endowment for both men and women.[40]

In describing her early endowment, Lucy M. Smith, married to Joseph's cousin, George A., revealed the intermingling of Masonry with it. "The party who anointed me in Emma's bedroom . . . poured oil on my head and blessed me. . . . I had different clothing on from what I wore when I went to the house first. This anointing was for the purpose of initiating me in the . . . endowments. The Order of Rebecca is a side degree of Masonry, for I think I had one or two degrees of it in that lodge . . . there was no curtain separating the ladies from the gentlemen. . . . Afterwards we promised not to reveal our endowments, or tell what it was."[41] Endowments would be given in Emma's house and in the Masonic Lodge room, but eventually they would take place in the temple. Building it took priority over all work projects.

8

In Search
of Iniquity

Spring–Summer 1842

The women of Nauvoo looked for ways to help build the temple. Sarah Melissa Granger had converted to Mormonism with her family in New York. She married Hiram Kimball, Heber C. Kimball's non-Mormon cousin, shortly after her arrival in Nauvoo. A plasterer and storekeeper by trade, he also had large landholdings in the city. As a well-to-do new bride, Sarah wanted to help build the temple. According to her own account, she and a friend, probably Margaret A. Cook, met in the Kimball living room and discussed ways to assist the temple project. These women recognized that some women had time but little means, others had money but little time. Sarah concluded to combine their efforts in a ladies' society. Several women met in her home and decided to organize formally, delegating Sarah Kimball to ask Eliza R. Snow to write a constitution and by-laws. Eliza obliged, but when the women took their efforts to the prophet for approval, Joseph said, "I am glad to have the opportunity of organizing the women, as a part of the priesthood belongs to them." He read the documents Eliza had written and pronounced them "the best he had ever seen," but, "this is not what you want. Tell the sisters their offering is accepted of the Lord, and He has something better for them than a written constitution." He asked the women to meet with him and several men of the church the following Thursday in the Masonic Lodge room on the second story of the red brick store. Then he stated, "I will organize the sisters under the priesthood after a pattern of the priesthood."[1]

On March 17, 1842, one day after Joseph "rose to the sublime degree" in Masonry, Emma entered the lodge room with nineteen other women.[2] Joseph, John Taylor, and Willard Richards were also present. The first order of busi-

ness was to signify by vote if all were satisfied with the character and reputation of each woman present. When the vote was positive, Emma introduced
seven additional names, bringing the official membership to twenty-seven.

Joseph proposed that the sisters elect a president and two counselors and
said he "would ordain them to preside over the Society—and let them preside
just as the Presidency preside over the Church; . . . If any Officers are wanted
to carry out the design of the Institution, let them be appointed and set apart,
as Deacons, Teachers, & etc. are among us."

Elizabeth Ann Whitney moved that Emma be president. The support
was unanimous. Emma then chose Elizabeth Ann and Sarah Cleveland, her
friend from Quincy days, as counselors. Eliza R. Snow would be secretary and
Elvira Cowles treasurer. Joseph read the Elect Lady revelation, explaining that
Emma "was called an Elect Lady . . . because [she was] elected to preside."
He explained that Emma was ordained at the time the revelation was given to
expound the scriptures to all. Then John Taylor "ordained" Sarah Cleveland
and Elizabeth Ann Whitney as Emma's counselors,[3] then "laid his hands on
the head of [Emma] Smith and blessed her, and confirm'd upon her all the
blessings which have been confer'd on her, that she might be a mother in
Israel and look to the wants of the needy, and be a pattern of virtue; and
possess all the qualifications necessary for her to stand and preside and dignify
her Office to teach the females those principles requisite for their future use-
fulness."

The women chose the name for their new organization, but not without a
challenge from Joseph and John Taylor. Sarah Cleveland moved to name it the
"Female Relief Society." Taylor suggested the word "Benevolent" instead of
"Relief." Sarah changed her mind and seconded Taylor's amendment, and the
motion passed unanimously. Emma asked for further discussion on the point;
then the newly elected president engaged her husband in a dignified debate.
She argued for the word "Relief" over "Benevolent," explaining, "The *popu-
larity* of the word 'benevolent' is one great objection—no person can think of a
word as associated with public Institutions, without thinking of the Washing-
tonian Benevolent Society which is one of the most corrupt Institutions of the
day. [I] do not wish to have it called after other societies in the world."[4]

"I have no objection to the word Relief," he said, and suggested that they
"deliberate candidly" all alternatives.

Sarah Cleveland changed her mind again and spoke in favor of "Relief."
Eliza Snow agreed with Emma, but only after Joseph had softened his stand.
"One objection to the word 'relief' is that the idea associated with it . . .
[suggests] some great calamity—that we intend appropriating on some extraordinary occasions instead of meeting the common occurences."

"We are going to do something *extraordinary!*" Emma challenged.
"When a boat is stuck in the rapids with a multitude of Mormons on board,

we shall consider *that* a loud call for *relief*. We expect extraordinary occasions and pressing calls."

Taylor finally conceded, "Your arguments are so potent I cannot stand before them—I shall have to give way." Joseph capitulated, and the women named their own organization the Female Relief Society of Nauvoo.

Joseph presented them with a five-dollar gold piece, Emma donated one dollar to the society, Sarah Cleveland twelve cents, Elizabeth Ann Whitney fifty cents, and Sarah Kimball, who had thought of the idea of a society in the first place, matched Emma's dollar, and John Taylor gave three dollars. The treasury of the first Relief Society stood at ten dollars and sixty-two cents.

Emma and Joseph together outlined the purposes of the society, which were "to provoke the brethren to good works . . . to save the elders the trouble of rebuking . . . to look after the wants of the poor . . . [to] do good . . . [to] deal frankly with each other," and to "correct the morals of the community." There would be no arguments about doing good and caring for the poor, but women dealing frankly with each other and correcting the morals of the community would become explosive issues in the city of Nauvoo.

A week later Emma called the second meeting of the Relief Society to order in the lodge room and offered the invocation.[5] Membership had increased by forty-two additional members. Emma addressed the women: "Measures to promote union in the Society must be carefully attended to. Every member should be held in full fellowship . . . divest[ing] themselves of every jealousy and ill feeling toward each other. . . . We will bring our conduct into respectability here and everywhere else. I rejoice in the prospects before me." She invited those wishing to join the society to do so.

When Vilate Kimball asked for a restatement of the purposes of the institution, Emma said, "No one need feel delicate in reference to inquiries about this society. There is nothing private. Its objects are purely benevolent." Emma organized the women to see to the poor. An employment committee sought work for women who needed it and supervised the purchase of goods rather than giving outright donations to the poor.

Emma reported that a young woman, Clarissa Marvel, "was accused of [telling] scandalous falsehoods on the character of Prest. Joseph Smith without the least provocation," and asked that "they would in wisdom, adopt some plan to bring her to repentance." She continued, "I presume that most of [you] know more about Clarissa Marvel than I."

There must have been silent consternation among a few in the group who were privy to the teaching of celestial marriage. Joseph's plural wife Louisa Beaman sat in the meeting as did Sarah Peake Noon[6] and Vilate Kimball. Did Emma know that her husband had approached some women and asked them to become his plural wives?

Agnes Coolbrith Smith, Don Carlos's widow, came to the accused girl's defense, apparently unaware that gossip linked her own name to Joseph's.[7]

"Clarissa Marvel lived with me nearly a year and I saw nothing amiss of her," she reported.

The women discussed the issue and agreed that someone should talk with Clarissa Marvel, but nobody wanted to do it. One Hannah Markham was given the task but she "objected on the grounds that she was unacquainted with the circumstances."

Emma acknowledged that the girl had no parents and needed friends, but "We intend to look into the morals of each other, and watch over each other. . . . All proceedings that regard difficulties should be kept among the members. . . . None can object to telling the good," Emma went on, "but withhold the evil." Given human nature, Emma was demanding an impossible commitment from her members. But gossip cannot be dismissed as a feminine predilection. Men also circulated tales. Gossip served both women and men as a means of transmitting information. Informal verbal accounts spread information for people who were barred from planning the course of the community either because they were women or because they had disagreed with their leaders. The inclination to gossip became even stronger when leaders were expected to be examples of piety.[8]

Undoubtedly word spread that the society was investigating Clarissa Marvel. The third meeting opened with "the house full to overflowing." Joseph was in front with Emma and rose to speak. He talked briefly about the society's organization and observed that "none should be received into the society but those who were worthy." He advised, "The society should grow by degrees, [it] should commence with a few individuals—thus have a select Society of the virtuous and those who will walk circumspectly. . . . The society should move according to the ancient Priesthood. . . . [I will] make of this Society a kingdom of priests as in Enoch's day—as in Paul's day."

Joseph also commented on the women's zeal to "purge out iniquity," but added that "sometimes [your] zeal is not according to knowledge." Emma proceeded with business after Joseph left the meeting: the case of Clarissa Marvel was still pending. As previous interviews with the girl seemed to prove her innocent, Sarah Cleveland moved that Elizabeth Durfee and Elizabeth Allred should investigate whoever had reported her. Unknown to Emma, Joseph had already taught these older women the principles of plural marriage. Sometimes referred to as "Mothers in Israel," they assisted Joseph by contacting women, explaining the new order of marriage to them, and occasionally delivering marriage proposals.[9] Thus Mrs. Durfee was uncomfortably caught between her role as Joseph's emissary and her assignment to investigate Clarissa Marvel. She objected. Emma encouraged, "We are going to learn new things, our way is straight, we want none in this society but those who *could* and would walk straight." Within three days Clarissa Marvel marked an X next to her name on the following statement: "This is to certify that I never have at any time or place, seen or heard any thing improper or unvirtuous in the conduct or conversation of either President Smith or Mrs. Agnes Smith. I also certify that I never have reported any thing derogatory to the characters of either of them." Apparently Emma took responsibility for closing the issue, for she told the women that the "disagreeable business of searching out those who were iniquitous seemed to fall on her." Emma obviously did not know that her widowed sister-in-law, Agnes Coolbrith Smith, had become a plural wife of Joseph.[10]

Mormon women found spiritual satisfaction in the gatherings. At the close of one meeting Emma, Sarah Cleveland, and Elizabeth Whitney laid their hands on the head of Elizabeth Durfee, who was ill, and blessed her. The next week Mrs. Durfee "said she never realized more benefit through any administration—that she was healed, and thought the sisters had more faith than the brethren."

This meeting became a prototype for Relief Society "testimony" meetings at which the women stood one by one to express individual feelings and spiritual experiences. Sarah Cleveland commented, ". . . as the Prophet had given us liberty to improve the Gifts of the Gospel in our meetings . . . [she] desired to speak in the gift of tongues, which she did in a powerful manner," and a second woman interpreted. Eliza Snow's minutes pronounced the meeting "interesting."[11]

During the ensuing week someone apparently questioned the propriety of women blessing the sick and speaking in tongues. Joseph addressed the subject on April 28, saying there was "some little thing circulating in this Society, that some persons were not going right in laying hands on the sick. . . . If the sisters should have faith to heal the sick let all hold their tongues, and let every thing roll on. . . . Who knows the mind of God? . . . Respecting the females, laying on hands . . . there could be no devils in it if God gave his sanction by healing—that there would be no more sin in any female laying hands on the sick than in wetting the face with water."[12] Elizabeth Ann Whitney wrote in 1878 that she and several other women were "ordained and set apart under the hand of Joseph Smith the Prophet to administer to the sick and comfort the sorrowful."[13]

Concerning speaking in tongues, Joseph cautioned, "If any have a matter to reveal, let it be in your own tongue. Do not indulge too much in the gift of tongues. . . . I lay this down for a rule that if any thing is taught by this gift of tongues, it is not to be received for doctrine."

Emma and the other women listened as Joseph spoke of "delivering the keys to this Society." The Relief Society was to receive "instruction thro' the order which God has established . . . and I now turn the key to you in the name of God and this Society shall rejoice and knowledge and intelligence shall flow down from this time." Years later, as George A. Smith compiled a history of the church, he changed Joseph's words from "I now turn the key *to you*" to "I turn the key *in your behalf*."[14] From that time it would appear in error in church publications. Whatever Joseph's intent, his words were ambiguous concerning the women's relationship to priesthood authority and the issue would be questioned in the future.[15]

Before adjourning the meeting Emma read a document that Joseph and the church leaders had prepared for the Relief Society in March. It stated that some men were approaching women to "deceive and debauch the innocent," saying they had authority from Joseph or other church leaders. "We have been informed that some unprincipled men . . . have been guilty of such crimes— We do not mention their names, not knowing but what there may be some among you who are not sufficiently skill'd in Masonry as to keep a secret. . . . Let this epistle be had as a private matter in your Society, and then we shall learn whether you are good masons. We are your humble servants in the Bonds of the New & Everlasting Covenant." Joseph Smith, Hyrum Smith, Heber C. Kimball, Willard Richards, Vinson Knight, and Brigham Young signed their names.[16]

One of the "unprincipled men" whom Joseph declined to name was John C. Bennett. By the spring of 1842 Bennett's political power in Nauvoo was almost as great as Joseph's. In eighteen months he had become major general of the Nauvoo Legion, president of the Agriculture and Manufacturing Association, chancellor of the proposed university in Nauvoo, mayor of the city, and de facto counselor to Joseph as Sidney Rigdon was too ill to function.

Bennett had learned of plural marriage, maybe from Joseph himself, and plunged in with alacrity. But, unhampered by any moral or theological framework, Bennett approached women with his own rationale: where there was no accuser, there was no sin; pregnancy would be taken care of with an abortion. When refused, Bennett stated he came with Joseph's approval.[17] He and his friends called their system of seduction "spiritual wifery," a term that had been used in the early establishment of plural marriage. The city rocked with tales that connected Joseph with Bennett's scandals, and Emma undoubtedly heard the rumors.

In mid-April Joseph had asked Sidney Rigdon's nineteen-year-old daughter Nancy to become his plural wife. Bennett had his own eye on the girl and forewarned her, so she refused Joseph. The following day Joseph dictated a letter to her with Willard Richards acting as scribe. It read in part, "Happiness is the object and design of our existence; and will be the end thereof, if we pursue the path that leads to it; and this path is virtue, uprightness, faithfulness, holiness, and keeping all the commandments of God. . . . That which is wrong under one circumstance, may be, and often is, right under another. . . . Whatever God requires is right, no matter what it is, although we may not see the reason thereof till long after the events transpire."[18]

Nancy Rigdon showed the letter to her father. Rigdon immediately sent for Joseph, who reportedly denied everything until Sidney thrust the letter in his face. George W. Robinson, Nancy's brother-in-law, claimed he witnessed the encounter and said Joseph admitted that he had spoken with Nancy but that he had only been testing her virtue.[19]

Hyrum Smith discovered that Bennett had a wife and children in Ohio. When Joseph accosted Bennett, he acknowledged his guilt and begged Joseph's forgiveness. In a dramatic act of false contrition, Bennett swallowed sufficient poison to make himself sick enough for sympathy but not sick enough to die. Joseph and the others forestalled further action. The break between Joseph and Bennett came on May 7, 1842. Politician Stephen A. Douglas visited Nauvoo, and Joseph called out the Legion for mock maneuvers. Emma and several other women observed on horseback. Joseph suspected Bennett had plans to kill him with an "accidental" shot and accused him of such. On May 17, Bennett resigned as mayor; the church leaders excommunicated him on May 25. Brigham Young told him he was charged with "seducing young women, and leading young men into difficulty." Hyrum Smith said Bennett "wept like a child and begged like a culprit for forgiveness, and promised before God and angels to mend his life."[20] He also pleaded for mercy to "spare him from the paper, for his mother's sake." Public notice of the excommunication was never made.

Bennett acknowledged the Relief Society's role in his downfall when he predicted that its actions "would be the means of a mob forthcoming." Undaunted by Bennett's remarks, Emma announced that she could not be afraid of mobs and called on the women to send out a circular exposing Bennett's character. She challenged them to write convincing statements. Bennett had correctly assessed the power of the organization but he underestimated Joseph's influence with it.[21]

Shortly after Bennett left Nauvoo in late May or early June he attacked Joseph and the church in the newspapers and published a defamatory book. His accounts provided titillating reading for some and encouraged prejudice toward the Mormons, but others saw through his pious cover. Thomas Ford commented: "Bennett was probably the greatest scamp in the western country . . . he was everywhere accounted the same debauched, unprincipled, and profligate character."[22]

While John C. Bennett would continue to embarrass and frustrate the Mormons for some time, one last monument to him remained in Nauvoo. He and his comrades had built a house of ill repute near the grove where the Mormons congregated for meetings. A large sign announced its purpose. One Mormon observed, "We could not get [to meeting] without passing this house and looking right at it, and one or two thousand people would go . . . [past it] on a Sabbath and they didn't feel very good seeing that house there with great big letters facing them."[23] The city council eventually put the building on rollers and pitched the house, furnishings and all, into a deep gully behind it.

The demand for secrecy coupled with the need to warn others of unauthorized practices such as Bennett's led Joseph and the Twelve to develop a system of evasion. By employing "code words" the practitioners of the "new and everlasting covenant of marriage," as taught by Joseph, felt they could publicly deny one thing and privately live by another—and do it with a clear conscience. In an 1869 letter George A. Smith noted: "Any one who will read carefully the denials, as they are termed . . . will see clearly that they denounce adultery, fornication, brutal lust and the teaching of plurality of wives by those who were not commanded to do so; eschewing clearly that it was understood that such commandment would be given to others."[24] An 1886 article in the *Deseret News* detailed specific code words and the rationale for their use. "When assailed by their enemies and accused of practicing things which were really not countenanced in the Church, they were justified in denying those imputations and at the same time avoiding the avowal of such doctrine as were not yet intended for the world." Examples were, *"Polygamy, in the ordinary and Asiatic sense of the term, never was and is not now a tenet of the Latter-day Saints. That which Joseph and Hyrum denounced . . . was altogether different to the order of celestial marriage including a plurality of wives. . . .* Joseph and Hyrum were consistent in their action against the *false doctrines* of *polygamy* and *spiritual wifeism,* instigated by the devil and advocated by men who did not comprehend sound doctrine nor the purity of the *celestial marriage* which God revealed for the holiest of purposes."[25]

Denial of polygamy "in the Asiatic sense" perhaps meant that theirs was a spiritual requirement rather than a cultural practice. Other acceptable terms synonymous with plurality of wives were: "the true and divine order," "eternal marriage," and "the Holy order of celestial marriage." Phrases such as "live up to your privileges," "new and everlasting covenant," and "we may have different views of things" also referred to plural marriage. Speaking before non-Mormons, newspaper reporters, and the uninitiated, the leaders supported plural marriage under the very noses of the suspicious. Perhaps the most confusing of the code words was "spiritual wifery." Joseph and the Twelve used the term, and a few women who were plural wives later referred to themselves as "spiritual wives," but through Bennett's use the term came into disrepute. Emma, who had not yet been taught the doctrine, seemed oblivious to the code words.

During this time the Relief Society continued to meet. At the April 28 meeting Joseph counseled the women—and not incidentally his wife—how to treat a husband. "Let this Society teach how to act towards husbands, to treat them with mildness and affection. When a man is borne down with troubles— when he is perplexed, if he can meet a smile, not an argument—if he can meet with mildness it will calm down his soul and sooth his feelings. When the mind is going to despair it needs a solace."[26] If there was a pointed message for Emma, within twenty-four hours she forgot about mildness and long-suffering. Someone apparently told her about Joseph's involvement in plural marriage.

On April 29, 1842, the day after the Relief Society meeting, Joseph's history reads: "A conspiracy against the peace of my family was made manifest, and it gave me some trouble to counteract the design of certain base individuals, and restore peace. The Lord makes manifest to me many things, which it is not wisdom for me to make public."[27] The confrontation between Joseph and Emma was serious. It may have been the reason the Relief Society did not meet the following week, and two weeks after the incident, Joseph was present, but the minutes do not mention Emma's name. Joseph did not elaborate on the process by which he reestablished his peace with Emma, but a clue lies in the recollections of a then fifty-four-year-old spinster, Vienna Jacques, whose name had been linked with Joseph's by gossip in Kirtland. Many years later Joseph Smith III interviewed her when she was over ninety. She recalled "the subject of spiritual wifery" was discussed at a Relief Society meeting when Emma was not present. Miss Jacques claimed she did not believe it was being taught as doctrine and said she went to Emma against the protests of some of the women in the group:

She told me she had asked her husband, the prophet, about the stories which were being circulated among the women concerning such a doctrine being taught, and that he had told her to tell the sisters of the society that if any man, no matter who he was, undertook to talk such stuff to them in their houses, just to order him out at once, and if he did not go immediately, to take the tongs or the broom and drive him out, for the whole idea was absolutely false and the doctrine an evil and unlawful thing.[28]

A week later Elizabeth Ann Whitney spoke to the society, saying she was "burdened in mind in thinking of existing evils in the church—was desirous that this Society become more obedient to the gospel in keeping all the commandments," exhorted the members to "humility and watchfulness," and affirmed that "the gifts and blessings of the gospel [are] ours, if [the women are] found faithful and pure before God." Emma followed her counselor's train of thought but addressed the situation at hand. From her remarks it appears that Joseph had deflected her anger by explaining that he had neither sanctioned nor participated in Bennett's spiritual wife doctrine. Eliza Snow's minutes state, "Mrs. Prest. said this day was an evil day—that there is as much evil in this as in any other place—said she would that this society were pure before God—that she was afraid that under existing circumstances the sisters were not careful enough to expose iniquity—the time had been when charity had covered a multitude of sins—but now it is necessary that sin should be exposed." Emma said "that heinous sins were among us—that much of this iniquity was practiced by some in authority, pretending to be sanctioned by Pres. [Joseph] Smith. Mrs. Prest. continued by exhorting all who had erred to

repent and forsake their sins—said that Satan's forces were against this church
—that every Saint should be at the post."[29]

The speech must have confused those women already initiated into plural
marriage. If "some in authority" who said they were sanctioned and encouraged by Joseph were not, where did that leave a virtuous woman who had
accepted one of the Twelve when he assured her he came with Joseph's command and approval? Emma's blunt comments made the men's arguments
suspect. Her statements became a stumbling block to the spread of polygamy
because women not wishing to enter the "principle" could now quote the
prophet's wife.

Counselors Sarah Cleveland and Elizabeth Ann Whitney called the regular meeting to order on May 26. The house was full to overflowing. Emma was
late. To stall for time, Elizabeth Ann began a speech thanking the women for
their donations. Finally Emma and Joseph entered together. Emma found a
seat; Joseph immediately took the floor, and Eliza carefully recorded his
speech. He read the fourteenth chapter of Ezekiel and emphasized that the
people should stand firm on their own faith. Then he said, "There is another
error which opens a door for the adversary to enter. As females possess refined
feelings and sensitiveness, they are also subject to an overmuch zeal which
must ever prove dangerous, and cause them to be rigid in a religious capacity.
[You] should be arm'd with mercy notwithstanding the iniquity among us.
. . . Put a double watch over the tongue. . . . [You] should chasten and
reprove and keep it all in silence, not even mention them again." He addressed
Emma directly. "One request to the Prest. and society, that you search yourselves—the tongue is an unruly member—hold your tongues about things of
no moment. A little tale will set the world on fire. At this time the truth on the
guilty should not be told openly—Strange as this may seem, yet this is policy.
We must use precaution in bringing sinners to justice lest in exposing these
heinous sins, we draw the indignation of a gentile world upon us (and to their
imagination justly, too). It is necessary to hold an influence in the world and
thus spare ourselves an extermination." Joseph contradicted his previous
charge that the women watch over the morals of the community. Emma was
doing her job too well.

She rose as Joseph ended his remarks, and clarified one or two statements
that may have sounded ambiguous. "All idle rumors and idle talk must be laid
aside yet sin must not be covered, especially those sins which are against the
law of God, and the laws of the country," Emma stated, "All who walk disorderly must reform, and any of you knowing of heinous sins against the law of
God, and refuse to expose them, becomes the offender—I want none in this
society who have violated the laws of virtue!" She adjourned the meeting until
the following day, as the business was not finished.[30]

The next day the women assembled in the grove near the temple site.
Membership had grown to over six hundred. As usual the meeting opened

with singing. Emma offered the invocation, accepted the names of almost two hundred new members, then addressed the large congregation. She emphasized that the group should remain united in their efforts to assist the needy. In behalf of the society Emma had hired a poor man to plow and fence the lot of an elderly brother and remarked that donations toward the man's wages could be made in "provisions, clothing, and furniture."

At that point Elizabeth Ann's husband, Newel K. Whitney, and Joseph arrived. Whitney complimented the women on the lofty purposes of the society. Then he said, "In the beginning God created man male and female and bestow'd upon man certain blessings peculiar to a man of God of which woman partook, so that without the female all things cannot be restor'd to the earth—it takes all to restore the Priesthood. . . . God has many precious things to bestow, even to our astonishment if we are faithful. I say again I rejoice in the prospect of what lays before." The bishop continued, "If we are striving to do right, altho' we may err in judgment many times yet we are justified in the sight of God if we do the best we can. . . . It is our privilege to stand in an attitude to get testimony for ourselves—It is as much our privilege as that of the ancient saints. . . . If we understand all things we shall not be barren or unfruitful in the knowledge of God." Whitney added, "Far be it from me to harbor iniquity and outbreaking sins. We may have different views of things, still there is some criterion which all may come to, and by bringing our minds and wills into subjection to the law of the Lord, may come to unity. . . . I tell you, there are blessings before to be confer'd as soon as our hearts are prepar'd to receive them." Apparently satisfied, Joseph did not speak, and the women adjourned.[31] Undoubtedly the speech diffused some of the consternation caused by Emma's emphasis on virtue by assuring those women who had accepted the principle of plurality of wives that it was yet taught, supported, and considered a commandment by the leaders of the church. And it presaged the coming endowment.

On June 9 the women assembled in the grove. Joseph addressed them: "It is no matter how fast the Society increases if all are virtuous." He no longer seemed disturbed by the rapid growth of the organization, which now had eight hundred women, but he did lay down rules for admittance to insure the new members would "be of good report."[32] This was not the small select society wherein he could teach the female part of the endowment ceremony. He had thus concluded to begin the endowment for women in a separate setting.

The Relief Society meetings continued throughout the summer of 1842. Emma missed a meeting on July 7 but presided over the proceedings on July 14. She found that business from the previous meeting had been deferred, "Mrs. President not being present."[33] A Sister Brown had been the object of "scandalous tales" spread by an unnamed woman of the society. A discussion of her case continued into the next meeting. Emma called for a vote on whether or not she should be admitted to the society. When the vote was in the affirmative, Emma gave permission to trace down the source of the rumors.

She told the women, "We can govern this generation in one way if not another—if not by the mighty arm of power we can do it by faith & prayer." In summary, "God knows we have a work to do in this place—we have got to watch and pray and be careful not to excite feelings—not make enemies of one another." When one woman moved to extend a vote of thanks to Emma, she declined, saying, "I do not want the thanks but the pray'rs of the Society."[34]

The Relief Society disbanded at the coming of winter with eleven hundred women on the rolls. A few sought membership for social acceptance rather than purely benevolent and charitable motives, but others flocked to the meetings for additional reasons. The organization gave them a focus for their religious energy and spiritual communion. In Relief Society they expressed their opinions and became a part of the official church movement. Women healed the sick, and Joseph gave his approval. They seemed to understand that their organization was parallel in structure with the priesthood.

In addition the organization reached out to the poor in Nauvoo with extraordinary effectiveness. Under Emma's leadership, it formed a successful labor market. Motherless children found homes, a bushel of wheat donated weekly went to feed a needy family, two widows with young children had money to pay for their schooling, elderly women's gardens were plowed, shoes appeared in poor homes, and a family without bedding received blankets. When a group of widows came with a complaint that some heads of families were not paying them for their labors, the problem was solved through the Relief Society. Individuals donated funds at every meeting. The amounts came in as small as six cents and as large as seventy-one dollars. Emma herself donated fourteen dollars in June. Once the treasury gained $143.23 in a single meeting. These funds were amplified by material donations. Emma handled compassionate service in Nauvoo as if it were "an extraordinary occasion and special call." In only six months' time the Relief Society had become a very important part of the social fabric of Nauvoo and the original benevolent purposes of the society never lacked attention.

Another reason for the large membership was that the women had never had their own judiciary body. Although they were not totally at ease with the search for iniquity, Emma had a reputation for fairness and for not indulging in idle gossip. When she opened meetings to a discussion of the actions of other women, she stated she was uncomfortable in having to pursue the issue to its conclusion. But while the women probably trusted Emma to be fair, rumors flooded Nauvoo, and no one could be sure that slander would not swoop down upon her.[35] It was better to be at the meetings.

Significantly, Emma was an effective president. When she organized a committee, accepted an assignment, or learned of someone's plight, she led by example or directed the women in dealing with the problem. The women had loved her for her generosity and compassion: they now respected her leadership. An acquaintance wrote of her:

> Sister Emma was benevolent and hospitable; she drew around her a large circle of friends, who were like good comrades. She was motherly in her nature to young people, always had a houseful to entertain or be entertained. She was very high-spirited and the brethren and sisters paid her great respect. Emma was a great solace to her husband in all his persecutions and the severe ordeals through which he passed; she was always ready to encourage and comfort him, devoted to his interests, and was constantly by him whenever it was possible. She was a queen in her home, so to speak, and beloved by the people, who were many of them indebted to her for favors and kindnesses.[36]

The women's organization was important to Emma, but during its first six months other events occurred that caused Joseph to rely on her for his own safety. While this brought them closer together, the issue of polygamy was far from settled and Emma soon had to confront it head on.

9

Aid to the Fugitive

June–September 1842

Clouds had moved in on the sun in Nauvoo on June 29, 1842, pouring first heavy rain, then hail that beat upon the side of the house Eliza Snow shared with Sarah Cleveland. Inside Eliza mused over unusual events as she began her Nauvoo journal. She needed to make note of that day, for she had just become Joseph Smith's plural wife.[1] "This is a day of much interest to my feelings. Reflecting on past occurrences, a variety of thoughts have presented themselves to my mind with regard to events which have chas'd each other in rapid succession in the scenery of human life. As an individual, I have not passed altogether unnoticed by Change, in reference to present circumstances and future prospects." Eliza's words discreetly hinted at her marriage which the need for secrecy would not allow her to describe. She went on, "While I am contemplating the present state of society—the powers of darkness, and the prejudices of the human mind which stand array'd like an impregnable barrier against the work of God . . . I will not fear. I will put my trust in Him who is mighty to save; rejoicing in his goodness and determin'd to live by every word that proceedeth out of his mouth."[2]

Eliza had been living with Sarah Cleveland since her parents moved fifty miles east to Walnut Grove. The 1842 city and county tax records place Sarah's husband, John Cleveland, several blocks away. No date is known for Sarah Cleveland's own marriage to Joseph, but she stood as witness to Eliza's while Brigham Young performed the ceremony. This and her living apart from John Cleveland suggest she was probably already married to Joseph. Almost certainly Emma was not aware that both her secretary and her counselor in the Relief Society had become Joseph's plural wives.[3]

Sarah and Eliza knew that Emma regarded them with respect and affection. While women who became Joseph's wives were able to accept the principle of plural marriage as revelation from God, they still had to grapple silently and alone with their betrayal of Emma. To live as a secret wife to a friend's husband demanded evasion, subterfuge, and deception. For these sincerely devout and faithful women, their duplicity regarding Emma must have prompted guilt and anxiety.

Eliza contemplated Emma's reaction if she found her out, as evidenced by a poem she addressed to "President Joseph Smith; and his lady, Presidentess Emma Smith," and published six weeks after her marriage. Referring to phrenology[4] to identify her own confused feelings, the first verse asked that malice would bring no pain. She depicted an angel observing "things passing" and wrote:

> He'd be apt to conclude, from the medly of things;
>   We've got into a jumble of late—
> A deep intricate puzzle, a tangle of strings,
>   That no possible scheme can make straight.
>
> Tell me, what will it be, and O, where will it end?
>   Say, if you have permission to tell;
> Is there any fixed point into which prospects tend?
>   Does a focus belong to pell-mell:
>
> From the midst of confusion can harmony flow?
>   Or can peace from distraction come forth?
> From out of corruption, integrity grow?
>   Or can vice unto virtue give birth?
>
> Will the righteous come forth with their garments unstained?
>   With their hearts unpolluted with sin?
> O, yes; Zion, thy honor will be sustained.
> And the glory of God usher'd in.[5]

Frustration, doubt, and confusion are evident here, but the last verse became a justification for her own involvement.

Another source of confusion and threat came into Emma's and Joseph's life from Missouri this same spring. Porter Rockwell, whom one writer described as "a strange member for any church," was rough, often uncouth, and erratic. His devotion to Joseph tied him to the church though the wilderness beckoned with excitement. He had belonged to the Danite band in Missouri and sometimes served as Joseph's bodyguard. Oddly enough for someone of rough-and-tumble reputation, he was short and small-boned. His face had small, almost feminine features with magnetic blue eyes. He wore his long brown hair in two braids.

Rockwell had been in Missouri during the early part of May 1842 and had returned to Nauvoo on Saturday, May 14. The following morning, in the Sunday service of the community, Joseph announced that ex-Governor Lilburn Boggs of Missouri had been shot and seriously wounded. Boggs had made a number of enemies but none were stronger or more bitter than the Mormons. Thus the Missourians, who suspected the Mormons—and Joseph Smith in particular—of being responsible for the attack, renewed their efforts to arrest Joseph. Talk of extradition was everywhere in Nauvoo. The week after Frederick's sixth birthday, the child announced to all the house at breakfast that he had a dream and "the Missourians had got their heads knocked off."[6]

In addition, John C. Bennett's exposés and emotional rhetoric fueled anti-Mormon feelings in Illinois. Joseph wrote Illinois Governor Thomas Carlin a letter responding to Bennett's accusations and alerting the governor to the Missouri threats. Determined to help Joseph, Emma took Eliza R. Snow and Amanda Barns Smith with her to Quincy to see Carlin in July. Amanda Smith had lost her first husband and a son at the Haun's Mill massacre, while another son had had his hip shot away. Emma probably invited her to describe the Missouri mobs. Thomas Carlin greeted the women cordially and listened to Emma plead Joseph's case. With assurance and self-confidence, she explained that she did not ask for Joseph's safety alone, but observed that if Joseph's freedom was endangered by unlawful arrests and attempts were made on his life while incarcerated in Missouri, then hundreds of Mormon lives were equally threatened. Emma assured him that Joseph had not participated in the attempted assassination of Governor Boggs. When Carlin said he would not advise Joseph to trust himself to Missouri, Emma challenged him to protect Joseph by invoking the laws of Illinois and secured his statement that he would use full legal means to protect the Mormons. Of the meeting Eliza commented in her journal, "It remains for time and circumstance to prove the sincerity of his professions."[7]

The day after Emma and Eliza returned from Quincy, Joseph wrote to thank Carlin for his friendly treatment of Emma. "I shall consider myself and our citizens secure from harm," he wrote. "We look to you for protection in the event of any violence being used towards us."[8]

Soon after Emma's visit with Governor Carlin, her nephew Lorenzo Wasson wrote to her and Joseph from Philadelphia where he served a mission. He had come to Nauvoo the spring before and Joseph had baptized him three days after the organization of the Relief Society. Now Wasson wrote that John C. Bennett's accounts were circulating in that city. "If I can be of any service in this Bennett affair I am ready," he offered. "I heard you give J. C. Bennett a tremendous flagellation [last summer] for practicing iniquity under the base pretense of authority from the heads of the church. . . . There are many things I can inform you of, if necessary, in relation to Bennett and his prostitutes." Joseph asked Emma to write to Lorenzo and request a statement of all he knew about Bennett.[9]

Meanwhile Lilburn Boggs in Missouri accused Joseph Smith and Porter Rockwell of assault. The new Missouri governor, Thomas Reynolds, sent a requisition to Governor Thomas Carlin, who in turn issued warrants charging Porter Rockwell with the shooting and Joseph as accessory. A deputy sheriff arrested the two men but left them in Nauvoo in care of the marshal while he went to confer with Governor Carlin. When the deputy returned two days later, Joseph and Porter were gone. The sheriff threatened Emma with unspecified legal consequences if her husband did not return.[10]

Joseph hid at his Uncle John Smith's home across the river and sent word for Emma, Hyrum, William Law, and several others to meet him that night on an island. Emma waited until dark to slip out of the house, walk past the red brick store, and find her way down to the river. The group pushed silently off from shore in a skiff. A few minutes later they met Joseph and a friend, who approached from the opposite bank. Pulling the two skiffs together so they could talk easily, they discussed a rumor that the governor of Iowa had also issued a warrant for Joseph's arrest and decided that Joseph should go up the Mississippi from Nauvoo to Edward Sayers's home. A faithful Mormon, Sayers farmed north of Nauvoo. Reassured that her husband would be safe, Emma returned to Nauvoo with the others.

The next day she consulted with William Law, then sent a messenger to a lawyer named Powers in Keokuk, Iowa, to learn if the Iowa governor had a warrant for Joseph's and Porter's arrest. William Walker, who boarded with the Smiths, crossed the river from Nauvoo with Joseph's horse as a decoy, while Joseph remained on the east side of the river.[11]

The following day, August 13, Joseph sent for Emma again. Emma prepared to leave but thoughtfully attended to a last-minute detail. She knew that Sarah Cleveland was moving to her lot along the river about four blocks to the east of the Smiths, leaving Eliza Snow without a home. Emma sent for Eliza, having already offered her a place in her own house a day earlier. Eliza wrote in her journal: "My former expectations were frustrated, but the Lord has opened the path to my feet, and I feel dispos'd to acknowledge his hand in all things. This sudden, unexpected change in my location, I trust is for good; it seem'd to come in answer to my petitions to God to direct me in the path of duty according to his will."[12] Eliza's father, Oliver Snow, who had become disenchanted with Joseph and the church over polygamy, perhaps specifically over Eliza's marriage to Joseph, was in Nauvoo on business and had apparently asked her to return to Walnut Grove with him. But on the same day that Emma sent for Eliza he commented with a father's perception, "Eliza cannot leave our Prophet."[13]

Emma had to be cautious. Four men kept watch around the city for

Joseph. They paid close attention to Emma's whereabouts. As a ruse, she walked over to Mrs. Durfee's while Joseph's private secretary, William Clayton, and Lorin Walker took her carriage, drove past the sheriff, and continued downriver. They circled back across the prairie, picked up Emma, and drove upriver with the sheriff none the wiser. A short distance from the Sayers farm, Clayton and Walker stopped the carriage and let Emma out. They returned to Nauvoo while Emma walked through thick woods to the farmhouse. "I was in good spirits," Joseph remembered, "and was much rejoiced to meet my dear wife once more."[14]

Emma stayed the night with Joseph. They spent the next morning talking and reading over his history. "[We] both felt in good spirits and very cheerful," Joseph said.[15] In the afternoon Emma waited while Joseph wrote a letter to Wilson Law, major general of the Legion, instructing him what to do if the city was attacked or Joseph was taken prisoner. After dinner Emma left with Erastus H. Derby and William Clayton who had returned to escort her home. They planned to walk to Nauvoo but the rain-soaked ground had turned to mud, so they took a skiff downriver. A fierce wind forced the craft between the islands in the river and with effort they finally landed on the opposite bank where Clayton procured another boat to take Emma across. The wind abated, but before they were halfway across it gusted again. Emma had another dangerous ride but landed safely.

Emma came home to good news. The lawyer from Keokuk met her and said that the governor of Iowa had not issued a writ against Joseph. Two days later, August 16, Erastus Derby brought a letter from Joseph. "My Dear Emma: I embrace this opportunity to express to you some of my feelings this morning. First of all I take the liberty to tender you my sincere thanks for the two interesting and consoling visits that you have made me during my almost exiled situation. Tongue cannot express the gratitude of my heart, for the warm and true-hearted friendship you have manifested in these things towards me."

Apparently Emma and Joseph had discussed the possibility of her going to see Governor Carlin again. He asked her not to go but added, "You may write to him whatever you see proper." Joseph told her that several friends had advised him to leave and perhaps go north to the "Pine Woods," a Mormon settlement in Wisconsin where lumber was cut to be shipped to Nauvoo. "If I go to the Pine country, you shall go along with me, and the children; and if you and the children go not with me, I don't go. . . . It is for your sakes, therefore, that I would do such a thing. I will go with you, then, in the same carriage, and on horseback from time to time as occasion may require; for I am not willing to trust you in the hands of those who cannot feel the same interest for you that I feel." He ordered his horse, gear, clothing, trunks, writing materials, and household furnishings to be loaded on a boat. "We will wend our way like larks up the Mississippi until the towering mountains and rocks shall remind us of the places of our nativity, and shall look like safety and home; and then we will bid defiance to the world."

Joseph signed it, "Yours in haste, your affectionate husband until death, through all eternity; for evermore."[16] This plan may have represented more wishful thinking than reality. Surely the Smith family belongings could not be loaded on a riverboat without observation, and the sheriff would have followed the baggage.

After he wrote to Emma, Joseph composed a sentimental essay which named his trusted associates and thanked them for their faithfulness. In it he paid Emma tribute. "With what unspeakable delight, and what transports of joy swelled my bosom, when I took by the hand, on that night, my beloved Emma—she that was my wife, even the wife of my youth, and the choice of my heart. Many were the reverbations of my mind when I contemplated for a moment the many scenes we had been called to pass through." He recognized "fatigues and the toils, the sorrows and sufferings, and the joys and consolations, from time to time, which had strewed our paths and crowned our board. Oh what a commingling of thought filled my mind for the moment, again she is here, even in the seventh trouble—undaunted, firm, and unwavering—unchangeable, affectionate Emma!"[17]

Emma's home in Nauvoo became the way station for communications about church, business, and legal matters. Emma assumed much responsibility for Joseph's welfare. She answered his letter about fleeing to the pine woods the same day that Joseph wrote it and she received it.

Dear Husband:—I am ready to go with you if you are obliged to leave; and Hyrum says he will go with me. I shall make the best arrangements I can and be as well prepared as possible. But still I feel good confidence that you can be protected without leaving this country. There are more ways than one to take care of you, and I believe that you can still direct in your business concerns if we are all of us prudent in the matter. If it was pleasant weather I should contrive to see you this evening, but I dare not run too much of a risk, on account of so many going to see you.

General Adams sends the propositions concerning his land, two dollars an acre, payments as follows: Assumption of mortgage, say about fourteen hundred, interest included. Taxes due, supposed about thirty dollars. Town property one thousand dollars. Balance, money payable in one, two, three or four years.

Brother Derby will tell you all the information we have on hand. I think we will have news from Quincy as soon as tomorrow.

Yours affectionately forever,

Emma Smith[18]

Emma sent the letter with Erastus Derby, then on the following day, August 17, she composed a letter to Governor Carlin. The letter was written in dramatic language and made an emotional appeal for the governor to spare her and her helpless children, and to allow "our aged mother" to see Joseph live. The fluent writing style was Emma's, but the fine penmanship was Eliza's.[19]

This same day Emma learned that Harmon T. Wilson, the sheriff from the county seat at Carthage, had come to Nauvoo in disguise and had taken lodging in the Davis tavern. A rumor reached Emma that Carlin was ready to issue a new writ and that Joseph's hiding place was known. She slipped out of her home in the dark of night and made her way with the faithful Derby to the Sayers farm to warn Joseph. Emma and Joseph and Erastus Derby left the Sayers place immediately and traveled unnoticed to Carlos Granger's house in Nauvoo, where in spite of the hour they were "kindly received and well-treated." Emma returned home reassured that Joseph was safe.[20]

The following day, August 18, 1842, Joseph wrote another letter. Three weeks earlier, on July 27, in the presence and with the consent of Elizabeth Ann, Newel K. Whitney had performed the marriage ceremony uniting their seventeen-year-old daughter Sarah Ann to Joseph.[21] Now, from the Granger home, Joseph addressed a letter to "Dear and beloved Brother and Sister Whitney & C.," and began, "I take this opportunity to communicate, Some of my feelings, privately, at this time, which I want you three Eternaly to keep in your own bosams; for my feelings are So strong for you Since what has pased lately between us." He commented on his loneliness: "It would afford me great relief, of mind, if those with whom I am alied to love me, now is the time to afford me succour. . . . The nights are very pleasant, indeed, all three of you can come and See me in the fore part of the night, let Brother Whitney come a little a head and nock at the south East corner of the house, at the window; it is next to the cornfield; I have a room entirely by myself, the whole matter can be attended to with the most perfect safty." He warned them, "The only thing to be careful of, is to find out when Emma comes, then you can not be Safe, but when She is not here, there is the most perfect safty. . . . Burn this letter as soon as you read it. keep all locked up in your breasts, my life depends upon it. one thing I want to see you for, is to git the fulness of my blessing Sealed upon our heads. . . . I think Emma wont come tonight if she dont, dont fail to come to night."[22] No entry was made in Joseph's history for this day.

This letter clearly indicates that Emma was unaware of Joseph's marriage to Sarah Ann. Newel Whitney recorded that Joseph gave them a blessing three days later on August 21. The evening after Joseph wrote the letter he went home under cover of darkness and spent the night with Emma, returning to his hiding place after conducting some business the next day. Three days later, on August 22, Emma sent a note to Joseph saying that she believed she could take care of him better at home than elsewhere. Joseph slipped into his own house that same night.[23]

Since 1842 Joseph's secretary, William Clayton, had been privy to important incidents in Nauvoo and by summer he was aware of many of Emma's
and Joseph's private problems. An English convert, Clayton developed a "single minded devotion" to his prophet through daily association with him.[24]
Clayton kept a detailed diary that would become the most extensive firsthand
contemporary account of Emma's activities over the next five years.[25]

While Joseph was in hiding Emma had corresponded with Governor
Carlin. Clayton, who delivered Emma's letter, reported that Carlin "passed
high encomiums on Emma Smith, and expressed astonishment at the judgment and talent manifest in the manner of her address." But the governor's
answer revealed his dilemma concerning Joseph. He explained to Emma that
he could not determine the guilt or innocence of an individual, but his duty
demanded that he respect the requests from other states for the return of
fugitives from justice. He reminded her that if Joseph was innocent of any
crime there could be no cause for alarm. But he retracted his statement about
the Missouri officials. He said he had meant the mobs could not be trusted, not
the legal system.[26]

On the twenty-seventh of August Emma dictated again while Eliza wrote.
"[I] still hope you will avail yourself of sufficient time to investigate our cause,
and thoroughly acquaint yourself with the illegality of the Prosecution insti-
tuted against Mr. Smith. . . . We do believe that it is your duty to allow us in
this place, the privileges and advantages guarenteed to us by the laws of this
State and the United States; This is all we ask." Emma quoted the Nauvoo
charter provision allowing the city council to make ordinances not conflicting
with the constitution of the state. She stated that the procedure for writs of
habeas corpus was properly done under the provisions of the city charter, and
that those powers were positively guaranteed in the charter "over your own
signature."

"Now I intreat your honor to bear with me patiently, while I ask, what
good can accrue to this State or the United States, or to yourself, or any other
individual, to continue this persecution upon this people, or upon Mr. Smith
—a persecution that you are well aware, is entirely without any foundation or
excuse." Emma's determination to point out the Mormon viewpoint did not
obscure her instinctive warmth and she invited Carlin and his family to spend
some time in Nauvoo.

Carlin commented on Emma's untiring efforts in Joseph's behalf when he
answered her. "Every word of [your letter] evinces your devotedness to the
interest of your husband, and pouring forth the effusions of a heart wholly
his." Carlin pointed out that the writs of habeas corpus, which gave citizens of
Nauvoo the right to face the court in Nauvoo regardless of where they were
arrested, did not have power over writs issued by other courts or by the governor of the state. He called the Mormons' assumption of power "most absurd
and ridiculous" and asserted that "to attempt to exercise it is a gross usur-

pation of power that cannot be tolerated." He went on to explain that he judged Joseph neither guilty nor innocent but that he simply abided by the requirements of his office to see that justice be done.[27]

Joseph's interpretation was that "Illinois gave unto Nauvoo her charters, ceding unto us our vested rights, which she has no power or right to take from us. All the power there was in Illinois, she gave to Nauvoo; and any man that says to the contrary is a fool."[28] Writs of habeas corpus issued by the Nauvoo court would often bring Joseph back to Nauvoo from other jurisdictions and would result in the charges against him being dismissed. The Mormons ignored the governor's warnings, sure that the legal system of Illinois was not effective and offered no protection against the Missouri writs. Joseph's experiences in Kirtland and Missouri would not let him trust any system except one that he controlled.

On August 29 Joseph surprised his followers at a conference in Nauvoo, when he walked up to the stand and greeted them. Rumor had him placed from Washington to Europe, but his presence in Nauvoo delighted both his friends and his enemies. Joseph believed the extradition efforts were prompted by Satan and not by the regular procedures of law. He publicly defied the sheriff when he announced in the Relief Society meeting two days later that he believed that "my Heavenly Father has decreed that the Missourians shall not get me into their power." In effect he challenged the authorities to prove his prophetic announcement false.[29]

Emma spearheaded a petition to send to Governor Carlin, and approximately a thousand women signed it through the Relief Society. Admitting that in ordinary cases "it would be more consistent with the delicacy of the female character to be silent," the women asked for protection from the Missouri mobs. The petition affirmed their belief in Joseph as a man "of integrity, honesty, truth and patriotism" and requested that he not be extradited to Missouri.[30] Joseph appeared with Emma at the August 31 meeting of the society. "I shall triumph over my enemies," he told the women. "I have begun to triumph over them at home and I shall do it abroad— . . . Altho' I do wrong, I do not the wrongs that I am charg'd with doing—the wrong that I do is thro' the frailty of human nature like other men. No man lives without fault. . . . I would to God that you would be wise, I now counsel you, if you know anything, hold your tongues, and the least harm will be done."[31]

Within three days the sheriff was after Joseph again. Around one o'clock Emma served dinner to the family—her own four children, Eliza, the Partridge sisters, assorted Walker children, Joseph, and perhaps others. Armed with requisitions from Iowa and Illinois, the sheriff and two deputies surreptitiously maneuvered their horses along the riverbank until they stood below the unfinished foundations of the Nauvoo House. They walked quietly to the Smiths' house and were in the building before an alarm could be given. They stumbled onto John Boynton, who was visiting the Smiths. While the sheriff asked for Joseph, Boynton stalled him with evasive answers. Joseph ran out of the back door of the large kitchen room, slipped through the high rows of corn in his garden, and hid in Newel and Elizabeth Whitney's apartment over the brick store.[32]

Emma confronted the officers when they wanted to search the house. "I have no objection if you have the proper authority," she told them. The sheriff said he did not but was going to search the premises anyway. Having delayed long enough for Joseph to get away, Emma asked Dimick Huntington to show him through the house.

After sundown another deputy approached the house and asked for Joseph. Emma spoke to him at the door; Eliza listened from inside. Emma asked again about a search warrant. Irascible at Joseph's disappearance, the deputy stated: "My will is good enough."

"Surely you could not object to telling me what you want with Mr. Smith," Emma commented.

King growled back, "There will be time enough to tell *that* afterward." Emma faced the man down and he rejoined his friends at Amos Davis's tavern. Joseph went into hiding again, this time with the Edward Hunter family.[33]

Joseph's followers were tireless in their efforts to clear his name. William Marks, president of the ecclesiastical association of several congregations in Nauvoo (termed a Stake by the Mormons), published his support of Joseph in August 1842 in the *Times and Seasons*. Marks attacked John C. Bennett: "I believe him to be a vile and wicked adulterous man, who pays no regard to the principles of truth or righteousness." Joseph had not taught the doctrine of plural marriage to Marks. Truthfully, Marks said he *knew* of "no order in the church which *admits* to a plurality of wives" and did not *"believe"* that Joseph Smith ever taught such a doctrine."[34]

The *Times and Seasons* reprinted the statement on marriage from the Doctrine and Covenants: "Inasmuch as this church of Christ has been reproached with the crime of fornication, and polygamy: we declare that we believe, that one man should have one wife; and one woman, but one husband, except in case of death, when either is at liberty to marry again." The article ended with a signed declaration from some of the leading men of the community stating, "We know of no other rule or system of marriage than the one published from the Book of Doctrine and Covenants, and we give this certificate to show that Dr. J. C. Bennett's secret wife system is a creature of his own make as we know of no such society in this place nor never did." Out of twelve men who lent their name to the document, Newel K. Whitney and John Taylor had already taken other wives. A similar statement carrying the names of nineteen Relief Society members followed. Emma's name headed the list. Two others, Eliza Snow and Sarah Cleveland, were plural wives of Joseph, as was Elizabeth Ann Whitney's daughter. A fourth woman, Leonora Taylor, knew her husband also practiced plural marriage.[35] Years later Eliza Snow was asked how she could have signed such a statement. She replied that they were putting down John C. Bennett's spiritual wifery. "At the time the sisters of the Relief Society signed our article I was married to the Prophet. We made no allusion to any other system of marriage than Bennett's. His was prostitution, and it was truly *his*, and he succeeded in pandering his course on the credulity of the unsuspecting by making them believe that he was thus authorized by the Prophet. In those articles there is no reference to divine plural marriage. We aimed to put down its opposite."[36]

John Taylor would echo the same sentiments in defense of the signed statement in the *Deseret News*, May 20, 1886. "So with that spiritual-wife doctrine which lustful men attempted to promulgate at that period. Joseph the prophet was just as much opposed to that false doctrine as any one could be. It was a counterfeit." Then Taylor employed code words to argue, "The true and divine order is another thing."

While friends worked in Joseph's behalf, he hid at Hunter's home. Emma made him a "very interesting" visit on September 9, 1842, at ten o'clock at night. After talking with friends, Joseph went home with Emma. Proud parents, they stood looking a moment at their sleeping children, then Joseph blessed them before he returned in the night to his quarters with the Hunter family.

The following day Emma again sent a messenger with a request that Joseph come home, saying "she thought [he] would be as safe there as anywhere." Assured by her evaluation of his safety, Joseph went home to Emma— and Eliza.[37]

10

More Wives
and a Revelation

September 1842–July 1843

Because Joseph's attempts to avoid imprisonment forced him to be absent, many of the family business responsibilities fell to Emma. On September 23, 1842, she sold $343.30 worth of store goods. In June Hiram Kimball sold to Emma and Joseph a three-quarter section of land and Emma and Joseph together sold a city lot to a newcomer. By October Emma bought and sold land without Joseph's supervision, but with his encouragement and approval.[1]

Emma interacted with church leaders in business. She wrote to Sidney Rigdon in September 1842 about the way he ran the post office. The letter began with a polite but no-nonsense comment: "I have noticed for some time back with feelings of regret that there is not that care and particularity in the Post Office in regards to the papers and letters belonging to Mr. Smith and the printing establishment that the nature of the case requires." Emma charged that unauthorized persons had been given Joseph's mail and had been seen "examining, overhauling, and handling both letters and papers belonging to Mr. Smith and opening and reading the papers, etc." She told Rigdon, "If this continues we shall feel in duty bound to make complaint to the proper authorities, considering it absolutely and indespensably necessary for the peace and interest of the community at large, as well as my husband's public and private interests. With sentiments of respect . . . Emma Smith."

Rigdon answered that he gave papers only to persons asking for them from the printing office and he declined to take responsibility for what happened to them afterward. Thus, Emma acted in behalf of Joseph and approached the problems directly. While some men deigned to respond to her, they did not always do so civilly. Rigdon's letter lacked the warmth of even the most formal salutation or closing.[2]

Throughout the summer and early fall of 1842 Emma's concern had been for Joseph, but in September she became ill. For seven days Joseph watched over her. The news that Governor Carlin had offered a reward of three hundred dollars each for Joseph and Porter Rockwell did not distract him from his vigil. The brief history entries for those days express his deep concern: "Emma is no better. I was with her all day. . . . Emma a little better, I was with her all day. . . . Emma is very sick again. I attended with her all day, being somewhat poorly myself." Although he did not become seriously ill, his own feelings of well-being rose and fell with Emma's.

By Wednesday, October 5, Joseph wrote, "My dear Emma was worse, many fears were entertained that she would not recover." Vilate Kimball described Joseph's anguish: "Emma was brought down nigh unto death; Bro. Joseph dispaired of her life, he mourned over her and refused to be comforted." His sorrow was not only for himself. "Oh dear," he cried. "What will become of my poor children. . . . [Emma] was baptized twice in the river, which evidently did her much good," he reported. "She grew worse again at night and continued very sick indeed. I was unwell and much troubled on account of Emma's sickness."

The following day Joseph was more optimistic. "Emma is better, and although it is the day on which she generally grows worse, yet she appears considerably easier. May the Lord speedily raise her to the bosom of her family, that the heart of His servant may be comforted again. Amen. My health is comfortable." And the day after: "Emma is some better. I am cheerful and well." Joseph's hopes were premature. Emma may have had typhoid fever or malaria and the disease would not run its course until January.[3]

Eliza Snow made no entry in her journal during Emma's illness until Sunday, October 9. Then two sheriffs came for Joseph, who, having been warned of a new writ, had gone into hiding two days earlier. "It was a sorrowful time," she wrote. "Sister Emma had been sick eleven days,—still confined to her bed—but he must go or be expose'd to the fury of the merciless!" When word came that Joseph was safe, Eliza wrote him:

> Sir, for your consolation permit me to tell
> That your Emma is *better*—she soon will be well;
> Mrs. Durfee stands by her, night & day like a friend
> And is prompt every call—every wish to attend;
> Then pray for your Emma, but indulge not a fear
> For the God of our forefathers, smiles on us here.[4]

Subtly Eliza had introduced herself into the poem. If the rhyme were entirely about Emma, the word "her" would have fitted nicely in place of "us" in the last line. Emma had received more than the usual amount of attention from Joseph since her illness. Perhaps Eliza felt somewhat left out.

Emma's recovery progressed slowly. When she saw Joseph three weeks later he reported with some satisfaction that "Emma is still getting better, and is able to attend to a little business, having this day closed contract and received pay for a quarter section of land."[5] He stayed with her overnight, then went back to his hiding place. He returned home at daylight a week later to find Emma worse and stayed at home. Joseph remained with her for several full days throughout the following weeks. His scribes noted that he frequently took her to the temple site[6] or for a ride in the carriage. Still her health seesawed over a period of four months.

For some time workers had been building a new home for Emma and Joseph across Main Street from the old Homestead. Young Joseph remembered that his parents' home "was generally overrun with visitors. There was scarcely a Sunday in ordinary weather that the house and yard were not crowded—the yard with teams and the house with callers. . . . About 1842 a new and larger home was built for us." Two stories high, this new house had a stairway dividing the parlor and living room on the main floor that led up to four rooms. Joseph had a hideaway built into the north upstairs bedroom. In the closet an ingenious hinged cleat with pins for hanging clothing disguised a ladder that led to the attic. After they had lived in the house for a while "some friends suggested that it should be expanded into a hotel, large enough to accommodate the usual crowds of visitors and an adequate force of domestic helpers as well."[7] A large back wing, composed of hotel rooms, would eventually extend to the east.

Some confusion exists over the date the family moved into the home. Latter-day Saint sources have traditionally placed the move in the summer of 1843 when the hotel wing was completed and Joseph hung the sign Nauvoo Mansion out front. Architectural studies of the building confirm that it was constructed in two stages. On November 2, 1842, Joseph moved his desk, books, and papers from the red brick store "to my house." Since the old Homestead was already overcrowded, he apparently referred to the new home where he could have an office on the first floor. People would sometimes call this the "Prophet's House" until August 31, 1843, when Joseph said they "commenced removing into the Nauvoo Mansion," or the hotel wing. From that time the building would be called the "Mansion House."[8] Eliza R. Snow, Eliza and Emily Partridge, two young sisters named Sarah and Maria Lawrence, several of the Walker children, including Lucy, William, and Lorin, and Lucy Mack Smith probably moved with them.

Shortly after the move Eliza Snow began teaching school in the lodge room over Joseph's store. The thirty-seven scholars included Emma's children. Alexander, at age four, was one of the youngest. Frederick was two years older, young Joseph was ten, and Julia eleven. Other children came from the Whitney, Partridge, Knight, and Marks families.

Eliza approached teaching school with some reluctance. The weather was cold and she dreaded the chilly room. She commented wryly in her diary, "In undertaking the arduous business with my delicate constitution, at this inclement season of the year, I was entirely governed by the wishes of Prest. and Mrs. Smith. . . . I desire and aim to be submissive to the requirements of those whom [God] has plac'd in authority over me."[9]

The students occasionally found an obstacle on the steps of their school in the form of Joseph's clerk, Willard Richards. A man of medium height, Richards weighed nearly three hundred pounds and his size intimidated the schoolchildren. Ordinarily he had a pleasant manner, but the boisterous youngsters who scrambled up and down the stairs disturbed his work. According to young Joseph, Richards would sometimes plant his stocky body firmly on the steps and growl at the children for being rude and noisy.[10]

The political scene changed in the fall of 1842. Thomas Ford replaced Thomas Carlin as governor of Illinois. His inaugural address concerned the Nauvoo charters, which for the most part were similar to those of other towns, but the Mormons interpreted theirs differently. A motion to repeal the Nauvoo charters was in front of the legislature by December 9, 1842, but repeal would have applied to other towns in the state as well and the matter rested.

Joseph decided to test his case in court after a summer and fall in hiding. On December 26, by prearrangement, Wilson Law arrested Joseph. Accompanied by forty men, they traveled to Springfield for the trial. His reputation preceded him and people flocked to the courtroom. Judge Nathaniel Pope was on the bench; Justin Butterfield represented Joseph. Butterfield won the audience with his opening remarks: "It is a momentous occasion in my life to appear before the Pope"—he made an appropriate bow to the judge—"in defense of a prophet of God"—a bow to Joseph—"in the presence of all these angels"—a last deep bow to the ladies. The courtroom was his. Butterfield defended his client on the grounds that Boggs's affidavit contained improper information. Joseph was discharged from his arrest.[11]

The jubilant party arrived home in Nauvoo on January 10 and a celebration seemed in order. On Tuesday, January 17, Emma's house overflowed with guests who met for a day of fasting, praise, and prayers of thanksgiving for Joseph's release. At ten o'clock on Wednesday morning they assembled again at the Smiths' to celebrate. Eliza had written a new song which the group sang "with the warmest of feelings." Friends milled through the front rooms while Emma and the girls in the kitchen made final preparations. At two o'clock in the afternoon Emma and Joseph served twenty-one guests a hearty meal assisted by the Partridge sisters, the Lawrence sisters, and some of the Walker children. The table was cleared and another group of twenty sat down to eat,

Emma and Joseph still serving. Eighteen people ate at the third table, including Emma and Joseph, then another fifteen, including the Smith children and the household members, were at the fourth. Joseph watched Emma move among the guests and supervise the work in the kitchen, then commented to the group, "This is not only a Jubilee but commemorates my marriage to Emma just fifteen years ago this day."[12]

The issues accompanying plural marriage seemed to disappear from Emma's life during the late summer, fall, and winter of 1842 and 1843. Joseph quietly solemnized at least two more marriages without her knowledge.[13] But the peace was not destined to last. Whether the new quarters created a false sense of security for Eliza and Joseph, or whether it simply was beyond their power to remain discreet indefinitely, Emma somehow discovered the liaison between the two, probably in February 1843.

When the full realization of the relationship between her friend Eliza and her husband Joseph came to her, Emma was stunned. She unquestionably reacted strongly, but the incident is so shrouded in Mormon folk tale and legend that it becomes difficult to determine what actually happened. Although no contemporary account of the incident between Emma and Eliza remains extant, evidence leads to the conclusion that some sort of physical confrontation occurred between the two women.[14] In 1886 Wilhelm Wyl published the first known version of the incident in his anti-Mormon book, *Joseph Smith the Prophet: His Family and His Friends:* "They say . . . there is scarcely a Mormon unacquainted with the fact that Sister Emma . . . soon found out the little compromise arranged between Joseph and Eliza. Feeling outraged as a wife and betrayed as a friend, Emma is currently reported as having had recourse to a vulgar broomstick as an instrument of revenge; and the harsh treatment received at Emma's hands is said to have destroyed Eliza's hopes of becoming the mother of a prophet's son."[15]

A second account is found in an undated entry that Mary Ann Barzee Boice made in her husband's patriarchal blessing book. Mary Ann Boice recorded Mrs. Aidah Clements as saying she worked for the prophet's family in Nauvoo and that Joseph Smith "was a going from home one day when she saw Emma go up to him and she was in a Passion jirked him by the collar and talked to him about going after other Women." Aidah also told Mary Ann that "once when she was at her work Emma went up stairs pulled Eliza R. Snow down stairs by the hair of her head as she was staying there." Written at the bottom of the page was, "this is the testimony of Aidah Clements," but Mary Ann crossed it out and added, "but this I give as a rumer only."[16]

A third account was related in 1931 by John R. Young, one of Brigham Young's sons. He reported a talk he had heard years earlier given by Solon Foster, who was Joseph's and Emma's carriage driver. Young said that Foster told of meeting with Joseph Smith III as an adult; he recalled, "The night your Mother turned Eliza R. Snow outdoors in her night clothes and you, and all the children stood out in the street crying, I led you back into the House and took you into Bed with me, and you said 'I wish Mother wouldn't be so cruel to Aunt Eliza.' "[17]

A fourth story, attributed to LeRoi C. Snow, Eliza's nephew, is an oral family tradition that tells of Emma knocking Eliza down the stairs with a broom, the fall resulting in a miscarriage for Eliza.[18] LeRoi Snow was eleven when his Aunt Eliza Snow died at age eighty-three, so it is unlikely that he heard the story from her. In his adult years he did research for intended biographies of his father, Lorenzo, and his Aunt Eliza, and his notes reveal a fifth account which he attributes to Charles C. Rich.

> Charles C. Rich called at the Mansion House, Nauvoo, to go with the Prophet on some appointment they had together. As he waited in the main lobby or parlor, he saw the Prophet and Emma come out of a room upstairs and walk together toward the stairway which apparently came down center. Almost at the same time, a door opposite opened and dainty, little, dark-haired Eliza R. Snow (she was "heavy with child") came out and walked toward the center stairway. When Joseph saw her, he turned and kissed Emma goodbye, and she remained standing at the bannister. Joseph then walked on to the stairway, where he tenderly kissed Eliza, and then came on down stairs toward Brother Rich. Just as he reached the bottom step, there was a commotion on the stairway, and both Joseph and Brother Rich turned quickly to see Eliza come tumbling down the stairs. Emma had pushed her, in a fit of rage and jealousy; she stood at the top of the stairs, glowering, her countenance a picture of hell. Joseph quickly picked up the little lady, and with her in his arms, he turned and looked up at Emma, who then burst into tears and ran to her room. Joseph carried the hurt and bruised Eliza up the stairs and to her room. "Her hip was injured and that is why she always afterward favored that leg," said Charles C. Rich. "She lost the unborn babe."[19]

This account appears to be fourth-hand and came over a hundred years after the incident would have occurred.[20] With the telling and retelling of this particular rendition some errors and family prejudices appear. "Dainty, little, dark-haired Eliza" may have seemed frail and small in her old age, as LeRoi Snow would have remembered her, but she stood five feet, six inches tall. The image of a tiny, defenseless woman being attacked by a hulking shrew is not valid. The Rich story also suggests that Emma should have watched her husband "tenderly kiss" Eliza and not be angry. Eliza had lived in her home in Kirtland and she was now living with the Smiths at Emma's invitation. The two women had worked together in the Relief Society organization and in

Joseph's behalf by visiting and writing to Governor Carlin. No matter how exalted Eliza viewed her marriage to Joseph to be, Emma could only be shocked and deeply hurt.

Another problem with the Rich account becomes evident. On July 12, 1869, Rich swore under oath that, in May of 1844, "Hyrum Smith taught him the principle of polygamy or celestial marriage."[21] This statement implies that Rich had not previously been taught plural marriage and therefore would not have been privy to the intimate scene some fifteen months earlier. No account places Eliza in the Smith household in 1844.

The statement that Eliza carried Joseph's unborn child and lost it is brought into question by Eliza's own journal. While her Victorian reticence probably would have precluded mention of her own pregnancy, if she were indeed carrying Joseph's child, other evidence in the journal indicates that she may not have been pregnant. Eliza's brother Lorenzo indicated that by the time she married Joseph, she was "beyond the condition of raising a family." Also if she was "heavy with child" as the Rich account states, she would not have been teaching school, for even legally married women usually went into seclusion when their pregnancies became obvious. Eliza continued to teach school for a month after her abrupt departure from the Smith household. Her own class attendance record shows that she did not miss a day during the months she taught the Smith children,[22] which would not have been probable had she suffered a miscarriage. This does not mean that Eliza was not Joseph's wife "in very deed," however. Years later, when asked if she had been Joseph's spiritual wife, Eliza retorted, "I certainly shall not acknowledge myself of having been a *carnal* one." She explained that "spiritual wife" was an epithet used to stigmatize "those of us who valiantly moved forward in obedience to the commands of God, in establishing the practice of plurality." Eliza testified that other women also were "the *bona fide* wives of Pres. Joseph Smith,"[23] implying that they were physically intimate with Joseph and enjoyed full conjugal rights. Heber C. Kimball is said to have told her it was his understanding that she was Joseph's wife in name only. "I thought you knew Joseph better than that,"[24] Eliza answered.

Whether Eliza fell down the stairs or whether Emma pushed her or pulled her down by the hair, or whether Emma only turned her out of the house, the result seems to be documented in Eliza's terse journal entry for February 11, 1843: "Took board and had my lodging removed to the residence of br. [Jonathan] Holmes."[25] Both Emma and Eliza had known Holmes's wife, Elvira Cowles, since they had arrived in Kirtland. Elvira Holmes was treasurer of the Relief Society and she would become Joseph's wife in less than three months.[26] Eliza did not make another entry in her journal for five weeks and wrote no explanation for either the gap in her diary or her abrupt departure from Emma's home.

To assume that Emma would not be angry at Joseph as well as at Eliza would be absurd. An undated poem in Eliza's journal is undoubtedly addressed to Joseph. Titled "Who Needs Consolation," it asks in part,

> I feel thy woes—my bosom shares
>   Thy spirit's agony:—
> How can I love a heart that dares
>   Suspect *thy* purity?
>
> I'll smile on all that smile on *thee*
>   As angels do above—
> All who in pure sincerity
>   Will love *thee*, I will love.
>
> Believe me, thou hast noble friends
>   Who feel and share thy grief;
> And many a fervent pray'r ascends
>   To heav'n, for thy relief.[27]

Except for unavoidable, formal occasions, the separation between the two women was permanent. Eliza had often referred to Emma by name in her journal during her residence in the house throughout the summer, fall, and winter. But references to Emma after this time reverted to the formal "Prest. Smith and lady."

Eliza taught the school until March 17, 1843, then confided to her diary, "This day clos'd my school much to my *own* satisfaction; having the pleasure of the presence of Prest. J. Smith, his lady—Mrs. Allred, Mrs. Durfee and others." Eliza read several "beautiful parting pieces, addressed to myself by the scholars," and her own farewell speech. She and the students sang a song she had composed,[28] Joseph ended the occasion with a prayer, and Eliza closed the school.

The incident between Emma and Eliza forced the issue of plural marriage into the open. Emma could no longer believe that Joseph was not involved, and he could no longer deny it. Emma had not acted with violence before; now her determined opposition might show up again with unexpected force. Joseph resolutely tried to bring Emma around.

After Eliza Snow's abrupt departure from Emma's house in February 1843, Joseph apparently resolved to pursue the establishment of plural marriage in spite of Emma's strong feelings. He approached Bishop Edward Partridge's daughters, who had lived for two years in his home. Emily was nineteen on February 28, 1843; Eliza would be twenty-three on April 20. "The first intimation I had from Brother Joseph that there was a pure and holy order of plural marriage," Emily wrote, "was in the spring of 1842, but I was not married until 1843."[29] Emily recorded the events of that year in her reminiscences. "Joseph said to me one day, 'Emily, if you will not betray me, I will tell you something for your benefit.' Of course I would keep his secret, but no opportunity offered for some time to say anything to me . . . he asked me if I would burn it if he would write me a letter."[30] Emily promised to do as he wished. "I began to think that was not the proper thing for me to do and I was about as miserable as I ever would wish to be for a short time. I went to my room and knelt down and asked my father in heaven to direct me in the matter. . . . I could not speak to any one on earth." Emily remembered, "I received no comfort till I went back and watched my opportunity to say I could not take a private letter from him."

"Do you wish the matter ended?" he asked.

"I do," she replied. But as time passed Emily wished that she had listened and felt "as miserable" as she was before.

Soon after Emily refused Joseph's letter she and her sister Eliza received an invitation from Mrs. Elizabeth Durfee to spend the afternoon at her home. Emily described this visit: "She introduced the subject of spiritual wives as they called it in that day," and wondered "if there was any truth in the report she heard." Emily thought to herself, "I could tell her something that would make her open her eyes if I chose." Not one to be drawn out by gossip, Emily said nothing. But on the way home she told her sister about Joseph's conversation, which disturbed Eliza also. "But it served to prepare her to receive the principles that were revealed soon after," Emily noted. Word that Emily would not betray Joseph was probably carried back to him by Mrs. Durfee. "I learned afterward," Emily wrote, "that Mrs. [Durfee] was a friend to plurality and knew all about it."

At a later date Mrs. Durfee told Emily that Joseph wanted an opportunity to talk to her. Emily asked, "Do you know what he wants?"

The woman's response was that she thought he wanted Emily "for a wife."

Emily agreed to meet Joseph at Heber Kimball's house in the evening. Some Kimball family members were present when she arrived. Heber explained to her, "Vilate is not at home, and you had better call another time."

Emily wrote, "I started for home as fast as I could so as to get beyond being called back, for I still dreaded the interview." Then she heard Kimball softly call, "Emily, Emily." When he was about to overtake her she turned and went with him. "I cannot tell all Joseph said, but he said the Lord had commanded [me] to enter into plural marriage and had given me to him and although I had got badly frightened he knew I would yet have him." Emily continued, "My mind was now prepared and would receive the principles." In a reflective moment she added, ". . . that was the only way that [it could] be done then. Well I was married there and then. Joseph went home his way and I going my way alone. A strange way of getting married wasn't it?" The date was March 4, 1843.[31]

Four days later Eliza Partridge married Joseph. She kept a journal but burned it later because it was "too full."[32] Her reminiscences contain the terse statement that while she lived with Emma and Joseph "he taught us the plan of Celestial marriage and asked us to enter into that order with him. This was truly a great trial for me but I had the most implicit confidence in him as a Prophet of the Lord."[33] The two sisters did not state how they reconciled their divided loyalties between Joseph and Emma. Emily's appreciation for Emma is apparent in her writings: "One day Emma said as we had been to so many parties, we ought to have one and invite the young people in to the home in return. Of course this pleased us very much."[34] But the young women would find that problems over their secret marriages would erode their friendship with Emma.

Late in April 1843 Emma boarded a riverboat bound for St. Louis. Because Joseph feared arrest he sent her to purchase store goods and supplies for the hotel wing under construction on the back of their house. Lorin Walker, who lived with the Smiths, traveled with her. His sister Lucy helped Emma with the housework and attended school with the Smith children. Young Joseph remembered her "marshalling" them to and from school like an elder sister. A second brother, William, reported that the prophet asked him for permission to marry Lucy. Joseph married seventeen-year-old Lucy Walker on May 1 with William Clayton officiating, while Emma and Lorin Walker were in St. Louis. Lucy said about her marriage, "Emma Smith was not present and she did not consent to the marriage; she did not know anything about it at all."[35] Joseph waited on the docks on May 2 until the *Maid of Iowa* brought Emma home.

Emma's return initiated two weeks of festivities. On May 6 Emma, on horseback, led a dozen women who rode to the parade ground with Joseph and his military staff to review the Legion's new uniforms. The brass band marched smartly ahead. On May 11 Emma and Joseph accepted a new carriage, then she drove it south to Quincy to visit friends. Joseph went to Yelrome for a conference where Emma met him four days later. They made the return trip together on May 15.[36]

Nearly a year had passed since Joseph had introduced a select group of men into a ceremony first called "the holy order" and later referred to as the "endowment." Hyrum Smith, William Law, Brigham Young, Heber C. Kimball, Willard Richards, Newel K. Whitney, George Miller, William Marks, and James Adams had met "in Joseph's private office, where [he] taught the ancient order of things for the first time in these last days, and [they] received [their] washings, anointings and endowments."[37] The participants wore white clothing that was not part of their daily apparel. Probably before Eliza Snow left in February, Joseph designed an undergarment for the endowment ceremonies that would be worn beneath regular clothing afterward. Elizabeth Allred, Emma's associate in the Relief Society, made the pattern. Her granddaughter, Eliza M. A. Munson, said they spread unbleached muslin out on a table and Joseph directed the cutting. Mrs. Allred made three patterns before she had designed it correctly. "The first garments were bound with turkey red and were without collars. Later on the Prophet decided he would rather they were bound with white." Noting the rough neckline, "Sister Emma proposed that they have a collar on and they would look more finished. . . . After Emma Smith had made the little collars [invisible under street clothing], Eliza R. Snow later introduced a wider collar of finer material to be worn outside the dress."[38] Eliza's design was not used.

Emma had heard Joseph and Heber C. Kimball address the Relief Society and allude to a time when women would participate in the endowment.[39] After being involved in the construction and design of the garments, the building of the temple, and hearing about their place in the endowment in the Relief Society, why had women not yet been admitted to the Endowment Council? Heber C. Kimball said it was because some women had led their husbands out of the church.[40] Joseph taught that a man must obey God to be worthy of the endowment and that a wife must obey a righteous husband to merit the same reward. Until Emma could be obedient to Joseph and give him plural wives, she could not participate in the endowment ceremonies, yet he taught her that the endowment was essential for exaltation—as opposed to salvation, which Joseph taught was available to all through the atonement of Christ.[41] Joseph wanted Emma to serve as the example, the Elect Lady, the "disseminator of the endowment blessing," to other women. Thus her rejection of plural marriage would have blocked her admittance into the Endowment Council, because she had not obeyed her husband, and therefore prevented other women from entering as well.[42]

Simultaneously with the endowment and plural marriage, Joseph formalized a third concept. He explained to Emma that husbands and wives could be married, "sealed," forever by proper priesthood authority. Couples who had been married in traditional ceremonies were considered to be married for "time," or until death separated them, but unions made in the new Mormon ceremonies were to last beyond the grave. These marriages were termed "eternal marriages" or "sealings" and could be performed for living couples as well as for a living spouse and a deceased one. Thus a man could be sealed to his dead wife and also to his living wife. Understanding this doctrine led to the next step, which was the marriage of a living husband to several living wives. This more gradual explanation of doctrine seemed to alleviate some of the repugnance when plural marriage was introduced. Although Joseph did not teach plural marriage in the meetings of the Endowment Council,[43] acceptance of the sealing ordinance enabled those whom he taught privately to accept polygamy.

Within the same few weeks, in the spring of 1843, both Hyrum Smith and Emma would accept plural marriage. Hyrum, who had disbelieved the rumors that linked Joseph's name with polygamy, had joined earlier with William Marks and William Law in condemning Bennett for his practice of spiritual wifery. They considered the rumors accusing Joseph of such practice to be attempts to blacken his reputation. Hyrum was patriarch to the church, Law was Joseph's counselor in the first presidency, and Marks was the Nauvoo stake president. Although the exact sequence of events is not clear, at some point the three became convinced that the rumors were founded in elements of fact. On May 14, 1843, Hyrum attempted to quash the stories in his Sunday sermon but his brother called on Brigham Young to respond.[44] Still believing that plural marriage would be destructive to the community and that it was against the standards of morality, Hyrum joined William Marks and William Law to "expose" Joseph and bring a stop to the practice. Heber C. Kimball learned of the effort and passed on his concerns to William Clayton, who recorded the incident in his diary on May 23.[45]

Hyrum had admitted to Ebenezer Robinson that he was opposed to the doctrine. He also told William Marks "he did not believe in it [plural marriage] and he was going to see Joseph about it, and if Joseph had a revelation on the subject, he would believe it."[46] But before Hyrum had an opportunity to speak to Joseph he found Brigham Young outside the Masonic Hall one day.

"Brother Brigham, I want to talk to you," he said. The two men eased down on a stack of rails near the fence. "I have a question to ask you," Hyrum continued. "I do know that you and the Twelve know something that I do not know . . . I know there is something or other which I do not understand that is revealed to the Twelve. Is this so?"

Brigham sidestepped the question. "I do not know anything about what you know, but I know what I know."

Hyrum pressed on. "I have mistrusted for a long time that Joseph had received a revelation that a man should have more than one wife, and he has hinted as much to me, but I would not bear it. . . . I am convinced that there is something that has not been told me."

"Brother Hyrum, I will tell you about this thing which you do not know if you will swear with an uplifted hand before God that you will never say another word against Joseph, and his doings, and the doctrines he is preaching to the people."

Hyrum was ready: "I will do it with all my heart. . . . I want to know the truth to be saved." According to Brigham, Hyrum then stood before him with an uplifted hand "and he made a covenant there, never again to bring forward one argument or use any influence against Joseph's doings."[47]

The same day that he talked with Brigham, Hyrum went to Joseph and confessed to him that he knew and he believed.

A year later Hyrum reported his conversation with Joseph—or at least a conversation on the same subject. Speaking on April 8, 1844, Hyrum recounted that he told Joseph he was troubled that his first wife, Jerusha, had died before God had shown him the concept of eternal marriage.

"You can have her sealed to you upon the same principle as you can be baptized for the dead," Joseph told him.

"What can I do for my second wife [Mary]?" he inquired.

"You can also make a covenant with her for eternity and have her sealed to you by the authority of the priesthood," Joseph responded.

Hyrum quoted Mary's reaction: "I will act as proxy for your wife that is dead, and I will be sealed to you for eternity myself. . . . I love you and I do not want to be separated from you nor be forever alone in the resurrection."[48]

From this logic, accepting plural marriage was not difficult. Hyrum's conversion was complete. On May 29 Mary Fielding and his dead wife, Jerusha Barden, were sealed to Hyrum with Mary acting as Jerusha's proxy. In August 1843 Hyrum Smith married his wife's sister Mercy and Catherine Phillips as plural wives.[49]

At the same time that Hyrum was struggling with plural marriage, so was Emma. Joseph had apparently been relentless in his efforts to convince her. He was not master in his own home so long as Emma opposed him, and since Emma had discovered his relationship with Eliza Snow, the subterfuge and deception in their lives loomed larger. He wanted Emma to practice plural marriage and to lead forth as the *example*. It was this setting the example for other women to follow that was the most difficult.

When Emma refused to accept plural marriage with the same faith shown by some of the other wives, Joseph apparently tried a variety of stratagems. William Carter Staines, a carpenter on the temple, saw Joseph and Emma standing in the doorway of their house on a spring day in 1843. As another man approached, "riding a very fine sorrel horse," Staines overheard Emma comment favorably on it.

"Would you like to have it?" Joseph asked.

"Oh yes, I should."

"Well, I will buy it for you on one condition," Joseph offered.

"What is it?"

"That you will never mention the words 'spiritual wife' to me any more, as long as you live—"

Emma agreed, "I will gladly do that." Staines added that Joseph purchased the horse for a hundred and fifty dollars.[50]

For two months, from March to May, Joseph appears to have talked with Emma about plural marriage. He apparently used their rides together to teach her the necessity of the endowment and sealing. There is no evidence that she ever opposed him on any doctrine but plural marriage. Convinced that it was necessary for her salvation and essential to their continued relationship, she may have decided to compromise with Joseph. In May 1843 she finally agreed to give Joseph other wives if she could choose them. Any of Joseph's other wives, who by now numbered at least sixteen,[51] would have been more comfortable if they had had Emma's approval. Emma chose the two sets of sisters then living in her house, Emily and Eliza Partridge and Sarah and Maria Lawrence.[52]

Joseph had finally converted Emma to plural marriage, but not so fully that he dared tell her he had married the Partridge sisters two months earlier. Emily said that "to save family trouble Brother Joseph thought it best to have another ceremony performed. . . . [Emma] had her feelings, and so we thought there was no use in saying anything about it so long as she had chosen us herself." Emily also remembered that Emma "helped explain the principles to us."[53]

How would Emma have explained the principles of plural marriage to young women who had been her wards for over two years? Merely that it was a law of God that had to be fulfilled? Did she try to allay any feelings of guilt or sin? Did she explain that marriage as Joseph intended it to be involved conjugal relations? Was she aware of that herself? Unfortunately no answers to these questions were recorded. One observation can be made: if Emma's explanation at this time differed from Joseph's earlier approach neither Emily nor Eliza mentioned it.

On May 23, 1843, Emma watched Judge James Adams, a high priest in the church who was visiting from Springfield, marry Joseph to Emily and Eliza Partridge in her home. Emily wrote, "We did not make much trouble, but were sealed in her presence." She noted "Emma was present. She gave her free and full consent."[54]

Emma had made the sacrifice; and within five days she had her reward. On a cold rainy day, May 28, 1843, Emma was sealed to Joseph for "time and all eternity."[55] On this same day she was the first woman admitted to the Prayer Circle. Joseph would initiate her into the endowment sometime before the early autumn of that year.[56]

Emma's capitulation, however, was only momentary. Emily wrote that "Emma seemed to feel well until the ceremony was over, when almost before she could draw a second breath, she turned, and was more bitter in her feelings than ever before, if possible, and before the day was over she turned around or repented what she had done and kept Joseph up till very late in the night talking to him." Understandably, Emily and Eliza, whose marriages Emma had sanctioned one moment and disapproved the next, had feelings of their own. "She had, as it were, bound us to the ship and carried us to mid ocean, then threw us over board to sink or swim, as the case might be."[57]

William Clayton's diary entry for that same day explains why Emma was angry. Joseph told Clayton that he "had had a little trouble with sis. E[mma]." He had been with Eliza Partridge in an upstairs room when he heard someone on the stairs and quickly shut the door "not knowing who it was and held it. [Emma] came to the door & called Eliza 4 times & tried to force open the door. Prest. [Smith] opened it & told her the cause etc. She seemed much irritated."[58] Why would Joseph have held the door until Emma had called Eliza Partridge's name four times? Did Emma believe that Joseph and Eliza were hiding something from her? Emily remembered that Emma "kept close watch on us. If we were missing for a few minutes and Joseph was not at home the house was searched from top to bottom and from one end to the other and if we were not found the neighborhood was searched until we were found."[59]

Emma was not successful in keeping Joseph from meeting with his wives. Emily Partridge would one day testify under oath that she "roomed" with Joseph on the night of her second marriage to him while Emma, she believed, was in the house at the time. She also testified that she had "slept with him" between her first marriage and the second ceremony.[60]

According to Emily, at about the time of her second ceremony, "Emma . . . gave her husband two other wives—Maria and Sarah Lawrence."[61] The Lawrence sisters had come to Nauvoo from Canada without their parents in 1840 when Maria was about eighteen and Sarah fifteen. Emma and Joseph offered them a home. According to William Law's account, the girls had inherited about eight thousand dollars in "English gold." Law said, "Joseph got to be appointed their guardian," and indicated that he and Sidney Rigdon were bondsmen to Joseph. After Emma approved of the Lawrence marriages, William Law accused her of doing so with an eye to helping Joseph secure the inheritance.[62] Joseph's history dated May 30, 1843, reads, "I superintended the preparation of papers to settle the Lawrence estate," and four days later the "accounts of the Lawrence estate were presented to the probate judge, to which he made objection."[63]

Apparently problems with the inheritance occupied Joseph for at least fifteen months. According to Joseph's history, the girls' stepfather, Josiah Butterfield, insulted him "so outrageously" on March 28, 1843, that Joseph "kicked him out of the house, across the yard and into the street." By June 4, 1844, Joseph was counseling John Taylor "to go on with the prosecution in behalf of Maria Lawrence. I concluded to go to Quincy with Taylor, and give up my bonds of guardianship as administrator of the Lawrence estate."[64]

Neither of the Lawrence sisters left any account of their marriages to Joseph, but their experiences were probably similar to those of the Partridge sisters. For almost a year the four young women would live with the Smiths, but the situation was most difficult. Emily wrote that Emma "said some very hard things" about the plural marriages and her "interviews were quite common."

Lucy Walker observed the difficulties surrounding her and learned to be discreet. She said Emma never knew about her own marriage, but emphasized that Emma gave her consent to the marriage of "at least four other girls to her husband, and that she was well aware that he associated with them as wives within the meaning of all that word implies. This is proven," Lucy went on, "by the fact that [Emma] herself, on several occasions, kept guard at the door to prevent disinterested persons from intruding, when these ladies were in the house."[65] Emma vacillated between reluctant acceptance and determined opposition to the marriages. Leonora Taylor said Emma "had received a testimony of the truthfulness of plural marriage." Orson Pratt in an 1869 discourse said that Emma would "at times fight against [Joseph] with all her heart; and then she would break down in her feelings . . . and would then lead forth ladies and place their hands in the hands of Joseph." When Zina Diantha Huntington Young was asked in 1895 "if Emma Smith was opposed to poligamy" her answer was an emphatic "No."[66] But the evidence seems clear that Emma gave her permission for plural marriages and immediately regretted that they had been performed. Emma began to talk as firmly and urgently to Joseph about abandoning plural marriage as he had formerly talked to her about accepting it.

Remembering this difficult year, Emily Partridge gave some insights into Emma's situation as well as her own:

She often made things very unpleasant, but I have nothing in my heart towards her but pity. I know it was hard for Emma, and any woman to enter plural marriage in those days, and I do not know as anybody would have done any better than Emma did under the circumstances. I think Emma always regretted having any hand in getting us into such trying circumstances. But she need not have blamed herself for that, in the least, for it would have been the same with or without her consent, and I have never repented the act that made me a plural wife . . . of Joseph Smith and bound me to him for time and all eternity.[67]

About the same time that Joseph married the Partridge and Lawrence sisters he initiated contacts for two more plural wives. The first was Almira Johnson and the second Heber and Vilate Kimball's daughter Helen. Joseph's history for Tuesday, May 16, 1843, states that he went to a nearby town named Ramus with Eliza Partridge, her younger sister Lydia, George Miller, and William Clayton. That evening they "went to Benjamin F. Johnson's with William Clayton to sleep. Before retiring, [Joseph] gave Brother and Sister Johnson some instructions on the priesthood." According to Johnson, Joseph "had come to Ramus to teach Me Plural Marriage" and while Joseph was in the Johnson home he shared a room with "the Daughter of the Late Bishop Patridge."[68]

Joseph visited the Johnson home several times through the spring. Soon he approached a delicate issue with Benjamin Johnson, who reported, "as he was again Required of the Lord to take more wives he had Come now to ask me for my Sister Almira—His words astonished me and almost *took* my *breath.*" Finally Johnson, "almost Ready to burst with emotion," looked his friend in the eye and said, "Brother Joseph This is Something I did not Expect & do not understand it—You know whether it is Right. I do not. I want to do just as you tell me and I will try. But if I ever Should know that you do this to Dishonor & debauch my Sister I will kill you as Shure as the Lord lives." Johnson explained why he granted Joseph's request. "I know that Joseph was Comanded to take more wives and he waited untill an angel with a drawn Sword Stood before him and declared that if he longer delayed fulfilling that Command he would Slay him." Joseph married Almira Johnson in the late summer. Johnson recorded that "the prophet again Came and at my house ocupied the Same Room & bed with my Sister [Almira] that the month previous he had ocupied with the Daughter of the Late Bishop Partridge as his wife."[69]

In much the same manner as Emma's friend Elizabeth Ann Whitney had given her daughter Sarah to Joseph a year earlier, Vilate Kimball and her husband Heber C. agreed to the marriage of their daughter—who was one month from her fifteenth birthday—to Joseph. Helen Mar Kimball told of her marriage in her 1881 autobiography.

Just previous to my father's starting up his last mission but one [June 10, 1843],[70] to the Eastern States, he taught me the principle of Celestial marriage, and having a great desire to be connected with the Prophet Joseph, he offered me to him; this I afterwards learned from the Prophet's own mouth. My father had but one lamb, but willingly laid her upon the alter: how cruel this seemed to the mother whose heartstrings were already stretched untile they were ready to snap asunder for he had taken Sarah Noon to wife & she thought she had made sufficient sacrifise but the Lord required more. I will pass over the temptations which I had during the twenty four hours after my father introduced to me the principle & asked me if I would be sealed to Joseph who came next morning & with my parents I heard him teach & explain the principle of Celestial marriage—after which he said to me, "If you will take this step, it will ensure your eternal salvation & exaltation and that . . . of your fathers household & all of your kindred." I willingly gave myself to purchase so glorious a reward. None but God & angels could see my mother's bleeding heart, when Joseph asked her if she was willing, she replied "If Helen is willing I have nothing more to say." She had witnessed the sufferings of others, who were older & who better understood the step they were taking, & to see her child, who had scarcely seen her fifteenth summer, following in the same thorny path, in her mind she saw the misery which was so sure to come as the sun was to rise and set; but it was all hidden from me.[71]

Apparently the Kimballs had not fully explained to Helen what the marriage would involve. "I would never have been sealed [married] to Joseph, had I known it was anything more than a ceremony," Helen later confided to her mother.[72]

Joseph's choice of women as plural wives gradually put a wedge between Emma and her friends as long as she remained either ignorant of the practice or opposed it. By late summer 1843 most of Emma's friends had either married Joseph or had given their daughters to him. Her sister-in-law, Agnes Coolbrith, was married to Joseph; another sister-in-law, Mary Fielding, had consented to the marriage of her husband Hyrum Smith and her sister Mercy. At least five women in her own household were Joseph's plural wives. Whether Emma knew about them or not, the women would not have been sympathetic to Emma while she opposed plural marriage. As a result, she became isolated from her friends and associates, and through the next four years this isolation would become more and more acute.

Secrecy circumscribed the role of Joseph's plural wives. He hid his relationship with them from the majority of the inhabitants of Nauvoo, as well as from Emma. Lucy Walker said that Joseph introduced her as his wife to Heber C. Kimball and Brigham Young, but she stressed that the marriage was never made public and she and the Lawrence sisters went by their maiden names.[73] Melissa Lott, daughter of the manager of Joseph's farm, stated, "I did not go to church . . . was never seen on the streets or in public places with him as his wife."[74] No evidence exists that he assumed the support of his wives in the traditional sense of providing them with food, clothing, and shelter, except for the young women in his house. Some remained with their parents; others lived with other plural wives; a few lived with other families where plural marriage was also practiced.[75] Their personal accounts attest that, for the most part, they felt Joseph cared for them deeply and they felt important to him. But if each wife secretly desired to be the first in Joseph's affections, she was destined for disappointment. Emma was sometimes harsh and angry, but when one of Joseph's plural wives complained about Emma to him he chided her, "If you desire my love you must never speak evil of Emma."[76]

One month after Emma witnessed Joseph's marriage to the Partridge and Lawrence sisters, she and Joseph concluded to visit some of her family members who had relocated to Lee County, Illinois. By 1843 seven of Isaac and Elizabeth Hale's children lived in Illinois. Emma's brothers Jesse, David, Alva, and Isaac lived with their families near the small towns of Dixon, Sublette, and Amboy. David Hale had married Rhoda Skinner, the midwife who helped deliver Emma's first child. Emma's Uncle Nathaniel and Aunt Sarah Lewis, and son Hiel, had also settled in Lee County. Elizabeth Hale and her husband, Benjamin Wasson, lived in an area of Amboy Township called Inlet Grove. Their son Lorenzo had joined the church. Apparently this would not be Joseph's first visit to this area, for the county history stated that Joseph preached in the schoolhouse occasionally and that gradually a group of people converted to the Mormon faith, some of whom came from "the most respectable families."[77]

Emma and Joseph had started to Amboy a year earlier but when Frederick fell out of the carriage and broke his leg the family immediately returned to Nauvoo. Now, on June 13, 1843, Emma, Joseph, and the children, accompanied by Lorin Walker, left Nauvoo in carriages to travel one hundred and fifty miles northeast.[78] Three days into their journey, Illinois Governor Thomas Ford issued a writ in Springfield for Joseph's arrest and extradition to the state of Missouri. William Clayton and Stephen Markham rode to warn Joseph.

Meanwhile Emma and Joseph arrived on June 20 at Elizabeth and Benjamin Wasson's home at Inlet Grove in Lee County unaware of any danger. After visiting a day, Emma and Joseph left for Dixon, but at four o'clock Markham and Clayton rode into the Wassons' yard, then wheeled their tired horses and caught up with Joseph. Joseph, Emma, Clayton, and Markham returned to the Wasson home. J. H. Reynolds, sheriff of Jackson County, Missouri, and H. T. Wilson, constable of Carthage, Illinois, arrived as the family sat down to dinner the following day. When Joseph walked toward the barn Wilson recognized him and yelled to alert Reynolds, who soon held cocked pistols to Joseph's chest. Reynolds cried out, "God damn if you stir one inch I'll shoot you, be still or I'll shoot you!"

"What is the meaning of this?" Joseph demanded. The excited men told Joseph he was under arrest. They forced him into a wagon and prepared to drive off. Markham grabbed the reins and held the horses while Joseph argued about a writ of habeas corpus and asked to say good-bye to his family. Emma ran out with a hat and coat. The officers rode to Dixon with Joseph under guard and Stephen Markham following. In Dixon, Markham obtained a writ against Reynolds and Wilson for threatening his own life, and the local constable took the two officers into his custody. Joseph sent William Clayton to catch the steamer *Amaranth* down the river to Nauvoo for help.

Cyrus Walker, a well-known criminal lawyer running for Congress, would not defend Joseph unless he could offer him the Mormon vote. Joseph agreed but would later regret it.

By ten o'clock on June 24 a writ from the circuit court of Lee County charged Reynolds and Wilson with private damage and false imprisonment. Cyrus Walker sent the sheriff of Lee County to travel with Joseph and his two arresting officers. The party headed toward Nauvoo with Reynolds and Wilson still hoping that they could spirit Joseph across the Mississippi River into Iowa or Missouri.

If Emma had hoped for relief from the stress in Nauvoo, Joseph's arrest in her sister's yard had not offered it. The Hales undoubtedly recalled Joseph's early arrest while they lived in Harmony, Pennsylvania. Emma's family had yet another excuse to look upon Joseph with derision.

Lorenzo Wasson drove Emma and the children in the carriage to Nauvoo where they arrived on June 27. Eliza R. Snow immediately found Emma and asked about the arrest. Emma learned that one hundred seventy-five men were traveling to Dixon, intent on saving their prophet. When Joseph met the men from Nauvoo, he turned to his captors. "Gentlemen, I think I will not go to Missouri this time! These are my boys!"[79] They brought a writ of habeas corpus which made the legal situation almost ludicrous. Joseph was a prisoner of Reynolds and Wilson, who were prisoners of Sheriff Campbell, who delivered the whole lot into the hands of Stephen Markham, who carried the writ of habeas corpus.

Word reached Emma that Joseph would arrive about noon on Friday, June 30, and the inhabitants of Nauvoo prepared to welcome their prophet home. A string of carriages, the Nauvoo Brass Band, the Martial Band, and whooping happy citizens escorted Emma to meet Joseph out on the prairie. She handed Joseph the reins to his horse; the band struck up "Hail Columbia" as Joseph embraced her. William Clayton watched Emma greet Joseph. "Such a feeling I never before witnessed when the Prest. took hold of the hand of his partner in sorrow & persecution. Surely it would have moved any thing but the heart of an adamantine."[80] Side by side on horseback, Emma and Joseph led the company of sheriffs and carriages to the door of the Mansion House. Lucy Mack Smith embraced her son; Julia, Joseph, and Alexander clung to their father. Little Frederick voiced the fears of them all when he piped, "Pa, the Missourians won't take you away again, will they?"

Emma served fifty people dinner, with Wilson and Reynolds uncomfortable at the head table. Joseph commented in his diary for that day, "I brought them as prisoners, not of chains, but of kindness to her from whom I was torn."[81]

Four days later, triumphant over their enemies, the Mormons celebrated the Fourth of July. Three steamboats brought eight hundred to a thousand people from Quincy, St. Louis, and Burlington. The Nauvoo Brass Band led the visitors to their seats on the hill, while cannons fired in salute.

In the Smith household, Emma and the young women prepared to feed a large group of guests. Emma ran to Mary Elizabeth Rollins Lightner's house to borrow a dining-room table for the officers and honored guests. Suddenly Joseph entered, dressed in his uniform. "I want you, and you," he said, pointing to four members of the Rollins family, "to go and be baptized."

"What, Joseph? Why is this? They have always been good members of the church," Emma reasoned. "And another thing, the officers will be for dinner soon."

"Never mind; they can wait."

"Well, you certainly are not going in those clothes," Emma responded, perhaps still hoping to salvage her dinner.

"No," Joseph answered. "But you all be ready by the time I return."

And in short order the group all trouped to the nearby riverbank where Joseph rebaptized Mary Elizabeth, her brother Henry and his wife, and an aunt.[82] In spite of the interruption the day went well and a visitor reported, "Nauvoo is destined to be, under the influence and enterprise of such citizens as it now contains, and her natural advantages, a populous, wealthy, and manufacturing city." Joseph was "highly gratified" with the day.[83]

While the Mormons celebrated, Emma again faced a personal challenge. She had come home to the same situation she had left two weeks earlier: Joseph's wives were still in the house. Inwardly, Emma struggled with the issue; outwardly, she was the loyal prophet's wife and participated in the social activities of Nauvoo.

Emma was of interest to the diary and journal keepers of Nauvoo. They described her as "a woman of commanding presence," only rarely losing self-control or giving way to tears. She was a "brilliant conversationalist" and "high spirited." A man once twitted her about "fishing for a compliment." Her prompt rejoinder, "I never fish in shallow water," took him aback. Young Henry Rollins appeared at Emma's house one day and offered his help. A friend had brought in a wagonload of hogs and Joseph asked Rollins to cut them up and salt them. "I want it done just as my wife Emma tells you," he instructed. Rollins remembered, "[Emma] came in the cellar after and told me to cut and salt them in the barrels . . . then put brine and then as much molasses to each barrel, and after laying for a certain length of time, take them out and hang them up in the carriage house and smoke them."

Rollins objected, "I am afraid as it is getting quite warm in the day [and] their being sweet the flies will spoil them."

"Fix them as I want it done [even] if they all spoil," Emma insisted. "And they did most of them spoil,"[84] Henry added laconically. Emma was apparently not as good at preserving meat as her hunter father had been, and the incident amused Henry Rollins for many years.

The Mormons discovered the delights of riverboating during the warm months of 1843. Joseph bought the *Maid of Iowa* from its captain, Dan Jones. Emma and Joseph boarded the boat for floating parties up and down the river with a hundred guests. These were daylong affairs. The band played intermittently, quantities of food were served, all were dressed in their best finery. "Much good humor and hilarity prevailed." The only shadow on the excursions fell when the boat docked on the Iowa or Missouri side of the river. Then Joseph kept himself concealed.

During this summer political activity increased as candidates began to campaign for the 1844 elections. Joseph had tried unsuccessfully to avoid being committed to a political party.[85] Judge Stephen Douglas, now quite well acquainted with Joseph, visited Nauvoo and dined at the Mansion. Joseph invited the leading men of Nauvoo to join them, but this invitation caught

Emma without a dessert. Quickly she made apple fritters and fried them to perfection. The men liked the fluffy morsel and one of them asked its name.

Emma smiled. "I call it a candidate."

"Why?" they all wanted to know.

"Why not?" she answered them. "Isn't it just a puff of wind?"[86]

The Mormon tendency to vote en bloc drew the politicians. Whig Cyrus Walker understood that Joseph had promised him the Mormon vote, but Hyrum announced that he had a revelation that the Mormons should vote for the Democratic candidate. Immediately preceding the election, Joseph announced that he would vote for Walker but that Hyrum had never had a false revelation. The Democrat Hoge won by a slim margin, and the Whigs felt betrayed. They enlisted some Democrats to their side, and the combined group vowed to repay the Mormons by driving them from the state.

In spite of the political tension, Emma celebrated her thirty-ninth birthday on July 10 by riding with Joseph out to their farm. Part of the following day, July 11, she also rode with Joseph in the carriage. No record exists of their conversation but events of the next several days suggest that they discussed Joseph's plural wives and that Emma voiced her opposition to them. William Clayton listed Sarah Ann Whitney, Helen Mar Kimball, Flora Woodworth, Louisa Beaman, and Desdemona C. Fullmer in his journal and stated, "Emma was cognizant of the fact of some, if not all, of these being his wives, and she generally treated them very kindly."[87] While Clayton's wording is ambiguous, he leaves the impression that Emma knew about the five women he listed. If she knew about Helen Mar Kimball's and Sarah Ann Whitney's marriages, then she probably knew that the girls' mothers had agreed to the arrangements, and she recognized the involvement of her adult friends. After describing her marriage in a 1904 letter, Mary Elizabeth Rollins Lightner stated, "Emma knew all about it."[88] These six women, and the Partridge and Lawrence sisters and Eliza R. Snow, numbered eleven women whom Emma may have known about. That was almost three times what Emma had agreed upon less than two months earlier, and she undoubtedly voiced her objections to Joseph.

On the morning of July 12, two days after Emma's birthday, Joseph and Hyrum entered the office in the brick store talking about plural marriage. William Clayton wrote that Hyrum said, "If you will write the revelation on Celestial Marriage, I will take and read it to Emma, and I believe I can convince her of its truth, and you will hereafter have peace."

Joseph retorted, "You do not know Emma as well as I do."

"The doctrine is so plain, I can convince any reasonable man or woman of its truth, purity and heavenly origin," said Hyrum.

"Well, I will write the revelation and we will see." Joseph asked Clayton to get paper and prepare to write. Hyrum urged Joseph to use the Urim and

Thummim, but Joseph said he did not need to, because he knew the revelation "perfectly from beginning to end."

Joseph "dictated the revelation on Celestial Marriage," while Clayton wrote it, "sentence by sentence, as he dictated."

Hyrum then took the document to Emma. Joseph and Clayton waited for his return. When Hyrum came back Joseph asked, "How did you succeed?"

"I have never received a more severe talking to in my life. Emma is very bitter and full of resentment and anger," Hyrum answered.

Joseph quietly remarked, "I told you you did not know Emma as well as I did." Joseph then put the paper in his pocket, and the brothers left the office.[89]

Joseph's journal for the following day records only, "I was in conversation with Emma most of the day,"[90] but William Clayton's diary for the same day records that Joseph called him into a private room with himself and Emma. They told Clayton about an agreement they had made with each other, which Clayton did not describe. Then both Emma and Joseph expressed their feelings about many subjects and "wept considerable." In this context their concern and discomfort could only have been about the plural marriage revelation, for Clayton then recorded, "O may the Lord soften her heart that she may be willing to keep and abide by his holy law."[91]

The revelation as it was subsequently published contained sixty-six verses.[92] It referred to Joseph's questions about the plural wives of Old Testament prophets. Joseph was told to "receive and obey" the instructions, "for all those who have this law revealed unto them must obey the same." The revelation stated, "If ye abide not that covenant, then ye are damned; for no one can resist this covenant and be permitted to enter into my glory."

In addition to the example of Abraham, the document singled out David, whose "wives and concubines were given unto him of me . . . and in none of these things did he sin against me save in the case of Uriah and his wife; and, therefore he hath fallen from his exaltation," emphasizing that God's sanction was necessary to enter the practice of plural marriage. Bringing together plural and eternal marriage, the revelation also explained that marriages contracted without the proper authority last only until death.

Although the modern Church of Jesus Christ of Latter-day Saints traces the revelation's beginning back to Kirtland in 1830–1831, it is clear that fifteen verses directed to Emma dealt with the Nauvoo period and particularly Joseph's immediate problem with Emma. One modern-day scholar states: "The burden of [the revelation] was to inform Emma that although she had been eternally married to her husband . . . the 'new and everlasting covenant' of marriage must be 'sealed unto them by the Holy Spirit of promise, by him who is anointed, unto whom I have appointed this power and the keys of this priesthood.' In other words, only by receiving the fullness of the priesthood could Emma Smith have claim on her husband in the eternities."[93] The "fullness of the priesthood" here refers to those ordinances of the endowment and second anointing that Emma would receive within two and a half months.

Contrary to the tone of the 1830 Elect Lady revelation, the new revelation was threatening and strident. First, Emma was commanded to ignore an unexplained previous instruction that seemed to have been given as a test. Then, "Let mine handmaid, Emma Smith, receive all those that have been given unto my servant Joseph, and who are virtuous and pure before me," the revelation continued, stating flatly that Joseph would receive from the Lord "an hundred-fold of this world, of wives" if she would not obey. Emma could either accept more wives willingly or she could have them forced upon her. Under the "law of the priesthood" a man "cannot commit adultery with that that belongeth to him and to no one else. And if he have ten virgins given unto him by this law, he cannot commit adultery, for they belong to him." The position of the first wife was addressed: "If any man have a wife . . . and he teaches unto her the law of my priesthood, as pertaining unto these things, then shall she believe and administer unto him, or she shall be destroyed, saith the Lord your God." And what of the husband whose wife refused to allow other wives? "It shall be lawful in me, if she receive not this law, for him to receive all things whatsoever I, the Lord his God, will give unto him, because she did not believe and administer unto him." The revelation exempted a man from the "law of Sarah," which law apparently required a husband to ask his wife for permission to take another wife. If the first withheld her consent, the revelation authorized the husband to proceed without it.

One paragraph directly instructed Emma. "And I command mine handmaid, Emma Smith, to abide and cleave unto my servant Joseph, and to none else. But if she will not abide this commandment she shall be destroyed, saith the Lord." This passage apparently reflects a conversation between Emma and Joseph that had taken place two and a half weeks earlier in Amboy. At that time, according to William Clayton, they had argued over plural marriage and Emma threatened to try a new form of pressure—"revenge" is what Clayton called it: she told him that if he continued to "indulge himself, she would too."[94] But the message of the revelation seemed clear: whatever discomfort might result, Emma's place was at Joseph's side.

William Clayton said that several of the leaders heard the revelation read during that same day and Joseph C. Kingsbury copied it. Joseph apparently took the original back, for Clayton wrote: "Two or three days after the revelation was written Joseph related to me and several others that Emma had so teased and urgently entreated him for the privilege of destroying it, that he became so weary of her teasing, and to get rid of her annoyance, *he told her she might destroy it* and she had done so, but he had consented to her wish in this matter to pacify her, realizing that he knew the revelation perfectly and could rewrite it at any time if necessary."[95] Isaac Sheen, a leader in a later church reorganization, wrote that Joseph "caused the revelation on that subject to be burned."[96] But other accounts involve Joseph more directly in its destruction. Emma told William McLellin in 1847 that after she and Joseph discussed the document they retired for the night. Joseph "wished her to get up and burn the revelation. She refused to touch it even with tongues [tongs]. He rose from his bed and pulled open the fire with his fingers, and put the revealment in and burned it up."[97] Again, in an 1856 interview, Emma said, "The statement that I burned the original of the copy Brigham Young claimed to have, is false, and made out of whole cloth, and not true in any particular." But Emma's oldest son pursued the question long after his mother's death. His diary entry for April 20, 1885, reads: "Visited James Whitehead had chat with him. He says he saw the Rev.—about 1 page of foolscap paper. Clayton copied it and it was this copy that Mother burned."[98] Apparently the incident later became talked about in the larger Smith family. Samuel Smith's daughter wrote to Don Carlos Smith's daughter: "I suppose you have heard that Aunt Emma burnt the revelation—which I suppose was so—I have heard my Aunt Lucy [Joseph's sister] say that Emma would not touch it with her fingers but took the tongs to put it in the fire."[99]

The incident raises several questions. Did Joseph burn the plural marriage revelation or did Emma? Did Emma deny that she put a paper in the fire at all, or was she saying that she did not believe that the paper she burned contained an authentic revelation from the Lord? One assumption can be made: if Emma destroyed the document, she did so with Joseph's permission.

One passage in the revelation that seems irrelevant on the surface reads: "And again, I say, let not my servant Joseph put his property out of his hands, lest an enemy come and destroy him." The position of this verse after the admonishments given to Emma suggests that she pressured Joseph to transfer deeds to some of his property. Joseph knew that open disclosure of plural marriage would endanger his life. Emma may have tried to punctuate that eventuality in Joseph's mind by insisting on financial security for her and the children. Whatever the reason, on Wednesday, July 12, the day Joseph dictated the revelation, he "directed Clayton to make out deeds of certain lots of land to Emma and the children." Nauvoo land records show that the transactions included transferring ownership of the Mansion House. The following day Joseph was "in conversation with Emma." His diary continued on July 14, "Deeded my half share in Steamboat *Maid of Iowa* and also sixty city lots to Emma."[100]

It was probably Saturday night, July 15, that the revelation was destroyed. On Sunday Joseph preached "all day A.M. & P.M. at the stand, in the grove near the west of the temple concerning a man's foes being they of his own house."[101] Whether it was a public rebuke of Emma, his choice of topic suggested that things were not as Joseph wanted them to be at home.

William M. Thompson later remembered going to Joseph and Emma's house between the two meetings. He found them eating Sunday dinner and joined them at the table. They discussed Joseph's sermon and Thompson recorded that Emma said, "You have made some statements that the brethren and sisters think applied to me that are not very complimentary." She asked that Joseph "apologise or explain in the afternoon."

After some discussion "backwards & Forwards Between Joseph Emma & others at the Table" Thompson reported that Joseph looked at him, pointed his finger at Emma, and "said that the woman was the greatest enemy I ever had in my Life . . . & My Bro Hyrum was always my best friend."[102] Thompson did not make his statement on the day it happened but wrote it from memory later. He dated it July 9, but because Joseph's sermon that day, if Willard Richards reported it correctly, did not contain any references that would give Emma offense, Thompson must have been at the Smith home one week later, on July 16, 1843. In fairness to both Emma and Joseph, Thompson's statement about her being the "greatest Enemy" may well have been his own invention.

During this summer most of the Twelve were on missions in the East. Brigham Young would not return to Nauvoo until October 22, more than three months after Clayton recorded the revelation. His knowledge of these events would be secondhand information, yet in future years he would speak about this period as though he had been a witness.

One week after Hyrum read the revelation to Emma, Eliza Snow received a visitor whom she did not identify in her Nauvoo diary:

Sister [blank in original] call'd to see me. Her appearance very plainly manifested the perturbation of her mind. How strangely is the human countenance changed when the powers of darkness reign over the empire of the heart! Scarcely, if ever, in my life had I come in contact with such forbidding and angry looks; yet I felt as calm as the summer eve, and received her as smilingly as the playful infant; and my heart as sweetly reposed upon the bosom of conscious innocence, as infancy reposes in the arms of paternal tenderness & love. It is better to suffer than do wrong, and it is sometimes better to submit to injustice rather than contend; it is certainly better to wait the retribution of Jehovah than to contend where effort will be unavailable.[103]

Was this visitor Emma? Probably. Eliza seemed unaware that her "heart sweetly reposing on conscious innocence" could be interpreted by her visitor as self-righteous smugness.

The temptation to compare Emma and Eliza, these two strong women, proved irresistible to those who knew of their troubled association. Brigham Young's daughter Susa Young Gates, born in 1856, penned her opinions of the two women in 1900. She never knew Emma but wrote: "Emma Smith was quite as dominant a character as Aunt Eliza and possessed splendid executive ability but she lacked the fundamental element of greatness," which was "the power to subordinate her own will to the will of those who had the right to direct her and the wisdom to counsel her; in this Eliza R. Snow was supreme."[104] In contradiction, she also wrote, "In times past, women have . . . done many improper things; and one of them is they often preferred men's opinions to their own and even yielded points of conscience for the sake of pleasing them, until, very naturally, they are looked upon by men as shallow, weak, and contemptible. . . . A course of self-reliance and self-assertion will restore our credit."[105] But Emma's self-reliance would further separate her from her friends.

On July 22, two days after Eliza Snow received her unnamed visitor, Joseph records that "Sister Maryann Holmes was brought to my house sick. She has been confined to her bed for upwards of two years."[106] Her compassion undeterred by her own problems, Emma began to care for the invalid woman.

11

The Poisoning

June–December 1843

While Emma was in Amboy with her sister at the time of Joseph's arrest, the Relief Society began its meetings for 1843. They met only from spring to fall as the weather permitted. The first meeting on June 16 "convened according to previous instruction of Prest. Emma Smith" even though she was not there and would be absent throughout the summer. Eliza Snow served as secretary for this meeting and the one following, then she moved to the Morley settlement and other women kept the minutes. Emma recommended through her counselor, Elizabeth Ann Whitney, that the women help the poor and actively raise money to build the temple. Several women offered to help. The membership was so numerous that the women divided into groups and met in rotation. Emma's continued absence may have affected attendance, for five weeks later, on July 28, the number of women at the meetings had fallen so abruptly the counselors worried that the Relief Society might be discontinued.

Some of Emma's absences might be explained by the disruption in her life over polygamy. The July 15 meeting was three days after Hyrum read the plural marriage revelation to her and Joseph's journal stated he spent the day at home. She was out of the city for several other meetings, and toward the end of the summer she was very ill for a long period. No explanation surfaces for her absence at other times. She maintained her position as leader, however, and was mentioned with warmth and concern almost every time the women met. Reynolds Cahoon, a friend of Joseph's, addressed the women in August and expressly emphasized Emma's line of authority over the Relief Society, saying that "the Relief Society was organized according to the mind of God, that Emma had directed to the appointment of this Comtee that Joseph had appointed Emma to direct the society."[1]

On August 6 Emma went a second time to St. Louis to conduct business for Joseph. While she was gone Joseph told William Clayton that Emma had left Nauvoo upset with Clayton for taking his first wife's sister, Margaret Moon, as a plural wife. Clayton began to watch Emma with a wary eye. She returned on August 12, 1843; the church High Council met that same day. William Marks, president of the Nauvoo Stake, his two counselors, Charles C. Rich and Austin Cowles, and twelve or thirteen other men were present. During the meeting Dunbar Wilson asked about the extent and practice of "a plurality of wives." He believed the rumors about it had some substance. Hyrum Smith walked across the street to his house and returned with a copy of the revelation Joseph had dictated a month earlier. He read it to the High Council. William Marks later said he "felt that it was not true but he saw the High Council received it." Hyrum's statement that those who believed and obeyed would be saved and those who did not would be damned divided the council. Three men rejected it out of hand. They were William Marks, Leonard Soby, and Austin Cowles, who may not have known that his daughter Elvira had married Joseph on June 1.[2] Marks would later struggle between rejecting the revelation and maintaining his loyalty to Joseph.

Word about the revelation spread quickly through Nauvoo. Ebenezer Robinson and his wife Angeline and Wilson Law and his wife left for a mission to New York. They hired William Marks to take them in his carriage to Chicago. On the way they discussed plural marriage. Marks reminded them that it came by revelation. Robinson summed up their anguish: "From Bro. Marks' testimony and what I had been told in Nauvoo, before leaving home, I as firmly believed that Joseph Smith had given a revelation on polygamy as that he had ever given one on any subject, in his life. Notwithstanding the revelation, every member of our party was opposed to the doctrine."[3]

Emma had already faced the same dilemma. No matter what its origin, she opposed the doctrine. She was not without power in the struggle with Joseph over it. Four days after her return from St. Louis Emma exerted her strongest leverage. She threatened divorce.

Clayton reported under the date of August 16, 1843, "This A.M. Joseph told me that sin[c]e Emma came back from St. Louis, she had resisted the P[rinciple] in toto, and he had to tell her he would relinquish all for her sake. She said she would give him E[liza] and E[mily] P[artridge] but he knew if he took them she would pitch on him, & obtain a divorce & leave him. He however told me he should not relinquish anything."[4] In the most serious crisis of their marriage, Joseph backed down. He told Emma that he would give up his wives. But he confided to Clayton that he did not intend to keep his word.

Five days after Joseph agreed to "relinquish all" Emma found two letters in his pocket from Eliza Snow, who was still at the Morley settlement. Emma confronted William Clayton with them and asked if he had delivered them to Joseph. Clayton denied being the courier; he said Emma "seemed vexed and angry."[5] He also recorded that Joseph told him Emma had said some "harsh words." Two months later Eliza would visit Nauvoo, on October 10, and would afterward confide to her diary, "Some circumstances of very peculiar interest occur'd during my visit to the City. Every thing connected with our *affections* is engraven on the heart, and needs not the perpetuating touch of the sculptor." The entry hints that Emma's suspicions about Eliza and Joseph were not unfounded. On August 19 Eliza Snow penned some verses for Eliza Partridge, who had begun to chafe under Emma's surveillance. The four stanzas indicated that the two Elizas knew of each other's marriages, but the final quatrain suggested how Eliza Snow viewed her situation.

> Our Heav'nly Father knows the best
> What way we must be tried:
> Stand still and his salvation test—
> *Thou shalt be satisfied.*[6]

Still smarting from finding Eliza's letters to Joseph the previous day, Emma went for a short carriage ride with her husband on August 22. She called on the Lucian Woodworth family while Joseph attended to some business at the temple. Emma apparently did not know that the Woodworths' sixteen-year-old daughter Flora had been Joseph's plural wife since spring. What probably began as a casual social visit resulted in a confrontation between Emma and Flora when Emma discovered that Joseph had given Flora a gold watch. She would have recognized the implications of such a gift, since he had also given one to Eliza Snow. Joseph returned just as Emma "was demanding the gold watch" from Flora, and he reprimanded her. Once in the carriage, however, Emma vented her own frustrations. Joseph told Clayton she continued "her abuse" after they arrived home, and said he finally had to employ "harsh measures" to stop her.[7]

The strain on both Emma and Joseph began to take its toll. Lucy Mack Smith had moved in with Emma and Joseph. When she became critically ill, Emma stayed by her bedside for five nights, until she herself collapsed and Joseph took her place at his mother's side. On September 11 he and friends prayed for the return of Emma's health. Elizabeth Ann Whitney expressed her concern "on account of Emma's sickness" to the Relief Society. By September 15 the women were praying that her life would be spared. She may have had malaria and did not improve until late fall.[8]

Since early spring Joseph had had frequent short illnesses, and his manner had begun to change. He now lost his temper more frequently, and his actions were abrupt. He "kicked [Josiah Butterfield] out of his house . . . and into the street" on March 28. On another occasion children playing in front of

Emma's house looked up startled to see a man coming out "into the street on the tow of Joseph's Boot. One good sender brought him from the door to the gate, another took him into the middle of the street." Aroet Hale, who reported the incident, said the man had called Joseph a liar. After preaching a sermon in July Joseph reported he was very sick, with his lungs "oppressed and over heated." His ill health nagged him for several days. He lost his temper again with a tax collector and "followed him a few steps and struck him two or three times." After the incident Joseph went home and tried to work but felt too sick.[9]

Completion of the new addition to her home in August offered Emma a diversion from the problems. The large extension transformed the house into a hotel. It had ten sleeping rooms on the second floor, and a kitchen, dining room, and space for meetings and socializing on the first floor. The new wing increased the size of Emma's home to seventeen or eighteen rooms.

On August 31, 1843, Emma and Joseph began moving furniture and supplies into the hotel portion of their house. Joseph put up a sign, Nauvoo Mansion, advertising his hotel. A commodious brick stable could house seventy-five horses along with the necessary tack and hay. Now the Homestead house offered space for meetings and conferences.

Emma and Joseph celebrated the completion of the hotel with an open house and dinner party a month later. One hundred couples met for "the luxuries of a well-spread board." After dinner Robert D. Foster assumed the duties of chairman and organized the drafting of suitable resolutions for the occasion. He spoke for Emma, thanking her guests for coming. Before the celebration ended Joseph performed the marriage ceremony for Emma's niece, Clara Wasson, and William Backenstos.[10] Perhaps the marriage drew some of Emma's relatives to Nauvoo, but no one kept a record of the guests.

The personal tension between Emma and Joseph may have eased toward the end of the summer when Emma seemed to have come temporarily to terms with plural marriage. Allen J. Stout, who served as Joseph's bodyguard, testified in an 1885 meeting that with "only a single door separating him from the family, he listened to a conversation which took place between Joseph and Emma Smith, on the much vaunted subject of plural marriage. This impulsive woman," Stout declared, "from moments of passionate denunciation would subside into tearful repentance and acknowledge that her violent opposition to that principle was instigated by the power of darkness; that Satan was doing his utmost to destroy her, etc. And Solemnly came the Prophet's inspired warning 'Yes, and he will accomplish your overthrow, if you do not heed my counsel.' "[11]

A young woman named Maria Jane Johnston told a similar story. Disowned by her family in Tennessee after joining the Mormons, she lived as a hired girl in Emma's home from 1841 to 1844. In 1843 she was nineteen, and, according to her reminiscences, she overheard a snatch of conversation between Emma and Joseph in the next room. Emma "was crying and in trouble about something." Joseph went to the door of the dining room where Maria Jane was working. He asked her to go to Hyrum's house with a request that he come to the Mansion. When Hyrum arrived with Maria Jane she heard him ask, "Well Sister Emma, what is the matter?" The door closed and the girl heard no more of the conversation.

The following day Emma found Maria Jane upstairs making beds and commented, "It was you that Joseph came to when he sent for Hyrum last night wasn't it?"

"Yes, Ma'am."

Emma invited the young woman to sit down on the bed. Emma "looked very sad and cast down," but remarked, "The principle of plural Marriage is right, it is from our Father in Heaven." Maria Jane reported, "Then she again spoke of her jealousy. . . . 'What I said I have got [to] repent of. The principle is right but I am jealous hearted. Now never tell anybody that you heard me find fault with that principle we have got to humble ourselves and repent of it.' "

Maria Jane remembered that Emma concluded the discussion by pondering, "I do not know why it is that Brother Hyrum holds such a controlling power over my spirit but when he comes to me and speaks to me I am melted to tears and cannot talk back to him."[12]

When William Law was asked if Emma talked to him about Joseph's wives, he answered, "She never came to my house for that purpose. But I met her sometimes on the street and then she used to complain especially because of the girls whom Joseph kept in the house, devoting his attention to them." Law added a further dimension to her predicament. He reported that Emma once said, "The revelation says I must submit or be destroyed. Well, I guess I have to submit." When Law saw her submit, he then concluded, "Emma was a full accomplice of Joseph's crimes."[13]

Emma's compliance seemed connected to her receiving the endowment. On September 28, 1843, Emma received the highest ordinance of the church, that of the second anointing.[14] This ordinance, also referred to as "the fullness of the priesthood," assured the recipient exaltation if he or she did not shed innocent blood or blaspheme against the Holy Ghost. In order to participate, Emma would have been endowed sometime between her sealing to Joseph on May 28 and the latter date. Joseph did not teach plural marriage in the Endowment Council; only first wives of male members and widows were admitted. His discretion on this matter was no doubt prompted by the opposition of William Law and William Marks to plural marriage; both men were members of the Prayer Circle, and although William Law would not receive all the ordinances of the group, William Marks would.[15] Emma found solace in this setting. In the language of the ordinance, she was Joseph's queen. She was the first woman to receive the ordinances and Joseph administered them to her.

Emma then initiated other women, who in turn initiated others, until Mormon women today trace their own endowments back to Emma Smith.

By October William Clayton found Emma "friendly and kind" toward him. She did an about-face in her attitude toward Clayton's marital situation and suggested that he take his pregnant plural wife, Margaret Moon, into his own home to care for her.[16]

Meanwhile a problem with Sidney Rigdon had been festering for some time. Joseph had addressed their differences earlier, and they had been temporarily resolved. William Marks reported that at that time "Sister Emma had a good many feelings against Elder Rigdon, but they are all done away. She has said within a few months, and in fact within one week, that she was on as good terms with Elder Rigdon as she had ever been since he was a member of the church."[17] But the strong feelings between her husband and Rigdon flared again.

Joseph called a special conference of the church on October 6 and charged his first counselor with interference with the mail in his management of the post office. But the real difficulty surfaced when Joseph accused Rigdon of giving information leading to his arrest near Dixon. Rigdon refuted the charges until inclement weather forced the conference to adjourn. On Sunday, October 8, Rigdon's eloquent affirmation of faithfulness turned the tide. The congregation voted that Sidney Rigdon be permitted to retain his position in the church presidency. Joseph chided his followers, "I have thrown him off my shoulders, and you have again put him on me. You may carry him, but I will not."[18]

Oblivious to the difficulties within the church leadership, new converts continued to arrive in Nauvoo in eagerness and anticipation. A young free black woman, Jane Elizabeth Manning, led a group of nine black Mormons to Nauvoo. As Jane and her family neared the Mansion House they saw a tall, dark-haired woman standing in the doorway. Emma welcomed them in and the household gathered to hear the newcomers' story. No one came to Nauvoo without a sense of adventure; Jane's account was indeed unusual.

Jane Elizabeth had been born in Connecticut about 1818. While a young girl, she lived as a servant, but not a slave, in a prosperous white farmer's home where she joined the church. Jane and eight members of her family joined a group immigrating to Nauvoo. In October 1843 white members of the party boarded a boat at Buffalo, New York, but the black members were refused passage. Eight hundred miles from Nauvoo, Jane recalled, "We walk until our shoes were worn out, and our feet became sore and cracked open and bled until you could see the whole print of our feet with blood on the ground . . . our prayers were answered and our feet were healed."[19]

Frightened at the threat of imprisonment in Illinois, they forded a river by walking into the stream until the cold water swirled around their necks. "We went on our way rejoicing, singing hymns, and thanking God for His infinite goodness and mercy to us in blessing us . . . protecting us . . . and healing our feet." Later, at the Mansion House, Joseph found Jane weeping. "The folks have all gone and got themselves homes, and I have got none."

"Yes, you have," he said, "you have a home right here if you want it. You mustn't cry, we dry up all tears here." Joseph left the room and returned shortly with Emma. "Emma," he said, "here is a girl that says she has no home; haven't you a home for her?"

Emma tendered to Jane the same hospitality that she had given others in similar need. Jane offered to wash and iron clothes and said she was a good cook and housekeeper. "When you are rested," Emma said, "you may do the washing, if you would just as soon do that."

Jane reported that Emma once asked if she would like to be adopted by her and Joseph as their child. Confused about the request, Jane later learned that the ordinance of sealing had been extended to include individuals who were not blood relatives. Jane Elizabeth Manning reported that Emma asked her again two weeks later. "I told her no mam! because I did not understand or know what it meant, they were always good and kind to me but I did not know my own mind. I did not comprehend."[20]

But Jane was quicker to comprehend other principles. She reported, "Brother Joseph's four wives, Emily Partridge, Eliza Partridge, Maria and Sara Lawrence, and myself, were sitting discussing Mormonism and Sarah said, 'What would you think if a man had more wives than one?' I said, 'That is all right!' Maria said, 'Well, we are all four Brother Joseph's wives!' I jumped up and clapped my hands and said, 'That's good.' Sarah said, 'She is all right, she believes it all now.' "[21]

Throughout the fall Joseph tried to strengthen the church and shore up Nauvoo's position in the Illinois community. On October 22 Brigham Young, Heber C. Kimball, and George A. Smith arrived in Nauvoo from missions in the eastern part of the United States. They had been absent from the city since July 7, five days before Hyrum read the plural marriage revelation to Emma. The citizens of Carthage and Warsaw had finished with rhetoric against the Mormons and turned to action. On December 2 a marauding party from Missouri, aided by anti-Mormons in Hancock County, captured a Mormon and took him across the Mississippi to be tried on a four-year-old charge of horse stealing. Several days later two ruffians went to a Mormon who lived on the prairie, robbed him of four dollars and fifty cents, and stabbed him in the abdomen. Later in the month David Holman's house near Ramus went up in flames. Two young messengers rode to Emma and Joseph's house at ten o'clock one night with the news that a mob was collecting at Warsaw.[22]

Although Emma's attempt to accept plural marriage brought temporary peace to the Smith household, neither Emma's resolve nor the peace lasted long. Emily Partridge commented that Joseph "would walk the floor back and forth, with his hands clasped behind him (a way he had of placing his hands when his mind was deeply troubled) his countenance showing that he was weighed down with some terrible burden."[23] The strain in his private life, coupled with threats from marauders and dissension within the church and community, began to affect Joseph's health. On Sunday, November 5, Joseph became suddenly sick at dinner and vomited so hard that he dislocated his jaw and "raised fresh blood." His self-diagnosis was that he had every symptom of poisoning. But he was well enough in the evening to attend an Endowment Council meeting in the room over the red brick store. According to current medical literature, no poison available in 1844 was caustic enough to pool blood in the stomach so rapidly after ingestion as Joseph's symptoms indicate and still be so ineffective as to allow the victim to pursue normal activities within a few hours.[24]

Twenty-two years later Brigham Young described a "secret council," probably the November 5 meeting, at which he said Joseph accused Emma of the poisoning and "called upon her to deny it if she could. . . . He told her that she was a child of hell, and literally the most wicked woman on this earth, that there was not one more wicked than she. He told her where she got the poison, and how she put it in a cup of coffee; said he, 'You got that poison so and so, and I drank it, but you could not kill me.' When it entered his stomach he went to the door and threw it off. He spoke to her in that council in a very severe manner, and she never said one word in reply. I have witnesses all around, who can testify that I am now telling the truth. Twice she undertook to kill him."[25] He did not elaborate on the alleged second occurrence, but in 1866 Brigham's rhetoric could well have been stronger than Joseph's actual words, for it came at a time when Brigham was particularly hostile toward Emma.

Evidence suggests that Joseph indeed accused Emma of poisoning his coffee. His diary records that he and Emma did not participate in the Prayer Circle at that meeting.[26] This is particularly significant because members were asked not to join in the Prayer Circle if they had feelings of antagonism toward anyone else in the group. Only unusual circumstances would have restrained them. Apparently Joseph *believed* at the time that Emma poisoned him, but strong evidence suggests that his self-diagnosis was mistaken and, therefore, so was his accusation of Emma.

Five weeks later Joseph again experienced sudden nausea and vomiting. "I awoke this morning in good health but was soon suddenly seized with a great dryness of the mouth and throat, and sickness of the stomach, and vomited freely. . . . I was never prostrated so low, in so short a time, before, but by evening was considerably revived." He mentioned being "somewhat out of health" on January 21, "somewhat unwell" on April 2, and "suddenly taken sick," on April 28.[27] Acute indigestion, food poisoning, ulcers, gallstones, and other diseases cause a reaction similar to Joseph's. Certainly Joseph's life was filled with the emotional tension and conflict that traditionally accompany ulcers. When he had his second attack of vomiting early in December, his diary states: "My wife waited on me, assisted by my scribe, Willard Richards, and his brother Levi, who administered some herbs and mild drinks."[28] In this instance Joseph portrayed Emma as a helper and nurse instead of the instigator of the attack. He apparently failed to correct the conclusions held by Brigham Young and John Taylor, for Emma remained forever suspect in their minds.

Stories of poisoning drew in another suspect. Samuel Smith's daughter Mary later wrote to her cousin Ina Coolbrith that Eliza R. Snow poisoned Joseph. She said that while Eliza resided in her Uncle Joseph's house Emma fixed Joseph a cup of coffee and Eliza poured something in it, then Joseph drank and vomited. Eliza had not lived in the house for nearly a year. Desdemona Wadsworth Fullmer, a plural wife married to Joseph by Brigham Young in July, wrote an autobiography in 1868 and related a bizarre dream that may have been prompted by rumors of Emma poisoning Joseph. She stated: "In the rise of poligamy in a dream [Emma] Smith was going to poison me. I told [the dream] to brother Joseph. He told me it was true, She would do it if she could." The talk of poisoning may have prompted Emily Partridge to say of this period: "There were times, one in particular that I was really afraid of my life."[29] She was far more likely to fear retribution from Emma than Emma was to administer it. But circulation of poisoning stories gave rise to apprehension and suspicion directed toward Emma.

Emma's personal appearance reflected her internal struggle. Visitors saw a "tall, austere woman, gaunt of form, and very plain of feature, but said to be of sensible, practical character." They described her as "stately and solemn" in her riding attire of "velvet with her hair dressed high with plumes."[30] Her costume and countenance were a marked contrast to her personal sorrow.

The Christmas season undoubtedly allayed tensions for both Emma and Joseph as the English immigrants brought their joyous customs into Nauvoo. At one o'clock on Christmas morning an English widow named Lettice Rushton and a dozen others gathered under Emma and Joseph's window, then suddenly began to sing "Mortals, Awake! With Angels Join." The household wakened to hear the carols ring through the still night air. The carolers then moved on to Hyrum Smith's residence.

At two o'clock on Christmas afternoon Emma in a new red velvet dress, with Joseph resplendent in his Legion uniform, hosted a dinner for fifty couples. The quadrille band played for dancing. Inspired by the music, one man danced a hornpipe with such dexterity that Emma and Joseph and the guests broke into applause.

Abruptly the door of the Mansion House burst open. The crowd looked in shock at an unkempt, ragged intruder whose hair fell around his shoulders: a Missouri "puke." The man entered in a drunken swagger and threatened the life of anyone who touched him. Joseph ordered him thrown out. As the men scuffled, the specter's sunken eyes caught his own in a full-face glance. The

"Missourian" was Porter Rockwell![31] Joseph joyfully welcomed his friend home and the music in the Mansion reached out again to the dark streets. Porter Rockwell had been in prison in Missouri, accused of the Boggs shooting.

At midnight on New Year's Eve the choir and William Pitt's Brass Band made their way on a dark rainy night to Emma and Joseph's home where they sang William W. Phelps's New Year's hymn to the delight of the inhabitants. The following day another large group took supper at Emma's table and the music and dancing continued until morning.

Helen Mar Kimball, now sixteen years old and married to Joseph for nearly eighteen months, watched Emma preside over the parties and dances. As an adult she remembered: "The last one that I attended there that winter, was on Christmas Eve [1843]. Some of the young gentlemen got up a series of dancing parties to be held at the Mansion once a week . . . but I had to stay home, as my Father had been warned by the Prophet to keep his daughter away from there, because of the blacklegs and certain ones of questionable character who attended there. His wife Emma had become the ruling spirit, and money had become her God."[32] Helen's evaluation of Emma reflected the jealousy of a young girl denied access to the parties and to Joseph. The parties were as much Joseph's as they were Emma's and he certainly occupied a position of authority over the "blacklegs and questionable characters" who entered his home. Helen Mar Kimball's comments may illustrate another aspect of Emma's life. Joseph had promised to put his other wives away when she came back from St. Louis, yet the girls were still living at the Mansion. Did Emma wonder which of the young women who joined Joseph on the dance floor had a secret association with her husband?

Emma and Joseph maintained an outwardly warm and loving relationship in spite of the tension. Joseph remarked to William Phelps that he had a kind, provident wife who would load the table with good things to eat until the sight destroyed his appetite when all he had asked her for was a little bread and milk. Emma came into the room in time to hear William Phelps say, "You must do as Buonaparte did,—have a little table just large enough for the victuals you want yourself."

With tact born of experience, Emma replied, "Mr. Smith is a bigger man than Buonaparte; he can never eat without his friends."

"That is the wisest thing I ever heard you say," Joseph commented.[33]

In 1903 Benjamin F. Johnson reminisced about a Sunday morning in Joseph's home. "Two of Emmas childr[e]n Came to him as just from there Mother—all So nice bright & Sweet." Joseph turned to his guest. "Benjamin, look at these Children. How Could I help loving thire mother; If Necessary I would go to *Hell* for Such a woman." Johnson added, ". . . altho at the time he had in the Mansion other wives younger & aparently more Brilliant—Yet Emma the wife of his youth—to me apeared the Queen of his *heart* & of his *home.*"[34] This pleasant story appears to be the root of later unfortunate anecdotes told by church leaders. After stating that Joseph said he would go to hell for Emma the rejoinder became, "Yes, and that's where he will find her."

But while the gentleness between Emma and Joseph enabled them to maintain an outward appearance of composure, their close association with William Law and his wife Jane became complicated and difficult. Emma, Joseph, William, and Jane had met in prayer meetings almost weekly. In September the men had prayed together for the health of Law's young daughter and Emma; William Law voted with other men in a unanimous decision to make Joseph president of a "special council"; the Laws were undoubtedly one of the hundred couples at the Mansion on October 3, and on the eleventh Emma and Joseph, William and Jane Law, and Hyrum and Mary Smith spent an afternoon together at a friend's house.[35] The friendship, however, would come to a close soon after Christmas.

A contemporary description of Joseph's thirty-three-year-old counselor in the church presidency stated, "No man could be better fitted to his station—wise, discreet, just, prudent—a man of great suavity of manner and amiability of character" and according to William Law's later recollection, he and his brother Wilson owned farms, lots, a flour mill, and other property valued at approximately thirty thousand dollars.[36]

William Law commented about the revelation on plural marriage. "The way I heard of it," he remembered, "was that Hyrum gave it to me to read. I was never in a High Council where it was read, all stories to the contrary notwithstanding. I took it home, read it, and showed it to my wife." Law said he also showed the paper, which he described as "two or three pages of foolscap," to Joseph, who said, "Yes, that is a genuine revelation."

"But in the Book of Doctrine and Covenants there is a revelation just the contrary of this," Law countered.[37]

Joseph explained that that revelation was given in the infancy of the church, but now the people were ready for stronger doctrine. William Law, like Heber C. Kimball before him, pleaded with Joseph to withdraw the requirement to enter plural marriage in an encounter he described as highly emotional. Joseph asserted that God had commanded him to teach the doctrine.[38] No doubt referring to this same conversation, Brigham Young later remembered Law's declaration: "If an angel from heaven was to reveal to me that a man should have more than one wife, if it were in my power I would kill him."[39] Yet Law's diary entry for January 1, 1844, also reveals his ambivalence. He wrote that he almost embraced the doctrine, then praised God that he and Jane had not trusted a man more than God.[40]

Law's protestations against plural marriage stemmed from intense belief that polygamy was contrary to the principles of virtue and justice. He was unable to reconcile his personal views and accept plural marriage, and he was not alone. Men and women began informally to take sides in Nauvoo. Some would oppose plural marriage through their own principles, others followed Joseph on equally strong principle, often through disruption of their own domestic peace. William Marks also opposed plural marriage but remained loyal to Joseph in spite of his doctrinal opposition. William Law would assume a more militant stance in respect to both Emma and Joseph.

On December 29, 1843, Joseph addressed a meeting of the policemen in Nauvoo. "My life is more in danger from some little doughhead of a fool in this city than from all my numerous and inveterate enemies abroad. I am exposed to far greater danger from traitors among ourselves than from enemies without."[41] Some concluded that he referred to Marks and Law. A member of the police force told William Marks, "Are you aware of the danger you are in?" When someone built a large fire near William Marks's house, he lay awake convinced Joseph thought he must be "the Brutus or the doughhead."[42]

Under pressure from the council five days after Joseph's speech, William Law named a policeman who admitted that it was his opinion that William Law was "the dough-head referred to." After a public reconciliation, Joseph said that Law agreed to "stand by me to the death."[43] Brigham Young commented, "I told some of the boys at that time, that [Law] knew he had done something he ought to die for, or he would not be so afraid of his best friends."[44] The public argument between Joseph and William Law may have foreshadowed a far deeper private matter between them that involved Emma.

12

"Voice of Innocence"

January–June 1844

Wednesday, January 17, 1844, dawned warm and clear. On this day George J. Adams hurried from the red brick store to the Mansion to find Emma. He exclaimed, "The matter is now settled. We now know who Joseph's successor will be: it is little Joseph, [for] I have just seen him ordained by his father."[1] The document authenticating the blessing would lie hidden among the scribe's private papers for a hundred and thirty-seven years, but the details of the ceremony were preserved by James Whitehead, financial clerk for Joseph. Whitehead told a friend, William W. Blair, in 1873 that he was in the outer office at the time, but he heard others discuss the ordination. Later, under oath, he remembered there were about twenty-five people in attendance.[2] Whitehead said "Hyrum Smith anointed [the boy] and his father blessed him and ordained him and Newel Whitney poured the oil on his head, and he was set apart to be his father's successor in office, holding all the powers his father held."[3] One of Joseph's scribes, Thomas Bullock, recorded the words.

> Blessed of the Lord is my son Joseph, who is called the third, for the Lord knows the integrity of his heart, and loves him, because of his faith, and righteous desires. And, for this cause, has the Lord raised him up; that the promises made to the fathers might be fulfilled, even that the anointing of the progenitor shall be upon the head of my son, and his seed after him, from generation to generation. For he shall be my successor to the Presidency of the High Priesthood: a Seer, and a Revelator, and Prophet, unto the Church which appointment belongeth to him by blessing and also by right.

Verily, thus saith the Lord: if he abides in me, his days shall be lengthened upon the earth, but, if he abides not in me, I, the Lord, will receive him, in an instant, unto myself.

Foreshadowing the pleasant relationship that Emma was to have with this son, it stated, "When he is grown, he shall be a strength to his brethren, and a comfort to his mother."[4]

As an old man Joseph III could not recall specifics of the blessing but wrote, "I was called into the room over my fathers store in Nauvoo . . . and was there anointed with oil and blessed by my father, and the privileges and callings to fit one to succeed him were confered by name upon me. I was publicly acknowledged by my father to be his successor, on the stand in Nauvoo in the presence of hundreds, possibly thousands of people." James Whitehead remembered Joseph announcing that "I am no longer their prophet," and described him "putting his hand on young Joseph's head" and saying, "This is your prophet, I am going to rest."[5]

Earlier Joseph had designated other successors: Sidney Rigdon on April 19, 1834; David Whitmer on July 8, 1834; Oliver Cowdery on December 5, 1834; and Hyrum Smith on January 19, 1841, and July 16, 1843.[6] In addition Joseph had continued to give the Twelve more responsibility and power. On August 16, 1841, during a special conference, Joseph said, "The Twelve should be called upon to stand in their place next to the first Presidency." Wilford Woodruff commented in his diary: "The temporal business of the Church is laid on the hands of the Twelve."[7]

Two months before Joseph blessed his son he administered the second anointing or "fullness of the priesthood," to Brigham Young, the senior member of the Quorum. By the end of January all but three of the Twelve had received the ordinance.[8] These men now held the authority to perform all ordinances of the church, as well as to administer the church's temporal business. Thus Joseph had given the "keys to the kingdom" to the Twelve and a blessing of succession to his oldest son.

Emma had ceased open opposition to plural marriage since receiving her second anointing. But now, with the blessing, she saw the possibility that young Joseph might be expected to perpetuate its practice. Although she had compromised her feelings, had concealed the practice, and had even cooperated with it in giving Joseph other wives, she apparently reached the limits of toleration as she envisioned her children's futures. Now she took steps to untangle the net.

Emily Partridge was the only plural wife who recounted the events. She said that interviews with Joseph, her sister, herself, and Emma occurred frequently. "She sent for us one day to come to her room. Joseph was present looking like a martyr. Emma said some very hard things. Joseph should give us up or blood would flow. She would rather her blood would run pure than be poluted in this manner." Emily did not say precisely that Emma threatened suicide, but perhaps Joseph's fear that Emma had reached the point of taking such a drastic step prompted this final confrontation. Emily "felt indignant towards Joseph for submitting to Emma. . . . His countenance was the perfect picture of despair." Emily wrote, "[Emma] insisted that we should promise to break our [marriage] covenants that we had made before God. Joseph asked her if we made her the promise she required, if she would cease to trouble us, and not persist in our marrying someone else. She made the promise. Joseph came to us and shook hands with us and the understanding was that all was ended between us. I for one meant to keep this promise I was forced to make."

The young women went downstairs. Soon Joseph followed. Finding Emily alone, he asked, "How do you feel, Emily?"

"I feel as anybody would under the circumstances."

"You know my hands are tied," Joseph responded.

Emily said he looked as if he would "sink into the earth"; her "heart was melted" and her anger left. But before she had time to speak Joseph was gone. Emma entered as he went out.

"Emily, what did Joseph say to you?" she asked.

"He asked me how I felt."

"You might as well tell me," Emma said. "I am determined that a stop shall be put to these things and I want you to tell me what he says to you."

"I shall not tell you," Emily retorted. "He can say what he pleases to me, and I shall not report it to you, there has been mischief enough made by doing that. I am as sick of these things as you can be."

Emily did not know how her words might affect Emma, but reported, "[I] learned afterwards that she gloried in my spunk."

The situation became intolerable for both Emma and the girls. Emily stated, "Emma could not rest till she had got us out of the house and then she was not satisfied, but wanted us to leave the city. She offered to give us money to pay our expenses if we would go. We consulted Joseph, he said we might make a visit to some of our relatives, who were living up the river two or three hundred miles. So we agreed to go, and she gave us ten dollars. Joseph said it was insufficient and for us not to go so we gave it up and returned the money to Emma."

Emily indicated that Joseph found her a place "with a respectable family."[9] Although the Lawrence sisters probably left the Mansion at this same time, Emily hinted in her history that Sarah and Maria received less severe treatment from Emma.[10]

Emma and Joseph celebrated their seventeenth wedding anniversary with a dancing party at the Mansion House on January 18. Five days later Joseph leased his hotel to Ebenezer Robinson, reserving several rooms for his family. One of Joseph's detractors stated that Joseph gave up the Mansion House to

Ebenezer Robinson because Emma made him turn out his spiritual wives who were living there. This allegation is supported by Jane Elizabeth Manning, the black girl who remembered staying with Emma and Joseph until after "they broke up the Mansion" early in 1844.[11]

Emma had continued to participate in the regular meetings of the Endowment Council throughout this stormy period. Joseph had never linked the endowment with plural marriage, and Emma didn't either. According to Heber C. Kimball, endowments for women were conducted in Emma's bedroom. Kimball recorded that "January, 1844, my wife Vilate and menny feemales was received into the Holy order and was washed and inointed by Emma." George A. Smith's wife Bathsheba remembered Emma saying, "Your husbands are going to take more wives, and unless you consent to it, you must put your foot down and keep it there." Bathsheba added that "Much more was said in regard to plural marriage at that time by Sister Emma Smith, who seemed opposed to the principle."[12]

In 1876 John Taylor recalled, "Emma Smith, at first professed having faith in the revelation on celestial marriage, but afterwards forsook it, using her influence to pervert the minds of the sisters and set them against it. She tried it with my wife." Taylor said Leonora "told me many things Emma Smith had told her. When I met Joseph I said, 'Brother Joseph, do you know that sister Emma has been talking thus and so to my wife, and telling her such and such things, and said that you have denied the revelation yourself?' "

"Brother Taylor," Joseph is reported to have answered, "Sister Emma would dethrone Jehovah himself, if she could, for the accomplishment of her purposes."[13]

Emma became increasingly outspoken. A young woman from Carthage reported:

> [My sister] went into the hotel parlor . . . to await the call to breakfast. Ten or twelve young women were assembled here, laughing and talking. Mrs. Emma Smith presently joined them, and recognizing my sister, whom she had met before, entered into conversation with her. Upon my sister asking, "Mrs. Smith, where does your church get this doctrine of spiritual wives?" her face flushed scarlet, and her eyes blazed as she replied, "Straight from hell, madam." Some of the young women blushed too, others giggled, and still others were stolid and indifferent.[14]

Emma was not alone in opposing plural marriage. Lucy A. Young, married to Brigham's brother Phineas, wrote, "With a sad heart I found all the married people at liberty to choose new companions if they so desired. There was marrying and giving in marriage for the first wife was expected to give others to her husband unless she rebelled as I did. There were queens and queens of

Queens in those days but I lost my queenship by not giving my husband the women he desired but he got them all the same." She voiced the dread of many women: that their men would take new wives in spite of their opposition. Cynthia Osborn's husband wrote, ". . . the doctrine of polygamy was repugnant to her and the thoughts of going to the body of the Church with her daughters she could hardly endure."[15]

Aroet Hale observed Emma's and Joseph's conflict over the issue and later recorded:

[A] grate meny of the Saints in these Days think that the Prophet wife Emma Hale Smith was a bad Woman that She tride to Poison the Prophet. Their never was a more Dutiful woman than Emma Smith was to her husband till after the Prophet had made publick the revelation of Seelestial marriage. He begun to take to himselve Other Wives. This proved a grate trial to her. How meny women is there in Our Day after 30 or 40 years . . . that it Dose not try to the Hartsbare. The propet Joseph Said that She was a good woman & that he would save her if he had to go into the bowels of Hell to get her. Emma wood & did go before Judges Rulers and Governors to Plead for her Husband. She would have Lade her life down for him.[16]

With the young wives gone from the Mansion House, Emma's love for Joseph, which was so evident to Aroet Hale, found room for expression. Within a month she became pregnant.

In late February an incident in the city court thrust Emma back into the public light. Hyrum Smith lodged a complaint that one Orsimus F. Bostwick had used "slanderous language concerning [Hyrum] and certain females of Nauvoo." Specifically, Bostwick said "he could take a half bushel of meal and get what accommodation he wanted with almost any woman in the city." Emma and the women of Nauvoo were irate. Francis M. Higbee, attorney for Bostwick, took the man's appeal to Carthage.[17] To counter the unfavorable publicity, Joseph relied on William W. Phelps for help. His diary entry for February 28, 1844, reads, "Phelps writing on O. F. Bostwick for women." Joseph called a general meeting at the temple and Phelps presented the document, titled "A Voice of Innocence from Nauvoo," which refuted Bostwick's accusations. The assembly approved it with two loud amens.[18] Joseph intended the statement to be for the women, and Emma soon presented it to the Relief Society.

At ten o'clock on March 9 Emma opened the first meeting of the Relief Society in 1844. She explained that the women had met to lend their collective voice to a proclamation that countered Orsimus Bostwick's slander of Hyrum Smith. Emma read the "Voice of Innocence from Nauvoo" aloud to the group. The flowery language condemned the *"blasting breath* and *poison-*

ous touch of debauchess, vagabonds, and rakes, who have jammed themselves into our city to offer *strange fire* at the shrines of infamy, disgrace and degradation." It called for "the whole virtuous female population of the city with one voice [to] declare that the Seducer of female chastity, the Slanderer of Female Character, or the Defamer of the Character of the Heads of the Church . . . The prostitute, or their pimps . . . shall have no place in our houses, in our affections, or in our Society." The people should view "with unqualified disapprobation and scorn the conduct of any man or woman, whether in word or deed, that reflects dishonor upon the poor persecuted mothers, widows, wives and daughters of the Saints of Nauvoo."[19]

Emma received a unanimous positive vote from the women, who were willing to "receive the principles of Virtue, keep the commandments of God, and uphold the Prest. in puting down iniquity." With a remark that may have seemed pointed toward Elizabeth Whitney and Vilate Kimball, whose young daughters had married Joseph, Emma told the women, "It is high time for Mothers to watch over their daughters and exhort them to keep the path of virtue." The meeting adjourned to reconvene at one o'clock.

The afternoon session differed from the earlier one only in the emphasis Emma placed on Joseph's public statements. "When he preaches against vice, take heed of it," she urged the women. "He means what he says." She concluded by asking everyone to use her "comon senses," forget what had passed, and reform.[20]

The meeting a week later, on March 16, convened for the same purpose as the former two. Emma again read the "Voice of Innocence" and told the women bluntly to "cleanse their hearts and Ears," adding, "We must throw the mantle of charity around to shield those who will repent and [sin] no more." Adeptly employing the system of public denial that others had used earlier, she stated that some still taught John C. Bennett's spiritual wife system as the doctrine of Joseph but reminded the women that if they wanted to know Joseph's doctrine they could find it in the Book of Mormon and the Doctrine and Covenants (which, at that time, did not contain the revelation on plural marriage). Then Emma read the church presidency's original letter to the Relief Society, written in 1842: "We therefore warn you, and forwarn you . . . we do not want anyone to believe anything as coming from us contrary to the old established morals & virtues, & scriptural laws . . . all persons pretending to be authorized by us . . . are and will be *liars and base imposters* & you are authorized . . . to denounce them as such . . . whether they are prophets, Seers, or revelators, patriarchs, twelve apostles . . . you are alike culpable & shall be damned for such evil practices."[21]

At one o'clock the Relief Society met again. Emma told the women that none should adopt the propositions she was about to read unless they were willing "to Maintain their integrity through time & Etirnity." She then presented both the "Voice of Innocence" and the presidency's letter, stating that the two documents contained the principles the society had started upon, but she "was sorry to have to say all had not adhere'd to them." Referring to Joseph's original charge to search out iniquity, Emma reminded the women that she was president of the society by the authority of Joseph. The minutes record, "If there ever was any Authority on earth [to search out iniquity] she had it—and had [it] yet." Emma urged the women to follow the teachings of Joseph Smith as he taught them "from the stand," implying that his private teachings should be disregarded. Reminding them that "there could not be stronger language than that just read," she emphasized that those were Joseph's words. The meeting adjourned until a more suitable place could be obtained to accommodate the "12 or 14 hundred members in all."[22]

The "Voice of Innocence" was published in the Nauvoo *Neighbor* March 20, but the Relief Society did not meet again in Nauvoo. In those last meetings Emma had reaffirmed the traditional Christian standards of marriage, using Joseph's public denials of polygamy, his own letter, and the "Voice of Innocence" to give every woman present a valid reason for avoiding plural marriage. When Emma had the women take a public oath with their hands raised in support of virtue, she caused enough consternation in the men's councils to stop the Relief Society meetings. The women would not have their own organization again for more than a decade.

The official history of the Relief Society erroneously states: ". . . the operations . . . were suspended in 1844 due to the various calamities which befell the saints."[23] Within a year Brigham Young would say, "When I want Sisters or the Wives of the members of the church to get up Relief Society I will summon them to my aid, but until that time let them stay at home & if you see Females huddling together, veto the concern, and if they say Joseph started it all tell them it is a damned lie for I know he never encouraged it."[24] John Taylor said the "reason why the Relief Society did not continue from the first organization was that Emma Smith the Pres. taught the Sisters that the principle of Celestial Marriage as taught and practiced by Joseph Smith was not of God." If the minutes are reasonably accurate, Emma did not teach this. She never mentioned "celestial marriage as taught and practiced by Joseph," but she did point out a rationale by which some women could come to that conclusion. Eliza R. Snow offered another view of the Nauvoo Relief Society when she later told a group of women in the Salt Lake Valley that "she wished to correct one erro[r]. It has been said that the Society in Nauvoo did more harm than good but it was not so. Emma Smith . . . gave it up so as not to lead the Society in erro[r]. The Society did a great deal of good—saved a great many lives."[25]

In the midst of the turmoil with the Relief Society, Emma watched Joseph launch a new effort by declaring himself a candidate for President of the United States in the 1844 election. Joseph needed a running mate and chose a man he had never met, James Arlington Bennet, who operated a school in New York. Interested in the Mormons, he frequently wrote favorable editorial comments about them under assumed names, but he claimed ineligibility for the vice-presidency.[26] Joseph eventually chose Sidney Rigdon and escaped meeting James Arlington Bennet in person, but Emma would not be so fortunate.

Meanwhile a traveler named Joseph H. Jackson returned to Nauvoo in March with the express intent of gaining the "confidence of the Prophet, that I might discover and disclose to the world his real designs and the nature of his operations."[27] To accomplish this, Jackson said he had to practice deception but felt "the end justified the means." In his exposé he said he presented himself to Joseph Smith as a fugitive from Georgia and sought Joseph's protection in return for "being of great service to him." But Joseph's diary for the date of their meeting indicates that Jackson introduced himself as a Catholic priest.[28] Although Jackson never joined the church, he claimed that Joseph "admitted [him] into all of his secret councils, and was confided in so far, that he disclosed to me every act of his life." Joseph's early opinion of Jackson was that he was "rotten hearted," but by Christmastime, when Jackson remarked that "he was almost persuaded to be one" with Joseph, the prophet's response was that "he was not only almost, but altogether."[29] But Jackson's name never appeared on any roll, in any minutes, or in any diary or journal entry referring to councils of the church, secret or otherwise.

Lucy Smith's history states that Jackson had asked Hyrum's permission to marry his daughter Lovina but was rebuffed, and when Joseph refused to intervene he entered into a "conspiracy" against the whole Smith family.[30] In the wake of Jackson's aborted courtship, he claimed that Joseph confided to him that he had been attempting to "get Mrs. William Law for a spiritual wife." He explained that "for the purpose of affecting his object [Joseph] got up a revelation that Law was to be sealed up to Emma, and that Law's wife was to be his; in other words there was to be a spiritual swop." Jackson commented that Joseph "had never before suffered his passion for any woman to carry him so far as to be willing to sacrifice Emma for its gratification."[31] As an old man in 1887, William Law said, "Joseph Smith never proposed anything of the kind to me or to my wife; both he and Emma knew our sentiments in relation to spiritual wives and polygamy; knew that we were immoveably opposed to polygamy in any and every form."[32] Yet while Law denied that Joseph offered him to Emma, he believed the rumor had its base in a story "that Joseph offered to furnish his wife, Emma, with a *substitute* for him, by way of *compensation* for his neglect of her, on condition that she would stop her opposition to polygamy and permit him to enjoy his *young wives in peace* and keep some of them in the house."[33]

Some writers have speculated that Joseph offered Emma a plural husband as a test of some sort. This view is based on a verse in the plural marriage revelation directed specifically to Emma: "A commandment I give unto my handmaid, Emma Smith, your wife, whom I have given unto you, that she stay herself and partake not of that which I commanded you to offer unto her; for I did it, saith the Lord, to prove you all, as I did Abraham."[34] This particular verse is ambiguous as it stands and was recorded nearly a year before the incident with the Laws reportedly occurred. Its meaning remains a mystery.

A contemporary named Alexander Neibaur reported that William Law wished to be sealed to his wife for eternity, but Joseph "Answered no because Law was a[n] Adulterious person." Neibaur wrote in his journal on May 24, 1844:

> Some days after Mr. Smith [was] going toward his office. Mrs. Law stood in the door [and] beakoned to him . . . as no one but herself [was] in the hous, she drawing her Arms around him [said] if you won't seal me to my husband Seal myself unto you, he Said stand away and pussing her Gently aside giving her a denial and going out, when Mr. Law came home to Inquire who had been [there] in his Absense, she said no one but Br. Joseph, he then demanded what had passed. Mrs. L[aw] then [said] Joseph wanted her to be married to him.[35]

Young Joseph, as an adult, remembered Jane Law being "petite, handsome, full of snap—energy and dash."

Joseph Lee Robinson's journal reported that his brother Ebenezer's wife Angeline "had some time before this watched Brother Joseph the Prophet, had seen him go into some house that she had reported to sister Emma." According to property records and early maps, Ebenezer and Angeline Robinson lived across the street within sight of the Laws. Ebenezer Robinson's brother reported that "it was at a time when [Emma] was very suspicious and jealous of [Joseph] for fear he would get another wife," and when Emma learned about Joseph's clandestine visits she "was determined he should not get another [wife]. If he did she was determined to leave and when she heard [of Joseph visiting another woman] she became very angry and said she would leave and was making preparations to go to her people in the State of New York. It came close to breaking up his family." Robinson noted that "he succeeded in saving her at that time but the Prophet felt dreadful bad over it."[36]

Joseph took immediate steps to stop the flow of information from Angeline Robinson to Emma. He went to Ebenezer Robinson and discussed the matter, but Angeline "did not give him any satisfaction" and Ebenezer refused to reprove his wife. Joseph sent Angeline and Ebenezer Robinson to Philadelphia for the purported purpose of Ebenezer's being Sidney Rigdon's printer. Joseph Lee Robinson summarized, ". . . there was something wrong or Joseph would not have sent him away that way and with that man, but Ebenezer thought sure his character stood clear in the eyes of the Prophet."[37] On this same day the church leaders excommunicated William and Jane Law for "unchristianlike conduct."

What was Emma's part in the incident with William and Jane Law? Did she ask for William as a "spiritual husband"? William Clayton indicated a year earlier that in an argument with Joseph over his wives Emma had countered that "if he would indulge himself" she thought "she might too,"[38] but no evidence, other than the word of the unprincipled Jackson, links her to William Law or anyone else. Law soon formed another church based on the Book of Mormon without the entanglements of plural marriage and with himself as head.[39] Plural marriage was not the only point of departure with Joseph. Law had begun to chafe under the church's increasing power over the social, economic, and political lives of the members. He saw these powers as overshadowing the members' freedom of choice in an ever widening sphere.

Word of Emma's and Joseph's domestic difficulties spread to outside sources. When Emma left on a steamboat for St. Louis on April 19, 1844, the day after the Laws' excommunication, Joseph wrote that she left to purchase goods, but the press discovered that Emma was traveling down the river alone. On April 23 the St. Louis *Republican* announced that "the Mormon prophet Joe Smith, has turned his wife out of doors for being in conversation with a gentleman of the sect which she hesitated or refused to disclose."[40] The news release was picked up and reprinted throughout the country. The Boston *Post* published a clarification, explaining that "Jo Smith's wife did not leave him for good; she only went to St. Louis on business and has returned to Mahomet." This account was not widely published, and the impression that Emma and Joseph had separated remained with many people. But the citizens of Nauvoo knew differently. One young woman, Almira Covey, wrote to her sister in Michigan: "Joseph's wife is not very well. The report . . . about her being turned out of doors is false. . . . Never could a man use a wife better than he has her. I presume you hear a great deal that is not true, but what I have written you is correct."[41]

After a five-day visit in St. Louis, Emma entered the main room of the Mansion House on April 24. A bar, complete with counter, shelves, and glasses for serving liquor, stood in the room. Porter Rockwell reigned supreme over it. Emma sent her eleven-year-old son into a meeting to tell Joseph she wished to speak with him; she waited in the hall.

"Joseph, what is the meaning of that bar in this house?" Emma asked with restraint obvious to her young son, who later recorded the confrontation. Joseph explained that a new building across the street was planned for Porter Rockwell's bar and barbershop, but until it could be completed Rockwell had set up the bar in the Mansion. "How does it look for the spiritual head of a religious body to be keeping a hotel in which a room is fitted out as a liquor-selling establishment?" she asked earnestly. Joseph countered that all hotels

Emma Hale Smith.
(Reorganized Church of Jesus Christ of Latter Day Saints RLDS Library-Archives)

Joseph Smith, Jr.
(RLDS Library-Archives)

Hyrum Smith, brother of Joseph Smith.
(Church of Jesus Christ of Latter-day Saints LDS Historical Department)

Lucy Mack Smith, mother of Joseph Smith . . .
(LDS Historical Department)

and her son, William Smith.
(LDS Historical Department)

her daughter, Lucy Smith Millikin . . .
(University of Utah Library Special Collections)

*Oliver Cowdery, baptized Emma
and acted as Joseph's scribe.*
(LDS Historical Department)

*William Wine Phelps, assisted
Emma in the publication of her first
hymnal.*
(LDS Historical Department)

William Clayton, Nauvoo diarist.
(University of Utah Library Special
Collections)

William Marks, Stake President and friend to Emma and Joseph.
(RLDS Library-Archives)

Brigham Young.
(LDS Historical Department)

Some of Joseph's plural wives . . .

Louisa Beaman, first plural wife of record in Nauvoo.
(Utah State Historical Society)

Helen Mar Whitney, daughter of Emma's friend and counselor in the Relief Society, who became a plural wife.
(Utah State Historical Society)

Emily Dow Partridge Young. She and her sister Eliza Maria Partridge lived in Emma's home when they became Joseph's plural wives.
(LDS Historical Department)

Eliza R. Snow, Emma's friend and secretary in the Relief Society.
(LDS Historical Department)

The Temple and Nauvoo in Emma's day.
(LDS Historical Department)

The Homestead, first home of Emma and Joseph in Nauvoo.
(By Jack W. Garnier, courtesy of RLDS Joseph Smith Historical Center)

The Mansion House, the home and hotel of Emma and Joseph in Nauvoo.
(By Jack W. Garnier, courtesy of RLDS Joseph Smith Historical Center)

The Riverside Mansion, built by Lewis C. Bidamon on the south wing of the old, unfinished Nauvoo house. Emma died in this home.
(LDS Historical Department)

Emma Hale Smith holding David Hyrum who was born five months after his father's death.
(RLDS Library-Archives)

Lewis C. Bidamon, Emma's second husband. (Courtesy of Marcia Vogel)

Emma's Children ...

*David Hyrum Smith just before his
ninth birthday.*
(LDS Historical Department)

*Joseph Smith III on his twenty-first
birthday.*
(LDS Historical Department)

Joseph Smith III as a young man.
(RLDS Library-Archives)

Alexander Hale Smith as a young man.
(RLDS Library-Archives)

Alexander Hale Smith as an old man.
(RLDS Library-Archives)

Julia Murdock Smith.
(RLDS Library-Archives)

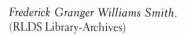

Frederick Granger Williams Smith.
(RLDS Library-Archives)

David Hyrum Smith as a young man...
(RLDS Library-Archives)

and in his later years.
(RLDS Library-Archives)

Emma in her later years.
(RLDS Library-Archives)

had their bars, the arrangement was only temporary, and he wanted to make up for Rockwell's months in prison. Unconvinced, Emma told Joseph he could hire someone to run the Mansion for him. "As for me," she continued, "I will take my children and go across to the old house and stay there, for I will not have them raised up under such conditions as this arrangement imposes upon us, nor have them mingle with the kind of men who frequent such a place. You are at liberty to make your choice; either that bar goes out of the house, or we will!"

Faced with an ultimatum he did not want to accept, Joseph answered, "Very well, Emma; I will have it removed at once."[42] Soon a frame structure, designed to house the bar and barbershop, began to rise across the street.

Had Joseph acquiesced so easily to halting plural marriages? He apparently did not take additional wives after November 1843,[43] but evidence is conflicting as to whether he intended to abandon the practice, as Emma believed, or whether he found it expedient to let his opponents *think* he was abandoning it. William Marks, who had never embraced the principle, said that Joseph approached him one day late in the spring and invited him to a secluded place to talk. "We are a ruined people," Marks quoted Joseph as saying. "This doctrine of polygamy or Spiritual-wife System, that has been taught and practiced among us, will prove our destruction and overthrow. I have been deceived, in reference to its practice; it is wrong; it is a curse to mankind, and we shall have to leave the United States soon, unless it can be put down." Marks further stated that Joseph asked him to go to the High Council and prefer charges against all who practiced the doctrine, while Joseph would "preach against it, with all my might, and in this way we may rid the church of this damnable heresy." But when Marks told others about these conversations with Joseph, rumors surfaced that he "was about to apostatize." His statements "were pronounced false by the Twelve, and disbelieved."[44]

The minutes of an 1867 meeting within the Reorganized Church refer to this issue. A man named Hugh Herringshaw had "heard Joseph tell the 12 that they must abandon polygamy and turned to Brigham Young and asked if he was willing to do so. Young said he had been asleep. Then Joseph spoke upon the matter as only he could talk denouncing the doctrine of polygamy. Brigham replied that he and Taylor had determined what course they would pursue."[45] A year earlier, in 1866, Brigham Young had conceded, "Joseph was worn out with it, but as to his denying any such thing I never knew that he denied the doctrine of polygamy. Some have said that he did, but I do not believe he ever did." Joseph's niece said he finally "awoke to a realization of the whole miserable affair [and] . . . tried to withdraw from and put dow[n] the Evil into which he had fallen."[46] Sarah Scott, a young immigrant from Massachusetts, wrote home to her mother about the situation. "Mr. Haven [her brother-in-law] told me . . . that those doctrines tried his faith very much till he heard Hyrum Smith explain them and now or then he thought it was right. But . . . [in late May or early June] Hyrum denied that he and Joseph had the revelation concerning it but said that it referred to ancient times; and was published so in the *Neighbor*. After I saw it I said to Mr. Haven: 'What do you think of that?' . . . He said that he supposed Hyrum saw what a disturbance it was making and thought he would say it on account of there being such excitement."[47] But whether or not Joseph *preached* against plural marriage, in June he would attempt a rendezvous with the Lawrence sisters in Cincinnati, evidence that he had not *abandoned* the practice.[48]

Emma became ill in the middle of May. By the seventeenth Joseph missed a caucus supporting his candidacy for President to be with her. Three days later she was described as "very sick" and Joseph spent most of the day with her. On the twenty-first Joseph rode out on the prairie with Porter Rockwell to escape an officer with a subpoena. William Clayton said Emma was angry because Joseph left her; Joseph's history reads, "I was at home towards night with Emma, who is somewhat better." On the twenty-third he optimistically noted, "Emma rather better."[49]

On the same day as Emma's improvement, Willard Richards came with the news that a grand jury in Carthage had a bill against Joseph for adultery that was established on the testimony of William Law. The charge was a blow, and it came only two days after Brigham Young, Heber C. Kimball, and a hundred other loyal men had left Nauvoo for the East to campaign for Joseph's presidency. The bill from Carthage coupled with his own nagging ill health seem to have pressured Joseph greatly.[50] In a speech on Sunday, May 26, he defended himself with angry exaggeration. He defied his opponents: "I have more to boast of than any man. . . . I am the only man that has ever been able to keep a whole church together since the days of Adam." Comparing himself to "Paul, John, Peter [and] Jesus," he asserted, "I boast that no man ever did a work as I . . . the Latter-day Saints never ran away from me yet. . . . This new holy prophet [William Law] has gone to Carthage and swore that I had told him that I was guilty of adultery. This spiritual wifeism! Why, a man dares not speak or wink, for fear of being accused of this."[51]

Joseph then produced a scapegoat for the predicament he faced. Although the "Voice of Innocence" was written in his office by W. W. Phelps, Joseph told the congregation that he never had any problems with the men who opposed him until "that Female Relief Society brought out the paper against adulterers and adulteresses."[52] In the rambling discourse Joseph alternately defended himself, scoffed at William Law, and pleaded for his people's loyalty. "I have set your minds at liberty by letting you know the things of Jesus Christ. When I shrink not from your defence will you throw me away for a new man who slanders you? I love you for your reception of me."[53]

During this period the men who supported William Law's attempts to reform the church had ordered their own printing press. William and Wilson Law, two brothers named Foster, and the two sons of Judge Elias Higbee opposed Joseph and they found other persons dissatisfied with the conditions in Nauvoo. They issued a prospectus for a new newspaper that promised to inform the readers of the *"many gross abuses exercised under the pretended authorities of the Nauvoo City Charter."* The publishers announced that they advocated the repeal of the Nauvoo charters and intended to "censure and decry gross moral imperfections wherever they may be found, either in the Plebian, Patrician, or self-constituted MONARCH."[54]

The first and only issue of the Nauvoo *Expositor* appeared on June 7, 1844. The front page stated, "We all verily believe, and many of us know of a surety, that the religion of the Latter Day Saints, as originally taught by Joseph Smith, which is contained in the Old and New Testaments, Book of Covenants, and Book of Mormon, is verily true." But "We have many items of doctrine, as now taught, some of which, however, are taught secretly and denied openly . . . [which] considerate men will treat with contempt." The *Expositor* disclosed the methods by which women were approached to become plural wives and described the general situation of polygamous women in Nauvoo as seen through the eyes of the publishers. To challenge them, Joseph would have had to make a public disclosure of plural marriage. The newspaper attacked Nauvoo's political system, criticized some church doctrines, and listed fourteen points of proposed reform.[55]

Law had underestimated the devotion of Joseph's followers, who now saw Law as an enemy rather than a reformer. Joseph called a city council meeting to consider what should be done about the *Expositor,* and on June 10 the council issued an order to Joseph to "abate the said nuisance."[56] Joseph ordered the marshal and the Legion to destroy the press. By eight o'clock in the evening a posse and a group of citizens gathered in front of the Mansion House to report that they had dumped the press, type, and printed sheets into the street. Joseph blessed them "in the name of the Lord" and promised that not a hair of their heads should be hurt. The publishers of the *Expositor* left town immediately.

It had been only a few months since Emma exacted a promise from Joseph to rid her home—and the church—of plural wives. The child she was now expecting seemed a confirmation of that reconciliation. But Emma's short-lived peace crumbled around her.

The day after the destruction of the press a mass meeting convened in Carthage. Indignant over the Mormon breach of the Bill of Rights, the crowd resolved "to *exterminate*—UTTERLY EXTERMINATE, the wicked and abominable Mormon leaders, the authors of our troubles. . . . A WAR OF EXTERMINATION SHOULD BE WAGED, to the entire destruction, if necessary for our protection of his adherents."

On June 12 Thomas Sharp published a frenzied editorial in the Warsaw *Signal:* "War and extermination is inevitable: CITIZENS ARISE, ONE AND ALL!!! Can you *stand* by and suffer such INFERNAL DEVILS: to ROB men

182

of their property and Rights, without avenging them? We have no time for comments; every man will make his own. LET it be made with POWDER AND BALLS!!!"[57] Joseph and the Nauvoo city council had unleashed a tornado which threatened to suck them into its vortex.

13

A Final Farewell

June 12–28, 1844

Details of Emma's role in events during the next few days are critical to understanding later accusations leveled at her. When Brigham Young and other leaders tried to reconstruct this period, they relied on reminiscences in which Emma's actions were often interpreted unfavorably.

On June 12 Joseph and seventeen others were arrested on charges stemming from the destruction of the press. Judge Daniel H. Wells, a friendly non-Mormon, acquitted them all. Word soon arrived at the Mansion House that ruffians had crossed the river from Iowa and Missouri in pursuit of Joseph, while crowds gathered at Warsaw and Carthage. Fiery speakers whipped emotions to a peak.

Vilate Kimball wrote to Heber, who was still on a mission: "I have ben thrown into such confusion I knew not what to write. . . . Nothing is to be heard of but mobs collecting on every side. The Laws and Fosters, and most of the [dissenting] party with their Families left here a day or two after their press was destroyed. . . . Betwene three and four thousand brethren have ben under arms here the past week."[1]

When men with eyes intent and jaws set rapped on Emma's door bearing news and messages for Joseph, the accounts were strikingly similar to those of past events in Missouri. She must have kept her home atmosphere calm, for the children later had difficulty remembering those days even though Julia, age thirteen, and young Joseph, eleven and a half, certainly were old enough to be aware of unusual events.

Joseph responded to lynching threats by declaring martial law and calling out the Legion. Dressed in his uniform, he reviewed his militia as they

marched past the Mansion on June 18 and stopped smartly in front of Porter
Rockwell's partially completed bar and barbershop. Joseph climbed up the
framework, then spoke for an hour and a half, warning the crowd of approaching danger. "Will you all stand by me to the death, and sustain at the peril of
your lives, the laws of our country, and the liberties and privileges which our
fathers have transmitted unto us, sealed with their sacred blood?"

The people shouted, "Aye!"

With a swift motion he drew his sword and thrust it up. "I have unsheathed my sword with a firm and unalterable determination that this people
shall have their legal rights, and be protected from mob violence, or my blood
shall be spilt upon the ground like water, and my body consigned to a silent
tomb."[2]

Emma saw little of Joseph in the following four days. He spent most of
his time sequestered in his office, planning a defensive strategy, aware that in a
short time he could be arrested again. He gathered affidavits in his behalf and
wrote to Governor Ford explaining his actions in the destruction of the Expositor. A second letter requested that Ford investigate the matter himself in
Nauvoo. At Joseph's request, Hyrum wrote Brigham Young on June 17, in-
forming him of the deteriorating situation in the city. He told the Twelve to
return immediately with "a little powder, lead and a good rifle" packed away in
their luggage. But Joseph waited three crucial days before he released Hyrum's
letter.[3]

When Joseph retreated to his office, he assigned Alpheus Cutler and
Reynolds Cahoon to guard the door. Emma moved into her usual role in times
of crisis: she acted as a liaison between him and anyone intruding into his
privacy, carried messages to him, and apprised him of the outside situation.
Some did not understand her assigned role. When Anson Call offered to help,
Joseph sent him and David Evans eighty miles to Knoxville to deliver an
affidavit and letter to Jesse B. Thomas, judge of the circuit court, requesting
clarification of Thomas's earlier instructions about Joseph's legal rights.

The two men returned to the Mansion on June 20 with a letter from
Judge Thomas, but the guards refused them entry to Joseph's office. When
Anson Call insisted, Cutler and Cahoon disappeared inside. After they returned, the four men argued sharply, but Call and Evans refused to leave until
they had personally delivered the letter. A few minutes later Lorenzo Wasson
appeared and said Emma would see them.

"You have a letter for Joseph, haven't you?" Emma asked. The two men
agreed and insisted they see Joseph. Anson Call remembered that "She used
many arguments and persuasions and we left the room and concilled together
and concluded to give her the letter." Emma broke the seal and read the
contents in the presence of the five men. Call later reconstructed the message
from memory: "I find that you were mistaken in the instructions that I gave
you while at Nauvoo, now sir I know of no course for you to pursue to answer

the requirements of the law but to suffer yourself to be taken by the officer holding the writ and go before the justice of the peace who issued the same and have an investigation of the matter. It is the officers duty to protect you." Call and Evans left the Mansion harboring the notion that Emma acted without Joseph's authority. In his autobiography, written years later, Call suggested that, because Willard Richards did not remember seeing the letter from Judge Thomas, Emma did not give it to Joseph.[4] Characteristically, Emma was steady in a crisis. Undoubtedly she gave Joseph the letter. He probably gave it a glance but chose not to give himself up.

Meanwhile Governor Ford decided to investigate the volatile situation himself and rode to Carthage. From there he wrote Joseph on June 22, "Your conduct in the destruction of the press was a very gross outrage upon the laws and the liberties of the people. It may have been full of libels, but this did not authorize you to destroy." Joseph had asked the governor in an earlier letter to call out the state militia in defense of Nauvoo before mobs attacked. Ford explained, "I can call no portion of the militia for your defense until you submit to the law." Having witnessed the lynching fever in Carthage, he told Joseph, "If you, by refusing to submit, shall make it necessary to call out the militia, I have great fears that your city will be destroyed, and your people many of them exterminated. You know the excitement of the public mind. Do not tempt it too far."[5] Joseph's answer reminded the governor that he had already been tried in Nauvoo for destroying the *Expositor:* "We would not hesitate to stand another trial . . . were it not that we are confident our lives would be in danger. . . . Some blood thirsty villain could find his opportunity to shoot. . . . We will make all things right if the Government will give us the opportunity. Disperse the mob, and secure to us our constitutional privileges, that our lives may not be endangered when on trial."[6]

On the evening of June 22 Emma, now four months pregnant, saw to the needs of her family and household. At about seven o'clock she heard John Taylor and others return from delivering Joseph's message to the governor. Joseph called Hyrum, John Taylor, Willard Richards, William Phelps, William Marks, and others to his room where one of them read Ford's letter aloud.

Joseph stalked back and forth across the room. "There is no mercy—no mercy here," he said.

"No," Hyrum responded, "just as sure as we fall into their hands, we are dead men."

"Yes; what shall we do, Hyrum?"

"I don't know."

Joseph did not speak for a moment, then his countenance brightened. "It is clear to me what to do. All they want is Hyrum and myself. . . . We will cross the river tonight." From the Iowa side of the river, he intended to travel east to Washington to place his appeal directly before President Tyler.[7] Joseph directed two men to take the *Maid of Iowa* to the upper landing, put Emma and the children and Hyrum's family on the steamer, and head down the Mississippi to the Ohio River, then upstream to Portsmouth, where he would contact them.

Although Joseph's own journal, which ends with this date, June 22, 1844, does not mention escaping to the West or the Rocky Mountains, others who later reconstructed the history added that Joseph changed his mind later and decided to "go west and all would be well." They also included his plan to meet Emma in Portsmouth, Ohio. If Joseph had intended to go west, he would not have sent Emma and the children eight hundred miles east to meet him. Portsmouth was the point of departure for Washington. Joseph may have discussed a sanctuary in the West, but two letters he wrote the following day clearly indicate that he had not planned to take a Western option.[8]

Around sunset Joseph asked Porter Rockwell to accompany him on a short journey. Porter, who would have followed his beloved prophet anywhere, promptly agreed. A friend had lent Joseph three hundred dollars. Joseph kept a hundred for himself, gave Hyrum a hundred, and split the remainder between Emma and Mary.[9]

Emma faced a difficult parting. She feared for Joseph's safety with mobs prowling on both sides of the river. They anxiously discussed escape plans for her and the children. Joseph's grief at leaving his family was deep. As he walked out of the house, Emma saw him pull his handkerchief from his pocket to cover his tears. Rockwell rowed Joseph, Hyrum, and Willard Richards in a leaky skiff across the rain-swollen Mississippi. They spent much of the pitch-black night bailing water with their boots. Rockwell returned as soon as Joseph had dictated a message to Emma. He probably arrived at her house before eight o'clock that morning. The letter informed Emma that three men owed Joseph money, including Heber C. Kimball, who had a thousand dollars. He told her she could sell any property in his name "for your support and children & Mother." Emma read on: "Do not dispair—If God ever opens a door that is possible for me I will see you again. I do not know where I shall go, or what I shall do, but shall if possible endevor to get to the city of Washington. May God almighty bless you & the children—& mother & all my friends. My heart bleeds." Joseph closed with a quick "No more at present. If you conclude to go to Kirtland, Cincinnati, or any other place, I wish you would contrive to inform me, this evening."[10]

Joseph wrote another letter from Montrose at nine o'clock that same morning. He intended to take at least two of his plural wives with him when he went east. Addressed to Maria and Sarah Lawrence, it read: "I take opportunity this morning to communicate to you two some of the peepings of my heart; for you know my thoughts for you. . . . I do not know what I shall do, or where I shall go, but if possible I will try to interview with President Tyler. Perhaps California or Austin will be more sympethetic." He urged the sisters to "Speak of this to no one I want you two to make arrangements with R.

Cahoon for passage at your earliest convenience. I want for you to tarry in Cincinnati untill you hear from me. Keep all things treasured up in your breasts, burn this letter as you read it. I close in hast. Do not dispair. Pray for me as I bleed my heart for you."[11] The letter documents the fact that Joseph intended to go to Washington and, if he did not have success there, would consider going to Texas or California. The letter also illustrates that he had a propensity to take his problems with him. He wanted Emma to inform him that evening if she decided to go to Cincinnati, because he did not want her and the Lawrence sisters in the same town.

Not long after Rockwell left Emma's door, Stephen Markham came and explained that Joseph wanted him to dismiss the Legion before dawn so anyone coming from Carthage would not know they were under arms. Markham was also to send Joseph's and Hyrum's horses across the river on the eight o'clock boat Sunday morning. Markham had gone home after disbanding the Legion the night before and apparently overslept because it was nine o'clock when he appeared at the Mansion—he should have had the horses on the boat an hour earlier. He found the barn door locked with the horses inside. It was locked for good reason. The night before a posse had ridden into Nauvoo to look for Joseph, promising they would return.[12] Emma saw that no unauthorized person could get to Joseph's horses. In the confusion of his departure, Joseph had given conflicting orders. He had told Porter Rockwell to take the horses across *that evening* under cover of darkness. Since Rockwell had delivered Joseph's letter before Markham arrived, she no doubt knew the horses were to leave that night and refused to give Markham the key which, he said, was in her pocket. When he threatened to chop the door down Emma told him, "You may go and deliver yourself up and rest contented that they will get the horses."[13]

Stephen Markham left Emma and walked toward the center of town, where a group of agitated men caught his attention. Alpheus Cutler, Reynolds Cahoon, and several others, including Hiram Kimball, were pursuing a heated conversation. Kimball told Markham that he believed Joseph should return to stand trial. "It is a bailable case and there is no danger." Hiram Kimball's concern was for his considerable property holdings in the city. "It will . . . lessen the value of property—also ruin a number of men for Joseph to leave," came the argument. They asked Markham to be part of a committee to invite Joseph to come back.

Markham refused. "Mind your own business, brethren, and let Joseph alone. I have my orders from him." He then stalked off to fulfill those orders by giving himself up.[14]

At Markham's departure, Reynolds Cahoon and Hiram Kimball headed toward the Mansion House. They met Wandle Mace and his brother in the street near Emma's home. Kimball and Cahoon were "very much excited, and thought it was absolutely necessary that Joseph should return," Mace related in his journal. "If Joseph don't come back the Governor will put the city under martial law, and then nothing can be brought into the city, neither can anything be taken out, and then what will all our property be worth?"

Wandle Mace countered, "We [should not] for the sake of a little property, be so selfish as to push him into the very jaws of death!"

Cahoon and Kimball turned toward the Mansion. The Mace brothers watched them stop outside the gate, absorbed in conversation. "We . . . both felt the impression that they were going to persuade Sister Emma, Joseph's wife, to write to him and prevail on him to return, this feeling came upon us so forcibly, we were very uneasy."[15]

Emma, meanwhile, had tried to make an accurate assessment of the situation because she needed to let Joseph know her plans by nightfall. The twenty-man posse from Carthage had returned shortly after Markham left the Mansion and told her that if Joseph and Hyrum did not give themselves up Governor Ford "would send his troops and guard the city until they were found, if it took three years to do it." Vilate Kimball's anxieties were as high as Emma's. "Some were tryed almost to death to think Joseph should leve them in the hour of danger. . . . I have not felt frightened . . . neither has my heart sunk within me untill . . . I heard Joseph . . . sent word back for his family to follow him, and Br Whitneys family were packing up, not knowing but they would have to go," she wrote Heber. "*Their* [Joseph's and Hyrum's] *giving themselves up, is all that will save our city from distruction.*"[16] Emma's sense of danger was also keen, but when James W. Wood, Joseph's trusted attorney, arrived with a pledge from Governor Ford for her husband's safety and a fair trial,[17] Emma's concern may have lessened. It was in this state of mind that Reynolds Cahoon and Hiram Kimball found her. She listened to them, then wrote to Joseph. She asked her nephew, Lorenzo Wasson, to go with the two men to find Porter Rockwell, who would take them across the river. The four men reached Joseph at one o'clock that same afternoon on June 23. Joseph read Emma's letter, then handed it to Hyrum. "I know my own business," he said, indicating that his course would be to leave.

Reynolds Cahoon snapped, "You always said if the church would stick to you, you would stick to the church, now trouble comes and you are the first to run." Hiram Kimball chimed in and the two men called Joseph a coward, reminding him that if mobs destroyed their property they would all be homeless.[18]

These were cutting words. "If my life is of no value to my friends, it is of none to myself," Joseph replied.

He turned to Rockwell, but Porter replied, "You are the oldest and ought to know best. As you make your bed, I will lie with you."

Joseph looked at Hyrum. "What shall we do?"

"Let's go back and give ourselves up, and see the thing out." Hyrum's daughter was to be married that night, and he wanted to be there.

Joseph stood silent for a few minutes, then looked at his older brother. "If you go back I will go with you, but we shall be butchered."[19]

Most historians have assumed that Emma's letter caused Joseph to return to Nauvoo, but only Joseph and Hyrum seemed to have read it. It has never been quoted, even in part. William Clayton's diary gives the only clue to the content: "Emma sent messengers over the river to Joseph & informed him what they intended to do and urged him to give himself up inasmuch as the Gov. had offered him protection."[20] But Emma's letter alone did not change his course. Hyrum Smith's desire to be at home and Cahoon's and Kimball's name-calling tipped the balance. But Joseph himself must also accept responsibility for his own decision. Obviously Emma had not expected his return, for she later told a friend, "When he came back I felt the worst I ever did in my life, and from that time I looked for him to be killed."[21]

Others in the city saw it differently. Vilate Kimball wrote to Heber: "Joseph went over the river out of the United States, and composed his mind, and got the will of the Lord concerning him, and that was, that he should return and give himself up for trial. . . . My heart said Lord bless those Dear men, and presurve them from those that thirst for their blood."[22]

Joseph stayed with Emma and the children that night. Julia at thirteen would never be a beauty, but her brown eyes and thick hair were assets. She was a sensitive girl with a streak of daring and a sense of humor that endeared her to her father. At eight years, blond, blue-eyed Frederick looked more like his father than the others. Six-year-old Alexander resembled his mother in coloring and features, as did young Joseph. Young Joseph remembered being called into the large north room of the Mansion where his father gave him a blessing similar to the one he had received in the red brick store a year earlier and said to the assembled group, "If anything should happen to me, you will know who is to be my successor. This, my son, has been blessed and set apart, and will in time succeed me."[23]

Brigham Young later alleged that Emma had Joseph remove his "garment of the priesthood" before going to Carthage to give himself up the next morning. Since these garments, worn by all the members of the Endowment Council, were seen as unspecified "protection" for the wearer, the insinuation is that Emma wished Joseph harm. Two other accounts refute Young's statement. Oliver Huntington lived at the Mansion at the time and in his autobiography he states: "Joseph pulled off his [priesthood] garments just before starting to Carthage to be slain and he advised Hyrum and John Taylor to do the same, which they did. . . . Joseph said before taking [them] off, that he was going to be killed . . . and he did not want his garments to be exposed to the sneers and jeers of his enemies."[24] Julia Bowen Dalton, who also resided at the Mansion at this time, said Joseph stated "that it was to be that he should lay down his life as a martyr to the testimony he bore but that his enemies could not take his life while he was wearing his garments. He took them off before leaving for Carthage."[25]

Joseph told members of the household, "I go as a lamb to the slaughter, but if my death will atone for any faults I have committed during my lifetime I am willing to die."[26] At six-thirty in the morning Joseph, Emma, and the children walked out into the fresh air. Joseph kissed each child good-bye. One witness said Joseph turned to his wife, "Emma, can you train my sons to walk in their father's footsteps?"

"Oh, Joseph, you're coming back!" Joseph repeated the question and Emma gave the same response, almost as though her saying it would make it so. The third time he asked, Emma's eyes filled with tears. "Oh, Joseph," she said again, *"you are coming back!"*[27]

Emma and the children stood together as Joseph hurried through the gate to meet the men who would accompany him and Hyrum to Carthage. In the party were John Taylor, Willard Richards, William W. Phelps, Dimick B. Huntington, Stephen Markham, Dan Jones, the lawyer James W. Wood, Lorenzo Wasson, and several others. Porter Rockwell started out with the group but Joseph insisted he return to Nauvoo for his own safety. At two-thirty Emma heard the horses return. Joseph had indeed come back, but he was not free. The men had returned to disarm the Nauvoo Legion, at the request of the governor. Leonora Taylor said Joseph tried to persuade his pregnant wife to go to Carthage with him, but she did not go because of her children and her delicate health. He again seemed resigned as he told her, "If they [do] not hang me, I do not know how they [will] kill me."[28]

A cousin of Joseph's wrote that "Joseph returned a third time to bid his family farewell. It seemed that he could hardly leave them but did it to appease the wrath of a wicked people."[29] It was now nearly 6 P.M. In a day filled with wrenching good-byes, Emma and Joseph said a final farewell.

Emma wanted a blessing from Joseph before he left for Carthage but there had been no time. Joseph told her to "write out the best blessing [she] could think of and he would sign the same on his return." Perhaps in the evening quiet of June 24 she wrote what she called "these desires of my heart."

First of all that I would crave as the richest of heaven's blessings would be wisdom from my Heavenly Father bestowed daily, so that whatever I might do or say, I could not look back at the close of the day with regret, nor neglect the performance of any act that would bring a blessing. I desire the Spirit of God to know and understand myself, that I desire a fruitful, active mind, that I may be able to comprehend the designs of God, when revealed through his servants without doubting. I desire a spirit of discernment, which is one of the promised blessings of the Holy Ghost.

I particularly desire wisdom to bring up all the children that are, or may be committed to my charge, in such a manner that they will be useful ornaments in the Kingdom of God, and in a coming day arise up and call me blessed.

I desire prudence that I may not through ambition abuse my body and cause it to become prematurely old and care-worn, but that I may wear a cheerful countenance, live to perform all the work that I covenanted to perform in the spirit-world and be a blessing to all who may in any wise need aught at my hands.

I desire with all my heart to honor and respect my husband as my head, ever to live in his confidence and by acting in unison with him retain the place which God has given me by his side, and I ask my Heavenly Father that through humility, I may be enabled to overcome that curse which was pronounced upon the daughters of Eve. I desire to see that I may rejoice with them in the blessings which God has in store for all who are willing to be obedient to his requirements. Finally, I desire that whatever may be my lot through life I may be enabled to acknowledge the hand of God in all things.[30]

This blessing, written in Emma's own hand, was a perceptive and candid self-evaluation. She probably placed the document in Joseph's desk with his other papers where he might find and sign it on his return.

The next day a messenger delivered a letter to Emma from Joseph. "Myself and Hyrum have been again arrested for treason because we called out the Nauvoo Legion," he wrote, "but when the truth comes out we have nothing to fear. We all feel calm and composed."[31] The first writ thirteen days earlier had been for destruction of the press, but Joseph explained in his June 22 letter to the Governor that the Nauvoo court had already acquitted him. The governor sidestepped legal entanglements by making treason the grounds for this second arrest. "I think the Governor has and will succeed in enforcing the laws," he assured her. In reality, the Governor introduced Joseph and Hyrum with their full military titles to the Carthage Grays, who threw up hats, drew swords, and shouted obscenities at Joseph and Hyrum.[32] Governor Ford should not have been surprised at the outcry; as state attorney from 1830 to 1834 he had attended circuit court in Carthage. He described the townspeople as "hard cases . . . with some honorable exceptions. . . . [They] were not horrified at the idea of taking the law into their own hands. That had been done before by neighbors and friends, and would be done again."[33]

Emma further learned from Joseph's letter that the governor planned to send troops "to Nauvoo to protect the citizens"; he told her to treat them kindly and ended the letter on a note of optimism: "Three o'clock—The Governor has just agreed to march his army to Nauvoo, and I shall come along with him. The prisoners, all that can, will be admitted to bail." The news encouraged Emma, but when a military unit arrived in Nauvoo early the following morning Joseph was not with them. The commander called a public meeting at ten o'clock. He assured the Mormons, "I see no cause of having a military force stationed here unless it is for the apprehension of your fears that a mob will come against you. . . . I was somewhat excited when I left home but am not now, for I see harmony and peace is with you, and I don't think the mob will make an attack upon you."[34] True to Joseph's request for kindness, Emma managed breakfast and a noon meal for forty men and supper for thirty.[35] In Carthage Joseph received a report that several men had said "the law could not reach them, but powder and ball would." Joseph and the others were not confined to a jail cell but rather to a room called the debtor's apartment on the second story of the gray stone building. That night Joseph and Hyrum slept on the only bed while the other five men slept on the floor. When a single shot shattered the night stillness, Joseph joined those on the floor. Dan Jones left early to determine the cause of the gunshot and encountered Frank A. Worell, the officer on duty for the Carthage Grays. "We had too much trouble to bring old Joe here to let him ever escape alive," Worell sneered; "unless you want to die with him you had better leave before sundown . . . you'll see that I can prophesy better than Old Joe, for neither he nor his brother, nor anyone who will remain with them will see the sun set today."[36] The guards allowed visitors and one smuggled a handgun to Joseph.

In Nauvoo Emma woke on the morning of June 27 with the clear sky promising another warm day. At noon Captain Singleton inspected the unarmed Legion, then told the three thousand men under his command that Ford would be arriving that afternoon. Emma expected Joseph to accompany the governor, but when Ford arrived about four o'clock Emma received a letter instead. Joseph had begun dictating it that morning. He told Emma that if the governor went to Nauvoo with his troops she would be protected. "I want you to tell Bro [Jonathan] Dunham [lieutenant general of the Legion] to instruct the people to stay at home and attend to their own business, and let there be no groups or gathering together unless by permission of the Gov."

He did not mention the unsettling shot the previous night or the antagonism of the Carthage militia. Instead he took the pen in his own hand and added, "I am very much resigned to my lot, knowing I am justified and have done the best that could be done give my love to the children and all my Friends . . . who inquire after me as for treason I know that I have not committed any and they cannot prove one apearance of any thing of the kind. So you need not have any fears that any harm can happen to us on that score. may God bless you all. Amen." He then added a postscript: "20 mi[nutes] to 10—I just learn that the Governor is about to disband his troops,—all but a guard to protect us and the peace,—and come himself to Nauvoo and deliver a speech to the people. This is right, as I suppose."[37]

This was ominous news, for in disbanding the Carthage Grays the governor left that anti-Mormon unit without any legal military supervision. Ford later insisted he released the troops for fear they would destroy Nauvoo,[38] but Thomas Gregg, a non-Mormon author of an early Hancock County history, related a conversation between Ford and Colonel Geddes of the Carthage Grays. "O, it's all nonsense; you will have to drive these Mormons out yet!" Ford said.

"If we undertake that, Governor, when the proper time comes, will you interfere?" Geddes asked.

"No, I will not," came the reply, "until you are through!"[39] With most of the Grays at liberty, Ford marched to Nauvoo with one small unit.

When he arrived in Nauvoo, he went directly to the Mansion where Emma received him with dignity and courtesy. Joseph's letter suggested giving him a room for a conference. Several members of the High Council and Legion staff had met a short time earlier in that same room. By mistake, Porter Rockwell had left his hat and returned to retrieve it. Inadvertently, he walked in on a conversation between the governor and several of his aides. One man said, "The deed is done before this time." Rockwell's abrupt entry terminated the conversation and the men stood in awkward silence. He lifted his hat from the rack and left. Only later that night would he realize the significance of the comment.[40]

When Ford emerged from the room he ordered the Mormons to gather outside the Mansion where he would address them. From the same platform Joseph had used nine days earlier the governor told the people: "You ought to be praying Saints, not military Saints. Depend upon it, a little more misbehavior on the part of the citizens, and the torch which is now already lighted, will be applied; the city may be reduced to ashes, and extermination would inevitably follow." Emma listened with increasing apprehension to the man who had taken the responsibility of safeguarding the Mormon prisoners. Governor Ford ended his speech, then immediately prepared to leave, declining an invitation to stay the night. At six-thirty he and his entourage rode out of Nauvoo, leaving a small unit behind.[41]

Emma returned to her work in the Mansion House. She fed members of her household and ten military men as well as several other paying guests who occupied rooms. Lucy Mack Smith and Emma's children prepared for the evening.

Porter Rockwell could not sleep that night. With an uneasy feeling, he remembered the statement he had overheard in the governor's conversation at the Mansion. Drawn to Carthage strongly enough to disobey Joseph's order to stay home, Rockwell saddled his horse and rode through the darkness. Part way to Carthage he met Lorenzo Wasson and George D. Grant coming toward him. After a brief exchange Porter wheeled his horse and raced back to Nauvoo.[42]

The sound of pounding hooves shattered Nauvoo's predawn silence and echoed from the closed house fronts. The steady, staccato beat and the sound of a raspy voice alerted the guard at the temple. As Rockwell drew closer, Anson Call heard his frantic voice screaming, *"Joseph is killed—they have killed him! Goddamn them! They have killed him!"*[43]

Moments later Lorenzo Wasson, breathless and covered with dust, told Emma that Joseph was dead. She reeled in horror. The disturbance woke young Joseph, who came through the house to find his cousin Lorenzo with his stunned mother. Emma turned to the boy. Her first difficult task as a widow was to tell the child his father was dead. Room to room, childish face to childish face, grandmother to hired girl, the news spread through the house.

Mary Fielding Smith answered a knock at her door at dawn. George Grant told her that Hyrum and Joseph had been killed. Mary stepped back and said simply, "It cannot be possible, can it?"

"Yes, it is true," Grant answered gently.

Mary felt her legs buckle and steadied herself against a bureau. Grant then helped her to a chair. A daughter remembered, "The news flew like wildfire through the house. The crying and agony . . . and the anguish and sorrow that were felt can be easier felt than described but . . . will never be forgotten by those who were called to pass through it."[44] It would be some time before the details were known, but in Carthage witnesses to the scene told their stories.

Sometime between four and five o'clock on June 27, Eudocia Baldwin, a girl with two brothers serving in the Grays, heard her brother-in-law exclaim, "A party of men are coming to take Joe Smith from jail, and hang him in the square." The news that something momentous was happening spread quickly through the town. One man told Eudocia, "A party of Mormons are coming to rescue the Smiths and take them to Nauvoo; we fear the guard will all be killed." Eudocia's elder brother was on duty at the jail. Someone shouted, "The Danites are coming for the Smiths!" The girl noticed that the men did not move toward the jail but only succeeded in adding to the confusion. In the square an officer attempted unsuccessfully to organize the men into a line. Eudocia's other brother, Tom, suddenly bolted with a shout, "Come on, you cowards, damn you, come on; those boys will be killed!" The girl and her mother followed. When Eudocia neared the jail a mob of men, their faces blackened with gunpowder and water, surged between the two women. Mrs. Baldwin believed the men were Mormons and rushed forward to save her sons, but the disguised men trapped her in place as an eyewitness. The guards on the front steps fired toward the attackers, who were less than twenty feet away, yet no one was hit. With no further resistance, the intruders threw the guards to the ground and started up the stairs.[45]

Only Joseph, Hyrum, John Taylor, and Willard Richards remained in the upper room of the jail. Joseph and Hyrum grabbed for hidden guns, then the four bolted the door and held it. Unable to gain entry, the mob fired through the wood. A ball hit Hyrum on the left side of his nose, shattering bone and flesh and knocking him backward to the floor. "I am a dead man!" he cried as another bullet entered his head from under his chin.

Joseph opened the door a crack and fired until the gun chamber clicked empty. Bullets from outside the window sprayed the room. Taylor fell against the window sill, wounded in the thigh. A shot from outside slammed into his vest-pocket watch, stopping the hands at five-fifteen. Spared by his own timepiece, John Taylor rolled under the bed just as a final bullet opened his hip. He lay half conscious while blood pooled under him.

Joseph leaped for the window as a mob burst through the door, pinning Richards behind it. Two bullets penetrated Joseph's back as a third entered his chest. With a cry of "O Lord, My God!" he lurched through the window, hung on the sill for a moment, then plummeted to the ground below. Only when Eudocia Baldwin's mother saw Joseph's body fall did she realize the attackers were not Mormons "and she turned away, heartsick and terrified." A witness said Joseph raised himself partly up against the side of a well, then slumped over dead.

Richards, with only a nick in one earlobe, had carried Taylor to the adjoining cell and covered him with straw. "This is a hard case to lay you on the floor," he explained, "but if your wounds are not fatal, I want you to live to tell the story." He could hear men on the stairs and expected to be killed any moment.

Then from outside came the shout, "The Mormons are coming! The Mormons are coming!" The mob fled from the jail and the streets emptied in the panic that followed. Richards and Taylor were alone in the eerie stillness.

Joseph's brother Samuel was one of the first to arrive at the scene of death. Joseph's body still rested against the well; Hyrum's lay upstairs. Samuel helped Richards carry the lifeless bodies to the Hamilton Hotel and helped John Taylor.

Although virtually every Mormon who kept a journal or wrote letters at the time of Joseph's and Hyrum's deaths mentions the murders, all felt their loss so deeply that they were unable to describe their grief. Only a stranger could write of the reactions of the dead men's families in detail. B. W. Richmond, a guest in the Mansion, went to comfort the family. When he entered Lucy Smith's room she approached him shedding no tears. Wrapping her stiff arthritic hands around his, she asked, "Why did they shoot my dear children?" then turned and gazed out the window.

Richmond found the children in another room. Julia and Joseph were on the floor with Alexander and Frederick, "leaning over them, mingling their grief in one wild scream of childish dispair." He then peered into the room where Emma sat in a chair, her face covered by her hands as she sobbed uncontrollably. A friend, John P. Greene, tried to comfort her. "Oh, Sister Emma, God bless you," he said, then laid his hands on her head and blessed her with "peace, protection, and resignation." When Emma asked the unanswerable whys—why was Joseph dead; why were her children fatherless, and she a widow—Green assured her that the sorrow she bore would be the crown of her life. Emma lifted her head. *"My husband was my crown."*[46]

Official word of the tragedy reached Emma soon after daybreak on June 28.

CARTHAGE JAIL, 8:05 o'clock, P.M., June 27th, 1844

Joseph and Hyrum are dead. Taylor wounded, not very badly. I am well. Our guard was forced, as we believe, by a band of Missourians from 100 to 200. The job was done in an instant, and the party fled towards Nauvoo instantly. This is as I believe it. The citizens here are afraid of the Mormons attacking them. I promise them no!

W. Richards,
John Taylor.[47]

John Taylor had requested that the seriousness of his wounds be minimized so as not to alarm his family.

The governor had returned to Carthage shortly before midnight. He told the curious few who still milled in the square to disperse as the Mormons would be so angry they would burn the town. Ford feared the county would erupt in civil war. Expecting Emma to be the intermediary, he had Richards write to the citizens of Nauvoo, *"Don't rush out of the city*—don't rush to Carthage." Richards told them he had pledged his word that the Mormons would "stay at home . . . and no violence will be on their part . . . in the name of the Lord, be still, be patient. . . ." When Emma received the letter from the men in Carthage, she issued a proclamation to the people to "remain quiet and peaceable."[48]

On Friday, June 28, two wagons carrying the bodies of the martyred brothers rolled into Nauvoo. In each wagon box lay a rough pine casket covered with boughs and leaves to shade it from the hot sun. The Nauvoo Brass Band led the cortege, and an honor guard of twelve men accompanied the wagons. Eight thousand people lined the streets as the procession wound through the city. Men and women wept openly. Allen Stout, a former Danite, ached for revenge as he stood with the crowd. "I there and then resolved in my mind that I would never let an opportunity slip unimproved of avenging their blood. . . . I knew not how to contain myself, and *when I see one of the men who persuaded them to give up to be tried,* I feel like cutting their throats yet."[49] Through strange twists in the writing of history it would be Emma, not Reynolds Cahoon and Hiram Kimball, who would bear the blame for bringing Joseph back.[50]

Emma waited at home. In the distance the faint sound of music from the Brass Band ushered Joseph home for the last time. Then willing hands carried the bodies inside and the doors were shut. The people would view the martyrs the next day. William Marks and William and Dimick Huntington prepared the bodies for burial in a final act of devotion. They dressed the lifeless forms in fine clothes with white neckerchiefs and shrouds, then the families came in. B. W. Richmond said Emma tried several times to walk across the room but each time she fainted. Finally a friend helped her from the room. Then Mary Fielding Smith entered with her four children. "She trembled at every step, and nearly fell, but reached her husband's body, and kneeled down by him, clasped her arm around his head, turned his pale face upon her heaving bosom, and then a gushing, plaintive wail burst from her lips: 'O! Hyrum, Hyrum! Have they shot you, my dear Hyrum? Are you dead? O! speak to me, my dear husband. I cannot think you are dead, my dear Hyrum.'" Richmond said, "Her grief seemed to consume her, and she lost all power of utterance. Her two daughters, and the two young children, clung some to her body, falling prostrate upon the corpse and shrieking in the wildness of their wordless grief."[51]

A few minutes later Dimick Huntington and another man assisted Emma back into the room. Dimick held his hat up to shield her view of Joseph. The two led her over to where Hyrum lay and Richmond took her hand and placed it on Hyrum's forehead. Emma stood for a minute, then said, "Now I can see him; I am strong now." Unassisted, she walked to Joseph where she "kneeled down, clasped him around his face, and sank upon his body. Suddenly her grief found vent, and sighs and groans and words and lamentations filled the room. 'Joseph, Joseph,' she said, 'are you dead? Have the assassins shot you?' Her children, four in number, gathered around their weeping mother, and the dead body of a murdered father, and grief that words cannot embody seemed to overwhelm the whole group."[52] Richmond said Emma spoke softly to Joseph and the only words he heard were the ones he recorded. Young Joseph remembered her saying, "Oh, Joseph, Joseph! My husband, my husband! Have they taken you from me at last!" Twenty-four years later Dimick Huntington claimed he heard Emma ask Joseph to forgive her.[53]

Lucy Smith entered then, sank back, and cried, "My God, my God, why hast thou forsaken this family!" She positioned herself between her dead sons, resting a hand on each body.[54]

Early the next morning the bodies were placed on the soft white cambric linings of coffins covered in black velvet and studded with brass nails. Squares of glass in the lids protected the faces. At eight o'clock the doors to the Mansion opened and throughout the day an estimated ten thousand mourners filed in the west entrance, through the dining room where the bodies lay, and out through the north door. Scattered among them were some of the brothers' plural wives. Eliza Snow wrote in her life sketch, "To look upon the noble, lifeless forms . . . was a sight that might well appal the heart of a true American citizen: but what it was for loving wives and children, the loyal heart may *feel."*[55] B. W. Richmond noticed "a lady standing at the head of Joseph Smith's body, her face covered, and her whole frame convulsing with weeping." He identified her as Lucinda Morgan Harris.[56]

Ironically, young Joseph stated in his memoirs: "It is a source of gratification to me now to remember that no other women bowed beside the bodies of these brothers . . . as wives to mourn and exhibit their grief . . . save my mother at my father's side and Aunt Mary at the side of my Uncle Hyrum. The scene was sacred to their grief and theirs alone."[57]

The day seemed endless. When Emma was not occupied with the children she paced the floor and went downstairs occasionally. "I saw Emma walking back and forth in [another part] . . . of the Mansion," one woman wrote to another, "she spoke to me, and I answered her, and then continued on my way."[58] At five o'clock the doors swung shut. Emma and Mary with their children and other family members came in for one final look at Joseph's and Hyrum's remains.

When the family could be ushered out, the cadence suddenly changed. Someone locked the Mansion doors. Joseph's head still carried a price in Missouri and rumors had already reached Nauvoo that enemies might try to mutilate his body to collect the bounty. Men lifted the coffins from outer pine boxes and placed them in a small bedroom to the northeast. Bags of sand quickly replaced the bodies, and Dimick Huntingon drove sand-filled coffins to a public funeral. At midnight the men carried the inner coffins containing the bodies of Hyrum and Joseph to graves in the open basement of the unfinished Nauvoo House. They replaced stones and debris and a heavy rain drenched the soil that night. By morning nothing remained to indicate the burying place to the bounty-hunting mobs.

14

The Lady
and the Lion

Fall 1844

Most widows follow rather predictable behavior as they work through their grief. While their actions are often out of character and may be misunderstood, they are not abnormal. Widows traditionally become extremely concerned about their financial well-being. Indecisive and compulsive, they are sometimes generous about giving away belongings of the deceased and on other occasions possessive of the most trivial items. Emma would exhibit all of these traits and in doing so would fit the profile of the "classic" widow[1] but would not suffer a mental breakdown or become an "empty shell," as some writers have suggested.

The next two years were emotionally taxing and difficult for Emma and Mary Fielding Smith, but no one has suggested that Mary went into "deep depression" or had a mental breakdown. Yet, at the death of the brothers, the two women reacted similarly. Three crucial differences set Emma apart from Mary as a widow. First, she had been *the* wife of *the* prophet. Second, her personal and financial affairs were intertwined with those of the church. Third, Emma unalterably opposed plural marriage. Mary approved when Hyrum married other wives and she would soon become a plural wife of Heber C. Kimball. These factors determined the separate paths the two women would follow.

While Emma and Mary began the adjustment to widowhood, an uneasy calm settled over Hancock County. Both sides remained cautious, the Nauvoo Legion paraded each afternoon at five, then stood guard around the city through the night, but no attack came. With John Taylor incapacitated by his wounds, Willard Richards as one of the Twelve and William Marks as Stake President represented the church leadership.

On the last day of June Willard Richards wrote to Brigham Young in Boston requesting the balance of the Twelve to return immediately and urging them to be cautious. "William Smith's . . . life," he warned, "is threatened with all the Smiths."[2] William Marks, on the other hand, wrote to Sidney Rigdon in Pittsburgh and asked him to come to Nauvoo and take control of the church. Marks may have seen Rigdon as his best hope to rid the church of plural marriage. Whether Marks informed Emma of his plan to bring Rigdon back is not known.

Apparently Lucy Smith worried about Joseph's estate, telling Emma that Joseph's "creditors will come forward & use up all the property there is." On July 2 William Clayton found Emma distressed that Lucy was "making disturbance" over property. Clayton warned Emma of "considerable danger if the family begin to dispute about the property. . . . If they will keep still there is . . . enough to pay the debts and plenty left for other uses."[3]

Joseph had left no will; he had made little distinction between his efforts to provide for his family and his efforts to accommodate the converts who flocked to Nauvoo. In buying the original Mormon land purchases in the city, Joseph, Hyrum, and Sidney Rigdon had pledged their personal credit, although they clearly intended them for church members. Joseph had also involved himself in business opportunities that ranged from operating stores to owning steamboats.[4] Emma knew that Nauvoo lands had been purchased on long-term credit and the debts were still outstanding at her husband's death. The family's resources were so low that Joseph had borrowed three hundred dollars before his death and had given Emma fifty. Five days after his death Emma gathered together three hundred dollars to pay off the debt, probably leaving her with very little money to operate her house.[5] On July 4 Clayton and the lawyer James W. Wood met at Emma's home and examined Joseph's finances. Afterward Clayton acknowledged that Emma's situation was indeed bleak. Most of the assets were in Joseph's name as trustee-in-trust for the church; the liabilities were in Joseph's name as private citizen and Emma was now accountable.

When Joseph had applied for bankruptcy in 1842 he listed his debts at $73,066.38. Although most of the eleven people who filed with him, including Hyrum, received discharge from all debts, Joseph did not. The others bought back their own property for a few cents on the dollar at the bankruptcy sales. Thus they retired their debts and still owned their property. When John C. Bennett charged in the local papers that Joseph intended to defraud his creditors, United States Attorney Justin Butterfield singled out his application. Joseph's case was still pending in March 1843 when Congress repealed the law on grounds that it allowed a misapplication of justice. By his own account, Joseph still owed approximately $70,000 (over $500,000 in today's dollars) when he and Hyrum were murdered.[6] Emma had inherited a debt that would plague her for years.

She also realized that the financial well-being of many church members, who had settled on much of the original Commerce, Illinois, land purchases, was related to Joseph's estate. As an initial step, James Wood advised Emma to have her deeds recorded in the county records at Carthage to insure their legality. William Clayton opposed this step.

When Clayton attended a meeting at William Marks's home in the afternoon of July 4, those present thought "that brother Marks place is to be appointed president & Trustee in trust and this accords with Emma's feelings." Clayton talked again with both Taylor and Willard Richards on this subject on July 7. They reversed themselves and agreed not to appoint a permanent trustee until the Twelve returned, and suggested Clayton be temporary trustee of the church, evidently without consulting Emma. The next day Emma received a letter from New York demanding six thousand dollars in payment for some old debts. Her financial situation was now becoming urgent. When she saw Clayton later in the day she told him she objected to an acting trustee and wanted a permanent appointment made that week.[7]

On July 12 William Marks and William Clayton discussed appointing a permanent trustee. After Marks left, Newel K. Whitney pointed out that Marks shared Emma's view of p[l]ral marriage, therefore, if Marks were appointed trustee, those "most important matters" would be removed from the church.[8] Unlike Emma, the men saw the office of trustee-in-trust as synonymous with that of church president. Emma and William Marks attended a three o'clock meeting upstairs in Emma's house. Parley P. Pratt, the first of the Twelve to arrive back in Nauvoo, spoke for the Quorum at the meeting. Emma asked the group to "nominate and appoint a trustee-in-trust for the whole Church," which was not a suggestion that they choose a successor to Joseph as church president. She argued that "a delay would endanger much property of a public and private character and perhaps cause a loss of scores of thousands."

Pratt protested that such an appointment "was the business of the whole Church, through its general authorities." He maintained that no such business could be conducted until the rest of the Quorum of Twelve returned. Someone reminded Pratt again of the members' precarious property situation. To this he replied, ". . . dollars and cents are no consideration with me . . . we cannot and will not suffer the authorities and principles of the Church to be trampled under foot, for the sake of pecuniary interest."[9] Pratt could afford his principles; since none of his property came from any of Joseph's land acquirements, he would lose nothing,[10] but he interpreted Emma's efforts to save her property as an intrusion into church affairs. The group did not have authority to choose a trustee and decided to meet again in two days.

Emma realized the outcome of the current situation would have long-term consequences for her and her children and wanted some voice in the matter. The following day she again insisted to William Clayton that a permanent trustee, who met with her approval, be appointed. She stated that if they did not consider her wishes she would keep the lots in her name, although it seems to have been understood that she held some for the church. She voiced her displeasure at not being treated fairly and stated flatly that she was capable of looking after herself if they were going to "trample on her."[11] Eventually Clayton was named acting, but not permanent, trustee for the church. Three weeks after Joseph's death Emma, Lorenzo Wasson, and James Wood rode to the courthouse in Carthage, where she filed papers designating her administratrix of her husband's estate and legal guardian of their four children. This satisfied her legal obligation as Joseph's widow.

In addition to legal matters, another concern occupied Emma. Samuel Smith was very ill. The day of his brothers' funeral he had complained of an intense pain in his side that persisted until he was confined to bed. In spite of Samuel's illness and her own pregnancy, the situation of the Lawrence estate made it necessary for Emma to travel to Quincy. Because Joseph had been legal guardian for Sarah and Maria Lawrence, their estate was connected to his. William Clayton as acting trustee accompanied Emma on the riverboat *Osprey*. The judge said he could not act on the Lawrence case until another guardian was appointed. Unable to complete their business, Emma and Clayton left at midnight, reaching Nauvoo just before noon the next day.[12]

Emma came home to a sorrowful household. Samuel Harrison Smith, thirty-six, had died July 30, the day she left.[13] Samuel's wife, Levira, became a widow on her twenty-ninth birthday. Pregnant with her third child, whom she lost three weeks later, she also cared for Samuel's three children. The oldest, Mary B., went to live with Emma and cared for her grandmother until shortly before Lucy died seven years later. Lucy Mack Smith had reared six sons to manhood; only William still lived, but because his wife was too ill to travel he remained in the East until the following May. In spite of her compounded losses, Lucy comforted her daughters-in-law. "I am convinced that no one but a widow can imagine the feelings of a widow,"[14] she told them.

When Brigham Young arrived in Nauvoo on August 6 he found Sidney Rigdon already claiming authority to act as "guardian" of the church because he was Joseph's remaining counselor. That afternoon Rigdon reminded church leaders of his long service and association with Joseph. Brigham told the group that "Joseph conferred upon our heads all the keys and powers belonging to the Apostleship which he himself held before he was taken away." This, he felt, gave him "the keys and the means of obtaining the mind of the Lord" about the presidency.[15] The next day Rigdon preached a sermon to a large crowd. He claimed to be the "identical man that the ancient prophets had sung about, wrote and rejoiced over . . . that the time was near at hand when he would see one hundred tons of metal per second thrown at the enemies of God, and that the blood would be . . . [as deep as] the horse's bridles; and that he expected to walk into the palace of Queen Victoria and lead her out by the nose."[16] The beleaguered Mormons had experienced enough violence. Rigdon's speech undermined his already questionable credibility.

William Marks, at Rigdon's request, called a special meeting to choose a guardian for the church, to be held in the grove on August 8. Rigdon spoke for ninety minutes in the morning. In the afternoon Brigham Young aligned the opposing factions when he stated: "Now, if you want Sidney Rigdon or William Law to lead you, or anybody else, you are welcome to them; but I tell you, in the name of the Lord, that no man can put another between the Twelve and the Prophet Joseph. . . . If the Twelve be the men to counsel you to finish the great work laid out by our departed Prophet, say so, and do not break you[r] covenants by murmering hereafter."[17]

As Brigham spoke, many in the audience believed they witnessed a miracle taking place. One said, "I Saw in . . . Brigham Young the Tall Straight, & portly Form of the Prophet Joseph Smith Clothed in a Sheen of Light Covering him to his feet and I heard the Real & Perfect Voice of the Prophet." This incident satisfied many people in the church that the "mantle of Joseph was on Brigham."[18] Not all of those gathered in the grove witnessed the "transfiguration," but most of them voted to accept the Quorum of the Twelve Apostles with Brigham Young at its head as the presiding authority. Emma did not attend this meeting.

Brigham's arrival in Nauvoo did not include a graceful reestablishment of ties with Emma. A letter he wrote to his fourteen-year-old daughter Vilate, who was attending school in Salem, Massachusetts, stated, "I cannot say much a bout the families of Brs. J[oseph] and H[yrum]Smiths for I have not had time to caul on them yet."[19] Brigham Young had gained control of the leadership of the church and appointed Newel K. Whitney and George Miller as trustees-in-trust, but he had neither visited nor consulted with Emma. Five weeks passed before he met with her to discuss the affairs of the church and Joseph's estate. No doubt he had talked with Clayton, Richards, and Pratt immediately upon his return, but Brigham was probably angered by their reports of Emma's activities in behalf of Joseph's estate. On September 13 Brigham paid his respects to Lucy Mack Smith. If Lucy was still living at the Mansion, one can assume that Brigham saw Emma on that occasion.

James Wood asked to see Joseph's bills and accounts along with a list of all lands and their titles both in Joseph's own name and as trustee-in-trust on August 12. This incensed Clayton, who believed Wood was probing into private church business, forgetting that Wood had been Joseph's trusted counsel. After conferring with Newel K. Whitney, Clayton and Brigham Young decided that Wood was inappropriately interfering with church matters. Clayton went to Emma and told her that church business would remain secret.

He said Emma's response was "warm," but she told him there was no need for secrets. She agreed with Wood that everything should be made public. A modern-day legal assessment of the accounts Wood wished to see reveals that Joseph's business transactions were legal;[20] Emma was correct in her assessment that they could stand investigation. She chided Clayton for neglecting her business and meeting in secret with the Twelve. "It was secret things which . . . cost Joseph and Hyrum their lives, and it will cost you and the Twelve your lives as it has done them," she argued.

"I would rather die than do anything to ruin the church," Clayton replied, still maintaining that transactions should be kept confidential. He suggested that Emma would not want all of her own actions made public. He neglected to detail in his diary what Emma would want kept secret but said only that she responded with anger and called him a liar. Clayton went directly to Brigham Young to make sure the church leader understood the position he had taken. Two days after the argument Emma discovered some money missing and blamed Clayton. Stung by the accusation, he concluded that Emma had invented the story to discredit him. Emma did not know he had used the money to pay one of Joseph's creditors. The incident destroyed any vestige of trust remaining between them.[21]

When Clayton insisted that Joseph's desk belonged to the church, Emma would not let him have it at first. He finally got it a week later, but Emma had kept the papers that were in it.[22] Brigham and the Twelve had Joseph's history, private records, manuscripts, and library. Emma assumed that Joseph's papers and other items belonged to her. When she pressed for their return she was told that "as her husband had been President of the church all his correspondence and public documents were the property of the organization."[23]

Brigham apparently kept Joseph's papers in his home and, suspecting that Emma might come for them, he told members of his household that she was not to have them. Emma did go to his house for the papers. Just as the person with whom she was talking was ready to let her have them, Harriet Cook, one of Brigham's plural wives with a reputation for being cantankerous, appeared at the top of the stairs and said, "I know these are Church records, not private records, and that they belong to the Church. I will see to it personally that they are kept in the possession of Brigham Young."

Emma remarked, "I guess I might as well give it up; I'm more afraid of Harriet than I am of the sheriff!"[24] Eventually Brigham returned a number of books to Emma.

By mid-September newspapers published stories about a rift between Emma and the church leaders. The Burlington, Iowa, *Hawkeye* reported that Emma "has given much dissatisfaction in consequence of her refusing to transfer some of the church property which was in the Prophet's name. . . . It is said she is weak in the faith."[25] Yet Heber C. Kimball noted, "Met in coucil at Sister Emma Smith . . . and expressed our feelings to her & [what] our intentions ware she seemed pleased with our course. it seemed like old times."[26]

Apparently when the leaders of the church met with Emma and informed her of their plans both sides reacted positively and without animosity.

Enmity between Brigham Young and Emma was not present the twelve years they had known each other. If Emma had any reservations about Brigham, she neither commented about him in a derogatory way nor influenced her young children to dislike him. By the time her son Joseph III wrote his memoirs, the temptation to discredit Young may have been very strong, but he remembered, "I often saw him upon the stand, in the streets, and in his home, and thought him a pleasant man to meet, neither liking nor disliking him particularly as I now recall, until a short time after my father's death."[27]

Brigham had offered support to Emma and Joseph on several occasions during the 1837 flight from Kirtland, when he prevailed on a church member to give Joseph two hundred dollars from the sale of a tavern stand. He had approved when Joseph deeded land to Emma and the children to provide them with an inheritance in Nauvoo,[28] and he had requested supplies for Joseph from church members in the outlying communities of Ramus and La Harp.[29]

Brigham's friendship had gone beyond his official capacity. A daughter born ten days before Brigham departed for the English mission was named Roxy Emma Alice after Emma. He wrote plaintively of his sixteen-month-old daughter as he expressed his homesickness to Mary Ann on January 15, 1841. "My little daughter Emma she dos not know eny thing a bout me." After 1847, when the relationship between Emma and Brigham had disintegrated, Roxy Emma Alice was known only as Alice.[30]

Both Brigham and Emma had a great affection for Joseph, although they differed about some of his actions. Emma recognized Joseph's prophetic calling, but the closeness of the marriage relationship forced her to deal more candidly with his failings. Brigham Young, in an 1857 speech, said, "Though I admitted in my feelings and knew all the time that Joseph was a human being and subject to err, still it was none of my business to look after his faults." Reflecting on the years in Kirtland, he confessed to only one uncertainty about Joseph and he quickly put the thought down. "A feeling came over me that Joseph was not right in his financial management, though I presume the feeling did not last sixty seconds."[31]

The first open conflict between Brigham and Emma probably came when Brigham's loyalty to Joseph led him to accept polygamy. Until Joseph complained about Emma's efforts to stop plural marriage, Brigham held his tongue and kept his feelings in check. After Joseph's death both Emma and Brigham contributed to the misunderstandings between them.

Brigham believed that his new role was to carry forth all that Joseph had taught him pertaining to the kingdom. His own journal and the writings of those who were closely associated with him indicate that he did so through frequent prayer. Brigham, often called "The Lion of the Lord," would become known in history as a great organizer and a highly competent administrator who usually had sound judgment and common sense.[32]

By September the Twelve were aware that Sidney Rigdon had been secretly ordaining "Prophets, Priests, & Kings," and claimed visions and revelations "at variance with those Given Prest. Joseph Smith."[33] On September 8 the Twelve excommunicated Rigdon, although William Marks spoke in his defense. In doing so, Marks sealed his own fate, for two days later he was dropped as a member of the High Council, although he retained his position as Stake President. Sidney Rigdon left for Pittsburgh. There he formed a "Church of Christ" and attacked polygamy, though he eventually instigated it within his own group. Only a few adherents remained after Rigdon's death in 1876.[34]

Emma stayed aloof from public debate over the question of leadership in Nauvoo. Only one fourthhand account linked her to Rigdon's cause. On September 12, 1844, Orson Hyde wrote to the Twelve from St. Louis that Rigdon had told a church member that he had talked with Emma the morning he left Nauvoo and she intended to go with him and give him Joseph's "new translation" of the Bible "and other important and sacred things."[35] Hyde's letter was full of gossip and hyperbole, and the story probably had been embellished.

A letter Emma wrote to a friend on October 18, 1844, indicated that she was attending to her own responsibilities. "I send by the stage twenty three bags, wishing brother Hollingshead to send some oats by the St[eam] B[oa]t Osprey as soon as is convenient. The Brick Store will be empty next week, and I would like well if You could find it advantageous to your interest to fill it with goods and groceries this fall, the rent will be low. I think it a good time to commence an establishment of that kind here now as there is a number of the merchants about to leave here soon." Expressing no hostility toward Brigham or the Quorum, she wrote, "My family are all in good health at present, and [the Twelve] are generaly well with the exception of Amasa Lyman who has been very sick, but is better now. My best respects to Your family and all our friends. Tell Sister Haywood I shall keep those shoes she gave to Mr. Smith as a memento both of her and my husband too, for I can never see them with[out] remembering them both."[36]

James Monroe, a young schoolteacher who lived with the Smith family, recorded the only known account of Emma's feelings about the succession to the presidency. His diary entry of April 24, 1845, reads, "My time has been occupied chiefly in conversing with Aunt Emma from whom I have obtained several new and interesting ideas concerning the organization and government of the church." Using an 1835 revelation[37] as the basis of her argument, Emma explained to Monroe, "Now as the Twelve have no power with regard to the government of the Church in the Stakes of Zion, but the High Council have all power, so it follows that on removal of the first President, the office would devolve upon the President of the High Council in Zion. . . . Mr.

Rigdon is not the proper successor of President Smith, being only his counselor, but Elder Marks should be the individual. . . . The Twelve . . . were
aware of these facts but acted differently."[38] Joseph had recommended in a
conference of the church on August 16, 1841, that "the time had come when
the Twelve should be called upon to stand in their place next to the First
Presidency, and attend to the settling of emigrants and the business of the
Church at the stakes."[39] Emma did not consider that announcement to be
tantamount to authority to become president of the church. Both Emma and
Marks believed that Joseph had abandoned plural marriage and meant to
remove it from the church at the time of his death. Knowing Brigham would
continue it, Emma supported William Marks. Polygamy was personally abhor-
rent to her, and she believed its abolition was necessary for the continuation of
the church. Unfortunately the church leadership would not come to that same
conclusion until 1890.

Meanwhile, an anonymous letter of August 19, 1844, to Emma brought
her into the effort to bring Joseph's and Hyrum's murderers to justice. "I have
been a strong Anti-Mormon but things has gone beyond humainity," the
writer told Emma. He said that Joseph H. Jackson had written a pamphlet "of
the most Slanderous nature" against the Mormons. "If you wish this man
exposed to the world as a notoreous villain you can have it done . . . he has
devulged things to me that would Sink him beneath the notice of every lowest
man."[40] It may have been this letter that prompted Emma and Mary to travel
to Quincy a few days later to see "what could be done to arrest the rascals who
had killed their husbands." One newspaper reporter did not believe the
women would be successful and "any attempt to bring them to justice will be
forcibly opposed by the Warsaw people."[41] The prediction was correct.

Governor Ford had made a special trip to Hancock County to examine
the slow-moving wheels of justice. One item of business on Ford's Nauvoo
agenda was to commission Brigham Young lieutenant general of the Nauvoo
Legion. Anticipating the event, it was probably on this day, September 27,
that Brigham sent a polite note to Emma requesting the use of one of Joseph's
horses, Joe Duncan, for the Legion parade. Emma asked her son Joseph to
prepare the horse. He rebelled at the request and reminded his mother that
the last time someone borrowed Joe Duncan he had overridden the animal.
Emma assured her son that Brigham Young would be careful with the horse
and only needed it for the two hours of the parade.

Joseph saddled Joe Duncan without further question and turned him over
to the messenger. Before long the same man came back and tersely informed
the lad that Mr. Young also wanted the animal in "full military housing . . .
including the . . . saddle, holsters and bridle." Resentment mounting, Joseph
complied. Four hours after the time Brigham had promised to return the
horse, Joseph caught sight of it racing along the river road, with Brigham's
clerk, George Q. Cannon, in the saddle. When the boy reported the scene to

his mother, Emma sent word that the horse had not been returned and she wanted it immediately. Another hour passed before Brigham's aide located the errant clerk and brought the horse home. Joe Duncan stood with legs splayed out, head drooping, and hair matted with heavy sweat. Tears streaked Joseph's face as he pulled the festive gear from the horse and sponged his coat with warm water. "I made a vow then and there . . . that never again would I put saddle or bridle upon him for Elder Young. Going to the house, I told Mother so, adding that if ever in the future she wished to lend one of our horses to that man she would have to get someone else to saddle it, for I would not do it."[42]

Meanwhile, dispute over the disposal of Joseph's real property and the payment of his debts continued. Emma wanted to preserve for herself and her family the inheritance that was rightfully theirs; Brigham wanted to preserve what rightfully belonged to the church. They were caught in the classic struggle over the disposal of a loved one's properties: Emma as widow and Brigham as successor each asserted dominion the other was unwilling to concede. The court replaced Emma as administratrix of Joseph's estate when she failed to post the bond required by law. Joseph W. Coolidge, who was also a creditor, inventoried the estate and started to process small claims. He sold various personal items in the estate, totaling about a thousand dollars, and paid funeral expenses and administrative costs. His settlement on behalf of Emma and her children was less than generous. She got her "household goods, two horses, two cows, her spinning wheels and one hundred and twenty-four dollars a year." Young Joseph said the family believed that while Coolidge "was, under ordinary circumstances, an honest man, in this matter was under the domination of others, [and Emma] was subjected . . . to a series of injustices at his hands and disagreeable experiences which became almost unbearable."[43] But Coolidge was actually dishonest. When he finally left Illinois after serving four years as a less than effective administrator, he apparently took with him some of the estate assets.[44] It became clear to Emma that no one else would look out for her interests.

Emma used the letter Joseph had written to her from the Iowa side of the river on June 23 to pursue her claims against the Twelve. Joseph had told her that Heber C. Kimball owed him a thousand dollars and named two others who owed him money as well. Kimball returned home after Joseph's death with thirteen hundred dollars in gold he had collected to pay Joseph's debts. The Twelve held a council to decide whether Emma should have the money. Kimball spoke up. "I want to pay Emma this money, and let her do as she pleases with it." William Clayton reported that when Kimball told her of the good feelings of the Twelve toward her, Emma seemed humble and kind. Brigham Young seemed to consider the money some sort of a gift.[45]

In the same letter Joseph also told Emma, "You may sell the Quincy Property—or any property that belongs to me . . . for your support and children & mother." But Brigham had the deed to the Quincy property, also known as the Cleveland farm. Brigham said she offered to trade the Bible containing Joseph's "new translation" for it. "She got the deed for the farm," he said, "but she was not ready yet to give up the Bible. She complained about her poor, little, fatherless children, and she kept up this whine until she got the farms she wanted . . . we gave her . . . the farm on the prarie by the burning ground."[46] The Quincy farm was Emma's to sell, and it must have rankled her to have to bargain with the Twelve for it. And nowhere did Brigham mention his refusal to let Emma's lawyer examine the papers concerning Joseph's estate only three days before Richards asked for the new translation. Surely that is why she refused to make the trade. She also felt a special "guardianship" over the Bible, for "it had been placed in her charge."[47]

Brigham said Emma "owned city property worth fifty thousand dollars." Joseph had deeded the Hugh White purchase to her before his death, but Brigham inflated its real value even at 1844–1845 prices. Joseph bought the one-hundred-twenty-three-acre plot in 1839 for five thousand dollars and divided it into thirty city blocks of four lots each. By the time he deeded it to Emma in July 1843, only twelve lots, the equivalent of three blocks, remained. Other property in her name at the time of her husband's death amounted to about sixteen city blocks.[48] She also owned six hundred fifty dollars' worth of personal property and five wells valued together at two hundred dollars. When she paid her taxes in 1847 her land was worth slightly over eight thousand dollars. By 1849 it was worth half of that.[49]

Brigham looked at Emma's holdings in terms of the equity the church so desperately needed and made his private judgments about her "wealth." But Emma was still responsible for approximately seventy thousand dollars of Joseph's debts. Neither Brigham nor Emma understood where the riches had gone, but Nauvoo had been built in a speculative economy. Five months before Joseph Smith's death Jacob Scott in Nauvoo wrote, "We confidently expect before long to witness the arrival of Saints from every country in Europe. And the time is not far distant when the *Arabians* will arrive with their tents & their camels & dromedaries, 'And *Etheopia* will soon stretch out her hands to God.' "[50] Such enthusiasm obscured the shaky financial base upon which Nauvoo's economy rested. Emma could not bring herself to leave the dream; Brigham believed he could take it with him. They both erred in assuming that Nauvoo could finance it.

15

Inherit the Legacy

October 1844–October 1845

While the ties between Emma and Brigham weakened, conflict between Brigham Young and William Marks sharpened. Marks had not endorsed the leadership of the Twelve. Emma had leased the Mansion House to Marks in August, retaining several rooms for her family.[1] When the new proprietor announced that he would give a ball on October 2, Brigham argued that such festivities were inappropriate when the floors were "still stained with the blood which flowed from Joseph and Hyrum, as their bodies lay in [the dining room] preparatory to burial."[2]

At the October conference the church members sustained "Brigham Young as president of the Quorum of the Twelve, as one of the Twelve and the First Presidency of the Church." The remaining church officers were approved, until John Smith moved that William Marks be sustained as President of the Nauvoo Stake. W. W. Phelps objected, arguing that Marks had acknowledged the authority of Rigdon over the Twelve. Brigham Young commented that Marks could be removed from office and still retain his membership. With two dissenting votes, William Marks was dismissed as Nauvoo Stake President, an office he had held since 1839.[3] Twice William Marks and his wife Rosannah appeared before the High Council to answer charges concerning their faith and lack of support of the Twelve but, contrary to popular belief, they were never excommunicated from the church.

Emma's own circumstances removed her from the incident with Marks. With her pregnancy approaching term, she decided to move her family back into the old Homestead house the week of November 4 to gain some measure of privacy.[4] At nine o'clock on the morning of November 17, 1844, four months past her fortieth birthday, Emma gave birth to a son. Old Mrs. Durfee, who professed some knowledge about everything, "intimated . . . that Joseph the prophet" had named the baby before he left for Carthage. He "was to be the David the Bible speaks of to rule over Israel forever."[5] Emma named the baby David Hyrum. Eliza Snow visited Emma, then composed a poem and published it in the *Times and Seasons:*

> Sinless as celestial spirits—
> Lovely as a morning flow'r,
> Comes the smiling infant stranger
> in an evil-omen'd hour.
>
> Thou may'st draw from love and kindness
> All a mother can bestow;
> But alas! on earth, a father
> You art distin'd not to know![6]

Perhaps in the birth of this child, fathered by the man they both had loved, the two women again found common ground. Emily Partridge also went to see Emma and the baby. "She was very gracious," Emily wrote, "for there was no Joseph to be jealous of then."[7]

The baby seemed to reflect the unsettled conditions of his birth. Oliver B. Huntington, who boarded at Emma's, remembered that when David was several weeks old, "as soon as it began to be dark at night, he would commence to cry and scream, and appeared to be afraid, and seemed as if he would go into fits. . . . Doctor Burnhisel and Emma, together, by medicine and management finally over came it in him."[8]

Dr. John M. Bernhisel boarded at the Mansion at the time. He was a competent physician with a medical degree from the University of Pennsylvania. He was one of the few who remained loyal to both Emma and Brigham Young, therefore remaining an impartial link between the two. Emma trusted him. She took the "Inspired Version" of the Bible from its secret hiding place under the false bottom of a blanket chest, and he spent weeks carefully copying Joseph's notes. Bernhisel passed many evenings talking with and instructing Emma's children.

Shortly after Joseph's death Emma had hired a twenty-seven-year-old woman, Lucy Messerve, to do the spinning for the family. A few months later Lucy became George A. Smith's plural wife. Knowing Emma's feelings about polygamy, she tried to keep her marriage secret. She later recalled, "[Emma] bore testimony to me that Mormonism was true as it came forth from the servant of the Lord, Joseph Smith, but . . . [said] the Twelve have made Bogus of it." According to Lucy, Emma admitted that plural wives were a reality in the church but "Joseph [had] taught [that] they were only sealed for eternity, they were not to live with them and have children, and now see. . . ." Lucy countered that she did not know what Emma was talking about.

"You do know," Emma retorted. "It's sticking out too plain." Lucy, no doubt, was pregnant. She reported her conversation with Emma to George A. Smith, who recounted another incident. He said he had gone to Joseph's home late one evening and found him washing his hands. "Joseph told him that one of his wives had just been confined and Emma was the Midwife and he had been assisting her." George A. told this to Lucy as proof "that the women were married for time" as well as eternity.[9] He implied that Emma knew that the child she helped deliver was Joseph's, but she may not have known. It is unlikely that Emma reconciled herself to plural marriage to the extent of delivering Joseph's child by another woman. Neither was Joseph so insensitive that he would expect that. Because children of plural marriages were concealed in a number of ways in Nauvoo, Emma could have acted as midwife, believing that the father was someone other than Joseph.[10]

Lucy Messerve Smith also related a conversation she overheard in the Smith home between two of Emma's children. During the winter of 1844–1845, Joseph was ill with fever, chills, and frequent nosebleeds. While he convalesced he often sat by Lucy's spinning wheel. One day he and Julia talked. "Julia was rehersing some of her mother's sayings," Lucy remembered. "There are two in this family," Joseph is said to have remarked, "that will be sorry for going against the Twelve as they do."[11]

Whether by Emma's choice or Brigham Young's, the social circle of the Twelve did not include her. She did not attend the Christmas party at Joseph Coolidge's as did Brigham, most of the Twelve, and their wives, nor was she present at the New Year's Day gathering at the home of Hiram and Sarah Kimball, where the conversation centered around the settlement of a "new country." As early as 1842 Joseph Smith had talked and prophesied of the church's movement to the Rocky Mountains. In February 1844 Joseph had met with the Twelve to choose a Western site for a new city.[12] The week following the party at the Kimballs' in January 1845, Brigham expanded on the discussion, and by March a small party of men left in search of a place for resettlement of the Mormon people.

Emma and Mary Smith were increasingly uneasy about the secret burial place of their husbands. The dirt basement of the Nauvoo House could not be a permanent resting place, for planned work on the building would disturb the graves. Sometime in the winter of 1844–1845 Emma and Mary decided to have the bodies moved. They agreed that the task should be accomplished under cover of darkness and set a time. Emma sent word to Mary that it had to be postponed, then for some unexplained reason proceeded at the scheduled time but neglected to tell Mary.

Mary found it difficult to sleep that night. Finally, around midnight, she wrapped a shawl around her shoulders and stepped outside. As she walked toward the river she recognized Emma, who stood supervising two men with shovels. Dimick and William Huntington, Jonathan Holmes, and Gilbert Goldsmith proceeded with the reburial. Mary stayed to oversee the rest of the process with Emma.[13] Joseph III remembered seeing the grave opened and watched as one of the men cut a lock of hair from his father's head and gave it to Emma. For the rest of her life she wore it in a locket.[14] About twenty-five paces from the southeast corner of the Homestead stood a small shed called the spring house. The men moved the structure, buried the two brothers side by side without disturbing the surrounding landscape, then placed the shed back over the graves.[15] Whether Emma's decision to move the bodies without including Mary was calculated or impulsive, Mary felt betrayed at not being told, and the incident became a wedge between the two women.

About this time newspapers published stories that several Mormon leaders had been ejected from the church and Emma Smith was soon to be among them. Accounts that she was "weak in the faith" were echoed in print across the country,[16] along with a rumor that Joseph Smith's widow would soon publish an exposé of Mormonism and its new leaders. In response to that rumor, the Twelve defended Emma in the *Times and Seasons.*

> [Emma] honored her husband while living, and she will never knowingly dishonor his good name while his martyred blood mingles with mother earth! Mrs. Smith is an honorable woman. . . . The very idea that so valuable and beloved a lady, could be coaxed into a fame of *disgrace* like the above, is as cruel and bloody as the assassination of her husband at Carthage.
>
> The fact is, the story must have been put in circulation to injure the Latter Day Saints; and as Mrs. Smith was one of them, to destroy or murder her reputation, and create division in the church.[17]

During the winter the legislators in Springfield attempted to repeal the Nauvoo charter. Almon W. Babbitt, an abrasive, impulsive man with some legal training, argued in vain before the legislature and on January 24 they voted two to one to repeal the charter. The action left Nauvoo without a city government, a judicial system, a militia, or legal protection. As Thomas Sharp began fanning old sparks of antagonism with his Warsaw *Signal,* Brigham Young organized the Nauvoo citizens for self-protection. The threat of mob violence increased and armed guards protected the church leaders' homes. Sometime that spring of 1845 the guard was expanded to include Emma and her family in the Homestead. Later reports by Joseph III and Samuel Smith's daughter Mary reveal that the Smiths regarded this action as hostile house arrest. Communication had disintegrated to the point that Brigham and Emma regarded one another with suspicion.[18]

A group designed to rid the city of undesirables called themselves the "whistling and whittling brigade." When an outsider became bothersome, he suddenly found himself surrounded by members of the brigade, whistling as they whittled, their jackknives and bowie knives passing precariously close to the victim's ears. Local people who were considered troublemakers received the same treatment. On March 12 William Marks said good-bye to a few friends and left Nauvoo. Brigham noted that he left "without being whittled out."[19]

Marks recalled his reasons for leaving. He claimed Joseph had asked for his help in ridding the church of polygamy. "I mentioned the circumstances of these conversations with Joseph, to many of the brethren, immediately after his death; but . . . my statement . . . was pronounced false by the Twelve and disbelieved. When I found that there was no chance to rid the church of that abominable sin, as I viewed it, I made my arrangements to leave Nauvoo."[20] Marks took his family to northern Illinois, but his life would again affect Emma's.

A month later the Nauvoo city police entertained at an evening party with a parody called "Father Marks' Return to Mormonism." Although Marks was gone from Nauvoo, he retained an unshakable faith in Joseph Smith and Mormonism. And contrary to later reports, he had never been a party to William Law's publication of the *Expositor* and other attempts to overthrow Joseph's leadership of the church, nor was Marks ever excommunicated from the church. A little over two weeks after Marks left, Brigham Young, the Twelve, and their families held a party at the Mansion House. The guests numbered one hundred forty, but no reference places Emma there.

One of Emma's concerns was the education of her children. In April she hired James Monroe as a private teacher for fifty cents a week. The class soon expanded to include John Taylor's children. Later in the spring Brigham Young also employed Monroe to teach, but at a different time of day.[21] James Monroe was a conscientious and well-respected instructor with considerable experience, yet he approached his new assignment with some apprehension. After his first day in the classroom he wrote, "I think I never felt my inability and incapacity of instructing children so much as I did today. . . . I sincerely pray that [the Lord] will enable me to do justice to the children of our lamented prophet." He then added, "I must own I have a selfish motive in view. . . . I think I shall not lose my reward for it in eternity."

Emma followed the scholastic progress of her children with interest, but some incidents took place that were not recounted to Emma. Although Julia was bright and learned easily, she had a streak of rebellion. When she and several other girls played during study time, James kept them after school and told them they would have to stay in the classroom until they made up all the time they had lost from their studies. At that, Julia stomped off into the next room and James overheard her complaining to someone, calling him "hard hearted" and saying he "had no more heart than a hog."

The day ended with Julia in tears and James missing a scheduled practice with his Legion unit—for which he was fined. When he returned to the Mansion that evening, feeling somewhat disgruntled, Julia sent word "that she was sorry for the way . . . she had acted." James sent for her and explained "that if she would . . . mind, behave herself and study in [the] future," he would let her come back into class. Furthermore, he would not report the incident to her mother. The schoolteacher did not record further trouble from his female scholar and her only absence occurred when she suffered from sunstroke. James reported that Julia grasped math quickly, "but Alexander don't seem to have any ambition at all," he said, "I must continue some way to excite it." Of young Joseph, James wrote: "He seems to be some different from most other boys, with more judgment, more manly and intellectual. I have great encouragements that he will make a very useful and highly talented man."

Oliver Huntington thought Joseph to be "very quick of understanding; and penetrating in discerning the feelings and thoughts of others. . . . He had a tender heart and uncommonly fine feeling. Knew how and when to grant a favour, and also how to receive one. Was very devout in all his actions and at all times and places, had the fear of God before his eyes." Oliver also noticed that "he was perfectly obedient . . . to his mother [and] tutor . . . and put great confidence in no one until he had well proven them. In short, he was the son of a prophet, and justly inherited his standing; and . . . his birthright."[22]

After William Smith arrived in Nauvoo on May 4, 1845, the subject of Joseph Smith III's "birthright" became another point of contention. William had been detained in the East for ten months after the death of his brothers because of his wife's heart ailment, "dropsy." Caroline had recovered enough to make the long journey but arrived at Emma's house dangerously ill.[23] While Emma nursed Caroline, William tried to retain his prominence in the church government. He had written to Brigham Young in August of 1844, petitioning the new leader for the office of presiding patriarch of the church.[24] Young had acknowledged William's right to that office at the October 1844 conference. On May 24, 1845, the Apostles ordained him presiding patriarch. Caroline died in Emma's home two days before her husband received his desired calling. William could not attend his wife's funeral or burial for the threats on his life became so intense that he had to stay hidden.

For Emma, Caroline's death came at an already difficult time. The trial of Joseph's assassins was in progress in Carthage. Nine men including Levi Williams, a minister; Jacob C. Davis, a state senator and attorney; William N. Grover, also an attorney; Mark Aldrich, captain of a Hancock County militia company; and Thomas C. Sharp, editor of the Warsaw *Signal*, faced murder charges, but when the trial ended all nine were acquitted.[25] Emma's husband

and his brother lay in an unmarked grave, while the men who killed them celebrated their freedom in the streets of Carthage. Brigham Young commented dryly that it was just what he had expected, even though "the court, attorneys, jury and bystanders [were] . . . all fully satisfied of their guilt."[26]

Thomas Ford sensed that his own name would long be linked to the death of the Mormon prophet and noted in his history of Illinois: "The author of this history feels degraded by the reflection that the humble governor of an obscure state, who would otherwise be forgotten in a few years, stands a fair chance, like Pilate and Herod, by their official connection with the true religion, of being dragged down to posterity with an immortal name, hitched on the memory of a miserable impostor."[27]

James Monroe, the schoolteacher for Emma's children, sometimes talked with William Smith about church issues when he recorded patriarchal blessings. William had decided that he should be president of the church. On the day the murder trial ended in Carthage, Monroe talked with Emma after he had dismissed the Smith children from school. He asked her opinion of William's new claims. Emma said William "talked well upon the subject and seemed to have correct principles." Monroe reminded her that William's character had been questionable. "It is rather difficult to expect a man to change his nature."

"It has been done," Emma replied, "and if a man wishes to change his course of conduct he should be encouraged."[28] She apparently had not heard the rumors that William had taken plural wives in Boston the previous year and had sanctioned others to follow suit. Brigham would disfellowship two of the men involved and tell William that there were ordinances that could not be administered by any person outside of Nauvoo. "Joseph said that the sealing power is always vested in one man . . . and that man is the president of the Church."[29]

Lucy Smith dreamed three times that her surviving son was already president of the church. As soon as a report of these "visions" reached Brigham Young, he dispatched Uncle John Smith and Cousin George A. Smith to persuade William to drop his claims, but to no avail. Two days later Brigham, the Twelve, and two bishops visited Lucy, who had previously supported the Twelve. They requested that William be there; he refused. Before leaving Mother Smith, Brigham composed a letter to William, explaining to him the bounds of his patriarchal responsibilities. The letter was cordial and to the point, and ended on a note of reconciliation: "We hope and trust there will be no feelings. . . . If you want peace so do we, and let us walk together in peace and help to build up the Kingdom. If this does not meet with your feeling brother William, write me again, or come and see me, and we will make all things right."[30] The letter was then read aloud. Brigham added a postscript saying that Mother Smith, her two daughters, and her son-in-law approved. Emma was not present at the discussion.

The June 30 visit with Lucy began a flutter of activity on the part of the church leaders to placate the Smiths and win their support. The Mormon people loved and revered the Smith family. William's bid for leadership probably made Brigham realize he could no longer ignore their concerns. Early in July 1845 Bishops Whitney and Miller gave a dinner in the Mansion for fifty of the Smith family, including seven widows, who were probably Emma, Mary, Levira, Agnes, Mother Smith, Mercy Thompson, and perhaps the widow of an uncle of the martyrs. The Twelve waited on the tables, serving the family members both food and kindness.[31]

Later that month the Twelve proposed to lease the Mansion House for three to five years and inquired as to the terms Emma might accept. Willard Richards reported that Emma vacillated about a decision, saying she might stay in Nauvoo and run the Mansion or might lease it out and move to Quincy. She did not lease the building to the Twelve at this time, but she did sell two blocks of land for five hundred fifty dollars to the trustees on August 2.[32] They invited Lucy Smith to inspect the recently purchased property and choose one block for herself and daughters. After careful inspection Lucy made her choice and requested "the Church build her a house like Brother Kimball's" fine one.[33] Owing to circumstances that developed in the next few months, Lucy never got her large, comfortable home, but Brigham did the best he could. He temporarily provided her with the spacious home of gunsmith Jonathan Browning. In April 1846 the church bought the small Joseph B. Noble residence and deeded it to Lucy.

Lucy had lived with or near Emma most of the seventeen years of Emma's and Joseph's marriage. She had seen her daughter-in-law respond to a variety of situations and had admired her. In her history, which she had dictated to Martha Corey the previous year, Lucy paid tribute to Emma. "I have never seen a woman in my life, who would endure every species of fatigue and hardship, from month to month, and from year to year, with that unflinching courage, zeal, and patience, which she has ever done; for I know that which she has had to endure—she has been tossed upon the ocean of uncertainty—she has breasted the storms of persecution, and buffeted the rage of men and devils, which would have borne down almost any other women."[34]

Lucy felt welcome in Emma's home but was, herself, independent by nature. Feeble as she was, she still desired a home of her own. With Samuel's daughter Mary as a companion, the two managed well. Emma's and Lucy's families would live in the vicinity.

Lawlessness had raged in and around Nauvoo since the time of the acquittal of Joseph's murderers and the repeal of the Nauvoo charter. The town became prey for petty criminals and fugitives. On the evening of September 9 a group of anti-Mormons were meeting in a home south of Warsaw to plan their strategy when a sudden gunshot shattered a window. No one was injured, but they blamed the incident on Mormons.

Soon men with blackened faces howled in nightly "wolf hunts," then descended on Mormon farms. Homes and crops went up in flames while mobs whipped the owners, tied to trees and fences. Before the week was out, marauders had burned forty-four Mormon buildings—barns, homes, and sheds. Brigham ordered all church members in outlying areas to gather into the city.

Hancock County sheriff Jacob Backenstos, described as "an active, energetic man, rather warlike in aspect, with a moustache on his upper lip . . . a man of courage,"[35] called for volunteers in Warsaw to halt the burning raids but could not find a single man willing to stop the plunder. When the citizens of Carthage learned of his attempt to raise a posse, they expelled him from town. He left in such haste that his family stayed behind and were harassed and abused by the house burners. The sheriff had asked Brigham for a posse earlier, but Brigham's policy was to let the mobs burn the houses "until the surrounding counties should be convinced that we were not the aggressors."[36] Now, with his life threatened, Sheriff Backenstos requested a posse of two thousand Nauvoo Legionnaires. Brigham finally responded. Although the number of men is in question, Backenstos had a small army. The Mormons retaliated with force. This time when houses went up in flames, they belonged to gentiles, and Mormons applied the torch.[37] "Napoleon Backenstos," the Warsaw *Signal* called the sheriff, and then in a frenzied tirade cried for the anti-Mormons to drive the Mormons out.

An exchange of letters between Brigham Young and Jacob Backenstos confirms Brigham's efforts to rein the sheriff in and defend the Mormons rather than attack. He did not want to corner the mob, for he knew they would fight to the death. He preferred to take the area as peacefully as possible, but he still warned his people that "if the mob come . . . give them *the cold lead* or obey the Sheriff's council."[38] Western Illinois teetered on the edge of civil war.

For months church leaders had talked of leaving Illinois. The two most likely places seemed the Great Basin in the Rocky Mountains and Vancouver Island in the Oregon Territory. On September 9 Brigham Young and the Twelve had decided that their only choice for survival as a church was to go west—and soon. On October 1, 1845, church leaders met with Stephen Douglas and General J. J. Hardin at the home of John Taylor and informed them of the plan. Relieved that the Mormons would go without being ordered out, Hardin wholeheartedly offered his help.[39] Brigham promised that if they could harvest their crops and have time to sell their property the Mormons would leave in the spring. The governor's committee warned: "Should you not do so . . . the end will be your expulsion from the state."[40]

Prior to the meeting with Douglas and Hardin, William Smith had renewed his demand for leadership of the church. He had written letters arguing that young Joseph was the successor contemplated by his father, and maintaining that the Twelve held their position of leadership only until the lad became of sufficient age to take his proper place.[41] Lucy Smith remembered a patriarchal blessing that her husband had given Joseph III when he was a small child in Kirtland. Not recorded until Martha Coray wrote it down for Lucy that summer of 1845, it said in part, "You shall have power to carry out all that your Father shall leave undone when you become of age."[42] In August William Smith published a pamphlet declaring that he should be guardian of the church and hold the presidency in trust for the young heir. At the fall conference on October 6 William Smith was dropped from the Quorum of the Twelve on the grounds that he was "an aspiring man" who planned to "uproot and undermine the legal Presidency of the Church" and "his doctrine and conduct" had been "unsavory." From a number of sources, it is clear that Joseph III's future role in the church was not at issue. Brigham would acknowledge that the sons of Joseph should one day have leadership positions in the church.[43]

Brigham feared for the safety of young Joseph and the Smith family. He told one church member "not to talk . . . of the possibility of young Joseph leading the church . . . for if the people . . . in Illinois thought that the saints expected that young Joseph Smith would be the head of the church . . . talk of such a thing would be like taking a knife and cutting the throats of the family."[44]

Two days after William's removal from the Quorum of the Twelve, Lucy Smith publicly supported Brigham Young. Almost five thousand people attended conference in the nearly completed temple. Brigham announced that the church would move west and the members should prepare for a migration. In response Lucy said, "If so be the rest of my children go with you, (and would to God they may all go), they will not go without me."[45]

Brigham responded with enthusiasm to Lucy's decision, then shifted to another topic. Joseph had built a family tomb near the temple. Brigham vowed to "petition sister Emma in the name of Israel's God, to let us deposit the remains of Joseph according as he commanded us. And if she will not consent to it, our garments are clear . . . when he awakes in the morning of the resurrection . . . the sin shall be upon her head, not ours."[46] His words suggest that Emma was not present, but the statement would have been repeated to her, awakening her fears that Joseph's grave might be robbed.

Sometime during the next week Brigham Young called William Smith to appear before the High Council. On his way to the meeting, William took his two daughters, Mary Jane and Caroline, to his mother. Many years after that night, Mary Bailey Smith recalled the experience: "Uncle William wore a large circular cloak . . . and a broad brimed slouch hat, drawn well down over his face, so as to conceal as much as possible his features as he suspected that he might be assassinated before he reached the hall. He told his mother to look after the children until he came back and if he never came back to care for them the best she could . . . my grandmother remained by the door to wait his return and I nestled beside her and laid my head upon her knee and went to sleep."[47] William returned sometime after midnight. The following Sunday, October 19, William Smith was "excommunicated by unanimous vote."[48]

William had been living in the Mansion and now he moved his mother, Mary Bailey, and two of his sisters, with their husbands (Lucy and Arthur Millikin and Katherine and Jenkins Salisbury), into the vacated William Marks home with him. Mary remembered that he was discouraged from public speaking when he went to the grove one morning and found the benches smeared with outhouse refuse. His house was guarded closely, according to Mary. "I can distinctly remember when the door was opened the lights would shine on the pistols and knives in the belts of the men standing each side of the door and under the trees in the yard."[49] A friend, William Hickman, helped William get out of the house unseen and accompanied him to the northern border of Iowa. From there William made his way back downriver to St. Louis.

He had expected Emma to support his claims against the Twelve and was affronted when she would not. From St. Louis he wrote, "Judge my serprise Emma when you now refuse to help me to reform the Church after the many times I have talked with you in this subject and asked what I should do to save my fathers family and all my friends and the answer was for me to come out and proclame against the spiritual wife doctrine [and] the urserpation of the 12. Now Emma I have done it and all hell is in rage and every lie that can be set on foot is on hand and you believe them."[50]

Emma's hope that William would change had evaporated. Since his public speech favoring plural marriage three months earlier, area newspapers accused him of practicing the "doctrine with an English girl in his family."[51] Emma had opposed Brigham over polygamy and would not now encourage William Smith. She refused to let her son be used as a pawn to forward someone else's personal ambitions. William's letter concluded with a defense of his own purity, and he swore he would never look at another woman again. His statement did not move Emma.

At this time James Arlington Bennet visited Emma. This was their first meeting, but Emma greeted him as Joseph's friend, not knowing he would use her name in a scheme that would adversely affect her reputation.

16

The *Sun* Casts a Shadow

Winter 1845–1846

Two years before his death, Joseph had been impressed with James Arlington Bennet's friendly writings about the Mormons. In June 1842 he had sent Willard Richards to request his help in stemming the unfavorable publicity directed toward the church. Sight unseen, the prophet conferred upon Bennet the title of inspector general of the Nauvoo Legion and awarded him an LLD degree from the University of Nauvoo, a dubious honor since the university never existed. When Joseph wrote to Bennet in September 1842 he explained that the honors had come solely on the recommendation of John C. Bennett.[1]

In August of the next year Brigham Young visited Bennet in New York and baptized him in the Atlantic Ocean, but Bennet downplayed the occasion in a subsequent letter to Joseph. "You are no doubt already aware that I have had a most interesting visit from . . . B. Young, with whom I have had a glorious frolic in the clear blue ocean." Bennet did not want his church membership made public. "It can be shown that a commission in the Legion was a *Herald* hoax, coined for the fun of it by me . . . in short, I expect to be yet, through your influence, governor of the State of Illinois."[2] Confident of Bennet's political prowess, Joseph had asked him to be his vice-presidential candidate, but the wily Easterner saw the futility of that campaign and claimed to be constitutionally ineligible by reason of foreign birth. Believing that no one would buy books by an American author, Bennet had posed as Irish-born to further sales of his manual on bookkeeping even though his parents had immigrated to America before his birth. He kept up a correspondence with Joseph until the prophet's death; and Emma wrote at least once to his wife.[3]

Two months after Joseph's death Bennet decided to seek a position of leadership in the church. On August 20 he wrote to Willard Richards that

Joseph and Hyrum had appeared to him in a vision. He described a grandiose spectacle of star-studded crowns, miters, seals, and an angel who "came forward and said to me *Kneel* which I did in great fear (which is contrary to any standard of mine) he placed on my head the crown of 30 stars . . . these dreams . . . have troubled me much and have almost moved me to go to Nauvoo."⁴ Young and the Twelve sent no invitation. By the next June Bennet was more explicit. He wrote to Willard Richards: "I feel very confident that if I were at Nauvoo I could reorganize the Legion & put it into such a state of defence, as would bid defience to any *MOB* that might be brought against it." He wanted to use the Legion to reenact Napoleon's battles. His "frolic in the ocean" with Brigham Young took on new meaning as he saw a way for it to serve his purpose. He wrote, "Brother Young's Blessing when naked in the Atlantic Ocean is now coming over me like a spell—[Brigham] said 'You Shall Conquer to your hearts desire' Doctor! It is neither ambition nor worldly glory that now moves me—It is inspiration in the Cause of the Saints. I will receive a commission from no Civil power—it must come from Heaven." Not understanding Brigham Young's propensity for handling his own affairs, Bennet reported that he had already written to President Sam Houston of the Texas Territory and asked for asylum for the Saints. Houston replied "that he would receive the 'Mormon Legion' as armed emigrants, with open arms . . . 'I am no bigot.' "⁵

Brigham Young's patience with Bennet was wearing thin. "This wild spirit of ambition," he commented, "has repeatedly manifested itself to us by many communications received from various sources. Suggesting schemes of blood and empire, as if the work of the Lord was intended for personal aggrandisement."⁶ Unaware of Brigham's displeasure, Bennet wrote that he had offered the Nauvoo Legion's services to the President of the United States as volunteers to defend Texas against the Mexicans,⁷ then he arrived in Nauvoo unexpectedly on October 20. He toured the temple, met with the Twelve, and discussed the Western plans, but made an untimely departure from Nauvoo. In a letter to President Young he explained, ". . . if you could appreciate the State of my health, you would not censure me for [leaving], as I was puking all round the City every hour I remained in it."⁸ Just before his abrupt exit Bennet had visited Emma.

Six weeks later, on December 9, 1845, an acid letter, allegedly signed by Emma Smith, appeared in the New York *Sun*. Editorial comment preceding the letter announced that it came by "private conveyance" from Mrs. Smith, widow of the Mormon prophet.

Nauvoo, Ill., Nov. 20th 1845

To the Editor of the New York Sun:

Sir:—I hope to be excused for addressing, for the first time in my life, a letter to the Editor of a newspaper, and this I have been induced to do, from seeing the letters of Gen. Arlington Bennett, published in the newspapers, urging the Mormon people to remove to the Pacific Ocean, and advocating the cause of the Tyrants, who have seized on the government of the Mormon Church. This church, such as it is, was formed by my lamented husband who was martyred for its sake, and whether true or false, has laid down his life for its belief!

I am left here, sir, with a family of children to attend to, without any means of giving them an education, *for there is not a school in the city,* nor is it intended there shall be any here, or at any other place, where the men who now govern this infatuated, simple-minded people, have sway. I have not the least objection that these petty tyrants remove to California, or at any other remote place, out of the world if they wish; for they will never be of any service to the Mormons, or the human family, no matter where they go. Their object is to keep the people over whom they rule in the greatest ignorance, and most abject religious bondage, and if these poor, confiding creatures remove with them, they will die in the wilderness! The laws of the United States are quite good enough for me and my children, and my settled intention is to remain where I am, take care of my property, and if I cannot educate my children here, send them to New York or New England for that purpose. Many of the Mormons will, no doubt, remove in the Spring, and many more will remain here; and nothing would give me greater pleasure than to have a *mixed* Society in Nauvoo; as in other cities, and all exclusive religious distinctions abolished.

I must now say, that I have never for a moment believed in what my husband called his apparitions and revelations, as I thought him laboring under a diseased mind; yet they may all be true, as a Prophet is seldom without credence or honor, excepting in his own family or country, but as my conviction is to the contrary, I shall educate my children in a different faith, and teach them to obey and reverance the laws and institutions of their country. Shall I not, sir, be protected in these resolutions against the annoyance of the men I now oppose, for they will no doubt seek my life?

What object Gen. Arlington Bennett has in advocating the cause of these petty tyrants, I am not able to understand, for he assured me, when at my house, that he had not the smallest intention of connecting himself in any manner with them, much less removing with them to the Pacific Ocean. But this is a strange world, and I would not be surprised if they had offered to anoint and crown him King or Emperor in the West! As I have something more to say, I will take the liberty to write you another letter.

With great respect,
I am, sir, your humble serv't

EMMA SMITH[9]

The editor commented briefly on the letter and added that General James Arlington Bennet of New York "pronounces it genuine." Emma's reaction was immediate. Eleven days after this issue of the *Sun* was off the press, Emma fired a letter to Bennet at Long Island.

General Bennett, Sir: The apology I have to offer for addressing you at this time is the unexpected appearance of a letter published in the New York *Sun* of Tuesday Morning, December 9. I never was more confounded with a misrepresentation than I am with that letter, and I am greatly perplexed that *you* should entertain the *impression* that the document should be a genuine production of mine. How could you believe me capable of so much treachery, as to violate the confidence reposed in me, and bring your name before the public in the manner that letter represents? If you thought I had committed such a breach of trust, you certainly valued my integrity much less than I did yours. Should you be now satisfied that I am not unworthy of your confidence you will please give me your opinion, if any you have formed, as to what quarter I am to look for the author of that forgery. By so doing you will greatly increase my obligations.

Yours with great respect,

Emma Smith[10]

Apparently John Bernhisel thought a private letter was not sufficient, for on December 27 he borrowed a copy of the *Sun* from Heber C. Kimball's office and presumably went to Emma with it.[11] Three days later Emma wrote:

"To the Editor of the New York Sun; Sir: I wish to inform you, and the public through your paper, that the letter published Tuesday morning, December 9th, is a forgery, the whole of it, and I hope that this notice will put a stop to all such communications.

Emma Smith.

Curiously, this denial never appeared in the *Sun* but was printed in the next issue of the *Times and Seasons*, dated January 15, 1846. Brigham Young, Heber C. Kimball, Orson Hyde, Parley P. Pratt, and Joseph Young discussed the whole matter in a council meeting and concluded Bennet was the true author of the letter.[12]

Why would Bennet use Emma in such a way? On the eighteenth of November 1845 he wrote to Young and Richards from New York. "Since I have been here I have endeavoured to place the Nauvoo affairs on the best foundation I could." He said his efforts had been met with indignation from the "Anties" and "priests & their adherents." He reported that he had met with Emma before leaving Nauvoo and had pretended to be against the Twelve so she would confide in him.[13] He believed that she had lost all favor with the Twelve and would eventually be cut off from the church, yet the Eastern press had been quite favorable to her and would consider her a reliable source of information. In Bennet's view, a public exchange of letters with Emma would establish a forum enabling him to put "the Nauvoo affairs on the best foundation" possible. He clearly intended to continue until he exhausted Emma as a tool, for the last line of the letter in question states: "As I have something more to say, I will take the liberty to write you another letter."

Perhaps pressure from his friends in New York was beginning to wear on Bennet and he sought a way to salvage his reputation. In that light, the more crucial paragraph in the letter is the last one, for coming from the respected Emma Smith was the statement: "What object Gen. Arlington Bennett has in advocating the cause of these petty tyrants, I am not able to understand, for he assured me, when at my house, that he had not the smallest intention of connecting himself in any manner with them, much less removing with them to the Pacific Ocean." With a stroke of the pen, Bennet publicly disassociated himself from the Mormons. At the same time he had a base for future dialogue with the *Sun* and a reason to speak out in favor of the church and its leaders as he countered "Emma's" letter.

Because the *Sun* editors were familiar with Bennet's handwriting and style, he most likely had an accomplice write the "Emma" letter. On December 19 the *Sun* carried his reply to the "Emma" letter. He stated that the letter either came from Emma or "some person in her confidence," then argued impressively for the church, praised Orson Pratt, defended the previous state of education in the community, and lauded Joseph Smith and the truthfulness of his revelations.[14]

Word of Brigham Young's displeasure must finally have reached Bennet, and he felt obligated to publish in the *Sun* the private letter Emma had written to him nearly two months earlier. With it, he offered this explanation: "The following letter is offered for publication in strict justice to Mrs. Emma Smith of Nauvoo, who appears to have no knowledge of the author of the letter published by you . . . in her name. . . . From this letter I am fully persuaded that the lady is incapable of betraying any confidence reposed in her,—She must look for its author among some of the seceders from the Mormon Church."[15]

Brigham Young and the Twelve had had enough of James Arlington Bennet and his schemes. But Bennet tried at least twice more to reestablish a relationship with Brigham. In 1851 Bennet wrote to him, "Your people did wrong to abuse me some years ago, for, what I wrote went to the praise of the Saints—I never wrote the paper purporting to have come from Mrs. Smith, that was written among the Methodest Priests at the Book Establishment of the Harper who are no better than they ought to be."[16] Interestingly, it was Harper's who had printed Bennet's bookkeeping manual. If any truth supported his allegation, the "Methodest Priests" most certainly got the information directly from their client.

Emma, too, saw through Bennet and seemed to be aware of his treachery toward her. When a letter of doubtful authorship arrived at the Mansion House in January 1870, Emma forwarded it to Joseph III, with this comment: "If I knew old Gen James Arlington Bennet was yet living, and I never heard of his dieing, I should believe the letter came direct from him. . . . Well now do not take it for granted that it is from that old arch hypocrite for it is only some of my disagreeable impressions, that will come sometimes unbidden, when I see such a guady cloak over any thing as the letter was over it."[17]

One of the prime efforts of the church leaders since Joseph's death had been to complete both the temple and the Nauvoo House. Emma listened to the workers across the street as the walls inched up to their full height. Then, with the announcement of the Western move, the temple became the building priority in the city and the Nauvoo House was left a roofless shell. To the restless anti-Mormons, the work on the temple meant duplicity on the part of the Mormons. If they promised to leave in the spring, why would they continue to build the temple? Government troops, aided by willing Hancock County locals, stepped up harassment of citizens in and around Nauvoo.[18] For Mormons, the completion of the temple meant they could receive the long-awaited endowment to which so few had had access previously.

Emma's children surveyed the work with interest. "I was over every foot of [the] building while it was being formed," Joseph remembered. "I stood by the workmen when with hammers and chisels they fashioned and polished the massive pieces which formed the outer wall from cellar to roof. . . . I watched the pillars grow from their moon-shaped pedestals to their star- and sun-crowned capitals, and the roof from its eaves to the gilded angel that swung at the top of the spire."[19]

By the tenth of December the upper rooms of the temple had been dedicated and temple ordinances were begun. Among the first forty were the Twelve and their wives and John Bernhisel, Reynolds Cahoon, William Clayton, Lucy Smith, Agnes Coolbrith Smith, Mary Fielding Smith, and her sister, Mercy Thompson.[20] Hundreds of church members donned sacred robes, received their endowments, and had marriages solemnized for eternity. The sessions went on day and night.

According to church records, Emma was never present in the temple. She had driven to the temple grounds with Joseph on many occasions and had appraised tithing that helped finance the building. The Relief Society over which she had presided began because women wanted to contribute to the effort. To many, the temple represented the final star in the crown of Joseph's prophetic reign. Perhaps Brigham Young and the Twelve had not invited Emma to participate in the ceremonies, or she may have avoided the temple knowing that Brigham intended to resolemnize and expand all the sealing ordinances to include polygamous unions since 1841. This he began in January 1846.

On January 29, 1846, Brigham received a disturbing letter from a church member in the East, Samuel Brannen, who told him of government plans to send troops to intercept the Mormons on their move west and confiscate firearms on the pretense that church members were going to join another nation. James Arlington Bennet's inflammatory letters to various government leaders and newspapers had caused the reaction.[21] This news came immediately after Brigham learned that some of Governor Ford's troops were searching the city for the leaders of the church with plans to arrest them.

On February 2, 1846, the Twelve, trustees, and a few others agreed that it was imperative to leave as soon as possible before government officials in the East were aware of their movements.[22] Brigham counseled the people to have everything ready to leave on four hours' notice. Those who could leave early were to do so. The city swarmed with people making preparations, selling, buying, and trading, and building wagons. Nauvoo became a "vast mechanic shop."

On February 6, 1846, the first wagons crossed the ice-choked Mississippi on skiffs under the supervision of the Nauvoo police. One flatboat nearly met disaster when "a filthy wicked man squirted some tobacco juice into the eyes of one of the oxen attached to Thomas Grover's wagon." The oxen plunged into the river. No one lost his life in the cold, swift current, but both oxen drowned and some of the wagon contents floated away; the rest were drenched and damaged. It would take a miracle to get the thousands of Mormons out of Nauvoo under such conditions.

The miracle came. A few days later the temperature plunged and the river froze solid. Wagons rolled over the bridge of ice by the hundreds and their occupants set up camp along Sugar Creek, nine miles into Iowa. But, in the rush to get across, many families left with inadequate provisions and the few who were prepared found their own families suffered as they shared food and shelter.

Wilford Woodruff called on Emma before he left, and talked freely and cordially. His concern for her well-being and safety touched Emma. She had had the rough oak from the box that carried Joseph's body from Carthage to the Mansion cut into cane-size strips and made a present of one of them to Woodruff, along with a pair of white cotton gloves. To his wife, Phoebe, she gave a handkerchief.

A visit from Heber C. Kimball did not end so cordially. He had been appointed to persuade her to go with the church. For Joseph's other wives, a similar offer meant help and security through marriage. Brigham Young had

married eight of Joseph's wives and Heber Kimball married at least five. Other
wives wed various church leaders. These marriages were performed "for time
only" as the women were sealed to Joseph "for eternity."[23] The only source
that suggests anyone in the church proposed to Emma comes through the
recollections of her family. "A certain red-haired elder came to Emma to plead
with her to take her family and go West. . . . He proposed marriage and
finally even used threats and said Emma would come to the time when she
would kneel to him and she said, 'Well, if I do it will be the first red-headed
Brighamite I ever bowed to.' "[24] Neither Brigham nor Heber C. Kimball had
red hair, but whoever the "red-haired elder" may have been, he didn't record
the rebuff.

In this light, Heber C. Kimball's mission may have been to offer Emma
assistance if she would move with the church. Benjamin F. Johnson, who
accompanied Kimball, remembered, ". . . nearly all night we labored with
her, and all we could learn was that she was willing to go with the Church on
condition she could be the leading Spirit. So we left her, and she did lead all
who would follow her so long as she lived."[25] Benjamin Johnson's choice of
words is misleading. If she had wanted to *head* the church, surely Johnson
would have plainly said so. Emma most likely said that she would go with the
church only if they abandoned plural marriage. In the eyes of Benjamin Johnson, for her to suggest doctrinal influence would have seemed an outrageous
attempt to lead the brethren.

Brigham Young would comment, "In Joseph's day she tried to throw me,
br. Heber, br. Willard Richards and the Twelve Apostles out of the Church,
and tried to distroy the whole church, and I know it."[26] Brigham made this
remark in 1863, and it reflects his anger at her opposition to plural marriage.
Emma had not used her position as Relief Society president as a springboard to
full church leadership. Besides, Brigham Young had effectively removed the
Relief Society organization from the church a year earlier.[27]

One church member who went west contemplated Emma's circumstances. Aroet L. Hale wrote in his journal: "If Emma had the right cours[e]
taken with her she would have com[e] to these valleys."[28]

Before Brigham crossed the river he sent for young Joseph to come to his
house. When the lad arrived, Brigham presented him with a small dueling
pistol. Joseph said of the gesture, "There were those who . . . suggested that
the weapon was given me with the idea in mind that I might possibly shoot
myself with it by accident, and thus rid the group of a possible annoyance in
after years. However, I never credited Elder Young with contemplating any
such exigency . . . I accepted the gift as an exhibition of good will." But the
gun proved to be dangerous. Because of its hair trigger, Joseph nearly wounded
himself with it twice. Emma finally forbade him to use it, so he traded it to his
Uncle Arthur Millikin, who threw it away after he barely missed shooting one
of his children when the gun went off accidentally.

Emma was further frustrated when George A. Smith gave her son a bowie knife with an eight- or nine-inch blade. The "Arkansas toothpick," as Joseph called it, was razor sharp and came with a belt scabbard. His first thought was that it was heavy enough to cut kindling for his mother. When he showed the gift to Emma she made no attempt to conceal her disgust.

"Pshaw! Why couldn't he have given you something useful?"

"Well, Mother, you can use this for cutting bread or for other things about the kitchen, can't you?"

"Joseph, it is too big and clumsy for such work," she told him.

Not especially enamored with the gift himself, Joseph replied, "I'll try to trade it to John Huntington for something we can use."

The boy returned from John Huntington's workshop with an extra-large cherry rolling pin and presented it to his mother. Emma remarked, "Now *that* is something useful."

Newel K. Whitney also called Joseph to his home to give him a beautiful writing desk.

"Elder Young and George A. have given you weapons of war," he told Joseph, "but the pen is mightier than the sword."[29]

Brigham Young and his family left Nauvoo on February 16. His wife Mary Ann stopped by to say a final farewell to Emma and to give her some dishes and housewares she was unable to take along. Other women did the same.[30] Emma offered to buy other household goods and traded or sold some of her own belongings that she knew would be useful to departing friends. But when Emma tried to do business with church leaders the transaction turned into conflict. The Saints in England had sent Emma and Joseph each a fine black wool cloak. When Heber C. Kimball wanted to buy the cloaks for himself and Vilate, a misunderstanding developed. He got Emma's cloak, but when he sent Joseph Heywood back across the river for Joseph's, Emma "said she would not give up the Cloak," and an argument developed. Kimball had apparently traded a bed, some chairs, and some cash for the cloaks. Heywood reported to Kimball that Emma said "she had been badly treated & intimated . . . that she would see you all damned before she would give up his [Joseph's] cloak to . . . an apostle. [She] said it would be settled at the Day of judgement—she knew where she stood."[31] Although Heywood usually tried to describe his dealings with Emma in fair and unbiased terms, he let his own frustrations color this encounter. For instance, he said Emma *intimated* that "she would see you all damned." The phrase, therefore, was Heywood's own interpretation of Emma's words.

Brigham Young had assigned Joseph L. Heywood, Almon W. Babbitt, John S. Fullmer, and John Bernhisel to stay in Nauvoo as agents for the church.[32] Their assignment was to sell land left by church members, to oversee the sale of church property and transact church business within the city. All the men were qualified for their task professionally but differed markedly in their ability to deal with people, particularly with Emma. John S. Fullmer had little contact with Emma in his new role, but Bernhisel continued to board at the Mansion and maintained his cordial friendship with her. Heywood was an intelligent, educated man with a tall, rather slender frame, a kind manner, and a sense of humor. He was usually considerate to Emma.[33]

Almon Babbitt's air, on the other hand, bordered on the pompous. Early in the Kirtland period Joseph had brought charges against him in the High Council for not keeping the word of wisdom. Babbitt's defense was that he was only following Joseph's example.[34] He later accused Joseph of extravagance for buying clothes for Emma and himself in Washington shortly after his escape from the Liberty jail. The following year Joseph disfellowshipped him after learning he was discouraging church members from gathering in Nauvoo.[35] Babbitt had earned a law degree from the state university at Cincinnati and eventually qualified for licenses to practice in six states. In 1843 Joseph's need for lawyers forced a reconciliation. Babbitt provided Joseph with legal advice that resulted in the destruction of the *Expositor*, then he refused to help when Joseph was jailed in Carthage, saying, "You are too late. I am already engaged on the other side."[36]

Either Brigham Young was not aware of Babbitt's propensity for alienating those around him or, like Joseph before him, he overlooked his faults because he needed his legal knowledge. In the future Brigham would have his own falling out with Babbitt and the rift would become so widely known that, when Indians killed Babbitt on the Western plains in 1856, Eastern newspapers erroneously reported that Brigham had ordered him killed.[37]

In the meantime, Emma assumed that because these men represented the Twelve they acted on direct orders from Brigham. And Brigham, his relationship with Emma strained at best, did not bother to separate the inflammatory rhetoric of Babbitt's letters from the less dramatic probabilities. Babbitt would make Brigham's requests to Emma sound abrupt and thoughtless, and her responses to him selfish and defensive.

17

War in Nauvoo

February–December 1846

Publication of the New York *Sun* letter prompted further insinuations that Emma Smith opposed the Twelve or had lost faith. Other newspapers used the story against the church as did men who challenged Brigham Young's leadership. Sidney Rigdon, William Smith, and fifteen others had led their followers into nearby states. Lyman Wight believed Joseph III to be the eventual leader and set up a colony in Texas. Emma dismissed Wight as a "disgrace to the community,"[1] and the rest she ignored.

James J. Strang decided not to ignore Emma and used the New York *Sun* letter to strengthen his position. Strang had been in the church little more than four months when Joseph died. He had traveled to Wisconsin, at Joseph's request, to scout the area for a possible location for a stake. After Joseph's death he produced a letter appointing him successor. He claimed Joseph had written it on June 18, 1844, less than a week before the martyrdom. It has been judged a forgery by those familiar with Joseph's handwriting and style, but Strang would eventually attract some two thousand followers. On February 11, 1846, he wrote to Emma, "I was not a little sorry to see the letter . . . by you . . . in the NY Sun—The many evil deeds done by those who usurp authority in the Church have shaken the faith of thousands, and it is not singular that your heart should be steeled against men who not only teach the abominable things now taught and practiced in Nauvoo but are all so ready to rob and plunder the widows and orphans of their benefactors." Strang offered to help Emma and assured her that he would "never teach such doctrines that it will be necessary to abolish schools in order to keep up the church." Finally he got to his main point: "Now Sister . . . if you intend to remain in

Nauvoo, you cannot well imagine how much I should rejoice in your full and hearty cooperation in my efforts for the regulation and salvation of the city."[2]

Emma answered Strang through John Bernhisel, who merely sent him a copy of her denial of authorship of the *Sun* letter. The matter would probably have ended there had William Smith not returned to Nauvoo. Strang had also written Mother Smith. William pored over both letters, discussed them with Emma and his mother, then investigated Strang's claims. On the first of March he sent separate petitions to the Twelve and to Strang.

Of the Twelve he demanded that they publish a statement recognizing his right as patriarch, return the Smith family to proper standing in the church, and provide them with an inheritance. He also wanted the Twelve to return to their place and "repent fourfold." With a wave of the olive branch, he closed: "If . . . they will grant me the above request, all warfare shall cease from this hour on my part, hatchet handle and all buried forever . . . and my influence shall be with all my energies to sustain the organization."[3]

To Strang he reported that he had talked with Emma and asked her what she knew of Strang's appointment by Joseph. He said that Emma remembered Joseph receiving a letter from him. "Hyrum was present . . . at first Joseph thought all was not right . . . but Hyrum thought otherwise. They talked over matters a while and came to the conclusion that Joseph would write a letter." William did not say that Emma knew the content or that she supported Strang, but he claimed "the whole Smith family of the Joseph stock join in sustaining J. J. Strang." He then added a postscript to that effect signed by William, his mother, his three sisters, and two brothers-in-law.[4] Katherine Salisbury, William's sister, later denied that she signed the letter, suggesting William manipulated his family members. Emma's name is conspicuous by its absence. William would later tell Strang that Emma would not "give her name and testimony to your appointment" and advised him that to pressure her would "most ashuredly . . . drive them further from the church." One of Strang's missionaries reported to a Cincinnati newspaper that "Emma . . . and her son, Joseph . . . acknowledge Strang as the Lord's annointed." Perhaps the persistent rumor that "all the Smith family" supported Strang was the claim that attracted William Marks to that fold. By April he had attended conference in Voree, Wisconsin,[5] and become bishop of that church. Although Marks would have problems with Strang, he would become an Apostle and counselor to him in August 1847.

In the meantime, Strang baited William Smith by offering him a coveted position as patriarch if William brought with him his mother, with the mummies and papyrus, together with the bodies of Joseph and Hyrum.[6] William realized he could not move his brothers' bodies without alienating Emma, but he tried to manage the rest. In June Strang's Voree *Herald* declared: "Our beloved brother Wm. Smith one of the Twelve and only surviving brother of the Martyred Prophet arrived in Voree with Bishop Wm Marks a few days since. He is in good health and spirits and is making arrangements to erect a house for his mother on a lot which a gentleman in the place [has donated] for that purpose." The article asks the members to send one dollar, so some of the brethren could "go and fetch her up from Nauvoo without charge."

Lucy Smith never followed her son to Voree; instead she settled into the small Joseph B. Noble house that the trustees of the church had finally deeded to her. But obtaining that house had not been easy for Lucy. Joseph Heywood and Almon Babbitt were aware that William would inherit his mother's property and they told Lucy they would not deed her a home unless William either gave his support to the Twelve or she refused to let him live with her.

Indignant, Lucy Smith responded immediately. "I am [wronged] out of a home, long promised to me by my son . . . you . . . put limits to my affections, threaten me with poverty, if I do not drive my children from my door." Lucy demanded that they deed her the house and advance to her the quarterly sum Brigham had promised her.[7]

By the middle of May approximately twelve thousand Saints had crossed the river into Iowa. Some six hundred still remained in Illinois, most of them in Nauvoo. Of those who waited to leave, some could not finance the needed equipment and supplies or were determined to wait until they were fully outfitted. Emma said good-bye to many who had been her friends for years. Later, as tales of hardships trickled back to her, she found it hard to pity them. "They might have known better than to have gone," she remarked to an acquaintance, "and many of them did know better, for I told them better."[8]

That spring a man from Ohio had offered to buy the unfinished Nauvoo House from the trustees. When John Bernhisel discovered that Emma held title to the lot on which it stood, he wrote to Brigham Young in Iowa, "I have had a conversation with [Emma] this morning in relation to it, but she would not give me a decisive answer, what she would do, or what she would take for her interest in it, in case it was concluded to sell it, she stated however that she had been offered a thousand dollars for it—She is not very well pleased that she did not receive the stock which she understood was purchased for her a little more than a year ago."[9] The stock incident was further evidence to Emma that church agents did not have her interests in mind.

Decisive answers were not easy for Emma now. She told Bernhisel that she planned to sell or lease her own property as soon as possible and move with her children to Quincy. Brigham answered Bernhisel's letter. "You can ascertain what terms [to] present," he told him, "and how sister Emma Smith's claim can be managed." But in the interim Emma had acted on her own. "She informed me, to my great surprise and deep regret," Bernhisel wrote to Brigham, "that she had sold the lot for five thousand dollars to a speculator in real estate named Furness, from Quincy, who has since taken possession of one or two of the basement rooms of the building."[10] With ownership of much of the property unclear, such transactions were inevitable, as were the ill feelings.

The previous spring Emma had voiced some of these frustrations in a letter to Thomas Gregg, who had asked for historical documents:

> I have no documents or papers in my possession of a historical charac-
> ter whatever. All the records of Mr. Smiths of that nature were left
> with Willard Richards and Wm Clayton and they have carried them
> off with them.
>   I do not know that I am acquainted with any event of importance
> that is not already before the publick.
>   Indeed Sir I do not know where or how I should begin even if I
> should undertake to give any information concerning events which
> have transpired in this community as I am Convinced that there is no
> confidence to be placed in the word of those who have acted conspic-
> uously in this place. For this reason, everything that has not come
> within my immediate observation remains doubtful in my mind untill
> some circumstance occurs to prove report either true or false.[11]

Throughout the spring and summer of 1846 Nauvoo attracted a variety of new citizens—fugitives, and a few anti-Mormons who came to harass and spy. Tensions between Mormon and anti-Mormon forces in Hancock County sometimes erupted into violence. Mobs attacked Mormons who ventured be-yond the city to plant crops or to retrieve their personal property. Officials from Carthage then arrested a number of men from Nauvoo and charged them with larceny and perjury. The prisoners were released when they proved they had been held under false arrest. Imprisoned with the Mormons were two new citizens of Nauvoo, Lewis and John Bidamon.[12] Emma would eventually marry Lewis C. Bidamon.

Unquestionably, Emma was acquainted with the Bidamon brothers be-fore Joseph's death. About 1843 they filled an order from Joseph and Hyrum for four carriages. Lewis Bidamon delivered two of the carriages to the Smith home before the martyrdom. When Joseph saw how well John Bidamon ran the carriage business, he hired him to go to Nauvoo and attempt to make a profit from the red brick store. Soon John was in Joseph's store. Saints walked in empty-handed and left with their arms full of merchandise. The only nod in the direction of the cash drawer was the statement, "My credit has always been good with Joseph." John Bidamon later had his own crockery shop in Nauvoo, and Emma bought dishes for the Mansion from him. Another brother, Christian, rented rooms in the Mansion House.[13]

Emma knew of some of Lewis's and John's activities in Nauvoo that summer of 1846, for when the diminished population banded together for protection, John Bidamon became a special constable.[14] By June Lewis was on the nine-member "New Citizens Committee" and negotiated with the anti-Mormon delegation from Carthage who proposed marching into the city to make sure the Mormons were actually leaving. Lewis and his committee objected but, in spite of their efforts, on July 14 the anti-Mormons gathered in force at Golden Point six or seven miles from Nauvoo. One witness wrote: "It seemed to be supposed that by threatening the reluctant . . . and working upon the fears of all they could clear the city in two or three days."

Fifty of the new citizens, including Lewis and John Bidamon, published a statement that the Mormons were "departing as fast as they can be ferried over the river and faster than is consistent with their means of subsistence, or their safety. . . . We can assure our fellow citizens, throughout the state, that there exists no cause for apprehension that Mormon emigration will be suspended."[15]

Raids on Mormon farms forced Governor Ford to attempt control measures. Lewis Bidamon represented the governor when he delivered instructions to the commander of the state militia to control the mobs.[16] One man in Quincy wrote to his brother in Nauvoo: "Maj. Bidamon succeeded in reaching this place on Tuesday, not without having been met by Brigadier Gen Stivers who intercepted them at Churchville and threatened to take them to [the anti-Mormon] Camp. . . . Maj. B[idamon] left that evening for Springfield with dispatches for the Gov."[17] From this time until his death Lewis Bidamon was known as "the Major." On September 2 he wrote his brother Christian and referred to himself as a "new citizen." He said the mob appeared to "respect neither person or property."

By September anti-Mormon forces, determined to drive the few remaining Mormons out, moved closer to the city. The troops, consisting largely of Carthage Grays commanded by John Carlin, indignantly rejected any more delays. One of their officers protested: "It is my opinion that men who rush into a situation of this kind hastily, and without due consideration, are damn fools."

"It is my opinion that men who deliberate too long and negotiate too much are damn cowards," snapped Carlin.

The group cheered loudly. Refusing to be a part of the bloodshed now inevitable, the officer resigned his command on the spot. The force of eight hundred men marched toward Nauvoo.[18] In a matter of days the number of men capable of defending the city dropped from three hundred to barely a hundred as families fled. Almon Babbitt, who had decided to run for political office in the upcoming election, quickly called a meeting in the temple to harangue the people into staying until after the election. To underscore his determination, Babbitt "took possession of the ferry boat," refusing passage to families camped on the riverbank in tents and wagons. Wandle Mace raised and repaired an old skiff that had sunk along the river edge. Once he had his wife and four children safely across, he returned to help plan and execute the city's defense.[19]

On September 8 Mary Fielding Smith, now a plural wife of Heber C.

Kimball, supervised the loading of her family belongings and provisions on skiffs. Her daughter Martha Ann remembered, "We left our home just as it was, our furniture, and the fruit trees hanging full of rosy cheeked peaches. We bid goodbye to the loved home that reminded us of our beloved father everywhere we turned. . . . We bid goodbye to our dear old feeble grandmother [Lucy Mack Smith]."[20] No description remains of Emma's and Mary's parting. Mary Fielding began her journey in a party of ten males and nine females, including her four children, her brother Joseph and sister Mercy. Her stepson, John Smith, heard his family had started west and rode back across Iowa to assist them.

If Emma ever corresponded with Mary or any of the other Smith widows, there is no record. Samuel Smith's widow, Levira, followed Brigham Young west, taking her own children and one of Mary Bailey's sons, Samuel H. B. Smith, with her. Don Carlos's widow, Agnes, married William Pickett and later moved to California. The children of these women had played together, and memories would compel some of them to seek out and correspond with each other as adults, though they would differ markedly in their religious attitudes.

Lucy Mack Smith had hinged her desire to go west on the condition "if the rest of my children go." Feeble and crippled by arthritis, the matriarch of the Smith family was dependent on Emma and Katherine, Sophronia, and Lucy. She had participated in the endowment ceremonies with Sophronia and her second husband, but both Lucy and Katherine accepted William's claim to the presidency. Whether it was this belief, or poverty, or other circumstances, the sisters and their families did not go west. Lucy Mack traveled about seventy miles north to Lucy and Arthur Millikin's home.[21]

Emma's immediate concern now became her own safety and that of her children. She received an anonymous threat, probably during this time: "if she did not move out of the house in three days it would be burned over her head." At the close of the third day Emma put her children to bed on the ground floor where they could get out quickly and propped the south door open. "I want you to be quiet," she cautioned the children. "If anything unusual occurs be sure and let me know. I'll just be overhead, upstairs." A bit frightened, the children said their evening prayers and asked God to keep them safe. The next morning the household awoke safely but, on inspection, Emma found a pile of charred sticks and leaves against the north side of the house. Flames had scorched the siding but had gone out before doing extensive damage. Obviously she had to leave Nauvoo.[22]

The anti-Mormon factions did not want supplies or reinforcements shipped into the city and warned riverboat captains up and down the Mississippi to avoid Nauvoo: none made their regular stops. Emma discussed her situation with John Bernhisel, explaining that once she left she did not plan to return. Although she had disposed of some property, she had not sold it all. At

Bernhisel's suggestion she left the Mansion in the care of Abram Van Tuyl, recently arrived from New York State, who had leased it from her in April.[23] Emma had earlier thought she would go to Quincy and live on property she owned there. Why she did not is a subject for speculation. Perhaps it was too close to Nauvoo to be safe. Perhaps she discovered that her friend and former counselor in the Relief Society, Sarah Cleveland, who had moved there, had secretly married Joseph as a plural wife.

Emma's brother, Jesse Hale, had written to her more than a year earlier, expressing his personal grief at Joseph's death and saying he "evinced a friendship unexpected and his memory will long be cherished." With the concern of an elder brother, he counseled Emma, "It has been my opinion for some time that you would enjoy your self far better out of Nauvoo than you can in it and if you can make it convenient to locate your self and family in this part of the country it would be highly gratifying to all of your friends and relatives in this part of the country."[24] By this time Rosannah and William Marks had settled in the river village of Fulton, to the west of Lee County, and had encouraged Emma to move there. If she went to Fulton she would be with friends and close to relatives.

Emma, always an early riser, had her household organized and was well into her day's task of packing by 7 A.M. on Friday, September 11, 1846, when the clang of the temple bell signaled an attack on the city. Anti-Mormons led by Colonel Thomas L. Brockman outnumbered Mormon forces almost eight to one, but two cannons Wandle Mace had helped restore in the basement of the temple, plus two more fashioned out of old steamboat parts, almost equalized the heavy artillery. Fifty Nauvoo sharpshooters, led by William Anderson, lay hidden in a cornfield along Parley Street, fingering the triggers of their guns, but they were discovered and fired upon. Curtis Edwin Bolton, a new citizen, described the skirmish. "We retreated into town as a last forlorn hope threw ourselves into some log houses, determined to do or die. Brockman . . . ordered his horses and men to move down and take possession of this valuable point. The men numbered 120. They charged gallantly down the gentle slope and then charged ungallantly back again for we were there with our repeating rifles, which would be fired 7 and 8 times without reloading."

Emma heard the gunfire throughout the day and undoubtedly spent an anxious night. The following morning one crusty riverboat captain by the name of Grimes defied the mob's threats and announced he was going into port at Nauvoo and would take anyone aboard who wanted to go. When the *Uncle Toby* docked on September 12, Emma was ready. The Lorin Walker and Wesley Knight families traveled with her on the boat while the men rode overland with the horses, carriage, and a wagon loaded with household goods. Wesley Knight left Nauvoo embittered over his own loss of property and disillusioned with his Mormon experience. "I do not pretend to any religion and do not think I shall again very soon. I have got enough of it to see the actions of the Twelveite party that went west. [It] is enough to make one shudder and stand agast at the actions and prosedings." He derided the practice of plural marriage and the new endowment and further criticized the Mormons who retaliated against the mobs by plundering and stealing. "I left Nauvoo in company with Mrs. Smith the wife of the prophet," he continued, "her feelings in relation to mormonism is the same as mine."[25]

Emma boarded the boat with her five children and her housekeeper, Savilla Durfee. David was not yet two, Julia had turned fifteen the previous spring, and Joseph would be fourteen in two more months; ten-year-old Frederick and Alexander, age eight, considered the trip an adventure. Two young girls, Jane and Nancy Carter, and William C. Clapp also traveled with Emma. The tall and dark William Clapp had been courting Nancy Carter with only limited success.

The *Uncle Toby* filled with other refugees as well. While passengers shouted last-minute good-byes and instructions to those who remained on shore, Captain Grimes eased the boat out into the Mississippi River. The craft chugged upstream at eight miles an hour. Emma watched the temple disappear as they rounded the bend out of sight of Nauvoo.

Emma did not leave any too soon. Before 11 A.M. Brockman's men marched into town, but William Anderson and his Nauvoo troops were ready. The men positioned a cannon ready to greet the approaching anti-Mormons, holding fire until the expected target was almost upon them. "Ready, fire!" came the command. The ball cut a road through the approaching ranks, causing a scattered retreat, while some stood firm. Anderson ordered the charge. Suddenly a bullet ripped into him and he sprawled to the ground, dead. Almost at the same instant the enemy fired their cannon through the corner of the house where Anderson's only son had been hiding, killing the boy.[26] By the time the Brockman forces retreated with their own casualties, eight or nine more were wounded. John Bernhisel cared for the injured.[27]

The two sides skirmished for several days and finally, on September 16, negotiated a treaty. The terms were: first, the city of Nauvoo would surrender and Colonel Brockman's forces would take possession; second, Mormon arms would be delivered to the Quincy Committee, who pledged to protect persons and property; third, Mormons were to cross the river as soon as possible; fourth, the sick and helpless would be treated with humanity; fifth, five men, including the trustees of the church, and five clerks with their families would be permitted to remain safely in the city to dispose of property; and, sixth, all hostilities were to cease immediately and ten men of the Quincy Committee would enter the city to perform their duties. Wandle Mace described events in the desolate city. "The mob led by Brockman immediately entered the city. They defiled the Temple in an outrageous manner, with drunkenness, gambling and ribald song, they paid no attention to the stipulations of the treaty, they ransacked wagons for arms, drove men across the river at the point of the bayonet, Father John Stiles . . . an old man, and others, were forced to the river to the point of the bayonet, and baptized face downward in the name of Tom Sharp the leader of the mob, and the editor of the Warsaw Signal."[28]

Eudocia Baldwin Marsh, who had stood in the streets of Carthage with her mother and witnessed Joseph's murder, recalled, "Many a house and lot were exchanged for a horse or a yoke of oxen. Sometimes a cow drew the wagon on which the family's all was loaded, while the family itself trudged along beside it on foot. It was not hard to realize that such an outfit would never reach the western border of Iowa, though its goal, with the rest of the caravan, was the far-distant Salt Lake Valley."[29]

Abram Van Tuyl, in possession of the Mansion he had leased from Emma, took note of those new citizens who aided the Mormons. When the occupation came, he pointed out to Brockman which ones should be expelled. One of those was William Pickett, Agnes Coolbrith's husband. He had fought alongside the Mormons and left town in disguise, taking shelter in Iowa with Wandle Mace, who remembered: "All through the night he rolled and tossed upon the bed, he would curse the mob, and every one who had brought about the surrender of Nauvoo . . . he moaned and swore, 'God Damn their souls to hell, they have done with pen ink and paper, *what they couldn't do with Gunpowder!!*' "[30]

Years later workmen in Nauvoo were tearing up the attic floor of an abandoned house and discovered a tintype of a little girl. Tucked away with the picture they found this note: "It is night almost and tomorrow we have to leave, for somewhere. I will hide the two little things I love, my kitten's plate and my little dog. I shall come back one day and find you again. Anne E."

Anne E. probably numbered among the six hundred souls bivouacked along the Iowa bank of the Mississippi River—part of the tattered remnants of a city that had once numbered nearly twelve thousand.[31] Some Illinois citizens were outraged at such inhumane treatment and reported, "The Mormons . . . are in need of all kinds of clothing, materials for tents, shoes & c., it is believed that half worn or old clothing if not too much worn would be acceptable to them. Some goods are to be sent them from this place by the first boat."[32] Food became scarcer than either clothing or shelter. Relief came when flocks of quail suddenly descended on the camp. They perched everywhere and even children could catch them with their hands. The beleaguered refugees considered it a miracle. Throughout the next month these people dispersed west across Iowa, south toward St. Louis, and north to small communities along the river. Those who looked back for a final glimpse of their homes, their temple, their city, perhaps had thoughts similar to Wandle Mace's: "Farewell Nauvoo, the Beautiful! The City of Joseph! The home of so much joy and happy contentment, and also of the most exquisite sorrow and anguish. . . . Farewell to the Temple upon which I have labored with so much pleasure. . . . The cost was so great . . . yet this was built by the energy, tithes and offerings of an honest although a poor persecuted people. . . . Farewell, Nauvoo."[33]

Meanwhile, Captain Grimes piloted the *Uncle Toby* slowly up the river. Emma and her family spent six days on the boat. One of the Bidamon brothers, probably Christian, and his family were among those with whom Emma passed the long hours in "pleasant conversation." The *Uncle Toby* stopped at every port to discharge cargo, passengers, and some of the fugitives from Nauvoo. On Friday, September 18, Emma and her group stepped onto the docks at the end of Cherry Street in Fulton, Illinois, about one hundred fifty miles upstream from Nauvoo. Situated on the east bank of the Mississippi River, Fulton was a "fractional" township or precinct that was not to gain full township status for six more years. A nearby quarry provided stone for many of the buildings in the community.

Emma and those in her party found temporary lodging among the townspeople. They had been in Fulton three days when two of the local women, Abbey Rice and Sarah Johnson, called on Emma to welcome her. Abbey Rice commented, "I like her appearance very well." Two weeks later, as Abbey packed for an extended trip to Chicago, she noted that "Mrs Emma Smith has rented this house and so I shall board out when I return."[34] The apartment was in the large white, two-story frame house of Dr. Daniel Reed, located at the corner of Base and Wall streets, four blocks from the river. Emma and her children shared rooms with the Knights, the Walkers, William Clapp, and the two Carter girls as well as Mrs. Durfee. Emma again lived in crowded conditions. That the residents accepted the Mormons as casually as any other settlers is evidenced by the local histories, for no mention is made of Emma or the others in either Fulton or Whitesides County histories. But one of Emma's friends wrote: "She won respect and esteem for herself dispite the prejudice many felt against the name 'Mormon.' I had more than a casual acquaintance with her, and knew her to be a rare good woman . . . a devoted mother. It seems to me that the rocky hills of Pennsylvania had developed in her a character of uprightness and integrity that carried her bravely through trials that would have overwhelmed women of more common mould."[35]

Emma's children found friends, attended school, and were included in social occasions. Before long Jane Carter married, and William Clapp finally won Nancy Carter. Their departure into their own homes eased the crowding in Emma's house. That fall and winter Emma contacted her brothers and sisters, who lived about forty miles east, in and around Amboy. She also kept abreast of the events in Nauvoo through her correspondence with John Bernhisel, who, with other men, had remained in the city to represent the church's interests. In turn, Bernhisel kept Brigham Young informed about the well-being of various church members, including Emma and Lucy Mack Smith.[36]

Bernhisel's colleague, Joseph Heywood, also wrote to Brigham from "Hell

Town formerly Nauvoo. . . . We wish to say a few words in relation to the bodies of the Smith family intered on Emma's place. It is known to some through Emma where they lie. We have thought if it was wisdom to remove them that it would be affected now especially as Emma is out of the way." Heywood stated that Emma's renter Van Tuyl had conspired with the anti-Mormons and he accused Emma of telling Van Tuyl the location of Joseph's and Hyrum's graves.[37] Emma would not have knowingly harbored a spy, nor would she have betrayed the secret burial to someone she thought would rob or molest graves. To Brigham Young's credit, he did not move on Heywood's request.

18

The Major

1846–1849

Emma received a letter in January 1847 that signaled a new era. Lewis C. Bidamon, who had retreated to his former home in Canton, Illinois, after the fall of Nauvoo, wrote to Emma with a business request.

> Dear Madam,
>   I Wright to you from this place where I have bin ever since our defeat at Nauvoo. I was taken Sick Shortley after I arived here with the Bilious Fever allmost dispared of recovery by my physician and friends. . . . I am only now able to walk about the House. My brother John and family have moved back and I shall returne as soon as my health will admit for traveling. They tell me there is nothing but peace and tranquility existing there. . . . Brother John and my Self are desirious to Rent the Mansion House of you if you intend letting it and if So, pleas inform me what will be your Termes per annum. We wish to Rent House Barne and Furniture, infine every thing that pertains to the Tavern. Pleas excuse this billit. I am verry nervis.
>
> Your Sincere Friend and well Wisher
>
> Lewis Bidamon[1]

Emma penned her answer on the back of Bidamon's letter. Her reply suggests that she did not intend to return to Nauvoo soon, if at all.

> Mr. Bidamon, Yours of the 1847—11th Jany to [me] was receved Yesterday, in answer to which I have to say, that I suppose I shall have to get

possession of the Mansion before I can rent it again, as I do not expect You would like to rent it and run the risk of getting possession as . . . Dr. Van T. [may not] be wiling to give up the property. . . . Indeed, I do expect Some trouble with him yet . . . though if Your brother is in Nauvoo perhaps he can find out on what conditions he will give up posession of the premises. . . . I want to rent the farm that is near Na[uvoo]. If you know some one that wants to rent it, you would do me a favor to let me know of it. Upland I have another farm between the Quincy roade and Warren near Marshes that I wish to rent or sell. I also have a number of city lots in Na[uvoo] I would like to sell. I am anxiously waiting to know what our new Gov. is agoing to do with regard to the affairs of hancock. I formed a very agreeable acquaintince with Your brother His family while on the boat with them and would be pleased to see them again and that *too* under more pleasant circumstances. You will please give them my best respects.

Yours Truly

Emma Smith[2]

Van Tuyl had not forwarded his rent money to Emma, and in February Bernhisel sent word confirming her suspicions of the renter: Van Tuyl had been building a houseboat which he intended to furnish with the contents of the Mansion. The rest of Emma's goods he planned to sell downriver on his way to Texas, hoping to get away before she learned of his plan. Perhaps with the aid of John Bidamon, Emma confirmed what Bernhisel had written, then packed her few belongings. Lorin Walker hitched old Charlie to the carriage and drove her and the five children back to Nauvoo. At first they moved rapidly over the frozen roads, but by the time they reached La Harpe the weather had warmed enough to turn the roads into thick mud. When the carriage entered the north end of town, Emma saw that many houses stood stark and empty against the sky, some boarded shut, others with doors and windows opened to the harsh weather.

Lorin Walker pulled Charlie to a halt in front of the Mansion "much to the astonishment and discomfort of the dishonest landlord," Joseph III recalled, for Emma caught Van Tuyl carrying furniture from the house. She was unable to collect any back rent from her tenant before he made his speedy exit from the city, and she failed to recover all her household furnishings, but in some ways she was fortunate. Van Tuyl had been collaborating with the anti-Mormon element, therefore the occupying troops did not pillage the house. Again mistress of the Mansion, Emma commented, "I have no friend but God, and no place to go but home."[3]

Like many river towns, Nauvoo was now rough and dangerous. John

Bernhisel continued to live at the Mansion, but many of Emma's boarders were coarse river travelers and land speculators. Emma's son recorded one apparently typical incident when a Dr. Stark tried to leave for New York without paying his bill. Joseph went to see him, but Stark ordered the boy out. The young man refused to budge until he got the money. Stark paid, leveled a series of crude insults about Emma, and concluded, "I will see that I never owe her anything again."

"Thanks, we will take care of that ourselves," Joseph retorted, then calmly shut the door behind him.

With few overnight travelers and fewer who paid, Emma often had no cash with which to run the Mansion and supply the table. Once when she had only twenty-five cents left she sent it with Joseph to the store for flour. The storekeeper offered to send a whole sack home and let Emma pay when she could. "No sir," he replied. "Mother told me to get only twenty-five cents worth, for that is all the money she has and she does not want to go into debt."[4]

In the absence of a police force, homes became frequent targets for burglary, and many citizens kept guns loaded and close at hand. One night a woman friend of Emma's had been out after dark. When she entered her home, her husband mistook her for an intruder and shot her, wounding her fatally. Emma spent long hours caring for the mother until she died. Several years later, when the father also died, Emma took the two orphaned boys into her home as part of the family until they were old enough to be on their own.[5]

During the six months that Emma had spent in Fulton, the main body of Mormons established camps along the Missouri River near present-day Omaha, Nebraska. They named the encampment Winter Quarters, and it grew to a population of several thousand people. In the early spring of 1847, at about the time Emma returned to Nauvoo, a vanguard wagon train of one hundred forty-eight people, including Brigham Young, other members of the Twelve, and William Clayton, left Winter Quarters for the trek westward. On July 22 an advance party entered the Great Basin of the Rocky Mountains and two days later Brigham Young, sick and feverish, reportedly gazed over the Great Salt Lake valley and said, "This is the right place, drive on."[6] From this time the church would be centered in Salt Lake City, but missionaries and travelers going to and from Utah would pass through Nauvoo out of nostalgia and curiosity. Some would visit Emma.

Emma turned forty-three the same month the Mormons entered the Salt Lake valley. A traveler through Nauvoo described her as "an intelligent woman . . . rather large and good looking, with a bright sparkling eye, but a countenance of sadness when she is not talking; she must have been a handsome woman when some years younger. She answered all our questions as we sat at dinner, although perhaps some of them might have been rather impertinent under a strict construction of the rules of etiquette, with a great readiness and great willingness."[7] According to Emma's son, an Irishman named James Mulholland found her still a "handsome woman" and began courting her. He may have been a relative of the James Mulholland who had died in Emma's home during that first year in Nauvoo. Although he frequently called on Emma, either he was not persistent enough or he did not interest her, for little more is known of him.

John Bernhisel, who had boarded in the Mansion since 1844, had now completed his work as a church agent and was ready to join his family in the West.[8] He had observed Emma in a variety of circumstances and respected her strong will and tenacity even when he came in conflict with them. He loved her children and admired Emma for her care of them. His farewell letter read:

Dear Sister Emma,

I cannot take my departure from this place, without acknowledging the debt of gratitude that I am under to you. And in making this acknowledgement, I especially desire to be understood that I am observing no mere form or idle custom, nor empty ceremony. During the three years that I was a member of your family, I found every necessary provided for my comfort, with much order and neatness, and from yourself and family I experienced not only kindness and respect, but such affectionate regard, tenderness and delicacy as to make me feel more than your grateful friend —I may never be permitted to pay you all; but the bond of obligation shall ever remain binding on my heart and life. And I beg you to accept my profound and grateful acknowledgments for your uniform kindness and attention to me, and for your trouble of me during so long a period; and I fervently pray that God may reward you in this world a thousandfold and in the world to come with life everlasting.

J. M. Bernhisel[9]

Bernhisel would visit Emma again as he traveled back and forth as a delegate to the United States Congress from the Utah Territory. He maintained a lifelong interest in her children, particularly Joseph and David. Joseph recalled his kindness: "he had frequently written me, and had greatly increased the value of my library by gifts of the various documents published by order of Congress, such as those on the exploration of the United States territory, reports of our dealings with foreign governments, the opening of commerce with China. . . . Indeed, there was little of importance . . . that he failed to send me."[10]

In contrast to Bernhisel's thoughtful diplomacy, Almon Babbitt's heavy-handed tactlessness offended Emma. Once as he left Nauvoo for Winter Quarters, he stopped his carriage in front of the Mansion. He had come to tell Emma that she should move to the Salt Lake valley with her children. As

Joseph tells the story, she refused, saying she could not live with the "false doctrines" preached there. "It has been determined to make you so poor that you will be willing and glad to go out there for protection," Babbitt threatened. "I have been appointed to accomplish that purpose and I propose to do so."

"Almon Babbitt," she retorted, "it may be possible for you to make me poor, but you could never make me poor enough to induce me to follow Brigham Young!"[11]

In the spring of 1847, Lewis C. Bidamon had returned to Nauvoo from his refuge in Canton, Illinois. The Major was forty-five. Joseph said he was "a fine-looking man, six feet tall, with a high forehead and splendid bearing. He usually dressed very well."[12] He was debonair and polished compared to many in Nauvoo, and had a quick sense of humor, the ability to laugh at himself, and a charm that made him attractive to women.

Lewis once said that he first became attracted to Emma Smith when he saw the beautiful darns in her stockings.[13] However she darned them, and whatever he observed along with the darns, it was enough to keep him interested in Emma as he settled down to storekeeping in the nearly deserted town. Their middle-aged courtship, however, was not without its problems. Joseph recalled that Lewis, wearing a high hat, came to call one evening. "Catching sight of Mother sewing at an upper window, he made her a very polite and widely sweeping bow. Regaining his erect posture after this elaborate ceremony, he replaced his hat upon his head and stepped forward briskly, when suddenly a clothesline he had failed to observe caught him across the forehead, just under the brim of his hat! Off flew the hat, but alas, along with it flew a very fine toupee." Both Emma and her son had seen the display and "laughed uncontrollably." Bidamon punctuated the recovery of both wig and hat with, "Damn that wig!" The "embarrassing situation . . . proved no handicap to the gallant gentleman," Joseph remembered, for he was made of "sterner stuff."[14]

Throughout the summer and fall of 1847 Emma continued to see Lewis Bidamon, who eventually proposed marriage. As his grandchildren later heard the story, he stated simply, "You are alone and I am alone. Let us live our lives out together." Who would perform the ceremony? The only Mormons left in the city were agents of Brigham Young with neither ecclesiastic nor legal authority. Lewis's and Emma's only choices were the Methodist circuit rider or a justice of the peace at the courthouse in Carthage. They chose the Methodist preacher.

No record is available to tell how often the Methodist minister, Rev. William Hany, came to Nauvoo, but Emma and Lewis set their wedding date to coincide with his regular visit, Thursday, December 23, 1847—the date of Joseph Smith, Jr.'s birth.[15]

Many Mormons were aghast that Emma would not remain a mourning monument dedicated to the memory of their dead prophet, but her remarriage argues that her association with Joseph was fulfilling enough to marry again. Curiosity about the wedding and speculation about Lewis Bidamon enlivened the otherwise dull social climate of Nauvoo during the 1847 Christmas season. Sarah M. Kimball, still in Nauvoo, gossiped in a letter to Nancy Marinda Hyde at Council Bluffs:

> The marriage of Mrs. Smith is the all-absorbing topic of conversation. She was married last Thursday eve, the groom, Mr. Bidamon, is, I believe, looked upon with universal contempt. He was a widower, wears a wig, has two daughters, young ladies. A Mrs. Kinney, who credits him with one child, says he still loves her, but married Emy for her property. Mrs. Smith manifested the confidence she has in her intended husband by employing attorneys to execute a marriage contract and secure to her all the Property. The ceremony was performed by the Rev. Methodist Mr. Hany. The bride was dressed in plum colored satin, a lace tuck handkerchief, gold watch and chain, no cap, hair plain.

Part of the sting in Sarah's report may be explained by her concluding remark: "We were not honored guests, but were told that things passed off very genteely."[16] Lewis Bidamon was attracted to women, but any link between him and Sarah's Mrs. Kinney remains unproven. Nauvoo land and population records fail to confirm the presence of any Kinneys in the city at that time. But Sarah's report that Emma had executed a marriage contract may have been correct. If so, she misunderstood the purpose. Marriage contracts could be made to relieve the spouse from responsibility for debt and Lewis Bidamon had made such an agreement with his previous wife, Mary Ann Douglas. Emma may have suggested such a contract to protect Bidamon from the debts she inherited from Joseph, rather than to constrain her new husband. Two days before her marriage she deeded the Mansion House to Mary Fielding's son-in-law, Lorin Walker, who deeded it back on the same day, an obvious attempt to clear the title.[17]

News of Emma's and Lewis's marriage was reported to Brigham Young. John Fullmer wrote this disparaging account on January 26, 1848:

> I suppose you know by this time that there was a certain widow in this place, who was lately given (and as the orthodoxy would say) "in holy matrimony" to one of his Satanic Majesty's high priests, to wit, one Lewis Bidamon. Now these twain being one flesh concocted a grand scheme by which they would effectually block our wheels and enrich themselves. They hit upon the idea that the church, according to a limited construction of one of our state laws, could only hold ten acres

of land, and that consequently, the deed from Emma and Joseph to
Joseph as a "Trustee" was illegal.[18]

Almon Babbitt told Heber C. Kimball and Brigham Young less than a
week later that Emma "had made a Quit Claim deed of all the lands . . . to
the Church" and added that it served as a "perfect estopel to the sale of any
more city property until the matter is tested in the courts of Law." Emma had
relinquished her claims and would settle for the widow's dowry that was hers
by law.[19] Unfortunately the issue was not so simple, and Emma would have to
deal with it later.

Probably because a Methodist minister performed the marriage ceremony, Babbitt reported that "Emma had joined the Methodist Church. . . .
She was taken in on trial of course (let them try her)." When he retold the
same story to Heber C. Kimball he added, "It is to be hoped that she will suit
them." The Methodists, he claimed, had their own interests and were trying
to get "possession of the Temple and other [church] property . . . through
Emma," but he told Brigham that "the temple has been sold since . . . and
bid in by Emma's husband on an execution in favor of William Backenstos."[20]

John Bernhisel returned to Nauvoo the following year and stated emphatically to Brigham Young that Emma "has not united with the Methodist
Church."[21] Still, the rumor would persist unfounded. Emma had been a member of the Methodist faith as a child and would have felt comfortable there,
but Nauvoo Methodist records did not list her as a member. But Emma did
give her family religious training. For example, a poem that David would write
as an adult described how she had taught her five children to pray with faith
and to read the Bible. "You know," he wrote, "how righteous she has been,
through all her weary years."[22]

Emma's union with Lewis Bidamon ended speculation that she might
someday accept the Twelve's offer of assistance to go west, and although her
name was never removed from the membership records, in their eyes it affirmed her separation from the church. It also united her for the second time
in her life to a man she loved—in spite of statements claiming the marriage
was one of convenience. A typical example is this thirdhand account written
thirty years after the event: "Sister Jemerson said that Emma Smith told her
mother that the reason she married Bidamon was that she promised the mob if
they would let her stay in Nauvoo and not molest her, she would hide the
Mormon books from her children and do all she could do to turn them against
the church and the works of their father. She thought that marrying Bidamon
would help the matter."[23]

Much of the gossip may have been prompted by the need to explain how
Emma could marry anyone after Joseph. An awareness of Lewis Bidamon's
personality is important in understanding the remaining thirty-two years of
Emma's life. Lewis was fourteen when the Bidamon family moved from his

birthplace in Smithfield, Virginia, to Highland County, Ohio. Little is known of him until his marriage at age twenty-five to Nancy Sebree in 1827.[24] Their first child was a boy, born in 1828. Lewis's second child was a girl, born in 1829, not to his wife but to one of Jeremiah Smith's daughters (no relation to the Joseph Smith family). This woman, probably Nancy Smith, left their illegitimate child, Almira, with her own parents to be raised. Almira knew who her father was, and when she was twenty-four began a remarkable correspondence with Lewis Bidamon that spanned at least twenty-five years.

Lewis and his wife, Nancy Sebree, moved to Canton, Illinois, where two more children were born. There, Nancy and the son died, leaving Lewis a widower with two daughters, Emma Zerelda and Mary Elizabeth. In 1842 Lewis married a widow named Mary Ann Douglas. Disillusioned with this marriage after two months, he composed a letter to Mary Ann's three brothers, a duty he found "paneful in the extreme." He told them that his "ardent affections" were not returned by his "coald hartless tyranical" wife. "I had my children under such command that if I had company at the table they would wait without a murmur but as a general thing children should eat with the family in order that they could be taught," he wrote. "My Dear companion made the quick reply with conciderable anemosatie that my children should not eat at hir table . . . she would as leaf set down with a passel of Cats. I told hir my children had always eat at the table when I eat and I further desired that hir children and mine should set at the same board." Mary Ann also made "long resittles" of his "imaginary falts . . . almost as regular as the earth made hir diurnal revolution she would reproch me on acount of my not being welthy and remark what a fool she was a woman like hir . . . to marry me in poverty. . . . I will not bost of my welth but them that has more than me is not in a sufering situation."[25] The marriage ended four months later. Mary Ann may have thought Lewis was wealthy because he owned an iron foundry in Canton, Illinois, and had converted a steam mill into a carriage factory which he later sold to the McCormick Company.

Joseph, who was fifteen, found his stepfather "a man of strong likes and dislikes, passionate, easily moved to anger." Bidamon had a taste for liquor and his absence of religious commitment bothered Joseph and would disturb his brothers as they became older. Although he had helped establish the first Congregational church in Canton, Illinois, in 1842, Lewis called himself a deist by the time he married Emma. He thought that Joseph Smith was an honest man, although perhaps deceived. "I believe in one God who has neither partner nor clerks," Lewis proclaimed.[26] A portrait of Joseph Smith always hung in the home, however, and Lewis would not allow anyone to speak against the dead prophet. Joseph III recalled of his stepfather, "While his moral character might not be considered to be of the highest quality, he did possess a certain pride of manhood, a deeply rooted dislike of being in debt or under obligation to anyone, and, so far as the ordinary transactions of life are concerned, a desire to deal honorably with his fellow men." Joseph continued with a remarkable analysis of "Pa Bidamon" that could easily have described his own father and suggests why Emma and her children seemed to adjust so readily to the presence of this colorful man in their lives: "There was much in the character of the man that called forth admiration. His house was open to all his friends and they came and went without reproach and at their own convenience. There was always room at the table for any who might be present when the meal was ready and his uniform sociability made everybody welcome. In some ways he made an excellent landlord, but was unfortunate in always having a number of 'human sponges' harboring about the place, feeding of his hospitality and rendering little in exchange therefor." Joseph wrote, "He was not a good judge of human character and was easily imposed upon. He had grown up with but little schooling and had been a hard and conscientious worker."[27] Emma accepted Lewis's daughters, Zerelda, thirteen, and Mary Elizabeth, eleven, as easily as she had accepted other motherless children. In return, Lewis would be the only father David, now three, would ever know.

At the time of Emma's marriage Lewis and a partner ran a store. When they dissolved the partnership Lewis suggested to Emma that they each put a thousand dollars' worth of goods in the red brick store and let Joseph run it. Emma agreed, thus giving her eldest son his first business opportunity. He converted one of the upstairs rooms, perhaps the same room his father had used as an office, into sleeping quarters and also acted as night watchman. Unfortunately he was no more successful at storekeeping than his father before him. He refused to dicker with the customers. Bidamon could easily mark down a bolt of fabric to move it off the shelf; Joseph hung on for the original price, and the cautious housewives never could feel they had struck a bargain.[28] The store did not make much money, but Joseph found some independence there until he became an adult.

Meanwhile a second business district had grown up on the north side of town near the temple, changing the face of the community. A New York company had agreed to lease the vacant temple for use as a school and a representative expected to start for Nauvoo on October 10, 1848. Shortly after 3 A.M. on October 9, the cry of "Fire, fire!" broke into Emma's sleep. From her window she could see the northern sky aglow with flames leaping from the roof of the temple. Lewis dashed toward the building nearly a mile away. The same alarm woke Joseph in his room above the store. He could see people running along the streets toward the center of town. One man called up to him that the temple was burning. Joseph ran to the Mansion and found that the Major had already gone. Afraid that an arsonist would strike next at the Mansion, Joseph stayed there with Emma and the younger children.[29]

The fire had started in the cupola, a news report later stated, "and as the flames shot up to the sky, they threw a lurid glare into the surrounding darkness. Great volumes of smoke and flame burst from the windows, and the crash

of falling timbers was distinctly heard on the opposite side of the river. The
interior of the building was like a furnace; the walls of solid masonry were
heated throughout and cracked by the intense heat. The melted zinc and lead
was dropping from its huge block."[30] Before daybreak the once beautiful
landmark stood smoldering with walls too hot to touch. Lewis Bidamon returned to Emma sometime after dawn, his face and hands black with smoke.
As he washed away the grime he recalled a biblical passage—"something about
a father's bowels yearning over his son."

"I never understood that passage before," said the Major, "but now I
seem to feel this loss, this terrible calamity, throughout my whole body. I
believe I begin to sense the meaning of that phrase in the Bible. I shall not
make light of it again."[31]

Area newspapers echoed the feeling of loss. The Nauvoo *Patriot* lamented, "To destroy a work of art, at once the most elegant and most re-
nouned in its celebrity . . . in the whole west, would . . . require a mind of
more than ordinary depravity." Two weeks after the fire the Keokuk *Register*
called on "Every good citizen [to] condemn this act . . . of the grossest bar-
barism. Situated on the bluff of the river, it commanded a prospect as far as
the eye could reach and as lovely as the eye ever rested upon. . . . The
citizens on both sides of the river reprobate the act as wanton and malicious in
the extreme." But others saw the burning of the temple as a final triumph over
the Mormons, for its destruction assured that they would not return. In Carthage some lauded those who had set the fire as "upright honorable men, not
vandals," and the Warsaw *Signal* called it a "benevolent act."[32]

Within a month the citizens of Nauvoo banded together to raise funds to
locate the arsonist. Lewis signed first on the subscription list and offered
twenty-five dollars. Eventually the blame centered on a man Joseph described
as a "river rat, a drunken lout" named Joseph Agnew. Lewis later told Mormon visitors from the West that some citizens of Carthage, Warsaw, and other
nearby towns had contributed five hundred dollars which they paid to Agnew
to burn the temple.[33]

Forty-seven years later, after the arsonist's death, a confidant published
Agnew's confession. He and two accomplices, posing as traveling strangers,
asked the temple guard to show them through the building. Agnew noticed a
key in the door and, unobserved, slipped it into his pocket. When the guard
left for his evening meal Agnew unlocked the heavy door and made his way to
the attic floor, then lit his tinder "where it would get a good start before it
would shed any light to be seen from the outside. . . . I began to retrace my
steps with joy and a light heart for I was sure that the Temple was as good as
burned."

Agnew made a wrong turn and became lost in the burning building. His
only way out lay through the fire. Wrapping his coat around his head, he dived
into the inferno and rolled out the other side. Badly burned and bruised, he

could barely make it back to his horse with the others. Agnew related, "After going about one-half mile I looked toward Nauvoo and I saw flickering light and the next minute flames burst through the roof."[34]

Lewis Bidamon believed that the loss of the temple was related to the drop in business at the Mansion House, for after the landmark burned, paying guests were not one fourth the number they had been before.[35] With Emma's and Lewis's financial situation precarious at best, the news that gold had been discovered in California pricked the Major's interest. He and his brother John decided to join the rush to riches by the overland route that took six thousand gold seekers across the plains and Western mountains in 1849. The Major and his brother crossed the Mississippi the last part of April to join a wagon train of forty-niners. By May 4 they had traveled well into Iowa. Lewis, still not distant enough from Nauvoo to be homesick, happily wrote to Emma, "Our Journey So far is verry pleasant. . . . I have nothing to regret in determining the undertaking this jant only being Seperated from hir—that I *love* and the Society of the Children. I have nothing of note to record except my Waggon is not made by gentleman and my horses got loose the first days traveling." Lewis then related an experience for Emma's amusement. One evening the travelers had apparently been late setting up their camp. By the time they had cooked "some fine browned squirl" for their evening meal it was dark. Someone accidentally knocked over the table along with the meat. John Bidamon groped in the grass for the squirrel with only the moon to light his search. "Thinking he had found a piece and applying it to his tasters to his great astonishment found it to be not bufelow chip but Cow chip. Dident he Spit! Good by for the presant Your dear Husband LC Bidamon."[36]

Emma and Lewis had been married about eighteen months when he left for California. He would be gone slightly over a year and their correspondence details events that happened to both of them during that time. Not all of their letters survive, although they apparently wrote monthly. Only one long letter from Emma, dated January 7, 1850, is extant.

The letters reveal much about Emma's and Lewis's relationship. From the Indian Territory Lewis wrote: "Dear Emma, ofttimes me mind hovers around the[e] and in amagination press the[e] tenderly to my bosom. O my Love! If I could only here from you and know that you was well and the family and you was injoying your Selfs, it would ease this akeing hart. It would over compare with the briliant prospects of my Success in california. Be cherefull *Dear*, if we live the day will arrive where we will again meet and press each other to our congenial brests."[37]

In spite of his apparent homesickness for Emma, Lewis Bidamon found the trip to California to be the great adventure he had anticipated. He noticed the emigrants were "kind and peaceable towards each other." One man gave him a pair of gum elastic boots which Lewis said "reaches to my but." "The account from the gold Regians is good and I think we will do well if we Should be so lucky as to get there," he wrote to Emma. In the late summer Lewis and John Bidamon arrived at the goldfields safely. In one letter to Emma, Lewis mentioned that he has not seen Emma's nephew, Lorenzo Wasson, who apparently left for California soon after Lewis. Whether Lewis met him in California is not known, but Lorenzo died en route home in February 1851.[38]

As Lewis traveled west it took up to six months for his correspondence to reach Emma. She described her loneliness as a reign of "gloomy solitude." She was concerned about eighteen-year-old Julia. A slender, fair-skinned, blue-eyed man of thirty-six named Elisha Dixon came to Nauvoo as an entertainer soon after Lewis's departure. Sometime in the summer of 1849 he and Julia married, despite Emma's disapproval of his occupation—or lack of one.[39] He soon went to St. Louis where he became involved in some sort of business for "forty dollars a month." Whether or not Julia went with him is not known but, when cholera hit St. Louis, Dixon retreated back to Nauvoo.

Emma, relieved that the cholera epidemic did not reach Nauvoo, speculated in a letter to Lewis that it was because the landings and wharf were now gone and the riverboats no longer stopped there. That summer had been one of the most disease-free in her memory, and she prayed it would last. "I earnestly hope that the allwise ruler of heaven will remember," she wrote, "that those beings that are in this place who would be humane if they had half a chance, have enough to contend with, without having the scourge of nations sent among them." Emma's boarders had dwindled to one. Paying her bills left her without cash, and she turned the operation over to Elisha Dixon. He invested about one hundred dollars and over the next few months did "better than I expected," Emma would reassure Lewis. She was also concerned about Lewis's fourteen-year-old daughter Mary Elizabeth, who married a Mr. Gibson on July 30. Shortly after their marriage the newlyweds left Nauvoo, taking Zerelda with them. Six months later Emma commented to Lewis with mingled worry and irritation, "I have not heard one word from them since."[40]

With Zerelda and Mary Elizabeth gone, Julia and her husband running the Mansion, and her children getting old enough that their care was not so demanding, Emma's life pace slowed and she began to gain weight. Although photographs of her during this time reveal that she was not obese, when John Bernhisel visited her in September he wrote to Brigham Young that the forty-five-year-old Emma had "become quite corpulent." Bernhisel also described Emma's reaction to his arrival. "Though Emma received me in the kindest, and entertained me in the most hospitable manner, yet she did not make a single inquiry in relation to the valley, the Church, or any of its members." Perhaps Emma's reticence can be traced to a letter her oldest son had received the previous spring.

Joseph had maintained a cordial correspondence with at least two of his cousins in the West, George A. Smith and John A. Smith. On March 13, 1849, George A. had written Joseph from Iowa: "It is my present calculation to move, with my family, to the Mountains this summer. I should be happy if you could find it convenient to accompany me. One great work accomplished by your father was the building up of the Church of Jesus Christ of Latter Day Saints. About five thousand of that body are already congregated in the Mountains, who would be much pleased to see you in their midst." Conscious of how Emma might feel, he told Joseph to "Consult your mother on this subject, and do as wisdom shall direct."[41] Emma would not have been pleased. She knew the thirty-two-year-old George A. had plural wives and she would have been reluctant to allow her seventeen-year-old son to observe polygamy at close range.

Bernhisel wrote news of others in the family as well. "Joseph has grown surprisingly, indeed so much so that I did not recognize him—his little brothers have also grown rapidly. Emma has employed a teacher, who is residing in the house and is instructing the children. Joseph is studying English, French, and Latin. Julia . . . has been joined in the silken bands of wedlock to a reformed gambler . . . who keeps the Mansion." He reported that "Mother Smith's health is very feeble and in all human probability she will not survive another winter." Lucy, he said, had asked about Brigham Young and others.

To John Bernhisel the city seemed "gloomy and desolate." He wrote, "The lots and trees with few exceptions are overgrown with weeds and grass. Few of the houses . . . are inhabited; the remainder are in a state of desolation and utter ruin. Though the walls of the Temple are standing, yet they are much cracked. . . . There has been nothing done to rebuild it except clearing away some rubbish. . . . [It] is enclosed with a rude fence and is used as a sheep fold and cow pen."[42]

Bernhisel did not mention Lewis Bidamon. Emma may have avoided talking about him. Lewis was already in California but she did not know that and feared that he might travel through the Salt Lake valley. Aware that some people there regarded him with suspicion, Emma felt apprehensive about his safety. When she did learn of his arrival in the goldfields, she would write, "My dear Lewis you cannot realize how thankful I was when I learned that you had got from the Bluffs safe and did not go by the valley."[43]

19

❧

Change in Nauvoo

1850–1860

A letter from Lewis arrived on December 29, 1849. Emma went to her room to read it in privacy before sharing it with her children. On January 7, 1850, she answered, "The satisfaction I enjoyed in persuing that letter none ever knew, or ever will know, but the truly faithful heart, that had waited in anxious suspence as long as I had." Emma had always expressed her feelings best in times of concern and now her writing was almost poetic.

> My dear Lewis, I have scarsely enjoyed any good thing since you left home, in consequence of the terrifying apprehension that you might be suffering for the most common comforts of life. I have never been weary without thinking that you might be much more so. I never have felt the want of food without fear that you might be almost, or quite starving, and I have never been thirsty without feeling my heart sicken with the reflection that perhaps you were sinking, faint, and famished for want of that reviving draught that I could obtain so easily and use so freely, and I have much feared that the heat of the sun on those burning plains might seriously affect you. But now these anxieties are over, and some may think that I might be content, but I am not, neither can I be untill you are within my grasp, then, and not till then shall I be free from fears for your safety, and anxieties for your wellfare.[1]

Emma included news of various family members and told Lewis of Julia and Elisha Dixon's attempt to run the Mansion Hotel. Then she added, "But the business and climate did not agree with his broken constitution, and his physicians told him he must go south or not live till spring. Accordingly, he started about the 10th of Dec. for Cuba, but only got to St. Louis where he had been confined to his bed for three weeks. This is the last news we have had yet of him. . . . Julia is with me and is almost as lonely as I am."

Emma assured Lewis that her children wanted him to know they remembered him. "It would have done your soul good if you could have seen how anxious they were to know if you were well, and then Joseph and Frederick and Alexander were not satisfied till they had all read your letter and Joseph copied it immediately for Mary Elizabeth." David, who had turned five in November, stood for a moment at his mother's side while she wrote, reminding Emma that he loved "his pa because he promised to bring him some gold in a little box and he is going to love him till he gets home."

Travelers through Nauvoo had been infrequent for over a year and Emma commented to Lewis that only one or two boarders came through in a week. "If business is no better here in the spring than it was last," she commented, "I think I shall take the sign down and do all we can on the farm." Emma expressed concern over property matters and although she did not mention names she spoke of the "treacherous designing knaves of a pack of cut-throat swindlers" that seemed to find their way to Nauvoo. "My chance of saving property is just as good as a woman's chance would be in the fifth story [window] of a burning building in Broadway N.Y. . . . holding her most precious goods . . . hesitating whether to throw [them] back into the flames, or throw them into the streets among the thieves." She told Lewis that since she could not always know the outcome of a situation beforehand he should not be surprised if she threw "some in the fire and some into the hands of the thieves." In spite of "lazy lawyers and treacherous hypocrites" she vowed she would save enough land to raise their potatoes and corn. "I do believe that you in the goodness of your generous soul will say that I have not done as bad as I might . . . you may rest assured that I shall do the best I can."

Emma's earlier dealings with Almon Babbitt and the other church representatives caused her to fear that Lewis might be in some danger from the Mormons in the West. She asked him to be cautious in dealing with them and wrote, "It may seem strange and ungrateful to you that they should even wish you harmed, and so it is, but I can tell you they are capable of an infamous ingratitude as any other beings." Because of Lewis's assistance in the Mormon war in Nauvoo, he might have expected gratitude, but Emma feared that their marriage had changed that: "All that I can find that they have against you is they think that you occupy a situation here that you have no business to. This is what Babbitt told me himself the day before he left here. . . . Babbitt [said] that you had no right to marry me, and of course on the same principle, I had no right to marry you." Babbitt, the last of the church trustees to leave Nauvoo, had taken his family to the valley the previous summer. "I believe they intend that I shall not enjoy anything without trial," Emma concluded. She had learned that some Mormon had met Lewis en route and asked him to return to Nauvoo, collect Emma and the children, and take them to the valley. Lewis declined and Emma told him, "I think you man[a]ged very prudently." At the close of her letter Emma asked, *"When O! when* can I begin to think about your coming home. . . . No more at present, only that I am as ever yours wholy."[2]

A messenger handed Emma's January 7, 1850, letter to Lewis while he was living in a tent a hundred miles southeast of Sacramento. "O the extacie of Joy in the perusal thereof, finding you alive and well and the family enjoy[ing] good helth," he wrote back to her.

I had allmost concluded that you existed not, and my friends, if I had any, had forgotten Such [a] beeing as I lived, but thank Heaven there is one Dear Solitary Angel Still bares me in mind. O my Dear Emma, that I could press you to my lonsome Hart and converce with you. . . . The antisipation or partisipation of emence welth Shall not keep me from your Dear imbrace. Untill then, my Love try to be content and happy. Greeve not if the infamous demons Should filch all of your property, they cannot destroy our love, and if we are blest with helth and strength we can live happy. *God* will protect the noble in Hart.

Lewis also had sobering news. "Gold is not as easy obtained nor in such abundance in California as was and is antisipated by the people of the States. It is obtained by the hardest of labour, harder than my constitution is able to bare." While some had found riches in a short time without working hard, he and John had managed to dig only thirty dollars' worth on their best day, some days as little as five, and "many days not any thing. . . . The amount of gold that John and I have on hand now and not indebt . . . is Something near 8 lbs pure gold."

Emma figured in Lewis's decision not to remain in the goldfields. "I do not like California. It affords no charms for me and especly in the absence of hir and only hir that can make me happy," he wrote. "Adeau, Dear Emma, for the present. Give my warmest affections to the children and all inquireing friends, and curses to my enmeys!"[3]

Emma saw the population of Nauvoo change considerably in that year. Étienne Cabet had led two hundred sixty émigrés from France, and their arrival in Nauvoo coincided with Lewis's departure. They called themselves Icarians and believed in equality, brotherhood, and communal property. In 1855 they would be a majority in Nauvoo with five thousand members, but their population dwindled and most had left in disillusionment or built other colonies by 1856. The Icarian era brought French customs into Emma's life, and for several years she and her children annually watched a miniature Mardi Gras parade. German immigrants soon joined the French and other new settlers. Before long Nauvoo became the largest German-speaking settlement in Illinois. Emma found friends among the new people. One day she sent her three youngest boys to tell a German friend that she and her family planned to spend the day with her. Six-year-old David piped up: "Mama sent us early so you'd have time to make a good ready."[4]

Early in 1850 Étienne Cabet and his men started to rebuild the interior of the gutted temple. Eleven men were working in the building on June 11 when a tornado struck. Seven were inside as the wind caught the north wall, knocking it inward. The sound of the crashing wall carried for three miles, but no one was killed. The temple was so weakened that the stones fell bit by bit until only the southwest corner was left standing. Finally the city council declared it a safety hazard and had it torn down. The citizens of Nauvoo used the temple stone to build workshops, a schoolhouse, and other buildings.[5]

Emma welcomed Lewis Bidamon home that same summer. Her boys liked Lewis and acknowledged his affection for them. Joseph would later tell a friend, "Our step father is as good as [a] step father can be. He loves us all as well as he does his own children."[6] Lewis had a tale of adventure to tell Emma and the boys. In California he had manufactured picks and shovels for the miners. John Bidamon became the sheriff of Hangtown, and Lewis served as his deputy for a while. In the spring Lewis left California and took a boat south to Panama, then hiked across the isthmus to the Gulf of Mexico where he secured passage to Havana, Cuba. There he took another boat to New Orleans, then came up the Mississippi River to Nauvoo. He managed to lose whatever funds he had been able to glean either from the goldfields or from merchandising products to the miners.[7]

While Lewis was gone, Emma had written to him about saving some of her property from "cut-throat swindlers." Lewis hardly had time to tell of his adventures in the West before court action threatened what Emma had salvaged. On August 9, 1850, the new United States attorney in Illinois filed a complaint to recover the debt Joseph Smith had owed from the 1840 purchase of the steamship Nauvoo.[8] He demanded that payment be made by selling all the land that Joseph Smith had owned at his death.[9] The court finally upheld the Illinois law that no church could legally hold more than ten acres of property. Judge Pope went a step further than the United States attorney's complaint and ruled that all the property that exceeded the allotted ten acres that Joseph held either personally or as trustee-in-trust after 1842 must be sold to pay the creditors. This included the Hugh White purchase and all the other property Joseph had conveyed to Emma or the children since that time.

By December 1850 the defendants in the case were Emma and her children, plus ninety-nine other people owning three hundred twelve lots plus twenty-nine tracts of land totaling more than four thousand acres. As surviving spouse, Emma was entitled to a one-third dower interest in what her husband owned and this took precedence over other claims. But because of Emma's age the court valued her widow's rights at only one sixth of Joseph's estate. The court did exempt from the sales the Mansion House, the Homestead, the Joseph Smith farm, and the Nauvoo House, which Emma had repurchased in 1848 from Lewis's brother Christian Bidamon and his wife Sarah for $805.

On April 8, 1851, the first of three public auctions took place on the front steps of the Mansion, to sell all but five lots that Joseph had conveyed to Emma and the children in 1843. A second sale was held at the Hancock County Courthouse on November 8, and a third one at the Adams County Courthouse in Quincy on May 3, 1852. Emma and Lewis repurchased twenty of the lots and one track of land at the April 1851 and May 1852 sales.[10]

The sale proceeds totaled $11,148.35. The United States Government received $7,870.23, which was full payment for the steamship debt plus court costs and interest. An additional $1,468.71 apparently went to pay legal fees and other court costs. Emma's widow's share of Joseph's estate was a mere $1,809.41. The rest of the creditors, with one exception, got nothing. Phineas Kimball, land speculator and brother to Hiram Kimball, had previously filed a claim for about $2,800. In March 1852 he refiled, asking for $5,000. On June 5 he received $3,000 from a judicial sale of the same property the court had earlier exempted.[11] Emma had to use the dower money plus more than $1,000 to buy back the Mansion House, the Homestead, the Nauvoo House, and the farm. Acting in her behalf at the federal sale, her lawyer, George Edmunds, Jr., had purchased another farm for $255. Kimball got the state court to agree to resell that property and Edmunds purchased it a second time for Emma, paying $700.[12]

Joseph III would remember "the kindness, the honesty, the courage, and the friendship" Edmunds exhibited in behalf of Emma and her family. "He interfered and saved certain pieces of property for Mother which would otherwise have been taken from her. . . . He voluntarily took it upon himself to defend our rights as a family and saved for us children the properties intended for us by father. . . . Mr. Edmunds simply said to our oppressors: 'You shall not do this thing! I will not submit to such an outrage being performed here!' "[13]

The circuit court ruled that Emma should be paid an additional $197.35 by "the proper Department at Washington." John M. Bernhisel would pursue Emma's claim for the next four years. On May 3, 1856, he informed her that the bill granting her the amount "has been this day considered in Committee of the Whole on the State of the Union, and was afterward passed by the House of Representatives. Now it goes to the Senate."[14] Before the year had ended Emma received her money through Bernhisel's persistence.

If Brigham Young realized Emma's financial plight, or if he knew the outcome of Joseph's estate and its effect on her, he never acknowledged it.

Instead he referred to Emma's wealth in public discourses, giving the impression that she had usurped it from the church. The church got nothing from the final settlement of the estate, but even the property Brigham thought he and the trustees had given Emma had to be repurchased by her with the money she received from the court. In 1847 Emma sold approximately $2,600 worth of property. The trustees for the church sold considerably more.[15] When much of this same property fell under the jurisdiction of the court sales, no church trustee witnessed the frustration of people who had bought land in good faith but no longer had title to it. But Emma was there. From the beginning she had warned that innocent people would lose their property. In the end she was right.

During this same time Orson Pratt in Utah announced on August 29, 1852, that polygamy was a doctrine of the Mormon church. Members had practiced it quietly since leaving Nauvoo, but the pressure of national rumors finally forced a public statement. With the news still fresh in Emma's household, William Holmes Walker came to see his brother Lorin, arriving on November 16. On his way to England as a missionary, he found that Lorin had moved to a nearby town so he spent two days with Emma and her family. "They all seemed glad to see me," he wrote in his journal, "and I had a good visit with them." William Walker brought up Joseph's possible future role in the Utah church, but Joseph had made up his mind about the doctrine of plural marriage and rejected Walker's invitation to go west.[16]

The public announcement of plural marriage coupled with pressures for her son to join the Saints in the West probably accounted for Emma's reluctance to talk freely with some Mormons traveling through. Hannah Tapfield King visited Nauvoo in May 1853 and was surprised when she saw Emma, for she had "heard much of her being a large vulgar woman." Mrs. King found Emma was not "coarse," but "Power is the principle that seems to be stamped on her, but it is like the lion when couchant. Her mind seemed to me to be absorbed in the *past* and lost almost to the present . . . neither does she seem to desire to form any intimacy. . . . She did not even seem to respond to kindness, but she looked as if she had suffered and as if a deep vein of bitterness ran through her system. I felt sorry for her." Emma did not need Mrs. King's sympathy, but the woman continued: "She seems to have shut her eyes to the light and knowledge she once possessed, and how great is the darkness that envelopes her. . . . I feel she is not worthy of the Prophet Joseph Smith, but I leave her. I am not her judge."[17] Mrs. King's letters have been quoted extensively to prove that Emma lived a deeply unhappy life and deserved to do so. However, other visitors over the next twenty years described Emma as a serene, articulate woman.[18]

Although Nauvoo had police by the early 1850s, violence was still a way of life for many who lived in or frequented the rough river towns. Julia described a fight during the summer of 1852. Two men got drunk, quarreled, and finally shot one another. One was brought to the Mansion. Julia wrote, "Well, you can imagine how we felt . . . four bullets in the back of his head. . . . They will take him away from here tonight they say, and I hope they will." The family deplored the opening of a new "liquor establishment." Julia commented, "We will have [fights] enough now. . . . I am so sorry about it, but what can't be cured will have to be endured."[19]

Joseph described another incident that happened while Lewis was away. A man from Nauvoo appeared at the Mansion House with "a strange woman." Emma, suspecting them of "improper conduct," ordered the couple to leave. "He went away, but soon returned, and boldly said the young woman should not leave. When Mother insisted, he drew a revolver and threatened her with it. This of course angered my mother and she firmly stated that both should go, and go at once." When Lewis returned he went after the man with a gun. Later Joseph found the two talking to each other over a drink.[20] While Bidamon's solution to the problem puzzled Joseph, Lewis probably found the intruder less angry several days later, and both men concluded they would not perpetuate a small-town feud over Emma's refusal to rent him a room.

The number of people in Emma's household seemed always in flux. In addition to the immediate family, the 1850 United States census listed a sixty-eight-year-old woman named Elizabeth Cole, an eight-year-old girl named Margaret, and the two orphan boys aged six and nine whose mother had died of a gunshot wound shortly after Emma returned to Nauvoo from Fulton. Lucy Mack Smith had been living for a time with her daughter, Lucy Millikin, in Fountain Green, near Sophronia McCleary and Katherine Salisbury, who would both be widows by the end of 1853.[21]

Julia and Elisha Dixon ran the Mansion House until the spring of 1852 when they moved to Galveston, Texas, where he served as a bookkeeper on a steamboat. Julia was homesick, and David's sketches and Emma's letters only made her more so. Julia cried over one of her mother's letters, then wrote, "The last time I saw you the Boyes and Zerelda were in the North Room and you were in the front Door and Joseph was beside the gate."[22] They "imprinted the last Kiss on one anothers Cheek" before she left. A year later she wrote Emma, "I wish I could just walk in to the front Door at home today and take you all by surprise. Would it not be delightful?—Tell Grandmother I want to see her very much." She wrote of her fortunate experience of being raised in Emma's home, then commented: "In childhood we see everything through a coulered Glass, as it were, and it coulers everything in the most brilyent light and pleases our eye, but as we grow older . . . it is a magnifying [glass] and we see things as they [really] are."[23] The following year the boiler exploded on the steamship on which her husband worked, throwing him into the ash pan. Badly burned, Elisha Dixon died after suffering three weeks. The young widow returned to Emma in 1853.

In the fall of that same year leaders of the Mormon church commissioned Frederick Piercy to illustrate the route from Liverpool, England, to the Salt Lake valley. He made fine drawings of Emma's family in Nauvoo. He sketched Joseph on his twenty-first birthday and described him as "a young man of a most excellent disposition and considerable intelligence," noting that Joseph held his mother in great affection and was always respectful and attentive to her needs. Young David, Piercy said, seemed to be happiest when he was drawing. Alexander and Frederick were "fine, strong, healthy fellows," and the "whole family had obtained a most excellent reputation for integrity and industry." Another visitor indicated that, while Emma was not young, she was still youthful in appearance and actions.[24]

Just as Emma had done, Lewis Bidamon made friends with the German and French people and learned from them how to grow grapes. When the wine from grapes grown on the sunny banks of the Mississippi became well known, Nauvoo had a new cash crop. Lewis eventually became a member of the Wine Growers Association and would one day be elected by his neighbors to represent them at a state meeting.

Creating businesses challenged Lewis; running them did not. After he sold the iron foundry in Canton to the McCormick farm machinery interests he started a match-manufacturing business which would become Diamond Match Company after he sold it.[25] By the early 1850s the Warsaw and Rockford Railroad planned a line to Nauvoo. Lewis provided services to the developers and when the line was completed he became the local agent and bookkeeper and attended some of the meetings as a stockholder. Hiring out his horse and buggy to visiting officials brought in additional income.[26]

Lewis also ran a ferry service with the packet boat *Lorna Doone*. Joseph commented, "I can but give Major Bidamon credit for considerable foresight in providing comfortably for the family from the resources at hand." He described "fair-sized gardens on our village home-lots," and the farm out of town where farm products were raised. "We had our own cows, chickens, and pigs, which helped to supply the table, and with our own horses did teaming to, from, and about the farm. . . . In all this work, under the direction of our stepfather, my brother Frederick and I shared as our abilities and capabilities permitted."[27]

Emma's small but regular income from the hotel bolstered the family's finances. One person said Lewis "was easy going, would lie late abed, was fond of liquor, was very profane, [and] would let her toil very hard."[28] But he was industrious and imaginative in devising ways to make a living. No item of correspondence from Emma implied that he was not carrying his share or that she believed he had taken advantage of her industry.

Emma and Lewis had settled into a routine with enough variety to make their lives interesting. In late December 1853 a letter arrived from Lewis's illegitimate daughter, Almira Smith. Raised by her grandparents, in 1850 she had married James M. Swiggart, who died nine months after the marriage. Four months later Almira gave birth to a daughter. Widowed and with a child to support, she had returned to her grandparents. Now at age twenty-four she sought out her natural father. Her first letter began hesitantly: "I avail myself of this opportunity of writing to you for the first time . . . and I feel at a great loss to know how to write at all." She mentioned a visit from Lewis when she was a schoolgirl in Ohio. He had tried to talk to her, but the presence of her friends had made her self-conscious and the visit was not a success. Now Almira told him, "I have oftimes looked back with sorrow upon the time that I Slited you[r] kind offers toward me but I do hope sincerely that you do not hold me accountable for my misbehavior towards you."[29] A subsequent letter mentioned her relatives' attempts to keep "me blinded so as not to Claim you as a Father but I was never so blind, I allways believed you to be my father. I never dare mention your name till since I was of age. . . . Dear Father, I love you dear as I love my soul. . . . That love has ever remained in my brest fro[m] my childhood to the present day but [I] allways kept it secreted from my relitives."[30] Lewis responded to his daughter's plea and answered her. He also helped her financially. Their correspondence lasted for at least twenty-seven years.

In 1855 another member of Emma's family began a correspondence. Joseph began writing to Emma Knight, a young woman whose family had spent the winter with the Smiths in Fulton. The two had not seen each other for nine years, so with some self-consciousness Joseph described himself. At age twenty-two, he said, "I am about 5 feet 8½ inches tall, weigh 178 pounds, and am as ugly as folks generally get to be in this country." He said nineteen-year-old Frederick was "nearly if not quite six feet high and very good looking, at least the girls all think him handsome." Alexander at seventeen was the same height as Joseph. "But David," Joseph wrote of his eleven-year-old brother, "is the boy of all boys, the pet of the family, and the very personification of gentleness and goodness. Mother has grown old [she was only fifty-one] though she bears up well she is just the same kind mother that she always was."[31]

During the spring of that same year Joseph became bored and restless with keeping the store. Emma had bought Gibbon's history of Rome and histories of Greece, England, the Continent, and the Reformation for her sons. The voluminous material John Bernhisel sent Joseph from Washington gave him a background in government. With his stepfather's encouragement, he prepared to go to Lewis's former home, Canton, Illinois, to study law. When he left at the end of May, Emma gave him a Bible and said, "My son, I have no charge to you as to what your religion shall be. I give you this Book with this admonition: Make it the man of your counsel; live every day as if it were to be the last, and you will have no need to fear what your future shall be."[32]

Joseph wrote to Emma, "Today I entered upon my duties as Clerk of the City Corporate of Canton. . . . I am studying as hard as I can, and will try to acquire the mysteries of the Law."[33]

"I know very well if your Father had been a little acquainted with the laws of the country he might have avoided a great deal of trouble," Emma later told her son. "Yet I have a horror of one of my children being entirely dependent upon being a lawyer for a living."[34]

After Joseph left, the letters that flew between Emma's children reveal delightful aspects of their personalities. Julia, though widowed, was still young enough at twenty-four to be an exuberant part of the local social activities. She nicknamed herself "Jute Dick" and gossiped to Joseph about who was taking whom for buggy rides and commented on the orations in English, French, and German, at the picnics. On the Fourth of July the young people went from picnic to supper to a dancing party. "We had flags aflying and the French band headed the procession. O, Could you have seen our town about 7 o'clock," Julia wrote, "everything was in motion. I had a good deal of fun that day at the expense of some of the country people coming in to see the elephant and you would have laughed too, could you have seen some of them. It was fun alive. After supper was over they all [wanted] to come down here and so Mother finally gave her consent for them to do so, and we went it on the light fantastic toes until daylight *caused us to part.*" The next day Frederick and Alexander arranged for a boat ride on the river. Some young women would not go because the water was too rough, but Julia reported that "we went at all hazards and had a delightful time of it." She teased her brother with news of a new girl in town. "One after my own heart," Julia said. "Wild as a March hare!"[35]

Emma's sons had also developed an affectionate camaraderie that becomes apparent in their correspondence. Joseph responded in breezy slang to a letter from Alexander. "Your thrice welcome epistle met my eyes this blessed morning and says I to myself, hey day what have I done to be brought up with a double envelope now? But *la,* bless my stars, it was a letter from my saucy brother and I just kicked the off heel of my *left* boot off trying to cut the double flying shuttle on the Larbaurd side of the Post Office step—when long come Jake Whistler, the *Marshall* . . . [he] slapped me on the back and said, 'Look here are you in fun or in liquor?'—I told him neither, just in sport.' "[36] Joseph wrote this letter with wide spaces between the lines, then filled in the spaces with the second half of the letter, a teasing trick that made his words make no sense until the reader caught on.

Julia's letters mentioned a John Middleton taking part in activities that summer. She married him soon after. Middleton was a Catholic, and Julia joined his church. Educated to become a priest, he failed to take his orders because of excessive drinking. He failed as a lawyer, and then as a farmer, before securing a position as a clerk in St. Louis. John Middleton's alcoholism eventually lost him his property, then his job, and finally his self-respect.[37]

Julia lived a sad and lonely life with him. She wrote colorless letters to her mother in an enduring attempt to make the best of an impossible situation but did not mention her husband's drinking or his cruelty. She only referred to him as being sick and expressed a continual hope that he would recover.

By the time Joseph returned to Nauvoo in the final months of 1855 he had become curious about the nationally popular practice of spiritualism. The phenomenon began in upstate New York in 1847 when the daughters of a Methodist farmer said the dead communicated with them by rapping and other noises. Interest in séances spread rapidly. People such as Mary Todd Lincoln, Horace Greeley, and Arthur Conan Doyle strongly advocated the practice. Authorities in the Mormon church preached against it. Late in November 1855 Enoch B. Tripp visited Nauvoo and wrote in his journal, "Joseph . . . is a very strong spiritual medium and claims that he through writing can converse with his father."[38] Joseph wrote to Emma Knight only ten days later. After "considerable experience" with the use of mediums he concluded: "I can scarcely see how we can have real tangible intercourse with departed spirits. I do not doubt their existence; I feel that it must be so, yet I feel we are cheating ourselves when we think that we are conversing with them."[39]

In 1851 Lucy Mack Smith came to live with Emma for the last five years of her life. Her memory and intellect seemed remarkable to many who visited her.[40] Hannah Tapfield King had found Lucy "pillowed up in bed" and noted: "She made a great impression on me for she is no ordinary woman. . . . She is a character that Walter Scott would have loved to portray and he would have done justice to her. . . . She blessed us with a mother's blessing, her own words, and my heart melted."[41] Another visitor found her "living in a lonely room in the eastern part of the house; she was in bed and very feeble. . . . She arose in bed and placing her hands around my neck, kissed me exclaiming, 'I can now die in peace since I have beheld your face from the valleys of the mountains.' "[42]

When Lucy could no longer walk Lewis made her a wheelchair. Finally her arthritic hands became so drawn out of shape that she was unable to feed herself. In spite of the difficulties Emma moved Lucy with the family to the farm several miles east of Nauvoo. Joseph corresponded with his friend Emma Knight on May 4, 1856: "Grandmother is not very well at present. We are afraid she cannot last much longer."[43] Ten days later, on Wednesday, May 14, Lucy Mack Smith died at age eighty-one and was buried the following day. No one described Emma's grief at the loss of her mother-in-law and friend of nearly thirty years.

Twelve days after Lucy's death Emma, Lewis, and Joseph sold the four Egyptian mummies. For years they had been in Lucy's care, and she had received a small income from showing them as a curiosity. A great-granddaughter of Lucy's, Jerusha Walker, remembered, "What fun we had with Aunt Emma's boys, Joseph, Frederick, Alexander and David. My favorite hiding place was in an old wardrobe which contained the mummies, and it was in here that I would creep while the others searched the house." The sale document indicated that Joseph Smith had paid twenty-four hundred dollars for them but did not record the price the collector paid on May 26, 1856.[44]

Around the time of his grandmother's death Joseph courted an attractive young woman named Emmeline—"Emma"—Griswold. Her family opposed the match because of Joseph's connection with the Mormons. Joseph discussed his beliefs with Emmeline and assured her that he had no particular interest in becoming actively engaged in church work, but should he ever choose to become an "advocate and defender" of Mormonism he "must be at perfect liberty to do so." He recorded in his memoirs that he solemnly promised that "I would have nothing to do with either the teaching or the practicing of polygamy or plural marriage, for I regarded the doctrine as utterly false and repulsive."[45] The couple married on October 22, 1856, becoming a second "Joseph and Emma Smith." They lived at the farm where Joseph had worked cooperatively with Frederick for several years instead of practicing law.

Ten days after the wedding George A. Smith and a missionary companion stopped by Nauvoo. Lewis politely greeted the men at the Mansion door. They followed him inside where Emma spoke to them coolly, then retreated, and Frederick and Alexander treated them with "stern reserve." When David tried to make conversation with the visitors he was "repeatedly called away." The two men stayed the night at the Mansion and lamented that the house needed paint and fixing up. George A. commented that their room was dirty.[46] The few boarders who came through Nauvoo did not generate enough income to hire help to keep a building as large as the Mansion clean or in repair. The two Mormon elders went to the farm to see Joseph, who described George A. as a "large, solidly built" man with sandy hair and beard. "His manners were very gentle, and he was active, good-natured, and a pleasant conversationalist. I liked him. . . . I know nothing of him to cause me to cherish personal dislike or ill will toward him."

George A. and his companion presented Joseph with a copy of the artist Frederick Piercy's finished volume. The gift pleased Joseph, for it contained sketches of various family members. The visitors expressed their desire that Joseph join with the church in the West. He politely refused.

"Well, you believe in the Bible and the Book of Mormon, do you not?" one of them asked him.

"Certainly I believe in the Bible and the Book of Mormon," Joseph answered, "but not as you people interpret them. I could not go out there and make my home with you while you are teaching and practicing as you are."

"I suppose you refer to polygamy?"

"Yes; I could never accept or countenance that doctrine," Joseph answered. In spite of their differences, the men parted friends.[47] But George A. recorded that Joseph had been "dyplomatic and evasive in the extreme" and somewhat cool although "far ahead of his mother and brothers." He also concluded that Joseph was "totally ignorant" of his father's teachings.[48]

Only a month passed before two more men stood at the Mansion House door asking for Joseph Smith. Lewis invited them inside where he introduced Emma to Samuel H. Gurley and Edmund C. Briggs. Emma also greeted these men with reserve and refused to be drawn into a conversation with them. They told her only that they were on a mission preaching the gospel but did not mention their special purpose for seeking out her son: to urge Joseph to become the prophet of a reorganized group of the Mormon church.[49]

20

Emma's Sons,
Lewis's Son

1860–1870

The 1846–1848 Mormon migration to Utah had left several thousand members of the church scattered throughout the Midwest. Some had drifted away from Mormonism; and others had first followed, then rejected other leaders. Some of these unattached members began to form branches of the church in Iowa, Illinois, and Wisconsin under the leadership of Jason Briggs and Zenas Gurley. As young Joseph grew to adulthood through the decade 1850–1860, their belief that he was the rightful successor to the original Mormon prophet was bolstered by spiritual manifestations among members of the group.[1] From 1851 to 1856 the church members waited with increasing anxiety until they became convinced that the spirit of God had signified the time had come. They sent Jason Briggs's brother Edmund and Zenas Gurley's son Samuel to call Joseph Smith III to be the head of their church and instructed the two men not to leave Nauvoo until he accepted.[2]

When Briggs and Gurley talked with Emma and Lewis Bidamon at the Mansion they learned that Joseph and his new bride, Emmeline, were living on the farm. They arrived there in the afternoon on December 6, 1856, and waited restlessly until Joseph came in from the fields. Samuel Gurley, new at this kind of diplomacy, blurted out that they were missionaries from the Reorganized Church of Jesus Christ of Latter Day Saints and thrust into Joseph's hand a letter containing a strongly worded exhortation to accept his responsibility to be their leader. The document read: "Through fasting and prayer, hath the answer from God come unto us, saying, 'Communicate with my servant Joseph Smith, son of Joseph the Prophet.' . . . We are assured that the same Spirit that has testified to us, has signified the same things to you.

. . . The good and the true are throughout the land waiting the true successor. . . . Arise in the strength of the Lord."[3]

Joseph read the letter, handed it back to Samuel Gurley, and said, "Gentlemen, I will talk with you on politics or any other subject, but on religion will not allow one word spoken in my house."

Gurley responded, "But we wish to tell you what we believe."

"I will not allow one word spoken on the subject to me in my house!" Joseph emphasized.

Samuel Gurley burst into tears, while Edmund Briggs pressed on. "We will not allow you to hinder us in doing our duty, as we have been sent by the command of God to tell you what we know and most surely believe in relation to your calling as the successor of your father."

Joseph rose to his feet. "When men come to my house and tell me what I must do, I tell them there is the door, and they can go out!"

Gurley turned to Briggs in defeat. "Come, let us go."

Edmund Briggs and Emmeline calmed the tempers enough that the four could eat together. Joseph agreed to meet the two men in Nauvoo the following morning. Briggs and Gurley again presented their case at the Mansion House. Joseph listened with more politeness but with no more conviction.

When Emma learned their purpose in coming, she explained, "I have always avoided talking to my children about having anything to do in the church, for I have suffered so much I have dreaded to have them take any part in it. . . . But I have always believed that if God wanted them to do anything in the church, the One who called their father would make it known to them." According to Briggs, Emma then said, "I never had confidence in Brigham Young," then gave her opinion that "Joseph did not for some time before his death."[4]

Samuel Gurley returned home, but Edmund Briggs stayed in Nauvoo for a year; part of the time he worked with Joseph on his farm. Briggs had been nine years old and living in Nauvoo at the time of the martyrdom, and was baptized into the Reorganization in 1852, at age seventeen. His knowledge of early Mormon doctrine was lacking, but he taught Joseph what he did believe. Joseph was not yet ready to lead the Midwestern church when Briggs left Nauvoo in 1857, but the seed had been planted. Contrary to tradition, Emma had not planted it, nor did she nurture it, although she apparently made no attempt to pluck it up.

By 1857 the Mormons in Utah had been practicing plural marriage as an openly avowed doctrine for five years. Newspapers continually publicized polygamy, which caused people to react toward the Utah Mormons with revulsion and disgust. Many of these reports undoubtedly reached Emma and her family. For well over a century the Eastern and Western Mormon churches would dispute Emma's role in influencing and teaching her son. While her decision not to go west with Brigham Young predisposed Joseph to remain in

Illinois, her refusal to join any of the other splinter groups also conditioned her son's attitudes. Joseph commented, "There was no opportunity or place for me in any of these groups . . . imbued as I was with certain ideals and standards irreconcilable with their doctrines." His tone indicated that he had thought about his own principles and found them to be at odds with what others were teaching. He singled out plural marriage as objectionable, but he also objected to the millennialism of Alpheus Cutler. He shrank from associating himself with any of the groups and laid "before the Almighty" the plain question: "To which body of believers shall I unite myself?"[5]

The repetitious news about the Mormons kept the memory of Brigham Young in Emma's mind, but the leaders in Utah remembered Emma without public prompting and used her as an example. On July 12, 1857, Heber C. Kimball preached in Salt Lake City. "What, sustain a woman, a wife, in preference to sustaining the Prophet Joseph, [or] brother Brigham," Kimball fumed, then pronounced his final sentencing on Emma. "That was the trouble with Emma Smith," he railed, "Joseph stood for the truth and maintained it, she stuck against it, and where is she? She is where she is, and she will not escape until Joseph Smith opens the door and lets her out."[6] Kimball's remarks sounded as if Emma were dead and consigned to hell and only Joseph could release her. In reality she was in Nauvoo happily awaiting the birth of a grandchild. But the image of Emma damned had been made public.

Joseph and Emmeline moved from the farm back to Nauvoo in 1857 and began to renovate the old Homestead house for their home. In July of that year Emmeline gave birth to a daughter and named her Emma Josepha.[7] Emma's granddaughter was called Emma J. to avoid confusion with the other Emmas in the family. Joseph took several jobs in Nauvoo. For seven years, from late 1856 until 1863, he was elected justice of the peace. The Major simultaneously served as the assistant marshal. In connection with the law firm of Morrill and Risse, Joseph established an office two blocks from his home. He championed the cause of many of the new German immigrants whose language barrier made them fair game for confidence men. But the financial struggle was difficult and he hired out as a day laborer when he could.[8]

Joseph and his wife had their second child in January 1859 and called her Eva. When the baby was nine months old she sickened and died. They buried the child in Nauvoo.

About the time of his daughter's death Joseph reconsidered his earlier opposition to leadership of the Reorganization. He gave as a reason for this decision that the promptings of the spirit of the Lord had answered his question about which church to join. He contacted his mother's old friend, William Marks, at Shabbona, Illinois, to say that he was ready to reconsider. "I am soon going to take my father's place at the head of the Mormon Church," Joseph wrote Marks, "and I wish that you and some others . . . [would] come and see me."[9]

William Marks had stayed with James J. Strang's church from 1846 until the summer of 1850. He left in disillusionment two years later to follow Charles B. Thompson, but by 1854 he had separated himself from that group and returned to Shabbona Grove, Illinois, where Zenas H. Gurley's group contacted him by 1859 and persuaded him to attend a church conference on April 10, 1859. He was standing at the pulpit with Gurley when a young woman approached with uplifted hands and said, "Thus saith the Lord; O thou man of God! In times past thou hast sat with my servant Joseph, the Seer; and in times near to come thou shalt sit in council with his son."[10] Deeply moved by the experience, Marks enthusiastically supported the Reorganization.

Marks and two other church leaders, Israel Rogers and William W. Blair, came to Nauvoo in March 1860. Emma probably had not seen William Marks since 1847 in Fulton. He told Joseph bluntly, "We have had enough of man-made prophets, and we don't want any more of that sort. If God has called you, we want to know it." Joseph promised that he would be present at the annual church conference in Amboy, Illinois, on April 6.[11] The following month Emma accompanied Joseph to Amboy. They arrived on the evening of April 5. Although her brothers and sisters lived in the area, Emma clearly was in Amboy to be with her son. A prayer meeting was held the night they arrived. This would be Joseph's first remembered testimony meeting and the experience left him singularly moved. "[I] heard the statements made by many who had received evidences concerning myself and the work God was calling me to do; I became fully aware of the fact that the same Influence and Power that had been at work with me, had determined my course of action, and had finally led me into their midst."[12] The following day, on the thirtieth anniversary of the church's founding, Emma and Joseph joined about one hundred and fifty people assembled in the Mechanics' Hall at ten o'clock for conference.[13]

Speakers at the morning session outlined general beliefs of the church and defined the differences between their doctrines and those of Brigham Young. They taught that a prophet would come to them by "right of lineage" and gather the scattered fragments of their group. When the afternoon session began, Joseph, twenty-seven years old, walked to the front of the hall. Zenas Gurley announced simply, "I present to you, my brethren, Joseph Smith."

Joseph addressed the group. "I come not here of my self, but by the influence of the spirit," he said. "For some time past I have received manifestations pointing to the position which I am about to take. . . . I have come in obedience to a power not my own, and shall be dictated by the power that sent me." He then outlined his reasons for accepting the position as head of the church and addressed the question of polygamy. "There is but one principle taught by the leaders of any fraction of this people that I hold in utter abhorrence. That is a principle taught by Brigham Young and those believing in him. I have been told that my father taught such doctrines. I have never believed it and never can believe it. If such things were done, then I believe they never were done by Divine authority. I believe my father was a good man, and a good man never could have promulgated such doctrines."[14]

His position indicated that he accepted his father as a prophet but that he was most ill informed about his father's involvement with plural marriage. Emma had not divulged to him his father's participation in its practice. She believed her husband had been a prophet but that his revelation on polygamy did not come from God, and therefore she broke no commandment by rejecting it. While Emma's conviction came from intimate knowledge of the practice of plural marriage, Joseph's stand was made in ignorance. Some people would tell him about his father's participation in polygamy, and others would reinforce his belief that Brigham Young was responsible for it.

For those at the Amboy conference, Joseph's speech was inspiring and to the point. He concluded, "If the same spirit prompts my coming, prompts also my reception, I am with you." When the motion was made that he be received as a prophet, the vote was unanimously affirmative.

Zenas Gurley, Samuel Powers, William W. Blair, and William Marks ordained Joseph president of the church and president of the high priesthood.[15] A second motion proposed that Emma Bidamon be received as a member of the Reorganization. Again the vote was unanimous in favor and Emma, age fifty-six, found herself united again with a Mormon church. Both she and Joseph came into the church by virtue of their earlier original baptisms and no subsequent ceremony was required.[16]

At the semiannual conference of the Reorganization the following October, Emma was appointed to make a selection of hymns and to work with a committee to publish the hymnbook. The actual extent of Emma's involvement is unknown, but this third hymnal came off the press in Cincinnati a year later, in 1861, without her name on it.[17] The format duplicated that of the 1841 hymnal published in Nauvoo with a reduced number of selections.

After Emma and Joseph returned to Nauvoo he decided that the church headquarters should be in the city founded by his father. Influenced by guilt and superstition, some people believed that the area would not prosper until the Mormons returned; others angrily recalled earlier Mormon interference in politics and the storm over plural marriage. Many communities drafted resolutions opposing the settlement, and a petition in Nauvoo told Joseph to go somewhere else to preach and practice his religion. The petition promised the Mormons "will not be allowed by the people of Hancock County to return." Joseph eventually convinced his neighbors that he led a more moderate Mormon group than his father had and gradually mollified public sentiment. His father's old antagonist, editor Thomas Sharp, wrote, "Young Jo is a different man from Old Jo, and don't seek to gather all the faithful together, that he may use them politically and financially, as the Brighamites do. There is noth-

ing objectionable in Young Joe's church, that we have heard of."[18] Joseph held
the first church meeting in the Homestead house, then used the house once
owned by William Marks. Finally, in an ironic circle, the Nauvoo branch of
the Reorganization met in the large room over the red brick store.[19]

While Emma was in Amboy in April she probably visited members of her
family. Tryal Morse, who was two years younger than Emma, had moved from
western New York to the outskirts of Amboy in 1859. Emma's visit to Amboy
in 1860 was the first known meeting of the two sisters since Emma had left
Harmony almost thirty years earlier. Shortly after Emma returned to Nauvoo a
tragedy struck the Morse family. On June 3 a tornado whipped through northern Illinois and touched down at Morse's farm, demolishing the house, trees,
fences, and outbuildings. The black funnel flung Tryal a hundred feet from
where the house had stood. She had lain for an hour with a splintered board
through her chest until she was found, then died within a few minutes. Her
twenty-nine-year-old daughter Emma had both legs broken and suffered nine
days until she, too, died from her injuries. The deaths of her younger sister and
her namesake coming so soon after they were reunited must have been especially difficult for Emma.[20]

During this summer Emma's private life was also changing. She took in
Lewis's daughter, Mary Elizabeth Gibson, and Mary's eight-year-old son
Charles. Another Bidamon relative, forty-eight-year-old Rosanna Bidamon,
also found a home with Emma.[21]

Two nephews from Utah, Joseph F. Smith and Samuel H. B. Smith,
stopped in Nauvoo to see Emma and have a reunion of cousins that summer.
After dinner the first evening Frederick brought the visitors into a room in the
Mansion House where Emma was working. She had not seen them for fourteen years. "Mother, do you know these young men?" he inquired. Joseph F.
Smith had to wait only a moment, but Emma's reply pleased him. With some
pride he soon wrote to his sister, "She appeared to have forgotten Samuel but
me She said she would have known anywhere because I looked so much like
father!!"[22]

When Joseph led the visiting cousins to their room he urged them not to
go any farther on their missions but to stop and reflect about the validity of
their own church. "Somewhat zealous" was Joseph F.'s summation of this
cousin. Samuel H. B. Smith wrote to George A. Smith about the visit and
blamed Emma for Joseph's position. "It is evident that Joseph has been under
the influence of his mother," he wrote home to Utah, "only he denies it." He
continued, "Aunt Emma was pretty much as she used to be. She had that
same way about her—which is very strange—I think we all have our ways and
especially her. Bidamon is the same blasphemer. If I were in the boy's places I
would be willing to dissolve partnership with him as he surely is a wicked man.
Anyhow what I call a wicked man."[23]

Joseph's acceptance speech at Amboy had been widely reprinted throughout the United States. In the ensuing year two ghosts from Emma's past rose up to haunt her son. James Arlington Bennet wrote to Joseph from New York City to announce that "your manefesto pleased me extremely." Bennet gushed forth, dropping names and assuming that Joseph now would accept his profusion of advice about how to set up his new Mormon kingdom. Bennet had the effrontery to ask Joseph to extend his respects to his "excellent mother."[24]

Joseph received another letter that raised difficult questions. William E. McLellin wrote:

> I do not wish to say hard things to You of your Father, but Joseph, if you will only go to your own dear mother, she can tell You that he believed in Polygamy and practised it long before his violent death! That he delivered a revelation sanctioning, regulating, and establishing it,—and that he finally burned the awful document before her eyes. . . . When I read your speech (taking it to be honest) I felt a pang wring my old heart. Joseph, You are but a youth, Do be admonished by one who has grown old, Take not your own dear Father for a pattern in your religious career . . . do carve out your own course.[25]

Thus from the commencement of his position as president of the church Joseph was urged to go to his mother for a full and accurate account of his father's polygamous activities. Evidence indicates that he did not. The question was an impossibly difficult one for a devoted and affectionate son to ask. It was far easier now to turn his full attention to solving the problems of the new church and immersing himself in concern for his family. His brother Frederick had become very ill.

Frederick had married Annie Maria Jones in September 1857, when he was twenty-one and she sixteen; they moved to the Smith farm outside Nauvoo. But the marriage went sour sometime after the birth of Alice Fredericka a year later.[26] Emma became anxious about Frederick's health in the fall and winter of 1861. In late December Joseph stopped to see him and found the house cold, the fire out, no wood chopped, and Frederick in bed too ill to care for himself. His wife had taken the child and gone to her mother's two days previously and had left no food or water near the bed. Angry at the obvious neglect, Joseph made his brother as warm and comfortable as he could. On Christmas Day Emma and Joseph moved Frederick into the Mansion. His wife and child did not return. Less than a month later Alexander's wife Elizabeth, whom he had married on June 23, 1861, gave birth to a son.[27] For several months after the birth Elizabeth was ill. Emma cared for the new baby, nursed her sixteen-year-old daughter-in-law, and tried to halt Frederick's steady decline.

In an April letter from St. Louis Julia wished spring would bring "health and healing on its wings" to her "poor invalid brother." With affection she encouraged, "Fred, I am truly sorry to hear of your continued ill health but I do still hope when I hear from you again you will be much improved."[28] Frederick died in the Mansion April 13, 1862. The church bells in Nauvoo announced his death to the community with twenty-six mournful peals, one for every year of Frederick Granger Williams Smith's life.[29]

From 1861 to 1865 the Civil War attracted many men and boys from Nauvoo, and Joseph made a rallying speech that drew seventeen names to the enlistment rolls within twenty minutes. But service in the forces posed a problem for the Smith brothers. As ordained ministers of a church whose doctrine prohibited the shedding of human blood except in the defense of their families or themselves, enlistment would make them accountable for bloodshed while in the service. But their spirits were also stirred by a call to serve their country. They solved the dilemma by deciding not to enlist but to go if they were drafted. Alexander was drafted and had spent two weeks in Quincy when General Robert E. Lee surrendered and the war was ended.[30]

Before the Civil War started, Lewis Bidamon had enthusiastically tried to introduce a new crop to the Nauvoo farmers to supplement their income from the grapes. He brought equipment into Nauvoo to process sugar cane, but with the advent of the war the project died. In 1864 sixty-two-year-old Lewis Bidamon was still a handsome man. His attraction to women would soon bring changes to the family.

A widow twenty-four years younger than Emma lived on a farm near Nauvoo. Nancy Abercrombie was born in Kentucky on November 16, 1828. She was seven years old when she was apprenticed to Mathew Baker. The terms of her indenture directed her "to serve until she attain the age of 18 . . . during which time [she] shall faithfully serve in all things demanded and behave herself to her said master . . . and the said Baker binds himself . . . that he will teach and cause to be taught said Nancy O the art of seamster and allow said apprentice sufficient meat and drink and apparel of every description . . . that she be of no charge to the county and at the end of her said service pay [her] 3 pounds 10 shillings and a new suit of clothes."[31] The Baker family moved from Kentucky to Illinois sometime prior to 1840, taking Nancy with them. At age seventeen, in 1845, she broke the terms of her indenture and married William Brooks. They had one son. Either the marriage failed or Brooks died, but Nancy married again. Her second husband, William Abercrombie, died in 1852 and left Nancy with a daughter.

Nancy Abercrombie had boarded with her children at the Thomas Luce tavern in Sonora Township adjacent to Nauvoo since sometime before 1859. Members of the Luce family had joined the Mormon church and immigrated to Nauvoo in the 1840s. Several Luce women were members of the Relief Society, but the family apparently dropped their connection with the church in the ensuing years.[32] During Nancy's stay with the Luce family she gave birth on September 9, 1859, to an illegitimate daughter named Mary whose father is unknown.

In years to come her grandchildren would remember her as petite with dark hair and eyes, a soft voice, and a self-effacing manner. She was "a sweet woman," although a little shy. In the fall of 1863 she became pregnant again and a son, Charles Edwin, was born March 16, 1864; Lewis Bidamon was the child's father.[33] Emma was fifty-nine years old and would turn sixty in July. While she left no record of her personal feelings, her subsequent actions indicate that with personal courage she accepted the facts as they existed and apparently did not dwell on them with rancor. That she opposed plural marriage but accepted Lewis's infidelity seems puzzling. But an important difference existed. Joseph insisted that Emma set the example for other women to follow, while Lewis expected no such action.

Nancy Abercrombie struggled to raise her young family alone for four years. In 1868 she asked Emma to take four-year-old Charles. Emma accepted and raised the child, treating the little boy with such love and affection that as an adult Charles Bidamon recalled, "I was raised in her home and knew what kind of a woman she was. . . . She was a person of very even temper. I never heard her say an unkind word, or raise her voice in anger or contention. . . . She had a queenly bearing, without the arrogance of a queen. A noble woman, living and showing charity for all, loving and beloved."[34]

One neighbor said of Emma, "Mrs. Smith Bidamon was awfully nice. There wasn't a better woman in Nauvoo. She was a good soul, a good christian woman. She was good to everyone. Everyone thought well of her. She was always busy, a great woman to work. She did a good job raising her children. Her boys, Joseph, Alexander, and David were good boys. She was good to Mr. Bidamon's son, Charles."[35]

The reaction of Emma's boys to Lewis's unfaithfulness seemed to follow their mother's example. Three years after Charles came to live with Emma, David Smith wrote to Lewis who was away on business. Teasing gently about the new city magistrate position, David called his stepfather "Illustrious Juror" and recounted events at the farm. In the same letter Emma addressed "Ever Dear Husband," signing it, "Affectionately yours allways in a hurry." When Joseph was forty-one he closed an 1873 letter to his mother, "With my kind love to all, Pa Bidamon, the first, I remain, Your son." Joseph wrote to his stepfather two years later, "So far as the $5 already received by you for rent is concerned, please do me the favor to lay the same out in the purchase of a hat to replace the one the wind and the waves stole from you last winter. It will give me pleasure to think that I have been instrumental in replacing your loss." And Alexander Smith remembered, "Give my kind regards to Pa Bidamon."[36]

Emma and Lewis continued to live together in a general atmosphere of kindness and consideration. When Emma expressed her love for blue damson plums, Lewis ordered plum trees from Massachusetts. A relative remembered that Emma regularly served Lewis his favorite corn bread. Emma's forthright personality was not diminished by her years with Lewis, however. She kept the milk cool in a low stone cellar with rickety stairs that Lewis kept promising to fix. He put off the repairs until Emma delivered an ultimatum: fix the steps or she would not carry any more milk down. He still delayed and in exasperation she threw the milk into the cellar, then quietly proceeded with the kitchen duties. The Major mended the steps.[37]

Emma's compassion was the moderating force in almost all of her relationships. In a surprising but characteristic manner, she extended it to Nancy Abercrombie, who ultimately benefited most from Emma's strength of character. As Charlie grew older, Emma employed Nancy, enabling her to be closer to her son.

The headquarters of the Reorganization had been in Nauvoo, Illinois, for five years when Joseph Smith III prepared to move his family to Plano, Illinois, in 1865. The move would enable him to supervise the church periodical, the *True Latter Day Saints' Herald*. In preparation for his editorial duties, Joseph learned shorthand. In his journal he commented that his mother saw "in phonography [shorthand] a multiplication of schools, and she wonders where she would find so much time as an excuse for the bad use we make of our time and talent." And in writing down her criticism Joseph slyly wrote in the newfangled shorthand at which Emma sniffed.[38]

By January 1866 Joseph, Emmeline, and their four children, three daughters and a baby son, had found a home in Plano, Kendall County, about one hundred seventy-five miles from Nauvoo. Not long after their move Emmeline became homesick for Nauvoo and returned with the children for a visit. The baby boy, Joseph Arthur, fell ill. Joseph arrived in Nauvoo on March 13, 1866, only to find that his son had died the day before. They held the funeral in Emma's dining room. Three years later, March 25, 1869, Emmeline followed her son to the grave.

During Emmeline's last illness Joseph hired a young woman to help with the house and care for his three young daughters, Emma J., Carrie, and Zaide. Bertha Madison agreed to stay on as housekeeper after Emmeline died, but Joseph became disturbed with the gossip of neighbors and church members who hinted at impropriety. After making the issue a matter of prayer, he proposed to Bertha Madison and married her on November 12, 1869, only to be criticized again for not letting the customary year of mourning pass. When one acquaintance chided him for marrying too soon, Joseph remembered, "I had the extreme satisfaction of reminding him that the gossipers had not waited the conventional year before using malicious and too-busy tongues upon my affairs." Bertha Madison Smith bore nine children, among them Frederick Madison, who would become the eldest living son and, as Joseph commented, "entitled to inherit the birthright."[39]

Emma's letters to Joseph after he left Nauvoo provide a record of her philosophy and her activities. In February she wrote that she had never "lived a winter with so little hard work to do." The cellar stored quantities of food for the winter and "I am blessed with a good appetite, and eat and sleep more than I ever did before." Content with the physical necessities of life, Emma turned her thoughts to more intangible things. "If there is anything in this world that I am or ever was proud of it is the honor and integrity of my children," she told her son. "But I dare not allow myself to be proud, as I believe that pride is one of the sins so often reproved in the good book. So I am enjoying the better spirit, and that is to be truly and sincerely thankfull and in humility give God the glory, not trying to take any of it to myself for it is him that has led my children in the better way." But Emma did feel a little unbidden pride in the accomplishments of her children. "No one knows the solid heartfelt pleasure I take in comparing my sons with others, and them too that has had fathers of their own to guard them."[40]

As her sons struggled to raise their families and keep them healthy, they turned to Emma. Joseph asked for her recipe for salve, and Emma sent him detailed instructions, commenting, "The first camphorated salve I ever made was just mutton tallow and beeswax and camphor alone and it was then thought to be an excellent article. If you have not the gymson and elder let me know and I will send you the salve ready made."[41]

When Chief Keokuk of the Sauk Indians visited Nauvoo in 1841 his wife had exchanged recipes for herbal medicines with Emma. One in particular, a tea made from squawberries and the juice from certain roots, was considered helpful for children's canker sores.[42] An undated note from David asked the owner of the local apothecary, "Please send the above articles to me for Mother, she seems to be in very poor health; tell us the cost." David had asked for two ounces of mandrake and golden seal and five cents' worth of gamboge. The pharmacist returned the note with the comment, "I did not send as much as you wanted. I thought you had no need for so much,"[43] indicating the personal interest shown by the small-town merchant.

Debts of the fledgling church worried Joseph from the time he assumed the presidency. He sold some of his own land to relieve the financial pressure but turned to Emma for advice. Emma suggested he sell the Kirtland temple. Joseph responded to his mother, "So much was your mind like my own upon the matter that I at once wrote to Kirtland, offering the temple for sale. Should I be able to sell for the price offered, I will be able to get out of debt. . . . However, I dare not build any air castles."[44]

Although Emma did not advise Joseph on points of doctrine, she encouraged her son in his efforts to keep the Reorganized Church financially solvent and knew that some old debts troubled him. She admitted that she did not desire riches—except when she thought of the financial struggles Joseph and Alexander and their young families faced. "Then I would like to straighten out all indebtedness and put the Bishop in possession of means to send out all on missions that are fit to go, then I feel I would willingly continue to keep tavern a long time yet."[45] Keeping a boardinghouse after the age of sixty-five was not an offer she made lightly. Emma knew how much work was involved.

Occasionally some of Joseph's other problems spilled over into Emma's life. She wrote, "Joseph I must tell you about a certain advent we had here . . . in the shape of two females announcing themselves as coming from Plano, direct from Brother Joseph's and the moment they said that I knew they were your undesirables you mentioned sometime ago." The women had not "thrown themselves on the church exactly," but, Emma noted, they "came down on us in the Mansion for a home." After telling them she could not employ them or take them in, she commented, "They appeared not to think as I did about the matter, and stayed three days and of course I lived and let live. I did not commit any outbreaking sin, but if they had not left after being told to every day I believe I would have committed some."[46] On another occasion when some of the church women in Plano apparently raised an issue with Joseph, Emma commented, "I think you must have had an interesting time in the excitement among the strong minded women. Well, I am not one of those strong minded ones. I have always found enough to do to fill up all my time in doing just what was very plainly and positively my duty without clamoring for some unenjoyed privilege which if granted would be decidedly a damage to me and mine."[47]

Emma rarely reflected upon her problems but in one letter to Joseph wrote: "How often I have been made deeply sensible that my pilgrimage had been an arduous one and God only knows how often my heart had almost sunk when I have reflected how much more arduous and trying your work was to be. I have often thought that I know just as well as any other person just how St. Paul felt when he said, 'If only in this life we have hope, we are of all men most miserable.' "[48]

Emma's daily routine changed slowly as she aged. According to a grand-daughter, she napped thirty minutes after the heavy noon meal and occasionally took time to read a copy of *Godey's Lady's Book*. While she tended the pansies and violets that bordered the rocks around the Mansion House she hummed, "There's a Feast of Fat Things for the Righteous Preparing," and "The Flowers That I Knew in the Wildwood." Her favorite flowers were lilacs —"lay-lacs" she called them—and the immense planting of them by the kitchen door helped to hide the peeling paint of the old house.[49]

Emma's eyesight began to fade in 1867, and she fussed in irritation when the press of duties did not allow her enough time to write to Joseph and Julia in the daylight and her broken spectacles were useless in the lamplight.[50] She thought she overtaxed her eyes with too much sewing. Emma always had boarders to care for, linens to wash, and meals to prepare. In years when the grapes were abundant Lewis sold them to large wineries. But when the price dropped Emma and the Major made their own wine. That year they prepared more than three hundred gallons of wine and a cask of cider because the price of grapes was so low.

Emma wrote to Joseph and asked for his help in extending a fence around the little family graveyard in front of the Homestead. Her baby son Don Carlos and the infant son who died at birth were buried near their father. She hoped the Smith relatives in Utah might help with an appropriate marker for Joseph and Hyrum and their parents. She also found time to be philosophical about the infirmities of her advancing age. In her sixty-fourth year, the year she took Charles Bidamon to raise, she wrote to Joseph, "I often find I have to yield my will to surrounding circumstances, so I am daily trying to learn St. Paul's lesson . . . to be contented with our *condition*, to pray always, and in *all things* to give thanks." Emma said she tried every day to feel contentment and found no difficulty praying regardless of the task at hand. "I can pray and work in the kitchen, or in the cellar, or up stairs," she commented. "My heart cannot prevent prayers." Yet she worried about not being thankful enough but lived in hope that she would be able to learn even that in time. "I have a promise," she wrote, "that my last days shall be my best days, and according to the years that is alloted to mankind, those days are not very far distant."[51]

After the Major had worked very hard on the vineyard and the garden in the summer of 1869 Emma philosophically remarked, "We shall have but very few grapes and perhaps none at all this fall, so he will not have the trouble of working them up." She was also sympathetic toward Lewis's advancing age and commented that after his steady work through the summer of 1869 he might have to allow himself some ease in the following years. But the relationship between her adult sons and the Utah church brought tension into her life.

21

Josephites
and Brighamites

1870–1877

Joseph struggled to increase the membership of the Reorganized Church from the time he became its president and reinstated a much-tested tool in his search for members. The Reorganization sent out proselytizing missionaries as frequently as the growing membership rolls would allow.[1] No area seemed more full of possibilities than Utah and its "Brighamites," because many of them remembered Joseph's father. They were already converted to the Book of Mormon and basic Mormon philosophy. Lurid newspaper accounts of the "evils of polygamy"[2] implied that many of the Western Saints would forsake Brigham Young's organization for a church headed by the prophet's son. Furthermore, virtually all visitors from Utah greeted the Smith boys with warmth and friendliness.

In the spring of 1863 Edmund C. Briggs and his companion, Alexander McCord, departed for Utah to preach. They arrived in Salt Lake City on August 7, 1863.[3] Four days after their arrival they met with President Young and twenty-five or thirty of his associates. The meeting was not cordial. The church leadership in Utah could see no place for an "apostate" group. Apparently feeling threatened by the Mormons' response to Joseph's presidency, Orson Hyde had earlier told a congregation in eastern Utah that the Joseph Smith who headed the Reorganization was not the son of Joseph Smith of Nauvoo.[4] Brigham Young now promised Briggs and McCord that no home or meeting house in Utah would welcome Reorganization missionaries. According to Briggs, Brigham then placed the blame for these missionary activities: "Emma Bidamon is a wicked, wicked, wicked woman and always was. . . . Joseph is led by his mother and is now acting under the direction of Emma.

. . . I know more of Emma, Joseph, Alexander, and David than they know of themselves."

"That is your opinion," Briggs refuted, "but I know better, that Emma knew nothing of this work untill it was brought to her, and I do know she has nothing to do with my mission here. We have come in obedience to a power not our own, nor of man, but in the name of the Lord of Hosts, and I know that my associates are not guilty of the crimes you charge them with."[5] But Brigham Young insisted on making Emma responsible for the presence of the Reorganization in Utah.

Briggs and McCord preached their message in spite of President Young's hostilities. They confronted the people of Utah with three main points: that young Joseph Smith was the true leader of Mormonism by virtue of his birthright; that Brigham Young had usurped the position of president; and that polygamy was an abomination introduced to the church by Brigham Young and not by the original prophet. Though their message won converts, Briggs's and McCord's attempts to build up local branches in Utah were frustrated by the migration of their people out of the Utah territory.

Three years later Joseph assigned his brother Alexander to take charge of the church's California mission. On May 20, 1866, Emma watched Alexander finish his preparations for traveling to the West Coast, then anxiously bade her son farewell, knowing he would spend some time in Utah on the way. Emma was uncertain about his influence on the Smith relatives in Salt Lake City. "I think it might be right for him to go and discharge his duty to them and leave them without excuse," she wrote Joseph. "I look upon their case as a hard one. I believe that God is able to do all that is for his glory and the good of those that truly serve him," she continued, and then she expressed her opinion of those members of the family who followed Brigham Young. "May be that God will consider them in their ignorance and convict and convert them and cleanse them from their abominations and make them fit for more decent society. I hope he will, that is those who were taken there when too young to know any better." To support Alexander, Emma resolved to take care of his family "as faithfully as I can."[6]

Alexander and his companions traveled without incident until they arrived at Fort Laramie. There they joined a Mormon immigrant train. Alexander mused about his unusual position—three "Josephite" missionaries "strongly antagonistic to the Utah church" in the midst of three hundred devoted Mormons on their way to Utah. He gave his name as Alex Hale instead of Alexander Smith.

"Where did you say you hailed from?" the captain, Thomas Ricks, asked.

Alexander sensed that the man knew him. "The state of Illinois."

"What county or town may I ask?"

"Certainly, sir," Alexander replied, "I came from Nauvoo, Hancock County."

"Ah! I thought so!" said Ricks and looked Alexander straight in the eye without another word.

"We understood one another," Alexander reported.[7]

The Mormon people had retained a special affection for Joseph Smith's children. A residual hope that the prophet's sons would eventually come west and join the Mormons had existed from the time of the exodus from Nauvoo. Brigham Young had remarked to his brother Phineas in February 1860, "Joseph . . . will be a good latter day saint; in time it may want a revelation from the Lord; but blessings will rest upon the posterity of Joseph Smith the Prophet."[8] Heber C. Kimball once told a congregation assembled in the outdoor Bowery in Salt Lake, "At present the Prophet Joseph's boys lay apparently in a state of slumber, everything seems to be perfectly calm with them, but by and by God will wake them up, and they will roar like the thunder of Mount Sinai!"[9] As Alexander approached Salt Lake City in a Mormon immigrant wagon train with his identity concealed, one of the ironies of Mormonism was now apparent. Ahead lay the sprawling domain of the Utah church with a burgeoning population and settlements scattered over a vast area of the West. The kingdom was in one church; the line of kings in the other.[10]

Hyrum Smith's oldest son, John, now patriarch of the Utah church, met his cousin Alexander at the mouth of Emigration Canyon and rode with him into Salt Lake City. The Mormon leaders understood that Alexander was on his way to California to advance his brother Joseph's claims and announced this in the local newspapers but did not mention that he might advocate those claims in the very midst of Utah.[11]

When Alexander Smith began to preach his message in Salt Lake City the "roaring of the thunder of Mount Sinai" Heber Kimball had predicted was not what the church leaders in Utah wanted to hear from Joseph's boys. Alexander spoke at Independence Hall, and at Fox's Gardens, and in Provo, and found that his cousin Joseph F. Smith was present to speak against him.[12] Alexander remained in the Salt Lake City area only fifteen days, but his brief stay aroused speculation. A month later, at October Semiannual Conference in Salt Lake City, President Young referred to the interest sparked by the Josephite missionaries. "I will speak upon a subject . . . for the benefit of a few who are inclined to be giddy-headed, unstable in their ways, and enthusiastic about something they do not understand." He then recognized Alexander's recent presence in the city and briefly rehearsed the birth dates and the names of Joseph Smith's sons. "The sympathies of the Latter-day Saints are with the family of the martyred prophet," he said, then turned his attention to Emma. "I never saw a day in the world that I would not almost worship that woman, Emma Smith, if she would be a saint instead of being a devil." He digressed for a moment to explain that "Young Joseph Smith does not possess one particle of this priesthood." Then he came back to Emma. "The Twelve apostles . . . would have been exceeding glad if the prophet's family had come with us when we left Nauvoo for the valleys of these mountains. We would have made cradles for them if they had required them, and would have fed them on milk and honey. . . . Emma is naturally a very smart woman; she is subtle and ingenious. . . . She has made her children inherit lies. To my certain knowledge Emma Smith is one of the damnedest liars I know of on this earth; yet there is no good thing I would refuse to do for her, if she would only be a righteous woman."

Brigham Young repeated the old story about her attempts to poison Joseph and said that Joseph had "told her that she was a child of hell, and literally the most wicked woman on this earth, that there was no one more wicked than she. He spoke to her . . . in a very severe manner and she never said one word in reply. . . . Twice she undertook to kill him."[13] He erred when he assumed that Emma was responsible for her son's being in Utah, and he erred in charging her with poisoning.

Unaware that she anticipated Brigham's angry speech by a month, Emma had written to Joseph in Plano while Alexander was in Utah. "Now you must not let those L.D.S.'s trouble you too much. If they are determined to do evil, they will do it, and such as are anxiously willing to make you trouble are not worth laboring very hard to save from the dogs. You may know you are not the first one that has been misunderstood or misapplied, or misquoted and misrepresented in every way, and in every conceivable shape."[14]

Alexander Smith traveled on to California where he preached for a year. On an evening late in December the sound of quick swinging steps in the Mansion's halls surprised and delighted his family. The Major's voice boomed from the office, "I knew your voice, Aleck!"[15]

In April 1868 Emma traveled to Plano for the spring conference. She had planned to make the visit two years earlier, and even though Lewis encouraged her—"Pa Bidamon quite insisted that I should fix up and go right off to Plano. . . . It was very kind of him and quite a temptation to me"—Emma had not been willing to leave Alexander's pregnant wife Lizzie while he was in Utah.[16] The baby had been born in November 1866.

Alexander moved his family from Nauvoo to Plano to be near Joseph and the church headquarters, but in 1869 Joseph again assigned Alexander to the mission field in Salt Lake City. This was to be no fifteen-day stopover but a regular preaching assignment, and Alexander was to take his brother David with him as his companion.

David was twenty-four and Alexander thirty-one when they sat at the table in Emma's dining room in the Mansion to eat one last piece of strawberry shortcake before they bade her farewell. They arrived in Utah early in July 1869. Patriarch John Smith welcomed them. David resembled his father more than the stocky Alexander did, and his personality was outgoing and ingratiating, but he had not counted on the expectations that met him in Salt Lake City. Brigham Young had hinted that David would someday lead the

Utah church, and on one occasion had said publicly, "Joseph [the prophet] said to me, 'I shall have a son born to me, and his name shall be called David; and on him, in some future time, will rest the responsibility that now rests on me.' "[17]

The first interview with Brigham Young, however, did not go smoothly. Alexander recorded that Brigham Young called them into a pleasantly appointed room, where John Taylor, Joseph F. Smith, Joseph and Phineas Young, and several other men waited. Brigham received them graciously until Alexander and David asked to use the newly completed tabernacle building for their meetings. Seeking to ease the tension, someone said, "We love these boys for their father's sake."

Alexander retorted, "That makes no impression on me. I expect to live long enough to make a name for myself and have the people of God love me for my own sake."

Alexander remembered that Brigham Young stood up, clenched his fists, and shook them down by his side. He rocked up on his toes and back down on his heels and exclaimed, "A name! a name! a name! You have not got God enough about you to make a name! You are nothing at all like your father. He was open and frank and outspoken, but with you there is something covering up, something hidden, calculated to deceive."

"Time will tell," countered Alexander.

Brigham's anger swept him on, and before Emma's sons he called her "a liar, yes, the damnedest liar that lives." Brigham repeated the old charge that their mother had tried to poison their father and accused her of stealing Hyrum's portrait and ring from Mary Fielding.[18]

David and Alexander struggled to contain their self-control in the face of insults to their mother. Alexander wrote, "I have had many trials in my short life of the power of control over my passionate temper, but never in that short life did I have need of strength more than I did yesterday." The two men eventually secured the use of the large Independence Hall. "Brigham did us a good turn when he refused us the Tabernacle, we do not want it now," Alexander remarked.[19]

In Nauvoo Emma's instincts about what might happen on the boys' trip to Utah were again quite correct. She wrote to Joseph about Alexander and David, "I tried before they left here to give them an idea of what they might expect of Brigham and all of his ites, but I suppose the impression was hardly sufficient to guard their feelings from such unexpected falsehoods and impious profanity as Brigham is capable of." Then Emma expressed at least one feeling of relief about Brigham's comments in Utah. "I do not like to have my children's feelings abused, but I do like that Brigham shows to all, both Saint and sinner, that there is not the least particle of friendship existing between him and myself."[20]

The most distinguishing aspect of the Reorganization's work in Utah continued to be the rapid migration of Josephite converts out of the territory. In spite of urging from Joseph in Plano to stay and build up the Reorganite congregations, these Utah converts did not heed the advice. Before the Reorganite thrust in Utah ended in 1890, three thousand new members would have left the Great Basin in wagon trains returning to the East or pushing farther west.[21]

After Brigham Young's public outbursts, visitors to Emma's home in Nauvoo sent increasingly negative descriptions back home to Utah. How Emma responded to them depended on the attitude they brought with them. If they were open and warm, she talked freely with them. If they came to challenge her, to prove points of doctrine, or to criticize, she withdrew.

While Alexander and David were still in the West, two men from Utah stopped at the Mansion in Nauvoo on November 29, 1869. They reported to the editors of the *Deseret News* in Salt Lake City that they found "Major Biderman, the husband of Emma Smith and proprietor of the House," playing cards. The report went on, "The fire having gone down, the Major, with sundry twists of the poker, assisted by some oaths too profane to be mentioned here, succeeded in arousing the fire." The visitors were "somewhat disappointed" in Emma's appearance.[22]

Joseph C. Rich visited in the Mansion House on Christmas Day that same year. His letter described his welcome to the Mansion House, where he "stepped into the office where perchance angels once visited and there sat . . . old Bidamon, the present husband of Emma, spitting tobacco on the stove." Rich described the premises as "old, unclean and decidedly shabby." When dinner was announced, Rich walked into the kitchen. "There I beheld for the first time that I can remember, Emma, the youthful wife of one of God's most honored prophets. . . . Emma looks very old and broken." Rich talked about his family at the table and waited expectantly for Emma to comment, "knowing that she was well-acquainted with my parents." When Emma remained silent, Joseph Rich thought, "What a change has come over that woman! Now she is the wife of a man who, even among his friends is reproached as a drunkard and an adulterer. Only recently an illegitimate child has been sent him that calls Emma grandmother. Holy God!"[23]

The letter in its entirety filled two columns in the *Deseret Evening News* on January 7, 1870, and must have been published immediately after its arrival in Salt Lake City. It was blatantly unfair for Rich to play upon Emma's age— she was sixty-five. By this time Lewis had begun construction of a home for himself and Emma on the foundations of the old Nauvoo House across the street, rather than keep up the old home. The unfinished walls of the Nauvoo House across the street from the Mansion offered large quantitites of building material. Lewis dismantled some of the structure and used the brick to erect a three-story house on the existing southwest corner of the old foundation. He worked slowly but steadily. David commented, "Pa Bidamon is still trying to build, but I am sore afraid he never will."[24] But it was finished in two years.

In December the Smith boys traveled westward to California, but David's health had broken. Early in the spring Alexander received word that his wife's health was failing rapidly, and he and David returned home.

All Emma's children but Joseph gathered in Nauvoo during the summer of 1870, and their activities kept her very much occupied. She also turned her attention to David's illness. "The trouble is in my left side near my heart, what ever it is, it is much lighter now and my general health is better," David wrote to Joseph in May. "Mother says I will come all right in a year or two more, perhaps less time." David was happy in other respects, however, for he married eighteen-year-old Clara Hartshorn on May 10 in Nauvoo. "Everybody seems well pleased with Clara," he wrote his brother, "and you may believe I am."[25]

Julia also came for a visit, finding refuge from the problems she faced with her alcoholic husband, John Middleton.[26] Six-year-old Charlie Bidamon scampered about the house, and Emma's granddaughter Emma J. came from Plano to spend the summer with her.

Two weeks after David's wedding a boatload of guests arrived at the Mansion on a pleasure excursion from Keokuk. David said their arrival created "considerable confusion" for his mother and he loathed seeing them come. "They are dancing now, and fluting. I am so weary with their folly and noise and of having the old home desecrated by them, the flowers destroyed, the trees barked, and the garden tramped, I would they were at home in better business."[27]

In spite of his health problems David was back in Utah by November 1870. The stay was brief, about two months. He wrote Joseph that the "Brighamites" were favorable toward "us" but that they were not trying to convert him.[28] David left Utah and went briefly to Michigan. From there he wrote to Emma, "You know Mother, Many stand by the vacant chair and lowly grave and regret that kinder words had not been spoken when the proper hour was given in which to speak, and now I feel an irresistible desire to tell you how much I love you." Mindful of his precarious health, he continued, "Dear Mother think of me as happy. Think of me as hoping for the dawning of that *new life* in which I hope to live again. . . . Think of me as talking with nature and warning my fellow man of good and evil. . . . I hope that you are well Mother, the people here pray for you and I pray that . . . you may dwell with us. You *know* that as regards my honor and all that you can trust me always, Mother. . . . If I could walk as I once did, I would send you means. I send a dollar for Clara."[29]

David returned to Nauvoo in the early spring and remained there with Clara throughout the summer. Their son Elbert Aoriul was born in March 1871. During this time the Major finished the new house, and he and Emma moved into the Riverside Mansion sometime in the latter half of the year.[30] Emma would run this house as a hotel also.

In the spring, 1871, David was ordained president of the Second Quorum of Elders and worked as assistant editor of the *Herald*. In addition he found time to be at his easel. He painted on commission but also painted Emma's portrait and placed himself in the picture as a young babe. David wrote to Joseph that an oil portrait of their mother "does not represent her, though father doubtless is a perfect picture as far as it goes."[31]

Emma received a letter from David early in 1872 stating: "I have not much time to write to you, only to state my love and respect to you is always and forever the same." He assured his mother that her old acquaintances remembered her with much kindness and commented that some of them had found ways to bring "shame upon themselves," then added, "Thank God there is no such disgrace attached to our family."[32]

Encouraged by many, including David himself, Joseph sent David and Alexander on another mission to the West.[33] While her sons were gone Emma, now sixty-eight years old, broke her arm. David wrote to Joseph, "I hear ill news from Mother, she has fallen down those ugly stone steps and broken her arm above the wrist, it is very touching to read her attempts to make light of it."

In Utah the brothers were the center of interest and controversy. John Smith as usual took them in, but David found Joseph F. Smith "uncongenial" and commented to his brother, "I retain too vivid a recollection of his abuses to Alexander to mingle freely with his spirit. . . . As for George A. [Smith] his false and slanderous assertions in regard to yourself are too much for my charity." David wrote Joseph, "He called you in public a drunkard, a horse-racer, and a gambler and a lawyer."[34]

This 1872 missionary trip to Utah brought David face to face with several disturbing issues, each of which requires examination because David could not deal rationally with his problems. First, he became friends with Amasa Lyman, the former Apostle of the Utah church who had married Eliza Partridge as one of his plural wives. Amasa Lyman had been excommunicated by the church in 1870 and had joined a liberal group in Salt Lake City led by William S. Godbe. The group founded a forum dedicated to free thought spiritualism. David became an unofficial member of the group but soon found his faith tested.[35] The concept of continuing modern revelation placed faith in both God and man. David saw the built-in possibility for deception inherent in the teaching. "The believe and be saved or disbelieve and be damned [teachings] of the churches . . . is a lever whereby designing men force the trusting ignorant and unreasoning to obey them." But he expressed his faith and trust in his brother when he told Joseph, "God bless you." David assured Joseph that he had a great chance for a good work to the people in Utah as well as in the East.[36]

David faced another major issue: his father's plural marriages. He apparently discussed plural marriage with Amasa Lyman and sought out Lucy Walker Kimball in Provo, Utah, to ask her directly if she had been his father's plural wife. "She told him she was, and gave him all the details pertaining to the marriage as well as the names and addresses of the man who married her and the two witnesses, all of whom were living in Salt Lake City." David went to each person named and corroborated her story.[37]

When a friend whom David addressed as "Bro. Sherman" inquired about plural marriage, David responded in a July 27, 1872, letter: "If I thought my brother was a deceiver I would save you from deception," he told Sherman, and then offered a defense of his mother. "I know my mother believes just as we do in faith, repentance, baptism and all the saving doctrines in the book of the church and all, but I do not wish to ask her in regard to polygamy for dear brother [Sherman] God forgive me if I am wrong—[but] . . . I believe there was something wrong. I don't know it, but I believe it, the testimony is too great for me to deny." Deeply disturbed over the conclusion he was forced to draw, David told Sherman, "If my father sinned I can not help it. The truth to me is the same—he must suffer for his sin. I do not know that he did and if I had not received such convincing testimony of the gospel my faith might fail, but it does not even though he did sin. . . . If I could tell you otherwise I would, ah how gladly. . . . I have prayed and suffered and can suffer no longer and so tell you what I think the truth is. . . . Trust me Sherman to tell you the truth hard or soft—be my dear friend still and please write me." David asked Sherman to burn the letter.[38]

Thus David struggled alone to reconcile his image of his father, whom he once described as having "all of manly and priestly truth and nobility," with the image of the father who had "sinned." He did not mention his turmoil in his letters to his family.

Toward the latter part of his visit to Utah David experienced a baffling recurrent mental illness that would continue to assault him. He recognized his problem in a letter to Joseph: "Should I break down again, please write to me. Of course I am well, but then how can it be ever repaired?"[39]

Through the rhyming stanzas of his poetry David described his inner confusion. Earlier this year he had written:

> I strive to win again the pleasant thought;
>   the Music only speaks in mournful tone;
> The very flowers wear a shade, and naught
>   can bring again the halo that is gone
> And every company my soul hath sought,
>   Though crowds surround me, finds me still alone.

I turn unto my tasks with weary hands,
    Grieving with sadness, knowing not the cause
Before my face a desert path expands,
    I will not falter in the toil, nor pause;
Only my spirit somehow understands
    This mournful truth—I am not what I was.[40]

David kept his symptoms secret from Emma. In November 1872 he told his mother, ". . . my health is so very well established that I have no fears." In spite of such assurances he had a severe bout with "brain fever," and he became more erratic. Unaware of the extent of his brother's problems, Joseph announced a revelation from the Lord calling David to be a counselor in the first presidency of the Reorganized Church.[41] David returned to Nauvoo. According to a 1930 Utah source, Emma is said to have met him at the door prepared to embrace him, but he extended his hand and stopped her with the comment, "Mother, why have you deceived us?"[42] Whatever the tone of the reunion might have been, family relationships seemed normal by the fall of 1873 when Emma went to Plano to help David and his family and took them some furniture. After she returned to Nauvoo David wrote to her of his appreciation. "I take my pen today to remember you in that spirit that I ever remember my Mother," he wrote. "The clouds that darkened my spirits have gone for a season . . . but wether they will remain away or return again as they so often have remains to be seen." He worried about the responsibility that Emma had accepted for his care. "If ever I have added sorrow to your heart, it has doubly troubled mine," he wrote her. "I know your reward in Heaven is sure, whatever mine may be. . . . Well, dear Mother, remember me as if I had been all to you I might have been."[43]

Throughout the years Emma had remained in correspondence with her own brothers and sisters. David Hale wrote to her at the time of his fiftieth wedding anniversary in 1873 and told her that her sister Elizabeth, her brother Jesse, and other members of the Hale family, most of them over seventy, were thriving in northern Illinois. David Hale sent Emma a circular describing a projected "history" of Harmony, Pennsylvania, to which he had contributed material. He prepared to send a detailed letter from his brother Jesse to the Pennsylvania historian and told Emma, ". . . your last letter may go in the same package."[44] Thus, in an indirect way, Emma contributed to the history of her hometown.

By the summer of 1872 Joseph Smith III had been president of the Reorganization for twelve years. Small branches were scattered throughout Illinois, the surrounding states, and the West. Emma's letters indicated that she regularly attended the congregation in Nauvoo, named the Olive Branch, although she once lamented to Joseph, "Our meetings are rather poorly attended. . . . The outsiders have left off attending. I think some of them are a little like myself, They miss my boys."[45] Gradually the church gained in membership and solidified its theological base but one problem refused to disappear. That was Joseph's recurring preoccupation with separating his church and family from the taint of plural marriage. His earliest known statement appeared in a letter to a friend in 1855 when he was twenty-three. "The Mormons of Salt Lake City are not the Mormons of my father's faith. They teach doctrines which are bound to carry those believing and practicing them to eventual destruction but my father never taught or believed them and so they [members of the Utah church] are well aware, but they have taken such precautions as keep the truth hidden. . . . I would that all understood this matter and could see it as I do."[46]

Though he reiterated his position about his father and plural marriage in his 1860 acceptance speech, other church leaders did not see the problem in the same light. In 1865 in a special council, "The question arose as to whether Joseph the Martyr taught the doctrine of polygamy," whereupon William Marks stated that Hyrum Smith had read "a revelation on it in High Council" in 1843. The minutes recorded no further discussion on it that day, but a year later the RLDS Council of Twelve discussed it again. After some discussion Jason Briggs moved that a motion stating that "Joseph Smith, the Martyr," was not the author of "the revelation . . . authorizing polygamy or spiritual wifery" be tabled. "President Smith then told us that the passage of the resolution would do more injury than good."[47]

Although Alexander and David had returned from missionary trips to Utah with accounts of their father's plural marriages, Joseph continued to deny it. But disturbing evidence mounted. W. E. McLellin, who had written to Joseph in 1861 cautioning him about overstating his father's innocence, wrote again in 1872. He reminded Joseph that he had visited with Emma in 1847 and for the second time admonished Joseph to ask his "own dear Mother for the truth." The events that McLellin recounted were damaging to a young man bent on salvaging the family name. Finally, quite sure that Emma would agree with him, McLellin asked the hardest question of all: "Can you dispute your dear Mother?" Emma had unknowingly reinforced McLellin's credibility when she wrote Joseph in 1866, "I hope that Wm. E. McLellin will unearth his long buried talents, and get them into circulation before it is everlastingly too late . . . for he is certainly a talented man."[48]

Joseph avoided the issue by not asking her at that time. "I never questioned her upon the subject [polygamy] until near the close of her life," he said. But nineteen years after Emma's death he reversed himself, implying more frequent discussions. An interview published in the *Saints' Herald* asked, "Did your mother ever deny that your father entered polygamy?" Joseph said, "Yes sir, more than once." Joseph's cousin Mary, who had cared for their grandmother for so many years, commented, "In regard to the guilt or innocence of his father [Joseph] knows comparatively but little—His mother of course said nothing to them to prejudice them against their father. She tried to hold his memory sacred."[49]

Many years earlier Emma had come to terms with the question of plural marriage and the process appeared to come in steps. When Lucy M. Smith, George Albert's wife, pressed Emma about women who were having children in plural marriage, Emma told her, "Joseph never taught any such thing, they were only sealed for eternity they were not to live with them."[50] Emma believed that Joseph had tried to rid himself and the church of plural marriage before his death. She had witnessed him telling the Partridge sisters their marriages were dissolved. Joseph Coolidge, onetime executor of Joseph's estate, told Joseph F. Smith that Emma "remarked to him that Joseph had abandoned plurality of wives before his death." Smith said Coolidge told her she was wrong. "She insisted that he had, Coolidge insisted that he . . . knew better." Coolidge told Joseph F. Smith that at this news Emma responded, "[Then] he was worthy of the death he died!"[51] This report, if accurately reported in its thirdhand form, was an impassioned statement that reflected her anger at Joseph's duplicity.

Sometime between Joseph's death and the adulthood of her sons, Emma began to either ignore or deny plural marriage in her own life. When she received her endowments she had taken upon herself covenants and promises that she swore never to reveal. She may have chosen to keep not only the forms and procedures of celestial marriage secret, but its very existence as well. She understood the code words the church leaders had used in Nauvoo to protect themselves and continued to use them throughout the remainder of her life. Her denials do not refute "the true order of marriage," the "new and everlasting covenant," "celestial marriage," or any of the other recognized terminology.

Whether Brigham Young forgot that church leaders had once used code words themselves, or whether he did not recognize Emma's use of them, he chastised her from the pulpit for her denials and publicly called her a liar.

Despite the shrewish reputation ascribed to Emma in the West, the women there seldom spoke of her in derogatory terms. Brigham Young's son John R. remembered, "[I] listened to the conversations of Eliza R. Snow, Zina D. Huntington, Emiline [Emily] Partridge, Precella Buel Kimball, wives of the Prophet Joseph Smith, and . . . during that year I never heard one of those noble women Say one unkind word against Emma Smith. To me, they were her truest, Best Friends." But Jesse Smith said Emma "dwarfed the minds of her children until the[y] were not the men that they should be."[52] When Emma decided not to tell her children about plural marriage, it was an attempt to remove problems from their lives. But once Joseph III decided that his father had nothing to do with polygamy, his position trapped both himself and his mother. He could not bring himself to listen to reasonable arguments that his father had founded plural marriage, and Emma, unaware of the continuing debate, did not disclose her knowledge of it to her son.

David Smith remained in Plano, Illinois, until he had a relapse in 1874, then he went to Nauvoo. Emma, at age seventy, cared for her thirty-year-old son during that summer and fall. In July Joseph acknowledged in an editorial in the *Herald* that David was ill again and "much disturbed mentally as well as bodily." In August Samuel H. B. Smith wrote to Joseph F. Smith, "I hear that David has entirely lost his mind and plays on the floor with the children," then reported from Nauvoo in December 1874 that "David is hopelessly insane, That he is with his Mother, I saw by one of the Heralds he was recommended to be prayed for."[53]

In a baffling change of condition, David improved enough to publish a volume of his poetry late in 1875. On the frontispiece he paid tribute to his mother: "To Emma, a most noble and devoted mother, her grateful son dedicates this, the child of his mind, wishing it more worthy her memory." David's illness was characterized by alternating relapse and recovery, and in 1875 he traveled to California on a mission with Alexander. Joseph worried about them in a letter to Emma: "I have no late word from David. Do not know how he is doing . . . whether ill or well. Nor have I any late news from Alex. At last he was not well, I wrote him to return." Emma was in Plano caring for Alexander's sick wife when Joseph telegraphed instructions to his brothers to come home. When the brothers arrived David was too ill to travel farther. Later, in March 1876, Emma took him to Nauvoo with her.[54]

Emma cared for David through the summer but his periods of clarity became shorter and his behavior increasingly bizarre. He slipped away from Emma to send numerous telegrams to buy and sell railroad lines. He believed that he had large deposits of money hidden away and that he was the architect and designer of many great buildings.[55] When Emma found that she could not control David, Alexander took him to Andover, Iowa, near Lamoni, to his farm.

While Joseph had sent his brothers to Utah on missions, he avoided going there himself for fifteen years after he became church president. Finally, in 1876, he left for a mission to California and Utah, ignoring David's arguments that travel there would give "more dignity to Utah than it deserves."[56] Joseph already had some hint of the challenge he might find awaiting him. In 1869 his cousin George A. Smith had written, listing the marriage dates and naming the men who performed the ceremonies for his father and seven women. He told of several polygamous marriages that Joseph Smith had performed for his brother Hyrum Smith, Brigham Young, and others. George A.'s comment that "the inauguration of these principles were a severe trial to your mother" did not make asking Emma about polygamy any easier.[57]

Joseph hoped to speak with two individuals in California who could tell him "something definite in regard to conditions at Nauvoo prior to my father's death, and as to whether polygamy or spiritual wifery was then known to exist or not." These were a Mr. Seeley and Carolyn Clark Huntington, the estranged plural wife of William Huntington. Mr. Seeley, who was not part of the inner circles in Nauvoo, could tell him nothing first hand, and Mrs. Huntington refused to discuss the matter at all.

After four months in California Joseph arrived in Utah the middle of November 1876. A facial neuralgia that would bother him the rest of his life flared up, but he made his first public speech in Utah on December 2, at the Liberal Institute in Salt Lake City. Joseph F. Smith invited his visiting cousin to dinner—but Joseph found himself feeling ill at the prospect of eating a complacent dinner with his cousin's three wives and a number of their children. Joseph also recalled visits with other cousins, John Smith and Samuel H. B. Smith, but specifically avoided asking any straightforward questions.

Although the Smith family welcomed Joseph, he remembered, "I had walked about their streets without recognition or friendly overtures from many, even from those who by family ties were not very distantly related to me."[58] Brigham Young had already taken pains to inform his people that "While the sun shines, the water runs, the grass grows, and the earth remains, young Joseph Smith never will be the leader of the Latter day Saints!" Three years before Joseph's visit Brigham had called him a "pettifogger" and accused him of associating with his father' murderers.[59] "Every person who hearkens to what they say, hearkens to the will and wishes of Emma Bidamon," he stormed. "The boys themselves, have no will, no mind, no judgement independent of their mother." Brigham still could not refrain from making Emma responsible for the activities of her sons. In the same 1873 speech in which Brigham had denied Joseph's right to lead the church, he opened up a new avenue. "But David, who was born after the death of his father, I still look for the day to come when the Lord will touch his eyes."[60] It was an unfortunate simile. David's eyes again saw the world in a strange and distorted light. Joseph left Salt Lake City on December 11, 1876, after spending only three weeks in Utah. On his way home he picked up David at Alexander's.

Emma, in Nauvoo, searched for a reason for David's problem. She confided to Junius F. Wells as he visited from Salt Lake in March 1876 that "David's imbicility was her greatest trouble." She blamed David's visits to Salt Lake for his illness and said they "neither did him nor the family any good." She had warned David not to go to Utah.[61]

Immediately after Joseph's return he set in motion the process for committing David to the Illinois State Hospital for the Insane in Elgin. David had threatened to injure Joseph's wife. Julia, who was visiting Emma, wrote to Joseph that it might be best to take David to the asylum. An undated letter from David to Emma, which seems to have been written around this time, suggests that Emma went to Plano to help sort out the difficult situation. The letter said, "When you were here, Mother, they made you to say that I was not your son. I saw it in a moment. You simply went up to the corner of that office square and touched it and they set it down against me. . . . You did not mean that I was a post. You were under their influence too much," David rambled. "I never say grace comfort any longer."[62]

Joseph wrote to the director of the asylum asking that David be accepted and describing his condition. A warrant for David's commitment directed Joseph Smith to take David to the hospital. On January 22, 1877, Emma's youngest son entered the Illinois State asylum. "I was forced to take David to the Hospital for treatment," Joseph confided to a friend. For years he harbored hope that David could be helped. After eight years, on April 11, 1885, Joseph released David from his position in the first presidency of the church.[63]

Some Utah church members worried that David had returned to Illinois converted to their beliefs and Emma and Joseph institutionalized him to avoid embarrassment. Some RLDS people suspected that something had happened to David in Utah and that he was poisoned while away from his regular boarding place.[64] Neither view is based on any evidence. Joseph believed that David could have willed away his illness. When the subject of a church-wide fast and prayer day came up a year after David's commitment, Joseph commented, "The one thing that has operated in my mind against it, was the thought that he gave himself up to the influence that took him captive." Joseph wrote, "God pardon me; how I have rebelled when I have thought of David's condition. . . . God forgive me if I have staggered under it all."[65]

Emma also sorrowed at the fate of her son. Joseph offered the hope expressed by one of the hospital physicians that "David might at any time return to himself, suddenly, and be returned of his difficulty."[66] In Nauvoo Emma became old and tired, and waited for a miracle that would cure her son. It never came.

22

The Last
Testimony

1873–1879

Emma had just passed her sixty-eighth birthday when a writer from New York visited Nauvoo. She greeted Julius Chambers graciously and arranged for his room and evening meal. "My eye-memory of the face and figure of the distinguished old lady is quite distinct," Chambers wrote. "She was tall, for her sex; her hair was gray, not white and was combed straight over her temples. Her face was thin; her nose lean, aquiline, and pointed. Her mouth was small; her chin was badly shaped and protruded; her eyes were very noticeable. . . . . I also remember her hands, which were small and had well-cared-for nails." After the evening meal Emma and Chambers sat in chairs near the edge of the bluff. He quizzed her on the city and the Mormons and, like many of the curious who came to Emma's door, he asked her about polygamy. He said she called it "vile and infamous" and that "it had blighted and dishonored a beautiful doctrine that came direct from an angel of God, inscribed upon plates of gold." He continued, "The dear old woman put me to shame with her dignified forbearance when I asked if she ever had seen those plates, or the miraculous pair of spectacles, known in Mormon history as 'Urim and Thummim.' She had not; but they veritably existed." They talked late into the evening. Emma, who had few visitors of intellect and experience, asked her own questions, a thousand of them, Chambers said, many of which he admitted he could not answer. "My last sight of this venerable woman occurred next forenoon," he wrote, "as she stood upon the bluff in front of the red hotel and waved her hand."[1]

Emma received many visitors toward the end of her life. One remarked, "Mrs. Smith's conversation is very memorable . . . especially to the excellence of its English." Another described her as "a picture of a fine woman, stranded on the lee-shore of age . . . among people who did not appreciate her intellect or her innate refinement." This member of the Reorganization said he did not believe that Emma's "pride of living" was as Lewis Bidamon's wife. "What earthly honor and renown she claimed was solely as the widow of Joseph Smith, a sincere believer, a devout man, and a loving husband." While her spirited personality had mellowed over the years, Emma could still respond sharply to rudeness. When a woman pressed her too far she retorted, "Madam, my husband was but a man except when the spirit of God was upon him."[2]

Many missionaries from Utah passed through. Two came in the early spring of 1876 and the record they left is a study in contrast. Junius F. Wells, the son of Daniel H. Wells, and Joseph Edward Taylor arrived in Nauvoo together. Taylor said he made the trip for the express purpose of learning "from Emma's own lips some things in relation to the 'Reorganized Church,' " and he subjected Emma to an interrogation. "Why did you use your influence to have your son Joseph installed as the president of the Re-organization, knowing, as you must have done, that the men who would confer upon him this authority were apostates and some of them had been cut off from the church?" Taylor said Emma was "somewhat evasive . . . but from her remarks he discovered her intense dislike for Pres. Brigham Young, whom she accused of entirely ignoring Joseph's family. She claimed that the family had a right to not only recognition but to representation." Emma had not influenced the men who persuaded her son, and she knew it. At that point Taylor thrust a photograph of Brigham Young at Emma. "After all, Emma, he appears to be pretty well preserved personally, and the Church has not lost any of its strength either numerically or otherwise from the opposition which I think you have unwisely aided and abetted." That comment ended the conversation.[3]

"Favorably impressed with her appearance," Wells noted that "she seemed to be considerable affected by our presence, and expressed an interest in some of the people in Utah whom she would like to see. [She] said she would like to see the President [Brigham Young] & tell him she still thought she was right about a certain subject of controversy between them several years ago." Wells continued, "She seems to have lost much of her bitterness towards the Twelve and the Saints, and though 72 years of age, would go to Utah yet, if she could do so in her own way."[4] Thus, both Wells and Taylor interpreted the same visit with Emma in opposite ways.

Emma did not always withdraw from pointed questions nor were her answers always considered evasive by others who came with specific inquiries. Within a year Parley P. Pratt, Jr., visited her and asked a number of questions. Emma's answers were forthright and to the point.

"Do you believe that your husband, Joseph Smith died true to his profession?" he asked.

"I believe he was everything he professed to be," Emma replied.

"Did he have any more wives than you?"

"Not to my knowledge."

"Did he receive the revelation on plural marriage?"

"Not to my knowledge," she repeated.

"Did he receive the plates from which he claimed to have translated the Book of Mormon?"

"Yes, they lay in a box under our bed for months but I never felt at liberty to look at them."

Emma also "stated emphatically that . . . Joseph Smith could not have written such a book without inspiration."

Pratt recorded an additional remark that Emma made to them: "You may think I was not a very good Saint not to go West, but I had a home here and did not go because I did not know what I should have there." Pratt said he did not detect any bitterness in Emma.[5]

Similarly, William Adams from the Utah Territory found Emma pleasant and communicative when he saw her that same winter. Emma greeted him warmly and they spent much of the day discussing mutual acquaintances. Emma asked many questions, but one Adams remembered most vividly. She wanted to know how she and her family would be received if they returned to the church in Utah. Adams told her, "They would be received with open arms by President Young and the whole body of the church and you'd want for nothing to make you comfortable and [your] family happy." Adams did not confront Emma but said he "reasoned with her." Consequently, "I was invited very kindly to stop and get dinner which I accepted having a very pleasant time." He recalled that Emma had "unpleasant feeling against President B. Young particularly as she wanted her son Joseph to be president of the church as she considered it to be his right."[6]

On August 29, 1877, Brigham Young died in Salt Lake City. Emily Partridge, who had become his plural wife after the martyrdom, commented, "I believe Pr. Young has done his whole duty towards Joseph Smith's family." She placed no blame on him for the difficulties Emma and her children had faced through the years.[7]

Not long after Brigham's death Emma received a letter from James Burgess in Salt Lake City. "I wish to ask of you as a private matter between you and me if supposing you can be furnished with the means to come out here if nothing more than to make a visit would you come?" the former acquaintance of David's asked. "In regards to the manuscript of the New Translation of the Bible would you give it to us for a season supposing it could be fully secured for its preservation?"[8] As to the Joseph Smith revisions of the Bible, Emma had already given it to the Reorganized Church. She had kept it hidden in her home until 1867, believing that "the reason why our house did not burn down when it has so often been on fire was because of [the Bible and its notes] and I still feel a sacredness attached to them."[9] Joseph immediately prepared it for publication. "I am very thankful that you are getting along so well with the manuscripts," Emma told him in 1867. "It is true that every L.D.S. cannot be trusted to copy them . . . if I had trusted all that wished for that privelege you would not have had them in your possession now."[10] Joseph thanked his mother through the *Herald*, and she responded, "Those lines in the Herald caused me to retrospect those years of mine portrayed in them and I find not one thing in them that I [had] done, which was not just simply my duty to do." Emma commented that "the happiness I now am enjoying is all new and unexpected" and expressed her gratitude that the "good and sincerely honest" people had what they had so long waited for in the translation.[11]

Outsiders were not the only ones who came to Emma's door. One day several boys scuffled along the riverbank and one fell in. His friends fished him out, then took him to Emma, who removed his wet clothing, dressed him in some old clothes, then gave them all cookies. From that time on, falling in the river became a frequent occurrence. After treats in Emma's kitchen, the children followed the Major around his vineyards. "Grandpa Bidamon was the only Grandpa I ever knew," one grown-up child remembered. "I often trooped with a bevy of children at his heels to gather grapes when they were just beginning to ripen." Until the last few years of Lewis's life he led the Fourth of July parade because, a neighbor said, he was the only one in town who owned a military uniform.[12]

Emma occasionally received letters from David. In one letter, written January 22, 1879, the hesitant style and difficulty with expression indicated that he was still not himself.

"I desire very much to hear from my dear mother again," he wrote. "I have often thought of you at old Nauvoo of late and wondered how you have got along. If you had been well enough to enjoy Christmas this year." David wrote poignantly of Nauvoo, "We used to have some very good times, some, well, I may say almost precious times together in dear old Nauvoo. . . . I remember the columbines and wild honeysuckle, and well, the violets; and I sometimes long for the comforts of a home more exclusive." In this January of her seventy-fifth year Emma read, "I may say again that I am thankful for good health and the blessing of a dear pious Mother at Nauvoo, who is still spared to bless and comfort me by continuing to live in the good council of almighty God."

David indicated that he had social contact with other people and a Bible to read. "Well, Mother hold on to the faithe and continue in the way of life we Long have found to lead to peace, and make for peace. Be sure and write as I wish to know how you are very much—and how you prosper in real or temperal affairs. . . . Good by dear Mother."[13] Apparently Emma's letters to David were not preserved at the institution.

Julia had returned to Nauvoo to live with Emma and Lewis two years earlier, in 1877. Her hope that John Middleton could overcome his alcoholism never materialized. He headed to New Mexico, a vagabond. Emma worried about the sores appearing on her daughter's back and breasts.[14] Julia suffered from painful cancers. Emma had outlined her philosophy about suffering and adversity in a statement to Joseph. "I have seen many, yes very many, trying scenes in my life in which I could not see any . . . place where any good could grow out of them," she wrote, "but yet I feel a divine trust in God, that all things shall work for good."[15]

As Emma grew older, Joseph needed one more thing from his mother. He had published a strongly worded editorial condemning plural marriage in the *Herald* late in 1873. Zenas H. Gurley, Jr., now an Apostle in the Reorganized Church, wrote, "Your editorial . . . has just been read by me, and I notice that you have taken very Ultra grounds in relation to the 'Polygamy' question. You state that 'neither Joseph nor Hyrum . . . *ever* built-up polygamy.' Will you please inform me why Hyrum Smith *did* teach it?" Gurley further stated in an 1879 letter: "You absolutely refuse to believe the evidence which would convict [your father]."[16]

William W. Blair, who had encouraged Joseph in his pronouncements, had an unsettling conversation with James Whitehead in April 1874. He recorded the conversation in his journal. Whitehead told him that "J[oseph] did te[ach] p[olygamy] and pr[actice] too. That E[mma] knos it too that she put [the] hand—of wives [in] Jos. hand. W[hitehead] says Alex. H. Smith asked him . . . if J[oseph] did P[ractice] and tea[ch] P[olygamy] and he, W[hitehead] told him he did."[17] Blair apparently confronted both Joseph and Alexander with the information, but theirs was a more personal dilemma. Joseph believed that his own reputation rested on that of his father's, and he continued a campaign to clear the stain of polygamy from the Smith name. By 1878 he declared with some triumph to his uncle, William Smith, "The prestige of my father's name belongs to me; and it is now assured to me; hence it could not be wrested from me."[18]

As the pressure about plural marriage grew, Joseph and Alexander stated in the *Saints' Advocate* that they had often been challenged, "Ask your mother, she knows." "Why don't you ask your mother; she dare not deny these things." "You do not dare to ask your mother!" They explained, "Our thought was that if we had lacked courage to ask her, because we feared the answers she might give, we would put aside that fear; and, whatever the worst might be, we would hear it." Early in 1879 Joseph and Alexander met with other leaders of their church in the *Herald* offices to discuss polygamy and their mother's knowledge of it. They "decided to present to her a few prominent questions, which were penned and agreed upon."[19]

In February 1879 Alexander and Joseph Smith traveled to a cold, snowy Nauvoo to interview their mother. Lewis Bidamon, who regarded Emma as "one of the noblest and best women that ever graced the earth,"[20] was present in the sitting room of the Riverside Mansion when the two sons came for the interview.

The original notes of the interview are still extant. They include two pages of questions written in ink in Joseph's hand and were most likely the questions prepared earlier at the *Herald* offices. Two questions at the end are in pencil, suggesting that they were added during the interview. The notes also include eight pages of answers written again in Joseph's hand, but in pencil. They show signs of being written in haste as Emma spoke and have additions between the lines, some words abbreviated, and others crossed out. Basically the version which was eventually printed after Emma's death, and from which the following summary is taken, is true to the handwritten notes. The published questions and answers do appear in a reordered and more organized form.[21]

Apparently Joseph eased into the conversation with the more benign subjects, asking about Emma's marriage to his father, the translation and publication of the Book of Mormon, and the deaths of her first three children. Emma's sons listed twenty-six questions, Lewis asked another one; of those, only six were about plural marriage. Emma's conflicting loyalties were to the truth and to her sons. Her answers indicate that she chose her words in an attempt to satisfy both. Joseph was either not aware of her selective terminology or he chose not to recognize it.

"What about the revelation on polygamy? Did Joseph Smith have anything like it? What of spiritual wifery?"

"There was no revelation on either polygamy or spiritual wives." Emma easily denounced the old John Bennett term. The question had not been about "patriarchal marriage" or the "new and everlasting covenant" or any of the other code words for the system early church leaders instigated. Her answer continued, "There were some rumors of something of the sort which I asked my husband. He assured me that all there was of it was, that, in a chat about plural wives, he had said, 'Well such a system might possibly be, if everybody was agreed to it, and would behave as they should; but they would not; and, besides, it was contrary to the will of heaven.' " She continued, "No such thing as polygamy, or spiritual wifery, was taught, publicly or privately, before my husband's death, that I have now, or ever had any knowledge of."

"Did he not have other wives than yourself?"

"He had no other wife but me; nor did he to my knowledge ever have."

The answer is partly in keeping with Emma's view, if she believed Joseph when he told her he would "forsake all for her." It is also true in a legal sense, for no plural marriage could be seen as legal in the eyes of the law.

Joseph pressed her more closely. "Did he not hold marital relations with women other than yourself?"

"He did not have improper relations with any woman that ever came to my knowledge." Years earlier Emma had established that she did not pretend to have knowledge of anything that she did not witness herself.[22] The choice of "improper relations" rather than "marital relations" also indicates that she may have been sidestepping her sons' questions very adeptly.

"Was there nothing about spiritual wives that you recollect?" they asked.

"At one time my husband came to me and asked me if I had heard certain rumors about spiritual marriage, *or anything of the kind;* and assured me that if I had, that they were without foundation; that there was no such doctrine, and never should be with his knowledge, or consent. I know that he had no other wife or wives than myself, in any sense, either spiritual or otherwise." Joseph, in recording the interview, could possibly have given strength to the answer (and his argument) by adding the phrases emphasized in the reply without foreseeing the potential injury to his mother's reputation by doing so.

The questioning then turned from plural marriage to safer realms.

"What of the truth of Mormonism?" one of them asked and recorded her answer as, "I know Mormonism to be the truth; and believe the Church to have been established by divine direction. I have complete faith in it." They asked about the translation process of the Book of Mormon and then asked:

"What was the condition of feeling between you and father?"

"It was good," Emma reportedly answered.

"Were you in the habit of quarreling?"

"No. There was no necessity for any quarreling. . . . He usually gave some heed to what I had to say. It was quite a grievous thing to many that I had any influence with him."

In response to a query about joining the Methodist Church, Emma said, "I have been called apostate; but I have never apostatized, nor forsaken the faith I at first accepted."

Joseph said he read the questions and answers to his mother before he left Nauvoo. "Major Bidamon stated that he had frequently conversed with her on the subject of the translation of the Book of Mormon, and her present answers were substantially what she had always stated in regard to it." Interestingly, Joseph did not record whether the Major confirmed the consistency of Emma's answers about plural marriage. At last Joseph and Alexander Smith had interviewed their mother. Later accounts of Joseph's interviews and conversations with people in Utah show that, as a lawyer, he knew how to ask questions that would supply him with the answer he sought. He also knew when not to cross-examine so as not to get more information than he wanted.[23]

A few weeks after Joseph's and Alexander's February interview with Emma, Zenas Gurley responded to one of Joseph's *Herald* articles: "Can it be shown the cause of Christ, the triumph of truth, depends upon your father's innocence or guilt? And if not pray tell me, what right have you or anyone else in placing the matter before the world as part of church policy?" Gurley continued his argument in a subsequent letter: "I can safely say that I never publicly or privately charged you with 'knowing' that your father was guilty—

or that you 'must know' but to the contrary I have always denied you that knowledge (as I now do) upon the ground that you were too young to *know* and from the very nature of things you could not be a competent witness." The issue between the two men came to an uneasy rest when Gurley insisted that polygamy was "wrong" and to dwell on who established it was a waste of time.[24]

A month after the interview the son of Thomas B. Marsh, an early Apostle in the church, stopped to see Emma. When he asked her if Joseph had been a polygamist, Emma "broke down and wept, and excused herself from answering directly, assigning as a reason . . . that her son Joseph was the leader of the Re-organized Church." Marsh interpreted Emma's response as a "tacit acknowledgement to him that her husband was a polygamist."[25] Emma was weary. The old ghosts still haunted her.

As spring came, Emma had a dream that she related to a friend, who told it to Alexander. Emma dreamed that the prophet came and took her to a beautiful mansion. In one of the rooms was a baby, whom Emma recognized as her child, Don Carlos. She dreamed she caught the child up in her arms and wept. When she regained her composure, she asked Joseph where the rest of the children were. He assured her that if she would be patient, she would have them all. According to Alexander's account, Emma said she also saw "a personage of light, even Jesus Christ," in her dream.[26]

Emma became weak as the spring progressed, but she greeted Joseph and her granddaughter Emma J. early in April. With some reservation, Joseph wrote to his wife that his mother's health was "comparatively good."[27] A few weeks later Alexander came unannounced to the Riverside Mansion. "I felt like a boy coming home. I went in at the front door, and through the hall, and into the kitchen, where I knew my mother was usually be to be found." Instead of Emma, he saw another woman, probably Nancy Abercrombie.

"Where is Mother?" he inquired.

"Don't you know that your mother is sick? She is in the other room."

Alexander entered: Emma lay in bed. "I had the testimony from God that my mother was dying," he remembered.

The Major assured Alexander, "Your mother is not serious, she'll soon be well," but Alexander's premonition was compelling. He sent a wire to Joseph: IF YOU EXPECT TO SEE MOTHER ALIVE, COME QUICK.

Joseph arrived twenty-six hours later. "Are you surprised?" Alexander asked.

"No," Joseph said, "I have been waiting for that summons."[28]

Emma sensed that her time was short. Concerned about the stigma of illegitimacy that surrounded fifteen-year-old Charles Edwin Bidamon, she called Nancy Abercrombie and Lewis to her bedside. In an extraordinary act of compassion, she asked them to marry and provide the boy with proper parentage after she died. They did so a year after Emma's death.[29]

For the next two weeks Julia, Joseph, Alexander, Lewis, and young Charles Bidamon cared for Emma and waited. Joseph kept a day-by-day account.

Tuesday, April 22: Found Alex here at Nauvoo and Julia in care of mother. Mrs. Abercrombie doing the work of the house.
Wednesday, April 23 . . . Mother apparently failing. . . . Slight rain. . . . Cherries in blossom. The old place looks lovely but oh! how desolate.
Thursday, April 24 . . . Slept splendidly so still, so pleasant. Clouds over the sky this am. . . . Mother continues to fail. Food fails to stimulate her.
Friday, April 25 . . . Mother fails more rapidly. Has taken no nourishment for some hours, her pulse grows feeble constantly . . . her breath labored.
Saturday, April 26 . . . Mother quite bad.
Sunday, April 27 . . . Was up with mother till 4:30. She was very bad. Did not think she would live till morning.[30]

That same day Alexander began a letter to his wife, "Dearest Lizzie: Once more I write to you from this place. Mother is still alive, but oh, how she suffers. . . . [She] needs someone constantly by her, she must be lifted up about every fifteen or twenty minutes. Night before last I sat up all night and lifted her. Joseph sat up last night until four o'clock this morning and then called me. Mr. Bidamon is very kind and gentle to her, but is nearly worn out." Two days later Alexander continued with his letter. "Tuesday, April 29. Mother is gradually failing, she cannot recognize anyone now. Her mind wanders constantly. Poor mother, Oh, Lizzie, it is hard to see her suffer so. We do all we can for her and still she suffers fearfully. . . . We are simply waiting the end, and it seems to be near, only God knows how near. I think sometimes I have passed through the worst, yet I know how hard it will be to give mother up."[31]

During the night Joseph and Alexander alternated turns at Emma's bedside. Alexander heard her call, "Joseph, Joseph, Joseph," and wakened his brother. Joseph hurried into the room to see his mother raise herself up and extend her left arm. "Joseph!" they heard her say. "Yes, yes, I'm coming."

Alexander slipped his arm behind her shoulders and grasped her hand. "Mother, what is it?" he asked. But Emma did not answer. He folded her hand against her breast and laid her back. At twenty minutes after four in the early dawn of April 30, 1879, Emma was dead.[32]

23

Epilogue

Funeral services for Emma began at two o'clock in the afternoon on Friday, May 2, 1879. Her body lay in the parlor of the Mansion House. A minister in the Reorganization, J. A. Crawford, took his funeral text from Job 14:14, "If a man die, shall he live again?" At the close of the service, Elder J. H. Lake paid tribute to her faith and hope. The community of Nauvoo mourned Emma and a large crowd attended her last rites.[1] She was buried in a dress brocaded with leaves and magenta flowers. Before her death she had given her sons specific instructions to dig her grave twenty-five paces from the southeast corner of the old Homestead in the area of an underground brick vault.[2] This was the unmarked burial place of Joseph Smith. Emma's remains rested there until 1928 when her grandson, Frederick M. Smith, then president of the Reorganized Church, opened the graves of Emma, Joseph, and Hyrum Smith and reburied them with Joseph in the center, Hyrum on his left, and Emma on his right. He placed markers over each of the graves.[3]

On July 15, 1879, the Reorganization held a memorial service for Emma in Plano where Elder Mark H. Forscutt delivered a two-hour eulogy. Notice of Emma's death appeared in publications throughout the Utah Territory. The *Woman's Exponent* spoke of her briefly: "Mrs. Emma Bidamon, died in Nauvoo on the 30th of April. Among the Latter-day Saints, in days gone by, she was familiarly known as 'Sister Emma,' wife of the Prophet Joseph Smith. She was considered rather a remarkable woman, possessing great influence and unusually strong characteristics, which if properly directed, as in the early days of this Church, would have made her name illustrious in the history of the women of the Latter-day Saints down to the end of time."[4]

As soon as Joseph returned to Plano he wrote to David's doctor at Elgin and informed him of Emma's death. He enclosed a note, "David, my brother . . . Our dear mother was sick for a long time and the other day went to her eternal sleep with Alexander, Julia, and I watching with her. Quietly and peacefully she went to sleep, we buried her over to the hillside and there among the locusts and the lilacs she is resting from her long journey of life. It was so that we could not come nor send for you or we would have done so."[5]

David continued to correspond with and receive periodic visits from members of his family. His wife Clara moved near her father's family in northwestern Iowa, where she raised their only son, Elbert. She talked with Joseph about her husband. "He may recover. If he does, he will find me his wife, as I was when he left me. His leaving was the result of misfortune for which neither of us was responsible, so far as my knowledge goes, and I wish to remain faithful to him." David spent the rest of his life in the Elgin, Illinois, institution and died there August 29, 1904, at the age of fifty-nine.[6]

Julia, who never had children, went home with Alexander after her mother's death but returned to Nauvoo later that year to live with friends until cancer took her life on September 12, 1880.

Lewis Bidamon, who had been married to Emma for thirty-two years, was seventy-two. He lived with Charles in the Riverside Mansion, then a year after Emma's death, on May 15, 1880, he married Charles's mother, Nancy Abercrombie, who was then fifty.[7] In the last three years of his life, "when he fell into senility and dotage and was practically helpless," Nancy cared for Lewis. He remembered her in his will in a delightful manner when he left her "the East half of the . . . Riverside Mansion. . . . One half of the garet . . . equal priveleges of the halls and stairs below and above . . . one half of the cellar . . . and full ingress and egress to and from the privy on the premises."[8]

In his memoirs Joseph reported that his stepfather changed his feelings toward religion in his final years, often asking visitors to read to him from the Bible and Book of Mormon and wanting hymns sung to him. Joseph said he took the opportunity to ask Lewis if he would not like to repent and be baptized. Joseph reported, "He . . . looked me squarely in the face . . . with tears trickling over his whitened cheeks."

"Joseph, *it is too late!*"

"Too late, Major?"

"Yes, my boy; it is too late." When Joseph offered a prayer in his behalf, Lewis responded, "Lord be merciful to me, a sinner." Lewis C. Bidamon died in 1891.[9]

Perhaps the controversy that surrounded him was inevitable. No man could have stepped into the place Joseph Smith occupied without being unfavorably compared to the prophet. For the most part, RLDS historians and writers have ignored Lewis Bidamon's existence. Among LDS writers, vilification of Lewis Bidamon easily became a subtle means of establishing that something must have been wrong with Emma Smith.

Joseph and Alexander never indicated whether they had initially intended to publish the interview with their mother or merely use it to satisfy their critics within the leadership of the church. But several months after Emma's death they received requests for the interview. "Members of the 'Josephite' church in Utah are wondering why the dying testimony of Mrs. Emma Smith Bidamon in regard to the truth or falsity of the Mormon work has not been published, or what her latest testimony was respecting Mormonism. If the *Herald* could answer, it would be interesting."[10]

Joseph and Alexander used their mother's "Last Testimony" to silence their critics. In October 1879, six months after her death, they published the "Last Testimony of Sister Emma."[11] This same year Joseph would publish his own theory of plural marriage.

> I believe that during the later years of my father's life . . . persons who might believe that there was a sufficient degree of spiritual affinity between them as married companions . . . might be "married" for "eternity," pledging themselves while in the flesh unto each other for the rights of companionship in the spirit; that this was called spiritual marriage . . . That this was not authorized by command of God or rule of the Church; but grew out of the constant discussion had among the elders. . . . From this: if one, why not two, or more, and plural marriage, or the plurality of wives was the growth. . . . That my father may have been a party to the first step in this strange development, I am perhaps prepared to admit though the evidence connecting him with it is vague and uncertain; but that he was in any otherwise responsible for plural marriage, plurality of wives, or polygamy, I do not know, nor are the evidences so far produced to me conclusive to force my belief.[12]

This account was written around the time that Emma's sons interviewed her and reflects what appears to have been Emma's final understanding of plural marriage. The publication of the "Last Testimony of Sister Emma" caused little concern among the general membership of the Reorganization, but for men like Zenas Gurley and Jason Briggs it widened the gap between them and their prophet, until they eventually left the Reorganization.[13]

When copies of Emma's last testimony appeared in the Great Basin, those who knew Emma best put responsibility for it back on her sons. Eliza R. Snow responded publicly through the *Woman's Exponent.* "I once dearly loved 'Sister Emma,' and now, for me to believe that she, a once honored woman, should have sunk so low, even in her own estimation, as to deny what she knew to be true, seems a palpable absurdity. If . . . [this] was really her

testimony she died with a libel on her lips—a libel against her husband—
against his wives—against the truth, and a libel against God; and in publishing
that libel, her son has fastened a stigma on the character of his mother, that
can never be erased." Eliza continued, "So far as Sister Emma personally is
concerned, I would gladly have been silent and let her memory rest in peace,
had not her misguided son, through a sinister policy, branded her name with
gross wickedness."[14]

Judge George Edmunds who had been a friend to Emma as well as her
legal counsel reflected on the paradox of Emma's position in an interview some
years later. "I tell you, sir," he said, "No man could look Emma Smith in the
face and tell a lie! She would detect it at once, and he knew it!" When asked
how he viewed what he had heard about polygamy and Emma's denial of it the
judge shifted in his chair then with an odd smile replied, "That's just the h[ell]
of it! I can't account for it nor reconcile her statements. . . . Nevertheless,
she was just the kind of a woman I have said she was."[15]

Joseph and Alexander worked together for the remainder of their lives in
the Reorganized Church of Jesus Christ of Latter Day Saints. It had grown
from a scattered group of three hundred in 1860 to a membership of seventy
thousand in 1914.[16] By either eliminating or downplaying the more controversial doctrines of Mormonism, such as baptism for the dead, eternal marriage,
plural marriage, and the Word of Wisdom, Joseph III gave an alternative
religious home to many believers in the Book of Mormon, the restoration of
the gospel, and the prophetic calling of his father.[17]

Alexander served as presiding patriarch, then Apostle, and finally counselor to his brother. He and his wife, Elizabeth Kendall, had nine children.
The couple spent their final years in Lamoni, Iowa, home of Graceland College. On August 12, 1909, Alexander died in the Mansion House while visiting
Nauvoo.

Joseph outlived his brother by six years. His quest to clear his father's
name followed him through the rest of his life. In 1882 when his aging Uncle
William Smith began to write his recollections of his martyred brothers, Joseph reminded him that "I have long been engaged in removing from father's
memory and from the early church, the stigmas and blame thrown upon him
because of polygamy; and have at last lived to see the cloud rapidly lifting." He
said that he would not consent to see further blame attached to him now by a
blunder. "Therefore, Uncle," the nephew commanded, "bear in mind our
standing today before the world as defenders of Mormonism from Polygamy
. . . and if you are the wise man I think you to be, you will fail [to] remember
anything [except] referring lofty standard of character at which we esteem
those good men."[18]

William accommodated his nephew's wishes in an undated letter, stating,
"Neither your father nor any member [of the] Quorum of the Twelve ever said
anything to me about a plural marriage revelation either before or since your

father's death . . . the plural marriage doctrine was taught and practiced in
Nauvoo by the Brigham party." But Joseph wanted more. Six weeks before
William's death in 1893 he asked him for a written statement before a magistrate declaring that in his father's lifetime no revelation on plural marriage was
ever read before the Quorum of the Twelve.[19]

Joseph traveled to Utah three more times after his mother's death and
interviewed women who had been plural wives of his father. He concluded,
"Whether my father was or was not the one through whom the practice was
introduced . . . and was or was not guilty of teaching and practicing it, both
the dogma and the practice" were wrong, and he, Joseph III, was under no
obligation to continue it.[20] The official position of the RLDS Church became
one of denial, proclaiming that "Joseph the Martyr" had not been a part of the
introduction of plural marriage in Nauvoo. But later church leaders also added
the provision that if he did teach and practice polygamy it was wrong. Ironically, the pressure put on the Utah church brought forth the massive collection
of affidavits, statements, and recollections from people who had firsthand experience with Joseph and the practice in Nauvoo that might never have existed
had Joseph III not been so persistent.

Joseph's second wife, Bertha Madison, died of injuries suffered in a carriage accident in 1895. Two years later he married Ada Clark, who was thirty-
nine years his junior. Joseph fathered seventeen children by his three wives,
and died at his home in Independence, Missouri, on December 10, 1914, at
age eighty-two.

Emma did not live to see the Utah church officially abandon plural marriage as a practice in 1890. But neither did her sons live to see the Reorganized
Church form policy that would allow polygamists in developing nations to
come into the church *without* giving up their plural wives, although they were
not allowed to take more wives after baptism. The irony of Emma's life was
that, in spite of her opposition to the issue of polygamy, the shadow of it
loomed over her until her death. Controversy over her relationship to it would
obscure the accomplishments of a good and productive life.

Emily Partridge perhaps expressed the sentiments of many who knew
Emma when she wrote in 1883, "After these many years I can truly say; poor
Emma, she could not stand polygamy but she was a good woman and I never
wish to stand in her way of happiness and exaltation. I hope the Lord will be
merciful to her, and I believe he will. It is an awful thought to contemplate
misery of a human being. If the Lord will, my heart says let Emma come up
and stand in her place. Perhaps she has done no worse than any of us would
have done in her place. Let the Lord be the judge."[21]

Abbreviations in Notes

The following abbreviations refer to frequently used names and sources in the notes.

BYU	Harold B. Lee Library, Brigham Young University, Provo, Utah.
BYU Studies	*Brigham Young University Studies.*
Dialogue	*Dialogue: A Journal of Mormon Thought.*
HC	Joseph Smith, *History of the Church of Jesus Christ of Latter-day Saints,* 7 vols. (Salt Lake City: Deseret Book Co., 1978).
Saints' Herald	*The True Latter Day Saints' Herald,* an early Reorganized Church of Jesus Christ of Latter Day Saints periodical now referred to as the *Saints' Herald.*
Huntington Library	Henry E. Huntington Library and Art Gallery, San Marino, California.
JD	*Journal of Discourses, Reports of Addresses by Brigham Young and Others* (Liverpool and London: F. D. and S. W. Richards, 1853–86).
LDS Archives	History archives of the Church of Jesus Christ of Latter-day Saints, Salt Lake City, Utah.
LDS D & C	*The Doctrine and Covenants of the Church of Jesus Christ of Latter-day Saints* (Salt Lake City, 1958).
RLDS D & C	*Book of Doctrine and Covenants* (Independence, Missouri: Herald House, 1978).
RLDS Library-Archives	Reorganized Church of Jesus Christ of Latter Day Saints, Library-Archives, Independence, Missouri.
Lucy Smith, Prelim. Ms.	The preliminary manuscript from which Lucy Smith prepared her book, *Biographical Sketches of Joseph Smith the Prophet and His Progenitors for Many Generations.*
ES	Emma Hale Smith.
ESB	Emma Smith Bidamon.
JS	Joseph Smith, Jr., husband of Emma Smith.
Joseph III	Joseph Smith III, son of Emma Smith.
OC	Oliver Cowdery.

CHC   *Comprehensive History of the Church of Jesus Christ of Latter-day Saints*, 6 vols. (Deseret News Press, 1930).

Temple Lot Suit   United States Circuit Court (8th Circuit) Testimony (1892), carbon copy manuscript transcript, LDS Archives.

Univ. of U.   Marriott Library, Special Collections, University of Utah, Salt Lake City, Utah.

USHS   Utah State Historical Society.

Yale University   Beinecke Rare Book and Manuscript Library, Yale University, New Haven, Connecticut.

Notes

AUTHORS' NOTE: The original manuscript submitted for publication was a thousand pages. To lower the cost we deleted more than three hundred pages. Copies of the longer manuscript are available in the libraries of the University of Utah, Brigham Young University, Utah State University, and the Reorganized Church of Jesus Christ of Latter Day Saints, Independence, Missouri.

CHAPTER 1

1. Inez Kennedy, *Pioneers of Lee County*, p. 96.
2. Joseph Smith III, "Last Testimony of Sister Emma," p. 49.
3. W. L. Hines statement in Arthur B. Demming, ed., *Naked Truths About Mormonism*, No. 1 (Oakland, Calif., January 1888). Hines gave the day incorrectly as Sunday. The Methodist circuit rider held services on Wednesdays, which accounts for Isaac Hale's absence.
4. Joseph III, "Last Testimony of Sister Emma," p. 49.
5. Emily C. Blackman, *History of Susquehanna County*, p. 103.
6. Ibid., p. 101.
7. Mark H. Forscutt, "Commemorative Discourse on the Death of Mrs. Emma Bidamon," p. 1. This story was disputed by some members of Emma's family. The Amboy (Ill.) *Journal* quoted Edwin Cadwell in the spring of 1879: " 'It was under the influence of her (Mrs. Joseph Smith) secret prayers, when but seven or eight years of age, that her deistical father, who accidently overheard her, was converted to faith in the divine mission of Christ.' Mr. Alva Hale says: 'There is not a word of truth in this statement of Elder Cadwell. That his father, Isaac Hale, was converted, joined the church, and he believes was class-leader, before his daughter Emma (the wife of Joseph Smith) was born' " (Joseph Lewis, "Review of Mormonism," Amboy *Journal*, 11 June 1879). William W. Blair entered the dispute and used Michael Morse, who married Emma's sister Tryal, as his source to assert that "[Isaac] Hale always claimed that he was converted from deism to faith in Christ . . . by a secret prayer of Emma's," (W. W. Blair, letter, 22 May 1879, published in *Saints' Herald* 20, No. 12 [15 June 1879]).
8. Blackman, *History of Susquehanna County*, pp. 100–10, as cited in Raymond T. Bailey, "Emma Hale, Wife of the Prophet Joseph Smith" (Master's thesis), p. 11.
9. Mary Audentia Smith Anderson, *Ancestry and Posterity of Joseph Smith and Emma Hale*, pp. 293–308, 350–55, 423–25, and 429–33, gives the basic reconstruction of Emma's ancestry. The author, Emma's granddaughter, became historian of the RLDS Church.
10. Ibid., p. 428.
11. Vesta Crawford notes, Univ. of Utah.

12. Rhamanthus M. Stacher, *Susquehanna County Centennial History—Pennsylvania*, p. 573.

13. Wesley P. Walters, *Joseph Smith's Bainbridge, N.Y., Court Trials*, p. 123.

14. Amboy *Journal*, Wednesday, 30 April 1879.

15. Lucy Smith, *Biographical Sketches of Joseph Smith the Prophet and His Progenitors for Many Generations*, p. 92. Hereafter cited as *Joseph the Prophet*. Lucy Smith dictated her manuscript to Martha Corey shortly after Joseph's death in 1844. It was published in England in 1853, but Brigham Young called it "a tissue of lies from beginning to end" and suppressed it. Modern scholars consider the book basically accurate. See Richard L. Anderson, "Reliability of the Early History of Lucy and Joseph Smith." A "corrected edition" was edited by Preston Nibley and published by Bookcraft in 1958. We have used a 1969 reprint of the 1853 edition. The original manuscript is in the LDS Archives and contains more information than the 1853 book. Most of the pages are unnumbered. The manuscript is hereafter cited as Lucy Smith, Prelim. Ms.

16. Amboy (Ill.) *Journal*, Wednesday, 30 April 1879. Josiah Stowell was acquainted with Joseph Smith before he hired him to work.

17. Lucy Smith, *Joseph the Prophet*, pp. 62–65.

18. As quoted in *The Pearl of Great Price*, Joseph Smith 2:16–20. This description is also found in *HC* 1:2–8. See Dean C. Jessee, "The Early Accounts of Joseph's First Vision," 275–94. See also Marvin S. Hill, "The First Vision Controversy: A Critique and Reconciliation," 31–46.

19. Lucy Smith, Prelim. Ms.; punctuation added.

20. Jessee, "The Early Accounts of Joseph's First Vision," p. 291.

21. *Saints' Herald* 28, No. 11 (June 1881):102–67.

22. Richard Anderson, "Gold Plates and Printer's Ink," p. 72.

23. *HC* 1:11–12.

24. Lucy Smith, *Joseph the Prophet*, pp. 89–99.

25. Ibid., pp. 91–92. Emma Smith described the stone. See ES to Mrs. Pilgrim, 27 March 1876, RLDS Library-Archives. For further details of the seer stone and its history, see Richard S. Van Wagoner and Stephen C. Walker, "Joseph Smith: The Gift of Seeing," *Dialogue* 15, No. 2 (Summer 1982):48–68.

26. Richard L. Bushman, unpublished Ms., "The Beginnings of Mormonism," used by permission of author, p. 46.

27. Statement of Isaac Hale, *Susquehanna Register* (Montrose, Pa.), 1 May 1834; reprinted in Eber D. Howe, *Mormonism Unvailed*, p. 263.

28. Stowell to J. S. Fullmer, 17 February 1843. Original in LDS Archives.

29. Marietta Colwell to Wilford C. Wood, 19 October 1946, Wilford C. Wood collection, microfilm, LDS Archives. The letter says, "It was here that the Mormon Prophet Joseph Smith boarded and lived while working in the woods getting out timber."

30. Hines, *Naked Truths About Mormonism*.

31. Statement of Isaac Hale in Howe, *Mormonism Unvailed*, p. 263.

32. Daniel S. Tuttle, "Mormonism," *New Shaff-Herzog Encyclopedia of Religious Knowledge* 2 (New York: n.p., 1883):1576. A discussion of this court trial is in Walters, *Joseph Smith's Bainbridge, N.Y. Court Trials*, pp. 128–155.

33. See W. D. Purple, *Chenango Union*, New York, 3 May 1877; *Latter-day Saints' Messenger and Advocate*, October 1835, p. 201; and *Evangelical Magazine and Gospel Advocate* 2 (9 April 1831). For a discussion of the three possible results of the trial, see Donna Hill, *Joseph Smith: The First Mormon*, p. 66.

34. JS to OC, published in *Messenger and Advocate*, December 1834, as cited in

Richard L. Anderson, "The Reliability of the Early History of Lucy and Joseph Smith,"
p. 18.

35. Donna Hill, *Joseph Smith: The First Mormon*, p. 68.

36. Lucy Smith, Prelim. Ms.

37. Reminiscences of Joseph Knight, LDS Archives, n.p.

38. Lucy Smith, *Joseph the Prophet*, p. 94.

39. Statement of Isaac Hale in Howe, *Mormonism Unvailed*, p. 234.

40. Statement of Peter Ingersoll, ibid., p. 235.

41. Lucy Smith, *Joseph the Prophet*, p. 99. The account that follows of Emma's
and Joseph's visit to the hill Cumorah is also found here, pp. 100–106.

42. *Saints' Herald* 28, No. 2 (June 1881):167.

43. Lucy Smith, *Joseph the Prophet*, p. 109.

44. Ibid., p. 113.

<h2 style="text-align:center">CHAPTER 2</h2>

1. Statement of Isaac Hale in Eber D. Howe, *Mormonism Unvailed*, p. 264.

2. Amboy *Journal*, 11 June and 30 April 1879. In 1879 Joseph and Hiel Lewis,
sons of Uncle Nathaniel Lewis, debated with a Mormon named Edwin Cadwell over
events in Harmony while Emma and Joseph lived there. The Amboy *Journal* reproduced their letters.

3. Interview of Emma Smith Bidamon by Nels Madson and Parley P. Pratt, Jr.,
1877, LDS Archives.

4. Joseph III, "Last Testimony of Emma Smith," *Latter-day Saints' Messenger
and Advocate*, pp. 49–52; Joseph III to Mrs. E. Horton, 7 March 1900, RLDS Library-
Archives.

5. *Saints' Herald* 31, No. 2 (21 June 1884):396; E. C. Briggs to Joseph III, 4
June 1884.

6. "Last Testimony," *Messenger and Advocate*, pp. 49–52.

7. Statement of Isaac Hale in Howe, *Mormonism Unvailed*, p. 265.

8. Joseph Knight, Sr., "Manuscript of the early History of Joseph Smith Finding
of Plates," n.p., LDS Archives. See also Dean C. Jessee, "Joseph Knight's Recollection
of Early Mormon History," pp. 29–30.

9. Donna Hill, *Joseph Smith: The First Mormon*, p. 75.

10. In 1980 this document was presented to the LDS Church by a young collector
named Mark Hoffman and is presently in the LDS Archives. This is not the version
traditionally published in the Book of Mormon.

11. Lucy Smith, *Joseph the Prophet*, pp. 115–117.

12. Most accounts refer to this child as Alva. Emma's Bible in the Buddy Youngreen private collection records the name in her own hand as Alvin. The birth date is
sometimes disputed also. The Bible lists it as 16 June but is not in Emma's hand and
was written later. The gravestone and the Preface section of the Latter-day Saints
Manuscript History (Book A-1) in the handwriting of Oliver Cowdery date it 15 June.

13. Amboy *Journal*, 6 August 1879. Years later Rhoda Skinner, who married Emma's brother David, signed an affidavit that appeared in Howe, *Mormonism Unvailed*.
The two accounts were given years apart and in separate locales, giving credence to the
women's claims.

14. Lucy Smith, Prelim. Ms.

15. Lucy Smith, *Joseph the Prophet*, pp. 118–21.

16. Ibid., pp. 126–31. Dean Jessee of the LDS Archives has examined fragments
of the original manuscripts of the Book of Mormon. Most of the manuscript is in

Oliver Cowdery's handwriting. A number of unidentified scribes wrote for Joseph but none of the handwriting can be definitely identified as Emma's. She may have acted as scribe for part of the one hundred sixteen pages Martin Harris lost, or she could have written some sections that are missing from the original manuscript. A third possibility is that Oliver Cowdery may have recopied some parts of it. See Dean C. Jessee, "The Original Book of Mormon Manuscript," pp. 272–73. For Joseph's parents' visit see Lucy Smith, *Joseph the Prophet*, pp. 146–50, and Lucy Mack Smith to Mary Pierce, 23 January 1829, photocopy of original LDS Archives.

17. Blackman, *History of Susquehanna County*, pp. 104–5.

18. Lucy Smith, *Joseph the Prophet*, p. 139.

19. David Whitmer to William H. Kelley and G. A. Blakeslee, 15 September 1882, as cited in Roberts, *CHC* 1:131.

20. David Whitmer, *An Address to All Believers in Christ* (Richmond, Mo., 1887), p. 31, published version.

21. Statement of Lucy Harris in Howe, *Mormonism Unvailed*, pp. 154–255.

22. LDS D & C 21:1–5; RLDS D & C 19:1–2b. These books are published by both branches of the Mormon church and are considered scriptural; therefore they are cited without an author. Joseph Smith originally compiled his revelations into the *Book of Commandments*, which went through several revisions until the book was renamed. The LDS Church published its book however the revelations fitted upon the page; the RLDS Church published its book in somewhat chronological order. Both citations will be used.

23. "Remarks," Mary Elizabeth Rollins Lightner, given at BYU, 14 April 1905; typescript, BYU.

24. *HC* 1:88–96; *HC* 6:395; Walters, *Joseph Smith's Bainbridge, N.Y., Court Trials*, pp. 123–28.

25. LDS D & C 25; RLDS D & C 24.

26. LDS D & C 3:6; RLDS D & C 2:36.

27. Carter E. Grant, "An Angel Visited This Home," pp. 168–72.

28. LDS D & C 27:3; RLDS D & C 26:1; *HC* 1:108.

29. *Saints' Herald* 28, No. 11 (June 1881):163.

30. Keith E. Melder, *Beginnings of Sisterhood*, pp. 49–61. We are indebted to Thayne Anderson of Dillingham, Alas., for bringing this conflict to our attention.

31. *Saints' Herald* 28, No. 11 (1 June 1881):167.

32. *HC* 1:108.

33. Lucy Smith, *Joseph the Prophet*, p. 163.

34. Lucy Smith, Prelim. Ms.

35. Joseph and his followers never considered the church to be Protestant because they had not broken away. They believed they were restoring Christ's church.

36. Joseph was preaching at his parents' home but apparently still living at the Whitmer farm in Fayette. Joseph, Sr., and Lucy, according to local tradition, were living in a small unincorporated village between Waterloo and Seneca Falls called The Kingdom. The meeting was a small gathering as opposed to the central group in Fayette.

CHAPTER 3

1. LDS D & C 38:18, 32–42; RLDS D & C 38:4d–f, 7–10.

2. Elizabeth Ann Whitney, "A Leaf from an Autobiography," *Woman's Exponent* 7, Nos. 7–15 (June–December 1878):51. This is a lengthy article that ran over several issues of the *Exponent* and was written after the Mormons immigrated to Utah.

3. Reminiscences of James Henry Rollins, 1888, LDS Archives.

4. Statement of Mary Elizabeth Rollins Lightner, 8 February 1902, original in Mary Lightner collection, BYU.

5. LDS D & C 41:8; RLDS D & C 41:3a.

6. Journal of John Murdock, 1792–1851, LDS Archives.

7. Lucy Smith, *Joseph the Prophet*, pp. 172–84, gives the full account of this voyage to Ohio.

8. *HC* 1:215–17.

9. Sue Foster, "How the Baking Heat Was Determined on up into the Mid-1800's," *Western Reserve Magazine*, November–December 1976. Thanks to Mr. and Mrs. O. Glen Chapman for this article.

10. Ezra Booth to Rev. I. Eddy, 21 November 1831, LDS Archives.

11. Roberts, *CHC* 1:280–82; *HC* 1:261–65; Luke Johnson, "Autobiography of Luke Johnson," *Latter-day Saints' Millennial Star* 26:835; John Wycliff Rigdon, "The Life and Testimony of Sidney Rigdon," Karl Keller, ed., *Dialogue* 1, No. 4:24–25; and "History of Luke Johnson," *Deseret News* (Salt Lake City), vol. 8. See also *HC* 1:261–65 for an account of the tar and feathering. Additional information regarding Emma and also the role of Dr. Dennison comes from Luke Johnson.

12. Statement of John D. Barber, 21 March 1902, LDS Archives. Two Mormon missionaries met a Mr. Silas Raymond in Grand Rapids, Michigan, 24 March 1902, who "stated that his father was one of the leaders of the mob" and produced the tar bucket and lantern which had been handed down in his family.

13. Inez A. Kennedy, *Recollection of the Pioneers of Lee County*, p. 98; see also journal of Aroet L. Hale, p. 3 of small tablet titled "First Book or Journal of the life and Travels of Aroet L. Hale," LDS Archives.

14. Elizabeth Ann Whitney, "A Leaf from an Autobiography," *Woman's Exponent* 7, No. 7:51.

15. Lucy Smith, Prelim. Ms.

16. JS to ES, 6 June 1832, original in Beinecke Rare Book and Manuscript Library, Yale University, New Haven, Conn.

17. Lucy Smith, Prelim. Ms.

18. JS to ES, 6 June 1832.

19. Ibid. For the revelation, see *HC* 1:381.

20. JS to ES, 13 October 1832; original in RLDS Library-Archives.

21. *HC* 1:297 and note. See also Scott C. Dunn, "The Tongue of Angels? Glossolalia in the Mormon Church," unpublished paper in possession of the authors.

22. George D. Watt, ed., *JD* 7:158 (Brigham Young address, 8 February 1868).

23. A discussion of the events of this period is found in Paul H. Peterson, "An Historical Analysis of the Word of Wisdom" (Master's thesis). The quotations from David Whitmer are from the Des Moines *Daily News*, 16 October 1886, p. 20.

24. LDS D & C 89; RLDS D & C 86.

25. Vesta Crawford notes, Univ. of U.; see also Watt, ed., *JD* 2:214–15 (George A. Smith address, 18 March 1855).

26. Fawn Brodie in her revised edition of *No Man Knows My History* evaluated the statements Philastus Hurlbut collected concerning the Spaulding-Rigdon theory of the origin of the Book of Mormon. She concludes that Hurlbut wrote the affidavits himself, putting to rest the theory that the Book of Mormon was a product of Solomon Spaulding or Sidney Rigdon (Brodie, Appendix B, pp. 442–56). But she used the same Hurlbut statements concerning the reputation of the Smith family as evidence that they were *"destitute of moral character and addicted to vicious habits"* (italics in Brodie; see pp. 17–18 and Appendix A, pp. 432–41). She mentioned only briefly another

collection of statements by the Smiths' neighbors attesting to their upright character (RLDS Library-Archives). Brodie's analysis of those affidavits dealing with the Spaulding-Rigdon theory throws doubt on many others Hurlbut collected. We have used only those statements that we, through our own research, have been able to authenticate.

27. Statement of Isaac Hale, Eber D. Howe, *Mormonism Unvailed*, pp. 265–66.

28. *HC* 1:379.

29. Ibid., 374–376.

30. Reminiscence of Emily Dow Partridge Young. Typescript in LDS Archives, Univ. of U. and BYU.

31. Edward and Nancy Larkey, "Personal Reminiscence," *Saints' Herald* 26, No. 11 (1 June 18—):165.

32. Donna Hill, *Joseph Smith: The First Mormon*, pp. 170–71.

33. Franklin D. Richards, "Bibliography of Utah," p. 3, as quoted in Dean C. Jessee, "The Writing of Joseph Smith's History," p. 458.

34. JS to ES, 18 May 1834; original in RLDS Library-Archives.

35. JS to ES, 4 June 1834, Joseph Smith letterbooks, LDS Archives.

36. The erroneous announcement of Joseph's death was repeated in the *Western Courier* (Ravenna, Oh.) 24 July 1834; the *Telegraph* (Painesville, Oh.) 18 July 1834; and the *Ohio Atlas and Elyria Advertiser*, 17 July 1834.

CHAPTER 4

1. Journal of Aroet Lucius Hale, p. 2, LDS Archives.

2. Edward W. Tullidge, *Women of Mormondom*, p. 76.

3. Lucy Smith, Prelim. Ms.

4. Journal of Caroline Barnes Crosby, 1851–82, USHS.

5. Oliver Cowdery to Elizabeth Cowdery, 1 January 1834, Huntington Library.

6. Joseph Smith, Sr., blessing given to ES, photocopy, RLDS Library-Archives; a copy was given to the authors by Paul M. Edwards.

7. *HC* 2:294; tense changed to facilitate dialogue.

8. This argument is scattered in the *HC* 2:294–355.

9. Ibid., 290, 304.

10. Jonathan Crosby, "A Biographical Sketch," p. 15, LDS Archives.

11. Journal of Caroline Crosby, LDS Archives.

12. Statement of W. R. Hines, Arthur B. Demming, ed., in *Naked Truths About Mormonism*, No. 1. Letters extant from Emma's brothers to her indicate that they communicated, supporting Hines's comment about carrying letters. Hines described an argument between Sidney Rigdon and Joseph over Emma that has no support either in accounts of Rigdon's and Joseph's lives, or in our study; therefore it has not been mentioned here.

13. Jonathan Crosby, "A Biographical Sketch," December 1834, LDS Archives.

14. Joseph III, *Joseph Smith III and the Restoration*, p. 27.

15. We thank Peter Crawley for his help in dating the publication. Several hymns published in the *Latter-day Saints' Messenger and Advocate* were printed in February or March of 1836 from the same type as the ones in the hymnbook, indicating that they were still printing the book.

16. Nancy Naomi Alexander Tracy, "Incidents, Travels, and Life," typescript at BYU.

17. *HC* 2:428.

18. George D. Watt, ed., *JD* 2:215 (George A. Smith address, 18 March 1855).

19. Vesta Crawford notes, Univ. of U.

20. Tullidge, *Women of Mormondom,* p. 207.

21. JS to ES, 19 August 1836, *Saints' Herald* 26 (1 December 1879):357.

22. LDS D & C 111; not in RLDS D & C. Ebenezer Robinson, *The Return* 1 (Davis City, Ia., July 1889):105.

23. *Latter-day Saints' Millennial Star,* 50:2. Descriptive details are supplied by Snow's biographer, Maureen Ursenbach Beecher. Family background, her conversion story, and descriptions of Smith family life can be found in Eliza R. Snow, "Sketch of My Life," unpaged, Bancroft Library, UC, Berkeley, Calif., microfilm at LDS Archives.

24. Mary Fielding to Mercy Thompson, 8 July 1837, LDS Archives. Joseph's illness and Emma's prayers are in this letter.

25. *HC* 2:519.

26. Richard Van Wagoner and Stephen C. Walker, "A Book of Mormons," unpublished ms., in possession of the authors.

27. ES to JS, 25 April 1837, Joseph Smith letterbooks, LDS Archives.

28. ES to JS, 3 May 1837, Joseph Smith letterbooks, LDS Archives.

29. Richard L. Anderson, "Methods Used in Discovering Joseph Smith's Family History," speech delivered to World Conference on Records, Salt Lake City, Ut., 12–15 August 1980, p. 5.

30. Joseph III, *Joseph Smith III,* p. 12.

31. Hiel Lewis, "The Mormon History," Amboy *Journal,* 6 August 1879. Lewis was the son of Emma's uncle, Nathaniel Lewis.

32. Book of Mormon, Jacob 2:22–30.

33. Brigham Young would tell a story many years later that also dates the revelation on plural marriage in 1831. He "Said that while Joseph and Oliver were translating the Book of Mormon they had a revelation that the order of Patriarchal Marriag[e] and the Sealing was right. Oliver said unto Joseph, 'Br Joseph why dont we go into the Order of Polygamy, and practice it as the ancients did? We know it is true, then why delay?' Joseph's reply was 'I know that we know it is true, and from God, but the time has not come.' " Charles Lowell Walker recorded Brigham Young's speech in his diary, 26 July 1872, LDS Archives. Dating the revision of the Bible is in Danel W. Bachman, "A Study of the Mormon Practice of Plural Marriage Before the Death of Joseph Smith" (Master's thesis), p. 56.

34. Watt, ed., *JD* 13:193 (Orson Pratt address, 7 October 1869).

35. Joseph F. Smith to Editor, *Deseret Evening News* (Salt Lake City), 18 February 1882, as quoted in Bachman, "Plural Marriage," p. 67.

36. Lawrence Foster, *Religion and Sexuality,* pp. 134–35, and notes, p. 299.

37. Mary Elizabeth Rollins Lightner to Emmeline B. Wells, summer 1905, LDS Archives.

38. Orson Pratt, *Latter-day Saints' Millennial Star* (Liverpool, England), 40 (16 December 1878):788.

39. Donna Hill, *Joseph Smith: The First Mormon,* p. 146.

40. McLellin to Joseph III, n.d. July 1872, RLDS Library-Archives.

41. Dean R. Zimmerman, *I Knew the Prophets, An Analysis of the Letter of Benjamin F. Johnson to George F. Gibbs, Reporting Doctrinal Views of Joseph Smith and Brigham Young,* p. 38.

42. *Salt Lake Tribune,* 6 October 1875; McLellin to Joseph III, July 1872.

43. Danel W. Bachman's "A Study of the Mormon Practice of Plural Marriage Before the Death of Joseph Smith," p. 83, discusses Fanny Alger's pregnancy and gives two sources: Wilhelm Wyl, *Mormon Portraits,* p. 57, and Ann Eliza Young, *Wife Number 19, or, The Story of a Life in Bondage, Being a Complete Expose of Mormon-*

ism, and Revealing the Sorrows, Sacrifices and Sufferings of Women in Polygamy, pp. 66–67.

44. Fanny Alger, Levi Hancock's niece, moved to Indiana and never confirmed or denied her association with Joseph. The Church Records of the Lima, Ill., Branch (1830–45) list several Algers (Samuel, Clarissa, John, Alva, Samuel, Jr., Thomas, and another Clarissa) and directly following them is a Fanny Carter, which in old handwriting was probably "Custer." Thomas Milton Tinney, in his "The Royal Family of the Prophet Joseph Smith, Junior: First President of the Church of Jesus Christ of Latter-day Saints" (typescript, 1963; USHS and Univ. of U.), states that Fanny Alger married Solomon Custor, as do other family and church sources.

45. OC to Warren Cowdery, 21 January 1838, original in Huntington Library. Oliver copied a letter he had written to Joseph Smith on this same day into this letter to Warren Cowdery. After Oliver left the church, Brigham Young commented that on 26 July 1872 Oliver had taken a plural wife named Annie Lyman, but at the present we can find no documentation that supports this. Brigham Young's remarks are repeated in a number of sources such as the Charles L. Walker journal, 8:18 (or p. 444 of the typescript in the BYU library). George Q. Cannon reprinted the comment in "History of the Church," *Juvenile Instructor* 16, No. 18 (15 September 1881):206.

46. Statement of Mrs. Warner Alexander, LDS Archives. Mrs. Alexander recorded that her parents became Mormons in New York and moved to Kirtland in 1836. Polly Beswick "made her home with her sister, Mrs. John Tanner, who lived next door to ours," reported Mrs. Alexander. Her statement is an example of the gossip circulating in Kirtland. In the LDS D & C 90:28–31 and RLDS D & C 87:7 a revelation dated 8 March 1833 states in part, "Vienna Jacques should receive money to bear her expenses, and go up to the land of Zion," a commandment that she should leave Kirtland and go to Missouri. As an old woman in Utah, Vienna Jacques seemed to have been recognized as a plural wife of Joseph Smith, but a 20 July 1869 affidavit to that effect is unsigned by her. One source linking her in marriage to Joseph is a 28 March 1858 sealing date, fourteen years after Joseph's death. Brodie, *No Man Knows My History,* p. 486, claims that descendants of Vienna Jacques's neighbors in Utah maintain "that the marriage took place while the prophet was alive."

47. ES to JS, 25 April 1837, and ES to JS, 3 May 1837, Joseph Smith letterbooks, Joseph Smith collection, LDS Archives. Italics added.

48. *HC* 2:246–47; RLDS D & C 111:4b. This statement is no longer in the LDS edition.

49. McLellin to Joseph III, n.d. July 1872, RLDS Library-Archives.

50. Hepsibah Richards to Willard Richards, 18 January 1838, LDS Archives.

51. Eliza R. Snow, "The Gathering of the Saints, and the Commencement of the City of Adam-ondi-ahman," *Poems, Religious, Historical, and Political,* 2 vols. (Liverpool: R. James, 1856), 1:10.

52. Journal of Caroline Barnes Crosby, USHS. Hepsibah Richards to Friends, 23 March 1838, LDS Archives.

53. Hepsibah Richards to Willard Richards, 19 January 1838, LDS Archives.

CHAPTER 5

1. Elden Jay Watson, ed., *Manuscript History of Brigham Young, 1801–1844,* pp. 24–26.

2. Ibid.

3. Vesta Crawford notes, Univ. of U.

4. The High Council meeting, 10 March 1838, in *HC* 3:8–10. The charges against Oliver Cowdery are in *HC* 3:16, 17.

5. William Swartzell, *Mormonism Exposed, Being a Journal of a Residence in Missouri From the 28th of May to the 20th of August, 1838* (Pekin, Oh., 1840), pp. 22–23; as quoted in Harold Schindler, *Orrin Porter Rockwell: Man of God, Son of Thunder*, p. 45.

6. Joseph had this speech reprinted under the name *Oration Delivered by Mr. S. Rigdon on the 4th of July, 1838, at Far West, Missouri* (Far West, Mo.: The Journal Office, 1838), Chicago Historical Society.

7. Lucy Smith, *Joseph the Prophet*, p. 227.

8. Crawford notes.

9. Lucy Smith, *Joseph the Prophet*, pp. 225–30.

10. Crawford notes.

11. *HC* 3:175. David Patten was buried 27 October 1838, the same day Governor Boggs of Missouri issued his extermination order against the Mormons.

12. Helen Mar Whitney, "Early Reminiscences," *Woman's Exponent* 8, No. 24 (15 May 1880):185.

13. *HC* 3:175. Missouri Governor Christopher S. Bond, at the suggestion of Lyman Edwards, rescinded the order in 1976 and apologized to the LDS and RLDS churches.

14. William Holmes Walker, *The Life Incidents and Travels*. Various sources reflect the strong emotions and recount the details of this attack. See Joseph Young's narrative, *HC* 3:183–87; Alma R. Blair, "The Haun's Mill Massacre," an unpublished paper, 15 April 1972, copy in possession of the authors; Ida Blum, *Nauvoo, Gateway to the West*, pp. 10–12.

15. Diary of William Huntington, p. 23, typescript at BYU.

16. *HC* 3:17–213. The execution order and Doniphan's response are on pp. 190–99.

17. The introduction to *HC* 3 mentions the incidence of rape in Far West.

18. *Saints' Herald* 26, No. 14 (15 July 1879).

19. Donna Hill, *Joseph Smith: The First Mormon*, pp. 245–46.

20. JS to ES, 4 November 1838, RLDS Library-Archives.

21. JS to ES, 12 November 1838, RLDS Library-Archives.

22. JS to ES, 1 December 1838, Joseph Smith papers, LDS Archives.

23. These first two visits are described by Joseph III in *Joseph Smith III and the Restoration*, pp. 13–14.

24. Journal of John Lowe Butler, LDS Archives, p. 20; punctuation added and tense changed to accommodate dialogue; see also *HC* 3:286–88.

25. Don Cecil Corbett, *Mary Fielding, Daughter of Britain*, pp. 82–87; Joseph III to A. V. Gibbons, 1 June 1893, and Joseph III to J. W. Davis, 10 June 1893, both in Joseph III Letterbook No. 4, RLDS Library-Archives. See also Lyman Wight to James J. Strang's *Northern Islander*, July 1855, Lyman Wight letterbook, RLDS Library-Archives. The letter said in part: "If you [had] been presant when Joseph called on me shortly after [we] came out of jail to lay hands with him on the head of a youth and heard him cry aloud you are my successor when I depart and heard the blessings pored on his head I say had you heard all this and seen the tears streaming from his eyes you would not have been led by blind fanaticism or zeal without knowledge."

26. Joseph III notes of interview with Emma Smith Bidamon, February 1879. RLDS Library-Archives.

27. Journal of David Pettigrew, p. 17, BYU.

28. Mormons' total losses in Missouri were of sufficient value that Joseph would confront the federal government over a period of years in an attempt to secure redress.

29. F. M. Cooper, "Spiritual Reminiscences in the Life of Sister Ann Davis," Marietta Walker, ed., in *Autumn Leaves* (Lamoni, Ia.: RLDS), p. 18.

30. ES to JS, 9 March 1839, Joseph Smith letterbooks, LDS Archives.

CHAPTER 6

1. ES to JS, 9 March 1839, Joseph Smith letterbooks, LDS Archives.

2. *HC* 3:293.

3. JS to ES, 21 March 1839, Joseph Smith papers, LDS Archives.

4. LDS D & C 121:7–9.

5. JS to ES, 21 March 1839, Joseph Smith papers, LDS Archives.

6. Agnes Smith to Hyrum and Joseph Smith, 11 April 1839, as reprinted in *HC* 3:314; Don Carlos Smith to Hyrum and Joseph, 6 March 1839, LDS Archives.

7. Statement of Dimick B. Huntington, LDS Archives, as quoted in David E. Miller and Della S. Miller, *Nauvoo: The City of Joseph*, p. 26.

8. *HC* 3:320–22.

9. Journal of Wandle Mace, p. 37, LDS Archives.

10. Robert Bruce Flanders, *Nauvoo: Kingdom on the Mississippi*, pp. 23–56, describes the acquisition of the townsite in detail.

11. Galland to "My very dear Sir," 22 July 1839, RLDS Library-Archives.

12. JS and ES to Mr. and Mrs. Cleveland, 24 May 1839, Joseph Smith letterbooks, LDS Archives.

13. Joseph III, *Joseph Smith III and the Restoration*, pp. 20–21.

14. Oliver B. Huntington, "History of the Life of Oliver B. Huntington, Also His Travels and Troubles Written by Himself," carbon copy of typescript at LDS Archives.

15. Elizabeth Ann Whitney, "A Leaf from an Autobiography," *Woman's Exponent* 7, No. 7 (1878):91.

16. Journal of Wandle Mace, p. 41, LDS Archives.

17. Charles Lowell Walker, "Ode to the Ague," from *Book of Verse*, LDS Archives.

18. Ida Blum, *Nauvoo, Gateway to the West*, pp. 70–71. The information on pioneer cooking and utensils all comes from this source.

19. Edwin F. Parry, compiler, *Stories About Joseph Smith the Prophet*, pp. 34–35.

20. *HC* 3:16.

21. ES to JS, 6 December 1839, Joseph Smith letterbooks, LDS Archives.

22. JS to ES, 9 November 1839, photocopy in LDS Archives, original at RLDS Library-Archives.

23. ES to JS, 6 December 1839, Joseph Smith letterbooks, LDS Archives.

24. *HC* 4:40.

25. *HC* 4:80.

26. A letter in rhyme sent by Abigail Pitkin to her sister, Rebecca Raymond, statement of John D. Barber, LDS Archives.

27. *HC* 4:3, 17.

28. Brigham Young to Mary Ann Angell Young, 12 June 1840, Univ. of U., Philip Blair collection.

29. Ibid., 12 November 1840. The Twelve had made every effort to communicate with Joseph about publishing. Orson Hyde, John Page, Parley Pratt, Brigham Young, and Willard Richards had all written to Joseph about the matter between December of 1839 and the fall of 1840.

30. *HC* 4:14.

31. Ibid., pp. 105–106; Peter Crawley, "A Bibliography of the Church of Jesus Christ of Latter-day Saints in New York, Ohio, and Missouri," pp. 524–26.

32. Crawley, "A Bibliography of the Church," pp. 521–31; see also S. A. Burgess, "Latter Day Saint Hymns," *Journal of History*, 18, No. 3 (July 1925):257–60.

33. BY to Mary Ann Angell Young, 15 January 1841, Univ. of U.

34. William Holmes Walker, *The Life Incidents and Travels*, p. 8.

35. Lucy Walker Holmes, "A brief Biographical Sketch of the life & Labors of Lucy Walker Kimball Smith," LDS Archives. See also William Holmes Walker, *The Life Incidents and Travels*, p. 10.

36. Emily D. P. Young, "Incidents in the Early Life of Emily Dow Partridge," p. 4, Univ. of U.; Emily Dow Partridge Young, "Autobiography," *Woman's Exponent* 14.

37. Joseph III, *Joseph Smith III*, p. 24.

38. Blum, *Nauvoo, Gateway to the West*, pp. 58–60.

39. Vesta Crawford notes, Univ. of U. Crawford calls the Rigdon child "Lacy" as does Rigdon family genealogy. The 1842 Nauvoo census listing the Rigdon children gives the name of this girl as Lucy, which is probably an error.

40. Ibid.

41. Joseph III to Mrs. D. C. Chase, 5 May 1893, RLDS Library-Archives.

42. Harold Joseph Mellen, Herbert Mellen, and Maybelle Winegar, "History of Pioneers—John Mellen and Jane Ramsden Mellen," unpublished history. Our thanks to Stuart Poelman for providing us a copy.

43. Lucy Smith, *Joseph the Prophet*, pp. 264–70.

44. Flanders, *Nauvoo*, p. 120.

45. Joseph III, *Joseph Smith III*, pp. 58–59.

46. See Flanders, *Nauvoo*, pp. 92–106.

47. Emmeline B. Wells, "LDS Women of the Past: Personal Impressions," *Woman's Exponent* 36, No. 7 (February 1908); see also the Journal History, LDS Archives, 4 July 1842.

48. Joseph III, *Joseph Smith III*, p. 46.

49. Crawford notes, Univ. of U.

50. Mary Bailey Smith Norman to Ina Coolbrith, n.d. [ca. March 1908], RLDS Library-Archives.

CHAPTER 7

1. Sources for this are numerous. They include: Joseph B. Noble, address, 11 June 1883, at Stake Conference in Centerville, Ut.; Journal History, LDS Archives; Joseph Bates Noble, deposition, Circuit Court Testimony, 1892; Andrew Jensen, compiler, *Historical Record* 6:232; journal of Franklin D. Richards, January 1869 (loose sheet), Franklin D. Richards papers, LDS Archives; journal of Wilford Woodruff, 22 January 1869, microfilm of original, LDS Archives; Joseph F. Smith, "40 Affidavits on Celestial Marriage," Book 1, p. 38, as cited in Andrew F. Ehat, "An Overview of the Introduction of Eternal Marriage in the Church of Jesus Christ of Latter-day Saints," unpublished paper, pp. 7–9, used with author's permission. Also see Fawn M. Brodie, *No Man Knows My History*, p. 465, for composite accounts of the Noble-Beaman story. LDS accounts of this marriage usually refer to it as the first plural marriage performed in Nauvoo. Evidence links Joseph to at least three previous ones in the city: Prescindia Huntington Buell, Nancy Marinda Johnson Hyde, and Clarissa Hancock.

2. Journal of Joseph Lee Robinson, pp. 12–13 of typescript, LDS Archives. Helen Mar Whitney "Pamphlet," 1882, published by Salt Lake Public Library, LDS

Church Archives, dated this speech as "previous to the return of the Apostles from Europe in 1841."

3. Journal of Joseph Lee Robinson, typescript, pp. 12–13; Ebenezer Robinson, *The Return* 2 (1890):287, and 3 (1891):28; Helen Mar Kimball Whitney, *Plural Marriage as Taught by the Prophet Joseph; a Reply to Joseph Smith, Editor of the Lamoni (Iowa) Herald*, p. 11.

4. Lawrence Foster, *Religion and Sexuality*, pp. 125–28.

5. Ibid., pp. 142–51.

6. JS to ES, 13 October 1832, RLDS Library-Archives; JS to ES, 18 May 1834, RLDS Library-Archives; JS to ES, 20 January 1840, Chicago Historical Society; JS to ES, 16 August 1842, *HC* 5:103 and in William Clayton, Book of the Law of the Lord, pp. 173–75.

7. Parley P. Pratt, *Autobiography of Parley Parker Pratt*, pp. 197–98.

8. For Brigham Young's reaction, see *Journal of Discourses* 3:266; for Heber C. Kimball's reaction, see Orson F. Whitney, *Life of Heber C. Kimball*, p. 336, and Stanley B. Kimball, *Heber C. Kimball*, pp. 86–105; John Taylor's reaction is recorded in *Comprehensive History of the Church* 2:102; and for Joseph Smith's reaction, see Helen Mar Whitney, "Life Incidents," *Woman's Exponent* 22 (1 August 1882):39.

9. Journal of Joseph Lee Robinson, typescript, p. 33.

10. Andrew Jenson's work is printed in the *Historical Record* 6, Nos. 3–5:233–34; Danel W. Bachman, "A Study of the Mormon Practice of Plural Marriage Before the Death of Joseph Smith" (Master's thesis), pp. 107–12, concludes that "scholars have not adequately contested sixteen ill-supported names" from Brodie in *No Man Knows My History*, which lists forty-eight; Stanley S. Ivins's collection is in the USHS. Further documentation for Joseph's involvement in plural marriage is extensive and varied. In the RLDS Library-Archives see letters from William McLellin to Joseph III, 10 January 1861 and July 1872; also High Council minutes. Other sources are readily available to the reader in Donna Hill, *Joseph Smith: The First Mormon;* Foster, *Religion and Sexuality;* Charles A. Shook, *The True Origins of Mormon Polygamy;* Joseph Fielding Smith, *Blood Atonement and the Origin of Plural Marriage;* and in personal accounts reprinted throughout the *Woman's Exponent.*

11. Fanny Alger, Eliza R. Snow, Mary Elizabeth Rollins Lightner, Eliza Partridge, Emily Partridge, Sarah Lawrence, and Maria Lawrence.

12. Diary of William Clayton, as reprinted in Jenson, *Historical Record* 6, Nos. 3–5 (May 1887):225.

13. "Remarks," Mary Elizabeth Rollins Lightner, given at BYU 14 April 1905, typescript BYU; Josephine R. Fisher, affidavit, 24 February 1915, LDS Archives. Foster, *Religion and Sexuality*, pp. 157–58, discusses possible children of Joseph.

14. Ida Blum, *Nauvoo, Gateway to the West*, p. 63.

15. Helen Mar Whitney, "Life Incidents," *Woman's Exponent* 10 (15 August 1881):85–86.

16. Foster, *Religion and Sexuality*, p. 153.

17. Vilate Kimball to Heber C. Kimball, 24 June 1843, Winslow Whitney Smith collection, LDS Archives.

18. *HC* 5:265.

19. George Q. Cannon, *The Life of Joseph Smith, The Prophet*, pp. 25–26.

20. Journal of Joseph Lee Robinson, p. 22; see also Foster, *Religion and Sexuality*, p. 148.

21. Sarah Melissa Granger Kimball affidavit in Jenson, *Historical Record* 6:232.

22. Three women in particular, Martha Brotherton, Sarah Pratt, and Nancy Rigdon, voiced their objections to plural marriage. Brotherton's story is recounted in Mrs.

T. B. H. Stenhouse, *Expose of Polygamy in Utah*, pp. 154–62; Sarah Pratt's and Nancy Rigdon's accounts are in Hill, *Joseph Smith: The First Mormon*, pp. 300–1.

23. Brigham Young officiated at the marriage between Joseph and Mary Elizabeth in the room over the red brick store in February 1842. Mary Elizabeth Rollins Lightner's entire account is found in Mary Elizabeth Lightner to Emmeline B. Wells, summer 1905; "Remarks," Mary Elizabeth Rollins Lightner given at BYU, 14 April 1905, typescript, BYU, and "The Life and Testimony of Mary E. Lightner," *Utah Genealogical and Historical Magazine*, July 1926, pp. 1–44.

24. Lucy Smith, Prelim. Ms., Chap. 18, p. 9; Lucy Smith, *Joseph the Prophet*, p. 271. For Smith family information, see biography of Samuel H. B. Smith, p. 1, LDS Archives.

25. Audentia Anderson, *Ancestry and Posterity*, pp. 303–5; for Isaac's tombstone see Vesta Crawford notes, Univ. of U.

26. Blum, *Nauvoo, Gateway to the West*, p. 120.

27. JS to Edward Hunter, 21 December 1841, as quoted in *HC* 4:482–83.

28. *HC* 4:501.

29. The birth date was eventually printed in error in *HC* 5:209. The "Manuscript History of the Church," from which the *HC* date was taken, states on December 26, 1842: "Home Sister Emma sick had another chill." The word "chill" apparently was mistaken for "child" in later years. Two letters from that period confirm that the baby was born early in 1842: Jacob Scott to Mary Warnock, 24 March 1842, RLDS Library-Archives, and Almira Covey to Harriet Whittemore, 24 February 1842, typescript in LDS Archives. Emma's family Bible in possession of Buddy Youngreen gives the date of the son's birth and death as 7 February 1842.

30. Margarette McIntire Burgess, "Reminiscence," *Juvenile Instructor* 27 (1892):67.

31. *HC* 4:548.

32. Joseph committed this doctrine to writing on 6 September 1842. It now appears in the LDS D & C 128:15–18. The RLDS Church does not include it.

33. "Baptisms for the Dead Performed in the Mississippi 1840–1841," LDS Genealogical Library, Salt Lake City, Ut. Isaac Hale's name appears first and is dated 1841. Phoebe Root's name also carries an 1841 year. The rest are undated but since they were recorded after Isaac Hale we have assumed that they were also done in 1841.

34. *HC* 4:550–52; see also Mervin B. Hogan, "What of Mormonism and Freemasonry?" unpublished paper, p. 9, LDS Archives.

35. Andrew F. Ehat discovered the date of Emma's sealing to be 28 May 1843. The specific documentation for this and her involvement in other ordinances will be discussed in the appropriate chapters. D. Michael Quinn in his article, "Latter-day Saint Prayer Circles," pp. 86–87n., lists alphabetically those who received their endowments between 1842 and 1844. He cites as his sources the "Meetings of the anointed Quorum," journal of Wilford Woodruff, 2 December 1842 to 26 February 1844; diary of Joseph Smith, in Roberts, *History of the Church*, and the "Manuscript History of the Church" for September 1843 to May 1844; journal of Heber C. Kimball, 7 and 10 December 1845, all in the LDS Archives; list of the members of the Quorum of the Anointed in the Newel K. Whitney 1833–45 Account Book, Newel K. Whitney family collections, BYU, and the less than complete Nauvoo Temple Supplemental Record of Endowments in the LDS Genealogical Library, Salt Lake City, Ut., Microfilm # 183, 371, pp. 66–67.

36. Extensive literature suggests that there are often important similarities in both the specific practices that have developed and in the social functions that those practices serve. These similarities can be quite striking even when two different ritual or

religious systems have developed independently of each other. For a discussion of initiation rites, a classic starting point is Arnold Van Gennep, *The Rites of Passage*, trans. Monika B. Vizedom and Gabrielle L. Caffe (Chicago: University of Chicago Press, 1960). Victor W. Turner, in *The Ritual Process: Structure and Anti-structure* (Chicago: Aldine Publishing Co., 1969), further explores and extends many of Van Gennep's insights. On the similarities between religious belief systems and practices in many different cultures, see the extensive writings of Mircea Eliade, including his *Rites and Symbols of Initiation: The Mysteries of Birth and Rebirth* (New York: Harper & Row, 1965).

Through Alexander Neibaur, Joseph Smith had access to ancient Jewish rites called cabalism at the same time he claimed to be translating the papyri from the Egyptian mummies purchased from Michael Chandler. The Book of Abraham published by the Mormons as coming from those papyri contains parallels to the endowment. For discussions on the Joseph Smith papyri and Book of Abraham, see *Dialogue* 3, No. 2 (Summer 1968):66–105. This issue devoted six articles to that topic. See also Benjamin Urrutia, "The Joseph Smith Papyri," *Dialogue* 4, No. 2 (Summer 1969):120–34, and Klaus Baer, "A Translation of the Apparent Source of the Book of Abraham," *Dialogue* 3, No. 3 (Autumn 1968):109–33.

37. Heber C. Kimball to Parley P. Pratt, 17 June 1842, Parley P. Pratt papers, LDS Archives.

38. Diary of Joseph Fielding, a private Smith family publication, June 1963, typewritten from five volumes of original diary. This letter is from Book 5, p. 22, of the original; statement of Jesse C. Little, as cited in Richard F. Burton, *The City of The Saints*, pp. 350–51.

39. Albert G. Mackey, *A Lexicon of Freemasonry*, 7th ed., pp. 9–12; Albert G. Mackey, *An Encyclopedia of Freemasonry* 1:26–27; II John 1:1.

40. These phrases appear throughout "A Record of the Organization and Proceedings of The Female Relief Society of Nauvoo," microfilm of original, Joseph Smith collection, LDS Archives.

41. Lucy M. Smith testimony, "Latter Day Saints Abstract of Evidence: Temple Lot Case," LDS Archives.

CHAPTER 8

1. "Story of the Organization of the Relief Society," *Relief Society Magazine* 129; and see the *Woman's Exponent* 7, No. 3 (1 July 1878):18.

2. *HC* 4:552. All the information for the meetings from 17 March to 28 September 1842 is from the minutes, "A Record of the Organization and Proceedings of The Female Relief Society of Nauvoo," microfilm of original, Joseph Smith collection, LDS Archives. Hereafter cited as RS Minutes. The Susa Young Gates collection, LDS Archives, has a typescript of these minutes. This copy contains errors, but they do not vary widely from what is cited here. The Reorganized Church of Jesus Christ of Latter Day Saints Library-Archives in Independence, Mo., has a microfilm copy of the original minutes.

3. Questions in regard to ordaining women would continue to surface. Finally in 1880 John Taylor explained in a general conference of the church that "some of the sisters have thought that these sisters mentioned were, in this ordination ordained to the priesthood. . . . I will say, it is not the calling of these sisters to hold the Priesthood, only in connection with their husbands, they being one with their husbands." *JD* 21 (8 August 1880), p. 367.

4. Keith E. Melder, *Beginnings of Sisterhood*, discusses the rise of women's societies and other organizations to which Emma probably referred.

5. Unless cited otherwise, all information for this meeting is from the RS Minutes, 2nd meeting, 24 March 1842, LDS Archives.

6. The name in question is most likely Sarah Noon, Heber C. Kimball's first plural wife.

7. RS Minutes, 18th meeting, 28 September 1842. The Clarissa Marvel statement of 2 April 1844, naming Agnes Smith, was added at the close of the Relief Society year because it was omitted earlier.

8. Mary P. Ryan, *Womanhood in America*, p. 36.

9. The term "Mother in Israel" seemed to have two meanings, one referring to the fulfillment of a woman's destiny in the church and to her faith, as when John Taylor blessed Emma to be a Mother in Israel in the first Relief Society meeting. Joseph H. Jackson, in the article titled, "Wonderful Disclosures Respecting Mormons," New York *Herald*, 5 September 1844, as quoted in Stanley Ivins's notebooks, states that a "Mrs. Tailar, old Madam Durfee and old Madam Sessions" were "Mothers in Israel" employed by Joseph to convert young girls to polygamy. Further documentation that these women contacted plural wives for Joseph is found in Emily D. P. Young, "Incidents in the Early Life of Emily Dow Partridge," Univ. of U. This is further discussed in Chapter 10.

10. For Clarissa Marvel's statement, see RS Minutes, 18th meeting, 28 September 1842. For Emma's statement, see 6th meeting, 28 April 1842. Agnes Coolbrith Smith, widow of Don Carlos Smith, is not included on any list of Joseph's wives. Fawn Brodie in *No Man Knows My History*, p. 469, lists a Mrs. A**** S**** and gives John C. Bennett's *History of the Saints: Or an Expose of Joe Smith and Mormonism* as her source. That the woman in question is a "Mrs." and the number of asterisks in the name match "Agnes Smith" suggest that it is she to whom he alluded. Willard Richards and Joseph dined with Agnes Smith 17 January 1842, *HC* 4:494; see also D. Michael Quinn, "Latter-day Saint Prayer Circles," 79–105.

11. RS Minutes, 5th meeting, 19 April 1842.

12. RS Minutes, 6th meeting, 28 April 1842.

13. Elizabeth Ann Whitney, "A Leaf from an Autobiography," *Woman's Exponent* 7, No. 12 (15 November 1878):91.

14. RS Minutes, 6th meeting, 28 April 1842, italics added. For further detail on George A. Smith's role in rewriting the history of the church, see Dean C. Jessee, "The Writings of Joseph Smith's History," p. 458.

15. For a discussion of these questions and their periodic resurfacing over the remainder of the nineteenth century, see Linda King Newell's essay, "Gifts of the Spirit: Women's Share," in a forthcoming book on historical and theological traditions of Mormon women, Lavina Fielding Anderson and Maureen Ursenbach Beecher, eds.

16. This article does not appear in the 30 March minutes but is inserted after the last meeting of the year on 28 September. The secretary was absent "at the time of it's reading else it would have appear'd in its proper place."

17. *Times and Seasons* 3 (1 August 1842):868–76. Affidavits concerning John C. Bennett's, Chauncey Higbee's, and Darwin Chase's proposals to women for sexual intercourse were apparently published in the Nauvoo *Neighbor (HC* 6:407). Originals of these affidavits are in the LDS Archives.

18. The letter appears in *HC* 5:134–36 as an "essay." Van Hale in "The Purported Letter of Joseph Smith to Nancy Rigdon," unpublished paper in possession of the authors, authenticates the letter as being from Joseph Smith to Nancy Rigdon and

places the date around 15 April 1842, instead of the *HC* date of 27 August 1842. Hale also gives convincing evidence that Willard Richards was the scribe.

19. George W. Robinson to James Arlington Bennett, 27 July 1842, as cited in Brodie, *No Man Knows My History*, p. 311n. George W. Robinson was married to Nancy Rigdon's sister Athalia.

20. Brigham Young's statement is in *Times and Seasons* 5 (15 May 1844):539; Hyrum Smith's statement is in *Times and Seasons* 3 (1 August 1842):868; and Bennett's reaction is in *HC* 5:18.

21. RS Minutes, 12th meeting, 23 June 1842. Slight changes in Emma's words facilitate the dialogue.

22. The Ford comment is found in Harry M. Beardsley, *Joseph Smith and His Mormon Empire*, pp. 107–8.

23. Vesta Crawford notes, Univ. of U.

24. George A. Smith to Joseph III, 9 October 1869, RLDS Library-Archives.

25. *Deseret News,* 20 May 1866, reprinted in *Woman's Exponent* 15, (1886):10, italics added. The author was probably Joseph F. Smith.

26. RS Minutes, 6th meeting, 28 April 1842.

27. *HC* 4:607–8.

28. Vienna Jacques told her story to Joseph III when he visited her in the Utah territory in 1876. Joseph III said of that interview, "I need not attempt to relate all the communication which passed between us," then proceeded with his account of the conversation that supported his position against plural marriage, *Joseph Smith III*, p. 263–64. Several other women interviewed by Joseph III left statements of their meetings with him. Some were taken under oath in the Temple Lot Suit.

29. RS Minutes, 8th meeting, n.d., 1842.

30. Ibid., 9th meeting, 26 May 1842; verb tense and pronouns changed to facilitate dialogue.

31. Ibid., 10th meeting, 27 May 1842.

32. Ibid., 11th meeting, 9 June 1842.

33. Ibid., 14th meeting, 14 July 1842.

34. Ibid., 15th meeting, 4 August 1842.

35. Ibid., 14th meeting, 14 July 1842. The minutes for the year 1842 name only ten women who were denied membership or investigated. Among these were Clarissa Marvel on 24 March, and Harriet P. Decker, C. Wood, and Angeline Robinson on 28 April. A committee was formed to look into the cases of the latter three and Harriet P. Decker's name was cleared by the next meeting (13 May) as the women accepted her into the society. The other two apparently never received membership; at least their names do not appear on the rolls. At the 23 June meeting "objections were remov'd against" Elizabeth Garlick, Mary Garlick, Hannah Garlick, and Talithacuma Garlick. On 7 July "The case of Sis Nightman, wishing admittance, was also presented and objected." This was the same day the debate over Sis. Brown began. There may have been more women who were rejected but were never brought before a vote of the society, for a committee was appointed to review names submitted for membership.

36. Emmeline B. Wells, "LDS Women of the Past: Personal Impressions," *Woman's Exponent* 36, No. 7 (February 1908):1.

CHAPTER 9

1. The inscription reads, "This Album was politely presented to Eliza R. Snow By Mrs. Sarah M. Kimball City of Nauvoo, March 1842." Maureen Ursenbach [Beecher], ed., "Eliza R. Snow's Nauvoo Journal." Hereafter cited as Beecher, "E. R.

Snow's Nauvoo Journal." Sources for the marriage are Eliza R. Snow, "Sketch of My Life," original at Bancroft Library, University of California, microfilm at LDS Archives; Eliza R. Snow, *Biography and Family Record of Lorenzo Snow*, p. 68; affidavit of Lorenzo Snow, 28 August 1869, LDS Archives. Eliza's brother stated that in April 1843 Joseph Smith "further said that my sister Eliza R. Snow had been sealed to him as his wife for time and eternity," Jenson, *The Historical Record*, 6, Nos. 3–5 (May 1887):222; Eliza R. Snow's letter to Daniel Munns, 30 May 1877, RLDS Library-Archives, reads in part, "I trust that my word may be sufficient. I was married to Joseph Smith the Prophet, more than two years previous to his death"; Eliza R. Snow to Joseph F. Smith, n.d., LDS Archives, "At the time the sisters of the Relief Society signed our article I was married to the Prophet."

2. Beecher, "E. R. Snow's Nauvoo Journal," 29 June 1842, p. 394.

3. Nauvoo city tax records, 1842, and Hancock County tax records; Nauvoo Restoration, LDS Archives. Both Mormon and anti-Mormon sources name Sarah Cleveland as a plural wife. See Jenson, *The Historical Record* 6, Nos. 3–5 (May 1887):234; Fawn Brodie in *No Man Knows My History*, p. 449, quotes Sarah Pratt in Wyl's *Mormon Portraits*, p. 90, as saying, "Sarah Cleveland kept a kind of assignation house for the Prophet and Eliza R. Snow." Angus M. Cannon, 12 October 1905 interview with Joseph III. Cannon was Eliza's stake president at the time of his conversation with her. (A stake in the Mormon church is comparable to a Catholic diocese in that it is composed of several congregations under the direction of an ecclesiastical leader called a stake president.) He also took the aged woman for rides in his carriage three times a week "when she was helpless as a child," (p. 12) and quotes her as saying, "Sister Emma . . . took my hand and put it in the hand of her husband, Brother Joseph, and gave me to him to wife." This is improbable. On the surface the account seems reliable, but a closer look at the entire interview reveals some problems in memory for the sixty-one-year-old Angus Cannon on other matters. Eliza's own sworn affidavit does not mention Emma. It states "She was married or sealed to Joseph Smith . . . by Brigham Young . . . in the presence of Sarah M. Cleaveland." Affidavit of Eliza R. Snow Smith, Joseph F. Smith affidavit collection, Book 1, p. 25, LDS Archives. None of Eliza's own writings ever mentions that Emma was present at the marriage or gave her consent. It must be assumed then that Cannon was in error in his report.

4. Davis Bitton and Gary L. Bunker, "Phrenology Among the Mormons," pp. 43–61.

5. *The Wasp* (Nauvoo, Ill.), 20 August 1842.

6. *HC* 5:45.

7. Beecher, "E. R. Snow's Nauvoo Journal," p. 394.

8. *HC* 5:83.

9. Lorenzo Wasson to JS and ES, 30 July 1842, *Times and Seasons*, 15 August 1842, pp. 891–92; Joseph's request that Emma write to Wasson, *HC* 5:105.

10. *HC* 5:89.

11. Ibid., 91–92; Danel Bachman, "A Study of the Mormon Practice of Plural Marriage Before the Death of Joseph Smith" (Master's thesis), Appendix C, and Fawn Brodie, *No Man Knows My History*, p. 450, both list Edward Sayers's wife, Ruth Vose, as a plural wife of Joseph.

12. Beecher, "E. R. Snow's Nauvoo Journal," p. 396.

13. Journal History, 13 August 1842, LDS Archives.

14. *HC* 5:86–92.

15. Ibid., 92.

16. Ibid., 103–5.

17. Ibid., 107.

18. Ibid., 110.

19. ES to Gov. Thomas Carlin, 17 August 1842, RLDS Library-Archives.

20. *HC* 5:117–18.

21. *Latter-day Saints Biographical Encyclopedia* 1:226; see also Jenson, *Historical Record* 6:225–26. For the published affidavits of both Sarah Ann Whitney and her mother, see Joseph Fielding Smith, *Blood Atonement and the Origin of Plural Marriage*, pp. 73–74.

22. JS to Brother and Sister Whitney, & C., 18 August 1842. George Albert Smith family papers at Univ. of U., photocopy; church manuscripts compiled by Alan H. Herber, Reel E 2:18, BYU. For further details on this incident, see Bachman, "Plural Marriage Before the Death of Joseph Smith," pp. 161–62; Lawrence Foster, *Religion and Sexuality*, pp. 155–56, and Dean C. Jessee, *Personal Writings of Joseph Smith*, pp. 538–42.

23. Newel K. Whitney recorded that Joseph gave them a blessing 21 August. Andrew F. Ehat, "An Overview of the Introduction of Eternal Marriage in the Church of Jesus Christ of Latter-day Saints," unpublished paper, p. 16. Used with permission. See *HC* 5:119 for Joseph's visit to Emma on 19 August, and *HC* 5:128–29 for reference to Emma's letter and Joseph's decision to return home. James B. Allen, "One Man's Nauvoo: William Clayton's Experience in Mormon Illinois," *Journal of Mormon History* 6 (1979):39–42, 50.

24. Clayton Family Association, *Journal of William Clayton* (Salt Lake City: The Deseret News, 1921), pp. vi–vii.

25. Information from the William Clayton diary will be cited in several ways because it comes from a number of different sources. The diary is in the vault of the First Presidency of the Church of Jesus Christ of Latter-day Saints and not in the LDS Church Archives; therefore, the Historical Department of the church has no jurisdiction over it. Few scholars have been given permission to see the diary, but those who have had access to it for historical purposes have quoted from it in books, pamphlets, or articles. Where possible, we cite the diary as it has been published in these works. By referring to his own notes on the diary, James B. Allen, who is William Clayton's biographer, has answered specific questions we have had concerning events recorded in the diary. We have cited these as: James B. Allen notes on the diary of William Clayton. In addition Dr. Allen has shared part of his forthcoming William Clayton biography. Chapter Eight, "Aftermath of Tragedy," deals extensively with Emma after Joseph Smith's death. This we have cited as: James B. Allen, Biography of William Clayton, forthcoming. Andrew F. Ehat has given us permission to cite his notes on the diary and we cite those as "Diary of William Clayton, Excerpts."

26. Carlin to ES, 24 August 1842, as published in *HC* 5:130–31.

27. ES to Carlin, 27 August 1842; original in RLDS Library-Archives; Carlin to ES, 7 September 1842, as published in *HC* 5:154–55.

28. *HC* 5:466–68.

29. Ibid., 137–41; RS Minutes, 16th meeting, 31 August 1842.

30. Ladies Relief Society Petition to Governor Thomas Carlin, 5 September 1842, LDS Archives.

31. RS Minutes, 16th meeting, 31 August 1842.

32. Joseph III, *Joseph Smith III and the Restoration*, pp. 24–25.

33. For the accounts of Emma's confrontations with Pitman and King, see Journal History, 3 September 1842, and Beecher, "E. R. Snow's Nauvoo Journal," p. 398. We have made slight changes in the wording for style and dialogue.

34. *Times and Seasons*, Monday, 1 August 1842, p. 875.

35. Ibid., Saturday, 1 October 1842, pp. 939–40.

36. Eliza R. Snow to Joseph F. Smith, n.d., Joseph F. Smith collection, LDS Archives.

37. *HC* 5:150–61.

CHAPTER 10

1. *HC* 5:21, 25, 172, etc.

2. ES to Sidney Rigdon, 12 September 1842, and Rigdon to ES, 12 September 1842; both in LDS Archives.

3. Emma's illness began 29 September and was of such severity that Joseph's history makes note of it on nine different days: October 3–7, 10, 20, November 1, and December 1, 1842. *HC* 5:166–67. For Vilate Kimball's letter, see Vilate Kimball to Heber C. Kimball, 16 October 1842, as published in "Helen Mar Kimball, Scenes and Incidents in Nauvoo," *Woman's Exponent* 11, No. 1 (1 June 1882):1–2.

4. Maureen Ursenbach [Beecher], "Eliza R. Snow's Nauvoo Journal," pp. 400–1. Hereafter cited as Beecher, "E. R. Snow's Nauvoo Journal." Only the first stanza of the poem is reproduced here.

5. *HC* 5:172.

6. Ibid., 182.

7. Joseph III, *Joseph Smith III and the Restoration*, p. 73.

8. *HC* 5:183, 556. Lucy Walker Kimball in the Temple Lot Suit papers, LDS Archives, identified the house as the "Prophet's House" before the expansion.

9. Beecher, "E. R. Snow's Nauvoo Journal," p. 402.

10. Joseph III, *Joseph Smith III*, pp. 28–29. His weight is given as "over 300 pounds" in Richard S. Van Wagoner and Stephen C. Walker, *A Book of Mormons*, p. 231.

11. *HC* 5:211–245; Inez Smith Davis, *The Story of the Church*, p. 319; Donna Hill, *Joseph Smith: The First Mormon*, p. 321.

12. Diary of Joseph Smith, 17 January 1843, LDS Archives. Tense changed to facilitate dialogue. See also *HC* 5:253. The marriage date was 18 January 1827. It was their sixteenth anniversary rather than the fifteenth.

13. Danel Bachman, "A Study of the Mormon Practice of Plural Marriage Before the Death of Joseph Smith" (Master's thesis), Appendix C, p. 334. The wives were thirty-eight-year-old Martha McBride Knight and probably Ruth Vose Sayers, thirty-five.

14. For an analysis of the incident and sources, see Maureen Ursenbach Beecher, Linda King Newell, and Valeen Tippetts Avery, "Emma, Eliza, and the Stairs: An Investigation," pp. 86–96.

15. Wilhelm Wyl (Wymetal), *Joseph Smith the Prophet: His Family and His Friends* (Salt Lake City: Tribune Printing and Publishing Co., 1886), p. 58. On page 57 Wyl recites another tale about Emma, only the Eliza involved was Eliza Partridge. He said, "Eliza Partridge . . . used to sew in Emma's room. Once, while Joseph was absent, Emma got to fighting with Eliza and threw her down the stairs," thus confusing the two Elizas.

16. Patriarchal Record Book and Family History of Mary Ann B. Boice; John Boice, blessing book, 1884–1885, LDS Archives.

17. John R. Young to Vesta P. Crawford, April 1931, John Ray Young scrapbook, 1928–30, LDS Archives.

18. Fawn Brodie, *No Man Knows My History*, pp. 345–46, 447–48.

19. LeRoi C. Snow, "Notes," in possession of Cynthia Snow Banner, as cited in Beecher et al., "Emma, Eliza, and the Stairs," pp. 86–94.

20. LeRoi C. Snow cited an 11 August 1944 letter from W. Aird Macdonald as

his source for the Rich account. Charles C. Rich's son, Ben E., was the mission president of Macdonald in 1906–8. Since the letter has not been found, we can only assume that Ben Rich may have heard the story from his father, then passed it on to his mission president, who told it in a letter to LeRoi Snow, who then recorded it in his papers. Snow told his own version of the story before he received the Rich account.

21. Joseph F. Smith affidavit book 1, p. 54, Vault, LDS Archives.

22. Discourse by Lorenzo Snow, 8 May 1899, St. George, Utah, *The Latter-day Saints' Millennial Star*, 61, no. 35: (August 1899): 548. Nauvoo School Records, LDS Archives.

23. Eliza R. Snow to Daniel Munns, 30 May 1877, RLDS Library-Archives. Eliza indicated that Emma knew that she was married to Joseph, although she never said at what point Emma knew. Sometime in 1885 or 1886 David McKay (father of David O. McKay) drove Eliza Snow from Huntsville to Eden and had a conversation with her which he recalled in a letter of 16 March 1916 to Mrs. James Hood, Glasgow, Scotland. He asked Eliza, "Did Emma Hale Smith know that you were married to her husband, Joseph Smith?" Her reply was, "Just as well as you know that you are sitting by my side in this buggy." The original of this letter is in private possession, and the authors were shown a copy of it by Maureen Ursenbach Beecher.

24. Statement, "Interview with Joseph Smith, President of the Reorganites," by Elder Angus M. Cannon, 12 October 1905, LDS Archives.

25. Beecher, "E. R. Snow's Nauvoo Journal," p. 402.

26. Brodie, *No Man Knows My History*, p. 450, places this marriage in 1842, probably June, but Bachman, "Plural Marriage Before the Death of Joseph Smith," Appendix C, p. 334, lists a "known" date as 1 June 1843.

27. Beecher, "E. R. Snow's Nauvoo Journal," p. 407.

28. Ibid., p. 403; later published under the title "As I Believe," and dedicated to Heber C. Kimball when he was president of the church.

29. Emily D. P. Young, "Autobiography of Emily D. P. Young," *Woman's Exponent* 14:37–38.

30. Emily D. P. Young, "Incidents of the Early Life of Emily Dow Partridge," December 1876, Salt Lake City, typescript Univ. of U. and LDS Archives. Tense changed to facilitate dialogue.

31. Ibid.

32. Eliza M. Partridge, "Reminiscences," in private possession.

33. Eliza M. Partridge Smith Lyman, "Life and Journal," photocopy in Mormon collection, Huntington Library.

34. Emily Partridge, "Emily Dow Partridge Young—From Her Writings," in private possession.

35. Joseph III, *Joseph Smith III*, pp. 32–33; William Holmes Walker, *The Life Incidents and Travels*, p. 9. Affidavit of Lucy Walker Smith Kimball, Journal History, 2 May 1843; dated 17 December 1902, LDS Archives. See also Lucy Walker's testimony in the Temple Lot Suit papers.

36. *HC* 5:386–90.

37. See Elden Jay Watson, ed., *Manuscript History of Brigham Young, 1801–1844*, p. 116, as quoted in D. Michael Quinn, "Latter-day Saints Prayer Circles," pp. 83–84. *HC* 5:1–2 lists the men included in this first group and does not include William Law and William Marks. This error is evident when the names are checked against the journal of Heber C. Kimball (1840–45) ("Strange Events" section) and his 1845–46 journal, 21 December 1845. For publication of these accounts, see Quinn, "Latter-day Saint Prayer Circles," p. 83, n. 21. Contemporary diary and journal references called the group the Quorum of the Anointed, the Anointed Quorum, or abbrevi-

ations of those titles. Historians have more recently called it "Joseph Smith's Prayer Circle" (Quinn, "Latter-day Saint Prayer Circles").

38. Statement of Eliza M. A. Munson, Church Manuscript collection, compiled by Alan H. Gerber, microfilm, BYU.

39. RS Minutes, 10th meeting, 27 May 1842.

40. Journal of Heber C. Kimball, 1845–46, 21 December 1845, p. 159, LDS Archives.

41. Latter-day Saints clearly separate exaltation and salvation in their doctrine. They teach "that through the atonement of Christ all mankind may be saved" in the kingdom of God. Only those who have received temple ordinances of washing, anointing, endowment, and marriage for eternity can be exalted with the potential, through the principle of eternal progression, to become like God.

42. For further discussion of this thesis, see Andrew F. Ehat, "Joseph Smith's Introduction of Temple Ordinances and the 1844 Succession Question," (Master's thesis) pp. 59–62.

43. Ibid.

44. Diary of Levi Richards, 14 May 1843, BYU, states: "A.M. Hyrum Smith addressed the people—subjects from Book of Mormon 2nd chapt. Jacob . . . said there were many that had a great deal to say about the ancient order of things as Solomon & David having many wives & Concubines—but its an abomination in the Sight of God."

45. The plan to expose Joseph and the others in plural marriage is from William Clayton's diary, 23 May 1843, as cited in Lyndon W. Cook, "William Law: Nauvoo Dissenter." Brigham Young confirmed that it was William Marks and William Law who were working in concert with Hyrum. See Brigham Young address, 8 October 1866, Brigham Young papers, LDS Archives.

46. Hyrum's statement to Ebenezer Robinson is found in Ebenezer Robinson, "Affidavits," 12 December 1873 and 24 October 1885, reprinted in Charles A. Shook, *The True Origins of Mormon Polygamy*, p. 164. William Marks's account of his conversation with Hyrum Smith is in the Council of the Twelve Minutes, Book A, 6 April 1865 to 12 April 1889, p. 11, RLDS Library-Archives.

47. Brigham Young address, 8 October 1866. Young began this speech by correcting the church historian, George A. Smith, on some details of history. He said, "It is important that history should go down to our children divested of all mistakes as far as possible." However, he apparently remembered the year of his conversation with Hyrum incorrectly. Contemporary accounts such as William Clayton's diary place the incident on 26 or 27 May 1843.

48. Address of Hyrum Smith at the General Conference of the Church, 8 April 1844, Miscellaneous Minutes collection, LDS Archives. Also in the "Manuscript History of the Church of Jesus Christ of Latter-day Saints." Although the published *History of the Church* has parts of Hyrum's address, the portions quoted here are not included.

49. Statement of Mercy Rachel Fielding Thompson, 20 December 1880, LDS Archives. Affidavit of Catherine Phillips Smith, November 1902, LDS Archives.

50. William C. Staines told his story to Joseph's scribe, Thomas Bullock, who wrote it on a small scrap of paper, probably sometime between 1845 and the mid-1850s. Bullock, during this time, collected bits of history pertaining to Joseph Smith for the "Manuscript History of the Church" begun in 1838 and finished in 1856. In the Joseph Smith collection is found another item from Staines entitled, "Proverbs of Joseph Smith." Heber C. Kimball mentions Staines reminiscing of Joseph Smith in the

Deseret News, 23 November 1854, and the *Contributor* printed his reminiscences. Van Hale pointed this out to us.

51. Bachman, "Plural Marriage Before the Death of Joseph Smith" (Master's thesis), Appendix C, pp. 333–36, lists forty-eight women who were possibly married to Joseph Smith. Although Bachman claims that a number of these are questionable, most can be documented. The dates of marriages that took place before the time now under discussion are listed by Bachman as follows: Prescindia Huntington (11 December 1841), Marinda Johnson (May 1843), Louisa Beaman (5 June 1841), Zina Huntington (27 October 1841), Mary Rollins (February 1842), Patty Sessions (9 March 1841), Eliza Snow (29 June 1842), Sarah Whitney (27 July 1842), Ruth Vose (February 1843), Lucy Walker (1 May 1843), Eliza Partridge (8 March 1843), and her sister Emily Partridge (4 March 1843). These last two women will be discussed in detail in the text of this chapter.

Bachman also included a Mrs. A.S. with no known date. This is Agnes Coolbrith Smith, widow of Joseph's brother Don Carlos. She became Joseph's plural wife early in 1842. See Chapter 8, n. 10, for documentation of this marriage. Bachman named twelve more women who were presumed to have been married to Joseph by the spring of 1843, but for whom there are no known dates. They are: Fanny Alger, Lucinda Morgan, Delcena Johnson, Mrs. Durfee, Sally Fuller, Sarah Cleveland, Flora Woodworth, Hannah Ells, Olive G. Frost, Sylvia Sessions, Sarah Lawrence and her sister Maria Lawrence (listed incorrectly by Bachman as Mona Lawrence). The rest were either married after the spring of 1843, or their date of marriage is not known, or they have questionable documentation as plural wives of Joseph Smith. For short biographical sketches of most of the above women, see Brodie, *No Man Knows My History*, Appendix C, pp. 457–88.

52. Lucy Walker Kimball, "Affidavit"; Shook, *The True Origins of Mormon Polygamy*, p. 137.

53. The three short quotations in this paragraph come from Jenson, *Historical Record* 6:240; Temple Lot Suit, p. 251 (answer to question 31), LDS Archives, and Emily D. P. Young, "Incidents of the Early Life of Emily Dow Partridge," p. 5 of typescript, Univ. of U.

54. The first quotation is taken from Emily D. P. Young, "Incidents of the Early Life," p. 5 of typescript, Univ. of U.; the second appears in her "Autobiography," *Woman's Exponent* 14:37. Emily recorded her marriage as 11 May. Judge James Adams was not in Nauvoo on that date but he did arrive in Nauvoo on 21 May 1843. Under cross-examination in the Temple Lot Suit she realized that she had not remembered the date correctly but swore under oath to the rest of the information surrounding her marriages to Joseph. Joseph's diary entry for 23 May, two days after Adams's arrival, states, "At home. In conversation with Judge Adams, and others." Judge Adams probably married her to Joseph on 23 May 1843 instead of 11 May.

55. For Emma's and Joseph's sealing date, see diary of Joseph Smith, 28 May 1843, LDS Archives. Part of this entry is written in the now defunct Taylor shorthand. La Jean Purcell of the Harold B. Lee Library aided Andrew F. Ehat in transcribing portions of Joseph's diary that Willard Richards wrote, thus revealing the sealing date for Emma and Joseph (Ehat, "Joseph Smith's Temple Ordinances," pp. 61–62).

56. Currently the temple ordinances of washing, anointing, and the endowment precede the eternal marriage ceremony in the Church of Jesus Christ of Latter-day Saints. This was not the case in 1843. Emma's endowment will be discussed more fully in the following chapter.

57. Emily Dow Partridge Smith Young, "Testimony That Cannot Be Refuted,"

Woman's Exponent 12:164–65, and Emily D. P. Young, "Incidents of the Early Life," typescript, p. 5.

58. James B. Allen notes on the diary of William Clayton, 23 May 1843. The full quote can be found in Beecher et al., "Emma, Eliza, and the Stairs: An Investigation," pp. 86–96. According to Clayton's diary, Joseph was inquiring about Joseph Jackson's conduct toward Eliza Partridge. Jackson was a traveler who had come to Nauvoo, by his own admission, to expose Joseph. On this particular day Joseph told Clayton that Jackson was "rotten hearted." From the tone of the conversation, Jackson may have made advances toward Eliza Partridge. That Joseph was capable of jealousy is illustrated in another of Clayton's diary entries less than a week later. On May 29 Joseph told William Clayton that he felt as though William had not been treating him "exactly right," and asked if he had "used any familiarity with E[mma]." Clayton told him "by no means," and this answer satisfied Joseph. Joseph did not question Clayton again on the subject, so the entry should be taken as a momentary misunderstanding between the two men. Courtesy of James B. Allen.

59. Emily D. P. Young, "Incidents of the Early Life," p. 5 of typescript.

60. Temple Lot Suit, Emily D. P. Young testimony, pp. 363–64, questions 309–24, and p. 371, questions 480–84.

61. *Woman's Exponent* 14:38. Also see the affidavit of Lovina Walker, *Historical Record* 6:223 and the court testimony of Lucy Walker, Temple Lot Suit, p. 371.

62. "The Mormons in Nauvoo," *Daily Tribune*, Salt Lake City, Ut.; interviews with William Law, "Letters," 7, 20, 27 January 1886. Sarah and Maria Lawrence inherited the money from their father's estate. The Aaronic Priesthood census of 1842 listed their mother, Margaret Lawrence, with Josiah Butterfield and several of the Lawrence children. On 20 May 1843 she sold lot 4 in the block 47 to Hiram Dayton and his wife. In that transaction she is referred to as "Margaret Butterfield, late Margaret Lawrence." Nauvoo Restoration, LDS Archives.

63. *HC* 5:415, 418. Diary of Joseph Smith entry for this same day does not include this statement. It was reconstructed later, probably from a diary entry of William Clayton.

64. For the incident with Butterfield, see *HC* 5:316. For Joseph's conversation with John Taylor, see: *HC* 6:427. Diary of Joseph Smith correlates with this history entry.

65. Testimony of Lucy Walker Kimball in Jenson, *Historical Record* 6, Nos. 3–5 (May 1887):229–30.

66. Mary Alice Cannon Lambert, "Leonora Cannon Taylor," *Young Women's Journal* 19 (1908):347. For Orson Pratt's statement, see his discourse of 7 October 1869, *JD* 13:194. For Zina Young's comment, see Minutes, "Sister's Meeting Held in Creation Room," 22 November 1895, LDS Archives.

67. Emily Dow Partridge Smith Young, "Testimony," *Woman's Exponent* 12:165.

68. *HC* 5:391, and Benjamin F. Johnson to George F. Gibbs, n.d. This letter published in full with an introduction, notes, and comments by Dean R. Zimmerman, *I Knew the Prophets, An Analysis of the Letter of Benjamin F. Johnson to George F. Gibbs, Reporting Doctrinal Views of Joseph Smith and Brigham Young*, pp. 40–44. By 1902 or 1903, when the letter is believed to have been written, Johnson was an old man and although his story is supported by other documents such as Joseph's diary and Emily Partridge's testimony in the Temple Lot Suit, his memory of dates is not so clear. He said it was only a month after Joseph visited with the Partridge woman that Joseph shared the same bedroom with Almira. It was more likely closer to three months later, for Almira's marriage did not take place until August 1.

69. Zimmerman, *I Knew the Prophets*, p. 44.

70. Stanley B. Kimball, *Heber C. Kimball, Mormon Patriarch and Pioneer*, p. 104.

71. Helen Mar Kimball Whitney, "Autobiography," 1881, LDS Archives.

72. Catharine Lewis, statement, Stanley S. Ivins collection, USHS. At least two other couples who were friends of Emma and Joseph—Cornelius and Permilla Lott, who ran the farm, and Isaac and Lucy Morley, who had offered the Smiths a home years earlier in Kirtland when Emma gave birth to the twins—would agree to give their daughters to Joseph in marriage. The Lotts recorded Melissa's marriage of September 1843 in the family Bible, LDS Archives; the Morleys' daughter Cordelia Calista refused to marry Joseph but after his death agreed to be sealed to him for eternity. "Cordelia Morley Cox's Book," BYU. Thus, some women listed as Joseph's wives in the Nauvoo Temple Records may have accepted a sealing after his death and not necessarily been his wives before. See also Andrew Ehat, "Joseph Smith's Temple Ordinances." Foster, *Religion and Sexuality*, pp. 150–51, discusses the tests of loyalty that Joseph Smith asked of his followers.

73. Affidavit of Lucy Walker Smith Kimball, 17 December 1902, sworn before James Jack, Journal History, 2 May 1843, LDS Archives.

74. Melissa Lott testimony, Temple Lot Suit, p. 97.

75. Diary of William Clayton, 27 April, 1 May, 13 May 1843, as quoted in James B. Allen, "One Man's Nauvoo," *Journal of Mormon History* 6 (1979):37–40; see also John Benbow's affidavit, 28 August 1869, Temple Lot Suit.

76. Lucy M. Wright, *Woman's Exponent* 30:59.

77. *History of Lee County*, p. 400.

78. For the carriage accident, see Lucy Smith, Prelim. Ms.; also Lucy Smith, *Joseph the Prophet*, p. 347. *HC* 5:431–60, gives account of the entire trip in some detail. All quotations are taken from this source.

79. Journal of Wandle Mace, p. 88, LDS Archives.

80. Diary of William Clayton, 30 June 1843, as cited in Allen, "One Man's Nauvoo," p. 44.

81. Diary of Joseph Smith, 30 June 1843, LDS Archives.

82. "The Life and Testimony of Mary Elizabeth Rollins Lightner," pp. 20–23, typescript at BYU.

83. *HC* 5:490–91. See also diary of Joseph Smith, 30 June 1843, LDS Archives.

84. Description of Emma comes from Emmeline B. Wells, "LDS Women of the Past: Personal Impressions," *Woman's Exponent* 36, No. 7 (February 1909); the "fishing" incident is in Vesta Crawford notes, Univ. of U.; and the story about the meat is in James Henry Rollins, "Reminiscences," 1888, LDS Archives.

85. *HC* 5:259.

86. Crawford notes.

87. William Clayton, statement, Salt Lake City, 16 February 1874, published in Jenson, *Historical Record* 6, Nos. 3–5:224–26. Tense changed to facilitate dialogue.

88. Stanley Ivins index, 7:167, Mary E. Lightner to A. M. Chase, 20 April 1904, USHS.

89. William Clayton, statement. Tense changed to facilitate dialogue. Although this statement of Clayton gives more detail to the event, his short diary entry for that day (12 July 1843) gives contemporary evidence for the incident. It states, "This A.M. I wrote a Revelation consisting of 10 pages on the order of the priesthood, showing the designs in Moses, Abraham, David and Solomon having many wives & concubines &c. After it was wrote Prest. Joseph & Hyrum presented it and read it to E[mma] who said

she did not believe a word of it and appeared very rebellious." William Clayton diary as quoted in Lyndon W. Cook, *The Revelations of the Prophet Joseph Smith*, p. 294.

90. Diary of JS, 13 July 1843.

91. Allen, "One Man's Nauvoo," p. 44n.

92. All quotations from Section 132, LDS D & C. This revelation does not appear in RLDS D & C. Contemporary evidence for the existence of the revelation in Nauvoo and that Joseph Smith authored it will be presented throughout the next three chapters of the book. For an in-depth analysis of the handwriting of the two manuscript versions, see Bachman, "Plural Marriage Before the Death of Joseph Smith" (Master's thesis), pp. 208–11.

93. Lyndon W. Cook, *The Revelations of the Prophet Joseph Smith*, p. 347. The women who were married to Joseph before his death were sealed to him again by proxy at the time they received their own endowments in the Nauvoo temple after 1844.

94. William Clayton statement in Jenson, *Historical Record*, p. 226.

95. Ibid. Italics added.

96. Isaac Sheen became editor of the *Saints' Herald* in 1860. In the March 1860 issue, p. 64, he discussed the doctrine of plural wives, saying, "Joseph Smith repented of his connection with this doctrine and said that it was of the devil," and then discussed the burning of the revelation. Cited in Shook, *The True Origins of Mormon Polygamy*, pp. 152–55.

97. William E. McLellin to Joseph III, July 1872, RLDS Library-Archives.

98. For Emma's statement, see Edmund C. Briggs, "A Visit to Nauvoo in 1856," *Journal of History* 9, No. 4 (October 1916):462; for Whitehead conversation, see diary of Joseph III, 20 April 1885, RLDS Library-Archives.

99. Mary Bailey Smith Norman to Ina Coolbrith, 27 March 1908, RLDS Library-Archives. Ina Coolbrith was Don Carlos Smith's daughter but took her mother's maiden name after moving to California.

100. "Manuscript History of the Church"; diary of JS, 21 December to 10 March 1843; see notations for 12, 13, 14 and 15 July 1843, LDS Archives.

101. Diary of JS, 16 July 1843.

102. William M. Thompson, statement, LDS Archives. Thompson may well have been currying favor among the Utah leaders by this time.

103. Beecher, "E. R. Snow's Nauvoo Journal," pp. 408–9.

104. Susa Young Gates collection, "My Recollections of Brigham Young's Wives," USHS. Susa was born to Brigham Young and his twenty-second wife, Lucy Bigelow, on 18 March 1856 and was Young's forty-first child. She became a prominent and well-known woman in Utah.

105. Richard Van Wagoner and Stephen C. Walker, "A Book of Mormons," unpublished manuscript in possession of authors, p. 75.

106. *HC* 5:515.

CHAPTER 11

1. "A Record of the Organization and Proceedings of The Female Relief Society of Nauvoo," 7th meeting, Second Ward, 13 August 1843. Microfilm of original JS collection, LDS Archives. Hereafter cited as RS Minutes.

2. Clayton's reaction is in James B. Allen, "One Man's Nauvoo: The Mormon Experience in Illinois as Seen and Felt by William Clayton," p. 44, n. 17. A week later, on August 18, Newel K. Whitney told Clayton that Aaron Farr, a young man who had courted Margaret Moon, was plotting with the Walker boys and girls and Emma to bring about Clayton's downfall. Clayton does not name the Walker children who

Whitney said were involved. Margaret Moon had told Aaron Farr of her polygamous marriage to Clayton and in his hurt and angry state Farr could have turned to friends like Emma and the young Walkers for sympathy and help. But either the plotting was no more than a rumor or nothing came of it; Clayton does not mention it again, although he does remain suspicious toward Emma. (Information courtesy of James B. Allen.) William Marks's comments are found in Minutes of the Council of Twelve of the RLDS, Book A, p. 11, line 14, RLDS Library-Archives. The date is listed as "Wednesday Morning," probably 3 May 1865. The division of the council is documented in David Fullmer and Leonard Soby, affidavits, which are published in Charles A. Shook, *The True Origins of Mormon Polygamy*, pp. 97–101. Austin Cowles is sometimes referred to as "Coles." His daughter Elvira had married Joseph 1 June 1843 in the presence of Vilate Kimball and Eliza Partridge. Elvira A. C. Holmes, affidavit, 28 August 1869, LDS Archives.

3. Ebenezer Robinson, statement, published in Shook, *Mormon Polygamy*, p. 101.

4. Diary of William Clayton, Excerpts, 16 August 1843.

5. Allen, "One Man's Nauvoo," p. 45, n. 17.

6. Maureen Ursenbach [Beecher], "Eliza R. Snow's Nauvoo Journal," p. 412, under the date 10 October 1843. Emphasis Eliza's. Hereafter cited as Beecher, "E. R. Snow's Nauvoo Journal."

7. Diary of William Clayton, Excerpts. Joseph's marriage to Flora Woodworth is documented from Jenson, *Historical Record* 6:225. See also Fawn Brodie, *No Man Knows My History*, p. 481. The gold watch that Joseph gave to Eliza Snow is in possession of the LDS Church. For more information on Eliza's watch, see Mary Belnap Lowe, statement, Ogden, Ut., 12 May 1841, LDS Archives.

8. The information about Emma's health during this period can be found in Vesta Crawford notes, Univ. of U.; Lucy Smith, *Joseph the Prophet*, p. 274; *HC* 6:31; diary of JS, 11 September 1843; RS Minutes, 11th and 12th meetings, 15 September 1843.

9. For incident with Butterfield, see *HC* 5:316. See also journal of Aroet Lucius Hale, p. 24, LDS Archives; diary of JS, 30 July 1843, LDS Archives; and *HC* 5:522, 524. This last incident does not appear in Joseph's diary and was either reconstructed later for the published history or taken from a contemporary account.

10. *HC* 6:42–43.

11. "Allen J. Stout's Testimony," Jenson, *Historical Record* 6, Nos. 3–5 (May 1887):230–31.

12. We are indebted to several of Maria Jane Johnston Johnson Woodworth's descendants, Roselyn W. Slade, Bea Mendenhall Jenson, Mac K. Johnson, and Mildred Johnson. Maria Jane did not learn to read and write until after she arrived in the Utah Territory. She dictated her memoirs to a relative in her later years wherein she said she "learned to dearly love the Prophet, Emma, and Hyrum." The incident with Emma is attached to a letter from George H. Brimall to Joseph F. Smith, 21 April 1902, LDS Archives.

13. Salt Lake City, *Tribune*, 1886.

14. Andrew F. Ehat, "Joseph Smith's Introduction of Temple Ordinances and the 1844 Succession Question" (Master's thesis), pp. 94–96. See also David John Buerger, "The Fullness of the Priesthood: The Second Anointing in Latter-day Saint Theology and Practice, *Dialogue* 16, No. 1 (Spring 1983): 10–44.

15. Ibid.

16. See Allen, "One Man's Nauvoo," pp. 44–45, n. 17. Joseph also confided to Clayton that Emma had been "annointed" and agreed with her that Clayton should

take Margaret into his own home. Clayton recorded Joseph's solution to any trouble that might result from such an action: ". . . if they raise trouble about it and bring you before me I will give you an awful scourging & probably cut you off from the church and then I will baptise you & set you ahead as good as ever" (diary of William Clayton, Excerpts, 19 October, 21 November 1843). Clayton's relief over Emma's change in attitude was short-lived. A month later Hyrum Smith told him that "E[mma] had power to prevent [his] being admitted to J's Lodge [or Prayer Circle] for the present." How much influence Emma had in determining who would be admitted to Joseph's Prayer Circle or Endowment Council is questionable. Surely Joseph invited whom he wanted but may have hesitated to choose Clayton because he did not want to upset Emma any further.

17. *Times and Seasons* 5 (15 September 1844):665.

18. *HC* 6:49.

19. The basic information for this account is taken from the "Life Sketch of Jane Elizabeth Manning James," Wilford Woodruff papers, LDS Archives. Dictated by Jane later in her life, this manuscript contains a few errors; i.e., historical evidence indicates Jane arrived in Nauvoo in late fall 1843 rather than 1840. Others in her group were her brothers Isaac and Peter, her sisters Angeline and Sarah, Sarah's husband, Anthony Stebbings, and a sister-in-law, Lucinda Manning, Jane's small son Sylvester, and her mother, Eliza. All the dialogue is taken from Jane's "Life Sketch." See also Henry J. Wolfinger, "A Test of Faith: Jane Elizabeth James and the Origins of the Utah Black Community," *Social Accommodations in Utah* (American West Center Occasional Papers), No. 6 (1975):128–29.

20. Henry J. Wolfinger, "A Test of Faith." Documents relating to Jane E. James (pp. 16–19) established that Jane repeatedly asked to receive her endowments and sealings around the turn of the century and was denied because of her race. That policy in the LDS Church was changed in 1978 and Jane's temple work has been done.

21. Jane Elizabeth James, "Life Sketch," p. 19, and Jane E. James to Joseph F. Smith, 7 February 1890, Joseph F. Smith papers, LDS Archives.

22. *HC* 6:100–54.

23. Statement of Emily D. P. Young Smith, Salt Lake City, 27 June 1893, LDS Archives.

24. Diary of JS, 5 November 1843; see also *HC* 6:65. For medical literature, see "Poisons and Poisoning Appendix," *Taber's Cyclopedic Medical Dictionary*, 12th ed. Revised and edited by Clayton L. Thomas (Philadelphia: F. A. David Co., 1973), pp. 108–28.

25. Brigham Young address, 7 October 1866, in Semi-annual Conference, Brigham Young papers, LDS Archives. Young had mentioned the poisoning on at least two previous occasions other than the speech quoted here: 25 February 1855 and 7 October 1863. Charles Lowell Walker recorded in his diary that Solon Foster said that Emma tried to poison Joseph. Walker's diary entry is dated 17 December 1876, ten years after Brigham Young's speech, and was probably hearsay.

26. Diary of JS, 5 November 1843, LDS Archives.

27. Ibid., 15 December 1843, LDS Archives; see also *HC* 6:115–16, 183, 285, 346.

28. H. Winter Griffith, M.D., *Instructions for Patients*, 2nd ed. (Philadelphia, London, Toronto: W. B. Saunders Co., 1975), pp. 235–36. When the authors described Joseph's symptoms to modern physicians, they universally rejected poisoning as a cause. They disclaim absolute diagnosis one hundred and forty years after the patient's death, of course, but they indicate that the factors of the symptoms together with the stressful life-style Joseph followed point most clearly to peptic ulcers. Personal

interviews with George Yard, M.D., and Corwin DeMarse, M.D., Flagstaff, Ariz. *HC* 6:66, 116; diary of JS, 6 November 1843, and 15 December 1843.

29. For the Eliza story, see Mary Bailey Smith Norman to Ina Coolbrith, n.d., RLDS Library-Archives. Eliza did not not live at the Smith home at this time nor would she live there again. The charges were without foundation. For the Fullmer account, see autobiography of Desdemona Wadsworth Fullmer, 1868, LDS Archives. According to the 1869 affidavit, Brigham Young married her to Joseph in July 1843, Temple Lot Suit. See also Emily Partridge, "Incidents of the Early Life," December 1876, p. 5, Univ. of U.

30. Description from Eudocia Baldwin Marsh, "When the Mormons Dwelt Among Us," pp. 374–75.

31. *HC* 6:134.

32. Helen Mar Whitney, *Woman's Exponent* 2:9.

33. Diary of JS, 4 January 1844; *HC* 6:165–66.

34. Dean R. Zimmerman, *I Knew the Prophets, An Analysis of the Letter of Benjamin F. Johnson to George F. Gibbs, Reporting Doctrinal Views of Joseph Smith and Brigham Young,* p. 18.

35. *HC* 6:31, 39, 42, 53, and see references to prayer meetings from 1 September to 27 December 1843. William Law's service to the church is impressive. He became a counselor to Joseph in the first presidency in January 1841. (JS Nauvoo Day Book [1 July 1841–July 1843] Cedar Rapids, Ia., Masonic Lodge, microfilm copy in LDS Archives; and William Law Day Book [27 April 1841–9 July 1842], Beinecke Rare Book and Manuscript Library, New Haven, Conn.) From June to August 1841 Law served a mission to Philadelphia *(HC* 4:284–86 and 5:37). During 1840–43 many church meetings were held in the Law home and William preached often in the Iowa Territory. (Nauvoo High Council Minutes, LDS Archives, has references to meetings at Law's house; also *HC* 4:340–53, the journal of Wilford Woodruff [10 April 1842], LDS Archives, and James B. Allen and Thomas G. Alexander, eds., *Manchester Mormons: The Journal of William Clayton* [1840–1842], p. 212.) In 1842 William Law publicly defended Joseph's character in the wake of John C. Bennett's charges (Lyndon W. Cook, "William Law: Nauvoo Dissenter"). In September 1842 he left on a second mission to the Eastern states and this time preached against John C. Bennett and "regulate[d] church affairs" *(Times and Seasons* 3 [1 August 1842]:872–73, and *HC* 5:149, 160, 183). In May 1842 William Law received his endowments with eight others. (Journal of Heber C. Kimball, 1840–45, "Strange Events" entry, LDS Archives, and Ehat, "Joseph Smith's Temple Ordinances" (Master's thesis), pp. 102–3.) During Joseph's period of hiding from August to December 1842, Law assisted him in a variety of ways *(HC* 5:103, 119). Both William and his brother Wilson also aided Joseph financially in the January 1843 trial at Springfield.

36. Description of Law is in *Latter-day Saints' Millennial Star* 3 (3 May 1842):9. Salt Lake City *Tribune,* 1886, for Law's properties and his conversation with Joseph.

37. This section of the 1835 D & C remains in the RLDS D & C today as Section 111.

38. Joseph W. McMurrin, "An Interesting Testimony," *Improvement Era* 6:507–10.

39. Brigham Young address, 8 October 1866, Brigham Young papers, LDS Archives.

40. Cook, "William Law: Nauvoo Dissenter," p. 65, n. 80.

41. *HC* 6:151–52.

42. Ibid., 67–70. *HC* 6:165 adds the following comment attributed to Joseph: "What can be the matter with these men? Is it that the wicked flee when no man

pursueth . . . that my remarks should produce such an excitement in their minds? Can it be possible that the traitor whom Porter Rockwell reports to me as being in correspondence with my Missouri enemies, is one of my quorum?" This editorializing is not in Joseph's diary. Possibly it was written after Joseph's death in an effort to implicate Marks as a conspirator with Law—which he was not.

43. Ibid., 165.

44. George D. Watt, ed., *JD*, 2:217.

CHAPTER 12

1. George J. Adams was a high priest and served several missions between his conversion in 1840 and Joseph's death. Emma related the incident with Adams to William W. Blair, who recorded it in his journal. His entry in Journal No. 7 for 14 May 1865 states, "Sister E. [Smith] Bidamon said in the spring of 1844 G. J. Adams rejoiced that the matter was now settled—that they now knew who Joseph's successor would be. Would,—it was Little Joseph—he had just seen him ordained." The tense is changed in the text. Blair's account was also published in the *Saints' Herald* 8 (1 October 1885). Emma mistakenly placed the time in the spring of 1844 rather than January 1844.

2. D. Michael Quinn, "Joseph Smith III's 1844 Blessing and the Mormons of Utah," *John Whitmer Historical Association Journal*, 1(1981): 14. Those present included Joseph and Hyrum Smith, John Taylor, Willard Richards, Newel K. Whitney, Reynolds Cahoon, Alpheus Cutler, Ebenezer Robinson, George J. Adams, and John M. Bernhisel.

3. Temple Lot Suit, p. 28, as quoted in Quinn, ibid.

4. "A blessing given to Joseph Smith, 3rd, by his father, Joseph Smith, Junr. on Jany. 17, 1844," manuscript at RLDS Library-Archives, photocopy in LDS Archives. For a complete discussion of the surfacing of this document, see D. Michael Quinn, "Joseph Smith III's Blessing and the Mormons of Utah," and Paul M. Edwards and Richard P. Howard, "Responses," *John Whitmer Historical Association Journal* 1 (1981):12–29.

5. Joseph III to Mr. A. V. Gibbons, 1 June 1893, Joseph III Letterbook No. 4, RLDS Library-Archives. Joseph's speech is in *HC* 6:183–85. See also Andrew F. Ehat and Lyndon W. Cook, *The Words of Joseph Smith*, pp. 317–19. James Whitehead's statement is in the Temple Lot Suit, pp. 28, 33, 37. For a carbon copy of the trial, see "Temple Lot Case," LDS Archives. For a more complete discussion of the meeting as it pertains to Joseph III, see D. Michael Quinn, "Joseph Smith III's 1844 Blessing," pp. 14–15.

6. Quinn, "Joseph Smith III's 1844 Blessing," p. 13.

7. Ronald K. Esplin, "Joseph, Brigham, and the Twelve: A Succession of Continuity," pp. 310–11.

8. For a discussion of Brigham Young and the Twelve and their involvement in the ordinances of the endowment, see Esplin, "Succession of Continuity," pp. 314–18. See also Andrew F. Ehat, "Joseph Smith's Temple Ordinances and the 1844 Succession Question" (Master's thesis).

9. Emily D. P. Young, "Incidents of the Early Life of Emily Dow Partridge," December 1876, p. 5, Univ. of U. Tense change to facilitate dialogue.

10. Emily Partridge Young, "Life of a Mormon Girl," n.d., p. 54, typescript, LDS Archives.

11. Jane M. James, "The Life Sketch of Jane Elizabeth Manning James," p. 20, Wilford Woodruff papers, 1893, LDS Archives. Jane reported this happening near the

time she learned that the Partridge and Lawrence sisters were Joseph's plural wives. Jane did not arrive in Nauvoo until late in October 1843.

12. Journal of Heber C. Kimball, 17 January 1844, LDS Archives, and affidavit of Bathsheba W. Smith, 19 November 1903, LDS Archives.

13. John Taylor, "Report of the Dedication of the Kaysville Relief Society House, 12 November 1876," *Woman's Exponent* 5, No. 19 (1 March 1877).

14. Eudocia Baldwin Marsh, "When the Mormons Dwelt Among Us," *The Bellman*, 1 April, 1916, p. 375.

15. Lucy A. Young to Joseph III, 22 May, no year, RLDS Library-Archives; and journal of David Osborn, 1835–1860, typescript, BYU.

16. Journal of Aroet Lucius Hale, p. 3, LDS Archives.

17. *HC* 6:225; "The Voice of Innocence," manuscript copy, LDS Archives.

18. *HC* 6:242.

19. "Voice of Innocence."

20. "A Record of the Organization and Proceedings of The Female Relief Society of Nauvoo," 1st meeting, 9 March 1844, LDS Archives.

21. JS and others to the Relief Society. This letter was first read 30 March 1842 but was not recorded in the minutes until 28 September 1842.

22. RS Minutes, 2nd meeting, 16 March 1842.

23. Statement of Amy Brown Lyman concerning history of the Relief Society, 20 October 1872, LDS Archives.

24. Speech dated 9 March 1845, Seventies Record, LDS Archives. The Relief Society did not meet again for ten years and did not formally organize for twenty-two years, when Brigham Young called Eliza Snow to become president in 1867. According to Maureen Ursenbach Beecher, Eliza's biographer, Eliza's date of 1866 in her "Sketch of My Life" is off by one year.

25. Statement of John Taylor, 29 June 1881, LDS Archives; Statement of Eliza R. Snow, "A Book of Records Containing the Minutes of the Organization and Proceedings of the Female Relief Society of West Jordan Ward." 12 April 1868, LDS Archives.

26. See *HC* 6:231–32 for Willard Richards to James Arlington Bennet. Bennet explained his reasons for not running on the ticket in a letter to Willard Richards a month later. James Arlington Bennet to Willard Richards, 14 April 1844, LDS Archives.

27. Joseph H. Jackson, *A Narrative of the Adventures and Experience of Joseph H. Jackson in Nauvoo: Disclosing the Depths of Mormon Villany Practiced in Nauvoo*, Introduction. Hereafter cited as *Adventures and Experience*.

28. Diary of JS, 18 May 1843, LDS Archives.

29. Jackson, *Adventures and Experience*, p. 20. See also diary of JS, 29 December 1842; *HC* 6:149.

30. Lucy Smith, *Biographical Sketches of Joseph Smith the Prophet and His Progenitors for Many Generations*, pp. 275–76.

31. Jackson, *Adventures and Experience*, p. 21. Neither Jackson nor any other of the sources cited give a date for Joseph's alleged interactions with Jane Law. It is probable that it occurred in the spring 1844.

32. William Law to Dr. W. Wyl, 7 January 1887, printed in the Salt Lake City *Daily Tribune*, January 1887. Italics in *Tribune*.

33. Ibid. See also diary of William Law, 1 January 1844, as cited in Lyndon W. Cook, "William Law: Nauvoo Dissenter," p. 65.

34. LDS D & C 132:51–52. A discussion of a different interpretation of this

342

passage is in Danel Bachman, "A Study of the Mormon Practice of Plural Marriage Before the Death of Joseph Smith" (Master's thesis).

35. Journal of Alexander Neibaur, 1841 to 1862, 24 May 1844, LDS Archives.

36. Ebenezer Robinson owned the southeast corner of lot 149; William Law owned the southwest corner of lot 148. The two properties faced each other across Granger Street. For the Robinson account, see journal of Joseph Lee Robinson, p. 27, LDS Archives; Joseph III's description of Jane Law is in Joseph III to E. C. Brant, 26 January 1894, Joseph III Letterbook No. 4, RLDS Library-Archives.

37. Journal of Joseph Lee Robinson, p. 27, LDS Archives.

38. Journal of William Clayton, Excerpts, 6 June 1843.

39. Brodie, *No Man Knows My History*, p. 372.

40. St. Louis *Republican*, 23 April 1844, as reprinted in Boston *Post*, 24, No. 108 (6 May 1844).

41. Boston *Post*, 24, No. 117 (16 May 1844), and Almira Covey to Harriet Whittemore, Nauvoo, 30 July 1844.

42. Joseph III, *Joseph Smith III and the Restoration*, pp. 74–75.

43. Bachman, "Plural Marriage Before the Death of Joseph Smith" (Master's thesis), Appendices C and H, pp. 333–36, 346–54.

44. William Marks, *Zion's Harbinger and Baneemy's Organ* (St. Louis, Mo.) 3, No. 7 (7 July 1853):53. Isaac Sheen stated that "[Joseph] abhorred and repented of this eniquity." Statement reprinted in Charles A. Shook, *The True Origins of Mormon Polygamy*, p. 155.

45. Council of the Twelve Minutes, Book A, 6 April 1865–12 April 1889, RLDS Library-Archives. In the minutes E. Ells quotes Herringshaw. E. Ells may have been a son of Josiah Ells, a physician whose daughter, Hannah Ells, served as secretary to the Relief Society in 1844 and was Joseph's plural wife. Ells followed James J. Strang after Joseph's death and later joined the Reorganization. Hugh Herringshaw was a member of the church and owned a tract of land in Nauvoo. Like Ells, Herringshaw followed Strang after Joseph's death.

46. Brigham Young address, 8 October 1866, Brigham Young papers, LDS Archives; and Mary Bailey to Ina Coolbrith, n.d., ca. January to March 1908, RLDS Library-Archives.

47. Sarah Scott to mother and father, Nauvoo, Ill., 22 July 1844, published in George R. Partridge, ed., "The Death of a Mormon Dictator: Letters of Massachusetts Mormons, 1843–1848," *New England Quarterly* 9, No. 4 (December 1936):598. Sarah Scott dates Hyrum's denial as "a few weeks before the murder." Joseph and Hyrum would be killed 27 June 1844.

48. JS to Sarah and Maria Lawrence, 23 June 1844. This letter will be discussed in detail in Chapter 13.

49. Diary of JS, 23 May 1844, LDS Archives; *HC* 6:397–402.

50. Diary of JS, 25 May 1844, LDS Archives; *HC* 6:405.

51. Sections of this speech have been distributed by some persons in an attempt to embarrass the LDS Church without explaining the circumstances surrounding Joseph's discourse. It may be found in its entirety in *HC* 6: 408–12, and in Andrew F. Ehat and Lyndon W. Cook, *The Words of Joseph Smith*, pp. 373–78.

52. Ibid. At the organization of the West Jordan Relief Society the minutes read: "She [Eliza R. Snow] wished to correct one erro[r] it has been said that the Society in Nauvoo did more harm than good but it was not so Emma Smith was Presidentess. She gave it up so as not to lead the Society in error[r]. The Society did a great deal of good saved a great many lives &c." ("A Book of Records Containing the Minutes of the

Organization of Proceedings of the Female Relief Society of West Jordan Ward," 12 April 1868 [LR 10051 Series 14 Reel #2].)

53. *HC* 6:411.
54. Nauvoo *Expositor,* 7 June 1844, p. 4.
55. Ibid., p. 2.
56. *HC* 6:432.
57. Ibid., 7:123.

CHAPTER 13

1. Vilate Kimball to Heber C. Kimball, Nauvoo, Ill., 9 June 1844, LDS Archives, published by Ronald K. Esplin, "Life in Nauvoo, June 1844: Vilate Kimball's Martyrdom Letters," pp. 231–40.
2. *HC* 6:479–500.
3. Ibid., 486–519.
4. "The Life and Record of Anson Call, Commenced in 1839," typescript USHS, BYU, and Huntington Library, pp. 11–12.
5. Ford to JS, 22 June 1844, *HC* 6:535–37.
6. JS to Thomas Ford, 22 June 1844, *HC* 6:539.
7. *HC* 6:545.
8. JS to ES, 23 June 1844, original in RLDS Library-Archives. This letter and a similar letter from JS to Sarah and Maria Lawrence dated the same day confirm that Joseph intended to go to Washington rather than "away to the west." Copies of both letters are in LDS Archives.
9. Statement of John A. Wolf, Wilford Wood collection, Bountiful, Ut., microfilm of collection Reel 7, LDS Archives.
10. JS to ES, 23 June 1844, RLDS Library-Archives.
11. JS to Sarah and Maria Lawrence, 23 June 1844, LDS Archives.
12. *HC* 6:548, 549.
13. Stephen Markham to Wilford Woodruff, 20 June 1856, LDS Archives. Henry G. Sherwood places himself in company with Alpheus Cutler on that morning. He said that Emma wanted him and Cutler to go across the river and bring Joseph back to Nauvoo, but he refused (Henry G. Sherwood statement, Joseph Smith collection, LDS Archives). Markham, on the other hand, said the group of men, with Cutler included, solicited *his* help in getting Joseph to come back to Nauvoo. Two of the group, Kimball and Cahoon, would later have to answer to Brigham Young for their part in Joseph's surrender at Carthage, and apparently said Emma made them do it. Sherwood may have taken a similar position and signed his own statement against Emma to vindicate himself. The direct quotations are taken from Markham's statement. For Joseph's instructions to Porter Rockwell, see *HC* 6:548; for Emma's statement to Markham, see Markham to Woodruff, 20 June 1856, LDS Archives.
14. Markham to Woodruff, 20 June 1856. Cutler's and Cahoon's overriding interest in property is corroborated by a statement in the *HC* 6:427 that is attributed to Joseph: "Alpheus Cutler and Reynolds Cahoon are so anxious to get property, they will all flat out as soon as the Temple is completed and the faith of the Saints ceases from them &c." *HC* 6:238 relates a conflict between Joseph and Hiram Kimball over ownership of the wharves where the riverboats docked.
15. Journal of Wandle Mace, LDS Archives, typescript BYU.
16. Vilate Kimball to Heber C. Kimball, 9 June 1844, LDS Archives. Italics added.
17. William Holmes Walker, *Life Incidents and Travels.*

344

NOTES

18. Lorenzo Wasson, Emma's nephew, was present because Emma trusted him, not because he was concerned about his property. He owned only a small lot—6 × 22 rods—that he purchased from Brigham Young in 1844. The *HC* 6:549 says he joined in the name-calling with Cahoon and Kimball. Other evidence, such as Joseph's reliance on him in the following days, suggests that Wasson was implicated falsely in this incident, probably because he was Emma's relative.

19. *HC* 6:549.

20. James B. Allen notes on the diary of William Clayton, 23 June 1844.

21. Edmund C. Briggs, "Visit to Nauvoo in 1856," *Journal of History* 9:453–54, RLDS Library-Archives.

22. Vilate Kimball to Heber Kimball, 9, 16, and 24 June 1844, LDS Archives.

23. Joseph III to J. M. Stubbart, 19 May 1896, Joseph III letterbook, 6:458, RLDS Library-Archives.

24. Historian's Office Journal, 24 July 1869, LDS Archives. This journal entry tells briefly of Brigham Young's address to the School of the Prophets on this day. Oliver B. Huntington, "History of the Life of Oliver B. Huntington," p. 406, LDS Archives.

25. Statement of Sarah Louise Dalton Elder, Church Manuscripts collection compiled by Alan H. Gerber, Microfilm Reel 2, Vol. 9, p. 85, BYU. The statement was given on or about 10 October 1931.

26. Mary B. Smith Norman to Ina Smith Coolbrith, 27 March 1908, RLDS Library-Archives. Joseph apparently made similar statements to others throughout the day. For a full account of Joseph's statements foreshadowing his death, see Richard L. Anderson, "Joseph Smith's Prophecies of Martyrdom," unpublished paper delivered at the Sidney B. Sperry Symposium, Brigham Young University, 26 January 1980.

27. Edwin Rushton, "Bridge Builder and Faithful Pioneer," Pioneer Journals, n.d., p. 3. Italics added. Church Manuscripts, BYU.

28. Leonora C. Taylor, statement, n.d., LDS Archives.

29. Almira Covey to Harriet Whittemore, 18 July 1844, Nauvoo, Ill., original in private possession, typescript LDS Archives.

30. The blessing is undated but external evidence suggests that she wrote it while Joseph was at Carthage. Juanita Brooks found this document in the possession of Ralph DeLong of Panguitch, Ut., in the 1930s. It had been part of Joseph Smith's papers, which Joseph Heywood, acting on behalf of the leaders of the church, took west. Somehow it remained in Heywood's possession. Brooks described both the blessing and a letter from Emma to Joseph Heywood as being in the same handwriting. Raymond T. Bailey, in his 1952 Master's thesis, "Emma Hale: Wife of the Prophet Joseph Smith," said the "blessing was folded, and worn along the folds, but was repaired and the original sent in to the office of the Church Historian of the Latter-day Saint Church." Apparently the document was misplaced, for only typescripts of both the letter and the blessing are there now. Edythe Houston Hindley, a descendant of Joseph Heywood, located the original letter from Emma Smith to Joseph Heywood dated 18 October 1844, and provided the authors with a photocopy. By authenticating the letter, which is, indeed, in Emma's hand, there can be little doubt that the blessing Brooks described as being with it is also authentic. Brooks's description of the documents and typescripts of each can be found in the USHS.

31. JS to ES, 25 June 1844, original in Joseph Smith collection, LDS Archives.

32. Samuel O. Williams to John A. Prickett, 10 July 1844, Mormon manuscripts collection, Chicago Historical Society, as quoted in Donna Hill, *Joseph Smith: The First Mormon*, p. 407.

33. Thomas Ford, *History of Illinois, from its Commencement as a State in 1818 to 1847*, p. 406.

34. Journal of Samuel W. Richards, LDS Archives. Tense changed to facilitate dialogue.

35. An itemized bill for the expenses of the military men at the Mansion from 24 to 28 June is in the Wilford Wood collection, Wilford Wood Museum, Bountiful, Ut., and is signed by Emma Smith.

36. *HC* 6:602.

37. JS to ES, 27 June 1844, original in RLDS Library-Archives.

38. Journal History, 29 June 1844, LDS Archives.

39. *HC* 6:586–87n.

40. Harold Schindler, *Orrin Porter Rockwell: Man of God, Son of Thunder*, pp. 134–35.

41. For the detailed accounts of Ford's visit, see journal of Wandle Mace, p. 146, LDS Archives, typescript at BYU; journal of Samuel W. Richards, LDS Archives.

42. Journal of Wandle Mace, p. 134. LDS accounts do not mention Emma's nephew, Lorenzo Wasson, being with Grant but it was he who delivered the news to Emma about the same time Grant told Mary. Wasson returned to Carthage the next day and was among the honor guard that escorted the bodies home.

43. Anson Call, "Life and Record," p. 27, typescript at BYU.

44. Martha Ann Harris to her posterity, Centennial Jubilee letter, 22 March 1881, as quoted in Don C. Corbett, *Mary Fielding, Daughter of Britain*, pp. 162–63.

45. Eudocia Baldwin Marsh, "When the Mormons Dwelt Among Us," 8 April 1816, p. 402.

46. B. W. Richmond's statement, "The Prophet's Death!" *Deseret News*, 27 November 1875, reprinted from the Chicago *Times;* Inez Smith, "The Elect Lady," *Autumn Leaves*, pp. 530–43; Ivan J. Barrett, "Emma Smith, the Elect Lady," Extension Publication Division of Continuing Education, BYU, 1966.

47. *HC* 6:621–22.

48. Ibid., 624–25. *Western Sun and General Advertiser* (Vincennes, Ind.) 35, No. 29 (13 July 1844) reports Emma's proclamation. This story was reportedly taken from the Quincy *Whig*. Other newspapers carried the same story. LeGrand Baker and Paul Ellsworth gave us this information.

49. Journal of Allen Joseph Stout, pp. 13–14, LDS Archives. Italics added.

50. By the 1870s, when Emma's sons had served missions to Utah on behalf of the Reorganized Church of Jesus Christ of Latter Day Saints, stories had begun to appear that blamed Emma for bringing Joseph back across the river to his death. Some of these accounts follow. All italics are ours.

"It was now revealed to the Prophet that his only safety was in flight to the Rocky Mountains, and he crossed the river with a few faithful friends with a full purpose not to return. But through the *PERSUASION and REPROACHES of his wife, Emma*, and others he was induced to return and give himself up to the slaughter. With all the persons who induced him to return I was well acquainted, and I know that fearful has been the hand of the Lord to follow them from the day they sought to steady the Ark of God, which resulted in the martyrdom of his servents." (Benjamin F. Johnson, *My Life's Review*, p. 102.)

"The instructions of Joseph's wife, *Emma*, to the men whom she requested to cross the river and *intreat him to return* to Nauvoo were well carried out. She had sent the same message by Bro. O. P. Rockwell; but he knew his duty too well to attempt to use any influence of that kind with Joseph. Not so with the others, they felt as Emma

did about Joseph's return, and were earnest advocates of HER SUGGESTION."
(George Q. Cannon, ed., *Juvenile Instructor* 5 (5 February 1870):21–22.)

"Went to the tabernacle. Elder Woodruff . . . referred to the time when the
Prophet Joseph crossed the River from Nauvoo and sent for his horses, *his wife Emma
LOCKED THE STABLE DOOR and refused to let them go.* Said that if Bro. Brigham
had been there at that time he would have smashed the doors into kindlings and sent
the horses to Joseph." (Diary of Charles L. Walker, 12 November 1876, LDS
Archives.) "1) What move did the Prophet Joseph make late in the evening June 22nd,
1844? A. He left Nauvoo and crossed the Mississippi River. 2) By whom was he
accompanied? A. Hyrum Smith and Willard Richards. 3) What object had they in thus
leaving Nauvoo? A. To flee to the west and thus escape from their enemies. 4) Did they
pursue their journey? A. No; *through the solicitations of Emma Smith and other SUP-
POSED friends,* Joseph and his companions returned to Nauvoo." *(Juvenile Instructor*
13 [15 March 1888]:86.)

51. B. W. Richmond's statement, "The Prophet's Death!" *Deseret News,* 27
November 1875, reprinted from the Chicago *Times.*

52. Ibid.

53. Significantly, Huntington kept a detailed journal at the time, but did not
remember Emma's words until 1868 when the missionary efforts of Emma's sons, on
behalf of the Reorganized Church, had become an issue in Utah. Denunciations of her
became a popular topic throughout the Utah Territory. The climate and the inflamed
rhetoric of the time cast serious questions on Huntington's account.

54. Lucy Smith, *Biographical Sketches of Joseph Smith the Prophet and His
Progenitors for Many Generations,* pp. 354–55.

55. Eliza R. Snow, "Sketch of My Life," p. 13 of typescript, LDS Archives.

56. B. W. Richmond's statement, "The Prophet's Death!" *Deseret News* 27 November 1875, reprinted from the Chicago *Times.* W. Wyl wrote that Sarah Pratt told
him, "Mrs. Harris was a married lady, a very great friend of mine. When Joseph made
his dastardly attempt on me, I went to Mrs. Harris to unbosom my grief to her. To my
utter astonishment, she said laughing heartily, 'How foolish you are! Why I am his
mistress since four years.' " (W. Wyl, "Mormon Portraits," p. 60, as cited in Brodie,
No Man Knows My History, Appendix C, pp. 436–37.) This statement was made in
1842, dating the Smith-Harris relationship to Far West, Mo., ca. 1837–38. Quite possibly Joseph had taken her as a plural wife and the label "mistress" was an embellishment
by either Sarah Pratt or W. Wyl. Mormon scholars prefer to list her as a plural wife.
Lucinda Morgan Harris was sealed by proxy, 22 January 1846, to Joseph Smith, Jr., for
eternity and the next day, 23 January 1846, to George Harris for time. Around that
time the same proxy ordinance was done on behalf of Joseph and the other women he
had taken as plural wives. (Nauvoo Temple Sealing Record: Temple Sealings, LDS
Archives.)

57. Joseph III, *Joseph Smith III and the Restoration,* p. 85.

58. Sarah Griffith Richards to Zina D. Young, 17 July 1889, LDS Archives.

CHAPTER 14

1. Lynn Caine, *Widow* (New York: Bantam Books, Inc., 1974).

2. Richards to Young, 30 June 1844, Journal History, LDS Archives.

3. James B. Allen, "One Man's Nauvoo: The Mormon Experience in Illinois as
Seen and Felt By William Clayton," pp. 57–58, fn. 58; diary of William Clayton,
Excerpts, 2 July 1844.

4. Dallin H. Oaks and Joseph I. Bentley, "Joseph Smith and Legal Process: In

the Wake of the Steamship *Nauvoo,*" pp. 750–66. This article was also reprinted in *BYU Studies* 19 (Winter 1979):167–99. All citations come from the *BYU Law Review.*

5. Statement of John A. Wolf, 22 June 1844, 2 July 1844, Wilford Wood collection, Microfilm Reel 7, LDS Archives. Emma clearly did not want further debts adding to her financial burden. Willard Richards had recovered twenty-five dollars of the hundred Joseph took to Carthage, and he paid Emma about half of that. Mary returned the fifty dollars Joseph had given her, which helped Emma pay John A. Wolf, the man from whom Joseph had borrowed the three hundred dollars.

6. For a list of debts and a full discussion of the bankruptcy case, see Oaks and Bentley, "Joseph Smith and Legal Process," pp. 750–67. In 1984 dollars the $70,000 would be approximately $500,000.

7. James B. Allen, Biography of William Clayton, forthcoming; Diary of William Clayton, Excerpts, 4, 7, 8 July 1844; Willard Richards, Journal, 8 July 1844, LDS Archives.

8. Diary of William Clayton, Excerpts, 6 July 1844 and 12 July 1844.

9. Parley P. Pratt, *Autobiography of Parley Parker Pratt,* p. 335.

10. Nauvoo land records, LDS Archives. Thanks to James L. Kimball for helping us locate this information.

11. James B. Allen, forthcoming Biography of William Clayton, and Diary of William Clayton, Excerpts, 14, 15 July 1844.

12. James B. Allen notes on Diary of William Clayton.

13. Several possibilities exist for the cause of Samuel's death. The traditional story is that he received some kind of injury while fleeing the mobs near Carthage. Exhausted physically and emotionally from the ordeal, the theory goes, he finally died. Another story that persists among some of Samuel's descendants is that he suffered from alcoholism. This could explain why he did not live in Nauvoo and why he did not gain prominence in church government as did William and Hyrum. The *History of the Church* 7:222 states that Samuel Smith died from bilious fever, which suggests a gall bladder or liver disorder that may well have been alcohol-related. Another possibility that his daughter, Mary B. Norman, suggested later in her life is that he became the victim of foul play.

14. Lucy Smith, Prelim. Ms., LDS Archives.

15. *HC* 7:229–30.

16. Journal History, 3 August 1844.

17. Journal of Wandle Mace, p. 159, LDS Archives.

18. Benjamin F. Johnson to George F. Gibb, published in Dean R. Zimmerman, *I Knew the Prophets,* p. 66; and "A short Sketch of the History of John Pulsipher," in Alan H. Gerber collection, Film 298 #98, Reel 2, 11:8, BYU.

19. Brigham Young to Vilate Young, 11 August 1844, LDS Archives.

20. For a complete discussion of Joseph Smith's legal transactions in Nauvoo, see Oaks and Bentley, "Joseph Smith and Legal Process."

21. James B. Allen, forthcoming Biography of William Clayton; and Diary of William Clayton, Excerpts, 5, 17 August 1844.

22. *HC* 7:260; Diary of William Clayton, Excerpts, 18 August 1844.

23. Joseph III, *Joseph Smith III and the Restoration,* p. 86.

24. Diary of Leonard J. Arrington, 19 March 1979. The story was told to Dr. Arrington by Phyllis Phillips and is used here with his permission. First person is used here to facilitate the dialogue.

25. Burlington (Ia.) *Hawkeye* 6, No. 17:2. Examples of other presses that ran the story are: Brookville *Indiana American,* 20 September 1844, p. 2; Boston *Post,* 20 September 1844, p. 2; New Bedford (Mass.) *Morning Register,* 21 September 1844, p.

348

NOTES

2; Northhampton (Mass.) *Hampshire Gazette,* 24 September 1844, p. 2. All of the articles apparently originated with the St. Louis *Republican.* LeGrand Baker and Paul Ellsworth collection.

26. Journal of Heber C. Kimball, 1844–45, 4 October 1844, as cited by D. Michael Quinn, "Latter-day Saint Prayer Circles," p. 85. See also Journal History, 4 October 1844.

27. Joseph III, *Joseph Smith III,* p. 50.

28. *HC* 4:412–13.

29. Twelve to the church at La Harp, 18 February 1843, LDS Archives; Twelve to Ramus, 23 February, LDS Archives.

30. Brigham Young to Mary Ann Angell Young, 15 January 1841, Philip Blair collection, Univ. of U.; Dean C. Jessee, "Brigham Young's Family: Part I 1824–1845," *BYU Studies* 18, No. 3 (Spring 1978):321.

31. Brigham Young address, George D. Watt, ed., *JD* 5:297–98.

32. For an in-depth study of Brigham's use of prayer, see Ronald K. Esplin, "Defending the Kingdom Through Prayer," *Eighth Annual Sidney B. Sperry Symposium: Sesquecentennial Look at Church History, January 26, 1980* (Provo, Ut., Church Educational System, 1980), pp. 102–22. The Twelve in 1844 had some elegant names: Brigham Young, the Lion of the Lord; Heber C. Kimball, the Herald of Grace; Orson Hyde, the Olive Branch of Israel; Willard Richards, the Keeper of the Rolls; John Taylor, the Champion of Right; William Smith, the Patriarchal Jacob's Staff; Wilford Woodruff, the Banner of the Gospel; Parley P. Pratt, the Archer of Paradise; George A. Smith, the Establisher of Truth; Orson Pratt, the Gauge of Philosophy; John E. Page, the Sun Dial; Lyman Wight, the Wild Ram of the Mountains *(HC* 7:435).

33. Journal of George A. Smith, 3 September 1844, LDS Archives, as quoted in D. Michael Quinn, "The Mormon Succession Crisis of 1844," p. 191.

34. Ibid.

35. Orson Hyde to the Twelve, 12 September 1844, LDS Archives.

36. ES to Joseph L. Haywood, 18 October 1844, original in private collection. Typescript copies are in the USHS and LDS Archives but those contain minor errors. The family name was Heywood; Emma misspelled it.

37. LDS D & C 107; RLDS D & C 104.

38. James Monroe diary, 24 April 1845, Beinecke Rare Book and Manuscript Library, New Haven, Conn.; microfilm copy at the USHS.

39. *HC* 4:402.

40. "Humanity" to ES, 19 August 1844, LDS Archives.

41. Greensburg *Pennsylvania Argus,* 23 August 1844.

42. Joseph III, *Joseph Smith III,* pp. 51–53.

43. Ibid., pp. 86–87.

44. Oaks and Bentley, "In the Wake of the Steamship *Nauvoo,"* p. 190.

45. James B. Allen notes on Diary of William Clayton, 8 August 1844; Brigham Young address, 1 April 1867, Liverpool, England, Brigham Young collection, LDS Archives.

46. JS to ES, 23 June 1844, RLDS Library-Archives. Brigham Young's side of this conflict is found in two documents: Brigham Young address, 1 April 1867, Liverpool, England, and "Remarks by President Brigham Young at the Semi-annual Conference, Great Salt Lake City, 7 October 1866," reported by G. D. Watt. Both documents are in Brigham Young collection, LDS Archives.

47. Joseph III, *Joseph Smith III,* p. 86; ES to Joseph III, 2 February 1866 [1867], RLDS Library-Archives.

48. Nauvoo land records, Nauvoo Restoration papers, LDS Archives.

49. Tax receipts for 1847 and 1849, Lewis C. Bidamon collection, RLDS Library-Archives. Joseph III, in a letter to John H. Hansen on 19 May 1875, detailed Emma's holdings at the time of his father's death and said her entire estate "was probably worth, at that time, not far from $10,000.00 a liberal estimate might send it up to $12,000.00." The letter also tells what property was later sold at auction, what the courts allowed his mother to keep, and what her children eventually received. RLDS Library-Archives.

50. Jacob Scott to Mary Scott Warnock, 5 January 1844, RLDS Library-Archives.

CHAPTER 15

1. A lease between ES and William Marks, 25 August 1844, RLDS Library-Archives.

2. *HC* 7:280.

3. Ibid., 293–96.

4. Joseph III, *Joseph Smith III and the Restoration*, indicates that during the period that Marks leased the Mansion the family lived "much of the time in the old house," but the Nauvoo *Neighbor*, 13 November 1844, reports that she moved "last week," which would be the week of 4 November. Joseph III also says they moved back into the Mansion after Marks left on 12 March, but it is clear from a number of sources that the Twelve were "in control" of the Mansion for a while after that. Although they did not lease it from her, according to the Nauvoo *Neighbor*, 7 May 1845, Emma still lived in the Homestead. She leased it to a Mr. Stringham later.

5. Journal of Oliver Huntington, p. 53, LDS Archives.

6. "Lines, Written on the Birth of an Infant Son of Mrs. Emma, Widow of the Late General Joseph Smith," *Times and Seasons* 5 (1 December 1844):735.

7. Emily D. P. Young, "Incidents of the Early Life of Emily Dow Partridge," December 1876, Univ. of U.

8. Oliver B. Huntington, "History of the Life of Oliver B. Huntington also His Travels and Troubles Written by Himself," typescript, LDS Archives.

9. Statement of Lucy Messerve Smith, 18 May 1892, George A. Smith collection, Univ. of U.

10. Most frequently the plural wife and the woman of the house in which she was staying went together into confinement and the child was presented as being the child of the mistress of the house. Joseph was also sealed to some women who were already married to living husbands (for example, Sarah Cleveland and Zina Huntington Jacobs) which introduces another possibility for concealing children that he may have fathered. For an in-depth discussion of women being married to more than one man at a time see Richard Van Wagoner, "When Is a Wife Not a Wife? Mormon Polyandry in Theory and Practice," forthcoming in *Dialogue*.

11. Statement of Lucy Messerve Smith, 18 May 1892, George A. Smith collection, Univ. of U.

12. For the 1842 accounts, see *HC* 5:85 and note, also "The Life and Record of Anson Call," Huntington Library. For the 1844 meeting, see "Minutes of the Twelve," 21 February 1844, as reprinted in *HC* 6:223.

13. Don C. Corbett, *Mary Fielding, Daughter of Britain*, pp. 173–74.

14. Joseph III, *Joseph Smith III and the Restoration*, p. 85.

15. S. O. Bennion to Heber J. Grant and Counselors, 21 January 1928, LDS Archives.

16. Rumors to this effect circulated since before Joseph's death and long after her

marriage to Lewis Bidamon in 1847. A. W. Babbitt to Heber C. Kimball, 31 January 1848, LDS Archives; John Fullmer to Brigham Young, 26 January 1848, LDS Archives.

17. *Times and Seasons* 5 (15 January 1845): 776–77. William Lawrence Foster, in his doctoral dissertation, "Between Two Worlds: The Origins of Shaker Celibacy, Oneida Community Complex Marriage, and Mormon Polygamy," p. 329, states that the tone of the above statement "is similar to the tone of other statements which tried to discourage Rigdon from writing expose," indicating that it was a move to counter Emma, rather than support her.

18. Joseph III, *Joseph Smith III*, p. 87; Mary B. Norman to Ina Coolbrith, 24 April 1908, RLDS Library-Archives; and diary of Allen Joseph Stout, November 1844 to March 1845, LDS Archives, gives detail on homes guarded and duties of the guards.

19. *HC* 7:387.

20. Statement of William Marks in *Zion's Harbinger and Baneemy's Organ* (St. Louis, Mo.) 3, No. 7:53.

21. Diary of James Monroe, Yale University, microfilm copy in USHS. All the quotations concerning Monroe in this section are taken from that diary, unless cited otherwise. James Monroe met an untimely death in Utah. A man by the name of Howard Egan became irate after his wife had given birth to Monroe's child. The journal of Lorenzo Brown, 26 January 1856, recorded that "Egan went east about 70 miles to meet Monroe who had charge of [a] Merchang train, took him aside & while in conversation cooly & deliberately drew a revolver & blew out his brains. The pistol not being more than six or eight inches from his head."

22. Journal of Oliver Huntington, pp. 54–55, LDS Archives.

23. Caroline suffered from congestive heart failure. The information about Caroline Grant Smith's relationship with Emma is a firm impression garnered by Gene A. Sessions while researching the life of Caroline's brother, Jedediah Morgan Grant. Sessions's work resulted in the book, *Mormon Thunder, a Documentary History of Jedediah Morgan Grant* (Urbana: University of Illinois Press, 1982).

24. William Smith to Brigham Young, 24 August 1844, Brigham Young collection, LDS Archives.

25. For the best account of the acquittal of those accused of Joseph's and Hyrum's murders, see Dallin H. Oaks and Marvin S. Hill, *Carthage Conspiracy: The Trial of the Accused Assassins of Joseph Smith.*

26. *HC* 7:420.

27. Thomas Ford, *History of Illinois, from its Commencement as a State in 1818 to 1847*, p. 360.

28. Diary of James Monroe, 30 May 1845. Tense change to facilitate the dialogue.

29. Brigham Young to William Smith, 10 August 1845, LDS Archives. This letter has particular significance for the twentieth-century Mormon church since the president of the church who "holds the keys" no longer authorizes plural marriage. Therefore anyone who either preaches it as a current practice or practices the doctrine is excommunicated from the church.

30. Brigham Young to William Smith, 30 June 1845, LDS Archives.

31. *HC* 7:433. The Twelve also offered to publish Lucy's history around this same time.

32. *HC* 7:434.

33. Brigham Young Conference address, 7 October 1866, and *HC* 7:434.

34. Lucy Smith, *Joseph the Prophet*, p. 169.

35. New York *Sun*, October 1845, Library of Congress copy.

36. *HC* 7:443.

37. Thomas Ford, *History of Illinois*, p. 408.

38. The letters exchanged between Brigham Young and Jacob B. Backenstos are dated 18–19 September 1845 and are cited in Ronald K. Esplin, "Brigham Young and the Power of the Apostleship: Defending the Kingdom Through Prayer, 1844–45," *Sidney B. Sperry Symposium, 26 January 1980*, LDS Library.

39. *HC* 7:449.

40. Ibid., 450.

41. William Smith to Brother Little, 20 August 1845, USHS.

42. Joseph III blessing recorded summer 1845 by Martha Corey, LDS Archives. The idea that Joseph III was the successor to his father was not a new one. Immediately following Joseph's death newspapers across the country printed stories to that effect. The *Adams Sentinel* in Gettysburg, Pa., suggested that the story had been perpetrated by anti-Mormons in an attempt to injure the church.

43. George D. Watt, ed., *JD* 4:6. Also statement of John H. Carter, Complainant's Abstract, p. 181, and John D. Lee, *Mormonism Unveiled; or the Life and Confessions of the Late Mormon Bishop, John D. Lee* (St. Louis, Mo.: Bryan, Brand & Co., 1877), pp. 155, 161–62, 164. There are numerous similar statements by Brigham Young that will be discussed in a later chapter.

44. Statement of John H. Thomas, Vesta Crawford notes, Univ. of U.

45. *HC* 7:471. At this same time the Twelve offered to publish Lucy Smith's *History.* One small section of the notes for the history contains names and dates of Emma's and Joseph's children and is in Emma's handwriting. Lucy Mack Smith, Prelim. Ms., LDS Archives.

46. *HC* 7:472–73.

47. Mary Bailey Norman to Ina Coolbrith, 27 March 1908, RLDS Library-Archives.

48. *HC* 7:403.

49. Mary Bailey Norman to Ina Coolbrith, 24 April 1908, RLDS Library-Archives.

50. William Smith to ES, 21 November 1845, LDS Archives.

51. Warsaw *Signal,* 3 September 1845. A reference to William's wife leaving him is in Willard Richards's diary, 31 August 1845, LDS Archives. She may have been Mary Ann Sheffield, whom Brigham Young sealed to William, date unknown.

CHAPTER 16

1. JS to James Arlington Bennett, 30 June 1842, Joseph Smith letterbooks, JS collection, LDS Archives. In most published sources his name appears "Bennett." His signature is "Bennet." James Arlington Bennet, James Gordon Bennett (editor of the New York *Herald),* and John C. Bennett could be related, perhaps distant cousins. They knew each other well and had periodic contact. *HC* 4:593; 5:157.

2. *HC* 6:72–73.

3. James Arlington Bennet to Willard Richards, 1 February 1844, 14 April 1844, LDS Archives. Having been told five weeks earlier that Bennet was Irish, Joseph had already chosen Sidney Rigdon to share the ticket. Reference to Emma's correspondence with Mrs. Bennet is in *HC* 5:162.

4. James Arlington Bennet to Willard Richards, 20 August 1844, LDS Archives.

5. James Arlington Bennet to Willard Richards, 4 June 1845, LDS Archives.

6. *HC* 7:429.

7. James Arlington Bennet to Willard Richards, 1 September 1845, LDS Archives.

8. James Arlington Bennet to Brigham Young, 18 November 1845, LDS Archives.

9. "Mrs. Smith, widow of the Mormon Prophet," New York *Sun*, 9 December 1845, p. 2. Photocopy of original *Sun* article was given to the authors by Donna Hill. See also Raymond T. Bailey, "Emma Hale," pp. 142–43.

10. "Some facts Concerning Emma Smith," *Saints' Herald*, October 1905, p. 268. Reprinted from the New York *Sun*, 25 January 1846.

11. Journal of Heber C. Kimball 1844–45, 27 December 1845, LDS Archives.

12. Ibid., 4 January 1846.

13. Bennet to Young, 18 November 1845, LDS Archives. Interestingly, this letter is dated two days before the date on the "Emma" *Sun* letter.

14. "The Mormons—Emma's Letter," New York *Sun*, 19 December 1845, p. 2. Photocopy of this New York *Sun* letter was given to the authors by Donna Hill. See also *Saints' Herald*, October 1905, pp. 167–68.

15. New York *Sun*, 25 January 1846. See also *Saints' Herald*, October 1905, p. 168.

16. James Arlington Bennet to Brigham Young, 22 June 1851, LDS Archives.

17. ESB to Joseph III, 21 January 1870, RLDS Library-Archives. Buddy Youngreen located this letter and provided us with a typescript of it. For a discussion of other possible authors of the *Sun* letter that we considered, then discarded, see Linda K. Newell and Valeen T. Avery, "New Light on the *Sun*: Emma Smith and the *New York Sun* Letter," pp. 23–35.

18. For a more detailed description of the problems between the Mormons and anti-Mormons, see Ronald K. Esplin, "Brigham Young and the Power of Apostleship: Defending the Kingdom Through Prayer, 1844–1845," *Sidney B. Sperry Symposium, 26 January 1980*, LDS Archives.

19. Joseph III, *Joseph Smith III and the Restoration*, p. 100; *HC* 7:537.

20. *HC* 7:542. Eliza R. Snow acted as secretary in the temple. See *Young Women's Journal* 4:295.

21. *HC* 7:577.

22. Journal History, 2 February 1846.

23. The five known widows of Joseph Smith who married Heber C. Kimball were Prescindia Huntington, Lucy Walker, Sarah Lawrence, Martha McBride, and Sarah Ann Whitney. Kimball family genealogy was provided by Stanley Kimball. The eight wives whom Brigham Young married were Olive Andrews, Emily D. Partridge, Louisa Beaman, Mary Elizabeth R. Lightner, Zina D. Huntington, Rhoda Richards, Olive G. Frost, and Eliza R. Snow. See Dean Jessee, "Brigham Young and the Wilderness Years," *BYU Studies* 19, No. 4 (Summer 1979):476. Some of these women were wives in name only.

24. Vesta Crawford notes, Univ. of U.

25. Benjamin F. Johnson, *My Life's Review*, p. 107.

26. Addresses of Brigham Young, October 1863–64, reported by G. D. Watt, 7 October 1863, Brigham Young collection, LDS Archives.

27. Some of the women had apparently approached Brigham Young about commencing the Relief Society meetings again. Brigham remarked: ". . . relative to things in which any of our Sisters have been engaged they have no right to meddle in the affairs of the kingdom of God . . . the[y] never can hold the keys of the Priesthood apart from their husbands, When I want Sisters or the Wives of the members of the church to get up Relief Society I will summon them to my aid but until that time let them stay at home & if you see Females huddling together veto the concern and if they say Joseph started it tell them it is a damned lie for I know he never encouraged it.

. . . I am determined to stay these proceedings for by it our best men have been taken from us. One ounce of prevention is better than one pound of cure" (Seventies Record, 9 March 1845, LDS Archives). The Relief Society would not organize again under church direction until Brigham Young called Eliza R. Snow to be president in 1867. For several years before that women would meet in sporadic, informal meetings and a few wards or congregations would organize their own Relief Societies but without official church direction *(History of the Relief Society 1842–1966*, pp. 27–30).

28. Journal of Aroet Lucius Hale, LDS Archives.

29. All three of the gift stories are related by Joseph III in his memoirs. The desk he used until 1866, at which time he gave it to his brother David (Joseph III, *Joseph Smith III and the Restoration*, pp. 54–57). It remains today in the home of David's grandson, Lynn E. Smith, in Independence, Mo.

30. Brigham Young address, 7 October 1866, Brigham Young collection, LDS Archives.

31. Joseph L. Heywood to Heber C. Kimball, 17 March 1846, LDS Archives.

32. Journal History, 18 January 1846. Heywood, Babbitt, and Fullmer had been elected as trustees on 4 January, replacing Newel K. Whitney and George Miller. ("Certificate of George Miller," 4 January 1844, *History of Hancock County, Documents, Petitions, and Excerpts, 1841–1905*, RLDS Library-Archives.

33. Joseph L. Heywood background comes from an unpublished Heywood family history. Our thanks to Edythe H. Hindley for sharing this information.

34. *HC* 2:252.

35. Journal History, 10 August 1842.

36. For Babbitt's legal background, see Kate B. Carter, compiler, *Our Pioneer Heritage* 11 (1968):520–21. For his refusal to help Joseph at the time of the martyrdom, see *HC* 6:600.

37. Crescent City *Oracle*, 22 May 1857, attributed Babbitt's death to "Mormon maurauders sent from Salt Lake City for that purpose . . . under direct orders of the presidency of the Church of the Latter-day Saints," but a band of Cheyenne Indians killed him, then tried to sell or trade the bounty from Babbitt's wagon and some of his personal effects at nearby trading posts. See also Richard S. Van Wagoner and Stephen C. Walker, *A Book of Mormons*, p. 9.

CHAPTER 17

1. Diary of James Monroe, 30 April 1845, LDS Archives.

2. James J. Strang to ES, 22 February 1846, original in Bienecke Rare Books and Manuscript Library, New Haven, Conn.

3. William Smith, Propositions to the agents of the Twelve, March 1846, RLDS Library-Archives.

4. Although one name is listed as Nancy Millikin it is very likely Lucy, probably a printer's error. William Smith to James J. Strang, 1 March 1846, as published in the *Saints' Herald*, 26 March 1899. Original in Strang collection, Yale University.

5. William Smith to James J. Strang, 25 December 1846, Strang Collection, Yale University. Voree (Wis.) *Herald*, March 1846, reprinted the story of Emma and Joseph III from the Cincinnati *Daily Commercial*. Voree *Record*, 6 April 1846, reports Marks's activities at the conference.

6. John C. Bennett often advised Strang and later became a counselor to him. In a 2 April 1846 letter, Bennett told Strang to offer William Smith the office of Patriarch if he would take to Voree *"his Mother*, with the *Mummies and papyrus*—the bodies of *Joseph and Hyrum*—etc. etc."

7. Voree (Wis.) *Herald*, August 1846, published Lucy Smith's letter.

8. Jonathan C. Wright to Brigham Young, 11 February 1848, Journal History.

9. John M. Bernhisel to Brigham Young, 10 June 1846, LDS Archives.

10. John M. Bernhisel to Brigham Young, 3 August 1846, LDS Archives.

11. ES to Thomas Gregg, 21 April 1846, copy in RLDS Library-Archives.

12. Miscellaneous Mormon Papers, Bancroft Library, University of California, Berkeley.

13. The information about John, Lewis, and Christian Bidamon came from a personal interview with Lewis C. Bidamon's grandson, Tom Bidamon, 28 November 1978, Nauvoo Restoration papers, LDS Archives, and Edward Luce, "The Bidamon Story," unpublished manuscript. Original in possession of Mr. Luce, who kindly shared a copy with the authors.

14. Thirty-three Mormon Broadsides, Chicago Historical Society; microfilm copies in Stanley Kimball's Mormon collection at Southern Illinois University. In this collection is a proclamation from John C. Bidamon, Special Constable, calling for "all Law abiding Citizens of Hancock County, to meet . . . on the Public Square, East of the Temple," and form a posse whose purpose was to arrest more than forty anti-Mormons, including Francis M. Higbee.

15. Journal History, 1846, LDS Archives.

16. Luce, "The Bidamon Story."

17. John M. Ferris to Hiram G. Ferris, 3 September 1846, Bancroft Library, University of California at Berkeley.

18. Eudocia Baldwin Marsh, "When the Mormons Dwelt Among Us," *The Bellman*, 8 April 1916, p. 406.

19. Journal of Wandle Mace, pp. 200–03, LDS Archives.

20. Martha Ann Harris, Centennial Jubilee letter, 22 March 1881, to her children. As quoted in Don C. Corbett, *Mary Fielding, Daughter of Britain*, p. 195.

21. John M. Bernhisel to Brigham Young, 14 October 1846, LDS Archives.

22. Joseph III, *Joseph Smith III and the Restoration*, p. 88. Minor changes made in the quotation to facilitate the dialogue.

23. John M. Bernhisel recorded his conversation with Emma in a letter to Brigham Young, 14 October 1846. Emma's decision to leave the Mansion is found in Joseph III, *Joseph Smith III*, p. 91. See Nauvoo Restoration records for the date of the lease, LDS Archives; also Hancock Ill. *Eagle* 10 and 24 April 1845, and 1 May 1845.

24. Jesse Hale to ES, 30 March 1845, typescript at BYU.

25. Knight to R. Fisk, 23 February 1847, original in private possession. Mr. Ralph M. McGrath supplied us with a photocopy of the letter.

26. Journal of Curtis Edwin Bolton, as quoted in Ida Blum, *Nauvoo, Gateway to the West*, p. 89.

27. Ibid.

28. Journal of Wandle Mace, p. 207. Terms of the treaty are also from this source.

29. Eudocia Baldwin Marsh, "When the Mormons Dwelt Among Us," *The Bellman*, 8 April 1916, p. 406.

30. Journal of Wandle Mace, p. 206; emphasis in original. For a more detailed account of the treaty at Nauvoo and the occupation by Brockman's troops, see David E. Miller and Della S. Miller, *Nauvoo: The City of Joseph*, pp. 185–212.

31. Most sources, including the *Times and Seasons* and the Nauvoo *Neighbor*, put the peak population at 20,000 to 25,000. Census records indicate that number is too high. A more accurate count places the number between 11,000 and 12,000 for Nauvoo, and if we include the immediate area around the city, the number is around 14,000.

32. Thirty-three Mormon broadsides, Chicago Historical Society; microfilm copies in Stanley Kimball's Mormon collection, Southern Illinois University.

33. Journal of Wandle Mace, pp. 207–8.

34. Diary of Abbey Jenks Rice, 1838–83. The diary is owned by June Gustafson, who graciously shared excerpts with the authors.

35. Fulton (Ill.) *Journal*, 30 May 1879.

36. John M. Bernhisel to Brigham Young, 14 October 1846, and John M. Bernhisel to Heber C. Kimball, 13 January 1847. Both letters are in LDS Archives.

37. Joseph L. Heywood to Brigham Young, 2 October 1846, LDS Archives.

CHAPTER 18

1. Lewis Bidamon to ES, 11 January 1847, RLDS Library-Archives.

2. ES to Lewis Bidamon, n.d., RLDS Library-Archives.

3. Vesta Crawford notes, Univ. of U.

4. Ibid. Both the incident with Mr. Stark and the one about the flour came from information Crawford obtained from Audentia Smith Anderson, a daughter of Joseph III.

5. Caroline R. Smoot account, as quoted in Crawford notes.

6. James B. Allen and Glen M. Leonard, *The Story of the Latter-day Saints*, p. 247. For more details of the migration, see pp. 217–90.

7. An account of a visit to Nauvoo in July or August 1847 by J. H. Buckingham, in Harry E. Pratt, ed., *Papers in Illinois History and Transactions for the Year 1847*, p. 169. Typescript of this account is in the Illinois State Historical Society and indicates the book by Pratt is in the Nauvoo Public Library. No further information is given.

8. The Nauvoo temple records confirm that John Milton Bernhisel was married to Melissa Lott. See also Ada M. Earle to Audentia Smith Anderson, Inez Smith Davis collection, RLDS Library-Archives. Mrs. Earle is a granddaughter of John M. Bernhisel and discusses one of his plural wives in the letter.

9. John M. Bernhisel to ES, 9 October 1847, photocopy of the original at RLDS Library-Archives.

10. Joseph III, *Joseph Smith III and the Restoration*, pp. 265–66.

11. Ibid., pp. 88–89. Tense change to facilitate dialogue.

12. Ibid., p. 94.

13. Personal interview by Valeen Avery with Lewis Bidamon's granddaughter, Nancy Bidamon Kalk, 29 November 1978.

14. Joseph III, *Joseph Smith III*, pp. 94, 95.

15. Nancy Bidamon Kalk interview. A number of sources, particularly RLDS writings, give the marriage date as 27 December 1847. The marriage certificate and the Hancock County marriage records establish the date as 23 December 1847. The clerk, however, wrote the wrong date in the record book. It appears there as 13 December 1847.

16. Kimball to Hyde, 2 January 1848, LDS Archives. Sarah was only twenty-two years old at the founding of the Relief Society. She initiated the idea of the Nauvoo Relief Society in 1842, then watched Emma Smith become president, and other women her counselors, secretary, and treasurer. Sarah may have felt some resentment. She distinguished herself in Utah as a Relief Society president for thirty years, an advocate of women's rights, and a suffragist. (For a more complete account of Sarah M. Kimball, see Jill C. Mulvay [Derr], "The Liberal Shall Be Blessed: Sarah M. Kimball." This article is the source for the information concerning Sarah M. Kimball after she left Nauvoo.)

356

17. For Lewis Bidamon's marriage contract with Mary Ann Douglas, see Lewis C. Bidamon to Armstrong, Joel C., and John Walker, 29 December 1842, Huntington Library. Deeds, ES to Lorin Walker, Lorin Walker to ES, 21 December 1847, RLDS Library-Archives.

18. Fullmer to Brigham Young, 26 January 1848, Crawford notes.

19. Almon Babbitt to Brigham Young, 31 January 1848, and Almon Babbitt to Heber C. Kimball, 31 January 1848. Both letters are in the Journal History. The authors thank Dale Whitman, attorney, for calling our attention to a misinterpretation of this issue in Valeen T. Avery and Linda K. Newell, "The Lion and the Lady: Brigham Young and Emma Smith," p. 95. Mr. Whitman assisted us in unraveling the issue in question here.

20. Babbitt to Young, 31 January 1848, and Babbitt to Kimball, 31 January 1848. Both letters are in the Journal History.

21. John M. Bernhisel to Brigham Young, 10 September 1848, LDS Archives.

22. Diary of David H. Smith, 1853–64, 17 February [1862], RLDS Library-Archives.

23. Diary of Alonzo Winters, 21 January 1877, original in possession of Alvira Alonzo Winter.

24. Nancy Abercrombie Bidamon's great-grandson, Edward Luce, has collected Bidamon family information. His unpublished compilation of information is called "The Bidamon Story." Much of Lewis Bidamon's background is from this source.

25. Lewis Bidamon to Armstrong, Joel C., and John Walker, 29 December 1842, Bidamon collection, Huntington Library.

26. Joseph III, *Joseph Smith III*, pp. 94–96.

27. Ibid., p. 465.

28. Ibid., pp. 86–98.

29. Ibid., pp. 99–101. Joseph III says the temple burned the night of 8 October; HC says November 19. The actual date is early morning on 9 October.

30. From the Keokuk (Ia.) *Register*, as quoted in E. Cecil McGavin, *Nauvoo the Beautiful*, p. 283.

31. Joseph III, *Joseph Smith III*, p. 99.

32. For the three newspaper reports, see: Nauvoo *Patriot*, as quoted in E. Cecil McGavin, *Nauvoo the Beautiful*, p. 282; Keokuk (Ia.) *Register*, ibid., p. 283; Ida Blum, *Nauvoo, Gateway to the West*, p. 76.

33. Nauvoo subscription list, 10 November 1848, Wilford Wood collection, microfilm, LDS Archives. For Lewis's statement, see HC 7:618.

34. Confession of Joseph Agnew as told to George Rudsill of Bowling Green, Fla., and reproduced in McGavin, *Nauvoo the Beautiful*, pp. 285–87.

35. HC 7:618.

36. Lewis Bidamon to ESB, 4 May 1849, RLDS Library-Archives.

37. Lewis Bidamon to ESB, 5 July, 16 July, 16 August 1849, RLDS Library-Archives.

38. Ibid. Lorenzo Wasson's death is described in Audentia Anderson, *Ancestry and Posterity of Joseph Smith and Emma Hale*, p. 305.

39. Crawford notes.

40. ESB to Lewis C. Bidamon, 7 January 1850, RLDS Library-Archives. In this letter Mary Elizabeth's married name appears to be "Gleason" but other sources indicate that her married name was "Gibson" as appears in the text. Emma stated that she had already written Lewis four letters, but because she was not sure he had received them she briefly recapped for him "the most important items." Unfortunately, the first four letters are not extant.

41. George A. Smith to Joseph III, 13 March 1849, RLDS Library-Archives.

42. Bernhisel to Young, 10 September 1849, LDS Archives.

43. ESB to Lewis C. Bidamon, 7 January 1850, RLDS Library-Archives.

CHAPTER 19

1. ESB to Lewis Bidamon, 7 January 1850, RLDS Library-Archives. All information in this section came from this letter.

2. Emma also noted that she had received two letters from Lewis that had been written in July. One had been mailed in Kanesville, Ia., and had reached her in a short time. The other had a Salt Lake City postmark of October 11. She received it in December. Kanesville was a small Mormon settlement on the western edge of Iowa and Emma concluded that someone there had seen the letter and sent it on to Salt Lake to be examined, or even copied, before sending it on to her. Lewis, however, explained to her when he answered on 20 April 1850 that he had not finished the letter at the time it was dated and when he arrived at Goose Creek, 1,100 miles from Nauvoo, he gave it to a Mormon there who promised to mail it from Salt Lake City. Thus the delay. (ESB to Lewis Bidamon, 7 January 1850, and Lewis Bidamon to ESB, 20 April 1850, RLDS Library-Archives.)

3. Lewis Bidamon to ESB, 20 April 1850, RLDS Library-Archives.

4. Ida Blum, *Nauvoo, Gateway to the West,* pp. 102–8. Emma's friend was Ida Blum's grandmother.

5. James Linforth, ed., *Route from Liverpool to Great Salt Lake Valley,* pp. 62–63; Blum, *Nauvoo, Gateway to the West,* p. 78; Joseph III, *Joseph Smith III and the Restoration,* pp. 191–92.

6. Joseph III to Emma Knight, 14 April 1855, USHS.

7. "Bidamon Story" in possession of Edward Luce; Vesta Crawford notes, Univ. of U.

8. In 1834 Robert E. Lee was given governmental orders to survey the Mississippi rapids between Warsaw and Nauvoo, then widen the passage and make the river navigable year around. Lee purchased a small steamboat and blasting equipment and, with a crew, worked during the summers of 1838 and 1839. Lee sold his equipment at a government auction in Quincy, 10 September 1840, to a Mormon businessman named Peter Haws. Bishop George Miller, his brother Henry, and Joseph and Hyrum Smith signed a surety for Haws, who paid with a $4,866.38 promissory note signed by the five men. The note would come due 10 May 1841. Charles B. Street bought into the proposed hauling business with a note for the same amount as Haws. The captain wrecked the steamboat, now rechristened the *Nauvoo,* within a month or two of its purchase. The Millers and the Smiths sued Street for his "$4,000 due on the boat." Street and his associates refused on the grounds that the boat no longer existed. The due date on the note passed, and the solicitor general of the U. S. Treasury had the U.S. attorney in St. Louis try to arrest Haws, the Millers, and the Smiths, but he did not find them. He then told Justin Butterfield, the U.S. attorney in Illinois, to collect. Butterfield summoned the men to appear in court on the first Monday in June 1842 and subsequently assigned three more dates, but no one appeared, so Judge Nathaniel Pope entered a default judgment of $7,870.23 against the defendants. This figure represented interest and court costs and was almost twice the original purchase price. The judgment became a lien on all real estate owned by Joseph Smith. (Dallin H. Oaks and Joseph I. Bentley, "Joseph Smith and the Legal Process: In the Wake of the Steamship *Nauvoo,*" pp. 735–72.)

9. By the end of 1849 thirty-one creditors had filed claims totaling $25,023.45

against the estate. The administrators of the estate had earlier paid approximately $1,000 for additional small claims and funeral costs. Four claimants asked for $21,500 or 82 percent of the total. They were Phineas Kimball, who had notes from Joseph amounting to about $2,800; Halstead Haines and Co. for a debt left over from the Kirtland days totaling $7,349; Almon Babbitt acting in behalf of the Lawrence sisters' estate, $4,033.87; and the United States Government, which now asked for $5,184.31 for the boat debt (see Oaks and Bentley, "Joseph Smith and Legal Process," p. 769).

10. Ibid., pp. 768–69. See also Record of the United States Circuit Court for the District of Illinois, No. 1603, 18 June 1841 through 17 July 1852. This volume is located at the Federal Records Center in Chicago; a copy of this case is filed in the BYU Archives, Mss/SC 174.

11. Oaks and Bentley, "Joseph Smith and Legal Process," pp. 778–80 and notes.

12. Record of United States Circuit Court.

13. Joseph III, *Joseph Smith III*, pp. 89–90.

14. John M. Bernhisel to ESB, 3 May 1856, LDS Archives.

15. Oaks and Bentley, "Joseph Smith and Legal Process," pp. 780–81; see also Nauvoo land records, Nauvoo Restoration papers, LDS Archives.

16. William Holmes Walker, *Life Incidents and Travels*, p. 18; Joseph III to L. O. Littlefield, 14 August 1883, Joseph III Letterbook No. 4, RLDS Library-Archives, as cited in Robert D. Hutchins, "Joseph Smith III: Moderate Mormon" (Master's thesis), p. 56.

17. Journal and Reminiscences of Hannah Tapfield King, 12 May 1853, original and typescript in LDS Archives; see also the section titled "Excerpts from letters."

18. Accounts of those visitors will be discussed in later chapters.

19. Julia Smith Dixon to Joseph III, 10 July 1855, RLDS Library-Archives.

20. Joseph III, *Joseph Smith III*, pp. 228–29.

21. United States Census for 1850; Audentia Anderson, *Ancestry and Posterity of Joseph Smith and Emma Hale*, pp. 74–75.

22. Julia Dixon to ESB, 25 March 1852, RLDS Library-Archives.

23. Julia Dixon to ESB, 18 March 1853, Bidamon collection, Huntington Library. Julia mentions a baby who was probably a visiting relative's, for she comments: ". . . they want me to Stop and See the Baby how She can walk and I Suppose I must for she is a great Baby—So we all think, and her Aunty Dick among the rest, as they call me." Julia would later refer to herself as "Jute Dick." She would remain childless.

24. For descriptions of Emma's children, see Linforth, ed., *Route from Liverpool,* pp. 63–66. For description of Emma, see Brenda Angell, "My Walton History," copy in possession of Tauna Navalta.

25. Interview by Valeen T. Avery with Lewis Bidamon's grandchildren, Thomas Bidamon, Leah McLean, and Nancy Kalk, 29 November 1978.

26. Lewis Bidamon expense list, Lewis C. Bidamon papers, Huntington Library.

27. Joseph III, *Joseph Smith III*, p. 96.

28. Vesta Crawford notes, Univ. of U.

29. Almira Swiggart to Lewis Bidamon, 11 December 1853, Huntington Library.

30. Almira Swiggart to Lewis Bidamon, 3 March 1855 and 24 March 1854, Huntington Library.

31. Joseph III to Emma Knight, 14 April 1855, Knight family papers, USHS.

32. Crawford notes.

33. Joseph III to ESB, 15 June 1855, RLDS Library-Archives.

34. ESB to Joseph III, 11 October 1866, RLDS Library-Archives.

35. Julia Smith Dixon to Joseph III, 10 July 1855, RLDS Library-Archives.

36. Joseph III to Alexander Smith, 25 September 1855, RLDS Library-Archives.

37. Joseph III to E. L. Kelly, 7 August 1884, RLDS Library-Archives.

38. Journal of Enoch B. Tripp, 25 November 1855, as cited in Crawford notes.

39. Joseph Smith to Emma Knight, 4 December 1855, Knight family papers, USHS.

40. William Holmes Walker, *Life Incidents and Travels;* diary of Hannah Tapfield King, 12 May 1853; Raymond T. Bailey, "Emma Hale, Wife of the Prophet Joseph Smith" (Master's thesis), pp. 153–54.

41. Journal and reminiscences of Hannah Tapfield King, 12 May 1853, LDS Archives.

42. Journal of Enoch B. Tripp, 25 November 1855; Crawford notes; and Journal History, LDS Archives.

43. Joseph III, *Joseph Smith III*, p. 17; Joseph III to Emma Knight, 4, 16 May 1856, Knight family papers, USHS.

44. Sale certificate, Deseret News Photo, *BYU Studies* 8, No. 2 (1968):202; see Stanley B. Kimball, "New Light on Old Egyptiana: Mormon Mummies 1848–71," 72–90, for background of the papyra and mummies. Jerusha Walker Blanchard, as told to Nellie Story Bean, "Reminiscences of the Granddaughter of Hyrum Smith," *Relief Society Magazine*, January 1922, pp. 8–9.

45. Joseph III, *Joseph Smith III*, p. 107.

46. Address book and journals of George A. Smith (1856–57), 30 October 1856, LDS Archives.

47. Joseph III, *Joseph Smith III*, p. 62; George A. Smith to Joseph F. Smith, 17 July (no year), LDS Archives; Joseph III to L. O. Littlefield, 14 August 1883, Joseph III Letterbook No. 4, RLDS Library-Archives.

48. Address book and journals of George A. Smith (1856–57), 1 November 1856, LDS Archives.

49. Edmund C. Briggs, "A Visit to Nauvoo in 1856," *Journal of History* 9 (October 1916): 446–62, RLDS Library-Archives.

CHAPTER 20

1. Inez Smith Davis, *Story of the Church*, pp. 390–404.

2. Information and quotations concerning this visit are from Edmund C. Briggs, "A Visit to Nauvoo in 1856," *Journal of History* 9 (October 1916):446–62, RLDS Library-Archives.

3. Davis, *Story of the Church*, pp. 425–29.

4. Briggs, "Visit to Nauvoo," pp. 446–62.

5. Joseph III, *Joseph Smith III and the Restoration*, pp. 154–55.

6. Raymond T. Bailey, "Emma Hale, Wife of the Prophet Joseph Smith" (Master's thesis), p. 100; Journal History, 12 July 1857, LDS Archives.

7. Audentia Anderson, *Ancestry and Posterity of Joseph Smith and Emma Hale*, pp. 578–80.

8. Joseph III, *Joseph Smith III*, pp. 113–18; Vesta Crawford notes, Univ. of U.

9. Edward W. Tullidge, *Life of Joseph the Prophet*, p. 773.

10. Davis, *Story of the Church*, pp. 422–23.

11. Tullidge, *Life of Joseph the Prophet*, p. 774.

12. Joseph III, *Joseph Smith III*, p. 161.

13. Richard Lyle Shipley, "Voices of Dissent: The History of the Reorganized Church of Jesus Christ of Latter Day Saints in Utah, 1863–1900" (Master's thesis), p. 10, n. 22. Joseph III testified that about 150 people were in attendance; other RLDS historians claim 300.

14. Amboy (Ill.) *Times*, 12 April 1860, reported Joseph III's speech in full.

15. Robert D. Hutchins, "Joseph III: Moderate Mormon" (Master's thesis), p. 64. Hutchins disagrees on the order of the ceremony. Here we follow the Amboy *Times* account. Hutchins discusses the LDS-RLDS argument over the priesthood authority of Gurley, Blair, and Marks in ordaining Joseph III: "The ordination of Joseph III by these men has long been attacked theologically and emotionally by the Utah Mormon Church. Joseph . . . attempted to explain . . . that holders of a lesser priesthood can ordain someone to a higher priesthood by stating: 'The objector [the Utah Mormons] sometimes uses the argument that a stream cannot rise higher than its foundation. It is answered, that to locate the fountain of the priesthood in the man ordaining, is a mistake. . . . The fountain is God. . . . Hence as God is higher than the President of the Church, the objector does not prove by this analogy what he seeks to prove.' "

16. Joseph III was baptized by his own father at the age of ten (Joseph III to A. V. Gibbons, 1 June 1893, Joseph III Letterbook No. 4, RLDS Library-Archives; Joseph III, *Joseph Smith III*, p. 166).

17. *Saints' Herald* 1, No. 10 (1860):238, "Minutes of the Semi-Annual Conference of the Church of Jesus Christ of Latter Day Saints," 6–7 October 1860.

18. Hutchins, "Joseph III: Moderate Mormon," pp. 71–72.

19. Davis, *Story of the Church*, p. 457.

20. Amboy *Times*, 7 June and 14 June 1860; Amboy *News*, 15 December 1893; Anderson, *Ancestry and Posterity*, pp. 3–5. This tornado took a hundred lives throughout Illinois, but the Morses were the only fatalities in the Amboy-Dixon area.

21. Hancock County, Ill., U. S. Government, Ninth DECENNIAL CENSUS, copy in the Genealogy Library, Church of Jesus Christ of Latter-day Saints, Salt Lake City, Ut.

22. Joseph Fielding Smith to Levira Smith, 28 June 1860, LDS Archives. Emma's comment to her nephew went through some interesting changes as years passed. By 1895 it was "Why as I live it is Joseph. Why Joseph, I would have known you in hell, you look so much like your father!" ("Shining Lights," *Contributor*, 16:169–70, January 1895; Church Manuscripts compiled by Alan H. Gerber, on microfilm at BYU). By 1980 a woman who lived in Utah and claimed to have researched Emma's life said that Joseph F. walked up to the Mansion House and saw a hard-looking old woman sitting in a rocking chair on the front porch with a corncob pipe clenched in her teeth. Squinting, she examined Joseph. Suddenly she pulled the pipe from her mouth and cackled, "Why, if it ain't Joseph F. I'd a knowed ya in hell!" Joseph F. Smith's own account, written to his sister within days of the event, is undoubtedly correct.

23. Samuel H. B. Smith to George A. Smith, July 1860, LDS Archives.

24. James Arlington Bennet to Joseph III, 6 May 1860, RLDS Library-Archives. See also Linda K. Newell and Valeen T. Avery, "New Light on the *Sun:* Emma Smith and the *New York Sun* Letter," pp. 23–35.

25. McLellin to Joseph III, 10 January 1861, RLDS Library-Archives.

26. Anderson, *Ancestry and Posterity*, p. 580.

27. Joseph III, *Joseph Smith III*, pp. 202–3; Anderson, *Ancestry and Posterity*, p. 580. On 23 June 1861 Alexander had married Elizabeth Kendall in the parlor of the Mansion House when he was twenty-three and Elizabeth was sixteen. Alexander's and Elizabeth's first baby arrived six and a half months after their marriage. The baby seemed well and healthy, and thus probably was not premature.

28. Julia M. Middleton to Frederick Smith, 4 April 1862, Inez Smith Davis papers, RLDS Library-Archives.

29. Ida Blum, *Nauvoo, Gateway to the West*, pp. 113–14.

30. Joseph III, *Joseph Smith III*, pp. 196–200. Several sources refer to Lewis

Bidamon's service as a major and colonel in the Illinois militia during the war, but Bidamon is not listed in the *Official Record of the War of the Rebellion.*

31. Indenture, Transcript of Cumberland County, Kentucky, Court Order, Book H, p. 445. We are indebted to Edward A. Luce for much information about his great-grandmother, Nancy Abercrombie.

32. Harriet, Mary, and Lydia Luce were received into the Relief Society (RS Minutes, 1842–44). In addition David, Stephen, Sarah, Ruth, Malatiah, John, Daniel, Lorena, and Samuel Luce's names appear on the membership records of the Mormon church in Nauvoo from 1840 to 1848. Wilford Woodruff baptized many of the Luces in Maine and one of the children was named Wilford W. after him.

33. Personal interview by Valeen T. Avery with Nancy Abercrombie's grandchildren, Leah McLean, Nancy Kalk, and Thomas Bidamon, 30 November 1978. Personal correspondence with Nancy's great-grandson, Edward A. Luce. Lewis Bidamon himself acknowledged his son.

34. Charles E. Bidamon to L. L. Hudson, 10 August 1940, RLDS Library-Archives.

35. Statement of Joseph S. Jemison, 29 August 1940. See also statement of Charlotte J. Stevenson, 31 August 1940, courtesy of Buddy Youngreen; Warren Van Dine collected statements about Emma's character which are in the RLDS Library-Archives.

36. David's comment can be found in "Titus" [David Smith] to "Illustrious Juror" [Lewis Bidamon], 24 June 1871, Lewis C. Bidamon papers, Huntington Library. Joseph's first comment is in Joseph III to ESB, 8 March 1873, RLDS Library-Archives. Joseph's daybook entry for 22 April 1879 reads, "Gave the Major $12 to finish paying his taxes. He says he will return it. Don't expect it" (RLDS Library-Archives). That statement could be interpreted to mean that the Major didn't repay his debts, or that there were not sufficient funds for him to pay it back, or that Joseph reminded himself not to expect the money when figuring his own finances. There is evidence for the latter. The following excerpt in the text is in Joseph III to Major Lewis C. Bidamon, 4 September 1874, LDS Archives. Alexander's statement is in Alexander Smith to ESB, n.d., Kalk-Boes collection, LDS Archives.

37. Interview with Leah Bidamon McLean, 30 November 1978; and Crawford papers.

38. Journal of Joseph III, 26 March 1865, RLDS Library-Archives.

39. Joseph III, *Joseph Smith III*, pp. 118–24.

40. ESB to Joseph III, 2 February 1866, RLDS Library-Archives.

41. ESB to Joseph III, 20 January 1867, RLDS Library-Archives.

42. Crawford notes, Univ. of U.

43. Undated note signed by David H. Smith, Marcia Vogel collection.

44. Joseph III to ESB, 8 March 1873, RLDS Library-Archives. Emma was not the first to contemplate offering the LDS temple for sale. Under the signatures of Babbitt, Heywood, and Fullmer, who were Brigham Young's attorneys, the temple at Nauvoo had been advertised for sale in 1846, being "admirably designed for Literary or religious purposes." In the same newspaper the Kirtland temple, "this splendid edifice," was also offered on "advantageous terms" *(Hancock Eagle* [Nauvoo, Ill.], 10 April 1846).

45. ESB to Joseph III, 27 December 1868, RLDS Library-Archives.

46. ESB to Joseph III, 22 October 1866, RLDS Library-Archives.

47. ESB to Joseph III, 1 August 1869, RLDS Library-Archives.

48. ESB to Joseph III, 19 August 1866, RLDS Library-Archives.

49. Crawford notes.

50. ESB to Joseph III, 2 December 1867, RLDS Library-Archives. Information in next two paragraphs from same source.

51. ESB to Joseph III, 27 December 1868, RLDS Library-Archives.

CHAPTER 21

1. ESB to Joseph III, 1 August 1869, RLDS Library-Archives; Inez Davis, *The Story of the Church*, pp. 459–485.

2. Gary L. Bunker and Davis Bitton, "Illustrated Periodical Images of Mormons, 1850–1860," *Dialogue* 10 (Spring 1977):82–94.

3. Journal of Edmund C. Briggs, No. 2, 1863–64 (11 August 1863), RLDS Library-Archives. The full account of this visit, including information and quotations in the next two paragraphs, is from this journal.

4. *Saints' Herald* (Plano, Ill.), 15 December 1866.

5. Journal of Edmund C. Briggs, No. 2, 1863–64 (11 August 1863). We have corrected spelling and changed the tense to facilitate dialogue.

6. ESB to Joseph III, 11 October 1866, RLDS Library-Archives; ESB to Joseph III, 19 August 1866 and 20 January 1867, RLDS Library-Archives.

7. Alexander Smith's journal was the basis for an account titled "The Story of Alexander Smith," written by his daughter Vida E. Smith. Unpublished Ms. courtesy of Gracia Denning, Alexander's great-great-granddaughter. His trip to Utah is described in Vol. 4, 1911.

8. Journal of Brigham Young, 1858–63, 28 February 1860, LDS Archives.

9. *JD*, 4:6.

10. Robert Flanders first used this phrase in his address, "Brother Brigham and Sister Emma." It is so apt that it should become a classic statement about the dilemma of the Mormon churches and it is gratefully acknowledged here.

11. Journal History, 29, 30 August 1866.

12. Vida Smith, "Story of Alexander," pp. 25–29; Richard Lyle Shipley, "Voices of Dissent: The History of the Reorganized Church of Jesus Christ of Latter Day Saints in Utah, 1863–1900" (Master's thesis), pp. 33–34.

13. Brigham Young address, 1 October 1866, recorded by G. D. Watt, Brigham Young collection, LDS Archives.

14. ESB to Joseph III, 19 August 1866, RLDS Library-Archives.

15. Vida Smith, "Story of Alexander," 5 (1912):6

16. ESB to Joseph III, 19 August 1866, RLDS Library-Archives.

17. "Addresses of Brigham Young, October 1863–1864: Remarks by President Brigham Young, G.S.L. City Bowery," 7 October 1863, as reported by G. D. Watt, Brigham Young collection, LDS Archives.

18. Vida Smith, "Story of Alexander," 5 (1912):8–11; Vesta Crawford notes, Univ. of U; *Saints' Herald* 16 (9 July 1869):85–86. These sources describe in detail this encounter between Alexander and David Smith and Brigham Young. Each of the two successive years, in General Conference addresses, Brigham Young had stated that Emma had taken from the widows of Hyrum and Don Carlos rings that had belonged to their husbands. "I *think* she also took a portrait of Hyrum," he said. Brigham charged that Emma "surreptitiously" obtained the jewelry "by misrepresentation." The statement suggests that Mary and Agnes gave the rings to her for a purpose which she, for some unknown reason, did not carry through. (Brigham Young address, 7 October 1866; and Brigham Young address, 1 April 1867, both documents in Brigham Young collection, LDS Archives. Emphasis added.) On 11 June 1889 Joseph III visited his cousin Ina C. Coolbrith in Oakland, California. He reported that "during her father's

[Don Carlos Smith] lifetime some admirer of the Smith brothers had presented them with heavy gold rings . . . In some manner her father's ring at his death was placed in my mother's care. She kept it until my brother Frederick was about grown, and then had confided it to him. At his death it came into my hands. His widow tried to claim it, but knowing whose it had been originally, I determined to deliver it sometime to the only surviving child of that Uncle Don Carlos, should I ever have the opportunity. Consequently, once when my brother Alexander went through to the coast, I sent the ring by him to his cousin [Ina]. Joseph III, *Memoirs of Joseph III, Photo-reprint*, pp. 282–83.

19. Vida Smith, "Story of Alexander," 5 (1912):8–11.

20. ESB to Joseph III, 1 August 1869, RLDS Library-Archives.

21. Shipley, "Voices of Dissent," p. 97.

22. W. W. Riter to editors, *Deseret News*, 19 December 1869, Journal History.

23. *Deseret Evening News* (Salt Lake City, Ut.), 7 January 1870. Rich's view of Lewis Bidamon is balanced by the accounts of his associates and Emma's sons. An example is a letter from Alexander written from California: "I find many who remember to have seen my Mother and they all desire to be remembered to her in loving kindness. . . . Give my kind regards to Pa Bidamon." (Alexander H. Smith to Emma Bidamon, n.d., Kalk-Boes collection, LDS Archives.)

24. David Smith to Joseph III, 26 May 1870, RLDS Library-Archives.

25. Ibid.

26. Joseph III to E. L. Kelly, 7 August 1884, RLDS Library-Archives, discusses Julia's life with John Middleton.

27. David Smith to Joseph III, 26 May 1870, RLDS Library-Archives.

28. David Smith to Joseph III, 12 November 1870, RLDS Library-Archives.

29. David Smith to ESB, 5 December 1870, Kalk-Boes collection, LDS Archives.

30. Joseph III to ESB, 29 December 1871, RLDS Library-Archives.

31. David Smith to Joseph III, 3 May 1871, RLDS Library-Archives.

32. David Smith to ESB, 25 January 1872, Marcia Vogel collection, LDS Archives.

33. Paul Edwards, "Sweet Singer of Israel: David Hyrum Smith," p. 174, says Alexander went with David. Shipley, "Voices of Dissent," pp. 73–76, says Josiah Ells went.

34. For the reference to Emma's fall, see David Smith to Joseph III, 23 July 1872, RLDS Library-Archives. David Smith to Joseph III, 14 March 1872, RLDS Library-Archives.

35. David Smith to Joseph III, 19 November 1872, RLDS Library-Archives; Ronald W. Walker, "The Liberal Institute: A Case Study in National Assimilation," and Ronald W. Walker, "When the Spirit Did Abound: Nineteenth-Century Utah's Encounter with Free Thought Radicalism," 304–24.

36. Quotations throughout this section are from David Smith to Joseph III, 22 October 1872, and from the collection of undated, unsigned letters of this period in David's hand, RLDS Library-Archives.

37. Statement by Judge D. H. Morris given in the office of Samuel O. Bennion, 12 June 1930, LDS Archives.

38. David Smith to Bro. Sherman, 27 July 1872, RLDS Library-Archives. Two possible people could be "Sherman." William Shearman was a leader in the Godbeite and spiritualist movement in Utah (see Ronald Warren Walker, "The Godbeite Protest in the Making of Modern Utah" [Ph.D. dissertation], pp. 133–35). Ford K., or Frederick (unclear), Sherman signed the commitment papers to the insane asylum in Elgin,

Ill., but his name does not appear as a member of the RLDS Church nor can we identify him other than as signer of the papers.

39. David Smith to Joseph III, 22 October 1872, RLDS Library-Archives. See also F. Mark McKiernan, "David H. Smith: A Son of the Prophet," pp. 233–45. McKiernan's thesis is that David did suffer from hypoglycemia, but we have not been able to confirm or refute his conclusions.

40. David H. Smith and Elbert A. Smith, *Hesperis*, p. 103. The original *Hesperis* published by David in 1875 was incorporated in this work by his son Elbert.

41. David Smith to ESB, 2 November 1872, Kalk-Boes collection, LDS Archives. For the revelation, see RLDS D & C 117:3a.

42. Statement of Judge D. H. Morris, 12 June 1930, given in the office of Samuel O. Bennion, LDS Archives.

43. David Smith to ESB, 4 January 1874, Marcia Vogel collection, LDS Archives.

44. David Hale to ESB, 12 February 1873, RLDS Library-Archives.

45. ESB to Joseph III, 22 October 1866, RLDS Library-Archives.

46. Joseph III to Emma Knight, 24 May 1855, USHS.

47. Council of the Twelve Minutes, Book A, 6 April 1865–12 April 1889, p. 11, line 15 (Wednesday Morning, apparently 2 May 1865), and p. 34, line 21 (Tuesday, 9 April 1867), RLDS Library-Archives.

48. McLellin to Joseph III, July 1872, RLDS Library-Archives; and ESB to Joseph III, 2 February 1866, RLDS Library-Archives. The contents of this letter indicate that Emma did not write the year, 1867, correctly.

49. Joseph Smith, *Autobiography*, p. 763, as quoted in Robert Bruce Flanders, "The Mormons Who Did Not Go West" (Master's thesis), p. 112; *Saints' Herald*, 29 July 1896; Mary Smith Norman to Ina Coolbrith, n.d., RLDS Library-Archives.

50. Statement of Lucy M. Smith, George A. Smith collection, Univ. of U.

51. Joseph F. Smith interview with Joseph W. Coolidge, Joseph F. Smith diary, 28 August 1870.

52. John R. Young to Vesta P. Crawford, April 1931. The Precella Buel Kimball referred to is Prescindia Huntington Buell. For Jesse Smith's comments, see Minutes, Parawan School of the Prophets, 22 July 1871, p. 113, LDS Archives.

53. Samuel H. B. Smith to Joseph F. Smith, 13 August 1874, LDS Archives; Samuel's information about David came from conversations with Alexander in California (Samuel H. B. Smith to Joseph F. Smith, 18 December 1874, and 5 September 1874, LDS Archives). Joseph F. Smith was in Liverpool, England, but his letters to Samuel H. B. Smith request any information available about David.

54. Joseph III to ESB, 13 November 1875, RLDS Library-Archives; ESB to Mrs. Pilgrim, 27 March 1876, RLDS Library-Archives.

55. Joseph III to Dr. E. A. Kilbourne, 4 January and 11 January 1877; Joseph III to Charles Derfy, 24 January 1877, RLDS Library-Archives.

56. David Smith to Joseph III, 14 March 1872, RLDS Library-Archives.

57. George A. Smith to Joseph III, 9 October 1869, RLDS Library-Archives.

58. Joseph III, *Joseph Smith III and the Restoration*, p. 247. An account of this 1876 visit to Utah is in pp. 237–71.

59. Journal of W. W. Blair, 25 November 1873, RLDS Library-Archives.

60. George D. Watt, ed., *JD* 15:136.

61. Diary of Junius F. Wells, 13 March 1876, LDS Archives; *Deseret News Weekly*, 3 July 1878; *Deseret News Daily*, 12, 22 June 1878.

62. Julia Middleton to Joseph III, 5 January 1877, in possession of Lynn Smith; and David Smith to ESB, n.d., Buddy Youngreen collection, used with permission.

63. Joseph III to Dr. E. A. Kilbourne, 4 January and 11 January 1877; Joseph III

to Charles Derfy, 24 January 1877, RLDS Library-Archives. Photocopies of thirteen legal documents dealing with David's commitment are in the LDS Archives and RLDS Library-Archives. For David's release from the First Presidency, see RLDS D & C 121.

64. Shipley, "Voices of Dissent," pp. 73–75, discusses the controversy between the two churches over David's commitment.

65. Joseph III to J. C. Jensen, 23 February 1878, RLDS Library-Archives.

66. Joseph III to ESB, 15 May 1878, RLDS Library-Archives.

CHAPTER 22

1. Julius Chambers, Brooklyn *Eagle*, n.d., as reprinted in *Saints' Herald*, 54 (1907):541–42.

2. The first and third accounts can be found in the Vesta Crawford papers, Univ. of U., the second account is in "Recollections of Nauvoo," *Saints' Herald*, 54 (1907):541–42.

3. Andrew Jensen, *Latter-day Saint Biographical Encyclopedia*, pp. 255–96.

4. Diary of Junius F. Wells, 13 March 1876, LDS Archives.

5. Statement of Nels Madsen, 27 November 1831, LDS Archives. Madsen accompanied Pratt on his visit to Nauvoo.

6. William Adams, "History of William Adams," LDS Archives. Several other less interesting accounts of visitors from Salt Lake City include Eli H. Pierce, who saw Emma late in 1877 and said Emma "was not at all communicative, but enough was elicited to know that she felt keenly the one false and fatal step of her life—that of leaving the Church and uniting herself, heart and hand, with an infidel, after having raised a family to one of the greatest and noblest of the creations of God" (as printed in Eliza R. Snow, *Biography and Family Record of Lorenzo Snow). Woman's Exponent* 5, No. 3:23, published a letter from Nathoni Wood Pratt that he had written after being in Nauvoo in 1877. He only mentioned that he visited Emma and "took dinner at her place."

7. Diary of Emily Dow Partridge Young, 29 August 1877, LDS Archives.

8. James Burgess to ESB, 30 January 1878, Kalk-Boes collection, LDS Archives. Emma never visited Utah.

9. ESB to Joseph III, 2 December 1867; Edmund C. Briggs to R. J. Hawkins, 28 March 1908, RLDS Library-Archives.

10. ESB to Joseph III, 20 January 1867, RLDS Library-Archives.

11. ESB to Joseph III, 2 February 1866 (correct date is 1867), RLDS Library-Archives.

12. Frederick M. Smith, "The Contribution of Emma Hale Smith," a sermon at the Campus, Independence, Mo., 9 July 1944, RLDS Archives; Mrs. Heman C. Smith to Mrs. L. C. Bidamon [Nancy Abercrombie Bidamon], 29 May 1905, LDS Archives; interview with grandchildren of Lewis Bidamon.

13. David Smith to ESB, 22 January 1879, RLDS Library-Archives.

14. ESB to Joseph III, 17 (no month) 1869, RLDS Library-Archives.

15. Ibid.

16. Zenas H. Gurley to the *Saints' Herald*, 5 December 1873, RLDS Library-Archives; Zenas H. Gurley, Jr., to Joseph III, 6 April 1879, RLDS Library-Archives.

17. Journal of W. W. Blair, 13, 17 June 1874, RLDS Library-Archives. Only five years earlier, on 16 June 1869, Hyrum Smith's daughter in Utah signed an affidavit that Emma had discussed the marriage of the Lawrence and Partridge sisters with her. It states: "I Lovina Walker hereby certify, that while I was living with Aunt Emma Smith, in Fulton City, Fulton Co., Illinois, in the year 1846, that she told me, that she, Emma

Smith was present and witnessed the marrying or sealing of Eliza Partridge, Emily Partridge, Maria Lawrence, and Sarah Lawrence to her husband, Joseph Smith, and that she gave her consent thereto." Joseph F. Smith Affidavit Book No. 1, vault, LDS Archives.

18. Joseph III to William B. Smith, 12 January 1878, RLDS Library-Archives.

19. *Latter-day Saints' Messenger and Advocate,* 4 (October 1879):2.

20. Mark H. Forscutt, "Commemorative Discourse on the Death of Mrs. Emma Bidamon," pp. 211–17.

21. *Saints' Advocate* 2, No. 4:49–52; *Saints' Herald* 26:289–90. All questions and answers quoted directly or paraphrased during this interview are as they appear in these sources. Joseph III's notes of the interview are in the RLDS Library-Archives.

22. ESB to Mr. Gregg, 21 April 1846, Buddy Youngreen collection. Used with permission. In this letter Emma responded to questions about historical events in Nauvoo, ". . . everything that has not come within my immediate observation remains doubtful in my mind until some circumstance occurs to prove report either true or false."

23. Zenas Gurley, Jr., to Joseph III, 6 April 1879, RLDS Library-Archives. In this letter Gurley charged: "You absolutely refuse to believe the evidence which would convict [your father] . . . evidence by witnesses who would readily be accepted by any court in the land and who stand unimpeachable by the Church."

24. Gurley to Joseph III, 7 August 1879, RLDS Library-Archives.

25. Lorenzo Snow to Francis M. Lyman, 10 August 1901, "Correspondence to the First Presidency, January 1901–May 1902," Vol. 36, LDS Archives.

26. Alexander Smith retold this dream in an article in *Zion's Ensign,* 31 December 1903, twenty-four years after it happened.

27. Joseph III to Bertha Smith, 4 April 1879, RLDS Library-Archives.

28. *Zion's Ensign,* 31 December 1903.

29. Interview with Leah Bidamon McLean, Lewis Bidamon's granddaughter.

30. Journal of Joseph III, April 1879, RLDS Library-Archives.

31. Alexander Smith to Lizzie Smith, 28–29 April 1879, Vesta Crawford papers, Univ. of U. The time of Emma's death is also in this letter.

32. *Zion's Ensign,* 31 December 1903.

CHAPTER 23

1. Accounts of Emma's funeral are found in the Nauvoo *Neighbor* as quoted in *The History of the Reorganized Church of Jesus Christ of Latter Day Saints,* 8 vols. (Independence, Mo.: Herald House, 1973), 4:268–70; diary of Joseph III, 2 May 1879, RLDS Library-Archives; Vesta Crawford notes, Univ. of U.

2. *Deseret News* (Salt Lake City, Ut.), 31 January 1928.

3. Ibid., and S. O. Bennion to President Heber J. Grant and Counselors, 21 January 1928, LDS Archives. The descendants of Hyrum Smith and leaders of the Utah church were angered that Frederick M. Smith would disturb the graves, particularly without notifying relatives in the West. S. O. Bennion, a Utah Mormon, witnessed the reburial. In his report to the First Presidency, he wrote, "It is my impression Brethren that he had heard the reports that Brigham Young took the bodies of Joseph and Hyrum to Utah and that he wanted to prove it untrue. He did not mention that but in an indirect way he did. I said to him didn't your Father tell you where these bodies were laid and he answered yes. I told him his Father had told me where they were and that I was convinced that they were close to the foot of Emma Smith's grave."

4. *Saints' Herald* 26, No. 14 (15 July 1879):209–17; *Women's Exponent* 7, No. 24:243.

5. Joseph III to E. A. Kilbourne, 6 May 1879; Joseph III to David Smith, 6 May 1879, both in RLDS Library-Archives.

6. Joseph III, *Joseph Smith III and the Restoration,* p. 273.

7. Photocopy of the marriage license of Lewis Bidamon and Nancy Abercrombie in possession of authors. In later years Emma's descendants were embarrassed by Charlie's illegitimacy. In a letter from a Brother Davey to J. A. Bailey, 22 July 1937 (RLDS Library-Archives), Mr. Davey asked who Charles Bidamon was. A handwritten note up the margin reads, "Inez Davis [a great-granddaughter of Emma] says . . . child of Lewis Bidamon and servant girl—illegitimate. Family does not discuss." Three of Charles Bidamon's children and one of his grandchildren have given access to private papers of Lewis and Emma Bidamon that they have inherited.

8. Joseph III, *Joseph Smith III,* pp. 464–67; L. C. Bidamon, Last Will and Testament, n.d., LDS Archives, as quoted in Dean C. Jessee, "The Original Book of Mormon Manuscript," 265–66. Mrs. Sarah M. Kimball, the onetime resident of Nauvoo who had written in 1847 to her friend in Winter Quarters of Emma's and Lewis's marriage, returned to visit her former home in Nauvoo and called on Lewis Bidamon. She remembered the box deposited in the cornerstone and asked Lewis about it. He said the box "had been so long exposed to the wet and weather that its contents were nearly ruined." He had given Joseph III a coin and "the manuscript of the Book of Mormon; but it was so much injured that he did not care for it." Bidamon's wife, Nancy Abercrombie, brought in a box with the decaying manuscript and gave it to Sarah, who asked, "Mr. B. How much for his relic?" He replied, "Nothing from you, you are welcome to anything you like from the box." This part of the original manuscript of the Book of Mormon is now in the LDS Archives.

9. Joseph III, *Joseph Smith III,* pp. 466–69. Italics in original.

10. Amboy (Ill.) *Journal,* 2 July 1879.

11. *Saints' Advocate* 2, No. 4 (October 1879):49–52.

12. Edward W. Tullidge, *Life of Joseph the Prophet,* pp. 798–800.

13. For a more complete analysis of Jason Briggs and Zenas Gurley, see Alma Blair, "Moderate Mormonism," *Essays in Mormon History* (Lawrence, Kans.: Coronado Press, 1973), and Robert D. Hutchins, "Joseph Smith III: Moderate Mormon" (Master's thesis).

14. *Woman's Exponent* 8 (1 November 1879):85.

15. Joseph III, *Memoirs of Joseph III, Photo-reprint,* p. 277.

16. Hutchins, "Joseph Smith III: Moderate Mormon."

17. Polygamy loomed large in the new Reorganization, but there were many other factors that shaped the doctrine and practices of the RLDS Church. Some ideas and practices can be traced back to the Kirtland era (see William McLellin to Joseph III, 10 January 1861 and July 1872). Alma Blair in his essay, "Reorganized Church of Jesus Christ of Latter Day Saints: Moderate Mormonism" (F. Mark McKiernan et al., *The Restoration Movement: Essays in Mormon History),* gives excellent background on the development of the Reorganization. See also Hutchins, "Joseph Smith III: Moderate Mormon."

18. Joseph III to William Smith, 11 March 1882, Joseph III, No. 3, p. 435, RLDS Library-Archives.

19. William Smith to Joseph III, n.d., and Joseph III to William B. Smith, 26 October 1893. Both in RLDS Library-Archives. Hutchins offers an explanation for Joseph III's quest to clear the family name. "The point was critical to Joseph III's way of thinking. He believed his father had to be a good man since the revelation of 1833

had promised him that the 'keys of the kingdom would never be taken from him.' It then followed that his father would never be guilty of such a heinous sin as plural marriage, then he would indeed have been a fallen prophet. If Joseph had been a fallen prophet, then his blessing of his son was not valid. Without a valid blessing and ordination, Joseph III would have no legitimate authority to lead the Reorganized Church. This fear forced Joseph to ignore weighty evidence that not only had his father introduced plural marriage to the church, but that he had also practiced it." Hutchins, "Joseph Smith III: Moderate Mormon," p. 76.

20. Joseph III to J. W. Rigdon, 24 July 1902, RLDS Library-Archives.

21. Emily D. P. Young, "Incidents of the Early Life of Emily Partridge," Univ. of U.

Selected Bibliography

Books, Pamphlets, and Articles

Ackerknecht, E. H. *Malaria in the Upper Mississippi Valley, 1760–1900.* Baltimore, 1945.

Allen, James B. "One Man's Nauvoo: William Clayton's Experience in Mormon Illinois." *Journal of Mormon History* 6 (1979):37–59.

—————, and Thomas G. Alexander, eds. *Manchester Mormons: The Journal of William Clayton (1840–1842).* Santa Barbara and Salt Lake City: Peregrine Smith Books, 1974.

—————, and Glen M. Leonard. *The Story of the Latter-day Saints.* Salt Lake City: Deseret Book Co., 1976.

Anderson, Mary Audentia Smith. *Ancestry and Posterity of Joseph Smith and Emma Hale.* Independence, Missouri: Herald House, 1929.

—————. "Emma Smith and the Church Hymns," *The True Latter Day Saints' Herald* 86 (6 May 1939):553–54.

Anderson, Richard Lloyd. "The Reliability of the Early History of Lucy and Joseph Smith," *Dialogue* 4, No. 2 (Summer 1969):12–28.

—————. *Joseph Smith's New England Heritage: Influences of Grandfathers Solomon Mack and Asael Smith.* Salt Lake City: Deseret Book Co., 1971.

—————. "The Impact of the First Preaching in Ohio," *BYU Studies* 11, No. 4 (Summer 1971):474–96.

—————. "Gold Plates and Printer's Ink," *The Ensign* 6 (September 1976):71–76.

—————. "The Whitmers," *The Ensign* 9 (August 1979):34–40.

Andrus, Hyrum. *Joseph Smith, Man and Seer.* Salt Lake City: Deseret Book Co., 1960.

Anonymous. *Free Masonry by a Master Mason.* New York: n.p., 1828.

Arrington, Leonard J. *Great Basin Kingdom: An Economic History of the Latter-day Saints 1830–1900.* Reprinted. Lincoln, Nebraska: University of Nebraska Press, 1966.

—————. "Why Did the Latter-day Saints Experience Persecution?" *Improvement Era,* August 1970, pp. 49–53.

—————. "Church Leaders in Liberty Jail," *BYU Studies* 13, No. 1 (Autumn 1972):20–26.

—————. *From Quaker to Latter-day Saint, Bishop Edwin D. Woolley.* Salt Lake City: Deseret Book Co., 1976.

—————. "The John Tanner Family." *The Ensign* 9 (March 1979):46–51.

—————, and Davis Bitton. *The Mormon Experience, A History of the Latter-day Saints.* New York: Alfred A. Knopf, 1979.

Austin, Emily M. *Mormonism: Or Life Among the Mormons.* Madison, Wisconsin: M. J. Cantwell, 1882.

Avery, Valeen T., and Linda K. Newell. "Lewis C. Bidamon, Stepchild of Mormondom," *BYU Studies* 19, No. 3 (Spring 1979):375–88.

—————. "The Elect Lady: Emma Hale Smith," *The Ensign* 9 (September 1979):64–67.

—————. "The Lion and The Lady: Brigham Young and Emma Smith," *Utah Historical Quarterly* 48, No. 1 (Winter 1980):81–97.

Backman, Milton V. "Awakening in the Burned-over District: New Light on the Historical Setting of the First Vision," *BYU Studies* 6, No. 3 (Spring 1969):301–20.

Barrett, Ivan J. *Heroines of the Church.* Provo, Utah: Brigham Young University Press, 1966.

Barrett, William E., and Alma D. Burton, eds. *Readings in L.D.S. Church History.* 3 vols. Salt Lake City: Deseret Book Co., 1953–58.

Bates, Irene M. "William Smith, 1811–93: Problematic Patriarch," *Dialogue* 16, No. 2 (Summer 1983):11–23.

Beach, Moses Yale, ed. *Wealth and Biography of the Wealthy Citizens of the City of New York.* New York: Sun Office, 1846.

Bean, Nellie Story. "Reminiscences of the Granddaughter of Hyrum Smith," *Relief Society Magazine,* January 1922, pp. 8–10.

Beardsley, Harry M. *Joseph Smith and His Mormon Empire.* Boston and New York: Houghton Mifflin Co., 1931.

[Beecher], Maureen Ursenbach. "The Eliza Enigma: The Life and Legend of Eliza R. Snow," *Charles Redd Monographs on American History: Essays on the American West,* Thomas G. Alexander, ed., No. 6, 1974–1975, Provo, Utah: Charles Redd Center for American History.

—————, ed. "Eliza R. Snow's Nauvoo Journal," *BYU Studies* 15, No. 4 (Summer 1975):391–415.

—————. "Leonora, Eliza, and Lorenzo: An Affectionate Portrait of the Snow Family." *The Ensign* 10 (June 1980):65–69.

—————, and James L. Kimball, Jr. "The First Relief Society," *The Ensign* 9 (March 1979):25–29.

—————, Linda King Newell, and Valeen Tippetts Avery. "Emma, Eliza, and the Stairs: An Investigation." *BYU Studies* 22, No. 1 (Winter 1980):51–62.

Bennett, John C. *The History of the Saints: Or an Expose of Joe Smith and Mormonism.* Boston: Leland and Whiting, 1842.

Bent, Charles, ed. *History of Whiteside County, Illinois.* Morrison, Illinois: n.p., 1877.

Bitton, Davis, and Gary L. Bunker. "Phrenology Among the Mormons," *Dialogue* 9, No. 1 (Spring 1974):43–61.

Blackman, Emily C. *History of Susquehanna County, Pennsylvania.* Philadelphia: Claxton, Remsen and Haffelfinger, 1873.

Blair, Alma. "The Haun's Mill Massacre," *BYU Studies* 13, No. 1 (Autumn 1972):62–67.

Blair, W. W. "The Ministry of Joseph's Sons," *One Wife or Many*. Lamoni, Iowa: Reorganized Church of Jesus Christ of Latter Day Saints, n.d.

Blum, Ida. *Nauvoo—An American Heritage*. Carthage, Illinois: Ida Blum, 1969.

——————. *Nauvoo, Gateway to the West*. Carthage, Illinois: Ida Blum, 1974.

A Book of Commandments, for the Government of the Church of Christ, Organized According to Law, on the 6th of April, 1830. 1833. Reprinted. Independence, Missouri: Herald House, 1972.

Book of Doctrine and Covenants. Independence, Missouri: Herald House, 1978.

The Book of Mormon, Joseph Smith, Jr., trans. New York: Egbert B. Grandin, 1830.

The Book of Mormon, Joseph Smith, Jr., trans. Salt Lake City: The Church of Jesus Christ of Latter-day Saints, 1958.

Brewster, James Colin. *Very Important to the Mormon Money Diggers*. Springfield, Illinois: n.p., 1843.

Briggs, Jason W. *The Basis of Brighamite Polygamy: A Criticism upon the (so called) Revelation of July 12th, 1843*. True Latter Day Saints Tract No. 28. Lamoni, Iowa: Reorganized Church of Jesus Christ of Latter Day Saints, 1875.

Brodie, Fawn. *No Man Knows My History: The Life of Joseph Smith, the Mormon Prophet*. 2nd ed. New York: Alfred A. Knopf, 1975.

Brooks, Juanita. *John D. Lee, Zealot—Pioneer-Builder—Scapegoat*. Glendale, California: Arthur H. Clark Co., 1962.

Buerger, David John. "The Fullness of the Priesthood: The Second Anointing in Latter-day Theology and Practice," *Dialogue* 16, No. 1 (Spring 1983):10–44.

Burgess, S. A. "Latter Day Saint Hymns," *Journal of History*, 18, No. 3 (July 1925):257–60.

——————. "The True Emma Smith," *The True Latter Day Saints' Herald* 88 (12 July 1941):873–74, 878, 885.

Burton, Richard F. *The City of the Saints*. London: Longman, Green, Longman & Roberts, 1861.

Call, Anson. "A Busy Life," *Gems of Reminiscence*. Seventeenth Book of the Faith Promoting Series. Salt Lake City: George C. Lambert, 1915.

Cannon, George Q. *The Life of Joseph Smith, The Prophet*. Salt Lake City: Juvenile Instructor Office, 1888.

Carmer, Carl. *The Farm Boy and the Angel*. Garden City, New York: Doubleday & Co., 1970.

Carter, Kate B. *Denominations That Base Their Beliefs on the Teachings of Joseph Smith*. 2nd ed. Salt Lake City: Daughters of the Utah Pioneers, 1969.

Caswall, Henry. *The City of the Mormons; Or, Three Days in Nauvoo, in 1842*. London: J. G .F. and J. Rivington, 1842.

Cheville, Roy A. *Joseph and Emma Smith, Companions*. Independence, Missouri: Herald House, 1977.

Cocheron, Augusta Joyce. *Representative Women of Deseret.* Salt Lake City: J. C. Graham and Co., 1884.

Collier, Fred C., compiler. *Unpublished Sermons of Brigham Young.* West Jordan, Utah: Mormon Underground Press, 1978.

"Communications," *The True Latter Day Saints' Herald* 8, No. 7 (1 October 1865):100–3.

Cook, Lyndon W. " 'A More Virtuous Man Never Existed on the Footstool of the Great Jehovah': George Miller on Joseph Smith," *BYU Studies* 14, No. 3 (Spring 1979):402–7.

——————. " 'Brother Joseph Is Truly a Wonderful Man, He Is All We Could Wish a Prophet to Be': Pre-1844 Letters of William Law," *BYU Studies* 20, No. 2 (Winter 1980):207–18.

——————. *The Revelations of the Prophet Joseph Smith.* Provo, Utah: Seventy's Mission Bookstore, 1981.

——————. "William Law: Nauvoo Dissenter," *BYU Studies* 22, No. 1 (Winter 1982):47–72.

Corbett, Don Cecil. *Mary Fielding, Daughter of Britain.* Salt Lake City: Deseret Book Co., 1966.

Corbett, Pearson H. *Hyrum Smith, Patriarch.* Salt Lake City: Deseret Book Co., 1963.

Cowdery, Oliver. *Defense in a Rehearsal of My Grounds for Separating Myself from the Latter-day Saints.* Norton, Ohio: Pressley's Job Office, 1939.

Cowley, Matthias F. *Wilford Woodruff, History of His Life and Labors As Recorded in His Daily Journals.* Salt Lake City: Deseret Book Co., 1901.

Cox, Harvey. *Understanding the New Religions.* Jacob Needleman and George Baker, eds. New York: Seabury Press, 1978.

Crawley, Peter. "A Bibliography of the Church of Jesus Christ of Latter-day Saints in New York, Ohio and Missouri," *BYU Studies* 12, No. 3 (Spring 1972):465–537.

——————, and Richard Lloyd Anderson. "The Political and Social Realities of Zion's Camp," *BYU Studies* 14, No. 4 (Summer 1974):406–20.

Cross, Whitney R. *The Burned-over District: The Social and Intellectual History of Enthusiastic Religion in Western New York, 1800–1850.* Ithaca, New York: Cornell University Press, 1950.

Daniels, William M. *A Correct Account of the Murder of Generals Joseph and Hyrum Smith at Carthage on the 27th Day of June, 1844.* Nauvoo: John Taylor, 1945.

Davis, George T. M. *An Authentic Account of the Massacre of Joseph Smith, the Mormon Prophet, and Hyrum Smith, His Brother.* St. Louis: Chambers and Knapp, 1844.

Davis, Inez Smith. "The Elect Lady," *The True Latter Day Saints' Herald* 62 (10 November 1915):1077–82.

——————. *The Story of the Church.* 9th ed. Independence, Missouri: Herald House, 1977.

Deen, Edith. *Great Women of the Christian Faith.* New York: Harper and Brothers, 1959.

[Derr] Mulvay, Jill C. "Eliza R. Snow and the Woman Question," *BYU Studies* 16, No. 2 (Winter 1976):250–64.

—————. "The Liberal Shall be Blessed: Sarah M. Kimball," *Utah Historical Quarterly* 44, No. 3 (Summer 1976):205–22.

The Doctrine and Covenants. Salt Lake City: The Church of Jesus Christ of Latter-day Saints, 1961.

Dow, George Francis. *History of Topsfield, Massachusetts.* Topsfield, Massachusetts: The Topsfield Historical Society, 1940.

Draper, Maurice L., ed. *Restoration Trials Studies 1,* Sesquicentennial Edition. Independence, Missouri: Temple School, 1980.

Durham, Reed C., Jr. "The Election Day Battle at Gallatin," *BYU Studies* 13, No. 1 (Autumn 1972):36–61.

Edmunds, John K. *Through Temple Doors.* Salt Lake City: Bookcraft, 1978.

Edwards, Paul. "Sweet Singer of Israel: David Hyrum Smith," *BYU Studies* 12, No. 2 (Winter 1972):171–84.

Ehat, Andrew F., and Lyndon W. Cook. *The Words of Joseph Smith.* Salt Lake City: Bookcraft, 1980.

"Emma Smith and Her Selection of Hymns," *The True Latter Day Saints' Herald* 52 (1905):386–87.

"Emma Smith, The Prophet's Wife," *Relief Society Magazine* 20, No. 4 (April 1933):237–41.

Esplin, Ronald K. "Sickness and Faith, Nauvoo Letters," *BYU Studies* 15, No. 4 (Summer 1975):425–33.

—————. "Life in Nauvoo, June 1844: Vilate Kimball's Martyrdom Letters," *BYU Studies* 19, No. 2 (Winter 1979):231–40.

—————. "Joseph, Brigham, and the Twelve: A Succession of Continuity," *BYU Studies* 21, No. 3 (Summer 1981):301–41.

Evans, John Henry. *Joseph Smith, An American Prophet.* New York: The Macmillan Co., 1933.

Fitzpatrick, Doyle. *The King Strang Story.* Lansing, Michigan: National Heritage, 1970.

Flanders, Robert Bruce. *Nauvoo: Kingdom on the Mississippi.* Urbana: University of Illinois Press, 1965.

Flint, B. C. *An Outline History of the Church of Christ (Temple Lot).* 2nd ed. Independence, Missouri: The Board of Publications, The Church of Christ (Temple Lot), 1953.

Ford, Thomas. *History of Illinois, from its Commencement as a State in 1818 to 1847.* Chicago: S. G. Griggs and Co., 1854.

Forscutt, Mark H. "Commemorative Discourse on the Death of Mrs. Emma Bidamon," *The True Latter Day Saints' Herald* 26, No. 14 (15 July 1879):209–17.

Foster, Lawrence. *Religion and Sexuality, Three American Communal Experiments of the Nineteenth Century.* New York, Oxford: Oxford University Press, 1981.

Garver, J. F. "Defending Smiths," *The True Latter Day Saints' Herald* 63 (3 May 1916):418–19.

Gibson, Margaret Wilson. *Emma Smith, The Elect Lady.* Independence, Missouri: Herald House, 1966.

Goodwin, S. H. *Mormonism and Masonry: A Utah Point of View.* Salt Lake City: Grand Lodge F. and A. M. of Utah, 1925.

Grant, Carter E. "Emma Hale Smith, the Prophet's Wife," *Juvenile Instructor* 63 (March 1928):123–25.

—————. "An Angel Visited This Home," *Improvement Era,* March 1963, pp. 168–72.

Gunn, Stanley R. *Oliver Cowdery.* Salt Lake City: Bookcraft, 1962.

Hancock, Mary Salisbury. "The Three Sisters of the Prophet Joseph Smith," *The True Latter Day Saints' Herald* 101, No. 2 (11 January 1954):34–35; No. 3 (18 January 1954):58–59; No. 4 (25 January 1954):82–83, 95.

Hansen, Klaus J. *Quest for Empire: The Political Kingdom of God and the Council of Fifty in Mormon History.* East Lansing: Michigan State University Press, 1967.

Hardy, John. *History of the Trials of Elder John Hardy Before the Church of "Latter Day Saints" in Boston.* Boston: n.p., 1844.

Harris, William. *Mormonism Portrayed.* Warsaw, Illinois: Sharp and Gamble, 1841.

Hartley, William G. "Mormon Sundays," *The Ensign* 8 (January 1978):19–25.

Hill, Donna. *Joseph Smith: The First Mormon.* Garden City, New York: Doubleday & Co., 1977.

Hill, Marvin S. "The First Vision Controversy: A Critique and Reconciliation," *Dialogue* 15, No. 2 (Summer 1982):31–46.

—————. "Joseph Smith and the 1826 Trial: New Evidence and New Difficulties," *BYU Studies* 12, No. 2 (Winter 1972):223–33.

—————, and James B. Allen, eds. *Mormonism and American Culture.* New York: Harper and Row, 1972.

—————, Keith C. Rooker, and Larry T. Wimmer. *The Kirtland Economy Revisited, a Market Critique of Sectarian Economics.* James B. Allen, ed. Provo, Utah: Brigham Young University Press, 1977.

Hinckley, Bryant S. "The Nauvoo Memorial," *Improvement Era,* August 1938, pp. 458–511.

History of Caldwell and Livingston Counties Missouri. St. Louis: National Historical Co., 1886.

History of the Church of Jesus Christ of Latter-day Saints. Period I. History of Joseph Smith, The Prophet, By Himself, vols. 1–6. *Period II From The Manuscript History of Brigham Young and Other Original Documents,* vol. 7. Introduction and notes by B. H. Roberts. Salt Lake City: Deseret Book Co., 1978.

The History of Daviess County Missouri. Kansas City, Missouri: Birdsall and Dean, 1882.

History of Jackson County, Missouri. Missouri: Union Historical Co., 1881.

History of Lee County. Chicago: H. H. Hill & Co., 1881.

History of the Relief Society 1842–1966. Salt Lake City: General Board of the Relief Society, 1966.

Hoffman, Mark William. "Finding the Joseph Smith Document," *The Ensign* 10 (July 1980):73.

Holm, Francis W., Sr. *The Mormon Churches: A Comparison from Within.* Kansas City, Missouri: Midwest Press, 1970.

Howard, Richard P. "Since Yesterday," *The True Latter Day Saints' Herald* 119, No. 5 (May 1972):45.

Howe, Eber D. *Mormonism Unvailed.* Painesville, Ohio: Published by the author, 1834.

——————. *Autobiography and Recollections of a Pioneer Printer.* Painesville, Ohio: Telegraph Steam Printing House, 1878.

Huntress, Keith. "Governor Thomas Ford and the Murderers of Joseph Smith," *Dialogue* 4 (Summer 1969):41–52.

Hyde, Orson. *Speech of Elder Orson Hyde, Delivered Before the High Priests' Quorum in Nauvoo, April 27th, 1845, Upon the Course and Conduct of Mr. Sidney Rigdon and Upon His Claims to the Presidency.* Liverpool, England: James and Woodburn, 1845.

——————. *A Voice from Jerusalem, or a Sketch of the Travels and Ministry of Elder Orson Hyde, Missionary of the Church of Jesus Christ of Latter Day Saints.* Liverpool, England: P. P. Pratt, Star Office, Printed by James and Woodburn, n.d.

An Illustrated Historical Atlas of Caldwell County, Missouri. Philadelphia: Edwards Brothers, 1876.

Jackson, Joseph H. *A Narrative of the Adventures and Experience of Joseph H. Jackson in Nauvoo: Disclosing the Depths of Mormon Villany Practiced in Nauvoo.* Warsaw, Illinois: n.p., 1844.

Jacob, Udney Hay. *An Extract from a Manuscript Entitled The Peace Maker, or the Doctrines of the Millennium: Being a Treatise on Religion and Jurisprudence. Or a New System of Religion and Politicks* [sic]. Nauvoo, Illinois: J. Smith, 1842.

Jenson, Andrew, compiler. *The Historical Record: A Monthly Periodical Devoted Exclusively to Historical, Biographical, Chronological, and Statistical Matters.* 9 vols. Salt Lake City: published by the author, 1887.

——————. *Church Chronology. A Record of Important Events Pertaining to the History of the Church of Jesus Christ of Latter-day Saints.* 2nd ed. Salt Lake City: Deseret News, 1899.

——————. *Latter-day Saint Biographical Encyclopedia.* 4 vols. Salt Lake City: Andrew Jenson History Company, 1902, 1914, 1920, 1936.

Jessee, Dean C. "The Early Accounts of Joseph's First Vision," *BYU Studies* 9, No. 3 (Spring 1969): 275–94.

——————. "The Original Book of Mormon Manuscript," *BYU Studies* 10, No. 3 (Spring 1970):259–78.

——————. "The Writing of Joseph Smith's History," *BYU Studies* 11, No. 4 (Summer 1971):439–73.

——————. "Kirtland Diary of Wilford Woodruff," *BYU Studies* 12, No. 4 (Summer 1972):365–99.

——————. "Joseph Knight's Recollection of Early Mormon History," *BYU Studies* 17, No. 1 (Autumn 1976):29–39.

————. "Joseph Smith's 19 July 1840 Discourse," *BYU Studies* 19, No. 3 (Spring 1979):390–94.

————, compiler and editor. *The Personal Writings of Joseph Smith.* Salt Lake City: Deseret Book Co., 1984.

————. "Steadfastness and Patient Endurance," *The Ensign* 9 (June 1979):41–47.

Johnson, Benjamin F. *My Life's Review.* Independence, Missouri: Zion's Printing and Publishing Co., 1947.

————. *"Mormonism as an Issue": An Open Letter to the Editor of the Arizona Republican.* Tempe: n.p., 1890.

Journal of History. 18 vols. Lamoni, Iowa, and Independence, Missouri: Board of Publication, Church of Jesus Christ of Latter Day Saints: 1908–25.

Kane, Thomas Leiper. *The Private Papers and Diary of Thomas Leiper Kane: A Friend of the Mormons,* Oscar Osburn Winther, ed. San Francisco: Gelber-Lilienthal, 1937.

Kelley, William H. *A Defense of Monogamic Marriage.* Copy in RLDS Library-Archives. Reorganized Church of Jesus Christ of Latter Day Saints: n.p., n.d.

Kennedy, Inez A. *Recollections of the Pioneers of Lee County.* Dixon, Illinois: n.p., 1893.

Kidder, Daniel P. *Mormonism and the Mormons: A Historical View of the Rise and Progress of the Sect Self-styled Latter Day Saints.* New York: G. Lane and C. B. Tipett, 1845.

Kimball, James L., Jr. "A Wall to Defend Zion: The Nauvoo Charter," *BYU Studies* 15, No. 4 (Summer 1975):491–97.

Kimball, Stanley B. "New Light on Old Egyptiana: Mormon Mummies 1848–71," *Dialogue* 16, No. 4 (Winter 1983):72–90.

————. *Sources of Mormon History 1939–48.* 2nd ed. Carbondale-Edwardsville: Southern Illinois University, 1966.

————. *Discovering Mormon Trails.* Salt Lake City: Deseret Book Co., 1979.

————. *Heber C. Kimball, Mormon Patriarch and Pioneer.* Urbana, Chicago, London: University of Illinois Press, 1981.

Knight, Newel. *Scraps of Biography.* Salt Lake City: n.p., 1883.

Lambert, Mary Alice Cannon. "Leonora Cannon Taylor," *Young Woman's Journal* 19 (1908):345–47.

Larson, Karl A., and Katharine Miles Larson, eds. *Diary of Charles Lowell Walker.* 2 vols. Logan, Utah: Utah State University Press, 1980.

Larson, Stan. "Changes in Early Texts of the Book of Mormon," *The Ensign* 6 (September 1976):77–82.

Lee, John Doyle. *The Mormon Menace: Being the Confessions of John Doyle Lee, Danite.* Introduction by Alfred Henry Lewis. New York: Home Protection Publishing Co., 1905.

————. *A Mormon Chronicle: The Diaries of John D. Lee, 1848–1876.* 2 vols. Robert Glass Cleland and Juanita Brooks, eds. San Marino, California: Huntington Library, 1955.

The Life and Labors of Eliza R. Snow Smith; with a Full Account of her Funeral Services. Salt Lake City: Juvenile Instructor Office, 1888.

Linforth, James, ed. *Route from Liverpool to Great Salt Lake Valley.* Liverpool: Franklin D. Richards, 1855.

Lyne, T. A. *A True and Descriptive Account of the Assassination of Joseph and Hiram Smith, The Mormon Prophet and Patriarch.* New York: C. A. Calhoun, 1844.

Lyon, T. Edgar. "Independence, Missouri and the Mormons 1827–1833," *BYU Studies* 13, No. 1 (Autumn 1972):10–19.

——————. "Doctrinal Development of the Church During the Nauvoo Sojourn, 1839–1846," *BYU Studies* 15, No. 4 (Summer 1975):435–46.

McGavin, E. Cecil. "Emma Smith's Collection of Hymns," *Improvement Era,* January 1936, pp. 38–39.

——————. *Nauvoo the Beautiful.* Salt Lake City: Stevens and Wallis, Inc., 1946.

Mack, Solomon. *A Narraitve [sic] of the Life of Solomon Mack, Containing an Account of the Many Severe Accidents He Met with During a Long Series of years, together with the Extraordinary Manner in which He Was Converted to the Christian Faith.* Windsor, Vermont: By the author, 1811?

Mackey, Albert G. *A Lexicon of Freemasonry.* 7th ed. London: Charles Griffin and Company, 1883.

——————. *An Encyclopedia of Freemasonry.* 2 vols. Chicago: Chicago Masonic History Co., 1924.

McKiernan, F. Mark. *The Voice of One Crying in the Wilderness: Sidney Rigdon, Religious Reformer, 1793–1876.* Lawrence, Kansas: Coronado Press, 1971.

——————. "David H. Smith: A Son of the Prophet," *BYU Studies* 18, No. 2 (Winter 1978):233–45.

——————, Alma R. Blair, and Paul M. Edwards, eds. *The Restoration Movement: Essays in Mormon History.* Lawrence, Kansas: Coronado Press, 1973.

Marsh, Eudocia Baldwin. "When the Mormons Dwelt Among Us," *The Bellman,* April 1, 8, 1916.

Matthews, Robert J. "Adam-ondi-Ahman," *BYU Studies* 13, No. 1 (Autumn 1972):27–35.

Melder, Keith E. *Beginnings of Sisterhood: The American Woman's Rights Movement, 1800–1850.* Gerda Lerner, ed. New York: Schocken Books, 1977.

Miller, David E., and Della S. Miller. *Nauvoo: The City of Joseph.* Santa Barbara and Salt Lake City: Peregrine Smith Books, 1974.

Moody, Thurmon Dean. "Nauvoo's Whistling and Whittling Brigade," *BYU Studies* 15, No. 4 (Summer 1975):480–90.

Mulder, William, and A. Russell Mortensen, eds. *Among the Mormons: Historic Accounts by Contemporary Observers.* New York: Alfred A. Knopf, 1958.

Newell, Linda K., and Valeen T. Avery. "Jane Manning James: Black Saint, 1847 Pioneer," *The Ensign* 9 (August 1979):26–29.

——————. "New Light on the *Sun:* Emma Smith and the *New York Sun* Letter," *Journal of Mormon History* 6 (1979):23–35.

——————. "Sweet Counsel and Seas of Tribulation: The Religious Life of the Women in Kirtland," *BYU Studies* 20, No. 2 (Winter 1980):151–62.

Newell, Linda King. "A Gift Given, A Gift Taken: Washing, Anointing, and Blessing the Sick Among Mormon Women," *Sunstone* 6, No. 4 (September/October 1981):16–26.

Nibley, Hugh. "A New Look at the Pearl of Great Price: Part 1, The Sacrifice of Sarah," *Improvement Era*, April 1970.

Nibley, Preston. *Joseph Smith the Prophet.* Salt Lake City: Deseret News Press, 1944.

Oaks, Dallin H., and Marvin S. Hill. *Carthage Conspiracy: The Trial of the Accused Assassins of Joseph Smith.* Urbana, Illinois: University of Illinois Press, 1975.

——————, and Joseph I. Bentley. "Joseph Smith and Legal Process: In the Wake of the Steamship *Nauvoo.*" *Brigham Young University Law Review*, 1976, No. 3:735–82.

O'Dea, Thomas F. *The Mormons.* Chicago: University of Chicago Press, 1957.

Palmyra: Wayne County, New York. Compiled by the Woman's Society of the Western Presbyterian Church, 1907.

Parry, Edwin F., compiler. *Stories About Joseph Smith the Prophet.* Salt Lake City: Deseret News Press, 1934.

Paxton, J. H. "Emma Hale Smith," *The True Latter Day Saints' Herald* 96 (26 February 1949):206–7, 214.

The Pearl of Great Price: A Selection from the Revelations, Translations, and Narrations of Joseph Smith. Salt Lake City: Church of Jesus Christ of Latter-day Saints, 1958.

Pearson, Carol Lynn. *Daughters of Light.* Salt Lake City: Bookcraft, Inc., 1973.

Perry, Grace L. "Emma Hale Smith," *The True Latter Day Saints' Herald* 87 (30 March 1940):396–98.

Phillips, Emma M. *Women of the Restoration.* Independence, Missouri: Herald Publishing House, 1960.

Porter, Larry C. "The Colesville Branch and the Coming Forth of the Book of Mormon," *BYU Studies* 10, No. 3 (Spring 1970):382.

——————. "The Joseph Knight Family," *The Ensign* 8 (October 1978):39–45.

——————. "Christmas with the Prophet Joseph," *The Ensign* 8 (December 1978):8–11.

——————. "Was the Church Legally Incorporated at the Time It Was Organized in the State of New York?" *The Ensign* 8 (December 1978):26–27.

——————. "Dating the Restoration of the Melchizedek Priesthood." *The Ensign* 9 (June 1979):5–10.

Pratt, Parley P. *Mormonism Unvailed.* 2nd ed. New York: O. Pratt and E. Fordham, 1838.

——————. *History of the Late Persecution Inflicted by the State of Missouri Upon the Mormons.* Mexico, New York: Reprinted at the Office of the Oswego County Democrat, 1840.

——————. *Late Persecution of the Church of Jesus Christ of Latter Day Saints. Ten thousand American Citizens Robbed, Plundered, and Banished.* Written in prison. New York: J. W. Harrison, 1840.

—————. *A Voice of Warning.* London: F. D. Richards, 1854.

—————. *An Address by a Minister of the Church of Jesus Christ of Latter Day Saints, to the People of England.* Manchester: James Jones, n.d.

—————. *Autobiography of Parley Parker Pratt: One of the Twelve Apostles of the Church of Jesus Christ of Latter-day Saints, Embracing His Life, Ministry and Travels, with Extracts, in Prose and Verse, from His Miscellaneous Writings.* Parley P. Pratt, Jr., ed. 1874. 3rd ed. Salt Lake City: Deseret Book Co., 1938.

Quaife, Milo. *The Kingdom of Saint James, A Narrative of the Mormons.* New Haven: Yale University Press, 1930.

Quincy, Josiah. *Figures of the Past.* Boston: Little, Brown & Co., 1901.

Quinn, D. Michael. "The Mormon Succession Crisis of 1844," *BYU Studies* 16, No. 2 (Winter 1976):187–233.

—————. "Brigham Young, Man of the Spirit," *The Ensign* 8 (August 1977):34–37.

—————. "Echoes and Foreshadowings: The Distinctiveness of the Mormon Community," *Sunstone* 3, No. 3 (March/April 1978):12–17.

—————. "Joseph Smith III's 1844 Blessing and the Mormons of Utah," *Dialogue* 15, No. 2 (Summer 1982):69–89.

—————. "The Newel K. Whitney Family," *The Ensign* 8 (December 1978):42–45.

—————. "Latter-day Saint Prayer Circles," *BYU Studies* 19, No. 1 (Fall 1978):79–105.

—————. "Joseph Smith III's 1844 Blessing and the Mormons of Utah," *John Whitmer Historical Association Journal* 1 (1981):12–27.

Rigdon, Sidney. *Oration Delivered by Mr. S. Rigdon on the 4th of July, 1838, at Far West, Missouri.* Far West, Missouri: The Journal Office, 1838.

Riley, Isaac Woodbridge. *The Founder of Mormonism.* New York: Dodd, Mead & Co., 1902.

Roberts, Brigham H. *Mormonism, Its Origin and History.* Independence, Missouri: Press of Zion's Printing and Publishing Co., 1923.

—————. *A Comprehensive History of the Church of Jesus Christ of Latter-day Saints.* 6 vols. Provo, Utah: Brigham Young University Press, 1965.

—————. *The Rise and Fall of Nauvoo.* Salt Lake City: Bookcraft, 1965.

Ryan, Mary P. *Womanhood in America; From Colonial Times to the Present.* 2nd ed. New York and London: Franklin Watts, 1975, 1979.

Schindler, Harold. *Orrin Porter Rockwell: Man of God, Son of Thunder.* Salt Lake City: University of Utah Press, 1966.

Shook, Charles A. *The True Origins of Mormon Polygamy.* Cincinnati: Standard Publishing Co., 1914.

Siegfried, M. H. "Tributes to Church Pioneers," *The True Latter Day Saints' Herald* 97 (24 April 1950):405.

Smith, Alexander H. *Polygamy: Was It An Original Tenet of the Church of Jesus Christ of Latter Day Saints?* Lamoni, Iowa: Reorganized Church of Jesus Christ of Latter Day Saints, n.d.

Smith, Bathsheba W. "Recollections of the Prophet Joseph Smith," *Juvenile Instructor* 27 (1 June 1892):344–45.

Smith, David H. *The Bible Versus Polygamy.* Plano, Illinois: Reorganized Church of Jesus Christ of Latter Day Saints. Nauvoo, Illinois, ca. 1870.

—————, and Elbert A. Smith. *Hesperis: Or Poems by Father and Son.* Lamoni, Iowa, and Independence, Missouri: Herald Publishing, 1911.

Smith, Elbert A. "Tribute to Hyrum Smith," *The True Latter Day Saints' Herald* 86 (19 July 1939):939.

—————. *Differences That Persist Between the Reorganized Church of Jesus Christ of Latter Day Saints and the Utah Mormon Church.* Independence, Missouri: Herald House, 1943.

—————. "Emma Hale Smith," *The True Latter Day Saints' Herald* 92 (1 September 1945):5–7.

—————. *Faith of Our Fathers.* Independence, Missouri: Herald House, 1972.

Smith, Emma, compiler. *A Collection of Sacred Hymns for the Church of the Latter Day Saints.* Kirtland, Ohio: F. G. Williams and Co., 1835.

—————. *A Collection of Sacred Hymns of the Church of Jesus Christ of Latter Day Saints.* Nauvoo, Illinois: E. Robinson, 1841.

Smith, E. Gary. "The Patriarchal Crisis of 1845," *Dialogue* 16, No. 2 (Summer 1983):24–36.

Smith, Heman C. "Distinguished Women," *Journal of History* 12, No. 1 (January 1919):93–110; and 12, No. 3 (July 1919):282–95.

Smith, Inez. *Autumn Leaves.* Lamoni, Iowa: Reorganized Church of Jesus Christ of Latter Day Saints, 1888–1931.

Smith, Jesse Nathaniel. *Six Decades in the Early West: The Journal of Jesse Nathaniel Smith; Diaries and Papers of a Mormon Pioneer, 1834–1906.* 3rd ed. Oliver R. Smith, ed. Provo, Utah: Jesse N. Smith Family Association, 1970.

Smith, Joseph III, ed. "The Elect Lady," *The True Latter Day Saints' Herald* 17, No. 3 (1 February 1870): 65–69.

—————. *Reply to Orson Pratt, By Joseph Smith, President of the Reorganized Church of Jesus Christ of Latter Day Saints.* 4 vols. Lamoni, Iowa: 1870.

—————. "Last Testimony of Sister Emma," *Saints' Advocate* (Plano, Illinois) 2, No. 4 (October 1879):49–52.

—————. "A Prophet Explains the Godhead," *The True Latter Day Saints' Herald* 45 (16 March 1898):162.

—————. *Joseph Smith III and the Restoration.* Mary Audentia Smith Anderson, ed. Independence, Missouri: Herald House, 1952.

—————. *The Memoirs of President Joseph Smith III (1832–1914): A Photo-Reprint Edition of the Original Serial Publication as Edited by Mary Audentia Smith Anderson and appearing in the Saints' Herald (November 6, 1934–July 31, 1937).* Richard P. Howard, ed. Independence, Missouri: Herald House, 1979.

—————. *One Wife, or Many.* Lamoni, Iowa: Reorganized Church of Jesus Christ of Latter Day Saints, n.d.

——————, and Heman C. Smith. *The History of the Reorganized Church of Jesus Christ of Latter Day Saints*. 4 vols. Lamoni, Iowa: Herald House, 1896–1903.

Smith, Joseph F., Jr. *Asahel Smith, of Topsfield, Massachusetts, with Some Account of the Smith Family*. Topsfield, Massachusetts: The Topsfield Historical Society, 1902.

Smith, Joseph Fielding. *Blood Atonement and the Origin of Plural Marriage*. Salt Lake City, Utah: Deseret News Press. Reprint of 1905 edition.

——————. *Essentials of Church History*. 13th ed. Salt Lake City, Utah: Deseret Book Co., 1975.

Smith, Lucy. *Biographical Sketches of Joseph Smith the Prophet and His Progenitors for Many Generations*. Liverpool, England: S. W. Richards, 1853.

Smith, William. *Defense of Elder William Smith, Against the Slanders of Abraham Curtis, and Others*. Philadelphia: Brown and Guilbert, 1844.

Snow, Eliza R. *Biography and Family Record of Lorenzo Snow . . . Written and Compiled by his Sister, Eliza R. Snow*. Salt Lake City: Deseret News Co., 1884.

——————. *Eliza R. Snow, an Immortal. Selected Writings of Eliza R. Snow*. Salt Lake City, Utah: Nicholas G. Morgan, Sr., Foundation, 1957.

"Some Facts Concerning Emma Smith," *The True Latter Day Saints' Herald* 52 (October 1905):267–68.

Spencer, Orson. *Letters Exhibiting the Most Prominent Doctrines of the Church of Latter-day Saints*. Salt Lake City: Deseret News Co., 1889.

Stacher, Rhamanthus M. *Susquehanna County Centennial History—Pennsylvania*. Philadelphia: R. T. Peck and Co., 1887.

Stanley, Reva. *Biography of Parley P. Pratt; The Archer of Paradise*. Caldwell, Idaho: Caxton Printers, Ltd., 1937.

Stegner, Wallace. *The Gathering of Zion, The Story of the Mormon Trail*. New York, Toronto, London: McGraw-Hill, 1964.

Stenhouse, Mrs. T. B. H. *Expose of Polygamy in Utah: A Lady's Life Among the Mormons*. New York: American News Company, 1872.

Stewart, John L. *Joseph Smith, The Mormon Prophet*. Salt Lake City: Hawkes Publishing Inc., 1966.

"The Story of the Organization of the Relief Society," *Relief Society Magazine* 6 (March 1919):129–42.

Stout, Hosea. *On the Mormon Frontier; the Diary of Hosea Stout, 1844–1861*. 2 vols. Juanita Brooks, ed. Salt Lake City: University of Utah Press, 1964.

Taylor, Samuel W. *Nightfall at Nauvoo*. New York: Macmillan, 1971.

Terry, Keith, and Ann Terry. *Emma: The Dramatic Biography of Emma Smith*. Santa Barbara, California: Butterfly Publishing, 1979.

Tullidge, Edward W. *Life of Joseph the Prophet*. 2nd ed. Plano, Illinois: The Reorganized Church of Jesus Christ of Latter Day Saints, 1880.

——————. *Women of Mormondom*. First printing, New York, 1877. Photo Lithographic Reprint, Salt Lake City, Utah, 1973.

"Unchristianlike Work," editorial, *The True Latter Day Saints' Herald* 51, No. 30 (27 July 1904):681–83.

Van Wagoner, Richard S., and Stephen C. Walker. *A Book of Mormons.* Salt Lake City: Signature Books, 1982.

——————. "Joseph Smith: 'The Gift of Seeing,' " *Dialogue* 15, No. 2 (Summer 1982):48–68.

Walker, Ronald W. "The Liberal Institute: A Case Study in National Assimilation," *Dialogue* 10, No. 3 (Autumn 1977):75–85.

——————. "When the Spirit Did Abound: Nineteenth-Century Utah's Encounter with Free Thought Radicalism," *Utah Historical Quarterly* 50 (Fall 1982):304–24.

Walker, William Holmes. *The Life Incidents and Travels of Elder William Holmes Walker and His Association with Joseph Smith, the Prophet.* n.p.: Elizabeth Jane Walker Piepgrass, 1943.

Walters, Wesley P. *Joseph Smith's Bainbridge, N.Y., Court Trials.* Salt Lake City: Modern Microfilm Company, 1974.

Watson, Elden Jay, ed. *Manuscript History of Brigham Young, 1801–1844.* Salt Lake City: Jay Watson, 1968.

Watt, George D., ed. *Journal of Discourses, Reports of Addresses by Brigham Young and Others.* 26 vols. Liverpool and London: F. D. and S. W. Richards, 1853–86.

Whitmer, David. *An Address to All Believers in Christ, by A Witness to the Authenticity of the Book of Mormon.* Richmond, Missouri: David Whitmer, 1887; photo reprint Concord, California: Pacific Publishing Co., 1959.

Whitney, Helen Mar Kimball. *Plural Marriage as Taught by the Prophet Joseph; a Reply to Joseph Smith, Editor of the Lamoni (Iowa) Herald.* Salt Lake City: Juvenile Instructor office, 1882.

——————. *Why We Practice Plural Marriage.* Salt Lake City: Juvenile Instructor Office, 1884.

Whitney, Orson F. *Life of Heber C. Kimball an Apostle: The Father and Founder of the British Mission.* Salt Lake City: Kimball Family, 1888.

Widtsoe, John A., ed. *Discourses of Brigham Young, Second President of the Church of Jesus Christ of Latter-day Saints.* Salt Lake City: Deseret Book Co., 1954.

Wirkus, Erwin E. *Judge Me Dear Reader.* Idaho Falls, Idaho: Erwin E. Wirkus, 1978.

Wyl, Wilhelm. *Joseph Smith, His Family, and His Friends.* Salt Lake City: Tribune Printing and Publishing Co., 1886.

——————. *Mormon Portraits, The Truth about the Mormon Leaders from 1830 to 1866.* Salt Lake City: Tribune Printing and Publishing Co., 1866.

Young, Ann Eliza. *Wife Number 19, or, The Story of a Life in Bondage, Being a Complete Expose of Mormonism, and Revealing the Sorrows, Sacrifices and Sufferings of Women in Polygamy.* Hartford, Connecticut: Dustin, Gilman, and Co., 1876.

Young, Kimball. *Isn't One Wife Enough?* New York: Henry Holt & Co., 1954.

Youngreen, Buddy. "The Death Date of Lucy Mack Smith: 8 July 1775, 14 May 1856," *BYU Studies* 12, No. 3 (Spring 1972):318.

——————. "Joseph and Emma: A Slide-Film Presentation," *BYU Studies* 14, No. 2 (Winter 1974):199–226.

——————. "Sons of the Martyrs' Nauvoo Reunion—1860," *BYU Studies* 20, No. 4 (Summer 1980):351–70.

Zimmerman, Dean R. *I Knew the Prophets, An Analysis of the Letter of Benjamin F. Johnson to George F. Gibbs, Reporting Doctrinal Views of Joseph Smith and Brigham Young.* Bountiful, Utah: Horizon, 1976.

Manuscript Collections

Berkeley, California: Bancroft Library, University of California at Berkeley. Mormon collection, including Daniel H. Wells narrative and Phoebe W. Woodruff reminiscence.

Edwardsville, Illinois: Southern Illinois University Library. Stanley B. Kimball collection.

Independence, Missouri: Library and Archives of the Reorganized Church of Jesus Christ of Latter Day Saints. Lewis C. Bidamon collection; William W. Blair journals; Edmund C. Briggs journals; F. M. Cooper reminiscences; Judge George Edmunds law office papers; Hancock County historical papers; Alexander Hale Smith collection; David Hyrum Smith collection; Emma Smith collection; Joseph Smith III journals, papers, and letterbooks.

New Haven, Connecticut: Beinecke Rare Books and Manuscript Library, Yale University, Western Americana collection, including the Oliver H. Olney papers, James M. Monroe diary (hand copy mislabeled as James Egan journal), Joseph Smith daybook for his store 1842–44, and James J. Strang papers.

Palo Alto, California: Stanford University Library. Thomas Kane papers and diaries.

Provo, Utah: Archives and Manuscripts at the Harold B. Lee Library, Brigham Young University. Howard Coray papers; Lewis Hudson papers; Alan H. Gerber collection, including Philo Dibble "Life History," John Pulsipher "Life Sketch," Zerah Pulsipher history, and Willard Richards' account of the arrest, imprisonment, and martyrdom of Joseph Smith; Mary Elizabeth Rollins Lightner collection; Wandle Mace journal; Cecil McGavin collection; Joseph Bates Noble journal; David Osborn journal; George A. Smith journal; Lucy Messerve Smith journal; Nancy Naomi Alexander Tracy papers; Newel K. Whitney papers.

Urbana, Illinois: Illinois Historical Society, University of Illinois Library. Minor Deming papers.

San Marino, California: Henry E. Huntington Library and Art Gallery. Mormon collection, including George Washington Bean diary; Lewis Crum Bidamon and Emma Smith Bidamon papers, 1830–90; Henry G. Boyle diary; Jesse W. Crosby diary; Oliver Cowdery letters; Isaac C. Haight diary; Sarah Leavitt diary; John Doyle Lee diary; Richards family correspondence; Erastus Snow diary.

Salt Lake City, Utah: The Historical Department of the Church of Jesus Christ of Latter-day Saints, Archives. Emma Smith Bidamon and Lewis C. Bidamon papers in the Marcia Vogel collection; Abraham H. Cannon diaries, 1879–95; Caroline Barnes Crosby memoirs and diary, 1851–82; Jonathan Crosby papers, 1871–75; Desdemona Wadsworth Fullmer autobiography, 1868; Aroet Lucius Hale journals and reminiscences, 1846–82; Oliver B. Huntington history; William Huntington diaries, 1841–46; Jane Elizabeth Manning James oral history recorded by J. D. Roundy, 1893; Benjamin F. Johnson papers; Journal History (a compilation of journal and diary entries arranged in chronological order), 750 vols., typed; Nancy Kalk historical collection, including Emma Smith Bidamon and Lewis C. Bidamon family papers; Heber Chase Kimball journal and record book, 1845–46; Lucy Walker Kimball biographical sketch; Hannah Tapfield King journal and reminiscences, 1849–60; Joseph Knight reminiscences; minutes of the Nauvoo Female Relief Society 1842–44; John Murdock journal and reminiscences; Nauvoo Restoration files, including newspaper accounts, property records; Mary A. Rich "Life of Mary Ann Rich Phelps" dictated by her; Willard Richards journals, 1836–53; Joseph Lee Robinson journal, 1883–92; James Henry Rollins reminiscences, 1888; Seventies Record; David Hyrum Smith papers, 1877–1904; George A. Smith papers; Joseph Smith, Jr., collection including letterbooks, correspondence, diaries, and items relating to his history; Joseph F. Smith affidavit books; Joseph F. Smith collection, 1869–76; Samuel H. B. Smith autobiography, 1856–63; William Smith papers; LeRoi C. Snow "Biographical Notes on Lorenzo Snow," 1876–1962; Mercy Rachel Thompson life sketch, 20 December 1880; Helen Mar Kimball Whitney autobiography; Wilford Woodruff journals, 1854–59; Brigham Young collection, including letters, journal excerpts, and diaries; Emily Dow Partridge Young autobiography and diary, 1874–99; Emmeline B. Wells papers.

Salt Lake City, Utah: Manuscripts Division, Special Collections of the University of Utah Libraries. Philip Blair papers; Fawn McKay Brodie papers; Vesta P. Crawford papers, including unfinished manuscript on Emma Hale Smith (with Fay Ollerton), correspondence, and notes; Joseph C. Kingsbury journal; Madeline Reeder McQuown papers including notes and documents on Brigham Young; George A. Smith papers; Brigham Young papers; Emily Dow Partridge Young papers.

Salt Lake City, Utah: Utah State Historical Society. Stanley S. Ivins collection; James Henry Rollins diary; Allen J. Stout diary.

Private Collections: Abbey Jenks Rice, Fulton, Illinois, journal in possession of June Gustafson; Prescendia L. Kimball Smith life sketch in possession of Tasma Pond Dansie; Buddy Youngreen collection of Joseph Smith, Sr., family and documents; Wilford C. Wood collection of Mormon papers and Mormon memorabilia; Maria Jane Johnston Johnson biography by and in possession of Roselyn Woodward Slade.

Unpublished Manuscripts

Avery, Valeen Tippetts. "Insanity and the Sweet Singer: A Biography of David Hyrum Smith, 1844–1904." Ph.D. dissertation, Northern Arizona University, 1984.

——————. "Last Years of the Prophet's Wife: Emma Hale Smith Bidamon and the Establishment of the Reorganized Church of Jesus Christ of Latter Day Saints." Master's thesis, Northern Arizona University, 1981.

Bachman, Danel W. "A Study of the Mormon Practice of Plural Marriage Before the Death of Joseph Smith." Master's thesis, Purdue University, 1976.

Bailey, Raymond T. "Emma Hale: Wife of the Prophet Joseph Smith." Master's thesis, Brigham Young University, 1952.

Barrett, Gwynn W. "John M. Bernhisel—Mormon Elder in Congress." Ph.D. dissertation, Brigham Young University, 1968.

Chessman, Paul. "An Analysis of the Accounts Relating Joseph Smith's Early Visions." Master's thesis, Brigham Young University, 1965.

Ehat, Andrew F. "Joseph Smith's Introduction of Temple Ordinances and the 1844 Succession Question." Master's thesis, Brigham Young University, 1982.

Fields, Clarence L. "History of the Kirtland Temple." Master's thesis, Brigham Young University, 1963.

Flanders, Robert Bruce. "The Mormons Who Did Not Go West, The Study of the Emergence of the Reorganized Church of Jesus Christ of Latter Day Saints." Master's thesis, University of Wisconsin, 1954.

Foster, William Lawrence. "Between Two Worlds: The Origins of Shaker Celibacy, Oneida Community Complex Marriage, and Mormon Polygamy." Ph.D. dissertation, University of Chicago, 1976.

Godfrey, Kenneth. "Causes of Mormon-Non-Mormon Conflict in Hancock County, Illinois: 1839–1844." Ph.D. dissertation, Brigham Young University, 1967.

Hill, Marvin S. "The Role of Christian Primitivism in the Origin and Development of the Mormon Kingdom, 1830–1844." Ph.D. dissertation, University of Chicago, 1968.

Hutchins, Robert D. "Joseph Smith III: Moderate Mormon." Master's thesis, Brigham Young University, 1977.

Luke, Kenneth O. "Nauvoo, Illinois, Since the Exodus of the Mormons, 1846–1973." Ph.D. dissertation, St. Louis University, 1973.

Parkin, Max. "Conflict at Kirtland." Master's thesis, Brigham Young University, 1966.

Peterson, Paul H. "An Historical Analysis of the Word of Wisdom." Master's thesis, Brigham Young University, 1972.

Shipley, Richard Lyle. "Voices of Dissent: The History of the Reorganized Church of Jesus Christ of Latter Day Saints in Utah, 1863–1900." Master's thesis, Utah State University, 1969.

Van Wagoner, Richard S., and Stephen C. Walker. "A Book of Mormons." In possession of the authors.

Walker, Ronald Warren. "The Godbeite Protest in the Making of Modern Utah." Ph.D. dissertation, University of Utah, 1977.

Newspapers

Adams Sentinel, Gettysburg, Pennsylvania.

Boston *Post,* Boston, Massachusetts.

Burlington *Hawkeye,* Burlington, Iowa.

Chardon *Spectator,* Chardon, Illinois.

Christian Advocate and Journal, New York, New York.

Church News, Salt Lake City, Utah.

Daily Missouri Republican, St. Louis, Missouri.

Deseret Evening News, Salt Lake City, Utah.

Deseret News Weekly, Salt Lake City, Utah.

Elders' Journal of the Church of Latter Day Saints, Kirtland, Ohio, and Far West, Missouri.

Evening and Morning Star, Independence, Missouri, and Kirtland, Ohio.

Evening News, Albany, New York.

Frontier Guardian, Kanesville, Iowa.

Hampshire Gazette, Northampton, Massachusetts.

Hancock Eagle, Nauvoo, Illinois.

Indiana American, Brookville, Indiana.

Latter-day Saints' Messenger and Advocate, Kirtland, Ohio.

Latter-day Saints' Millennial Star, Manchester, England.

Missouri Wigg, Palmyra, Missouri.

Mormon, The, New York, New York.

Morning Register, New Bedford, Massachusetts.

Naked Truths About Mormonism, Oakland, California.

Nauvoo *Expositor*, Nauvoo, Illinois.

Nauvoo *Independent*, Nauvoo, Illinois.

Nauvoo *Neighbor*, Nauvoo, Illinois.

New York *Daily Herald*, New York, New York.

New York *Evening Post*, New York, New York.

New York *Sun*, New York, New York.

New York *Weekly Tribune*, New York, New York.

Northern Democrat, Montrose, Pennsylvania.

Ohio Repository, Canton, Ohio.

Painesville *Telegraph*, Painesville, Ohio.

Pennsylvania Argus, Greensburgh, Pennsylvania.

Pittsburgh *Catholic*, Pittsburgh, Pennsylvania.

Public Leader, Philadelphia, Pennsylvania.

Quincy *Whig*, Quincy, Illinois.

Return, The, Davis City, Iowa; Richmond, Missouri; Denver, Colorado; Independence, Missouri.

St. Louis *American*, St. Louis, Missouri.

St. Louis *Daily New Era*, St. Louis, Missouri.

Salt Lake Tribune, Salt Lake City, Utah.

Seer, The, Washington, D.C., and Liverpool, England.

Tioga Eagle, Wellsboro, Pennsylvania.

Times and Seasons, Commerce and Nauvoo, Illinois.

Voree *Herald*, Voree, Wisconsin.

Warsaw *Signal*, Warsaw, Illinois.

Wasp, The, Nauvoo, Illinois.

Western Courier, Ravenna, Ohio.

Woman's Exponent, Salt Lake City, Utah.

Index

·A